PERSPECTIVES

ON POLITICAL

PHILOSOPHY

Thucydides through Machiavelli

Thucydides

through

Machiavelli

VOLUME I

PERSPECTIVES ON POLITICAL PHILOSOPHY

Edited by

JAMES V. DOWNTON, JR. *University of Colorado*

DAVID K. HART *University of Washington*

Holt, Rinehart and Winston, Inc.
New York   Chicago   San Francisco   Atlanta
Montreal   Toronto   London   Sydney

Library of Congress Catalog Card Number: 74–152768

SBN: 03–081404-9

Printed in the United States of America

1 2 3 4   0 9 0   9 8 7 6 5 4 3 2 1

For our children

Katherine Downton

Karen, Susan, David and *Andrea Hart*

PREFACE

This anthology of secondary source readings in political philosophy is the first of three similar volumes intended as supplements to accompany both the original works of the major political philosophers and the available textbooks in the history of political philosophy. The volumes, organized chronologically, offer perspectives on the great theories, some adding insight to our understanding of the general outlook of leading political philosophers, while others concentrate on more specific issues. By carefully studying textbooks, students can become familiar with a political philosopher's general perspective rather easily. However, in most standard survey courses it is possible for them to learn only the basic outlines of the great theories and they do not have the opportunity to sample the many essays that offer perspectives on a single aspect of thought or even a crucial term which could deepen their understanding and appreciation of those theories. Consequently, we have chosen to include numerous interpretative works that focus more sharply on certain fragments of a master work, thereby casting new light on the political philosopher's total view. We hope these essays will add new insights that may enliven and deepen the dialogue that has become a traditional part of political philosophy courses.

For the most part, the essays are drawn from the leading journals in the field. However, in some instances chapters from major books were included where they seemed appropriate and necessary, although limitations of space prevented us from including more numerous excerpts. Drawing heavily from the journals made it possible to include a more abundant and representative number of political philosophers as well as more numerous perspectives on each thinker. This comprehensiveness is crucial if the anthology is to function properly as a vehicle for study, discussion, and research.

In all, there are three volumes in this series. In the final offering of this set, a somewhat different orientation to the study of contemporary political philosophy was developed. Instead of looking exclusively at the work of strictly "political" philosophers, an attempt was made to convey an impression of the fragmentation of the enterprise through several autonomous academic disciplines. Major thinkers from Sociology and Psychology are included (as well as theologians arguing an existential point of view). From our perspective, this organizational scheme has many attractive features, conveying a sense of the origin of the social sciences, the development of the behavioral outlook, and some understanding of where political philosophers stand with respect to the development of science and the problems of this age.

Introductions to anthologies generally attempt to discuss what is included and why, but we have taken a different approach. Instead, we have explored perspectives on the general nature of political philosophy as introductory essays to Volumes I and II. In the third volume we have examined the philosophical roots and basic dilemmas of political action, both issues of importance in contemporary political philosophy. Our essays are intended to stimulate thinking and discussion as much as to convey information. By reading and arguing with these introductory essays, students should be better prepared to appraise specific political philosophies, to obtain a better sense for the continuity of the tradition, and to begin to see the relevance of political philosophy to the development of behavioral science and the problems of political change.

The reader will note that we use the term "political philosophy" instead of the more conventional usage of "political theory." There are many reasons for this, which are explained in greater detail in the introductory essay to Volume II. Briefly, however, the term "political philosophy" conveys a somewhat more realistic impression of the nature of the enterprise. Also, the term "political theory" has recently been pre-empted by the political behavioralists and used as the equivalent for scientific theory in political science. Therefore, in order to convey more adequately what we believe to be the traditional meaning and to avoid confusion, we use the term "political philosophy."

Finally, we wish to express our appreciation to a number of people whose assistance has been most valuable. Our colleagues pointed out omissions in our collection, they suggested more readings, they read our essays and they offered both encouragement and useful criticisms. Specifically we would like to thank Professors Thomas Landon Thorson, George

Smith, Gerald I. Jordan, Glen Dealy, and Matthew Stolz. A number of research assistants and typists spent long hours over the project. While we cannot mention all of them we would like to mention specifically Mr. Kent Anderson and Miss Pat Windust, at the University of Washington.

As is customary and correct, we wish to absolve all those mentioned from any responsibility for the volumes. They added greatly to the merits of the project, but must be held blameless for their flaws. Also, it should be obvious that the authors who have kindly allowed their essays to be included are not responsible for the ideas we express or for the arrangement of the volumes.

James V. Downton, Jr.
David K. Hart

November 1970

CONTENTS

PERSPECTIVES

ON POLITICAL

PHILOSOPHY

Thucydides through Machiavelli

Reflections on Political Philosophy: An Introductory Essay

JAMES V. DOWNTON, JR.

Although political philosophy appears to have had a somewhat sporadic development because of the cycles of political turmoil out of which it takes form, it is in fact a fairly constant enterprise. Even when political conflicts are at a low ebb, there will be men driven by their opposition to the existing political condition, and those who defend it, engaging in political philosophy. The invitation to build political philosophies is not exclusive, but is open to all those who have assessed the causes of political disorder and wish to reform political life accordingly. This is not to say, however, that all political philosophy is good philosophy, for individuals differ markedly in their capacities for careful observation, and only a small number are gifted with sufficient political insight and imagination to gather a circle of disciples. The importance of care in philosophical observation was emphasized by Hobbes, among others: "The best prophet naturally is the best guesser, he that is

1

most versed and studied in the matters he guesses at: for he hath most signs to guess by." [1] It is not surprising, therefore, that the recognized prophets in the history of political philosophy have been men who seemed as comfortable in the associations of active political life as they were among their literary and intellectual equals, for it seems that success in the guessing game of political philosophy is contingent on one's perceptivity in grasping the way the political game is played. In this vein, political philosophy cannot be considered the exclusive property of a single class, although it has traditionally been indulged in primarily by the intelligentsia, for the politically knowledgeable may be found in various walks of life—in purely academic circles, in legislative chambers, even in the politically rebellious sectors demonstrating against the excesses of constituted authority.

Political philosophy is, in part, a speculative process that seeks to increase the accuracy of guesswork pertaining to the best political arrangement. But to introduce the notion of "best," according to the behavioralist, is to contaminate a strictly scientific goal by adding an evaluation derived from subjective personal values relative to one's belief system. This criticism is valid, of course, for in addition to the empirical emphasis within political philosophy there is a transempirical aspect derived from the political philosopher's attempt to suggest either how political relations ought to be arranged, how men ought to behave politically, or both.[2]

Little benefit is to be gained from another analysis of the points of conflict between political philosophy and the behavioral school, since numerous accounts are already available for reference.[3] It would be foolish to contest the argument advanced by the behavioralist and clearly stated by Arnold Brecht that value-laden assertions cannot be scientifically proven true or false, nor can "ought" statements be logically derived from factually grounded premises.[4] The validity of these criticisms is not questioned, but we may wonder whether there are not other grounds for judging the value

---

[1] Thomas Hobbes, *The Leviathan*, edited by Michael Oakeshott (New York: Collier Books, 1962), p. 17.

[2] In a scientific age where the norm is to reject value judgments or "ought" statements out of hand because they cannot be proven true or false, the danger facing the political philosopher is not one of becoming irrelevant for his times, but lies rather in his own reluctance to discuss values in the face of a hostile scientific community, in his embarrassment at defending the importance of subjective evaluations which he increasingly accepts as a form of regression, and, most significantly, in his apparent disorientation arising from his belief that a large segment of his academic class are neither listening nor responding to what he has to say.

[3] See, for example, Vernon Van Dyke, *Political Science: A Philosophical Analysis* (Stanford, Calif.: Stanford University Press, 1960); Joseph S. Murphy, *Political Theory: A Conceptual Analysis* (Homewood, Ill.: Dorsey Press, 1968); Fred M. Frohock, *The Nature of Political Inquiry* (Homewood, Ill.: Dorsey Press, 1967); Eugene J. Meehan, *Contemporary Political Thought* (Homewood, Ill.: Dorsey Press, 1967); and George Kateb, *Political Theory: Its Nature and Uses* (New York: St. Martin's, 1968).

[4] Arnold Brecht, *Political Theory* (Princeton, N.J.: Princeton University Press, 1959), p. 48.

of political philosophy. In fact, one may question whether political philoso-phy is rightly judged when scientific standards are the basis of judgment. Perhaps the standard should be an artistic rather than a scientific one. Thus, political philosophy might be judged in the eyes of science for what it is, rather than for what it is not.

BUILDING HYPOTHETICAL CONSTRUCTS

In the most general sense, "political philosophy—whether in the hands of Plato, Hobbes, Mill, or Marx—is basically a recommendation on how men should conduct politics. These are not ordinarily recommendations cas-ually advanced to meet a specific problem, but recommendations that are *intended* to be valid for all time." [5] In this context there are essentially two directions open to the political philosopher as he considers the ways politi-cal life may be rearranged to make it bearable or better: Proposals may be made to change the structure of political institutions or to alter the basic nature of man. Comprehensive theories, often called "architectonic" be-cause they are total in scope, are likely to encompass both tendencies, a notable example being Plato's *Republic.*

When political structures are assumed to be the source of trouble, the political philosopher turns his attention to the construction of a hypotheti-cal political community where new arrangements are stipulated whose adoption will improve the quality of political life. In this way the political philosopher is able to depict how the behavior of men will be changed when the structural sources of violence and disorder are conceptually elim-inated or controlled. "If we could alter the political arrangement in the fol-lowing way," we are told, "then the problems we observe would be elimi-nated for all time." When the focus is on the deficiencies of the individual, on the other hand, the political philosopher may be tempted to experiment with man himself, purging the lustful and greedy and accentuating the noble and cooperative aspects of character. Here, the political philosopher constructs a hypothetical man, allowing himself greater freedom in experi-menting with political structures, and tells us: "Assuming that man is basi-cally cooperative and rational, the following new arrangements in political life are made possible." Implicit in both types of hypothetical constructs is the philosophical recommendation that the proposed changes be trans-formed into public policy. But how does the political philosopher persuade us to take his recommendations seriously? What tests can be applied to de-termine whether or not those recommendations should be made a part of our own course of action?

[5] Thomas Landon Thorson, *The Logic of Democracy* (New York: Holt, Rinehart and Winston, Inc., 1962), pp. 68–69.

EVALUATING HYPOTHETICAL CONSTRUCTS

Whether or not a political philosopher's recommendations are acceptable as a potential program for action hinges on the answers to four questions that may be posed each time a political philosophy is examined. First, Are the problems chosen by the political philosopher for treatment pressing ones and of concern to political communities in general? The greatness of a political philosopher is often the result of his ability to see serious political difficulties before others have become conscious of them. Marx's popularity in this century, for example, can be attributed in significant measure to his perceptivity in focusing on political, economic, and social problems that for many in various polities were only felt through a sense of "quiet desperation," to use Thoreau's expression. The fact that many of Marx's assessments and guesses were wrong has not diminished the sense of general deference we pay him as one who identified and understood the problems of the Industrial Revolution like few others.

If the problems chosen by a political philosopher are considered both pressing and significant to political communities in general, then a second question may be posed: Have the primary causes of these problems been located, or have only symptoms of the real causes been analyzed? Here, the student must decide whether the evidence offered to demonstrate the connection between the problems and their expressed causes is real and not simply a matter of speculation. Furthermore, he may consider whether the recommendations would actually eliminate those causes and subsequently eliminate the problems. By encouraging his critical capacity the student begins to get a sense of being engaged in the dynamics of political philosophy, questioning the assertions of the great thinkers as if they were tentative hypotheses. For example, he may wonder if there is evidence in the contemporary setting to substantiate Plato's hypothesis that the most responsible leadership is achieved where those who have no interest in ruling assume public office from a sense of citizen duty. Is it true, the student may ask, that choosing men for office who would rather contemplate the problems of philosophy than dirty their hands in politics would effectively and permanently reduce political corruption?

The third question pertains to the proposal's practicality: Can the recommendation be transformed into effective policy? If one of the motives for studying political philosophy is to change the world, as Marx tells us, then philosophical proposals must be evaluated from a pragmatic point of view, with a sensitivity to the concrete problems of transforming mere recommendations into laws that would produce the desired changes. In this mood students may well ask Plato to explain in practical terms how a political system encourages individuals to assume leadership when they have no interest in public office and how it closes off those same offices from the politically ambitious. (This is not to say that utopian theories are without value. Indeed, they have their practical side, as will be demonstrated later.)

Last, but of great significance, is the ethical question, Are the consequences of the recommended course of action defensible on moral grounds? Here one must consider whether there are bad residual effects that may offend one's moral system. For example, even if we assume that Plato's "philosopher king" will not misuse his authority, a student may criticize the establishment of a ruling class on the grounds that it is contrary to the ethical foundations of equality and the virtues of public participation. If one holds the belief that it is good for people to have a voice in the determination of public policy, an ethical judgment so prevalent today, then of course a recommendation that has the consequence of reducing public involvement would be judged as "bad" and rejected out of hand. In this instance a student may choose to tolerate selfish and politically corrupt leaders on occasion in order to defend the right of the citizen to determine who shall make the laws that affect his life.

To the extent that each of these questions produces an affirmative response, a philosophical recommendation can be accepted and become the basis for political action. When a collection of recommendations are acceptable on these grounds an individual may identify himself with a total philosophical system, calling himself a "Marxist," an "anarchist," and so on. When a political philosophy becomes a set of standards for selecting alternative courses of action in this way, it has been transformed by the actor into an ideology, for under these circumstances the political philosophy has become internalized as a part of his personality.

Answers to the foregoing questions will be relative to one's perception of the world, which can never be isolated from the nature of personality.[6] Therefore, debate is inevitable on each question because individual judgments will vary according to differences in personality and experience. For some with scientific pretensions, this debate is cause for ridicule because it does not appear to advance the cause of scientific knowledge. But during the disturbances generated by the pressures of social change, our attention focuses on this debate, as efforts are made to find the most appropriate philosophical recommendations for solving the crisis. It is also during such times that the scientific knowledge so important to the behavioralist seems diminished in significance, save as a source of information for carrying on an effective armed struggle for executing a new political arrangement or for judging results after the new changes have been made. During political crises our attention turns first to the hypothetical systems of political philosophy; only after a course is agreed upon do we come to realize and experience anew the impact of science.

[6] See Herbert McClosky, "Conservatism and Personality," *The American Political Science Review*, 52 (1958), pp. 26–45.

UTOPIAN THOUGHT IN POLITICAL PHILOSOPHY

Utopian theory is an integral part of political philosophy, although many are apt to reject utopian recommendations because they fail to meet the criterion of practicality. This is not universally true, of course, because there is always a small cadre of dreamers whose perceptions of the world are amenable to a type of political experimentation based on utopian proposals. Not all writers are willing to place the utopian dimension in the political philosophic tradition, however. Dante Germino is one who resists this openly, arguing that "political theory, whether ancient or modern, is aware that the world is as it is and not some other way. The task of political theory is to describe the *conditio humana* and not engage in the fallacious attempt to transform it into something which on principle it cannot be." [7] This view, if taken literally, would cut into the heart of many well-known theories from Plato to Camus, because the transformation of the human condition beyond what may appear to be possible has always been accepted as an extension of the philosophic enterprise, given the universal uncertainty about the limits of the possible. In essence, Germino diminishes the freedom of the political imagination by failing to appreciate the game utopian thinkers are playing and overlooks the role of utopian recommendations in setting the ultimate, although sometimes unrealistic, goals toward which political action is directed. In the latter case, utopian theorists are less interested in setting goals to be reached than in moving political communities closer to goals: Willing to fall short of their dreams, they are satisfied to improve the lot of man. Such theories can be likened to the Soviet five-year plans, which, although setting production goals difficult to reach, acted as accelerators of progress.

Besides setting goals toward which political communities may strive, utopian theorists are great experimenters, deriving hypothetical communities from hypothetical men. Much like the anarchist who destroys a political system in order to rebuild it, the utopian theorist destroys our picture of reality to experiment with new political forms. He says: "Forget what you know and imagine man as having different attributes. Instead of imputing selfish motives to him, for example, see him as basically cooperative and public spirited. Now, imagine the new political arrangements that may be derived from this hypothetically cooperative individual. If these arrangements seem desirable, consider next how man may be changed to fit this hypothetical model." A utopian theory, then, attempts to rearrange our factual images of man in order to expand our consciousness of new human and structural possibilities. The student who reads Plato's *Republic* and hurriedly rejects it as unrealistic and thus irrelevant has failed to play the game that is being proposed. Plato would say: "Consider first the relation-

[7] Dante Germino, *Beyond Ideology: The Revival of Political Theory* (New York: Harper and Row, 1967), p. 32.

ship between my hypothetical man (there are actually several hypothetical men) and the hypothetical community of which he is a part. Consider whether the fit is good. If you find it so, only then appraise the practical problems of transforming man into the creature who will make the new political arrangement possible. In this process, remember to judge my political community on the basis of the man I made, not on the basis of what you or others make of him." [8]

Plato is regarded as a great thinker not simply for his contributions to our understanding of the human condition, to return to Germino's point, but because, through the abundance of his political insight and imagination, he was willing and able to experiment with the architecture of government and of political man. Would his political insight and imagination have been nourished and *The Republic* written had Plato accepted the view that political theory must not attempt to transform the human condition into something that in practice it cannot be? The answer is obvious.

DISTINGUISHING UTOPIAN FROM PRAGMATIC THEORIES

Utopian elements are not the exclusive property of utopian theories, for on closer inspection they are scattered, unobtrusively at times, across the history of political philosophy. Even those theories that accept the world as it is and offer pragmatic recommendations to manipulate it often cannot control the tendency to move beyond the possible into the gravitational field of the utopian. But before utopian elements can be located in a political philosophy a more systematic examination of those elements is imperative. What are the unique properties of utopian theory, and how can our understanding of those properties sharpen our comprehension of the more clearly pragmatic political philosophies of such men as Aristotle, Machiavelli, and Hobbes?

A unique feature of utopian philosophy is to be found in the apparent reworking of man's basic nature.[9] In the process of making a hypothetical man a distillation treatment is set into operation where the impurities of

---

[8] Those who have called Plato a "totalitarian" theorist have failed to heed this advice. See, for example, Karl R. Popper, *The Open Society and Its Enemies* (Princeton, N.J.: Princeton University Press, 1950) and R. H. S. Crossman, *Plato Today* (London: George Allen and Unwin, 1959). For a balanced view of the issues involved consider Thomas Landon Thorson (ed.), *Plato: Totalitarian or Democrat?* (Englewood Cliffs, N.J.: Prentice-Hall, 1963).

[9] All political philosophers operate from a conception of human nature, that is, the persistent and generalized behavioral patterns of man. However, utopian theorists tend to consciously reject the universally accepted evidence concerning the substance of man in order to experiment with less familiar political forms. Much like the behavioralist, the utopian thinker resists the view that there is an unalterable substance called "human nature." Seeing the individual as malleable, he feels a greater sense of freedom than others in considering numerous imaginative structural possibilities.

nature that give rise to political struggle are removed. A purified man is made—an unbelievable man at times—who must live up to the norms of the utopian community, for to construct a hypothetical community that resembles the "City of God" requires a man truly in His image. Thus, according to George Kateb, "utopian theorists have assumed either that a few men were (or could be made) close enough to angels to be entrusted unchecked with the great power required by the perfect social order; or that the great mass of men were (or could be made) close enough to the angels, and hence would live in such a way that the coercive tasks of government could lapse. . . ." [10] For example, both Plato in *The Republic* and B. F. Skinner in *Walden Two* rework man into a different substance than we observe at play in the many aggressive games available to modern man. In the distillation process, where men become angels, there is the subsequent feeling that politics has been dehumanized; that the madness in the human condition, which can be linked so closely to the aggressive instincts of other animals,[11] has suddenly vanished with the same ease and feeling of relief as a bad dream. Thus, Plato's "philosopher king" and Skinner's "manager" appear as incomplete men, for neither is aggressive in assuming power to reap the benefits that fall to those in authority. The "philosopher king" would rather bathe in the light of pure philosophy, while his counterpart, the "manager," is anxious to fulfill his leadership obligation to return to the creative arts.

Followers are no less incomplete, for in both communities they are no longer motivated to make the upward move to the status of power. Plato establishes an elaborate socialization scheme that would eliminate the lust for power as it more generally reduced the influence of private passions in public life. In this sense, it is clear that Plato did not wish to completely transform men into angels, although he apparently was confident that education could do so. The same may be said for Skinner's communal nursery, where children are taught to control aggressive impulses and to tolerate the novel and strange.

Where no one aspires to positions of power, Plato and Skinner hope, only the knowledgeable and obligated will assume public offices, provided that the masses will remain occupied with commerce and the creative arts rather than political conspiracy. The lustful, selfish, and brutish tendencies in real men are not to be found, then, in the utopian man; the utopian theorist either assumes man to be what he is not or promises to perfect him. Either way, madness is eliminated from politics, which is to say that political aggression in man is ended.

The elimination of sources of conflict that encourage factional political struggles is the second important feature of utopian thought. The uto-

[10] George Kateb, *Utopia and Its Enemies* (New York: Free Press, 1963), p. 69.
[11] See Konrad Lorenz, *On Aggression*, translated by Marjorie Kerr Wilson (New York: Bantam Book, 1966); and Desmond Morris, *The Naked Ape* (New York: Dell, 1969).

pian theorist does not stop after removing the negative characteristics of man, but the negative structural conditions—the sources of political conflict and disorder—are isolated and then banished from the body politic. Consequently, political harmony and public happiness are enhanced, even guaranteed. Thomas More abolishes private property in *Utopia,* believing that private ownership was the source of considerable injustice and public misery that could be the undoing of English society. Speaking to the leaders of his day, More sets up his utopian colony to illustrate how conditions could be improved if private property—the major manifestation of man's greedy nature—could be ended.[12]

If we assume that political struggle is the essence of politics (putting aside what we would like it to be), then utopian theorists may be viewed as being antipolitical, not simply apolitical. The emphasis given to political harmony and the attendant condemnation of conflict and violence set the utopian theorist in opposition to politics. Thus Marx, the advocate of political violence as a means of breaking the deadlock between the irreconcilable forces of history, ultimately chooses a utopian course, ending the state —but only after he eliminates the sources of conflict that are the basis of politics. Socialism was to remove the inequities that made politics necessary; communism was to be an arrangement where politics was no longer required.

Although the utopian theorist's preference for harmony may limit the scope of allowable political change, one should avoid the incorrect conclusion that utopias are static. All utopias include mechanisms for change, albeit changes in public policy rather than basic political structures. But all political philosophers, whether utopian or pragmatic, tend to offer their recommendations as if they would solve the problems of disorder for all time; consequently, changes in basic political structure would be unnecessary. The credibility of a political philosophy would probably be questioned if we were told, "What I have laid out before you is the best arrangement for creating civic harmony. If it fails to achieve the expected result I have wisely included a procedural device for altering everything." Because persuasion is so crucial in selling philosophical recommendations, the philosopher's seemingly arrogant testimony that he has discovered the way to eliminate disorder is understandable, even admirable, given the nature of his task.

If utopias are not unique in failing to allow for basic structural change, then how are they set off from other, more pragmatic, theories? It is not in the reliance on gradual policy changes, as this is a typical feature in most philosophical systems; rather, it is in the way the policy alternatives are developed. By eliminating political interests and subsequent political struggles, the utopian theorist guarantees the development of policy al-

---

[12] Thomas More, *Utopia* (New Haven, Conn.: Yale University Press, 1964), p. 53.

ternatives within a special class. Thus, the changes that are necessary for adaptation to the environment result from the careful thought and appraisal of experts, selecting the courses of action that would be best for the community as a whole. Hence, when a thinker—be he a Plato or a Hobbes —seeks to prevent political interests from affecting policy formation, the utopian inclination has gained ascendence. When we speak of "the end of politics," then, it is to suggest the abolition of such interests as catalysts of policy change—a utopian feature—whether present in pure utopian thought or found inconspicuously in more pragmatic philosophies.

In setting utopian thought off from more pragmatic considerations, one should avoid the view that utopias are "dream worlds" completely removed from the "real world" of politics. It would be wiser to join Kateb in asserting that "utopia carries (certain) tendencies to their conclusions." [13] Certain aspects of the "real world" of politics are given special emphasis at the expense of other things. The tendency toward cooperation, for example, is carried to its ultimate conclusion; it is expanded into many more facets of political life in the utopian system than is the case in actual fact. So, for example, the occasional aid one man gives to another for altruistic reasons becomes the dominant mode of behavior in Marx's communist system, while the competition between men, which is habitual in fact, is repressed as an important factor. Taking what he sees to be positive factors within the human condition, Marx simply overthrows the decadent and evil. Revolution is carried out in its simplest and most economical form—by the pen.

If the utopian thinker reworks man's basic nature and abolishes political interests from the body politic, then his counterpart—the pragmatic political philosopher—accepts man as he is, sees political interests and struggle as natural, and proceeds to arrange political life accordingly. While the utopian theorist achieves civic harmony by purging man of his aggressive instincts, the pragmatic thinker sees this madness as political energy that needs to be controlled or redirected into beneficial channels. But of course what man "is" will vary in relation to the philosopher's experience and personal ideology. It is not surprising, for instance, that "the state of nature," used as a conceptual starting point by Hobbes, Locke, and Rousseau, could lead to such different philosophical recommendations. Each theorist describes man in a somewhat different way; each offers a somewhat different estimate of the abuses of freedom; consequently, their recommendations for limiting those abuses must vary, as they do. In each case personal ideology shares some honor for the recommended political arrangement, for the level of trust in man's ability to govern and control his passions is directly related to the extent of political freedom we are willing to grant him.[14]

---

[13] Kateb, *Utopia and Its Enemies*, p. 19.
[14] Support for this assertion can be found in Morris Rosenberg, "Misanthropy and Political Ideology," *American Sociological Review*, 21 (1956), pp. 690–695.

Unlike the utopian theorist who achieves civic harmony by abolishing political interests, the pragmatic thinker builds hypothetical communities where conflict between political interests is possible but limited. Machiavelli's *Prince* is a clear example of this tendency, for the leader is not advised to do away with political interests but rather to learn how to manipulate them. Accepting the morality of the world around him, the prince could become both a founder and preserver through the cultivation and application of political intelligence and intuition. By applying cunning or force as the situation required, the political struggle between the Italian city-states would be limited, consequently violence and bloodshed would be reduced. It is in this sense that Sheldon Wolin correctly describes Machiavelli's theory as one based on "an economy of violence." [15] Here, the goal of Machiavelli, as with pragmatic theorists in general, is to reform politics not eradicate it. The excesses of factional struggle are reduced, but political factions are left intact. In this specific context Machiavelli was no totalitarian, for totalitarian regimes seek not to control political interests but to end them if possible—a goal with a very strong utopian tendency.[16]

So far we have separated the utopian and pragmatic for analytic reasons, but in fact both tendencies may be found together in a single philosophy. Even those theorists who appear to us as hardheaded realists may include a utopian feature in their thinking. Let us illustrate this point by discussing Machiavelli and Hobbes, philosophers who apparently accepted man as he is and constructed pragmatic recommendations accordingly. Both Machiavelli and Hobbes develop hypothetical men who are changed in some special way, so that we begin to suspect they are not real men, but imaginary creatures of the mind. Machiavelli's prince is such a figure, for a man who can know when and how to use cunning and force to make and then preserve a state for any length of time is not to be found. Even men who are often identified as archetype Machiavellians, such as Hitler or Mussolini, developed weaknesses in judgment that led to their fall. Actual limits of political intelligence and intuition, even among historical heroes, make states based on the leadership principle very tenuous indeed, as Machiavelli himself came to realize. Thus, Machiavelli unknowingly alters man's nature in *The Prince*, making him capable of a level of political competence that cannot be observed in fact. As in utopian thought, tendencies in the real world—political intelligence and intuition—are taken to their most developed state. The prince must be infinitely wise in choosing the correct course of action, just as Plato's "philosopher king" must be absolutely honest in his capacity as guardian of the political conscience. Both are decidedly unreal and unbelievable men.

Hobbes's *Leviathan* lays down the best possible arrangements to en-

---

[15] See Sheldon Wolin, "Machiavelli: Politics and the Economy of Violence," in *Politics and Vision* (Boston: Little, Brown, 1960).
[16] This point is substantiated very clearly in Hannah Arendt, *The Origins of Totalitarianism* (New York: Meridian Books, 1958).

sure civic peace, arrangements that depend on certain changes in the nature of man. To create a political community where citizens will be content to accept their sovereign, he joins Plato in changing man to fit a hypothetical model. According to Hobbes, subjects should be taught not to love the governments of neighboring countries, not to follow other leaders who might "shine in the commonwealth," not to "speak evil of the sovereign representative," and so forth.[17] Hobbes apparently hopes to make man into a submissive and apolitical animal, a first step to ending political interests and securing for the leader the silence that makes good political judgments possible. Here the two features of utopian thought are coupled, making Hobbes far less pragmatic than many may be willing to admit.

If most political philosophies contain utopian features, as we suspect, then it may not be possible to dissociate utopian thought from the main body of political philosophy, as Germino recommends. Rather, the utopian and pragmatic tendencies should be located in each philosophical system. Political philosophy is not restrictive but expansive: The upward movement to utopian thought is a liberating experience, except for those who are embarrassed at contemplating the impossible. Furthermore, it is a natural extension of thought because the political imagination frees itself from the known and the tested.

ART IN POLITICAL PHILOSOPHY

For the contemporary student of politics art often has a narrow and limited meaning—the capturing of images on canvas, the creation of forms in sculpture, the weaving of impressions into designs. Most students have failed to recognize or fully appreciate the artistic dimension that runs through the historical spectrum of political philosophy. The preference for harmony, balance, integration, and form in constructing hypothetical architectonic systems was an artistic preference that cannot solely be considered a means for attaining some higher ideal, but should be recognized as an end in itself. Pleasure in contemplation of an architectonic model was significantly no different from an artist's gratification upon seeing the aesthetic harmony of line and form in a finished painting.[18] This dimension is clearly fundamental for Hobbes, "for by art is created that great *Leviathan* called a commonwealth. . . ."[19] But how has the artistic dimension influ-

---

[17] Hobbes, *The Leviathan*, pp. 249–252.
[18] Striving for the balance of political forms, the political philosopher was compelled to consider the total set of arrangements related to the task of structuring harmonious states. This preference for the total view—the architectonic preference—has been a dominant tendency in the Western political tradition, although some noted theorists, for example, Thucydides, Polybius, Cicero, and Tocqueville, chose not to follow the architectonic route.
[19] Hobbes, *The Leviathan*, p. 19.

enced the general character of political philosophy? Has the artistic temperament diminished or disappeared entirely in the twentieth century? If so, can an explanation be offered that may usefully distinguish the mood of contemporary political philosophers from the dominant tendency of the past?

The artistic feature is no stranger to the political philosopher. In the centuries before the Renaissance, art was generally understood and accepted as "any activity concerned with making." [20] "Making," which was synonymous with art, was clearly distinguished from "doing," an enterprise associated with prudence—the essence of moral science. The "maker" judged only the good of the thing that was made, that is, the end product, while the prudent man considered the morality of means a crucial issue. Does this imply that artists may be uninterested in the ethical boundaries of action? Thomas Aquinas answers: "Art does not require of the craftsman that his act be a good act, but that his work be good. . . ." [21] According to this argument, we should avoid asking whether the ends justify the means, recognizing that, for the artist, the "means are judged from and by the end." [22] Rejecting the morality of means as relevant to his enterprise, the artist restricts his attention to the efficiency of the means in producing the result he seeks. Casting the prince into the mold of the artist, for example, Machiavelli clearly dispenses with moral considerations: "In five years Cesare Borgia lays his foundations admirably well. And as we follow him, it is the edifice to be built, the soundness of the structure, that concerns. Any question of the good—of the moral good—is completely excluded." [23]

The fabrication of architectonic systems was the result of the artistic preference in political philosophy. Given his artistic disposition, the builder of the architectonic structure failed to focus his attention on serious ethical consequences that arose when one gauged the means necessary to actualize his hypothetical political community. From "the perspective of art" this conduct was amoral, if we consciously assume the artistic perspective of the political philosopher. To think Plato a "totalitarian theorist," once a popular fashion, or to see Machiavelli as an immoral practitioner in the political struggle is to lose sight of the artistic preference in their philosophical temperaments: Appreciation of the end product dominated their minds, the morality of means having been left to bother the prudent in the moral sciences. Across the historical field from Plato through Marx, making has been the dominant philosophical tendency: Building architectonic structures was the common practice. Yet, in the twentieth century there has been a decided rejection of the artistic preference, casting out utopian

[20] Charles S. Singleton, "The Perspective of Art," *The Kenyon Review*, 15 (1953), p. 169.
[21] Singleton, "The Perspective of Art," p. 173.
[22] Singleton, "The Perspective of Art," p. 179.
[23] Singleton, "The Perspective of Art," p. 178.

and pragmatic architectonic constructions alike. Without alluding to the popularly ascribed influence of science, can a new angle of vision be offered to account for the diminishing importance of the artistic dimension?

The twentieth century ushered in a new epoch in national and international politics—a period which may rightfully be called the century of engineered violence. This condition was fundamental for the development of contemporary political philosophy, because organized terror and dehumanization were associated with the construction of totalitarian systems, and the formation of totalitarian structures demonstrated the price of actualizing architectonic systems. With the technological innovations of the twentieth century the means for "making" actual states fell into the hands of "princes." Quite in conformity with the artistic preference, totalitarian dictators judged only the good of the thing to be made, abandoning any responsibility for the brutish means that were strategically employed. Accepting the invitation of the political philosopher to follow artistic guidelines in constructing architectonic systems, the totalitarian dictator became a "maker"—an artist. Contemporary political philosophers witnessed the horrible consequences when the hypothetical architectonic structures in political philosophy became standards for political experimentation.

A rising emphasis on prudence in political philosophy—the political philosophy of means—appears to have developed, roughly in correlation with the loss of philosophical innocence, that is, the recognition of the human costs that may have to be paid when political leaders take the recommendations of political philosophers seriously. The decline of the artistic emphasis in political philosophy, made manifest by a drastically reduced interest in the construction of architectonic structures, seems to have resulted from this loss of innocence. Examining the work of two contemporary political philosophers—Hannah Arendt and Albert Camus —one is struck by their mutual rejection of "making." Both affirm the central role of "doing" by emphasizing the moral limits of action. By restricting the influence of force and violence in political life and by expanding the level of toleration for unpopular causes and ideas, both hope to extend the spaces in which creative politics is possible. Their rejection of the artistic (architectonic) approach is predicated on their judgment that, in reality, it affirms an absolute standard that may oppress the individual and end politics, as they see it. Arendt speaks for a style of politics where political struggle is confined to persuasion and debate, guided by sensitivity to means and a commitment to the primacy of public issues. Camus writes to awaken man's consciousness, to work on his moral conscience, and to persuade the individual to accept nonviolence and moderation as standards for action. Unlike the revolutionary who is obsessed with the ends of action, Camus' "rebel" is sensitive to means, limited always by moral considerations. Camus asks: "Does the end justify the means? That is impossible.

But what will justify the means? To that question, which historical thought leaves pending, rebellion replies: the means." [24]

The audience of the contemporary political philosopher appears distinct from that of earlier thinkers. Others have written for academicians, the clergy, sovereigns, workers; Arendt and especially Camus write for and to the individual from any station and with any belief system. The political philosophy of means, for which Arendt and Camus speak, offers standards for guiding individual behavior that are critical for living and acting in a politically responsible manner. For students attempting to make sense out of a political environment that appears senseless, the work of Arendt and Camus offers direction and heightened self-consciousness. The behavioralist performs an important function in observing human behavior, but the contemporary political philosopher is not content with observation only, for, having observed the insanity of political behavior which appears to have no moral limits, he wants to fuse a moral conscience to the personal attitudes, disposition, and behavior of his audience.

THE VALUE OF POLITICAL PHILOSOPHY

There are some who would justify political philosophy on the grounds that it is personally gratifying. By providing room for creative analysis and political imagination, the argument goes, political philosophy creates an intimacy with ideas which is an end in itself. This position is not the best defense of the enterprise, however, because it fails to make political philosophy relevant to the hard facts of politics. What makes political philosophers "political" is their concern with issues related to the nature of politics and the organization of political life. This is true, as we have argued, for utopian and pragmatic thinkers alike.

Elites can be affected by the recommendations of political philosophers, whether in states undergoing revolutionary changes, newly formed states in former colonial territories, or stable societies. In this century alone, Marx's recommendations have had a remarkably great influence on the developing states of Africa. His artistic preference has greatly encouraged political leaders to be artists—to "make" states with an eye to ends rather than means. Who can fail to see the Soviet Union as an artistic representation of Marx's hypothetical political community, and the transformation of Che Guevara into the model revolutionary citizen as an effort by Castro to breathe life into Marx's hypothetical man?

A political philosopher's recommendations are accepted not because they are true in a scientific sense, but because they hold out promise that the persistent crises of politics may yet be solved if a new direction is

[24] Albert Camus, *The Rebel* (New York: Vintage Books, 1956), p. 292.

taken. The philosopher must find new ways of coping with the disorders he observes around him. His is a unique function—to propose how political relationships ought to be changed and how men ought to behave to keep up with the tempo of their age. When a new political direction is necessary, it is of little consequence that "ought" statements cannot be scientifically validated or logically derived from the facts. On the other hand, the political philosopher may find scientific knowledge indispensable when formulating his recommendations. For example, knowledge of the conditions that increase toleration may bear directly on the philosophical recommendations to expand opportunities for participation within the American community.[25]

In conclusion, political philosophy should be seen as more than a stimulating enterprise that excites the mind to flights of imagination. Whether in the tradition of "making" or "doing" in political philosophy, philosophical recommendations will be necessary as long as man is unable to control his passions or the affairs of state. While political philosophy is fairly constant, political crises create surges of interest and activity. The crisis of urban America, where so many are clamoring for greater participation and control, is an invitation to find a new direction. Thus, the desire to find new ways to revitalize democracy—to make the forms of democracy a matter of practice—may be seen as an important impetus of student activism. In a very basic sense, the tracts that are being written within the student movement—analyzing problems, setting goals, and making recommendations for reform—are clear proof that political philosophy does not have to originate among the elders of the academy.

[25] Consider the type of philosophical recommendations that could be based on data from Samuel A. Stouffer, *Communism, Conformity, and Civil Liberties* (Gloucester, Mass.: Peter Smith, 1963).

I

THE CLASSICAL ERA:

THUCYDIDES,

PLATO,

AND ARISTOTLE

1

Causal Theory in Thucydides'
Peloponnesian War

WILLIAM T. BLUHM

The "Great Books" of our culture never go out of print because they have something to say about the concerns of
every generation. When contemporary insight and imagination dull, scholars and laymen perennially recur to the
classics for a fresh point of departure, new directions. In
recent years the break in political science with an unima-
ginative empiricism and an effort at "retheoretization" has
been leading students of politics to the classics of political
thought in search of theories for our time, conceptual systems and hypotheses to give order and meaning to empirical research. For example, as far back as 1934 Charles
Sherman showed how Aristotle's theory of tyranny could
be used to explain the emergence and characteristic features of Nazism, and to predict the conditions of its overthrow. And in 1952 Fred Kort attempted the quantification
of Aristotle's theory of revolution.[1] Then in 1954 Andrew

This article was originally published in *Political Studies,* 9 (February
1962), 15–35. It is reprinted here with the permission of the author
and of the publisher, Clarendon Press, Oxford, England.
[1] Charles L. Sherman, "A Latter-Day Tyranny in the Light of Aristotelian Prognosis," *American Political Science Review (APSR),* June
1934; Fred Kort, "The Qualification of Aristotle's Theory of Revolution," *APSR,* June 1952.

Hacker, in a brilliant article on the use and abuse of the "Great Books," urged more students of political ideas to leave off their essentially biographical and historical pursuits and join the work of building operational theories by mining the wisdom of the "Greats."[2] This essay presents the results of one such "mining" operation.

My object is to show that in Thucydides' *Peloponnesian War* there is to be found a cluster of orienting concepts and hypotheses which are pregnant for the study of the dynamics of national power in our time. This is so because Thucydides was a genius, because his times were much like our own—an age of the "breaking of nations"—and because his method of political analysis has much in common with that of today's behavioural science.

As the expansion of Soviet power today poses the possibility of world war and a threat to the world state system, so in ancient Greece did the rise of the Athenian Empire (organized like the Russian satellite system as a league of states) bring on a world war and threaten to destroy the Hellenic state system. And then as now, scholars were led by these events to inquire into the causes of imperialism and war, and into the foundations of national power and weakness. What human motives are the causes of political activity, particularly of aggressive expansion? Are these motives and the foreign policies produced by them conditioned by political and social institutions, and if so in what way? What is the connexion between the form of a society's political system and the society's power position in international politics?

Thucydides' answers to these questions constitute an arresting psychological theory of empire. And they are set forth in a conceptual framework which is intelligible and meaningful to the modern political scientist. Like our own social scientists, Thucydides learned his method from the natural scientists of his time, the Hippocratic doctors and Sophistic "psychologists."[3] He saw politics as a naturalistic process, characterized by the exercise of power and influence by man over man. He excluded teleological and metaphysical ideas from his frame of reference, and studied this process with naturalistic concepts of causation, viewing political man in the category of necessity rather than that of freedom.[4] And he sought to

---

[2] Andrew Hacker, "Capital and Carbuncles: The 'Great Books' Reappraised," *APSR*, September 1954.

[3] See John H. Finley, Jr., *Thucydides* (Cambridge: Harvard University Press, 1942), p. 69, ch. III, esp. pp. 98–99, 109–110, and p. 294; George B. Grundy, *Thucydides and the History of His Age* (Oxford: Basil Blackwell, 1948, 2d edition), vol. ii, pp. 35–37; Charles N. Cochrane, *Thucydides and the Science of History* (London: Oxford University Press, 1929), pp. 8–9, 26, 31–32, 146; Eric Voegelin, *Order and History*, vol. ii (Baton Rouge: Louisiana State University Press, 1957), pp. 453–458.

[4] See Thucydides, *Peloponnesian War*, 1.75–76; 3.45, 82, 84; 5.89–105; 6.18. All citations of this work are from the unabridged Crawley translation, N.Y.: Modern Library, 1951.

delineate constant or universal factors in the political process which have predictive value.[5]

THUCYDIDES' INTENTION

Thucydides' chief purpose was to reveal the dynamics of empire, the inner workings of the process of imperial growth and decline, conceived as a recurrent natural event. And his *Peloponnesian War* is a case study[6] of a prime example of empire, that of the fifth-century Athenian democracy, one of the greatest empires the world had known to that time. It focuses on the period of the empire's crisis, the Peloponnesian War of 431–404 B.C., which Thucydides describes as "the greatest movement (*kinesis*) yet known in history, not only of the Hellenes, but of a large part of the barbarian world —I had almost said of mankind."[7] The greatest empire as it culminates and decays produces the greatest conflict. And a careful description, a case study of so classic, so full-blown a particular is a useful way of revealing the universal. As John Finley puts it, Thucydides displays "that profoundest of Greek abilities, apparent alike in their literature and their art, the ability to convey the generic without falsifying the unique."[8] One case proves nothing, of course, about the universal, but we are treating Thucydides' findings only as hypotheses to be checked by the examination of many cases.

THUCYDIDES' USE OF THE CASE METHOD

It was from the methodology of the Hippocratic school of medicine which flourished in the Athens of his day that Thucydides learned the case method for collecting and presenting his material. He examined imperial development in the way that doctors studied disease, that is, as a dynamic natural process which may work upon an organism under certain conditions, producing profound changes in the operation of the organism's life processes, rising to a climax, subsiding, and perhaps leaving certain after effects of its passage through the body. Like the doctors, he believed that the best way to develop an understanding of the process was through careful description of particular cases of it. From such analysis could be built

---

[5] *Peloponnesian War,* 1.22.
[6] Thucydides describes his work as a *syngraphe,* which means simply something which is written, a book. Eric Voegelin thinks the translation "write-up," a term not very different from "case study" or "case history," well expresses Thucydides' intention, *Order and History,* vol. ii, p. 350.
[7] 1.1.
[8] Finley, *Thucydides,* p. 67.

up a picture of the typical course of empire, which could serve as an instrument for predicting the course of future cases of the "disease," especially of the times and severity of periods of crisis. He even borrowed from the Hippocratic vocabulary, as in his use of words like *prophasis* (exciting cause) and symptom. And, like the doctors, his emphasis was on diagnosis and prognosis rather than on therapy—his book was to be primarily an instrument for interpretation rather than of manipulation and control.[9]

The study opens with an introductory section which students of Thucydides have dubbed the "Archaeology." [10] This constitutes a brief review of several mild cases of the "disease" of power, and takes the form of a survey of the development of power in Hellas, and the magnitude of past power, from Homeric times to the Persian Wars. Between the lines appears in summary form Thucydides' theory of the causes and structure of empire, or rather a preview of it. He then introduces the reader to the case which is to be examined in detail, the case of the Athenian Empire. He describes the onset of the "disease" as a result of the Persian Wars, and then speaks of the rapid development of Athenian power to a condition of crisis. Next he describes all the circumstances surrounding the beginning of the critical period, the Peloponnesian War, and he distinguishes the real causes from the apparent causes of the crisis.[11] He then goes back and describes in detail the early stages of the "sickness" up to the outbreak of the war. This is the section known as the "Pentekontaetia," the story of the development of Athenian power in the fifty years between the end of the Persian Wars and the beginning of the Peloponnesian War.[12] Then after a description of the opening movements of the war comes a lengthy treatise on the "symptoms" of the crisis period, all the events of the war, which constitutes the bulk of the book.[13] Finally comes the break in the "fever" and the gradual termination of the "disease" with the failure of the Sicilian expedition and the exhaustion of Athenian financial resources.[14] The case study is not complete and breaks off suddenly in the midst of a description of some of the "terminal symptoms" of the "disease"—changes in the structure of the government of the metropolis of the declining empire and various desultory military operations. The book ends abruptly in the midst of an account of the twenty-first year of the twenty-seven-year war. We have to turn to the work of Xenophon for a description of the final "cure" of the "patient," who came very close to dying of the malady.

[9] See citations in note 5.
[10] 1.1–19.
[11] 1.19–88.
[12] 1.89–1.118.
[13] 1.119–7.41.
[14] 7.42–end.

A POLITICAL PSYCHOLOGY

What are the organizing concepts and the causal hypotheses about empire with which Thucydides interlines, explicitly and implicitly, this case study of imperial symptoms? The basic theory is motivational, a political psychology. And on this foundation is built up a theory of the elements of imperial power and a theory of the causes of imperial development and decline.

Three impulses in particular, Thucydides believed, move all men to engage in political activity, that is, to seek control over others or to submit to another's control. These are (1) the desire for security or safety (*asphaleia*), (2) the drive for honour, prestige, or glory (*doxa, time*), and (3) the desire for gain or profit—wealth and the material well-being which it brings (*ophelia, kerdos*). Thucydides often employs the term "fear" (*phobos, deos*) interchangeably with the expressions "security" and "safety" (*asphaleia*) since the desire for security manifests itself as fear of the loss of this value. Similarly, when Thucydides speaks of vengeance (*timoria*) as a basic motive he appears to view it as a sub-class of the honour drive (*time*) —a hurt suffered at the hands of another constitutes a slight to my honour, which gives rise in my heart to the desire for revenge.[15]

The pages of the *History* are studded with references to these forces. They are the prime movers of the world of politics, and they appear over and over again, both in the speeches and in the words of the narrator. Thus in the Funeral Oration, Thucydides makes Pericles say that in the maintenance of law and order "fear is our chief safeguard."[16] In speaking of the causes of the war, Thucydides himself says that Spartan fear was the chief agent: "The real cause I consider to be the one which was formally most kept out of sight. The growth of the power of Athens, and the alarm which this inspired in Lacedaemon, made war inevitable."[17]

Ambassadors from Corcyra, seeking an alliance with Athens, tell the Athenians that there are few states which come asking for help that "can give in the way of security and honour as much as they hope to receive."[18] In relating in the "Archaeology" how the early states of Greece were formed, Thucydides says that "love of gain would reconcile the weaker to the dominion of the stronger."[19] All three motives are mentioned together by the Athenian envoys at Sparta before the war: "And the nature of the case first compelled us to advance our empire to its present height; fear being our principal motive, though honour and interest afterwards came

[15] See 2.42, 3.38, 3.40, 3.82, 4.62, 7.68.
[16] 2.37.
[17] 1.23.
[18] 1.33.
[19] 1.8.

in." [20] And in the passage immediately following this one they are referred to as "three of the strongest motives" (or, "the three strongest motives").

Is there a hierarchy amongst "fear, honour, and interest"? Is one more powerful than another? In the event of a conflict, which wins? In answer to these questions, Thucydides gives us two hierarchies—an irrational ordering and a rational ordering, which are posited as valid both for individuals and for groups of individuals organized as states. When the drives are irrationally ordered, honour, particularly in the form of vengeance, is more powerful than either desire for riches or safety. This pattern produces policies which ultimately frustrate all the drives, both of individuals, when they act only as individuals, and of groups. When reason, the calculating factor, conditions the drives, it induces a recognition that self-preservation and safety are necessarily prior to the enjoyment of wealth or honour, so in the rational hierarchy security is the most powerful drive. This produces policies which optimize all the values. For individuals acting as parts of a group, however, the rational and irrational orderings are the same. The individual seeks honour by risking personal safety for the security of the state. Reason dictates that the safety of the state is a precondition of individual safety, interest, and honour. In this case honour may be obtained by posthumous recognition by the group, e.g. by a funeral eulogy and magnificent burial, even though the safety drive be frustrated.[21]

Rational motivation depends on conditions in the social environment. Times of distress, and of violent conflict, in particular times of war and revolution, or plague, destroy reason and permit the irrational hierarchy to assert itself.[22] Also, excessive deprivation of a basic value, such as occurs in extreme poverty, will lead to a reckless pursuit of that value. And at the other extreme, satiety, or complete fulfilment of one of the basic drives, will lead to the irrational pursuit of the value next highest in the hierarchy. Thus "plenty fills [men] with ambition which belongs to insolence and pride," and the impulse arises "to drive men into danger." [23] The iron necessity of the passions in these circumstances replaces the freedom of reason. And the result is the final frustration of the passionate person or state.

It should be clear that in Thucydides' view of things power is a splendid instrument for obtaining the basic goods, but only this. Men do not seek power—control over the actions and resources of others—for its own sake, but for the security, wealth, and glory which it can bring. It is true that Thucydides describes the tendency for men to seek power in very strong terms, as "a necessary law of their nature." [24] But this is not because of a satisfaction inherent in the exercise of power, but because power is the

[20] 1.75.
[21] See 2.44, 1.75 & 76, 4.17, 4.87, 4.63, 4.65, and cf. 2.45 with 2.60 and 2.65.
[22] 3.82.
[23] See 3.45 & 46.
[24] 5.105.

surest safeguard of the basic goods. It is not always an available instrument, however. Sometimes rational policy requires submission rather than efforts at domination or resistance, if safety and wealth at least are to be protected.[25] Thus political activity of all kinds—the pursuit of power, resistance to power, submission to power—is derived from the three primary impulses.

The type of political activity which will result from any particular impulse, abstractly considered, is indeterminate. It will vary according to the circumstances. If unguided by reason there will be one result. If reason is present to channel the impulses, any one of a variety of actions may result, depending on the assessment of the possibilities in the situation. Thus, the safety drive may at one time result in behaviour aimed at the creation of imperial power, at another in behaviour aimed at the development of power by alliance, at still another in a policy of isolation and avoidance of alliances, at another in submissive behaviour. At one time it may result in a policy of peace, at another in a policy of war. It may lead either to the identification of an individual with a power group or to his opposition to the group.[26] Similarly, the behaviour produced by the desire for gain will vary, according to the circumstances, from submission to empire-building.[27] And the glory drive may lead to policies of empire or alliance, depending on the situation.[28] Unlike the other two impulses, however, at least when groups are concerned, the passion for glory can never produce submissive behaviour. Though, so far as individuals are concerned, if there is a close identity with the group, submission to the policies of the group may help the group to win glory which can be vicariously enjoyed by the individual.

Despite this indeterminacy of the behaviour resulting from any one motive taken alone, Thucydides believed, as we have shown, that the three motives taken together account for all the main types of political behaviour. Whether it is behaviour of domination, submission, resistance, or alliance, it can always be traced back to one or a complex of the three primary things—fear, honour, or interest.[29]

Thucydides' trilogy of political motives is, of course, no great

[25] 1.8.
[26] See 1.75, 1.76, 9.97, 6.83, 1.33, 1.123, 2.37, 4.62, 1.141, 3.70, 6.92.
[27] 1.8, 1.75, 1.76.
[28] 1.75, 1.76, 1.22.
[29] I have pieced together Thucydides' theory of motivation from his own statements and also from the things said about human motives by the various speakers in the book—Pericles, Diodotus, Alcibiades, etc. This is a proper way to proceed, of course, only if Thucydides and his speakers share the same psychological theory or if the speeches reveal psychological patterns which are also described in the narrative. On this point I accept the authority of John Finley and David Grene, who argue that this is a correct way to get at Thucydides' theory. See John H. Finley, *Thucydides*, pp. 100–104, 296–299, esp. p. 100, and David Grene, *Man in his Pride* (Chicago: University of Chicago Press, 1950), chaps. 3, 6, esp. pp. 34, 66.

revelation to the modern student of politics. "Fear, honour, and interest"
are well-known drives whose importance has been recognized in all the
"Great Books" of our political tradition from the fifth century B.C. to our
own time. Naturalists like Machiavelli and Hobbes in particular have
stressed their importance and have used them as foundation stones in their
own theoretical structures. In the writings of modern social scientists like
Harold Lasswell and Gardner Murphy they appear with such labels as
"safety, income, and deference," and "gain and prestige." [30] And in the effort of Shils and Parsons to construct a model for analysing human behaviour, Thucydidean "fear," renamed "anxiety," plays a most important role.[31]
What remains unique in Thucydides' theory, however, is the dual hierarchy he establishes amongst the motives, his description of the social
conditions under which the two patterns arise, and the connexion of these
patterns with both political forms and the rise and decline of national
power. Let us see now what Thucydides has to say about the relationship
of "fear, honour, and interest" to democratic institutions and to empire.

A THEORY OF IMPERIAL DEMOCRACY

Thucydides describes navies, capital, and commerce as the most important
material foundations of empire. But they are only the immediate or proximate causes of power. And all are radically dependent variables, dependent
not only on one another, but on a whole range of other more primary factors. These primary factors Thucydides believed to be those intangible,
often obscure, psychological traits—moral and intellectual qualities—
which we today usually label "national character." The roots of power are
in the minds and souls of men, and also in the political and social institutions which condition and influence these minds and souls.[32]

One complex of traits that is indicated by Thucydides as vital for the
citizens of a flourishing empire comprises all the things which Machiavelli,
writing twenty centuries later, summed up in the concept "virtu." Thucydides himself uses no label for this group of characteristics, but merely describes its elements individually in those portions of the History devoted to
a comparative analysis of the Athenian and Spartan characters.

The central qualities in this important group are a spirit of innovation, coupled with imagination, daring, optimism, high intelligence, energy,

[30] See Harold Lasswell, "World Politics and Personal Insecurity," in *A Study of Power*
(New York: The Free Press, 1950), p. 3; Gardner Murphy and others, *Human Nature and
Enduring Peace* (N.Y.: Houghton-Mifflin Co., 1945), p. 30.
[31] See Talcott Parsons and Edward A. Shils, eds., *Toward a General Theory of Action*
(Cambridge: Harvard University Press; London: Oxford University Press, 1951).
[32] See John H. Finley, "The Unity of Thucydides' History" in *Harvard Studies in Classical Philology*, supplementary vol. I (Cambridge: Harvard University Press, 1940),
pp. 225–297, which suggested several elements of the following analysis.

a capacity to act swiftly, and a capacity for hard work. At the outbreak of
the war the Corinthians chide their Spartan allies for their lack of these
qualities and for their ultra-conservative spirit as compared with the progressive mentality of their Athenian adversaries:

> The Athenians are addicted to innovation, and their designs are character-
> ized by swiftness alike in conception and execution; you have a genius for
> keeping what you have got, accompanied by a total want of invention . . .
> your wont is to attempt less than is justified by your power, to mistrust
> even what is sanctioned by your judgment, and to fancy that from danger
> there is no release. Further, there is promptitude on their side against pro-
> crastination on yours; they are never at home, you are never far from it; for
> they hope by their absence to extend their acquisitions, you fear by your
> advance to endanger what you have left behind. They are swift to follow
> up a success, and slow to recoil from a reverse . . . The deficiency created
> by the miscarriage of an undertaking is soon filled up by fresh hopes; for
> they alone are enabled to call a thing hoped for a thing got, by the speed
> with which they act upon their resolutions . . . to describe their character
> in a word, one might truly say that they were born into the world to take
> no rest themselves and to give none to others.[33]

The Corinthian speaker then adds that in times of change such a progressive spirit is not only important but essential for political success:

> It is the law as in art, so in politics, that improvements ever prevail; and
> though fixed usages may be best for undisturbed communities, constant ne-
> cessities of action must be accompanied by the constant improvement of
> methods.[34]

Pericles, in the Funeral Oration, is also made to praise the daring
and innovatory spirit of the Athenians as a significant power factor.[35] And
many of the successful Athenian strategies related by Thucydides, such as
the occupation of Pylos which resulted in a turning of the Spartan flank,
and innovations in the art of naval warfare, can be understood as illustrations of the effect of this quality. At the end of the book, even while re-
counting the decline of Athenian fortunes after the exhausting Sicilian disaster, Thucydides underlines once more the importance of Athenian "dash
and enterprise" and of Sparta's "slowness and want of energy," by showing
how these things were responsible for Sparta's failure to follow up an advantage gained by the capture of Euboea in the twenty-first year of the
war. Use of the opportunity so afforded would have put the whole Athenian empire in Sparta's power. But it was lost. And the Athenians by their
quick recovery were able to drag on the war for six more years. In this
context Thucydides makes the important point that it was after all not the

[33] 1.70.
[34] 1.71.
[35] 2.40.

Spartans but the Syracusans, "who were most like the Athenians in character," who, in their management of the defence of Sicily, were the real agents of Athenian defeat.

What we have said so far should not be taken to mean that Thucydides found no place in his catalogue of power for a wise spirit of moderation and conservatism. It was only excess of conservatism, unaccompanied by any fire or enterprise, that he called weakness. The most durable, as well as the greatest power comes to states which can combine "daring and deliberation," to use a phrase from the Funeral Oration.[36] Also, the qualities of liberality and generosity—doing for others as well as for yourself—which go along with moderation, or may be considered aspects of this quality, are described as elements of power, equally with daring, acquisitiveness, and the drive to "get ahead." [37]

Athens in the height of her power, in the Periclean period, combined both drive and moderation, or the ethos of progress and the ethos of conservatism, in an optimum fashion. Evidence of this is found in the policies pursued by Pericles as leader of the Ecclesia.

> As long as he was at the head of the state during the peace, he pursued a moderate and conservative policy; and in his time its greatness was at its height. When the war broke out, here also he seems to have rightly gauged the power of his country . . . He told them to wait quietly, to pay attention to their marine, to attempt no new conquests, and to expose the city to no hazards during the war, and doing this, promised them a favourable result.[38]

There was no "hybris," no overweening pride and arrogance, to be found in his policies. What Archidamus, the Spartan king, had pointed to as a key element of Spartan power—"a wise moderation; thanks to it we do not become insolent in success" [39] was also at this time an element of Athenian power, although it was combined with the daring and acquisitiveness which Sparta lacked.

In terms of Thucydides' psychological theory, during the Periclean period, Athenian policy flowed from a mentality characterized by a rational ordering of the primary motives—in the making of foreign policy cool calculation tempered the honour drive with the security drive, the result being the maintenance of commitments in balance with power, and hence the maximization of power. But Thucydides shows us that after the death of Pericles a new type of leadership asserted itself in Athenian affairs. After Pericles came Cleon and Alcibiades, and with them a spirit of acquisitiveness and recklessness unrestrained. The rational ordering of mo-

[36] 2.40.
[37] 2.40.
[38] 2.65.
[39] 1.84.

tives gave way to the irrational, and the blind drives of honour and interest took precedence over all considerations of security. And thus the decision on the Sicilian expedition, and disaster. Daring, unsupported by
moderation, from being the strong arm of Athenian power, became its
Achilles heel.

What caused this sudden change in Athenian policy and leadership
after the death of Pericles? Can the new kind of leadership be related to
some alteration in Athenian national character? If so, what were the foundations of Athenian mentality in the Periclean period, and what produced
the changes in that mentality in the post-Periclean period? Some commentators on the *History* have said that Thucydides treated leadership as a
random variable in politics. Thus Mortimer Chambers says that it was "the
inability of the Athenian leaders to work together that—in Thucydides'
view—ended the Athenian empire." [40] And Eric Voegelin tells us that
"such failure of personal leadership that lost a war which by military calculation should have been won, Thucydides is inclined to consider accidental, an unpredictable misfortune." [41] But others such as John Finley
have written that Thucydides viewed political leadership as a function of
the psychological tone of a community, and further that he believed that
the tone of a community in turn depends upon social and political institutions. Thus it is Athenian democracy which is singled out as the cause, at
one point in its development, of intelligent moderation in the Athenian
people, and hence of Periclean leadership; and as the cause, at another
point in its development, of frantic imperialism, and thus of Cleon and Alcibiades.[42] And the second I think is the better view; Thucydides quite
clearly derives the personalities of leaders from national character, and relates national character in turn to social, economic, and political institutions, as we shall see.

A significant statement of Thucydides' doctrine on this matter is
found in the famous Oration of Pericles at the funeral of the Athenian soldiers who died in the first year of the war. Only a part of the Oration, and
the smaller part at that, sings the praises of the dead. Most of it constitutes
a eulogy and analysis of the institutions of Athenian society. Pericles
speaks with praise of four Athenian institutions: (1) equality before the
law, (2) commerce, (3) individual freedom in manner of life and education,
(4) democratic policy-making processes. With these institutions he associates "refinement without extravagance," "knowledge without effeminacy,"
"liberality," "courage," the employment of wealth "more for use than for
show," "daring and deliberation," "generosity," "versatility,"—in short, the
mentality of moderate progressiveness, the character of the "golden mean."

[40] "Thucydides and Pericles," *Harvard Studies in Classical Philology*, lxii (Cambridge:
Harvard University Press, 1957), p. 87.
[41] "Thucydides and Pericles," p. 363.
[42] "The Unity of Thucydides' History," pp. 284–290.

And he winds up this portion of the Oration with the statement that these "habits"—institutions and traits of national character—were the foundation of the empire.[43] He seems to tell us that every member of the Athenian democracy could, because of the institutional pattern, hope for the satisfaction of the three principal drives: equality before the law gave him security against arbitrary treatment by his fellows; the "openness" of Athenian society gave opportunity to a man of talent to rise to the highest position, and to satisfy the honour drive; and Athenian commerce made jobs for all and a high standard of material well-being. From their recognition of these opportunities derived the acquisitiveness and initiative of Athenians, their great energy and optimism, and their capacity for hard work. Everyone was "on the make." Hence daring and a willingness to experiment and innovate—the poor boy on his way up has nothing to lose and all to gain; his life is a process of change in itself, from one social condition to another.

The system of free education coupled with the democratic decision-making process developed intelligence, initiative, and a capacity for careful calculation. Athenians acquired from these institutions the habit of reflecting on their situation, of thinking before acting. Their behaviour became based on thought rather than passion, on a rational appraisal of alternatives of behaviour as related to individual interest.

Out of the process of interest calculation the Athenian arrived at the realization that his individual good depended upon the good of the state —that the power and glory of Athens, and the strength of her democratic institutions were the source of his own satisfaction. And thus emerged a mentality of enlightened self-interest. Everyone recognized that his own success depended upon following the rules of the democratic game and co-operating with his fellows in the joint enterprise of building a powerful Athens. Thus individual aggressiveness became coupled with a spirit of moderation, of "live and let live" in civic relationships, with patriotism, co-operativeness, and a willingness to work hard for the state. And liberality arose from the self-confidence and ease which flow from wealth and power. In foreign affairs these same traits carried over into a policy of moderate imperialism. In sum, the result was a "golden mean" character in all things.

The personality and policies of Pericles himself epitomized the spirit of enlightened self-interest produced by the democracy. And his analysis of the Athenian democratic system was the natural product of that system. As leader of the state he made articulate the commonly-held understanding of the system's ideology which he expressed so eloquently in the Funeral Oration. The Oration was a reminder to Athenians of their own nature, of the kind of men they were. As he closed his eulogy of Athenian life Pericles said, "Such is the Athens for which these men, in the assertion of their resolve not to lose her, nobly fought and died." His picture of Athens was the

[43] 2.41.

same picture as that carried in the minds of the men who had perished. The death of these men on the battlefield was not an act of blind devotion to duty, but an act of enlightened interest—an act based on the knowledge that without it neither Athenian power, nor the democratic institutions which made life good could be secure; while in death glory, the greatest good, could still be theirs:

> For this offering of their lives made in common by them all they each of them individually received that renown which never grows old, and for a sepulchre, not so much that in which their bones have been deposited, but that noblest of shrines wherein their glory is laid up to be eternally remembered upon every occasion on which deed or story shall fall for its commemoration.[44]

In summary, the greatest power, supreme empire, according to Thucydides, rests on a foundation of democracy, "golden-mean" national character, commerce, wealth, and naval power, building blocks which rise one upon the other in the order given. Power resting on other bases cannot reach an equivalent magnitude. One might logically ask at this point what conditions give rise to democratic institutions—the primary building block. Surely they are not a random occurrence. But Thucydides' theory does not extend this far.

Athens' great rival, Sparta, an oligarchic, conservative, agrarian land power, though she finally won the war, never exercised as wide a sway as the imperial democracy. The Spartans, living as a small ruling class in the midst of subject peoples—the Perioeci and Helots—who performed the agricultural and commercial functions of the society, never developed the system of free education and the spirit of individualism that were so important in the making of Athenian power. A government which derives from an experience of tribal conquest, a rigid caste separation of the conquering from the conquered people, and the maintenance of control by sheer force of arms, cannot afford such freedom, but requires iron discipline—a regimented ruling class—in order to survive. Attica, because of the poverty of her soil in tribal times, was free of war and faction, and hence developed as a free association. In pre-democratic times her ruling aristocracy was not, as in the case of Sparta, a conquering warrior tribe. And by the fifth century, as we have seen, Athens became an "open" society. There was no ruling class.

Spartan education put a premium on rigid conformity to a model of dogged military courage and blind devotion to the state. The idea of the individual as independent, self-reliant, thinking, calculating, had no place in such a society. Hence intelligence and imagination were stultified and in contrast to the Athenian love of innovation the attitude that predominated

[44] 2.43.

was one of firm attachment to the status quo. Such power could be Sparta's as comes from a sense of order and from unthinking, habitual subordination of the individual to the group, from an ethos of self-control and courage deriving from military discipline. The higher flight is reserved for democratic power.

The highest flight is not necessarily the longest, however. Athenian power was short-lived, lasting in all about fifty years. To what did Thucydides attribute the loss of the war and destruction of the empire?

Paradoxically, Thucydides found in the very democratic institutions which were the ultimate source of her power the key to the instability of that power.[45] The *History's* implicit argument on this point may be reconstructed thus.—The immediate cause of the destruction of the Athenian empire was the failure of the Sicilian expedition and the attendant factionalism and civil disorders which exhausted the physical and moral resources of the state. The expedition failed for several reasons. In the first place it was an undertaking of very great magnitude which constituted a grave risk in view of the commitments of her power which Athens had already made. Pericles would not have dreamed of such a venture. It was undertaken without any clear knowledge of the resources of the opponent—"most of the [Athenians] being ignorant of [the island's] size and the number of its inhabitants, Hellenic and barbarian, and of the fact that they were undertaking a war not much inferior to that against the Peloponnesians." [46] And the logistics for the war were incorrectly calculated. What had happened to the famed Athenian intelligence and capacity for careful deliberation?

Rash as the scheme was, Thucydides says that the expedition might have succeeded had it been properly directed and supported.[47] Three generals were sent to conduct the war—Alcibiades, Nicias, and Lamachus. Of the three, Alcibiades and Nicias were the most important. Thucydides says nothing of the effect of Lamachus' actions on the course of events, and he records that he was killed early in the campaign. While both Alcibiades and Nicias had certain good qualities, these were offset in each case by a radical deficiency of character which made effective leadership impossible. Alcibiades was the abler of the two, a man of great intelligence, and a clever, imaginative, and daring strategist. But he was self-centred, of questionable patriotism, inordinately ambitious for personal power, wealth, and fame, ruthless, ostentatious, and licentious. His undesirable qualities

---

[45] Cf. Peter Fliess, "Political Disorder and Constitutional Form," *The Journal of Politics*, November 1959, esp. pp. 615–618, which parallels my exposition from this point to my summary below of Thucydides' theory of empire. Fliess stresses the connexion seen by Thucydides between democracy and Athenian moral decline and weakness, but he neglects the contribution of democracy to the *rise* of Athenian power. And he fails to show why demagogic leadership and moral decay set in only after Pericles' death rather than earlier.

[46] 6.1.

[47] 2.65.

gained him the hatred of many and the suspicion of all. At a critical moment in the Sicilian campaign, Alcibiades was recalled to Athens to stand trial for sacrilege and a conspiracy against the democracy, and the state was thereby deprived of his abilities. As Thucydides puts it, "his habits gave offence to every one, and caused them to commit affairs to other hands, and thus before long to ruin the city." [48]

Nicias was everything that Alcibiades was not. On the positive side he was honest, patriotic, just to his fellow citizens and religious. Thucydides tells us that "the whole course of his life had been regulated with strict attention to virtue." [49] He was also a man of some intelligence and foresight. But he did not have a forceful and persuasive personality. And he was entirely lacking in decision and daring, even when pressed into a corner. He thought constantly in defensive terms and fought a defensive war because of his unduly cautious nature. He had a passion for avoiding any dangerous enterprise. The difficulties involved in any offensive action always loomed larger in his mind than the possibilities of success. And he had little inventiveness and imagination. Thus each one of the chief leaders of the Sicilian expedition was badly balanced; in each, one aspect of the Athenian nature predominated at the expense of the contrasting and tempering qualities. And it was this imperfect leadership which caused the Athenians to lose the campaign and ultimately the war.

Can we go behind the factor of leadership to find a still more fundamental cause of the failure, the cause of the faulty leadership itself? Thucydides indicates that we should look for such a cause in the mentality of the Athenian society as a whole, that the perversions of the leaders reflected the perversions of the Athenian character as such.

In the last days of Pericles' leadership, and more especially after his death, Athenian national character underwent a disastrous transformation. The rational, balanced ordering of "fear, honour, and interest" in the private lives and public policies of the Athenians gave way to untempered passion—to honour, in the form of overweening pride, dominating action at one moment, excessive fear and attendant suspicion ruling the next. Now what appealed was any wild scheme, no matter how hazardous, which promised greater power and riches and glory. Thucydides depicts in detail the irrational "Castles in Spain" atmosphere of the Assembly which took the decision to invade Sicily. Nicias tried to bring Athenians out of their daydream by pointing out the grave risks and asking how often success was "got by wishing and how often by forecast." [50] Then, seeing that they were nevertheless intent on the venture, he attempted to spoil their taste for it by describing in great detail the enormous force and amount of money necessary for success. But to no avail. They became all the more

[48] 6.15.
[49] 7.86.
[50] 6.13.

anxious to try it.[51] And the decision was taken on the advice of Alcibiades, the man of pride and ambition.

Coupled with this megalomania was an equally irrational, indeed paranoiac, fear. Thucydides writes that after the expedition had departed, the Athenians conducted an investigation into the sacrilege and alleged anti-democratic plot in which Alcibiades was implicated. And they proceeded in an almost hysterical way. "Instead of testing the informers, in their suspicious temper [they] welcomed all indifferently, arresting and imprisoning the best citizens upon the evidence of rascals . . . They were always in fear and took everything suspiciously." [52]

Out of their fear they recalled Alcibiades to stand trial, and this removed their ablest man from the leadership of the expedition, and left in charge Nicias, the man of fear and excessive caution.

Thus irrational fear and irrational ambition alternately dominated Athenian policy. And with the new irrationalism came a narrow selfishness and complete loss of the old public spirit. As Thucydides put it, the Athenians allowed "private ambitions and private interests . . . to lead them into projects unjust both to themselves and to their allies—projects whose success would only conduce to the honour and advantage of private persons, and whose failure entailed certain disaster on the country in the war." [53] The new spirit was clearly reflected in the leaders who chose to occupy "themselves with private cabals . . . by which they not only paralysed operations in the field, but also introduced civil discord at home." [54] And the treason of Alcibiades, who defected to the enemy when recalled to Athens, was its most prominent symbol.

This corruption of character and loss of unity were the product of three things—the empire, the war, and the plague. We have already noted above [55] that according to Thucydides' theory, human rationality is always a tenuous and delicate affair. Two sets of conditions in particular threaten rational policy—great deprivation of the "three greatest things," or some one of them, and over-satisfaction of the three basic drives, or some one of them. In the case of Athens, both sets of conditions, paradoxically, seem to have existed at the same time. On the one hand the war, which forced the Attic yeomanry to abandon their homes and farms to the enemy and retreat within the walls of the city to live in crowded squalor, and the plague which followed upon this action, gave rise to an excessive and irrational fear, to an over-concern with the private good, and this led to moral breakdown and disunity. Thucydides speaks of the

[51] 6.24.
[52] 6.53.
[53] 2.65.
[54] 2.65.
[55] p. 120.

lawless extravagance which owed its origin to the plague. Men now coolly ventured on what they had formerly done in a corner, and not just as they pleased, seeing the rapid transitions produced by persons in prosperity suddenly dying and those who before had nothing succeeding to their property. So they resolved to spend quickly and enjoy themselves, regarding their lives and riches as alike things of a day . . . Fear of the gods or law of man there was none to restrain them.[56]

And with reference to the devastations of the war:

As private individuals they could not help smarting under their sufferings, the common people having been deprived of the little that they ever had possessed, while the higher orders had lost fine properties with costly establishments and buildings in the country.[57]

For a while, Pericles, by the weight of his personality, could force this frightened people to reflect and be calm, to face their fear, and recognize its irrationality—as long as the navy and empire were safe, Athens was secure and these private losses could be recouped. But after his death the irrational fear ran its course untrammelled. And since at the same time Athenians were enjoying an unheard-of national prosperity and the glory of being the first power in Hellas, *hybris* arose—overweening pride and arrogance, the feeling that, having won so much, anything was possible; so a wild passion for unlimited acquisition seized them. This new spirit is most graphically shown in the speeches of the Athenian envoys in the famous Melian dialogue.—"The strong do what they can and the weak suffer what they must." [58] And in his speech of warning about the Sicilian expedition Nicias makes reference to it. "Your unexpected success, as compared with what you feared at first, has made you suddenly despise [the Spartans and their allies], tempting you further to aspire to the conquest of Sicily." [59] Thus, just as Pericles had been the product of their reason, and had braced that reason by the power of his personality and rhetorical ability, so later leaders simply mirrored their unreason—Alcibiades their pride and ambition, Nicias their fear.

Now, why was it that only Pericles stood between Athenians and the abyss which their irrational passions were to plunge them into? Why was no other individual able to bring them back to reason? And why was Athenian reason so terribly dependent on an individual and on circumstances of peace, quiet, and moderate prosperity? Apparently because Athenian institutions offered no bulwark to reason. Democracy might facilitate the creation of great power, but it was helpless to maintain it. Athenian rational-

[56] 2.53.
[57] 2.65.
[58] 5.89.
[59] 6.11.

ity rested on enlightened self-interest, which the institutions of democracy could produce but not sustain. Such a conscious, calculated awareness of the relationship between the individual good and the common good, and of the need for social unity and for cool and moderate policies was too fragile a thing to stand up in the face of the pressures of fear and honour deriving from the empire, the war, and the plague.

An unthinking people like the Spartans, whose reason—that is, whose devotion to the common good and spirit of moderation—resided in habits inculcated from the cradle by the stern authoritarian institutions of their closed society rather than in the conscious self-control of individuals, was insulated from the disrupting effects of extreme fear and pride. In the light of the Sicilian disaster and its sequel, the words of Archidamus at the beginning of the war about Spartan traditions take on a special significance:

> The quality which they condemn is really nothing but a wise moderation; thanks to its possession, we alone do not become insolent in success and give way less than others in misfortune; we are not carried away by the pleasure of hearing ourselves cheered on to risks which our judgment condemns; nor, if annoyed, are we any the more convinced by attempts to exasperate us by accusation. We are both warlike and wise, and it is our sense of order that makes us so . . . We are educated with too little learning to despise the laws, and with too severe a self-control to disobey them, and are brought up not to be too knowing in useless matters . . . The superiority lies with him who is reared in the severest school. These practices, then, which our ancestors have delivered to us, and by whose maintenance we have always profited, must not be given up.[60]

The conscious self-control which goes with the kind of free or open society represented by Athens is possible only in the absence of extreme compulsions of fear or pride. It gives way before them like a house of cards. But the man in whom a rigid discipline has bred a habit of moderate and dutiful behaviour can stand such storms without faltering. Spartan power, although not as great as Athenian, proved in the end more durable—and Spartan institutions, according to Thucydides, were no insignificant factor in the result.

We may summarize this theory of empire in the following set of propositions:

1. The foundation of the material elements of the power of a commercial and naval state, and of the ability to use them efficiently in the creation of empire, is a complex of psychological traits which has been epitomized in the ancient Athenian national character (a spirit of innovation, coupled with imagination, aggressiveness and daring [tempered by a spirit of moderation], and with optimism, high intelligence, energy, a capacity to act swiftly, a capacity for hard work, and a spirit of unity).

[60] 1.84–85.

2. A national character of this kind is causally related to the institutions of open, democratic, commercial, and secular societies such as Athens. More specifically, the institution of educational freedom, coupled with commerce with the opportunity for men of capacity to rise without hindrance to places of social, economic, and political prominence, and with equality before the law and of access to public policy-making institutions, give rise to and/or increase a spirit of unity and dedication to the state based on enlightened self-interest, naval skills, and developed intellectual power throughout the society.

3. The dominant psychological traits of an open and democratic society, and any change in these traits, are directly and immediately reflected in the character of the society's leaders.

4. The imperial power potential of such states is greater than that of any other type of state.

5. The actual imperial power of such states is very precarious, because of the absence of "insulating" devices in its institutions against the demoralizing effects of conditions such as war, plague, and sudden power, which work adversely on individual rationality and hence tend to destroy the rationality of policy.

6. Overstimulated passions paralyse the rationality of such societies and produce unduly aggressive or demagogic leaders and/or unduly timorous leaders, civil factions and selfishness, and megalomaniac foreign policies, all of which result in the destruction of the imperial power. An incidental effect of civil discord and loss of empire may be the modification of the constitution in an oligarchical direction.

7. The actual imperial power of closed states and oligarchies such as Sparta is more stable than democratic power because of the "insulation" such societies provided against the demoralizing effects of external factors such as war, plague, and empire.

8. The foundation of the material elements of power of an agrarian land power, and of the ability to use them effectively in the creation and maintenance of modest empire is a complex of psychological traits which has been epitomized in the Spartan national character (a spirit of iron discipline and devotion to the state, coupled with martial courage, asceticism, conservatism, moderation, and caution).

9. A national character of this kind is causally related to stratified, oligarchic, agricultural, and religious institutions. More specifically, the institution of a compulsory, rigid, uniform system of education and military training designed to unculcate military skills and a spirit of civic loyalty and obedience, coupled with ascetic equality in the citizen body, a static social system, institutions of communal living, and with a system of divided, checked, and balanced governmental authority gives rise to and/or increases a spirit of unity and loyalty to the state based on unthinking habit, military skills, martial courage, and cautious foreign policies.

10. The imperial power potential of such societies is less than that of democratic societies such as Athens because of the society's ultra-conservatism, lack of imagination and drive, and under-developed intellectual power.

Not all of these hypotheses, of course, are unique to Thucydides. Pareto, for example, made substantially the same observation as that contained in the first and sixth hypotheses when he wrote that it was a lack of "balance between the combination-instincts [61] and the residues of group persistence" in Athenian character which caused the Athenian foreign policy disasters.[62] But he did not explain the social conditions which account for the imbalance, while Thucydides, as we have seen, supplies us with a theory which explains the development and destruction of such a balanced national character. Similarly, while Pareto observed a correlation between periods of transition to democracy and "economic and political prosperity," he refused to admit the causal connexions between these, as specified in hypotheses 1 and 2. He wrote, for example, that "if the prosperity in question were due to different systems of government, the prosperity should continue as long as the new regime endured. But that is not the case . . . The Athens of Pericles declined very soon, while the form of government was becoming more and more democratic." [63] Thucydides' theory shows how democracy was a cause *both* of prosperity *and* of decline. And it does so by tying together the three variables of national power, national character, and the political and social system, while Pareto related only the first two factors. More recent social psychological theory, for instance, the work of Cartwright and Zander and of Turner and Killian,[64] has begun to focus on the relationship between motivation and social environment. But Thucydides' psychological theory of national power has not been reformulated and put to use as a research tool. And it deserves the attention of social scientists who are interested in the foundations of power.

As summarized above, Thucydides' theory is not stated in operational terms. Rapoport, for example, would call the hypotheses "provisionally meaningless." [65] Before they can be tested they will have to be refined further and "operationalized." But that, of course, is not the first but the last stage in the development of a theory.

It is also clear that we cannot expect to measure the extent and the stability of the power of states today by identifying particular nations either with the Spartan or the Athenian model, because we cannot expect to find "Athenian" or "Spartan" societies today in anything like a pure form.

[61] Pareto's expression "combination-instincts" is a shorthand way of referring to such traits as creative imagination, daring, aggressiveness, self-seeking individualism, and a spirit of shrewd calculation taken as a group. The "residues of group persistence" are by contrast the conservative characteristics of discipline, dogged courage, self-abnegation, faith in established institutions, reliance on force rather than on wit.
[62] Vilfredo Pareto, *The Mind and Society* (New York: Harcourt, Brace, and World, 1935, vol. iv), para. 2424.
[63] *The Mind and Society,* paras. 2485, 2486.
[64] See Dorwin Cartwright and Alvin Zander, eds., *Group Dynamics* (2d edition, New York: Harper & Row, 1960); Ralph H. Turner and Lewis M. Killian, *Collective Behavior* (Englewood Cliffs, N.J.: Prentice-Hall, Inc., 1957).
[65] See Anatol Rapoport, *Operational Philosophy* (New York: Harper, 1954), chap. 3.

Ours is an age of world-wide transition from agrarian to commercial and industrial economy. And all states will in one degree or another resemble the Athenian model, while retaining fewer or more institutional and psychological remains of an earlier traditional or "Spartan" period. But one may nevertheless use Thucydides' theory to classify particular *institutions* as creators or stabilizers of national power.

Also, despite the fact that Thucydides' theories seem to describe only a particular kind of power, empire, rather than national power as such, they can be applied meaningfully to more than the formal empires of today. Any state which, because of the military and economic power it is able to wield, can significantly influence the policies of other nations, roughly fits Thucydides' working definition of empire, whether or not the lines of its influence are formalized. The *History* explains Spartan as well as Athenian power, though the Peloponnesian League was not called an empire. And even the Athenian Empire was officially a league of states. Both the USA and USSR exercise hegemony, or are capable of exercising hegemony, in a wide area beyond their borders, although the coalitions which form the Western and Soviet blocs are not formally called empires.[66] And although the Western bloc today is a much looser affair than the Soviet system, and the Peloponnesian League rather than the Delian League would be the parallel to such organizations as OAS, SEATO, and NATO, the power of both American and Russian leadership derives, although in different proportions, from essentially the same sources—the military, economic, institutional, and moral resources of these states.

CONCLUSION

I have tried to demonstrate that the conceptual framework of Thucydides' *Peloponnesian War* and the relationships which Thucydides posits between motivation, political forms, and power can be fruitful tools for contemporary political analysis. And I believe that careful consideration of others of the "Great Books" will reveal a similar utility in them. Certainly the greatest minds in our intellectual history should be widely consulted by modern political scientists, who have the same human concerns as they. Their only fee is the time required for the careful and receptive reading of their work.

[66] See on this point Reinhold Niebuhr, *The Structure of Nations and Empires* (New York: Scribner, 1959), chap. 1.

2

Plato

LEO STRAUSS

Thirty-five dialogues and thirteen letters have come down to us as Platonic writings, not all of which are now regarded as genuine. Some scholars go so far as to doubt that any of the letters is genuine. In order not to encumber our presentation with polemics, we shall disregard the letters altogether. We must then say that Plato never speaks to us in his own name, for in his dialogues only his characters speak. Strictly, there is then no Platonic teaching; at most there is the teaching of the men who are the chief characters in his dialogues. Why Plato proceeded in this manner is not easy to say. Perhaps he was doubtful whether there can be a philosophic teaching proper. Perhaps he, too, thought like his master Socrates that philosophy is in the last analysis knowledge of ignorance. Socrates is indeed the chief character in most of the Platonic dialogues. One could say that Plato's dialogues as a whole are less the presentation of a teaching than a monument to the life of Socrates—to the core of his life: they all show how Socrates engaged in his most important work, the awaken-

This article was originally published in Leo Strauss and Joseph Cropsey (eds.), *History of Political Philosophy* (Chicago: Rand McNally, 1963), pp. 7–63. It is reprinted here with the permission of the author and of the publisher.

ing of his fellow men and the attempting to guide them toward the good life which he himself was living. Still, Socrates is not always the chief character in Plato's dialogues; in a few he does hardly more than listen while others speak, and in one dialogue (the *Laws*) he is not even present. We mention these strange facts because they show how difficult it is to speak of Plato's teaching.

All Platonic dialogues refer more or less directly to the political question. Yet there are only three dialogues which indicate by their very titles that they are devoted to political philosophy: the *Republic*, the *Statesman*, and the *Laws*. The political teaching of Plato is accessible to us chiefly through these three works.

THE REPUBLIC

In the *Republic*, Socrates discusses the nature of justice with a fairly large number of people. The conversation about this general theme takes place, of course, in a particular setting: in a particular place, at a particular time, with men each of whom has his particular age, character, abilities, position in society, and appearance. While the place of the conversation is made quite clear to us, the time, *i.e.*, the year, is not. Hence we lack certain knowledge of the political circumstances in which this conversation about the principles of politics takes place. We may assume, however, that it takes place in an era of political decay of Athens, that at any rate Socrates and the chief interlocutors (the brothers Glaukon and Adeimantos) were greatly concerned with that decay and thinking of the restoration of political health. Certain it is that Socrates makes very radical proposals of "reform" without encountering serious resistance. But there are also a few indications in the *Republic* to the effect that the longed-for reformation is not likely to succeed on the political plane or that the only possible reformation is that of the individual man.

The conversation opens with Socrates' addressing a question to the oldest man present, Kephalos, who is respectable on account of his piety as well as his wealth. Socrates' question is a model of propriety. It gives Kephalos an opportunity to speak of everything good which he possesses, to display his happiness, as it were, and it concerns the only subject about which Socrates could conceivably learn something from him: about how it feels to be very old. In the course of his answer Kephalos comes to speak of injustice and justice. He seems to imply that justice is identical with telling the truth and paying back what one has received from anyone. Socrates shows him that telling the truth and returning another man's property are not always just. At this point Kephalos' son and heir, Polemarchos, rising in defense of his father's opinion, takes the place of his father in the conversation. But the opinion which he defends is not exactly the same as his father's; if we may make use of a joke of Socrates', Polemarchos inherits only half, and perhaps even less than a half, of his father's intellectual property. Polemarchos no longer maintains that telling the truth is essential to justice. Without knowing it, he thus lays down one of the principles of the *Republic*. As appears later in the work, in a well-ordered society it is necessary that one tell untruths of a certain kind to children and even to the adult subjects.[1] This example reveals the character of the discussion which occurs in the first book of the *Republic*, where Socrates refutes a number of false opinions about justice. This negative or destructive work, however, contains within itself the constructive assertions of the bulk of the *Republic*. Let us consider from this point of view the three opinions on justice discussed in the first book.

Kephalos' opinion as taken up by Polemarchos (after his father had left to perform an act of piety) is to the effect that justice consists in returning deposits. More generally stated, Kephalos holds that justice consists in returning, leaving, or giving to everyone what belongs to him. But he also holds that justice is good, *i.e.*, salutary, not only to the giver but also to the receiver. Now it is obvious that in some cases giving to a man what belongs to him is harmful to him. Not all men make a good or wise use of what belongs to them, of their property. If we judge very strictly, we might be driven to say that very few people make a wise use of their property. If justice is to be salutary, we might be compelled to demand that everyone should own only what is "fitting" for him, what is good for him, and for as long as it is good for him. In brief, we might be compelled to demand the abolition of private property or the introduction of communism. To the extent to which there is a connection between private property and the family, we would even be compelled to demand abolition of the family or the introduction of absolute communism, *i.e.*, of communism not only regarding property but regarding women and children as well. Above all, extremely few people will be able to determine wisely which things and which amounts of them are good for the use of each individual —or at any rate for each individual who counts; only men of exceptional wisdom are able to do this. We would then be compelled to demand that society be ruled by simply wise men, by philosophers in the strict sense, wielding absolute power. The refutation of Kephalos' view of justice thus contains the proof of the necessity of absolute communism in the sense defined, as well as of the absolute rule of the philosophers. This proof, it is hardly necessary to say, is based on the disregard of, or the abstraction from, a number of most relevant things; it is "abstract" in the extreme. If we wish to understand the *Republic*, we must find out what these disregarded things are and why they are disregarded. The *Republic* itself, carefully read, supplies the answers to these questions.

[1] Plato, *Republic*, 377 ff., 389b–c, 414b–415d, 459c–d.

Before going any further, we must dispose of a misunderstanding which is at present very common. The theses of the *Republic* summarized in the two preceding paragraphs clearly show that Plato, or at any rate Socrates, was not a liberal democrat. They also suffice to show that Plato was not a Communist in the sense of Marx, or a Fascist: Marxist communism and fascism are incompatible with the rule of philosophers, whereas the scheme of the *Republic* stands or falls by the rule of philosophers. But let us hasten back to the *Republic*.

Whereas the first opinion on justice was only implied by Kephalos and stated by Socrates, the second opinion is stated by Polemarchos, although not without Socrates' assistance. Furthermore, Kephalos' opinion is linked in his mind with the view that injustice is bad because it is punished by the gods after death. This view forms no part of Polemarchos' opinion. He is confronted with the contradiction between the two opinions according to which justice must be salutary to the receiver and justice consists in giving to each what belongs to him. Polemarchos overcomes the contradiction by dropping the second opinion. He also modifies the first. Justice, he says, consists in helping one's friends and harming one's enemies. Justice thus understood would seem to be unqualifiedly good for the giver and for those receivers who are good to the giver. This difficulty, however, arises: If justice is taken to be giving to others what belongs to them, the only thing which the just man must know is what belongs to anyone with whom he has any dealing; this knowledge is supplied by the law, which in principle can be easily known by mere listening. But if the just man must give to his friends what is good for them, he himself must judge; he himself must be able correctly to distinguish friends from enemies; he himself must know what is good for each of his friends. Justice must include knowledge of a high order. To say the least, justice must be an art comparable to medicine, the art which knows and produces what is good for human bodies. Polemarchos is unable to identify the knowledge or the art which goes with justice or which is justice. He is therefore unable to show how justice can be salutary. The discussion points to the view that justice is the art which gives to each man what is good for his soul, *i.e.*, that justice is identical with, or at least inseparable from, philosophy, the medicine of the soul. It points to the view that there cannot be justice among men unless the philosophers rule. But Socrates does not yet state this view. Instead he makes clear to Polemarchos that the just man will help just men rather than his "friends," and he will harm no one. He does not say that the just man will help everyone. Perhaps he means that there are human beings whom he cannot benefit. But he surely also means something more. Polemarchos' thesis may be taken to reflect a most potent opinion regarding justice—the opinion according to which justice means public-spiritedness, full dedication to one's city as a particular society which as such is potentially the enemy of other cities. Justice so understood is patriotism, and consists indeed in helping one's friends, *i.e.*, one's fellow citizens, and harming one's enemies, *i.e.*, foreigners. Justice thus understood cannot be entirely dispensed with in any city however just, for even the most just city is a city, a particular or closed or exclusive society. Therefore Socrates himself demands later in the dialogue that the guardians of the city be by nature friendly to their own people and harsh or nasty to strangers.[2] He also demands that the citizens of the just city cease to regard all human beings as their brothers and limit the feelings and actions of fraternity to their fellow citizens alone.[3] The opinion of Polemarchos properly understood is the only one among the generally known views of justice discussed in the first book of the *Republic* which is entirely preserved in the positive or constructive part of the *Republic*. This opinion, to repeat, is to the effect that justice is full dedication to the common good; it demands that man withhold nothing of his own from his city; it demands therefore by itself—*i.e.*, if we abstract from all other considerations—absolute communism.

The third and last opinion discussed in the first book of the *Republic* is the one maintained by Thrasymachos. He is the only speaker in the work who exhibits anger and behaves discourteously and even savagely. He is highly indignant over the result of Socrates' conversation with Polemarchos. He seems to be particularly shocked by Socrates' contention that it is not good for oneself to harm anyone or that justice is never harmful to anyone. It is most important, both for the understanding of the *Republic* and generally, that we do not behave toward Thrasymachos as Thrasymachos behaves, *i.e.*, angrily, fanatically, or savagely. If we look then at Thrasymachos' indignation without indignation, we must admit that his violent reaction is to some extent a revolt of common sense. Since the city as city is a society which from time to time must wage war, and war is inseparable from harming innocent people,[4] the unqualified condemnation of harming human beings would be tantamount to the condemnation of even the justest city. Apart from this, it seems to be entirely fitting that the most savage man present should maintain a most savage thesis on justice. Thrasymachos contends that justice is the advantage of the stronger. Still, this thesis proves to be only the consequence of an opinion which is not only not manifestly savage but is even highly respectable. According to that opinion, the just is the same as the lawful or legal, *i.e.*, what the customs or laws of the city prescribe. Yet this opinion implies that there is nothing higher to which one can appeal from the man-made laws or conventions. This is the opinion now known by the name of "legal positivism," but in its origin it is not academic; it is the opinion on which all political societies tend to act. If the just is identical with the legal, the source of justice is the

[2] *Republic*, 375b–376c.
[3] *Republic*, 414d–e.
[4] *Republic*, 471a–b.

will of the legislator. The legislator in each city is the regime—the man or body of men that rules the city: the tyrant, the common people, the men of excellence, and so on. According to Thrasymachos, each regime lays down the laws with a view to its own preservation and well-being, in a word, to its own advantage and to nothing else. From this it follows that obedience to the laws or justice is not necessarily advantageous to the ruled and may even be bad for them. And as for the rulers, justice simply does not exist: they lay down the laws with exclusive concern for their own advantage.

Let us concede for a moment that Thrasymachos' view of law and of rulers is correct. The rulers surely may make mistakes. They may command actions which are in fact disadvantageous to themselves and advantageous to the ruled. In that case the just or law-abiding subjects will in fact do what is disadvantageous to the rulers and advantageous to the subjects. When this difficulty is pointed out to him by Socrates, Thrasymachos declares after some hesitation that the rulers are not rulers if and when they make mistakes: the ruler in the strict sense is infallible, just as the artisan in the strict sense is infallible. It is this Thrasymachean notion of "the artisan in the strict sense" which Socrates uses with great felicity against Thrasymachos. For the artisan in the strict sense proves to be concerned, not with his own advantage, but with the advantage of the others whom he serves: the shoemaker makes shoes for others and only accidentally for himself; the physician prescribes things to his patients with a view to their advantage; hence if ruling is, as Thrasymachos admitted, something like an art, the ruler serves the ruled, *i.e.*, rules for the advantage of the ruled. The artisan in the strict sense is infallible, *i.e.*, does his job well, and he is only concerned with the well-being of others. This, however, means that art strictly understood is justice—justice in deed, and not merely in intention as law-abidingness is. "Art is justice"—this proposition reflects the Socratic assertion that virtue is knowledge. The suggestion emerging from Socrates' discussion with Thrasymachos leads to the conclusion that the just city will be an association where everyone is an artisan in the strict sense, a city of craftsmen or artificers, of men (and women) each of whom has a single job which he does well and with full dedication, *i.e.*, without minding his own advantage and only for the good of others or for the common good. This conclusion pervades the whole teaching of the *Republic*. The city constructed there as a model is based on the principle of "one man one job." The soldiers in it are "artificers" of the freedom of the city; the philosophers in it are "artificers" of the whole common virtue; there is an "artificer" of heaven; even God is presented as an artisan—as the artificer even of the eternal ideas.[5] It is because citizenship in the just city is craftsmanship of one kind or another, and the seat of craftsmanship or art is in the

---

[5] *Republic,* 395c; 500d; 530a; 507c, 597.

soul and not in the body, that the difference between the two sexes loses its importance, or the equality of the two sexes is established.[6]

Thrasymachos could have avoided his downfall if he had left matters at the common-sense view according to which rulers are of course fallible, or if he had said that all laws are framed by the rulers with a view to their apparent (and not necessarily true) advantage. Since he is not a noble man, we are entitled to suspect that he chose the alternative which proved fatal to him with a view to his own advantage. Thrasymachos was a famous teacher of rhetoric, the art of persuasion. (Hence, incidentally, he is the only man possessing an art who speaks in the *Republic.*) The art of persuasion is necessary for persuading rulers and especially ruling assemblies, at least ostensibly, of their true advantage. Even the rulers themselves need the art of persuasion in order to persuade their subjects that the laws, which are framed with exclusive regard to the benefit of the rulers, serve the benefit of the subjects. Thrasymachos' own art stands or falls by the view that prudence is of the utmost importance for ruling. The clearest expression of this view is the proposition that the ruler who makes mistakes is no longer a ruler at all.

Thrasymachos' downfall is caused not by a stringent refutation of his view of justice nor by an accidental slip on his part but by the conflict between his depreciation of justice or his indifference to justice and the implication of his art: there is some truth in the view that art is justice. One could say—and as a matter of fact Thrasymachos himself says—that Socrates' conclusion, namely, that no ruler or other artisan ever considers his own advantage, is very simple-minded: Socrates seems to be a babe in the woods. As regards the artisans proper, they of course consider the compensation which they receive for their work. It may be true that to the extent to which the physician is concerned with what is characteristically called his honorarium, he does not exercise the art of the physician but the art of money-making; but since what is true of the physician is true of the shoemaker and any other craftsman as well, one would have to say that the only universal art, the art accompanying all arts, the art of arts, is the art of money-making; one must therefore further say that serving others or being just becomes good for the artisan only through his practicing the art of money-making, or that no one is just for the sake of justice, or that no one likes justice as such. But the most devastating argument against Socrates' reasoning is supplied by the arts which are manifestly concerned with the most ruthless and calculating exploitation of the ruled by the rulers. Such an art is the art of the shepherd—the art wisely chosen by Thrasymachos in order to destroy Socrates' argument, especially since kings and other rulers have been compared to shepherds since the oldest times. The shepherd is surely concerned with the well-being of his flock—so that the

[6] *Republic,* 454c–455a; cf. 452a.

sheep will supply men with the juiciest lamb chops. As Thrasymachos puts it, the shepherds are exclusively concerned with the good of the owners and of themselves.[7] But there is obviously a difference between the owners and the shepherds: the juiciest lamb chops are for the owner and not for the shepherd, unless the shepherd is dishonest. Now, the position of Thrasymachos or of any man of his kind with regard to both rulers and ruled is precisely that of the shepherd with regard to both the owners and the sheep: Thrasymachos can securely derive benefit from the assistance which he gives to the rulers (regardless of whether they are tyrants, common people, or men of excellence) only if he is loyal to them, if he does his job for them well, if he keeps his part of the bargain, if he is just. Contrary to his assertion, he must grant that a man's justice is salutary, not only to others and especially to the rulers, but also to himself. It is partly because he has become aware of this necessity that he changes his manners so remarkably in the last part of the first book. What is true of the helpers of rulers is true of the rulers themselves and all other human beings (including tyrants and gangsters) who need the help of other men in their enterprises however unjust: no association can last if its members do not practice justice among themselves.[8] This, however, amounts to an admission that justice may be a mere means, if an indispensable means, for injustice—for the exploitation of outsiders. Above all, it does not dispose of the possibility that the city is a community held together by collective selfishness and nothing else, or that there is no fundamental difference between the city and a gang of robbers. These and similar difficulties explain why Socrates regards his refutation of Thrasymachos as insufficient: he says at its conclusion that he has tried to show that justice is good without having made clear what justice is.

The adequate defense or praise of justice presupposes not only knowledge of what justice is, but also an adequate attack on justice. At the beginning of the second book, Glaukon attempts to present such an attack; he claims that he restates Thrasymachos' thesis, in which he does not believe, with greater vigor than Thrasymachos had done. Glaukon also takes it for granted that the just is the same as the legal or conventional, but he attempts to show how convention emerges out of nature. By nature each man is concerned only with his own good and wholly unconcerned with any other man's good to the point that he has no hesitation whatever about harming his fellows. Since everyone acts accordingly, they all bring about a situation which is unbearable for most of them; the majority, *i.e.*, the weaklings, figure out that every one of them would be better off if they agreed among themselves as to what each of them may or may not do. What they agree upon is not stated by Glaukon, but part of it can easily be

[7] *Republic*, 343b.
[8] *Republic*, 351c–352a.

guessed: they will agree that no one may violate the life and limb, the honor, the liberty, and the property of any of the associates, *i.e.*, the fellow citizens, and that everyone must do his best to protect his associates against outsiders. Both the abstention from such violations and the service of protection are in no way desirable in themselves but only necessary evils, yet lesser evils than universal insecurity. But what is true of the majority is not true of "the real man" who can take care of himself and who is better off if he does not submit to law or convention. Yet even the others do violence to their nature by submitting to law and justice: they submit to it only from fear of the consequences of the failure to submit, *i.e.*, from fear of punishment of one kind or another, not voluntarily and gladly. Therefore every man would prefer injustice to justice if he could be sure of escaping detection: justice is preferable to injustice only with a view to possible detection, to one's becoming known as just to others, *i.e.*, to good repute or other rewards. Therefore since, as Glaukon hopes, justice is choiceworthy for its own sake, he demands from Socrates a proof that the life of the just man is preferable to that of the unjust man even if the just man is thought to be unjust in the extreme and suffers all kinds of punishment or is in the depth of misery, and the unjust man is thought to be of consummate justice and receives all kinds of reward or is at the peak of happiness: the height of injustice, *i.e.*, of the conduct according to nature, is the tacit exploitation of law or convention for one's own benefit alone, the conduct of the supremely shrewd and manly tyrant. In the discussion with Thrasymachos, the issue had become blurred by the suggestion that there is a kinship between justice and art. Glaukon makes the issue manifest by comparing the perfectly unjust man to the perfect artisan, whereas he conceives of the perfectly just man as a simple man who has no quality other than justice. With a view to the teaching of the *Republic* as a whole, one is tempted to say that Glaukon understands pure justice in the light of pure fortitude; his perfectly just man reminds one of the unknown soldier who undergoes the most painful and most humiliating death for no other purpose whatsoever except in order to die bravely and without any prospect of his noble deed ever becoming known to anyone.

Glaukon's demand on Socrates is strongly supported by Adeimantos. It becomes clear from Adeimantos' speech that Glaukon's view according to which justice is choiceworthy entirely for its own sake is altogether novel, for in the traditional view justice was regarded as choiceworthy chiefly, if not exclusively, because of the divine rewards for justice and the divine punishments for injustice, and various other consequences. Adeimantos' long speech differs from Glaukon's because it brings out the fact that if justice is to be choiceworthy for its own sake, it must be easy or pleasant.[9] Glaukon's and Adeimantos' demands establish the standard by

---

[9] Cf. *Republic*, 364a, c–d, 365c with 357b and 358a.

which one must judge Socrates' praise of justice; they force one to investigate whether or to what extent Socrates has proved in the *Republic* that
justice is choiceworthy for its own sake or pleasant or even by itself sufficient to make a man perfectly happy in the midst of what is ordinarily believed to be the most extreme misery.

In order to defend the cause of justice, Socrates turns to founding, together with Glaukon and Adeimantos, a city in speech. The reason why
this procedure is necessary can be stated as follows. Justice is believed to
be law-abidingness or the firm will to give to everyone what belongs to
him, *i.e.*, what belongs to him according to law; yet justice is also believed
to be good or salutary; but obedience to the laws or giving to everyone
what belongs to him according to law is not unqualifiedly salutary since
the laws may be bad; justice will be simply salutary only when the laws
are good, and this requires that the regime from which the laws flow is
good: justice will be fully salutary only in a good city. Socrates' procedure
implies, furthermore, that he knows of no actual city which is good; this is
the reason why he is compelled to found a good city. He justifies his turning to the city by the consideration that justice can be detected more easily
in the city than in the human individual because the former is larger than
the latter; he thus implies that there is a parallelism between the city and
the human individual or, more precisely, between the city and the soul of
the human individual. This means that the parallelism between the city
and the human individual is based upon a certain abstraction from the
human body. To the extent to which there is a parallelism between the city
and the human individual or his soul, the city is at least similar to a natural being. Yet that parallelism is not complete. While the city and the individual seem equally to be able to be just, it is not certain that they can be
equally happy (cf. the beginning of the fourth book). The distinction between the justice of the individual and his happiness was prepared by
Glaukon's demand on Socrates that justice should be praised regardless of
whether or not it has any extraneous attractions. It is also prepared by the
common opinion according to which justice requires complete dedication
of the individual to the common good.

The founding of the good city takes place in three stages: the healthy
city or the city of pigs, the purified city or the city of the armed camp, and
the City of Beauty or the city ruled by philosophers.

The founding of the city is preceded by the remark that the city has
its origin in human need: every human being, just or unjust, is in need of
many things, and at least for this reason in need of other human beings.
The healthy city satisfies properly the primary needs, the needs of the
body. The proper satisfaction requires that each man exercise only one art.
This means that everyone does almost all his work for others but also that
the others work for him. All will exchange with one another their own
products as their own products: there will be private property; by working

for the advantage of others everyone works for his own advantage. The reason why everyone will exercise only one art is that men differ from one another by nature, *i.e.*, different men are gifted for different arts. Since everyone will exercise that art for which he is by nature fitted, the burden will be easier on everyone. The healthy city is a happy city: it knows no poverty, no coercion or government, no war and eating of animals. It is happy in such a way that every member of it is happy: it does not need government because there is perfect harmony between everyone's service and his reward; no one encroaches on anyone else. It does not need government because everyone chooses by himself the art for which he is best fitted; there is no disharmony between natural gifts and preferences. There is also no disharmony between what is good for the individual (his choosing the art for which he is best fitted by nature) and what is good for the city: nature has so arranged things that there is no surplus of blacksmiths or deficit of shoemakers. The healthy city is happy because it is just, and it is just because it is happy; in the healthy city, justice is easy or pleasant and free from any tincture of self-sacrifice. It is just without anyone's concerning himself with its justice; it is just by nature. Nevertheless, it is found wanting. It is impossible for the same reason that anarchism in general is impossible. Anarchism would be possible if men could remain innocent, but it is of the essence of innocence that it is easily lost; men can be just only through knowledge, and men cannot acquire knowledge without effort and without antagonism. Differently stated, while the healthy city is just in a sense, it lacks virtue or excellence: such justice as it possesses is not virtue. Virtue is impossible without toil, effort, or repression of the evil in oneself. The healthy city is a city in which evil is only dormant. Death is mentioned only when the transition from the healthy city to the next stage has already begun.[10] The healthy city is called a city of pigs not by Socrates but by Glaukon. Glaukon does not quite know what he says. Literally speaking, the healthy city is a city without pigs.[11]

Before the purified city can emerge or rather be established, the healthy city must have decayed. Its decay is brought about by the emancipation of the desire for unnecessary things, *i.e.*, for things which are not necessary for the well-being or health of the body. Thus the luxurious or feverish city emerges, the city characterized by the striving for the unlimited acquisition of wealth. One can expect that in such a city the individuals will no longer exercise the single art for which each is meant by nature but any art or combination of arts which is most lucrative, or that there will no longer be a strict correspondence between service and reward: hence there will be dissatisfaction and conflicts and therefore need for government which will restore justice;

[10] *Republic,* 372d.
[11] *Republic,* 370d–e, 373c.

hence there will be need for something else which also was entirely
absent from the healthy city, *i.e.*, education at least of the rulers, and
more particularly education to justice. There will certainly be need for
additional territory and hence there will be war, war of aggression.
Building on the principle "one man one art," Socrates demands that
the army consist of men who have no art other than that of warriors.
It appears that the art of the warriors or of the guardians is by far
superior to the other arts. Hitherto it looked as if all arts were of equal
rank and the only universal art, or the only art accompanying all arts,
was the art of money-making.[12] Now we receive the first glimpse of
the true order of arts. That order is hierarchic; the universal art is the
highest art, the art directing all other arts, which as such cannot be
practiced by the practitioners of arts other than the highest. This art
of arts will prove to be philosophy. For the time being we are told
only that the warrior must have a nature resembling the nature of that philosophic beast, the dog. For the warriors must be spirited and hence iras-
cible and harsh on the one hand and gentle on the other, since they must
be harsh toward strangers and gentle to their fellow citizens. They must
have a disinterested liking for their fellow citizens and a disinterested
dislike for foreigners. The men possessing such special natures need
in addition a special education. With a view to their work they need
training in the art of war. But this is not the education with which Socrates
is chiefly concerned. They will be by nature the best fighters and the
only ones armed and trained in arms: they will inevitably be the sole
possessors of political power. Besides, the age of innocence having
gone, evil is rampant in the city and therefore also in the warriors.
The education which the warriors more than anyone else need is
therefore above all education in civic virtue. That education is "music" education, education especially through poetry and music. Not all poetry and
music is apt to make men good citizens in general and good warriors or
guardians in particular. Therefore the poetry and music not conducive to
this moral-political end must be banished from the city. Socrates is very far
from demanding that Homer and Sophocles should be replaced by the
makers of edifying trash; the poetry which he demands for the good city
must be genuinely poetic. He demands particularly that the gods be presented as models of human excellence, *i.e.*, of the kind of human excellence
to which the guardians can and must aspire. The rulers will be taken from
among the elite of the guardians. Yet the prescribed education, however
excellent and effective, is not sufficient if it is not buttressed by the right
kind of institutions, *i.e.*, by absolute communism or by the completest possible abolition of privacy: everyone may enter everyone else's dwelling at

[12] *Republic*, 342a–b, 346c.

will. As reward for their service to the craftsmen proper, the guardians do not receive money of any kind but only a sufficient amount of food, and, we may suppose, of the other necessities.

Let us see in what way the good city as hitherto described reveals that justice is good or even attractive for its own sake. That justice, or the observing of the just proportion between service and reward, between working for others and one's own advantage, is necessary was shown in the discussion with Thrasymachos by the example of the gang of robbers. The education of the guardians as agreed upon between Socrates and Adeimantos is not education to justice.[13] It is education to courage and moderation. The music education in particular, as distinguished from the gymnastic education, is education to moderation, and this means to love of the beautiful, *i.e.*, of what is by nature attractive in itself. Justice in the narrow and strict sense may be said to flow from moderation or from the proper combination of moderation and courage. Socrates thus silently makes clear the difference between the gang of robbers and the good city: the essential difference consists in the fact that the armed and ruling part of the good city is animated by love of the beautiful, by the love of everything praiseworthy and graceful. The difference is not to be sought in the fact that the good city is guided in its relations to other cities, Greek or barbarian, by considerations of justice: the size of the territory of the good city is determined by that city's own moderate needs and by nothing else.[14] The difficulty appears perhaps more clearly from what Socrates says when speaking of the rulers. In addition to the other required qualities, the rulers must have the quality of caring for the city or loving the city; but a man is most likely to love that whose interest he believes to be identical with his own interest or whose happiness he believes to be the condition of his own happiness. The love here mentioned is not obviously disinterested in the sense that the ruler loves the city, or his serving the city, for its own sake. This may explain why Socrates demands that the rulers be honored both while they live and after their death.[15] At any rate the highest degree of caring for the city and for one another will not be forthcoming unless everyone is brought to believe in the falsehood that all fellow citizens, and only they, are brothers.[16] To say the least, the harmony between self-interest and the interest of the city, which was lost with the decay of the healthy city, has not yet been restored. No wonder then that at the beginning of the fourth book Adeimantos expresses his dissatisfaction with the condition of the soldiers in the city of the armed camp. Read within the context of the whole argument, Socrates' reply is to this effect: Only as a member of a happy city can a man be happy; only within these limits can a man, or any other

---

[13] *Republic*, 392a–c.
[14] *Republic*, 423b; cf. also 398a and 422d.
[15] *Republic*, 414a, 465d–466c; cf. 346e ff.
[16] *Republic*, 415b.

part of the city, be happy; complete dedication to the happy city is justice. It remains to be seen whether complete dedication to the happy city is, or can be, happiness of the individual.

After the founding of the good city is in the main completed, Socrates and his friends turn to seeking where in it justice and injustice are, and whether the man who is to be happy must possess justice or injustice.[17] They look first for the three virtues other than justice (wisdom, courage, and moderation). In the city which is founded according to nature, wisdom resides in the rulers and in the rulers alone, for the wise men are by nature the smallest part of any city, and it would not be good for the city if they were not the only ones at its helm. In the good city, courage resides in the warrior class, for political courage, as distinguished from brutish fearlessness, arises only through education in those by nature fitted for it. Moderation on the other hand is to be found in all parts of the good city. In the present context, moderation does not mean exactly what it meant when the education of the warriors was discussed but rather the control of what is by nature worse by that which is by nature better—that control through which the whole is in harmony. In other words, moderation is the agreement of the naturally superior and inferior as to which of the two ought to rule in the city. Since controlling and being controlled differ, one must assume that the moderation of the rulers is not identical with the moderation of the ruled. While Socrates and Glaukon found the three virtues mentioned in the good city with ease, it is difficult to find justice in it because, as Socrates says, justice is so obvious in it. Justice consists in everyone's doing the one thing pertaining to the city for which his nature is best fitted or, simply, in everyone's minding his own business: it is by virtue of justice thus understood that the other three virtues are virtues.[18] More precisely, a city is just if each of its three parts (the money-makers, the warriors, and the rulers) does its own work and only its own work.[19] Justice is then, like moderation and unlike wisdom and courage, not a preserve of a single part but required of every part. Hence justice, like moderation, has a different character in each of the three classes. One must assume, for instance, that the justice of the wise rulers is affected by their wisdom and the justice of the money-makers is affected by their lack of wisdom, for if even the courage of the warriors is only political or civic courage, and not courage pure and simple,[20] it stands to reason that their justice too—to say nothing of the justice of the money-makers—will not be justice pure and simple. In order to discover justice pure and simple, it then becomes necessary to consider justice in the individual man. This consideration would be easiest if justice in the individual were identical with justice in the city; this

[17] *Republic*, 427d.
[18] *Republic*, 433a–b.
[19] *Republic*, 434c.
[20] *Republic*, 430c; cf. *Phaedo*, 82a.

would require that the individual or rather his soul consist of the same
three kinds of "natures" as the city. A very provisional consideration of the
soul seems to establish this requirement: the soul contains desire, spiritedness or anger,[21] and reason, just as the city consists of the money-makers,
the warriors, and the rulers. Hence we may conclude that a man is just if
each of these three parts of his soul does its own work and only its own
work, *i.e.*, if his soul is in a state of health. But if justice is health of the
soul, and conversely injustice is disease of the soul, it is obvious that justice
is good and injustice is bad, regardless of whether or not one is known to
be just or unjust.[22] A man is just if the rational part in him is wise and
rules,[23] and if the spirited part, being the subject and ally of the rational
part, assists it in controlling the multitude of desires which almost inevitably become desires for more and ever more money. This means, however,
that only the man in whom wisdom rules the two other parts, *i.e.*, only the
wise man, can be truly just.[24] No wonder then that the just man eventually
proves to be identical with the philosopher.[25] The money-makers and the
warriors are not truly just even in the just city because their justice derives
exclusively from habituation of one kind or another as distinguished from
philosophy; hence in the deepest recesses of their souls they long for tyranny, *i.e.*, for complete injustice.[26] We see then how right Socrates was
when he expected to find injustice in the good city.[27] This is not to deny of
course that as members of the good city the nonphilosophers will act much
more justly than they would as members of inferior cities.

The justice of those who are not wise appears in a different light
when justice in the city is being considered, on the one hand, and justice
in the soul on the other. This fact shows that the parallelism between the
city and the soul is defective. This parallelism requires that, just as in the
city the warriors occupy a higher rank than the money-makers, so in the
soul spiritedness occupies a higher rank than desire. It is very plausible that
those who uphold the city against foreign and domestic enemies and who
have received a music education deserve higher respect than those who
lack public responsibility as well as a music education. But it is much less
plausible that spiritedness as such should deserve higher respect than desire as such. It is true that "spiritedness" includes a large variety of phenomena ranging from the most noble indignation about injustice, turpi-
tude, and meanness down to the anger of a spoiled child who resents being
deprived of anything that he desires, however bad. But the same is also
true of "desire": one kind of desire is *eros*, which ranges in its healthy

[21] *Republic*, 441 a–c.
[22] *Republic*, 444d–445b.
[23] *Republic*, 441e.
[24] Cf. *Republic*, 442c.
[25] *Republic*, 580d–583b.
[26] *Republic*, 619b–d.
[27] *Republic*, 427d.

forms from the longing for immortality via offspring through the longing
for immortality via immortal fame to the longing for immortality via participation by knowledge in the things which are unchangeable in every respect. The assertion that spiritedness is higher in rank than desire as such
is then questionable. Let us never forget that while there is a philosophic
eros, there is no philosophic spiritedness [28]; or in other words that Thrasymachos is much more visibly spiritedness incarnate than desire incarnate.
The assertion in question is based on a deliberate abstraction from *eros*—
an abstraction characteristic of the *Republic.*

This abstraction shows itself most strikingly in two facts: when Socrates mentions the fundamental needs which give rise to human society, he is
silent about the need for procreation, and when he describes the tyrant, Injustice incarnate, he presents him as *Eros* incarnate.[29] In the thematic
discussion of the respective rank of spiritedness and desire, he is silent
about *eros.*[30] It seems that there is a tension between *eros* and the city and
hence between *eros* and justice: only through the depreciation of *eros* can
the city come into its own. *Eros* obeys its own laws, not the laws of the
city however good; in the good city, *eros* is simply subjected to what the
city requires. The good city requires that all love of one's own—all spontaneous love of one's own parents, one's own children, one's own friends and
beloved—be sacrificed to the common love of the common. As far as possible, the love of one's own must be abolished except as it is love of the city
as this particular city, as one's own city. As far as possible, patriotism takes
the place of *eros,* and patriotism has a closer kinship to spiritedness, eagerness to fight, "waspishness," anger, and indignation than to *eros.*

While it is harmful to one's soul to jump at Plato's throat because he
is not a liberal democrat, it is also bad to blur the difference between Platonism and liberal democracy, for the premises "Plato is admirable" and
"liberal democracy is admirable" do not legitimately lead to the conclusion
that Plato was a liberal democrat. The founding of the good city started
from the fact that men are by nature different, and this proved to mean
that men are by nature of unequal rank. They are unequal particularly
with regard to their ability to acquire virtue. The inequality which is due
to nature is increased and deepened by the different kinds of education or
habituation and the different ways of life (communistic or noncommunis-
tic) which the different parts of the good city enjoy. As a result, the good
city comes to resemble a caste society. A Platonic character who hears an
account of the good city of the *Republic* is reminded by it of the caste system established in ancient Egypt, although it is quite clear that in Egypt
the rulers were priests and not philosophers.[31] Certainly in the good city of

[28] Cf. *Republic,* 366c.
[29] *Republic,* 573b–e, 574e–575a.
[30] Cf. *Republic,* 439d.
[31] *Timaeus,* 24a–b.

the *Republic,* not descent but in the first place everyone's own natural gifts determine to which class he belongs. But this leads to a difficulty. The members of the upper class, which lives communistically, are not supposed to know who their natural parents are, for they are supposed to regard all men and women belonging to the older generation as their parents. On the other hand, the gifted children of the noncommunist lower class are to be transferred to the upper class (and vice versa); since their superior gifts are not necessarily recognizable at the moment of their birth, they are likely to come to know their natural parents and even to become attached to them; this would seem to unfit them for transfer to the upper class. There are two ways in which this difficulty can be removed. The first is to extend absolute communism to the lower class; and, considering the connection between way of life and education, also to extend music education to that class.[32] According to Aristotle,[33] Socrates has left it undecided whether in the good city absolute communism is limited to the upper class or extends also to the lower class. To leave this question undecided would be in agreement with Socrates' professed low opinion of the importance of the lower class.[34] Still, there can be only little doubt that Socrates wishes to limit both communism and music education to the upper class.[35] Therefore, in order to remove the difficulty mentioned, he can hardly avoid making an individual's membership in the upper or lower class hereditary and thus violating one of the most elementary principles of justice. Apart from this, one may wonder whether a perfectly clear line between those gifted and those not gifted for the profession of warriors can be drawn, hence whether a perfectly just assignment of individuals to the upper or lower class is possible, and hence whether the good city can be perfectly just.[36] But be this as it may, if communism is limited to the upper class, there will be privacy both in the money-making class and among the philosophers as philosophers, for there may very well be only a single philosopher in the city and surely never a herd: the warriors are the only class which is entirely political or public or entirely dedicated to the city; the warriors alone present therefore the clearest case of the just life in one sense of the word "just."

It is necessary to understand the reason why communism is limited to the upper class or what the natural obstacle to communism is. That which is by nature private or a man's own is the body and only the body.[37] The needs or desires of the body induce men to extend the sphere of the private, of what is each man's own, as far as they can. This most powerful striving is countered by music education which brings about moderation,

---

[32] *Republic,* 401b–c, 421e–422d, 460a, 543a.
[33] *Politics,* 1264a 13–17.
[34] *Republic,* 421a, 434a.
[35] *Republic,* 415e, 431b–c, 456d.
[36] Reconsider *Republic,* 427d.
[37] *Republic,* 464d; cf. *Laws,* 739c.

i.e., a most severe training of the soul of which, it seems, only a minority of men is capable. Yet this kind of education does not extirpate the natural desire of each for things or human beings of his own: the warriors will not accept absolute communism if they are not subject to the philosophers. It thus becomes clear that the striving for one's own is countered ultimately only by philosophy, by the quest for the truth which as such cannot be any-one's private possession. Whereas the private par excellence is the body, the common par excellence is the mind, the pure mind rather than the soul in general. The superiority of communism to noncommunism as taught in the *Republic* is intelligible only as a reflection of the superiority of philoso-phy to nonphilosophy. This clearly contradicts the result of the preceding paragraph. The contradiction can and must be resolved by the distinction between two meanings of justice. This distinction cannot become clear be-fore one has understood the teaching of the *Republic* regarding the rela-tion of philosophy and the city. We must therefore make a new beginning.

At the end of the fourth book, it looks as if Socrates had completed the task which Glaukon and Adeimantos had imposed on him, for he had shown that justice as health of the soul is desirable not only because of its consequences but above all for its own sake. But then, at the beginning of the fifth book, we are suddenly confronted by a new start, by the repetition of a scene which had occurred at the very beginning. Both at the very be-ginning and at the beginning of the fifth book (and nowhere else), Socrates' companions make a decision, nay, take a vote, and Socrates who had no share in the decision obeys it.[38] Socrates' companions behave in both cases like a city (an assembly of the citizens), if the smallest possible city.[39] But there is this decisive difference between the two scenes: whereas Thrasy-machos was absent from the first scene, he has become a member of the city in the second scene. It could seem that the foundation of the good city requires that Thrasymachos be converted into one of its citizens.

At the beginning of the fifth book Socrates' companions force him to take up the subject of communism in regard to women and children. They do not object to the proposal itself in the way in which Adeimantos had objected to the communism regarding property at the beginning of the fourth book, for even Adeimantos is no longer the same man he was at that time. They only wish to know the precise manner in which the communism regarding women and children is to be managed. Socrates replaces that question by these more incisive questions: (1) Is that communism possible? (2) Is it desirable? It appears that the communism regarding women is the consequence or presupposition of the equality of the two sexes concerning the work they must do: the city cannot afford to lose half of its adult popu-lation from its working and fighting force, and there is no essential differ-

[38] Cf. *Republic*, 449b–450a with 327b–328b.
[39] Cf. *Republic*, 369d.

ence between men and women regarding natural gifts for the various arts. The demand for equality of the two sexes requires a complete upheaval of custom, an upheaval which is here presented less as shocking than as laughable; the demand is justified on the ground that only the useful is fair or noble and that only what is bad, *i.e.*, against nature, is laughable: the customary difference of conduct between the two sexes is rejected as being against nature, and the revolutionary change is meant to bring about the order according to nature.[40] For justice requires that every human being should practice the art for which he or she is fitted by nature, regardless of what custom or convention may dictate. Socrates shows first that the equality of the two sexes is possible, *i.e.*, in agreement with the nature of the two sexes as their nature appears when viewed with regard to aptitude for the practice of the various arts, and then he shows that it is desirable. In proving this possibility, he explicitly abstracts from the difference between the two sexes in regard to procreation.[41] This means that the argument of the *Republic* as a whole, according to which the city is a community of male and female artisans, abstracts to the highest degree possible from the highest activity essential to the city which takes place "by nature" and not "by art."

Socrates then turns to the communism regarding women and children and shows that it is desirable because it will make the city more "one," and hence more perfect, than a city consisting of separate families would be: the city should be as similar as possible to a single human being or to a single living body, *i.e.*, to a natural being.[42] At this point we understand somewhat better why Socrates started his discussion of justice by assuming an important parallelism between the city and the individual: he was thinking ahead of the greatest possible unity of the city. The abolition of the family does not mean of course the introduction of license or promiscuity; it means the most severe regulation of sexual intercourse from the point of view of what is useful for the city or what is required for the common good. The consideration of the useful, one might say, supersedes the consideration of the holy or sacred[43]: human males and females are to be coupled with exclusive regard to the production of the best offspring, in the spirit in which the breeders of dogs, birds, and horses proceed; the claims of *eros* are simply silenced. The new order naturally affects the customary prohibitions against incest, the most sacred rules of customary justice.[44] In the new scheme, no one will know any more his natural parents, children, brothers, and sisters, but everyone will *regard* all men of the older generation as his fathers and mothers, of his own generation as his

[40] *Republic*, 455d–e, 456b–c.
[41] *Republic*, 455c–e.
[42] *Republic*, 462c–d, 464b.
[43] Cf. *Republic*, 458e.
[44] Cf. *Republic*, 461b–e.

brothers and sisters, and of the younger generation as his children.[45] This means, however, that the city constructed according to nature lives in a most important respect more according to convention than according to nature. For this reason we are disappointed to see that while Socrates takes up the question of whether communism regarding women and children is possible, he drops it immediately.[46] Since the institution under consideration is indispensable for the good city, Socrates thus leaves open the question of the possibility of the good city, *i.e.*, of the just city, as such. And this happens to his listeners and to the readers of the *Republic* after they have made the greatest sacrifices—such as the sacrifice of *eros* as well as of the family—for the sake of the just city.

Socrates is not for long allowed to escape from his awesome duty to answer the question regarding the possibility of the just city. The manly Glaucon compels him to face that question. Perhaps we should say that by apparently escaping to the subject of war—a subject both easier in itself and more attractive to Glaucon than the communism of women and children—yet treating that subject according to the stern demands of justice and thus depriving it of much of its attractiveness, he compels Glaucon to compel him to return to the fundamental question. Be this as it may, the question to which Socrates and Glaucon return is not the same one which they left. The question which they left was whether the good city is possible in the sense that it is in agreement with human nature. The question to which they return is whether the good city is possible in the sense that it can be brought into being by the transformation of an actual city.[47] The latter question might be thought to presuppose the affirmative answer to the first question, but this is not quite correct. As we learn now, our whole effort to discover what justice is (so that we would be enabled to see how it is related to happiness) was a quest for "justice itself" as a "pattern." By seeking for justice itself as a pattern we implied that the just man and the just city will not be perfectly just but will indeed approximate justice itself with particular closeness [48]; only justice itself is perfectly just.[49] This implies that not even the characteristic institutions of the just city (absolute communism, equality of the sexes, and the rule of the philosophers) are simply just. Now justice itself is not "possible" in the sense that it is capable of coming into being, because it "is" always without being capable of undergoing any change whatever. Justice is an "idea" or "form," one of many "ideas." Ideas are the only things which strictly speaking "are," *i.e.*, are without any admixture of nonbeing, because they are beyond all becoming, and whatever is becoming is between being and nonbeing.

[45] *Republic*, 463c.
[46] *Republic*, 466d.
[47] *Republic*, 473b–c.
[48] *Republic*, 472b–c.
[49] *Republic*, 479a; cf. 538c ff.

Since the ideas are the only things which are beyond all change, they are in a sense the cause of all change and all changeable things. For example, the idea of justice is the cause for anything (human beings, cities, laws, commands, actions) becoming just. They are self-subsisting beings which subsist always. They are of utmost splendor. For instance, the idea of justice is perfectly just. But their splendor escapes the eyes of the body. The ideas are "visible" only to the eye of the mind, and the mind as mind perceives nothing but ideas. Yet, as is indicated by the facts that there are many ideas and that the mind which perceives the ideas is radically different from the ideas themselves, there must be something higher than the ideas: "the good" or "the idea of the good" which is in a sense the cause of all ideas as well as of the mind perceiving them.[50] It is only through perception of "the good" on the part of the human beings who are by nature equipped for perceiving it that the good city can come into being and subsist for a while.

The doctrine of ideas which Socrates expounds to Glaukon is very hard to understand; to begin with it is utterly incredible, not to say that it appears to be fantastic. Hitherto we have been given to understand that justice is fundamentally a certain character of the human soul, or of the city, *i.e.*, something which is not self-subsisting. Now we are asked to believe that it is self-subsisting, being at home as it were in an entirely different place than human beings and everything else that participates in justice.[51] No one has ever succeeded in giving a satisfactory or clear account of this doctrine of ideas. It is possible, however, to define rather precisely the central difficulty. "Idea" means primarily the looks or shape of a thing; it means then a kind or class of things which are united by the fact that they all possess the same "looks," *i.e.*, the same character and power, or the same "nature"; therewith it means the class-character or the nature of the things belonging to the class in question: the "idea" of a thing is that which we mean by trying to find out the "what" or the "nature" of a thing or a class of things. . . . The connection between "idea" and "nature" appears in the *Republic* from the facts that "the idea of justice" is called "that which is just by nature," and that the ideas in contradistinction to the things which are not ideas or to the sensibly perceived things are said to be "in nature." [52] This does not explain, however, why the ideas are presented as "separated" from the things which are what they are by participating in an idea or, in other words, why "dogness" (the class character of dogs) should be "the true dog." It seems that two kinds of phenomena lend support to Socrates' assertion. In the first place the mathematical things as such can never be found among sensible things: no line drawn on sand or paper is a line as meant by the mathematician. Secondly and above all,

[50] *Republic*, 517c.
[51] Cf. *Republic*, 509b–510a.
[52] *Republic*, 501b; 597b–d.

what we mean by justice and kindred things is not as such, in its purity or perfection, necessarily found in human beings or societies; it rather seems that what is meant by justice transcends everything which men can ever achieve; precisely the justest men were and are the ones most aware of the shortcomings of their justice. Socrates seems to say that what is patently true of mathematical things and of the virtues is true universally: there is an idea of the bed or the table just as of the circle and of justice. Now while it is obviously reasonable to say that a perfect circle or perfect justice transcends everything which can ever be seen, it is hard to say that the perfect bed is something on which no man can ever rest. However this may be, Glaukon and Adeimantos accept this doctrine of ideas with relative ease, with greater ease than absolute communism. This paradoxical fact does not strike us with sufficient force because we somehow believe that these able young men study philosophy under Professor Socrates and have heard him expound the doctrine of ideas on innumerable occasions, if we do not believe that the *Republic* is a philosophic treatise addressed to readers familiar with more elementary (or "earlier") dialogues. Yet Plato addresses the readers of the *Republic* only through the medium of Socrates' conversation with Glaukon and the other interlocutors in the *Republic*, and Plato as the author of the *Republic* does not suggest that Glaukon—to say nothing of Adeimantos and the rest—has seriously studied the doctrine of ideas.[53] Yet while Glaukon and Adeimantos cannot be credited with a genuine understanding of the doctrine of ideas, they have heard, and in a way they know, that there are gods like *Dike* or Right,[54] and *Nike* or Victory who is not this or that victory or this or that statue of Nike but a self-subsisting being which is the cause of every victory and which is of unbelievable splendor. More generally, they know that there are gods—self-subsisting beings which are the causes of everything good, which are of unbelievable splendor, and which cannot be apprehended by the senses since they never change their "form." [55] This is not to deny that there is a profound difference between the gods as understood in the "theology" [56] of the *Republic* and the ideas, or that in the *Republic* the gods are in a way replaced by the ideas. It is merely to assert that those who accept that theology and draw all conclusions from it are likely to arrive at the doctrine of ideas.

We must now return to the question of the possibility of the just city. We have learned that justice itself is not "possible" in the sense that anything which comes into being can ever be perfectly just. We learn immediately afterward that not only justice itself but also the just city is not "possible" in the sense indicated. This does not mean that the just city as meant

---

[53] Cf. *Republic*, 507a–c with 596a and 532c–d, contrast with *Phaedo*, 65d and 74a–b.
[54] *Republic*, 536b; cf. 487a.
[55] Cf. *Republic*, 379a–b and 380d ff.
[56] *Republic*, 379a.

and as sketched in the *Republic* is an idea like "justice itself," and still less that it is an "ideal": "ideal" is not a Platonic term. The just city is not a self-subsisting being like the idea of justice, located so to speak in a super-heavenly place. Its status is rather like that of a painting of a perfectly beautiful human being, *i.e.*, it is only by virtue of the painter's painting; more precisely, the just city is only "in speech": it "is" only by virtue of having been figured out with a view to justice itself or to what is by nature right on the one hand and the human all-too-human on the other. Although the just city is decidedly of lower rank than justice itself, even the just city as a pattern is not capable of coming into being as it has been blueprinted; only approximations to it can be expected in cities which are in deed and not merely in speech.[57] What this means is not clear. Does it mean that the best feasible solution will be a compromise so that we must become reconciled to a certain degree of private property (*e.g.*, that we must permit every warrior to keep his shoes and the like as long as he lives) and a certain degree of inequality of the sexes (*e.g.*, that certain military and administrative functions will remain the preserve of the male warriors)? There is no reason to suppose that this is what Socrates meant. In the light of the succeeding part of the conversation, the following suggestion would seem to be more plausible. The assertion according to which the just city cannot come into being as blueprinted is provisional, or prepares the assertion that the just city, while capable of coming into being, is very unlikely to come into being. At any rate, immediately after having declared that only an approximation to the good city can reasonably be expected, Socrates raises the question, what feasible change in the actual cities will be the necessary and sufficient condition of their transformation into good cities? His answer is, the "coincidence" of political power and philosophy: the philosophers must rule as kings, or the kings must genuinely and adequately philosophize. As we have shown in our summary of the first book of the *Republic,* this answer is not altogether surprising. If justice is less the giving or leaving to each what the law assigns to him than the giving or leaving to each what is good for his soul, but what is good for his soul is the virtues, it follows that no one can be truly just who does not know "the virtues themselves," or generally the ideas, or who is not a philosopher.

By answering the question of how the good city is possible, Socrates introduces philosophy as a theme of the *Republic.* This means that in the *Republic,* philosophy is not introduced as the end of man, the end for which man should live, but as a means for realizing the just city, the city as armed camp which is characterized by absolute communism and equality of the sexes in the upper class, the class of warriors. Since the rule of philosophers is not introduced as an ingredient of the just city but only as a means for its realization, Aristotle is justified in disregarding this institu-

[57] *Republic*, 472c–473a; cf. 500c–501c with 484c–d and 592b.

tion in his critical analysis of the *Republic* (*Politics* II). At any rate, Socrates succeeds in reducing the question of the possibility of the just city to the question of the possibility of the coincidence of philosophy and political power. That such a coincidence should be possible is to begin with most incredible: everyone can see that the philosophers are useless if not even harmful in politics. Socrates, who had some experiences of his own with the city of Athens—experiences to be crowned by his capital punishment—regards this accusation of the philosophers as well-founded, although in need of deeper exploration. He traces the antagonism of the cities toward the philosophers primarily to the cities: the present cities, *i.e.*, the cities not ruled by philosophers, are like assemblies of madmen which corrupt most of those fit to become philosophers, and on which those who have succeeded against all odds in becoming philosophers rightly turn their back in disgust. But Socrates is far from absolving the philosophers altogether. Only a radical change on the part of both the cities and the philosophers can bring about that harmony between them for which they seem to be meant by nature. The change consists precisely in this: that the cities cease to be unwilling to be ruled by philosophers and the philosophers cease to be unwilling to rule the cities. This coincidence of philosophy and political power is very difficult to achieve, very improbable, but not impossible. To bring about the needed change on the part of the city, of the nonphilosophers or the multitude, the right kind of persuasion is necessary and sufficient. The right kind of persuasion is supplied by the art of persuasion, the art of Thrasymachos directed by the philosopher and in the service of philosophy. No wonder then that in our context Socrates declares that he and Thrasymachos have just become friends. The multitude of the nonphilosophers is good-natured and therefore persuadable by the philosophers.[58] But if this is so, why did not the philosophers of old, to say nothing of Socrates himself, succeed in persuading the multitude of the supremacy of philosophy and the philosophers and thus bring about the rule of philosophers and therewith the salvation and the happiness of their cities? Strange as it may sound, in this part of the argument it appears to be easier to persuade the multitude to accept the rule of the philosophers than to persuade the philosophers to rule the multitude: the philosophers cannot be persuaded, they can only be compelled to rule the cities.[59] Only the nonphilosophers could compel the philosophers to take care of the cities. But, given the prejudice against the philosophers, this compulsion will not be forthcoming if the philosophers do not in the first place persuade the nonphilosophers to compel the philosophers to rule over them, and this persuasion will not be forthcoming, given the philosophers' unwillingness to rule. We arrive then at the conclusion that the just city is not possible because of the philosophers' unwillingness to rule.

[58] *Republic*, 498c–502a.
[59] *Republic*, 499b–c, 500d, 520a–d, 521b, 539e.

Why are the philosophers unwilling to rule? Being dominated by the desire for knowledge as the one thing needful, or knowing that philosophy is the most pleasant and blessed possession, the philosophers have no leisure for looking down at human affairs, let alone for taking care of them.[60] The philosophers believe that while still alive they are already firmly settled, far away from their cities, in the Isles of the Blessed.[61] Hence only compulsion could induce them to take part in political life in the just city, *i.e.*, in the city which regards the proper upbringing of the philosophers as its most important task. Having perceived the truly grand, the human things appear to the philosophers to be paltry. The very justice of the philosophers—their abstaining from wronging their fellow human beings —flows from contempt for the things for which the nonphilosophers hotly contest.[62] They know that the life not dedicated to philosophy and therefore in particular the political life is like life in a cave, so much so that the city can be identified with the Cave.[63] The cave dwellers (*i.e.*, the nonphilosophers) see only the shadows of artifacts.[64] That is to say, whatever they perceive they understand in the light of their opinions, sanctified by the fiat of legislators, regarding the just and noble things, *i.e.*, of conventional opinions, and they do not know that these their most cherished convictions possess no higher status than that of opinions. For if even the best city stands or falls by a fundamental falsehood, although a noble falsehood, it can be expected that the opinions on which the imperfect cities rest or in which they believe, will not be true. Precisely the best of the nonphilosophers; the good citizens, are passionately attached to these opinions and therefore violently opposed to philosophy,[65] which is the attempt to go beyond opinion toward knowledge: the multitude is not as persuadable by the philosophers as we sanguinely assumed in an earlier round of the argument. This is the true reason why the coincidence of philosophy and political power is, to say the least, extremely improbable: philosophy and the city tend away from one another in opposite directions.

The difficulty of overcoming the natural tension between the city and the philosophers is indicated by Socrates' turning from the question of whether the just city is "possible" in the sense of being conformable to human nature to the question of whether the just city is "possible" in the sense of being capable of being brought to light by the transformation of an actual city. The first question, understood in contradistinction to the second, points to the question whether the just city could not come into being through the settling together of men who had been wholly unasso-

---

[60] *Republic*, 485a, 501b–c, 517c.
[61] *Republic*, 519c.
[62] *Republic*, 486a–b.
[63] *Republic*, 539e.
[64] *Republic*, 514b–515c.
[65] *Republic*, 517a.

ciated before. It is to this question that Socrates tacitly gives a negative answer by turning to the question of whether the just city could be brought
into being by the transformation of an actual city. The good city cannot be
brought to light out of human beings who have not yet undergone any
human discipline, out of "primitives" or "stupid animals" or "savages" gentle or cruel; its potential members must already have acquired the rudiments of civilized life. The long process through which primitive men become civilized men cannot be the work of the founder or legislator of the
good city but is presupposed by him.[66] But on the other hand, if the potential good city must be an old city, its citizens will have been thoroughly
molded by their city's imperfect laws or customs, hallowed by old age, and
will have become passionately attached to them. Socrates is therefore compelled to revise his original suggestion according to which the rule of philosophers is the necessary and sufficient condition of the coming into being
of the just city. Whereas he had originally suggested that the good city will
come into being if the philosophers become kings, he finally suggests that
the good city will come into being if, when the philosophers have become
kings, they expel everyone older than ten from the city, *i.e.*, separate the
children completely from their parents and their parents' ways and bring
them up in the entirely novel ways of the good city.[67] By taking over a
city, the philosophers make sure that their subjects will not be savages; by
expelling everyone older than ten, they make sure that their subjects will
not be enslaved by traditional civility. The solution is elegant. It leaves
one wondering, however, how the philosophers can compel everyone older
than ten to obey submissively the expulsion decree, since they cannot yet
have trained a warrior class absolutely obedient to them. This is not to
deny that Socrates could persuade many fine young men, and even some
old ones, to believe that the multitude could be, not indeed compelled, but
persuaded by the philosophers to leave their city and their children and to
live in the fields so that justice will be done.

The part of the *Republic* which deals with philosophy is the most important part of the book. Accordingly, it transmits the answer to the question regarding justice to the extent to which that answer is given in the *Republic*. The explicit answer to the question of what justice is had been
rather vague: justice consists in each part of the city or of the soul "doing
the work for which it is by nature best fitted" or in a "kind" of doing that
work; a part is just if it does its work or minds its own business "in a certain manner." The vagueness is removed if one replaces "in a certain manner" by "in the best manner" or "well": justice consists in each part doing
its work well.[68] Hence the just man is the man in whom each part of the
soul does its work well. Since the highest part of the soul is reason, and

[66] Cf. *Republic*, 376e.
[67] *Republic*, 540d–541a; cf. 499b, 501a,e.
[68] *Republic*, 433a–b and 443d; cf. Aristotle *Nicomachean Ethics*, 1098a 7–12.

since this part cannot do its work well if the two other parts too do not do their work well, only the philosopher can be truly just. But the work which the philosopher does well is intrinsically attractive and in fact the most pleasant work, wholly regardless of its consequences.[69] Hence only in philosophy do justice and happiness coincide. In other words, the philosopher is the only individual who is just in the sense in which the good city is just: he is self-sufficient, truly free, or his life is as little devoted to the service of other individuals as the life of the city is devoted to the service of other cities. But the philosopher in the good city is just also in the sense that he serves his fellow men, his fellow citizens, his city, or that he obeys the law. That is to say, the philosopher is just also in the sense in which all members of the just city, and in a way all just members of any city, regardless of whether they are philosophers or nonphilosophers, are just. Yet justice in this second sense is not intrinsically attractive or choiceworthy for its own sake, but is good only with a view to its consequences, or is not noble but necessary: the philosopher serves his city, even the good city, not, as he seeks the truth, from natural inclination, from *eros*, but under compulsion.[70] It is hardly necessary to add that compulsion does not cease to be compulsion if it is self-compulsion. According to a notion of justice which is more common than that suggested by Socrates' definition, justice consists in not harming others; justice thus understood proves to be in the highest case merely a concomitant of the philosopher's greatness of soul. But if justice is taken in the larger sense according to which it consists in giving to each what is good for his soul, one must distinguish between the cases in which this giving is intrinsically attractive to the giver (these will be the cases of potential philosophers) and those in which it is merely a duty or compulsory. This distinction, incidentally, underlies the difference between the voluntary conversations of Socrates (the conversations which he spontaneously seeks) and the compulsory ones (those which he cannot with propriety avoid). This clear distinction between the justice which is choiceworthy for its own sake, wholly regardless of its consequences, and identical with philosophy, and the justice which is merely necessary and identical in the highest case with the political activity of the philosopher is rendered possible by the abstraction from *eros* which is characteristic of the *Republic*. For one might well say that there is no reason why the philosopher should not engage in political activity out of that kind of love of one's own which is patriotism.[71]

By the end of the seventh book justice has come to sight fully. Socrates has in fact performed the duty laid upon him by Glaukon and Adeimantos to show that justice properly understood is choiceworthy for its own sake regardless of its consequences and therefore that justice is un-

[69] *Republic*, 583a.
[70] *Republic*, 519e–520b; 540b,e.
[71] Consider *Apology of Socrates*, 30a.

qualifiedly preferable to injustice. Nevertheless the conversation continues, for it seems that our clear grasp of justice does not include a clear grasp of injustice but must be supplemented by a clear grasp of the wholly unjust city and the wholly unjust man: only after we have seen the wholly unjust city and the wholly unjust man with the same clarity with which we have seen the wholly just city and the wholly just man will we be able to judge whether we ought to follow Socrates' friend Thrasymachos, who chooses injustice, or Socrates himself, who chooses justice.[72] This in its turn requires that the fiction of the possibility of the just city be maintained. As a matter of fact, the *Republic* never abandons the fiction that the just city as a society of human beings, as distinguished from a society of gods or sons of gods, is possible.[73] When Socrates turns to the study of injustice, it even becomes necessary for him to reaffirm this fiction with greater force than ever before. The unjust city will be uglier and more condemnable in proportion as the just city will be more possible. But the possibility of the just city will remain doubtful if the just city was never actual. Accordingly Socrates now asserts that the just city was once actual. More precisely, he makes the Muses assert it or rather imply it. The assertion that the just city was once actual is, as one might say, a mythical assertion which agrees with the mythical premise that the best is the oldest. Socrates asserts then through the mouth of the Muses that the good city was actual in the beginning, prior to the emergence of the inferior kinds of cities [74]; the inferior cities are decayed forms of the good city, soiled fragments of the pure city which was entire; hence the nearer in time a kind of inferior city is to the just city the better it is, or vice versa. It is more proper to speak of the good and inferior regimes than of the good and inferior cities (observe the transition from "cities" to "regimes" in 543d–544a). "Regime" is our translation of the Greek *politeia*. The book which we call *Republic* is in Greek entitled *Politeia. Politeia* is commonly translated by "constitution." The term designates the form of government understood as the form of the city, *i.e.*, as that which gives the city its character by determining the end which the city in question pursues or what it looks up to as the highest, and simultaneously the kind of men who rule the city. For instance, oligarchy is the kind of regime in which the rich rule and therefore admiration for wealth and for the acquisition of wealth animates the city as a whole, and democracy is the kind of regime in which all free men rule and therefore freedom is the end which the city pursues. According to Socrates, there are five kinds of regime: (1) kingdom or aristocracy, the rule of the best man or the best men, that is directed toward goodness or virtue, the regime of the just city; (2) timocracy, the rule of lovers of honor or of the ambitious men which is directed toward superiority or victory; (3) oligar-

---

[72] *Republic,* 545a–b; cf. 498c–d.
[73] *Laws,* 739b–e.
[74] Cf. *Republic,* 547b.

chy or the rule of the rich in which wealth is most highly esteemed; (4) democracy, the rule of free men in which freedom is most highly esteemed; (5) tyranny, the rule of the completely unjust man in which unqualified and unashamed injustice holds sway. The descending order of the five kinds of regime is modeled on Hesiod's descending order of the five races of men: the races of gold, of silver, of bronze, the divine race of heroes, the race of iron.[75] We see at once that the Platonic equivalent of Hesiod's divine race of heroes is democracy. We shall soon see the reason for this seemingly strange correspondence.

The *Republic* is based on the assumption that there is a strict parallelism between the city and the soul. Accordingly Socrates asserts that, just as there are five kinds of regime, so there are five kinds of characters of men, the timocratic man, for instance, corresponding to timocracy. The distinction which for a short while was popular in present-day political science between the authoritarian and the democratic "personalities," as corresponding to the distinction between authoritarian and democratic societies, was a dim and crude reflection of Socrates' distinction between the royal or aristocratic, the timocratic, the oligarchic, the democratic, and the tyrannical soul or man, as corresponding to the aristocratic, timocratic, oligarchic, democratic, and tyrannical regimes. In this connection it should be mentioned that in describing the regimes, Socrates does not speak of "ideologies" belonging to them; he is concerned with the character of each kind of regime and with the end which it manifestly and explicitly pursues, as well as with the political justification of the end in question in contradistinction to any transpolitical justification stemming from cosmology, theology, metaphysics, philosophy of history, myth, and the like. In his study of the inferior regimes Socrates examines in each case first the regime and then the corresponding individual or soul. He presents both the regime and the corresponding individual as coming into being out of the preceding one. We shall consider here only his account of democracy, both because this subject is most important to citizens of a democracy and because of its intrinsic importance. Democracy arises from oligarchy, which in its turn arises from timocracy, the rule of the insufficiently musical warriors who are characterized by the supremacy of spiritedness. Oligarchy is the first regime in which desire is supreme. In oligarchy the ruling desire is that for wealth or money, or unlimited acquisitiveness. The oligarchic man is thrifty and industrious, controls all his desires other than the desire for money, lacks education, and possesses a superficial honesty derivative from the crudest self-interest. Oligarchy must give to each the unqualified right to dispose of his property as he sees fit. It thus renders inevitable the emergence of "drones," *i.e.*, of members of the ruling class who are either burdened with debt or already bankrupt and hence disfranchised—of beggars

[75] Cf. *Republic,* 546e–547a and Hesiod *Works and Days,* 106 ff.

who hanker after their squandered fortune and hope to restore their fortune and political power through a change of regime ("Catilinarian exis-
tences"). Besides, the correct oligarchs themselves, being both rich and unconcerned with virtue and honor, render themselves and especially their
sons fat, spoiled, and soft. They thus become despised by the lean and
tough poor. Democracy comes into being when the poor, having become
aware of their superiority to the rich and perhaps being led by some
drones who act as traitors to their class and possess the skills which ordinarily only members of a ruling class possess, make themselves at an opportune moment masters of the city by defeating the rich, killing and exil-
ing a part of them, and permitting the rest to live with them in the
possession of full citizen rights. Democracy itself is characterized by freedom, which includes the right to say and do whatever one wishes: everyone can follow the way of life which pleases him most. Hence democracy is
the regime which fosters the greatest variety: every way of life, every regime can be found in it. Hence, we must add, democracy is the only
regime other than the best in which the philosopher can lead his peculiar
way of life without being disturbed: it is for this reason that with some exaggeration one can compare democracy to Hesiod's age of the divine race
of heroes which comes closer to the golden age than any other. Certainly
in a democracy the citizen who is a philosopher is under no compulsion to
participate in political life or to hold office.[76] One is thus led to wonder
why Socrates did not assign to democracy the highest place among the inferior regimes, or rather the highest place simply, seeing that the best regime is not possible. One could say that he showed his preference for democracy "by deed": by spending his whole life in democratic Athens, by
fighting for her in her wars, and by dying in obedience to her laws. However this may be, he surely did not prefer democracy to all other regimes
"in speech." The reason is that, being a just man, he thought of the well-
being not merely of the philosophers but of the nonphilosophers as well,
and he held that democracy is not designed for inducing the nonphilosophers to attempt to become as good as they possibly can, for the end of democracy is not virtue but freedom, *i.e.*, the freedom to live either nobly or
basely according to one's liking. Therefore he assigns to democracy a rank
even lower than to oligarchy, since oligarchy requires some kind of restraint whereas democracy, as he presents it, abhors every kind of restraint.
One could say that adapting himself to his subject matter, Socrates abandons all restraint when speaking of the regime which loathes restraint. In a
democracy, he asserts, no one is compelled to rule or to be ruled if he does
not like it; he can live in peace while his city is at war; capital punishment
does not have the slightest consequence for the condemned man: he is not
even jailed; the order of rulers and ruled is completely reversed: the father

---

[76] *Republic*, 557d–e.

behaves as if he were a boy and the son has neither respect nor fear of the father, the teacher fears his pupils while the pupils pay no attention to the teacher, and there is complete equality of the sexes; even horses and donkeys no longer step aside when encountering human beings. Plato writes as if the Athenian democracy had not carried out Socrates' execution, and Socrates speaks as if the Athenian democracy had not engaged in an orgy of bloody persecution of guilty and innocent alike when the Hermes statues were mutilated at the beginning of the Sicilian expedition.[77] Socrates' exaggeration of the licentious mildness of democracy is matched by an almost equally strong exaggeration of the intemperance of democratic man. He could indeed not avoid the latter exaggeration if he did not wish to deviate in the case of democracy from the procedure which he follows in his discussion of the inferior regimes. That procedure consists in understanding the man corresponding to an inferior regime as the son of a father corresponding to the preceding regime. Hence democratic man had to be presented as the son of an oligarchic father, as the degenerate son of a wealthy father who is concerned with nothing but making money: the democratic man is the drone, the fat, soft, and prodigal playboy, the lotus-eater who, assigning a kind of equality to equal and unequal things, lives one day in complete surrender to his lowest desires and the next ascetically, or who, according to Karl Marx's ideal, "goes hunting in the morning, fishes in the afternoon, raises cattle in the evening, devotes himself to philosophy after dinner," i.e., does at every moment what he happens to like at that moment: the democratic man is not the lean, tough and thrifty craftsman or peasant who has a single job.[78] Socrates' deliberately exaggerated blame of democracy becomes intelligible to some extent once one considers its immediate addressee, the austere Adeimantos, who is not a friend of laughter and who had been the addressee of the austere discussion of poetry in the section on the education of the warriors: by his exaggerated blame of democracy Socrates lends words to Adeimantos' "dream" of democracy.[79] One must also not forget that the sanguine account of the multitude which was provisionally required in order to prove the harmony between the city and philosophy is in need of being redressed; the exaggerated blame of democracy reminds us with greater force than was ever before used of the disharmony between philosophy and the people.[80]

After Socrates had brought to light the entirely unjust regime and the entirely unjust man and then compared the life of the entirely unjust man with that of the perfectly just man, it became clear beyond the shadow of a doubt that justice is preferable to injustice. Nevertheless the conversation continues. Socrates suddenly returns to the question of poetry, to a question which had already been answered at great length when he discussed

[77] See Thucydides VI. 27–29 and 53–61.
[78] Cf. Republic, 564c–565a and 575c.
[79] Cf. Republic, 563d with 389a.
[80] Cf. Republic, 577c–d with 428d–e and 422a,c.

the education of the warriors. We must try to understand this apparently
sudden return. In an explicit digression from the discussion of tyranny,
Socrates had noted that the poets praise tyrants and are honored by tyrants (and also by democracy), whereas they are not honored by the three
better regimes.[81] Tyranny and democracy are characterized by surrender
to the sensual desires, including the most lawless ones. The tyrant is *Eros*
incarnate, and the poets sing the praise of *Eros*. They pay very great attention and homage precisely to that phenomenon from which Socrates abstracts in the *Republic* to the best of his powers. The poets therefore foster
injustice. So does Thrasymachos. But just as Socrates, in spite of this, could
be a friend of Thrasymachos, so there is no reason why he could not be a
friend of the poets and especially of Homer. Perhaps Socrates needs the
poets in order to restore, on another occasion, the dignity of *Eros*: the *Banquet*, the only Platonic dialogue in which Socrates is shown to converse
with poets, is devoted entirely to *Eros*.

The foundation for the return to poetry was laid at the very beginning of the discussion of the inferior regimes and of the inferior souls. The
transition from the best regime to the inferior regimes was explicitly ascribed to the Muses speaking "tragically," and the transition from the best
man to the inferior men has in fact a somewhat "comical" touch [82]: poetry
takes the lead when the descent from the highest theme—justice understood as philosophy—begins. The return to poetry, which is preceded by
the account of the inferior regimes and the inferior souls, is followed by a
discussion of "the greatest rewards for virtue," *i.e.*, the rewards not inherent in justice or philosophy itself.[83] The return to poetry constitutes the
center of that part of the *Republic* in which the conversation descends
from the highest theme. This cannot be surprising, for philosophy as quest
for the truth is the highest activity of man, and poetry is not concerned
with the truth.

In the first discussion of poetry, which preceded by a long time the
introduction of philosophy as a theme, poetry's unconcern with the truth
was its chief recommendation, for at that time it was untruth that was
needed.[84] The most excellent poets were expelled from the just city, not because they teach untruth, but because they teach the wrong kind of untruth. But in the meantime it has become clear that only the life of the philosophizing man in so far as he philosophizes is the just life, and that that
life, so far from needing untruth, utterly rejects it.[85] The progress from the
city, even the best city, to the philosopher requires, it seems, a progress
from the qualified acceptance of poetry to its unqualified rejection.

In the light of philosophy, poetry reveals itself to be the imitation of

[81] *Republic*, 568a–d.
[82] *Republic*, 545d–e, 549c–e.
[83] *Republic*, 608c, 614a.
[84] *Republic*, 377a.
[85] *Republic*, 485c–d.

imitations of the truth, *i.e.*, of the ideas. The contemplation of the ideas is the activity of the philosopher, the imitation of the ideas is the activity of the ordinary artisan, and the imitation of the works of artisans is the activity of poets and other "imitative" artisans. To begin with, Socrates presents the order of rank in these terms: the maker of the ideas (*e.g.*, of the idea of the bed) is the God, the maker of the imitation (of the bed which can be used) is the artisan, and the maker of the imitation of the imitation (of the painting of a bed) is the imitative artisan. Later on he restates the order of rank in these terms: first the user, then the artisan, and finally the imitative artisan. The idea of the bed originates in the user who determines the "form" of the bed with a view to the end for which it is to be used. The user is then the one who possesses the highest or most authoritative knowledge: the highest knowledge is not that possessed by any artisans as such at all; the poet who stands at the opposite pole from the user does not possess any knowledge, not even right opinion.[86] In order to understand this seemingly outrageous indictment of poetry one must first identify the artisan whose work the poet imitates. The poets' themes are above all the human things referring to virtue and vice; the poets see the human things in the light of virtue, but the virtue toward which they look is an imperfect and even distorted image of virtue.[87] The artisan whom the poet imitates is the nonphilosophic legislator who is an imperfect imitator of virtue itself.[88] In particular, justice as understood by the city is necessarily the work of the legislator, for the just as understood by the city is the legal. No one expressed Socrates' suggestion more clearly than Nietzsche, who said that "the poets were always the valets of some morality. . . ."[89] But according to the French saying, for a valet there is no hero: Are the artists and in particular the poets not aware of the secret weakness of their heroes? This is indeed the case according to Socrates. The poets bring to light, for instance, the full force of the grief which a man feels for the loss of someone dear to him—of a feeling to which a respectable man would not give adequate utterance except when he is alone, because its adequate utterance in the presence of others is not becoming and lawful: the poets bring to light that in our nature which the law forcibly restrains.[90] If this is so, if the poets are perhaps the men who understand best the nature of the passions which the law restrains, they are very far from being merely the servants of the legislators; they are also the men from whom the prudent legislator will learn. The genuine "quarrel between philosophy and poetry"[91] concerns, from the philosopher's point of view, not the worth of poetry as such, but the order of rank of philosophy and poetry. According to Socrates, po-

[86] *Republic,* 601c–602a.
[87] *Republic,* 598e, 599c–e, 600e.
[88] Cf. *Republic,* 501a.
[89] *The Gay Science,* No. 1.
[90] *Republic,* 603e–604a,c, 607a.
[91] *Republic,* 607b.

etry is legitimate only as ministerial to the "user" par excellence, to the king who is the philosopher, and not as autonomous. For autonomous poetry presents human life as autonomous, *i.e.*, as not directed toward the philosophic life, and therefore it never presents the philosophic life itself except in its comical distortion; hence autonomous poetry is necessarily either tragedy or comedy since the nonphilosophic life understood as autonomous has either no way out of its fundamental difficulty or only an inept one. But ministerial poetry presents the nonphilosophic life as ministerial to the philosophic life and therefore, above all, it presents the philosophic life itself.[92] The greatest example of ministerial poetry is the Platonic dialogue.

The *Republic* concludes with a discussion of the greatest rewards for justice and the greatest punishments for injustice. The discussion consists of three parts: (1) proof of the immortality of the soul; (2) the divine and human rewards and punishments for men while they are alive; (3) the rewards and punishments after death. The central part is silent about the philosophers: rewards for justice and punishments for injustice during life are needed for the nonphilosophers whose justice does not have the intrinsic attractiveness which the justice of the philosophers has. The account of the rewards and punishments after death is given in the form of a myth. The myth is not baseless, since it is based on the proof of the immortality of the souls. The soul cannot be immortal if it is composed of many things unless the composition is most perfect. But the soul as we know it from our experience lacks that perfect harmony. In order to find the truth, one would have to recover by reasoning the original or true nature of the soul.[93] This reasoning is not achieved in the *Republic*. That is to say, Socrates proves the immortality of the soul without having brought to light the nature of the soul. The situation at the end of the *Republic* corresponds precisely to the situation at the end of the first book of the *Republic* where Socrates makes clear that he has proved that justice is salutary without knowing the "what" or nature of justice. The discussion following the first book does bring to light the nature of justice as the right order of the soul, yet how can one know the right order of the soul if one does not know the nature of the soul? Let us remember here also the fact that the parallelism between soul and city, which is the premise of the doctrine of the soul stated in the *Republic*, is evidently questionable and even untenable. The *Republic* cannot bring to light the nature of the soul because it abstracts from *eros* and from the body. If we are genuinely concerned with finding out precisely what justice is, we must take "another longer way around" in our study of the soul than the way which is taken in the *Republic*.[94] This does not mean that what we learn from the *Republic* about justice is not

[92] Cf. *Republic*, 604e.
[93] *Republic*, 611b–612a.
[94] *Republic*, 504b, 506d.

true or is altogether provisional. The teaching of the *Republic* regarding justice, although not complete, can yet be true in so far as the nature of justice depends decisively on the nature of the city—for even the transpolitical cannot be understood as such except if the city is understood—and the city is completely intelligible because its limits can be made perfectly manifest: to see these limits, one need not have answered the question regarding the whole; it is sufficient to have raised the question regarding the whole. The *Republic* then indeed makes clear what justice is. However, as Cicero has observed, the *Republic* does not bring to light the best possible regime but rather the nature of political things—the nature of the city.[95] Socrates makes clear in the *Republic* what character the city would have to have in order to satisfy the highest needs of man. By letting us see that the city constructed in accordance with this requirement is not possible, he lets us see the essential limits, the nature, of the city.

THE STATESMAN

The *Statesman* is preceded by the *Sophist,* which in its turn is preceded by the *Theaitetos*. The *Theaitetos* presents a conversation between Socrates and the young mathematician Theaitetos which takes place in the presence of the mature and renowned mathematician Theodoros, as well as of Theaitetos' young companion named Socrates, and which is meant to make clear what knowledge or science is. The conversation does not lead to a positive result: Socrates by himself only knows that he does not know, and Theaitetos is not like Glaukon or Adeimantos who can be assisted by Socrates (or can assist him) in bringing forth a positive teaching. On the day following Socrates' conversation with Theaitetos, Socrates again meets with Theodoros, the younger Socrates, and Theaitetos, but this time there is also present a nameless philosopher designated only as a stranger from Elea. Socrates asks the stranger whether his fellows regard the sophist, the statesman, and the philosopher as one and the same or as two or as three. It could seem that the question regarding the identity or nonidentity of the sophist, the statesman, and the philosopher takes the place of the question, or is a more articulate version of the question, What is knowledge? The stranger replies that his fellows regard the sophist, the statesman or king, and the philosopher as different from one another. The fact that the philosopher is not identical with the king was recognized in the central thesis of the *Republic,* according to which the coincidence of philosophy and kingship is the condition for the salvation of cities and indeed of the human race: identical things do not have to coincide. But the *Republic* did not make sufficiently clear the cognitive status of kingship or statesmanship.

[95] Cicero, *Republic* II.52.

From the *Republic* we can easily receive the impression that the knowledge required of the philosopher-king consists of two heterogeneous parts: the purely philosophic knowledge of the ideas which culminates in the vision of the idea of the good, on the one hand, and the merely political experience which does not have the status of knowledge at all but which enables one to find one's way in the Cave and to discern the shadows on its walls, on the other. But the indispensable supplement to philosophic knowledge also seemed to be a kind of art or science.[96] The Eleatic stranger seems to take the second and higher view of the nonphilosophic awareness peculiar to the statesman. Yet in the dialogues *Sophist* and *Statesman* he makes clear the nature of the sophist and of the statesman, *i.e.*, the difference between the sophist and the statesman, without making clear the difference between the statesman and the philosopher. We are promised by Theodoros that the Eleatic stranger will also expound (in a sequel to the *Statesman*) what the philosopher is, but Plato does not keep his Theodoros' promise. Do we then understand what the philosopher is once we have understood what the sophist and the statesman are? Is statesmanship not, as it appeared from the *Republic,* a mere supplement to philosophy, but an ingredient of philosophy? That is to say, is statesmanship, the art or knowledge peculiar to the statesman, far from being merely the awareness necessary for finding one's way in the Cave and far from being itself independent of the vision of the idea of the good, a condition or rather an ingredient of the vision of the idea of the good? If it were so, then "politics" would be much more important according to the *Statesman* than it is according to the *Republic.* Surely the conversation about the king or statesman takes place when Socrates is already accused of a capital crime for the commission of which he was shortly thereafter condemned and executed (see the end of the *Theaitetos*): the city seems to be much more powerfully present in the *Statesman* than in the *Republic,* where the antagonist of Socrates, Thrasymachos, only plays the city. On the other hand, however, whereas in the *Republic* Socrates founds a city, if only in speech, with the help of two brothers who are passionately concerned with justice and the city, in the *Statesman* Socrates listens silently to a nameless stranger (a man lacking political responsibility) bringing to light what the statesman is in the cool atmosphere of mathematics: the concern with finding out what the statesman is seems to be philosophic rather than political.[97] The *Statesman* seems to be much more sober than the *Republic.*

We may say that the *Statesman* is more scientific than the *Republic.* By "science" Plato understands the highest form of knowledge or rather the only kind of awareness which deserves to be called knowledge. He calls that form of knowledge "dialectics." "Dialectics" means primarily the art of

---

[96] Cf. Plato, *Republic* 484d and 539e with 501a–c.
[97] Cf. *Statesman,* 285d.

conversation and then the highest form of that art, that art as practiced by Socrates, that art of conversation which is meant to bring to light the "what's" of things, or the ideas. Dialectics is then the knowledge of the ideas—a knowledge which makes no use whatever of sense experience: it moves from idea to idea until it has exhausted the whole realm of the ideas, for each idea is a part and therefore points to other ideas.[98] In its completed form dialectics would descend from the highest idea, the idea ruling the realm of ideas, step by step to the lowest ideas. The movement proceeds "step by step," *i.e.*, it follows the articulation, the natural division of the ideas. The *Statesman* as well as the *Sophist* presents an imitation of dialectics thus understood; both are meant to give an inkling of dialectics thus understood; the imitation which they present is playful. Yet the play is not mere play. If the movement from idea to idea without recourse to sense experience should be impossible, if in other words the *Republic* should be utopian not only in what it states about the city at its best but also in what it says about philosophy or dialectics at its best, dialectics at its best, not being possible, will not be serious. The dialectics which is possible will remain dependent on experience.[99] There is a connection between this feature of the *Statesman* and the fact that the ideas as treated in the *Statesman* are classes or comprise all individuals "participating" in the idea in question and therefore do not subsist independently of the individuals or "beyond" them. However this may be, in the *Statesman* the Eleatic stranger tries to bring to light the nature of the statesman by descending from "art" or "knowledge" step by step to the art of the statesman or by dividing "art" step by step until he arrives at the art of the statesman. For a number of reasons we cannot here follow his "methodical" procedure.

Shortly after the beginning of the conversation, the Eleatic stranger makes young Socrates agree to what one may call the abolition of the distinction between the public and the private. He achieves this result in two steps. Since statesmanship or kingship is essentially a kind of knowledge, it is of no importance whether the man possessing that knowledge is clothed in the vestments of high office by virtue of having been elected, for example, or whether he lives in a private station. Second, there is no essential difference between the city and the household and hence between the statesman or king on the one hand and the householder or master (*i.e.*, the master of slaves) on the other. Law and freedom, the characteristically political phenomena, which are inseparable from one another, are disposed of at the very beginning because statesmanship is understood as a kind of knowledge or art, or because abstraction is made from that which distinguishes the political from the arts. The Eleatic stranger abstracts here from the fact that sheer bodily force is a necessary ingredient of the rule of men

[98] *Republic,* 511a–d, 531a–533d, 537c.
[99] Cf. *Statesman,* 264c.

over men. This abstraction is partly justified by the fact that statesmanship or kingship is a cognitive rather than a manual (or brachial) art. It is, however, not simply cognitive like arithmetic; it is an art which gives commands to human beings. But all arts which give commands do so for the sake of the coming into being of something. Some of these arts give commands for the sake of the coming into being of living beings or animals, *i.e.*, they are concerned with the breeding and nurture of animals. The kingly art is a kind of this genus of art. For the proper understanding of the kingly art it does not suffice to divide the genus "animal" into the species "brutes" and "men." This distinction is as arbitrary as the distinction of the human race into Greeks and barbarians, as distinguished from the distinction into men and women; it is not a natural distinction but a distinction originating in pride.[100] The stranger's training of young Socrates in dialectics or in the art of dividing kinds or ideas or classes goes hand in hand with training in modesty or moderation. According to the stranger's division of the species of animals, man's nearest kin is even lower than it is according to Darwin's doctrine of the origin of the species. But what Darwin meant seriously and literally, the stranger means playfully.[101] Man must learn to see the lowliness of his estate in order to turn from the human to the divine, *i.e.*, in order to be truly human.

The division of "art" leads to the result that the art of the statesman is the art concerned with the breeding and nurture of, or with the caring for, herds of the kind of animal called man. This result is manifestly insufficient, for there are many arts—*e.g.*, medicine and matchmaking—which claim as justly to be concerned with a caring for human herds as does the political art. The error was due to the fact that the human herd was taken to be a herd of the same kind as the herds of other animals. But human herds are a very special kind of herd: the bipartition of "animal" into brutes and men originates not merely in pride. The error is removed by a myth. According to the myth now told in its fullness for the first time, there is once a time (the age of Kronos) when the god guides the whole and then a time (the age of Zeus) when the god lets the whole move by its own motion. In the age of Kronos the god ruled and took care of the animals by assigning the different species of animals to the rule and care of different gods who acted like shepherds and thus secured universal peace and affluence: there were no political societies, no private property, and no families. This does not necessarily mean that men lived happily in the age of Kronos; only if they used the then available peace and affluence for philosophizing can they be said to have lived happily. At any rate, in the present age the god does not take care of man: in the present age there is no divine providence; men must take care of themselves. Bereft of divine care,

---

[100] *Statesman*, 262c–263d, 266d.
[101] Cf. *Statesman*, 271e, 272b–c.

the world abounds with disorder and injustice; men must establish order and justice as well as they can, with the understanding that in this age of scarcity, communism, and hence also absolute communism, is impossible. The *Statesman* may be said to bring into the open what the *Republic* had left unsaid, namely, the impossibility of the best regime presented in the *Republic*.

The myth of the *Statesman* is meant to explain the error committed by the Eleatic stranger and young Socrates in the initial definition of the *Statesman*: by looking for a single art of caring for human herds they were unwittingly looking toward the age of Kronos or toward divine caring; with the disappearance of divine caring, *i.e.*, of a caring by beings which in the eyes of everyone are superior to men, it became inevitable that every art or every man should believe itself or himself to be as much entitled to rule as every other art or every other man,[102] or that at least many arts should become competitors of the kingly art. The inevitable first consequence of the transition from the age of Kronos to the age of Zeus was the delusion that all arts and all men are equal. The mistake consisted in assuming that the kingly art is devoted to the total caring for human herds (which total caring would include the feeding and mating of the ruled) and not to a partial or limited caring. In other words, the mistake consisted in the disregard of the fact that in the case of all arts of herding other than the human art of herding human beings, the herder belongs to a different species than the members of the herd. We must then divide the whole "caring for herds" into two parts: caring for herds in which the herder belongs to the same species as the members of the herd and caring for herds in which the herder belongs to a different species than the members of the herd (human herders of brutes and divine herders of human beings). We must next divide the first of these two kinds into parts, so that we can discover which partial herding of herds in which the herder belongs to the same species as the members of the herd is the kingly art. Let us assume that the partial caring sought is "ruling cities." Ruling cities is naturally divided into ruling not willed by the ruled (ruling by sheer force) and ruling willed by the ruled; the former is tyrannical, and the latter is kingly. Here we receive the first glimpse of freedom as the specifically political theme. But at the very moment in which the stranger alludes to this difficulty, he turns away from it. He finds the whole previous procedure unsatisfactory.

The method which proves to be helpful, where the division of classes and into classes as well as the myth have failed, is the use of an example. The stranger illustrates the usefulness of examples by an example. The example is meant to illustrate man's situation in regard to knowledge—to the phenomenon which is the guiding theme of the trilogy *Theaitetos-Sophist-Statesman*. The example chosen is children's knowledge of reading. Start-

[102] *Statesman*, 274e–275c.

ing from knowledge of the letters (the "elements"), they proceed step by step to the knowledge of the shortest and easiest syllables (the combination of "elements"), and then to the knowledge of long and difficult ones. Knowledge of the whole is not possible if it is not similar to the art of reading: knowledge of the elements must be available, the elements must be fairly small in number, and not all elements must be combinable.[103] But can we say that we possess knowledge of the "elements" of the whole or that we can ever start from an absolute beginning? Did we in the *Statesman* begin from an adequate understanding of "art" or "knowledge"? Is it not true that while we necessarily long for knowledge of the whole, we are condemned to rest satisfied with partial knowledge of parts of the whole and hence never truly to transcend the sphere of opinion? Is therefore philosophy, and hence human life, not necessarily Sisyphean? Could this be the reason why the demand for freedom is not so evidently sound as many present-day lovers of freedom believe on the basis of very similar thoughts? (Perhaps this could induce one to consider Dostoyevsky's *Grand Inquisitor* in the light of Plato's *Statesman*.) After having compelled us to raise these and kindred questions, the stranger turns to his example, which is meant to throw light, not on knowledge in general or on philosophy as such, but on the kingly art. The example chosen by him is the art of weaving: he illustrates the political art by an emphatically domestic art and not by such "outgoing" arts as herding and piloting; he illustrates the most virile art by a characteristically feminine art. In order to find out what weaving is, one must divide "art," but divide it differently than they divided it at first. The analysis of the art of weaving which is made on the basis of the new division enables the stranger to elucidate art in general and the kingly art in particular before he applies explicitly the result of that analysis to the kingly art. Perhaps the most important point made in this context is the distinction between two kinds of the art of measurement: one kind which considers the greater and less in relation to one another, and another kind which considers the greater and less (now understood as excess and defect) in relation to the mean or, say, the fitting, or something similar. All arts, and especially the kingly art, make their measurements with a view to the right mean or the fitting, *i.e.*, they are not mathematical.

By explicitly applying to the kingly art the results of his analysis of the art of weaving, the stranger is enabled to make clear the relation of the kingly art to all other arts and especially to those arts which claim with some show of justice to compete with the kingly art for the rule of the city. The most successful and clever competitors are those outstanding sophists who pretend to possess the kingly art, and these are the rulers of cities, *i.e.*, the rulers lacking the kingly or statesmanly art, or practically all political rulers that were, are, and will be. Of this kind of political rule there are

[103] Cf. *Sophist*, 252d–e.

three sorts: the rule of one, the rule of a few, and the rule of many; but each of these three kinds is divided into two parts with a view to the difference between violence and voluntariness or between lawfulness and lawlessness; thus monarchy is distinguished from tyranny, and aristocracy from oligarchy, whereas the name of democracy is applied to the rule of the multitude regardless of whether the multitude of the poor rules over the rich with the consent of the rich and in strict obedience to the laws or with violence and more or less lawlessly. (The distinction of regimes sketched by the stranger is almost identical with the distinction developed by Aristotle in the third book of his *Politics;* but consider the difference.) None of these regimes bases its claim on the knowledge or art of the rulers, *i.e.,* on the only claim which is unqualifiedly legitimate. It follows that the claims based on the willingness of the subjects (on consent or freedom) and on lawfulness are dubious. This judgment is defended with reference to the example of the other arts and especially of medicine. A physician is a physician whether he cures us with our will or against our will, whether he cuts us, burns us, or inflicts upon us any other pain, and whether he acts in accordance with written rules or without them; he is a physician if his ruling redounds to the benefit of our bodies. Correspondingly, the only regime which is correct or which is truly a regime is that in which the possessors of the kingly art rule, regardless of whether they rule according to laws or without laws and whether the ruled consent to their rule or not, provided their rule redounds to the benefit of the body politic; it does not make any difference whether they achieve this end by killing some or banishing them and thus reduce the bulk of the city or by bringing in citizens from abroad and thus increase its bulk.

Young Socrates, who is not shocked by what the stranger says about killing and banishing, is rather shocked by the suggestion that rule without laws (absolute rule) can be legitimate. To understand fully the response of young Socrates, one must pay attention to the fact that the stranger does not make a distinction between human laws and natural laws. The stranger turns the incipient indignation of young Socrates into a desire on the latter's part for discussion. Rule of law is inferior to the rule of living intelligence because laws, owing to their generality, cannot determine wisely what is right and proper in all circumstances given the infinite variety of circumstances: only the wise man on the spot could correctly decide what is right and proper in the circumstances. Nevertheless laws are necessary. The few wise men cannot sit beside each of the many unwise men and tell him exactly what it is becoming for him to do. The few wise men are almost always absent from the innumerable unwise men. All laws, written or unwritten, are poor substitutes but indispensable substitutes for the individual rulings by wise men. They are crude rules of thumb which are sufficient for the large majority of cases: they treat human beings as if they were members of a herd. The freezing of crude rules of thumb into sacred,

inviolable, unchangeable prescriptions which would be rejected by everyone as ridiculous if done in the sciences and the arts is a necessity in the
ordering of human affairs; this necessity is the proximate cause of the ineradicable difference between the political and the suprapolitical spheres.
But the main objection to laws is not that they are not susceptible of being
individualized but that they are assumed to be binding on the wise man,
on the man possessing the kingly art.[104] Yet even this objection is not entirely valid. As the stranger explains through images,[105] the wise man is
subjected to the laws, whose justice and wisdom is inferior to his, because
the unwise men cannot help distrusting the wise man, and this distrust is
not entirely indefensible given the fact that they cannot understand him.
They cannot believe that a wise man who would deserve to rule as a true
king without laws would be willing and able to rule over them. The ultimate reason for their unbelief is the fact that no human being has that
manifest superiority, in the first place regarding the body and then regarding the soul, which would induce everybody to submit to his rule without
any hesitation and without any reserve.[106] The unwise men cannot help
making themselves the judges of the wise man. No wonder then that the
wise men are unwilling to rule over them. The unwise men must even demand of the wise man that he regard the law as simply authoritative, i.e.,
that he not even doubt that the established laws are perfectly just and
wise; if he fails to do so, he will become guilty of corrupting the young, a
capital offense; they must forbid free inquiry regarding the most important
subjects. All these implications of the rule of laws must be accepted, since
the only feasible alternative is the lawless rule of selfish men. The wise
man must bow to the law which is inferior to him in wisdom and justice,
not only in deed but in speech as well. (Here we cannot help wondering
whether there are no limits to the wise man's subjection to the laws. The
Platonic illustrations are these: Socrates obeyed without flinching the law
which commanded him to die because of his alleged corruption of the
young; yet he would not have obeyed a law formally forbidding him the
pursuit of philosophy. Read the *Apology of Socrates* together with the
Crito.) The rule of law is preferable to the lawless rule of unwise men
since laws, however bad, are in one way or another the outcome of some
reasoning. This observation permits the ranking of the incorrect regimes,
i.e., of all regimes other than the absolute rule of the true king or statesman. Law-abiding democracy is inferior to the law-abiding rule of the few
(aristocracy) and to the law-abiding rule of one (monarchy), but lawless
democracy is superior to the lawless rule of a few (oligarchy) and to the
lawless rule of one (tyranny). "Lawless" does not mean here the complete
absence of any laws or customs. It means the habitual disregard of the

[104] *Statesman*, 295b–c.
[105] *Statesman*, 297a ff.
[106] *Statesman*, 301c–e.

laws by the government and especially of those laws which are meant to restrain the power of the government: a government which can change every law or is "sovereign" is lawless. From the sequel it appears that, according to the stranger, even in the city ruled by the true king there will be laws (the true king is the true legislator), but that the true king, in contradistinction to all other rulers, may justly change the laws or act against the laws. In the absence of the true king, the stranger would probably be satisfied if the city were ruled by a code of laws framed by a wise man, one which can be changed by the unwise rulers only in extreme cases.

After the true kingly art has been separated from all other arts, it remains for the stranger to determine the peculiar work of the king. Here the example of the art of weaving takes on decisive importance. The king's work resembles a web. According to the popular view all parts of virtue are simply in harmony with one another. In fact, however, there is a tension between them. Above all, there is a tension between courage or manliness and moderation, gentleness, or concern with the seemly. This tension explains the tension and even hostility between the preponderantly manly and the preponderantly gentle human beings. The true king's task is to weave together these opposite kinds of human beings, for the people in the city who are completely unable to become either manly or moderate cannot become citizens at all. An important part of the kingly weaving together consists in intermarrying the children of preponderantly manly families and those of preponderantly gentle families. The human king must then approximate the divine shepherd by enlarging the art of ruling cities strictly understood so as to include in it the art of mating or matchmaking. The matchmaking practiced by the king is akin to the matchmaking practiced by Socrates,[107] which means that it is not identical with the latter. If we were to succeed in understanding the kinship between the king's matchmaking and Socrates' matchmaking, we would have made some progress toward the understanding of the kinship between the king and the philosopher. This much can be said safely: While it is possible and even necessary to speak of "the human herd" when trying to define the king, the philosopher has nothing to do with "herds."

The *Statesman* belongs to a trilogy whose theme is knowledge. For Plato, knowledge proper or striving for knowledge proper is philosophy. Philosophy is striving for knowledge of the whole, for contemplation of the whole. The whole consists of parts; knowledge of the whole is knowledge of all parts of the whole as parts of the whole. Philosophy is the highest human activity, and man is an excellent, perhaps the most excellent, part of the whole. The whole is not a whole without man, without man's being whole or complete. But man becomes whole not without his own effort, and this effort presupposes knowledge of a particular kind: knowledge

[107] Cf. *Theaitetos*, 151b.

which is not contemplative or theoretical but prescriptive or commanding [108] or practical. The *Statesman* presents itself as a theoretical discussion of practical knowledge. In contradistinction to the *Statesman*, the *Republic* leads up from practical or political life to philosophy, to the theoretical life; the *Republic* presents a practical discussion of theory: it shows to men concerned with the solution of the human problem that that solution consists in the theoretical life; the knowledge which the *Republic* sets forth is prescriptive or commanding. The theoretical discussion of the highest practical knowledge (the kingly art) in the *Statesman*, merely by setting forth the character of the kingly art, takes on a commanding character: it sets forth what the ruler ought to do. While the distinction of theoretical and practical knowledge is necessary, their separation is impossible. (Consider from this point of view the description of the theoretical life in the *Theaitetos* 173b–177c.) The kingly art is one of the arts directly concerned with making men whole or entire. The most obvious indication of every human being's incompleteness and at the same time of the manner in which it can be completed is the distinction of the human race into the two sexes: just as the union of men and women, the primary goal of *eros*, makes "man" self-sufficient for the perpetuity, not to say sempiternity, of the human species, all other kinds of incompleteness to be found in men are completed in the species, in the "idea," of man. The whole human race, and not any part of it, is self-sufficient as a part of the whole, and not as the master or conqueror of the whole. It is perhaps for this reason that the *Statesman* ends with a praise of a certain kind of matchmaking.

THE LAWS

The *Republic* and the *Statesman* transcend the city in different but kindred ways. They show first how the city would have to transform itself if it wishes to maintain its claim to supremacy in the face of philosophy. They show then that the city is incapable of undergoing this transformation. The *Republic* shows silently that the ordinary city—i.e., the city which is not communistic and which is the association of the fathers rather than of the artisans—is the only city that is possible. The *Statesman* shows explicitly the necessity of the rule of laws. The *Republic* and the *Statesman* reveal, each in its own way, the essential limitation and therewith the essential character of the city. They thus lay the foundation for answering the question of the best political order, the best order of the city compatible with the nature of man. But they do not set forth that best possible order. This task is left for the *Laws*. We may then say that the *Laws* is the only political work proper of Plato. It is the only Platonic dialogue from

[108] *Statesman*, 260a–b.

which Socrates is absent. The characters of the *Laws* are old men of long political experience: a nameless Athenian stranger, the Cretan Kleinias, and the Spartan Megillos. The Athenian stranger occupies the place ordinarily occupied in the Platonic dialogues by Socrates. The conversation takes place far away from Athens, on the island of Crete, while the three old men walk from the city of Knossos to the cave of Zeus.

Our first impression is that the Athenian stranger has gone to Crete in order to discover the truth about those Greek laws which in one respect were the most renowned, for the Cretan laws were believed to have had their origin in Zeus, the highest god. The Cretan laws were akin to the Spartan laws, which were even more renowned than the Cretan laws and were traced to Apollo. At the suggestion of the Athenian, the three men converse about laws and regimes. The Athenian learns from the Cretan that the Cretan legislator has framed all his laws with a view to war: by nature every city is at all times in a state of undeclared war with every other city; victory in war, and hence war, is the condition for all blessings. The Athenian easily convinces the Cretan that the Cretan laws aim at the wrong end: the end is not war but peace. For if victory in war is the condition of all blessings, war is not the end: the blessings themselves belong to peace. Hence the virtue of war, courage, is the lowest part of virtue, inferior to moderation and above all to justice and wisdom. Once we have seen the natural order of the virtues, we know the highest principle of legislation, for that legislation must be concerned with virtue, with the excellence of the human soul, rather than with any other goods is easily granted by the Cretan gentleman Kleinias who is assured by the Athenian that the possession of virtue is necessarily followed by the possession of health, beauty, strength, and wealth.[109] It appears that both the Spartan and the Cretan legislators, convinced as they were that the end of the city is war and not peace, provided well for the education of their subjects or fellows to courage, to self-control regarding pains and fears, by making them taste the greatest pains and fears; but they did not provide at all for education to moderation, to self-control regarding pleasures, by making them taste the greatest pleasures. In fact, if we can trust Megillos, at any rate the Spartan legislator discouraged the enjoyment of pleasure altogether.[110] The Spartan and Cretan legislators surely forbade the pleasures of drinking—pleasures freely indulged in by the Athenians. The Athenian contends that drinking, even drunkenness, properly practiced is conducive to moderation, the twin virtue of courage. In order to be properly practiced, drinking must be done in common, *i.e.*, in a sense in public so that it can be supervised. Drinking, even drunkenness, will be salutary if the drinkers are ruled by the right kind of man. For a man to be a commander of a ship it

[109] *Laws*, 631b–d; cf. 829a–b.
[110] *Laws*, 636e.

is not sufficient that he possess the art or science of sailing; he must also be free from seasickness.[111] Art or knowledge is likewise not sufficient for ruling a banquet. Art is not sufficient for ruling any association and in particular the city. The banquet is a more fitting simile of the city than is the ship ("the ship of state"), for just as the banqueteers are drunk from wine, the citizens are drunk from fears, hopes, desires, and aversions and are therefore in need of being ruled by a man who is sober. Since banquets are illegal in Sparta and Crete but legal in Athens, the Athenian is compelled to justify an Athenian institution. The justification is a long speech, and long speeches were Athenian rather than Spartan and Cretan. The Athenian is then compelled to justify an Athenian institution in an Athenian manner. He is compelled to transform his non-Athenian interlocutors to some extent into Athenians. Only in this way can he correct their erroneous views about laws and therewith eventually their laws themselves. From this we understand better the character of the *Laws* as a whole. In the *Republic* [112] the Spartan and Cretan regimes were used as examples of timocracy, the kind of regime inferior only to the best regime but by far superior to democracy, *i.e.*, the kind of regime which prevailed in Athens during most of Socrates' (and Plato's) lifetime. In the *Laws* the Athenian stranger attempts to correct timocracy, *i.e.*, to change it into the best possible regime which is somehow in between timocracy and the best regime of the *Republic*. That best possible regime will prove to be very similar to "the ancestral regime," the predemocratic regime, of Athens.

The Cretan and Spartan laws were found to be faulty because they did not permit their subjects to taste the greatest pleasures. But can drinking be said to afford the greatest pleasures, even the greatest sensual pleasures? Yet the Athenian had in mind those greatest pleasures which people can enjoy in public and to which they must be exposed in order to learn to control them. The pleasures of banquets are drinking and singing. In order to justify banquets one must therefore discuss also singing, music, and hence education as a whole: [113] the music pleasures are the greatest pleasures which people can enjoy in public and which they must learn to control by being exposed to them. The Spartan and Cretan laws suffer then from the great defect that they do not at all, or at least not sufficiently, expose their subjects to the music pleasures.[114] The reason for this is that these two societies are not towns but armed camps, a kind of herd: in Sparta and Crete even those youths who are by nature fit to be educated as individuals by private teachers are brought up merely as members of a herd. In other words, the Spartans and Cretans know only how to sing in choruses: they do not know the most beautiful song, the most noble

---

[111] *Laws*, 639b–c.
[112] *Republic*, 544c.
[113] *Laws*, 642a.
[114] Cf. *Laws*, 673a–c.

music.[115] In the *Republic* the city of the armed camp, a greatly improved Sparta, was transcended by the City of Beauty, the city in which philosophy, the highest Muse, is duly honored. In the *Laws*, where the best possible regime is presented, this transcending does not take place. The city of the *Laws* is, however, not a city of the armed camp in any sense. Yet it has certain features in common with the city of the armed camp of the *Republic*. Just as in the *Republic*, music education proves to be education toward moderation, and such education proves to require the supervision of musicians and poets by the true statesman or legislator. Yet while in the *Republic* education to moderation proves to culminate in the love of the beautiful, in the *Laws* moderation rather takes on the colors of sense of shame or of reverence. Education is surely education to virtue, to the virtue of the citizen or to the virtue of man.[116]

The virtue of man is primarily the proper posture toward pleasures and pains or the proper control of pleasures and pains; the proper control is the control effected by right reasoning. If the result of reasoning is adopted by the city, that result becomes law; law which deserves the name is the dictate of right reasoning primarily regarding pleasures and pains. The kinship but not identity of right reasoning and good laws corresponds to the kinship but not identity of the good man and the good citizen. In order to learn to control the ordinary pleasures and pains, the citizens must be exposed from their childhood to the pleasures afforded by poetry and the other imitative arts which in turn must be controlled by good or wise laws, by laws which therefore ought never to be changed; the desire for innovation so natural to poetry and the other imitative arts must be suppressed as much as possible; the means for achieving this is the consecration of the correct after it has come to light. The perfect legislator will persuade or compel the poets to teach that justice goes with pleasure and injustice with pain. The perfect legislator will demand that this manifestly salutary doctrine be taught even if it were not true.[117] This doctrine takes the place of the theology of the second book of the *Republic*. In the *Republic* the salutary teaching regarding the relation of justice and pleasure or happiness could not be discussed in the context of the education of the nonphilosophers because the *Republic* did not presuppose, as the *Laws* does, that the interlocutors of the chief character know what justice is.[118] The whole conversation regarding education and therewith also about the ends or principles of legislation is subsumed by the Athenian stranger under the theme "wine" and even "drunkenness" because the improvement of old laws can safely be entrusted only to well-bred old men who as such are averse to every change and who, in order to become willing to change

[115] *Laws*, 666e–667b.
[116] *Laws*, 643c, 659d–e; 653a–b.
[117] *Laws*, 660e–664b.
[118] *Republic*, 392a–c.

the old laws, must undergo some rejuvenation like the one produced by the drinking of wine.

Only after having determined the end which political life is meant to serve (education and virtue), does the stranger turn to the beginning of political life or the genesis of the city in order to discover the cause of political change and in particular of the change of regimes. There have been many beginnings of political life because there have been many destructions of almost all men through floods, plagues, and similar calamities bringing with them the destruction of all arts and tools; only a few human beings survived on mountaintops or in other privileged places; it took many generations until they dared to descend to the lowlands, and during those generations the last recollection of the arts vanished. The condition out of which all cities and regimes, all arts and laws, all vice and virtue emerged is men's lack of all these things; the "out of which" something emerges is one kind of cause of the thing in question; the primary lack of what we may call civilization would seem to be the cause of all political change.[119] If man had had a perfect beginning, there would have been no cause for change, and the imperfection of his beginning is bound to have effects in all stages, however perfect, of his civilization. The stranger shows that this is the case by following the changes which human life underwent from the beginnings when men apparently were virtuous because they were, not indeed wise, but simple-minded or innocent yet in fact savage, until the destruction of the original settlement of Sparta and her sister cities Messene and Argos. He only alludes with delicacy to the Spartans' despotic subjugation of the Messenians. He summarizes the result of his inquiry by enumerating the generally accepted and effective titles to rule. It is the contradiction among the titles or the claims to them which explains the change of regimes. It appears that the title to rule based on wisdom, while the highest, is only one among seven. Among the others we find the title or claim of the master to rule over his slaves, of the stronger to rule over the weaker, and of those chosen by lot to rule over those not so chosen.[120] Wisdom is not a sufficient title; a viable regime presupposes a blend of the claim based on wisdom with the claims based on the other kinds of superiority; perhaps the proper or wise blend of some of the other titles can act as a substitute for the title deriving from wisdom. The Athenian stranger does not abstract, as the Eleatic stranger does, from bodily force as a necessary ingredient of the rule of man over man. The viable regime must be mixed. The Spartan regime is mixed. But is it mixed wisely? In order to answer this question one must first see the ingredients of the right mixture in isolation. These are monarchy, of which Persia offers the outstanding example, and democracy, of which Athens offers the most out-

[119] *Laws,* 676a,c, 678a.
[120] *Laws,* 690a–d.

standing example.[121] Monarchy by itself stands for the absolute rule of the wise man or of the master; democracy stands for freedom. The right mixture is that of wisdom and freedom, of wisdom and consent, of the rule of wise laws framed by a wise legislator and administered by the best members of the city and of the rule of the common people.

After the end as well as the general character of the best possible regime have been made clear, Kleinias reveals that the present conversation is of direct use to him. The Cretans plan to found a colony, and they have commissioned him together with others to take care of the project and in particular to frame laws for the colony as they see fit; they may even select foreign laws if they appear to them to be superior to the Cretan laws. The people to be settled come from Crete and from the Peloponnesos: they do not come from one and the same city. If they came from the same city, with the same language and the same laws and the same sacred rites and beliefs, they could not easily be persuaded to accept institutions different from those of their home city. On the other hand, heterogeneity of the population of a future city causes dissensions.[122] In the present case the heterogeneity seems to be sufficient to make possible considerable change for the better, i.e., the establishment of the best possible regime, and yet not too great to prevent fusion. We have here the viable alternative to the expulsion of everyone older than ten which would be required for the establishment of the best regime of the Republic. The traditions which the various groups of settlers bring with them will be modified rather than eradicated. Thanks to the good fortune which brought about the presence in Crete of the Athenian stranger while the sending out of the colony is in preparation, there is a fair chance that the traditions will be modified wisely. All the greater care must be taken that the new order established under the guidance of the wise man will not be changed afterward by less wise men: it ought to be exposed to change as little as possible, for any change of a wise order seems to be a change for the worse. At any rate without the chance presence of the Athenian stranger in Crete there would be no prospect of wise legislation for the new city. This makes us understand the stranger's assertion that not human beings but chance legislates: most laws are as it were dictated by calamities. Still, some room is left for the legislative art. Or, inversely, the possessor of the legislative art is helpless without good fortune, for which he can only pray. The most favorable circumstance for which the legislator would pray is that the city for which he is to frame laws be ruled by a young tyrant whose nature is in some respects the same as that of the philosopher except that he does not have to be graceful or witty, a lover of the truth, and just; his lack of justice (the fact that he is prompted by desire for his own power and glory alone) does not do harm

[121] Laws, 693d.
[122] Laws, 707e–708d.

if he is willing to listen to the wise legislator. Given this condition—given a coincidence of the greatest power with wisdom through the cooperation of the tyrant with the wise legislator—the legislator will effect the quickest and most profound change for the better in the habits of the citizens. But since the city to be founded is to undergo as little change as possible, it is perhaps more important to realize that the regime most difficult to change is oligarchy, the regime which occupies the central place in the order of regimes presented in the *Republic*.[123] Surely, the city to be founded must not be tyrannically ruled. The best regime is that in which a god or demon rules as in the age of Kronos, the golden age. The nearest imitation of divine rule is the rule of laws. But the laws in their turn depend on the man or men who can lay down and enforce the laws, *i.e.*, the regime (monarchy, tyranny, oligarchy, aristocracy, democracy). In the case of each of these regimes a section of the city rules the rest, and therefore it rules the city with a view to a sectional interest, not to the common interest.[124] We know already the solution to this difficulty: the regime must be mixed as it was in a way in Sparta and Crete,[125] and it must adopt a code framed by a wise legislator.

The wise legislator will not limit himself to giving simple commands accompanied by sanctions, *i.e.*, threats of punishment. This is the way for guiding slaves, not free men. He will preface the laws with preambles or preludes setting forth the reasons of the laws. Yet different kinds of reasons are needed for persuading different kinds of men, and the multiplicity of reasons may be confusing and thus endanger the simplicity of obedience. The legislator must then possess the art of saying simultaneously different things to different kinds of citizens in such a way that the legislator's speech will effect in all cases the same simple result: obedience to his laws. In acquiring this art he will be greatly helped by the poets.[126] Laws must be twofold; they must consist of the "unmixed law," the bald statement of what ought to be done or forborne "or else," *i.e.*, the "tyrannical prescription," and the prelude to the law which gently persuades by appealing to reason.[127] The proper mixture of coercion and persuasion, of "tyranny" and "democracy," [128] of wisdom and consent, proves everywhere to be the character of wise political arrangements.

The laws require a general prelude—an exhortation to honor the various beings which deserve honor in their proper order. Since the rule of laws is an imitation of divine rule, honor must be given first and above everything else to the gods, next to the other superhuman beings, then to the

123 Cf. *Laws*, 708e–712a with *Republic*, 487a.
124 *Laws*, 713c–715b.
125 *Laws*, 712c–e.
126 *Laws*, 719b–720e.
127 *Laws*, 722e–723a; cf. 808d–e.
128 Cf. Aristotle *Politics*, 1266a 1–3.

ancestors, then to one's father and mother. Everyone must also honor his soul but next to the gods. The order of rank between honoring one's soul and honoring one's parents is not made entirely clear. Honoring one's soul means acquiring the various virtues without which no one can be a good citizen. The general exhortation culminates in the proof that the virtuous life is more pleasant than the life of vice. Before the founder of the new colony can begin with the legislation proper, he must take two measures of the utmost importance. In the first place he must effect a kind of purge of the potential citizens: only the right kind of settlers must be admitted to the new colony. Second, the land must be distributed among those admitted to citizenship. There will then be no communism. Whatever advantages communism might have, it is not feasible if the legislator does not himself exercise tyrannical rule,[129] whereas in the present case not even the cooperation of the legislator with a tyrant is contemplated. Nevertheless, the land must remain the property of the whole city; no citizen will be the absolute owner of the land allotted to him. The land will be divided into allotments which must never be changed by selling, buying, or in any other way, and this will be achieved if every landowner must leave his entire allotment to a single son; the other sons must try to marry heiresses; to prevent the excess of the male citizen population beyond the number of the originally established allotments, recourse must be had to birth control and in the extreme case to the sending out of colonies. There must not be gold and silver in the city and as little money-making as possible. It is impossible that there should be equality of property, but there ought to be an upper limit to what a citizen can own: the richest citizen must be permitted to own no more than four times what the poorest citizens own, *i.e.*, the allotment of land including house and slaves. It is impossible to disregard the inequality of property in the distribution of political power. The citizen body will be divided into four classes according to the amount of property owned. The land assigned to each citizen must be sufficient to enable him to serve the city in war as a knight or as a hoplite. In other words, citizenship is limited to knights and hoplites. The regime seems to be what Aristotle calls a polity—a democracy limited by a considerable property qualification. But this is not correct, as appears particularly from the laws concerning membership in the Council and election to the Council. The Council is what we would call the executive part of the government; each twelfth of the Council is to govern for a month. The Council is to consist of four equally large groups, the first group being chosen from the highest property class, the second group being chosen from the second highest property class, and so on. All citizens have the same voting power, but whereas all citizens are obliged to vote for councillors from the highest property class, only the citizens of the two highest property classes are obliged to vote for

[129] *Laws,* 739a–740a.

councillors from the lowest property class. These arrangements are obviously meant to favor the wealthy; the regime is meant to be a mean between monarchy and democracy [130] or, more precisely, a mean more oligarchic or aristocratic than a polity. Similar privileges are granted to the wealthy also as regards power in the Assembly and the holding of the most honorable offices. It is, however, not wealth as wealth which is favored: no craftsman or trader, however wealthy, can be a citizen. Only those can be citizens who have the leisure to devote themselves to the practice of citizen virtue.

The most conspicuous part of the legislation proper concerns impiety, which is of course treated within the context of the penal law. The fundamental impiety is atheism or the denial of the existence of gods. Since a good law will not merely punish crimes or appeal to fear but will also appeal to reason, the Athenian stranger is compelled to demonstrate the existence of gods and, since gods who do not care for men's justice, who do not reward the just and punish the unjust, are not sufficient for the city, he must demonstrate divine providence as well. The *Laws* is the only Platonic work which contains such a demonstration. It is the only Platonic work which begins with "A god." One might say that it is Plato's most pious work, and that it is for this reason that he strikes therein at the root of impiety, *i.e.*, at the opinion that there are no gods. The Athenian stranger takes up the question regarding the gods, although it was not even raised in Crete or in Sparta; it was, however, raised in Athens.[131] Kleinias strongly favors the demonstration recommended by the Athenian on the ground that it would constitute the finest and best prelude to the whole code. The Athenian cannot refute the atheists before he has stated their assertions. It appears that they assert that body is prior to soul or mind, or that soul or mind is derivative from body and, consequently, that nothing is by nature just or unjust, or that all right originates in convention. The refutation of them consists in the proof that soul is prior to body, which proof implies that there is natural right. The punishments for impiety differ according to the different kinds of impiety. It is not clear what punishment, if any, is inflicted on the atheist who is a just man; he is surely less severely punished than, for instance, the man who practices forensic rhetoric for the sake of gain. Even in cases of the other kinds of impiety, capital punishment will be extremely rare. We mention these facts because their insufficient consideration might induce ignorant people to scold Plato for his alleged lack of liberalism. We do not here describe such people as ignorant because they believe that liberalism calls for unqualified toleration of the teaching of all opinions however dangerous or degrading. We call them ignorant because they do not see how extraordinarily liberal Plato is

---

[130] *Laws*, 756b–e.
[131] *Laws*, 886; cf. 891b.

according to their own standards, which cannot possibly be "absolute." The standards generally recognized in Plato's time are best illustrated by the practice of Athens, a city highly renowned for her liberality and gentleness. In Athens Socrates was punished with death because he was held not to believe in the existence of the gods worshipped by the city of Athens— of gods whose existence was known only from hearsay. In the city of the *Laws* the belief in gods is demanded only to the extent to which it is supported by demonstration; and in addition, those who are not convinced by the demonstration but are just men will not be condemned to death.

The stability of the order sketched by the Athenian stranger seems to be guaranteed as far as the stability of any political order can be: it is guaranteed by obedience on the part of the large majority of citizens to wise laws which are as unchangeable as possible, by an obedience that results chiefly from education to virtue, from the formation of character. Still, laws are only second best: no law can be as wise as the decision of a truly wise man on the spot. Provision must therefore be made for, as it were, infinite progress in improving the laws in the interest of increasing improvement of the political order, as well as of counteracting the decay of the laws. Legislation must then be an unending process; at each time there must be living legislators. Laws should be changed only with the utmost caution, only in the case of universally admitted necessity. The later legislators must aim at the same commanding end as the original legislator: the excellence of the souls of the members of the city.[132] To prevent change of laws, intercourse of the citizens with foreigners must be closely supervised. No citizen shall go abroad for a private purpose. But citizens of high reputation and more than fifty years old who desire to see how other men live and especially to converse with outstanding men from whom they can learn something about the improvement of the laws are encouraged to do so.[133] Yet all these and similar measures do not suffice for the salvation of the laws and the regime; the firm foundation is still lacking. That firm foundation can only be supplied by a Nocturnal Council consisting of the most outstanding old citizens and select younger citizens of thirty years and older. The Nocturnal Council is to be for the city what the mind is for the human individual. To perform its function its members must possess above everything else the most adequate knowledge possible of the single end at which all political action directly or indirectly aims. This end is virtue. Virtue is meant to be one, yet it is also many; there are four kinds of virtue, and at least two of them—wisdom and courage (or spiritedness)— are radically different from one another.[134] How then can there be a single end of the city? The Nocturnal Council cannot perform its function if it cannot answer this question, or, more generally and perhaps more pre-

---

[132] *Laws*, 769a–771a, 772a–d, 875c–d.
[133] *Laws*, 949e ff.
[134] *Laws*, 963e.

cisely stated, the Nocturnal Council must include at least some men who
know what the virtues themselves are or who know the ideas of the various
virtues as well as what unites them, so that all together can justly be called
"virtue" in the singular: is "virtue," the single end of the city, one or a
whole or both or something else? They also must know, as far as is hu-
manly possible, the truth about the gods. Solid reverence for the gods
arises only from knowledge of the soul as well as of the movements of the
stars. Only men who combine this knowledge with the popular or vulgar
virtues can be adequate rulers of the city: one ought to hand over the city
for rule to the Nocturnal Council if it comes into being. Plato brings the
regime of the *Laws* around by degrees to the regime of the *Republic*.[135]
Having arrived at the end of the *Laws*, we must return to the beginning of
the *Republic*.

[135] Aristotle, *Politics*, 1265a 1–4.

3

Plato's Just Man:
Thoughts on Strauss' Plato

ROBERT HALL

The relationship of man to the state is one of the key points of the *Republic* whereby interpreters either praise or attack Plato's theory of man and the state as a whole. Usually the interpreters divide into two groups, doubtless after Plato's method of dichotomous division, Platophobes and Platophiles. The 'philes exalt the Greek philosopher to the skies, finding in him the source of all that is good in Western civilization—the doctrine of the immortality of the soul, the theory of natural law and perhaps even the American Declaration of Independence. The 'phobes darkly suggest that the *Republic* is the notorious harbinger of the "closed society." They roundly condemn its theory of the state as the ideological parent of fascism, totalitarianism, and all that is nasty and pernicious in Western political theory and practice. Passions for or against the *Republic*'s theory of man and the state run high among the 'philes and 'phobes. Sometimes it is difficult to imagine how the

This article was originally published in *The New Scholasticism*, 42 (Spring 1968), 202–225. It is reprinted here with the permission of the author and publisher.

same text can give rise to such violently conflicting interpretations. There is, however, a "majority opinion" interpretation of Plato's theory of man and the state in the *Republic*. This majority opinion cuts across the party lines of both those pro and contra Plato, with one approving, the other scorning the theory. It is the essentials of such a theory which are reproduced in textbooks of political theory and provide a guide to interpretations of Plato for the non-Plato specialist.[1]

The principal features of this interpretation, in brief, are that for Plato most men are incapable of self-government both individually and politically. In contrast, there just happen to be men who potentially are philosophers with knowledge of the world of ultimate reality, of what is eternal, unchanging, and true. But the masses, the *hoi polloi*, are forever within the shadows of the cave of ignorance, tradition and habit. Unreflectingly and apparently really wishing to let themselves go in a perpetual carnival atmosphere, they are forced to toe the mark by the austere philosopher king who rules the society autocratically, albeit benevolently. Under the philosopher's wings they will attain some measure of happiness and will lead at least outwardly orderly and stable lives. Their morality is naturally inferior to the morality or justice of the philosopher since they lack the knowledge of the forms.

The second-best morality of the citizens consists only in doing the particular job for which they are best suited by nature without interfering with the social activity of their colleagues. Such are the main lines of a view of the *Republic* held by both 'phobes and 'philes. It is the basis of most of our thought about Plato and it forms the basis of such accounts of Plato's *Republic* as are found in the histories of philosophy and of political thought. The difference among interpreters reduces to those who approve of this supposedly Platonic view of man and those who heartily despise it.

I would suggest that such an apparently "objective" statement of Plato's thought in the *Republic* is, in fact, highly evaluative. It rests on a misinterpretation of a central aspect of the *Republic*'s analysis. A careful reading of the text will reveal no real basis for such an interpretation. Because Professor Leo Strauss falls between the two stools of 'phile and 'phobe, I shall use his analysis of the *Republic* as it appears in *History of Political Philosophy* to illustrate my contention that a grievous, yet widespread misinterpretation of Plato's thought on man and the state in the *Republic*, which is approved or condemned, has become an accepted fact.[2] I want here to question whether the majority opinion is factually based on the *Republic*'s text.

The fundamental flaw in Strauss' analysis as well as in most such ac-

[1] For a more extensive statement of this majority opinion cf. my "Plato—A Minority Report" in *The Southern Journal of Philosophy*, 2 (1964), 7–64.
[2] "Plato," by Leo Strauss in *History of Political Philosophy* edited by Leo Strauss and Joseph Cropsey (Chicago, 1963).

counts of the relation between the state and the individual, is an interpretation of the famous political analogy between soul and state that throws the entire subsequent analysis of the relationship out of focus. Despite the fact that it is an analogy, the political analogy is interpreted by Strauss in the customary fashion as an identity between individual soul and state or, at the least as a strict analogy. In his analysis, Strauss interprets the relation between soul and state as an identity or a "strict parallelism," rather than, as I think it was intended to be, a rough and imperfect analogy which should not be pushed too far. Here is Socrates' statement of the political analogy whose genesis came as a result of the attempt to define the nature of the justice of the individual:

> The inquiry we are undertaking is no easy one but calls for keen vision, as it seems to me. So, since we are not clever persons, I think we should employ the method of search that we should use if we, with not very keen vision, were bidden to read small letters from a distance, and then someone had observed that these same letters exist elsewhere larger and on a larger surface. We should have accounted it a godsend . . . to be allowed to read those letters first, and then examine the smaller, if they are the same. "Quite so," said Adeimantus; "but what analogy to this do you detect in the inquiry about justice?" "I will tell you," I said: "there is a justice of one man, we say, and, I suppose, also of an entire state?" "Assuredly," said he. "Is not the state larger than the man?" "It is larger," he said. "Then, perhaps, there would be more justice in the larger object and more easy to apprehend. If it pleases you, then, let us first look for its quality in states, and then only examine it also in the individual, looking for the likeness of the greater in the form of the less. . . . If, then . . . our argument should observe the origin of a state we shall see also the origin of justice and injustice in it? . . . And if this is done, we may expect to find more easily what we are seeking?" [3]

The purpose is not so much an investigation into the nature of political institutions as it is an inquiry into the nature of the morality of the state conceived like the individual as a means to the discovery of the nature of the justice of the individual. The individual and the state are distinct, though similar, entities. Finally, the inquiry into the nature of the justice of the state does not end the search for the definition of the justice of the individual, which would be the case if the justice of the individual were the justice of the state. Socrates and his friends are to look for the quality of justice in the state, and then only to inquire into the justice of the individual and to find the likeness of the justice of the state in that of the individual. In terms of the analogy, then, Socrates distinguishes between justice of the state and justice of the individual, a distinction which will be referred to here as the distinction between communal justice and

[3] *Rep.*, 368d–369b. All references are to the Loeb Library Edition of Shorey with occasional modifications in the translation. Reprinted by permission of the publishers and the Loeb Classical Library from Plato's *Republic*, translated by Paul Shorey.

private justice. Most analyses of the political analogy, including that of Professor Strauss, submerge private justice by identifying it with communal justice.[4]

The basis for this assumption of an identity between communal and private justice is in the commonly held view, which Strauss shares, that for Plato men are inherently unequal. Such inequality is not only in terms of the individual's social talents or abilities, but apparently also in terms of either his manhood or ability to acquire virtue. The philosopher is at the top of the heap. Strauss seems to think, not that the non-philosopher is less of a man than the philosopher, but that he is naturally unequal in comparison to the philosopher in the ability to secure virtue. Thus Strauss observes of Socrates' founding of the city,

> The founding of the good city started from the fact that men are by nature different, and this proved to mean that men are by nature of unequal rank. They are unequal particularly with regard to their ability to acquire virtue.[5]

Strauss confuses private justice with communal justice because he assumes that the basis for private justice is the same as that for communal justice, a fundamental inequality in human nature. Consequently, it is reasonable for him to assume that only the philosopher can be truly just, because only the philosopher has the necessary knowledge of the forms which in Strauss' interpretation is the only way to acquire virtue.

Socrates does consider that in the formation of the good state, men are different in their social abilities and, as is well known, thinks that at least the logical basis of society is a division of labor based upon differing aptitudes: ". . . our several natures are not all alike, but different. One man is naturally fitted for one task, and another for another." [6] But this assumption of inequality extends only to the individual's social function, only to differences in external tasks. An indication of Strauss' preconceived view of Plato's theory of man is his passing over completely the important passage in the first book which, perhaps roughly yet clearly, sets forth a fundamental equality in man in the ability to achieve virtue or justice.[7] These two passages about inequality and equality are not contradictory, but complementary. They refer to different sides of man's nature. The above passage refers to "external differences" in human nature, differences among men in social abilities and aptitudes whose correct performance, as Socra-

---

[4] Professor Strauss does recognize a justice of the soul apart from the justice of the state. But he restricts it to the philosophers, leaving as the justice of all non-philosophers the justice of the state. CF. Strauss, p. 33.
[5] Strauss, pp. 22–23.
[6] *Rep.*, 370a–b.
[7] Cf. Strauss, p. 14, where he gives only fleeting mention to one aspect of the last part of Book I of the *Republic*. The passage I have in mind is 353a–354a.

tes establishes later, results in the justice of the state. The passage about to be considered, however, underlines a fundamental equality in human nature in the potentiality for virtue. Inequality of talents or aptitudes in human nature underlies communal justice, equality of capacity to achieve justice underlies private justice. The crucial passage for the interpretation of an equality in human nature as to the potentiality of attaining virtue, which Strauss ignores, is part of Socrates' argument to counter Thrasymachus' claim that injustice is superior to justice in itself and its consequences.

Despite the fact that Socrates concludes Book I with the rueful admission that as yet justice has not been defined, the equality of man for the acquiring of virtue has been stated as a virtual definition of man. In a series of examples, Socrates brings out the fact that every class of objects, whether it be a class of animate or inanimate objects, has a certain function or work which either only it can perform, or which it can do better than anything else. The description of such a function amounts to a definition of the class of objects concerned. When a member of a class of objects does its appropriate function well, it has, according to Socrates, achieved its peculiar excellence (arete). Whether we are considering axes, eyes, pruning hooks, or whatever, the general principle applies that "there is a specific excellence (arete) of everything for which a specific work or function is appointed." Applying this principle to man, Socrates assigns to man the distinctive, defining function of living, not in a biological sense, but in a moral sense. The kind of living characteristic of all men is living qualified by "management, rule, deliberation, and the like" in the soul.

> The soul, has it a work (ergon) which you couldn't accomplish with anything else in the world, as for example, management, rule, deliberation, and the like? Is there anything else than soul to which you could rightly assign these and say that they were its peculiar work . . . and again life? Shall we say that it too is the function (ergon) of the soul? . . . and do we not also say that there is an excellence or virtue of the soul? Will the soul ever accomplish its own work well if deprived of its own virtue . . . ? Of necessity, then, a bad soul will govern and manage things badly, while the good soul will in all these things do well. . . . And did we not agree that the excellence or virtue of the soul is justice and its defect injustice? [8]

Despite the fact that here is a preliminary, tentative definition of the nature of justice, this passage does disclose significant aspects of Plato's theory of man which would otherwise be missed. The context of the passage, the examples of the definition of the axe and of the eyes in terms of use, shows that the passage itself is presenting a definition of man in terms of the capacity to live in a certain way, in terms of the function of the soul

[8] *Rep.*, 353d–353e.

with regard to management, rule, and deliberation—a function that can be performed well or badly. The extension of man, the range of the application, is to all members of the class of man. Any man, because he is a man, has the potentiality for virtue. In that potentiality lies the very definition of man. To be incapable of virtue or to be less capable of virtue than another man would either be to be no man or to be less of a man.

The defining function of man, then, is the capacity to be just, a capacity which as the passage indicates, may or may not be realized. And to anticipate what will later appear in my argument, the purpose of the good or ideal state is to make possible the realization of this capacity for justice which all men because of their manhood equally share, diverse as their social talents and aptitudes may be. Rejected, then, is the common view shared by Strauss that according to Plato most men suffer from something like innate lobotomies, that they are naturally dull and stupid. For the qualities which apply to living well have to do with management, rule, and deliberation which entail the use of reason.

To say in answer to the above points that it does not follow that all men under any conditions will be able to attain virtue or with regard to living, be able to manage, rule, and deliberate is to go against the meaning of the passage. If a definition of man is intended and if most men are incapable of attaining virtue under any circumstances and of acting rationally in these above senses, then obviously the definition is faulty. It is a poor definition that does not cover most, if not all, members of the class denoted by the *definiendum*. Socrates did intend the definition of man's function to extend to all men as the function of the axe and the eyes extend to all axes and eyes, not merely to those of the philosophers!

The impact of this definition of man will become fully apparent in our discussion of the nature of private justice which Socrates takes up after the definition of the justice of the state. Justice of the state comes about when those individuals capable of doing those social tasks for which they are naturally suited do in fact discharge them without interfering with the activities of others in the society.

Justice of the state is a development of the principle underlying the origin of the state enunciated by Socrates early in the *Republic,* "that each man must perform one social service in the state for which his nature was best adapted." Fully orchestrated, this theme becomes the principle of justice of the state, communal justice, "the proper functioning of the money-making class, the helpers and the guardians, each doing his own work in the state. . . ." [9] The definition of the science (episteme) of the state as embodied in the guardians is worth quoting here: it is the "science which does not take counsel about some particular thing in the city but about the state as a whole and the betterment of its relations with itself and other

[9] *Rep.,* 434c.

states." [10] The state is wise "by virtue of its smallest class and minutest part of itself, and the wisdom that resides therein, in the part which takes the lead and rules, that a city established on principles of nature would be wise as a whole." [11]

After establishing the nature of the justice of the state, Socrates recapitulates the purpose of the entire inquiry in terms which unquestionably indicate a difference between communal justice and private justice:

> . . . let us work out the inquiry in which we supposed that if we found some larger thing that contained justice and viewed it there, we should more easily discover its nature in the individual man. And we agreed that this larger thing is the state, and so we constructed the best state in our power, and knowing that in the good state it would of course be found. What, then, we thought we saw there we must refer back to the individual, and if it is confirmed, all will be well. But if something different manifests itself in the individual, we will again return to the state and test it there. [12]

If private justice were identical with communal justice, Socrates would not after discovering the justice of the state have to "refer back to the individual" to see if his earlier analysis was correct. Obviously a similarity does exist between the justice of the state and that of the individual. Socrates does expect to apply the results of his investigation into the justice of the state to that of the individual. Socrates implies an identity of principle, rather than of content, underlying private and communal justice, the principle being that each part of a whole, whether individual soul or state, should do that job for which it is naturally suited.

As if to underscore the fact that personal justice can under proper conditions be realized by any man, Socrates in a necessary transition to the discussion of private justice establishes that every man has a soul with three aspects, rational, spirited, and appetitive. Any man, then, because he is a man has a rational aspect in his soul "whereby it (the soul) reckons and reasons." [13] According to Socrates, it is natural for reason to rule as he already has maintained in justifying the rule of the philosophers in the ideal state. And so it is with any man. Because the individual has a rational aspect it is natural for it to rule. But, unless the proper conditions exist for such rule, the soul may be under the domination of the spirited or appetitive aspects.

Just as any city contains individuals naturally suited for rule, for guarding, and for tending to the appetitive or economic needs of the society, so any soul contains a rational aspect naturally suited to rule, a spirited aspect to act as the ally of the rational aspect, and the appetitive to

---

[10] *Rep.*, 428d–e.
[11] *Rep.*, 428e.
[12] *Rep.*, 434d–e.
[13] *Rep.*, 439d.

take care of bodily needs. In the case of the state, only if those individuals naturally suited to rule do in fact rule and those naturally fit to guard and those capable of taking care of the economic needs of the city do in fact perform these functions, is the state just, wise, courageous, and temperate. Any state, Socrates suggests, contains men who are naturally suited to perform these three sorts of functions. The problem of the just state is to have its members doing that job for which they are best suited by nature. What the ideal state requires above all else for its institution is that philosophers become kings. The individual soul likewise has the three aspects of reason, spirit, and appetites. When these aspects function as they should according to reason, then the soul is just and has the other virtues as well.

What seems little recognized in Strauss' analysis of Plato's theory of man is that every man does have reason and that reason by nature ought to rule and under the proper conditions, i. e. living in the ideal state, *can* rule in any individual. But it is the reason of the individual man, not that of the philosopher which rules a man's own soul. What the political analogy establishes is that in the whole of the state as well as the whole of the individual soul, justice is secured when the rational aspect, whether of the few naturally suited to be philosopher rulers or of the individual soul, is in charge of the whole. To say that reason naturally should rule is to imply that reason *can* rule in the individual as well as in the state.

The discussion of the justice of the individual (441e–445e) like its preliminary statement in Book I refers to any man, not just to the philosopher. Standard English translations as well as the Greek text afford no basis for restricting the scope of the just individual to the philosopher. The definition of justice of the individual here is a further development and refinement of the distinctive function of man as living in a moral sense. Justice in the individual comes about when "the several parts within him perform each their own task." What such living entails is seen in the tripartite division of soul and the statement of each aspect's function. The text makes more specific the earlier passage on the distinctive function of man as living in the sense of deliberating, management, and rule.

Communal justice is inter-individual, it rests on the principle of the division of labor which assumes an inequality in social abilities among the citizens. Private justice is intra-individual. It is based on the right functioning of the three aspects of the soul, aspects which every man has. Merely because reason is in charge of the soul as well as the state does not mean that its objects have to be the same as those of reason in relation to the state. In fact, the very real difference between the individual and the state as the aggregate of citizens suggests a very real difference in the content of wisdom or the objects of reason. Underlying both communal justice and private justice is the principle of a hierarchical arrangement of the parts of a whole, with each part performing its natural function for the good of the whole. The different medium of application results in communal justice,

which depends upon the proper discharge of external function of many individuals, and in private justice, which requires the correct performance of
the parts of the soul of one individual. Socrates brings out this transference
of the division of labor principle from its application in particular cases to
the individual.

> Finished, then, is our dream and perfected—the surmise we spoke of, that
> by some Providence, at the very beginning of our foundation of the state,
> we chanced to hit upon the original principle and a sort of type of justice.
> . . . It really was . . . which is why it helps, a sort of adumbration of jus-
> tice, this principle that it is right for the cobbler by nature to cobble and
> occupy himself with nothing else, and the carpenter to practice carpentry
> and similarly all others. But the truth of the matter was, as it seems, that
> justice is indeed something of this kind, yet not in regard to the doing of
> one's own business externally, but with regard to that which is within and
> in the true sense concerns one's self, and the things of one's self—it means
> that a man must not suffer the principles in his soul to do each the work
> of some other and interference and meddle with one another, but that he
> should dispose well of what in the true sense of the word is properly his
> own.[14]

That all citizens are to be just in the sense described above, not
merely the philosophers, follows from the dependence of justice of the state
upon the justice of the individual. Only if the citizen has private justice,
justice within his soul, can he go about doing his appropriate social function in attaining communal justice. Only when the citizen has "made of
himself a unit, one man instead of many, self-controlled and in unison, he
should then and only then turn to practise if he finds aught to do either in
the getting of wealth or the tendance of body or it may be in political action or private business. . . ."[15]

The range of activities indicated here includes those of the appetitive
or money-making class. A mutual relation of dependence exists between
communal justice and private justice. Only if the citizen has private justice
can he, according to the passage above, perform well his natural function
in contributing towards the winning and maintenance of communal justice.
To attain private justice, the individual must live within a state that already
has communal justice.

What makes this interpretation of the text difficult to accept is the assumption that only the philosophers have wisdom or knowledge. But in
discussing the nature and function of the wisdom of the state, Socrates
notes the many other kinds of knowledge which exist in the state. The
knowledge of the philosopher is not the only knowledge in the state, but
that knowledge which is necessary for rule of the whole state. The philosopher rulers are proficient in that "science in the state . . . which does not

[14] *Rep.*, 443b–d.
[15] *Rep.*, 443e.

take counsel about some particular thing in the state but about the state as a whole and the betterment of its relations with itself and other states." [16]

Contrast this definition of the wisdom of the state with that of the individual. The individual is wise "by that small part that rules in him and handed down these commands (about what is or is not to be feared), by its possession in turn within it of the knowledge of what is beneficial for each and for the whole, the community composed of the three." [17] According to Socrates, the rational part of the soul rules, "being wise and exercising forethought in behalf of the whole soul." [18] Similarity exists between the wisdom of the soul and that of the state, in the reason of each guiding its respective whole. But the difference between the two wholes certainly affects the kind of wisdom which is exercised by the rational element in taking charge of the whole. It takes a heap more thinking, so to speak, to run the affairs of the state than to guide one's own activities.

To guide the state in its external and internal affairs, the philosopher ruler has knowledge of the forms. Significantly, the first real discussion of the forms comes after the analysis of the justice and other virtues of the individual. The purport of the discussion of the theory of forms is not that it produces a higher justice for the philosophers than for the ordinary citizen, but that it equips the philosopher with the ability to rule, in vindication of Socrates' dictum that society shall not be rid of evils until philosophers become kings or kings philosophers:

> Since the philosophers are those who are capable of apprehending that which is eternal and unchanging, while those who are incapable of this, but lose themselves and wander amid the multiplicities of multifarious things are not philosophers, which of the two kinds ought to be leaders in a state? . . . Whichever appear competent to guard the laws and pursuits of society, these we should establish as guardians. . . . Do you think . . . that there is any appreciable difference between the blind and those who are veritably deprived of the knowledge of the veritable being of things, those who have no vivid pattern in their souls and so cannot, as painters look to their models, fix their eyes on the absolute truth, and always with reference to the ideal and in the exactest possible contemplation of it establish in this world also the laws of the beautiful, the just, and the good, when that is needful, or guard and preserve those that are established? [19]

Knowledge of the forms, then, enables the philosophers to do that job for which they are naturally suited, a task which, in large measure, is implemented through the education of citizens to some awareness of justice. It is such knowledge rather than any more real justice which separates the philosophers from the ordinary citizen; at one point Socrates even suggests

[16] *Rep.*, 428d–e.
[17] *Rep.*, 442b.
[18] *Rep.*, 441e.
[19] *Rep.*, 484b–e.

that there is no real difference in the degree of virtue between the philosophers and the non-philosophers,

> Shall we . . . appoint those blind souls, as their guardians, rather than
> those who have learned to know the ideal reality of things and who do not
> fall short of the others in experience *and are not second to them in any part
> of virtue?* It would be strange indeed . . . to choose other than the philos-
> ophers, provided they were not deficient in these other respects, for this
> very knowledge of the ideal would perhaps be the greatest of superiori-
> ties.[20]

Knowledge of the forms, then, distinguishes the kind of job the philosopher performs from that of the members of the artisan class. But superiority in knowledge is not necessarily also in terms of a superiority in
private justice. Such knowledge enables the philosopher ruler to do his social task in part by educating the citizens to some awareness of justice. To
do so the philosopher rulers frequently glance at

> justice, beauty, sobriety and the like as they are in the nature of things, and
> alternately at that which they were trying to reproduce in mankind, min-
> gling and blending . . . the hue of flesh, so to speak, deriving their judg-
> ment from that likeness of humanity which Homer too called when it ap-
> peared in men, the image and likeness of God.[21]

Because of his knowledge of the realm of forms, the philosopher is
always "Stamping on the plastic matter of human nature in public and private the patterns that he visions there (in the world of forms), and not
merely to mold and fashion himself. . . ." [22]

The craft analogy here is metaphorical. The philosopher ruler cannot
create a moral individual as a builder builds a house. Socrates emphasizes
the moral responsibility of the individual with his definition of private justice as being "not in regard to the doing of one's business externally, but
with regard to that which is within and in the true sense concerns oneself
and the things of oneself." Through the kind of state and the cultural and
educational context which he creates, the philosopher ruler provides the
means for the individual citizen to acquire private justice through his own
efforts.

As I have already suggested, the ordinary citizen does not need to
have knowledge of the forms to be just, although such knowledge *is* necessary for teaching justice. Further, the average citizen from one standpoint
is hardly intellectually impoverished. The artisan class includes, as Socrates has already mentioned, many different kinds of knowledge and arts.[23]

[20] *Rep.*, 484d. Italics mine.
[21] *Rep.*, 501b.
[22] *Rep.*, 500d.
[23] *Rep.*, 428b–c.

The navigator, doctor, architect are just as much members of the appetitive class as the carpenter, shoemaker, and cook. Not merely intelligence, but only a certain type of intelligence, qualifies one for membership among the philosopher rulers. Although Socrates is primarily concerned with the kind of knowledge and education to be had by the philosopher rulers, he does provide some idea of the sort of knowledge which may be had by the citizens. What may be termed an "educated" right opinion appears as the cognitive source whereby the citizens become just.[24] Such right opinion is not merely a blind knack for doing the right thing as may be the case in the *Meno,* but knowing how to do the right thing because of education. Such right opinion is almost assimilated in value to knowledge in the *Republic.* Right opinion entails the awareness of standards and their foundations and ways of action in human nature, and their relevance to conduct.

I have suggested up to this point that Strauss identifies the justice of the state with that of the individual. It is true that he distinguishes between something like private justice and communal justice; but this distinction is nullified so far as the average citizen of the ideal state is concerned. For Strauss only the philosopher can be just in the sense of having reason ruling his soul.

> A man is just if the rational part in him is wise and rules, and if the spirited part, being the subject and ally of the rational part, assists it in controlling the multitude of desires for more and more money. This means, however, that only the man in whom wisdom rules the two other parts, i.e., only the wise man can be truly just. No wonder then that the just man eventually proves to be identical with the philosopher. The money-makers and the warriors are not truly just even in the just city because their justice derives exclusively from habituation of one kind or another as distinguished from philosophy: hence in the deepest recesses of their souls they long for tyranny, i.e. for complete injustice.[25]

[24] Cf. *Rep.,* 430b. What Socrates says of the courage of the state could be also applied to the courage of the individual, "you would consider right opinion about the same matters (relating to courage) not produced by education, that which may manifest itself in a beast or slave, to have little or nothing to do with law and . . . you would call it by any other name than courage." Also cf. 506c, ". . . have you not observed that opinions divorced from knowledge are ugly things? The best of them are blind. Or do you think that those who hold some true opinion without intelligence differ appreciably from blind men who go the right way."

[25] Strauss, p. 21. Strauss' reference for his assumption that the non-philosophers long for complete injustice is a passage from the Myth of Er, 619b–d. Because of the difficulty of the interpretation of the Platonic myths as such, it would seem appropriate to have such interpretations based on passages from the myth corroborated by statements made outside a mythic framework. The passage tells of a soul after death choosing for its next life the life of a tyrant because he was "one of those who had come down from heaven, a man who had lived in a well-ordered polity in his former existence, participating in virtue by habit and not by philosophy." The acceptance of this passage as evidence would require literal acceptance of the immortality of the soul as well as metempsychosis. But taken at face value the quoted passage does not necessarily support Strauss' contention that the non-philosophers long for injustice. The "well-ordered polity" is not necessarily the ideal state nor are the non-philosophers of the

The only sort of justice which the ordinary person can acquire is that of communal justice, of doing his task for the welfare of the whole society. He seems to think that communal justice is a lesser sort of justice because it is not "intrinsically attractive or choiceworthy for its own sake, but is good only with a view to its consequences, or is not noble, but necessary." [26] . . . The philosopher does display this sort of justice but has also private justice. The non-philosopher can only have such communal justice.

If this is so, then it becomes difficult to understand what Strauss means in the above passage by claiming that the money-makers and warriors are not truly just, even in the just city, because their justice derives exclusively from habituation of one kind or another as distinguished from philosophy. What can this possibly mean? Surely the non-philosophers must truly have communal justice if the state is to be really just. Perhaps Strauss means that the non-philosophers have a spurious form of private justice. But how can this be? What form could such spurious private justice take? One must assume that any approximation of private justice would entail the domination of soul by reason. But how can there be degrees of such rule? Either reason does or does not dominate the soul. If reason does, how can there be any degrees of such domination or justice? Clearly, private justice is a univocal term.

The possibility remains that Strauss means that the private justice of the average citizen is based on right opinion. Private justice based on right opinion may not be always maintained in the soul as is the case with justice based on knowledge of the forms. Still, when it is in the soul it would be like the justice of the philosopher, with reason ruling the other two parts. What seems to be left in Strauss' claim that the "money-makers and warriors are not truly just," is that their personal actions and observances of the laws are only from external compulsion and suggestion, not from within. Their souls are not ruled by reason but by appetites or desires. But

ideal state virtuous from habit alone. The definition of private justice and the activities of the privately just man surely require the use of reason, as the concomitant virtue of wisdom suggests.

[26] Strauss, p. 33. The real difference between the philosopher and the ordinary citizen is not in terms of a higher degree of justice for the philosopher. Nor is it even that a philosopher is wise and the individual citizen who has private justice is not. The unity of the virtues requires that the individual citizen be wise with regard to matters pertaining to moral action and standards. The philosopher has an entirely different kind of wisdom than that of the privately just citizen. It is something "greater than justice and the virtues," it is knowledge of the forms and the idea of the good (504d). And this constitutes the famous "longer way" around in the inquiry after the nature of virtue. The shorter way which began at 435d and culminated in the definition of the private justice of the individual in the ideal state was an outline for the purpose of describing the nature of the justice and other virtues attainable by the ordinary man. "The longer way" is necessary because for the philosophers to be able to teach the citizens how to be just, they, the philosophers, must have knowledge of the forms and the idea of the good. They must know the relation of justice and the other virtues to the forms and the idea of the good if they are to be able to rule.

at the same time they apparently do exhibit a real sort of communal justice. They do their social task well without interfering with the task of others, thus bringing about the justice of the state, communal justice. In short, Strauss seems to suggest that the average citizen is privately unjust although he is just in the sense of doing his allotted social function for the justice of the whole.

According to the text, this interpretation that the citizens are privately unjust but communally just is impossible. The correct performance of one's social function requires that one be inwardly just. If most of the citizens were not privately just, they could not perform their function appropriately so as to attain communal justice, for private and communal justice have been shown to be interdependent. Nor is it the case, as Strauss suggests, that the average man in the ideal state longs for tyranny, for complete injustice. On the contrary affirms Socrates, a just man may, among other things, be entrusted with a deposit of gold and silver without embezzling it, and would not engage in adultery or neglect of parents. Further, the just man may be "far removed from sacrilege and theft and betrayal of comrades in private life or of the state in public." [27]

Obviously these characteristics could not apply to the rulers. They have no parents in the ordinary sense whom they could neglect, nor wives whom they could be unfaithful to, or with. They would not be guilty of embezzling funds, not because they were reliable, but because they are not to have anything to do with gold or silver. They would not betray comrades in private life, not because they are always faithful to their friends, but because they have no private life. To whom can such characterization belong? Obviously to the non-philosophers, despite Professor Strauss' bold, sweeping statement of the *Republic*: ". . . only the wise man can be truly just. No wonder then that the just man eventually proves to be identical with the philosopher." [28] I have provided sufficient evidence for establish-

---

[27] *Rep.*, 442e–443a.

[28] Strauss, p. 21. I find it odd that Strauss should rely on 580d–583b for his interpretation that only the philosopher can be just. A far more pertinent reference not cited by Strauss on this point (though he uses it in another connection, p. 21, fn. 25), is Socrates' statement 517d, after the discussion of the meaning of the allegory of the cave, that without knowledge of the form of the good, no one can act wisely in private or public life. The grounding here of virtue upon knowledge of the forms is quite consistent with the *Phaedo's* assertion (69 ff.) that "true virtue cannot be without knowledge;" this is knowledge, as the context establishes, of the Forms. 517d is clearly in contradiction with the interpretation advanced here that the ordinary man can have private justice without knowledge of the forms. A possible explanation of this apparent contradiction is simply Plato's inability to discard the belief so firmly held in the earlier *Phaedo* that virtue requires knowledge of the forms. But the general character of the discussion of the *Republic* holds to the grounding of justice on "educated" right opinion, not merely on knowledge of the forms. The relevant later dialogues, especially the *Laws* maintain no necessary grounding of virtue on the theory of forms: "educated" right opinion is sufficient; cf. the Chapter on the *Laws* in my *Plato and the Individual* (The Hague, 1963). A central theme of the *Laws* is that despite the fact that no possibility exists for a philosopher king with knowledge of the forms, yet men can be virtuous if they live in a society based on the right sort of laws.

ing the fact that Strauss' first sentence is correct, but his second is quite probably false. Only the wise are the just. But the ordinary man can be wise, and hence just, without being a philosopher.

Strauss' citation of 580d–583b, the account of the three lives and their respective value as ways of lives, the money-making life, the life of honor, and the philosophic life, as the only evidence for his statement that "the just man eventually proves to be identical with the philosopher" is somewhat misleading. Inasmuch as Strauss and others have placed emphasis on this passage for justifying that only philosophers can be wise, I should like to consider it in its overall context as an instance in which a preconceived interpretation of what Plato has said has determined the interpretation of specific passages.

The passage cited above by Strauss is the second of three arguments to show the superiority of the just life over the unjust in respect to the happiness each brings.[29] The main purpose of this entire section is the advocacy of the life of private justice over injustice. It apparently suits Strauss' thesis because it shows the superiority of the philosophic way of life over the lives of money-making and honor, in a fashion that may lead the superficial reader to equate justice with wisdom. But a careful reading of the passage shows that Socrates is more concerned with identifying the rule of reason with the philosophic life. The contrast he draws is not between the philosopher and the just soldier or artisan in the ideal state, but between the philosopher and what the reader of the *Republic* has already come to know as the timocratic and oligarchic man. In contrast to the philosopher, the timocratic man, the man exhibiting the life of honor in the passage to which Strauss refers, is dominated by the spirited aspect of the soul; the individual stumping for the money-making life is under the dominance of certain of the appetites. But the just individual of the ideal state, whether he is an artisan or a carpenter, is ruled by reason, not by the spirited aspect nor by the appetites. But does this mean that the carpenter is a philosopher? Not in the least. Socrates is making use of the philosopher as a model or ideal which is to be approximated by the ordinary man as far as possible.

Throughout the three arguments stressing the superiority of the just way of life over the unjust, "rational" and "philosophical" appear as interchangeable terms. In the first argument Socrates emphasizes that for the individual to be happy is to be "king over himself," which is the case with the description of the ordinary just man in 442 ff. Reference in the same argument to "the royal, the timocratic, the oligarchic, the democratic, and the tyrannical man" to find out who among these is the happiest suggest again that the principal contrast is not between the philosopher and the ordinary man, but between the just man, including the philosopher and the

---

[29] On this point, cf. my *Plato and the Individual*, pp. 173–177.

artisan or soldier who has private justice, and the various types of unjust man.[30] Just as in the second argument, the one used by Strauss as evidence that only the philosophers can be just, it seemed implausible to take the descriptions of the lives of money-making and honor as applying to the artisan and soldier, so in the third and final argument presented by Socrates the following description is hardly applicable to the just citizen, as would be the case in Strauss' interpretation,

> those who have no experience of wisdom and virtue but are ever devoted to feastings and that sort of thing are swept downward . . . with eyes ever bent upon the earth and heads bowed down over their tables they feast like cattle, grazing and copulating ever greedy for more of these delights; and in their greed kicking and butting with one another with horns and hooves of iron they slay one another in sateless avidity, because they are vainly trying to satisfy with things that are not real the unreal and the incontinent part of their souls.[31]

It is difficult to imagine the ideal state existing if most of its inhabitants fit the above description as would be required in Strauss' interpretation. In the same argument Plato clearly distinguishes between a soul dominated by reason or right opinion and one by appetites.

> And which of the two groups of kinds (of nourishment of which the soul may partake) do you think has a greater part in pure essence, the class of foods, drinks, and relishes and nourishment generally, or the kind of true opinion, knowledge, and reason, and, in sum all things that are more excellent.[32]

With his placing right opinion on a par in excellence with knowledge and reason, Socrates is apparently showing that from the standpoint of private justice, right opinion, educated right opinion it may be assumed, is adequate. All three arguments show not that only the philosopher is the just man, that not only is the just life happier than the unjust, but that private justice means the rule of the rational part of the soul, that which is in every man and which is typified most vividly in the philosophic life.

The purpose of the ideal state, then, is the construction and maintenance of communal justice. It is to bring it about that every individual within the state has realized his innate capacity for private justice which is valuable for its own sake. There is no question of the individual citizen being subordinated to the interest of the communal justice of the state. Private and communal justice are mutually inter-dependent. Because of the rule of the philosophers, the citizen in the ideal state is able to be "gov-

[30] *Rep.*, 580b–c.
[31] *Rep.*, 586a–b.
[32] *Rep.*, 585c.

erned by the divine and intelligent, . . . indwelling and his own. . . ." [33] It is this analysis of the relation between the individual and the state which the placing of the political analogy affords. It does not follow from this that in the *Republic* Plato is a free-wheeling democrat, that the ideal state is a democracy. But the fact should not be obscured that for Plato the fundamental goal of the ideal state is to enable the individual citizen to choose rightly and justly in this life, and, if there is one, in the afterlife.

[33] *Rep.*, 590e. This passage provides a perspective, as does the Myth of Er, for viewing the relationship between the individual and the state. The myth suggests a moral responsibility for the individual that may very well transcend earthly life. His choices are his responsibility, no one else's (617e). During his narrative of the Myth of Er (618c–619a) Socrates exhorts his companions to seek out the man who will give one the "ability and knowledge to distinguish the life that is good from that which is bad" and to make "a reasoned choice between the better and the worse life" through considering "the effects of high and low birth and private station and office and strength and weakness and quickness of apprehension and dullness and all similar natural and acquired habits of the soul, when blended and combined with one another. . . ." The goal of all this is to avoid "the worse life which will tend to make it (the soul) more unjust and choose the better, which will make it more just." All other concerns Socrates affirms a man must reject, for "this (the just life) is the best choice, both for life and death."

Again the reference here extends to all men, not merely to the philosophers. Indeed low birth, differences in private station, weakness of apprehension, dullness, hardly apply to the philosopher rulers.

4

Aristotle–His Life and Times: The Place of the *Politics* in His System

SIR ERNEST BARKER

THE SOURCES OF THE *POLITICS*

To knowledge, as much as to the objects of knowledge, Aristotle applied the idea of development. Truth itself, or facts themselves, compel men to make a beginning of knowledge; and under the same compulsion it is developed, until the object of study is fully realised, and the development of knowledge comes to its "end." Aristotle thus conceived of his own contributions to knowledge, not as breaking fresh ground, but as developing the contributions of his predecessors. Not only so; but he also conceived himself to stand at the end of this process, and regarded his own development of his predecessors' work as marking

This article is reprinted from Sir Ernest Barker, *The Political Thought of Plato and Aristotle* (New York: Dover, 1959; originally published by Methuen and Co., London, England), pp. 208–263. It is reprinted here with the permission of Methuen and Co.

the final attainment of Greek knowledge. In the field of knowledge of the State, or political science, this eschatology is necessarily connected with a belief that the object of knowledge, which is also progressive like the knowledge itself, has come to *its* "end": the city-state is to Aristotle the goal of perfection, and in politics "almost everything has been discovered." It is easy to regard Aristotelian eschatology as arrogant. But if one confines oneself to Greece, it is true that Aristotle set the final form upon its political thought, and that at a time when the object of that thought, the autonomous city, was coming to its end. The *Politics* is the last word of Greece in political science: the Stoics, when they come, are the reflection and the teachers, not of Greece, but of a world-state created by the Macedonian conquest of the East; and it is to that, and to the Roman Empire which succeeded it, that their philosophy applies. As a matter of fact, his eschatology led Aristotle to regard himself rather as the systematiser of a given knowledge, than as the creator of an original philosophy. It led him to attach great importance to the results of previous thinkers; and in the *Politics* especially we are conscious of a constant reference, explicit or implied, to the teaching of his precursors in this field of inquiry. It seems at first sight inconsistent with this view, that Aristotle should, wherever he mentions his predecessors, appear to show a spirit of hostility to their views. Especially does his attitude to his own master, Plato, seem open to criticism. If Plato is his friend, truth, and a very candid truth, seems very much more of a friend. The answer to such an objection depends upon an appreciation of Greek habits of quotation and criticism. Where Aristotle agrees with the views of a predecessor, he adopts those views without mention; and it is the fact that he names when he criticises and is silent when he agrees, which makes him appear so critical and so combative. A new charge, that of plagiarism, may indeed emerge from this defence; but plagiarism in days before printing, plagiarism in books which look like the notes of a lecture, whether made in advance by the master, or taken down by pupils from his dictation, is not a serious charge. Pupils who had no libraries would count it for righteousness to a master that he should make them acquainted with views, which were no doubt matters of oral tradition rather than theses maintained in books—which, in that case, without the *litera scripta* to attest their authorship, would be (and were) regarded rather as tenets of this or that school, than as products of this or that thinker's mind. Nor indeed does Aristotle merely adopt; he tests before adoption. He first attempts to discover what amount of truth there is in a previous view, by means of a searching criticism; and then, and only then, as a rule, he assimilates into his system the truth which survives the criticism. And the criticism is on the whole sympathetic: even where he detects error, he often allows that the error is one of stating too generally what ought to be stated with limitation, or, at any rate, he shows "the cause of the error" into which a previous thinker has fallen.[1] On the other hand his criticism is often external and defective: he criticises Plato, for instance, in the *Politics*, for saying things which he had never said [2]; or he colours a Platonic view in order that it may be amenable to a criticism which will elicit the right view; or finally, though he states the conception to be criticised fairly, he criticises from some particular point of view, and entirely fails to do justice to the whole conception. But then—is this peculiar to Aristotle? If one knew the Sophists more thoroughly, one might discover that Plato had coloured their views to suit his purpose, or that he had criticised partially, and not sympathetically.

The respect which, whether by positive adoption or negative criticism, Aristotle thus showed, on the whole, to previous thinkers, was also paid by him, in the realm of practical science—of ethics and politics—to popular opinion and existing practice. In the *Ethics* he speaks of the respect to be paid to the sayings and opinions of the old and the wise [3]; and he even asserts that the *consensus mundi* constitutes ethical truth.[4] In the *Politics*, too, he shows a great respect for the judgment of the many: their collective virtue, their collective capacity, entitle them to rule, and enable them to see how to rule. His aim might be said to be the refining of common sense: he adopts, for instance, popular opinion on the subject of the classification of States, and then proceeds to refine it, by substituting a qualitative and causal for a quantitative and accidental differentia. This respect for popular opinion involves a certain Conservatism, which distinguishes Aristotle from Plato, the Radical innovator, despising popular opinion as the mere verdict of the cave. Aristotle it is true attempted to create an ideal State; but his wings soon flagged in the attempt to imitate the flights of Platonic fancy, and the books which treat of the ideal State are significantly incomplete.[5] The essence of the *Politics* is its justification of existing institutions like the State, slavery, the family; or again its practical discussion of the proper medicines for the diseases of actual States. The "divine right of things as they are" appealed to Aristotle. At the same time, it would be unjust to stop short at such a dictum, and not to admit that "things as they are" only appeal to Aristotle, when they are what they ought to be. The State whose natural character he justifies is no "perverted" State of ordinary life, but a "right" State whose members form an association in good life; and the slavery which he vindicates is one, which, while it sets the master free for a strenuous life, assures the slave of that moral guidance which he cannot find in himself. In a word, Aristotle "does

---

[1] Cf. *Metaphysics*, 989a 30 *sqq.*, on Anaxagoras: 985a 4 *sqq.*, on Empedocles.
[2] It is true that Plato had said things in his lectures which do not occur in his writings.
[3] 1143b 11–14.
[4] 1173a 1, ἅ . . . πᾶσι δοκεῖ ταῦτ' εἶναί φαμεν.
[5] Von Wilamowitz-Möllendorf, *Aristoteles und Athen*, i., 358.

not so much raise new points of view, as conceive given relations in their
ideal meaning." [6] The "given" upon which he works, the "data" of his politics, is indeed narrow: he rests upon Greek experience alone, and he does
not consider its last phase, the Hellenisation of Asia, any more than he
shows traces in his zoological writings of the new store of facts which Alexander's expedition had brought to light. But it could hardly be expected
that the Achillean escapade of Alexander should, especially by contemporaries, be regarded as a new datum of science.[7] And the fact that he confined his view to the limits of the Greek world made it possible for Aristotle to arrive at those conceptions of the functions of the State and its
various kinds, which are permanently true, but which nevertheless, if he
had included a wider area in the mass of details to be generalised, might
never have been attained. If he limited himself to the Greek in particular,
he generalised the experience of the Greek into laws of universal application.

Within the limits of the Greek world, the knowledge he had amassed
was singularly full. From Sicily to the Euxine, from Cyrene to Thrace, he
knows and can cite the constitutional development and the political vicissi-
tudes of each State. Diogenes Laertius assigns to Aristotle 158 *Polities of
States,* "general and particular, democratic, oligarchic, aristocratic, and tyrannical." Some have viewed these *Polities* as compilations intended for a
collection—as forming, along with a parallel collection of laws, a sort of
dictionary of politics to which reference could be made in writing the *Politics;* and some doubt has been thrown upon their Aristotelian authorship.
Others again have viewed them, arguing from the extant Aθηναιων
πολιτεία, as set works in the nature of political pamphlets, written with an
attempt, and a very successful attempt, at style, by a writer who was not
merely aiming at the collection of facts, but passing judgments on the character of each constitution, and suggesting reform along the lines of those
judgments to practical statesmen. This is a view which would make Aristotle physician in general to the States of Greece, and it is, to that extent,
consonant with the attitude adopted in the later books of the *Politics.*
Whatever view be taken of the character of these *Polities,* they at any rate
attest the width of Aristotle's knowledge. And that knowledge is still further attested by other lost works of Aristotle. Three of these, by their practical character, may seem to favour the view which assigns a practical purpose to the *Polities.* These are the treatise *On Monarchy,* the work called

---

[6] Eucken, *Die Methode der Aristotelischen Forschung,* p. 15.
[7] There are many omissions, however, in Aristotle, which cannot be explained in this
way. He never alludes to the Athenian empire: he never mentions the federations of
which there had been several examples in Greece. He only considers the πόλις, and refuses to look at any of its extensions. Similarly he never considers the subdivision of the
πόλις —the Attic deme, for instance; and hence he never discovers the principle of representation, which was to some extent present in the relations of the deme to the Council of 500.

Alexander, or Concerning Colonies, and the so-called δικαιώματα *of the Greek States.* The former discussed, in the form of a letter to Alexander, the problem of the proper treatment of Greeks and Persians in his new empire; and Aristotle, it would appear, suggested that the two should be treated differently, the former as friends, or constitutionally, the latter like animals and plants, or despotically, on the ground that they were naturally differentiated by their capacities for virtue—a suggestion reminiscent of Aristotle's view of slavery, and of his belief in the natural servitude of barbarians, as men incapable of virtue. The second work, *Concerning Colonies,* had an equally practical purpose; it was written in the form of a dialogue to advise Alexander upon the proper methods of colonising the East. And thus in these two works, if not in the *Politics,* Aristotle does, with the same practical bent which distinguishes his *Ethics* and *Politics,* pay very real heed to the last results of Greek experience. The last of these treatises, the δικαιώματα *of the Greek States,* seems to have discussed cases of law, and to have propounded decisions, according to which, our authorities say, Philip decided the disputes of the Greeks, possibly at the synod of Corinth in 338. A fourth work seems to have differed from these three in the absence of a practical purpose, and to have possessed something of the encyclopædic character which some authorities have assigned to the *Politics.* This is the work, in four books, on *Customs,* probably identical with another work on *Barbarian Customs,* which is also mentioned. The *Customs of the Etruscans,* to which Athenæus refers, would appear to be an excerpt from this work. It is interesting as showing Aristotle's acquaintance with the non-Hellenic world, and as explaining the references which we find in the *Politics* to customs like compurgation and compensation for murder.

THE LIFE OF ARISTOTLE

To complete this sketch of the background of the *Politics,* some mention must now be made of the facts of Aristotle's own life and the condition of contemporary Greece.[8] Stress has been laid on the fact that Aristotle was the son of an Asclepiad or physician, and that, as such, he was probably trained in anatomy. His practical knowledge of dissection, it has been said, explains the analytic method, by the use of which he begins the *Politics:* it explains the comparison between the State and the human body, which he occasionally draws.[9] But Plato also had spoken in the *Phædrus* of dividing a subject naturally by its joints: Plato also had used the comparison of the State to the body; and the use of analogies from the arts is the commonplace of Greek philosophy. Stress has again been laid, but probably with

[8] *Cf.,* for what follows, Von Wilamowitz-Möllendorf, i., c. x.
[9] Oncken, *Die Staatslehre des Aristoteles,* pp. 3–7.

no more truth, on his birth at Stagira in Chalcidice, whence, it is suggested, he derived a "strong aversion" to Macedonia, which led him to refuse to study its constitution in the *Politics*.[10] From Stagira he came to Athens to study under Plato; but he also studied the writings and the methods of Isocrates, though he did not sit under the great rhetorician himself. The influence of Isocrates explains his interest in rhetoric and poetry: it may also have helped to turn his mind to the study of logic.[11] But the influence of Plato was dominant, and it attracted him from the study of speech to the study of man, to that domain of ethics and politics, which, as the *Republic* and the *Laws* show, was perhaps the greatest interest of Plato's mind. Before, however, he began to lecture on these subjects himself, he lived for some twelve years, the twelve years which followed Plato's death, away from Athens. Three years (347–345) he stayed with Hermias, tyrant and ex-slave, in Asia Minor; and the problems of a tyrant's rule and the nature of slavery are subjects which would naturally be discussed between the two. He seems to have been a devoted friend of Hermias, and he proved his friendship, when Hermias was ruined and killed, by marrying his adopted daughter. In his friendship for Hermias, as in his still earlier friendship for Eudemus, one detects the basis of that theory of friendship which he preached in the *Ethics*, and which served him in the sphere of politics by helping to explain the unity of the State. In his marriage to a wife, who was by his own testimony "temperate and virtuous," we see the background in his life of that belief in the family as a natural institution, which is stated in the first book of the *Politics;* which leads him in the second to attack Plato's communism; and culminates, in the *Ethics*, in his view of the family as the sphere of a peculiar friendship, and as having, in virtue of that friendship, a great influence for good. In this, as in many other respects, one finds Aristotle acting in the easy, ordinary, natural way of any Greek gentleman: his life, as well as his doctrine, shows a belief in the natural character of the world's existing arrangements, and a respect for the popular opinion which gives such arrangements life. The philosophic livery of long locks and coarse cloak he never assumed: he dressed like an ordinary layman. Nor had he anything of the philosophic contempt for the goods of this world: he was himself a man possessed of comfortable means, and he believed that a man's perfect development demanded a material basis of wealth as its condition. And if the economic views of the *Politics* seem to us idealistic, yet his calm discussion of the acquisition of wealth and the functions of money stamps Aristotle's as an eminently practical intellect.

It accords with his practical genius, that we should find him, for the eight or nine years of his life after he left the court of Hermias, living in

[10] Von Wilamowitz-Möllendorf, i., 312.
[11] Von Wilamowitz-Möllendorf, p. 320.

the very centre of events and in contact with the greatest figure of his generation, as tutor of Alexander at Pella. He is no lonely professor like Kant, but, like Leibniz, a man of the world, acquainted with the courts of princes. When he writes of education, when he speaks of politics, he is discussing things of which he has been a part. It is not only the knowledge he has amassed, not only his quiet naturalism, not only his respect for popular opinion and the sayings of the elders, which command our respect for his *Politics:* it is, perhaps more than all these, the feeling that he knew from the inside the meaning of politics. There is evidence that he had some influence with Philip: the refounding of Stagira is attributed to his suggestion; and his δικαιώματα, as we saw, are said to have been Philip's guide in the solution of Greek disputes. His advice to Alexander on the treatment of the conquered Asiatics and on the settlement of colonies suggests something more than academical exercises after the Isocratic fashion. But the most important part of Aristotle's life is not that which he spent at Pella; and his relations to Philip and Alexander are perhaps not the most influential of his political relations. His life at Athens as the head of a school from 335 almost until his death in 322, and his connection with Antipater—these are the things which touch the *Politics* most closely.

During this period Antipater was regent of Macedonia, while Alexander was absent in the East. In that capacity he had the general superintendence of Greek affairs. Aristotle was his intimate friend; and remembering this fact, one feels that Aristotle's suggested emendations of actual States, and his proposal—as the practical ideal for Greece—of the "polity" or rule of the middle class in all her States, possess (or must to hearers who knew his relations to Antipater have seemed to possess) a very important contemporary meaning. For why should not Antipater use the *Politics* to solve constitutional difficulties, as Philip had used the δικαιώματα to settle judicial disputes? Yet it is not as meant for Greece at large, but as speaking to Athens, that the *Politics* is most eloquent; and some account of that Athens, in which Aristotle lectured on politics, seems indispensable, for it cannot but be that he spoke most directly to the city which he had learnt to know better than any other in Greece, the city in which he taught, the city whose constitutional history was the most instructive of any in Greece, the city which had in her day been the mistress of the Ægæan. During his stay in Athens as a pupil of Plato, Aristotle had seen Eubulus quietly repairing the finances and maintaining a policy of peace: he had seen the Radicals, on the other hand, advocating an imperial policy, coupled by the ruck of that party with pay for the citizens, though patriots like Demosthenes would gladly have used the pay to serve the imperial policy. But there were some, who, like the party which ruled Athens in 411, wished to sink the dream of a greater Athens in the strengthening of the real Athens, and, in order to do so, were willing to abolish or to limit the pay. But inasmuch as many of the citizens could only act as citizens because the pay furnished them with leisure, any limitation of the pay must diminish the number of citizens, and modify the constitution in the direction of that "polity," or government of the middle class, which Aristotle afterwards came to applaud. And here this party of "little Athenians" covered itself with the mantle of archaism, explaining the progress which it sought to achieve as retrogression to the old times of Solon or the Areopagus. While however, in its propaganda, it carried its archaism back to Solon, it really sought to recreate, what it really knew, the constitution established in 411, with its limited body of 5000 citizens. With this party Aristotle would seem to have identified himself; and in the light of its principles the "polity of Athens" may have been written in his later days. But new features had arisen to mark the Athens of the time when Aristotle taught there as a master. Archaism had applied itself to practice; and the revival which resulted was of a distinctly religious character, while its leader, Lycurgus, was a man of priestly descent and pious temper. The temples of the gods were restored, as in the Augustan age of revival: what is still more interesting is the treatment by the State of the Attic youth. That moral education of the individual, combined with the formation of a citizen army, which distinguished Plato's *Republic,* now appeared, and in the same connection, in actual Athens. The Attic youth, between the age of eighteen and twenty, were to be drilled in barracks: their initiation into this life was through a religious service. They fed together at common tables managed by "masters of discipline": a "moderator" presided over the whole system. The approximation to Platonic ideas, perhaps those of the *Laws* still more than those of the *Republic,* is striking. It is clear that the State was thrown into the melting-pot: this actual innovation, and the archaising tendencies of earlier years, are both significant proofs. But these are the conditions, in which the sketch of an ideal State is absolutely practical; and under these conditions Aristotle's ideal State, equally with his practical suggestions to diseased constitutions, acquires a contemporary meaning. Nor, living as he did in an Athens animated by a religious revival, an Athens supervising its youth by moral officials, whose very names represented moral qualities like self-discipline and moderation, could Aristotle do otherwise than insist on one of his cardinal lessons, the moral purpose of the State.

"Indeed, these are giant times, and in them Aristotle stands like a giant. In distant Susa the young lord of the world solemnises his marriage to Rhoxana, a symbol of peace and reconciliation in that ancient feud of the nations, which Homer and Herodotus had painted. It is the new-born Achilles' wedding to Polyxena; and yet again it is the dawn of Hellenism, for the child of the marriage of the nations is Christianity. In distant Athens rises undismayed the voice of the old man, wise, and yet of little faith for all his wisdom, denying the possibility of the union, and asserting relentlessly the superiority of the Hellenic race against the barbarians and the King of Macedon. In Athens herself, and in all Hellas, it lies like a mountain of lead upon all patriotic hearts, that the tiny States of their birth, which they love so well, should cease to mean the world. With redoubled ardour they cherish the sanctity of their domestic gods and customs and institutions, calling to remembrance the great deeds, which with these, and through these, their fathers had done before them." [12]

These then are the times in which Aristotle lived, and this is his attitude to the past and its thinkers. But to have considered these does not yet entitle us to say that we have sketched the background of the *Politics*. The *Politics* and the *Ethics* form practically one treatise: what then are the exact relations of the one part of this treatise to the other? Many terms from Aristotle's philosophic terminology are applied to express political conceptions, words like "nature," "association," "compound": must we not study these terms, if we are to understand the political conceptions which they are used to express? In a word, the *Politics* is by no means a detached treatise, but part of a system, a link of a chain: other parts throw light upon it, other links supplement it; and it must therefore be considered in the light of Aristotle's general method and as supplemented by his general philosophic attitude, but most of all as closely connected with his ethical views, if we are to understand its full meaning.

THE TELEOLOGY OF ARISTOTLE

Science,[13] according to Aristotle, deals with "forms": matter, as matter, is unknowable, because it is in a constant flux. Form, on the contrary, is permanent, and knowable because it is permanent. Here he was following Heraclitus and Plato; and in the *Politics* there occurs what seems a definite reference to the former. What is the identity, he asks, and what constitutes the permanence of a State? Not its matter, not, in other words, its citizens: true, you *might* "step twice into the same river," [14] so long as its particles consisted of water, and you *might* meet twice the same citizen-body, so long as its members were of one stock; but what makes the State's identity and constitutes its permanence, is not its particles or members but its form, that is to say its constitution, for the constitution is the form of the State. Science, then, is a science of forms: political science is a science of political forms, or constitutions. But while form is the subject of science, and not matter, yet, with the exception of the Divine Mind, form cannot exist apart from matter, as Plato had thought: on the contrary, the two are indissolubly connected. Therefore science, or knowledge of forms, demands sense-

---

[12] Von Wilamowitz-Möllendorf, *Aristotles und Athen*, i., 370, 371.
[13] In this section I follow Eucken, *Die Methode der Aristotelischen Forschung*.
[14] A contradiction of Heraclitus' saying that there is no stepping twice into the same river.

perception of matter for its basis; and the process of human inquiry is an ascent from the individual of matter to the general of form, or, in other words, induction. Investigation being thus directed towards facts will, Aristotle holds at the beginning of the *Politics*, attain the best results, if it follows the facts most closely, and if, when they develop, it follows their development from the beginning. It will attain a true conception of form most certainly, if it observes matter in its growth towards form.

The word development brings us to a new conception, that of "end," which is universal in Aristotle's philosophy, and is closely connected with the allied conception of "form." The conception of end is applied by Aristotle to the whole of Nature. His view of the world is teleological: [15] everywhere things are regarded as determined towards an end. If we ask why we should regard the world teleologically, we are only told that "if the products of art are determined to an end, obviously the products of Nature are also." [16] This anthropomorphic argument in its bare statement is not very conclusive; but perhaps Aristotle's teleology rested, not on any such argument, but on his whole conception of matter and form, and of their relation one to another. Form is an end towards which matter is determined; matter is the primary material necessary for the realisation of some end; and this primary material develops until the end is realised. There is thus a constant movement from matter to form, or from the "Potential," which is matter, to the "Actual," which is matter informed by form. This great general conception, of "movement" towards an "end," is applied by Aristotle, as we have already said, to knowledge or science itself: it is applied to poetry; it is applied to politics. In a science like astronomy there is a certain primary material consisting of obvious empirical generalisations about the stars made by the shepherd or sailor, which "moves" towards an "end" of scientific knowledge: in poetry, there is the primary material of impromptu imitations, which has "increased" until it reached "its own nature" in perfect tragedy: in politics there is the primary material of family association, which developed until it reached its "bound" in the State whose constitution is its final "form." This dynamic conception of the relation of matter and form is not indeed quite the same as the static. Dynamically, the matter of the State is the family association, while statically it is the individual citizen: dynamically the matter of tragedy is impromptu imitations, while statically it is the individual words, rhythms, and musical notes.

---

[15] *Cf.* what was before said of Plato, pp. 126, 154. Aristotle differs from Plato in not believing in a single end of all being, an Idea of the Good: each form is to him the end of whatsoever it shapes, but there is no single end of all existence. On the other hand, as we shall see, Aristotle believes in a single end of human action, the human good, which must be postulated, unless we are to fall into a *progressio ad infinitum. I.e.*, if it be said, Callias did *this,* in order to get at *that,* then we may ask, Why did he want to get *that?* and this process would continue *ad infinitum* unless it could be stopped, as Aristotle supposes that it is, by the final answer—"To attain the human Good."
[16] *Physics,* 199a 17–18.

In considering the dynamic conception of the relation of matter and form, we naturally inquire whether "the necessary" matter is always such as to develop into its form, and is always subordinate to its end; or whether, on the other hand, matter may not sometimes be incongruous with form, and possess an independent existence. Generally, it may be answered, Aristotle does assume congruity: the end for the sake of which "movement" arises finds a necessary material suited to itself and to movement towards itself. But it is not always so: a matter may exist which is not congruous with form, and that matter may limit the extent to which movement attains its form. In politics the primary matter may be so rude, that the movement from it never reaches a constitution, but stops at a tribal State; or again, it may be less rude, but yet so imperfect, that the movement, while attaining a constitution, attains a "perverted" constitution. Again, a second inquiry naturally arises, partly springing from this last. Does matter move towards form *sua sponte*, or are external agencies at work, which may, along with a rude or imperfect matter, explain occasional failures to reach a final form? A distinction has to be made. As regards "things possessing in themselves a source of movement," the movement does take place *sua sponte*. That is to say, Aristotle speaks of "Nature" as its cause; and "though Aristotle in countless passages speaks of Nature as a person, we soon learn to seek its agency rather in things themselves." [17] It might seem as if there were here two conceptions of Nature, which cannot be reconciled, one regarding it as an external thing, the other as an immanent force. But perhaps there is more consistency than at first sight appears. In one of the passages where Nature is treated as a person, it seems to be parallel with God: "God and Nature do nothing in vain." [18] Now God, we are also told, "causes movement as an object of love" [19]; that is to say, He does not cause movement actively, or as acting of Himself, but passively, and as being the cause of matter's acting. He is not an active, but an attractive force. But if He be an attractive force, He is not external, but immanent in things in the attraction which He inspires. Similarly Nature if it be parallel with God, is not an active, but an attractive force: it does not act on matter, but attracts matter, so that matter moves *sua sponte* towards Nature in response to its attraction. But, indeed, when pushed to its ultimate meaning, Nature is not merely parallel with God, but *is* God; and the "nature" of each thing is its immanent impulse to become as like God as possible. This being so, Nature is present as an agency in things, in the sense that the attraction towards itself which it inspires is present as the mainspring of movement. And it is present throughout, both in the primary material, and in its movement, and in the form in which that movement ends. Aristotle therefore applies the term "Nature" in

[17] Newman, *Politics*, i., 19.
[18] *De Caelo*, 271a 33.
[19] *Metaphysics*, 1072b 2.

the *Physics* to each of these three stages. Nature is "the primary material which is the substratum of all things possessing in themselves an impulse towards movement" [20]: secondly, "Nature, when the name is applied in the sense of development, is the path towards Nature" in the sense of form [21]: thirdly, "Nature is form," [22] or "end." Each of these three is called "Nature," because it is what it is "by nature," or, in other words, by the agency of Nature as immanent in it. But it is obvious that form or end is, as Aristotle says, Nature in a peculiar sense, because it means the final identification with Nature, attraction towards which is the root of the whole matter, and because in it the agency of Nature is therefore most vivid and close. The instance of human association, as the sphere of a movement of matter culminating in the form of the State, may serve to illustrate this view. Such association belongs to the class of things possessing in themselves a source of motion. It is therefore in the sphere of Nature's action, or rather, attraction. Its primary material, the family association, is "Nature," because it is "by nature," and it is by nature, because it is what it is through the agency of Nature,[23] attraction towards which determines in the first place its primary character, just as that same attraction causes, in the second place, its movement from that primary character towards ultimate form. But the State, the final goal or form of such movement, is most of all Nature, most of all by nature. And this brings us to one of the most fundamental things in Aristotle's political philosophy. While he holds primitive society to be natural (like Hobbes), he also holds the final State to be natural, and still more natural (whereas Hobbes would regard it as artificial). Nay, he would hold that primitive society was only by nature because it was an approximation to the State, and through the State to Nature itself.

But movement may also take place by art as well as by Nature, by external agencies as well as by an immanent force. Things not possessing in themselves a source of movement are changed by human agency: the marble becomes a statue by the hand of the sculptor. But human agency acts not only within this province: it also acts in the province of things which have in themselves a source of movement. It may act to thwart Nature: it may also act to realise Nature. Human agency may, like rude or imperfect material, be a reason for the failure of the movement of human association to find its proper haven, and may account for that movement's stopping short at an imperfect form, or going awry into a perverted constitution. But human agency is rather conceived by Aristotle as a force co-operative with Nature. Art, we may say, loves Nature, and Nature too loves art: man is animated in his action by that same attraction towards Nature, which inspires movement in the sphere of things which have in themselves

[20] *Physics*, 193a 28.
[21] *Ibid.*, 193b 12.
[22] *Ibid.*, 193a 30; *Politics*, 1252b 32.
[23] In the sense of God, or the purpose of all movement.

a source of movement. Art, in Aristotle's words, partly finishes what Nature fails to finish, and partly imitates what she actually does.[24] There is no necessary distinction between the artificial and the natural, such as the Sophists had made.[25] Poetry naturally grew—as men carried it forward [26]; and again the impulse towards a State existed by Nature—but the man who compounded the State was the greatest of benefactors.[27] That there should be this room for human co-operation obviously implies that there may be a certain defect in Nature. And Aristotle admits that this is the case.[28] Nature is indeed like "a prudent man," or "a wise steward": it does nothing in vain; "its product is perfection." It gives the proper tool along with the capacity for its use: to each capacity it gives its separate tool. Yet "where it is not possible to do otherwise, it uses the same tool for several purposes"; and it may fail of perfection; it may wish one thing, and the opposite may often happen.[29] And the reason is that matter, as we said, is not always congruous with form; and Nature, as the force impelling matter to form, may therefore, and indeed must therefore, sometimes fall short of its aim. But Nature's defects are man's opportunities: it is through them that art gets a new sphere of operation. It is because Nature does not always succeed in its political creations that "political art" can arise to offer its suggestions and apply its remedies. For Political Science, to Aristotle as much as to Plato, is an art as well as a science: it acts as well as analyses.

In what ways did this conception of teleological development, realising itself, or realised by man, determine the political theory of Aristotle? It helped him, as we have already incidentally seen, to an evolutionary view of the State: it saved him from any mechanical view of political origins. Believing in development, he naturally turned to an historical method: he traced the historical growth of the State from its first origin: he criticised Plato's theory of revolutions on the ground that it was unhistorical, and attempted an historical account himself. It is this evolutionary and historical character of his work which makes it appeal to modern minds. But it must always be remembered that his view of development *is* teleological, and as such, both free from defects that beset modern views of evolution when applied to politics, and liable, on the other hand, to errors of its own. Because his view is teleological, Aristotle emphasises, not the process of development, but the end. "Animals are not constructed as they are, because they have developed as they have: they have developed as they have in

[24] *Physics*, 199a 15.
[25] *Cf.* Plato, *Laws*, 709b: "God governs all things, and chance and opportunity co-operate with Him in the government of human affairs: and art should be there also."
[26] *Poetics*, 1449a 13.
[27] *Politics*, 1253a 30; *cf.* Plato's *Cratylus* (434–435), where Socrates says that language is both natural and artificial.
[28] *De Part. Animal.*, 683a 22.
[29] *Politics*, 1254b 27–34.

order to attain the construction which they show." [30] The end explains the development, and not the development the end. Asserted against Empedocles, and in another field than that of politics, this might still be asserted against Spencer, in the sphere of human "conduct." Because it explains the development, the end is in a sense prior to it, while yet, because it comes before the end in order of time, the development is also prior to the end. Thus Aristotle can both say in the *Politics* that the State is prior to the household and the individual, and assert in the *Ethics* that the household is prior to the State. The end, then, explains the development: the development does not explain the end. The immediate reasons which move a thing as it develops will not explain the reasons which underlie the thing as it stands completed. Mere life is the immediate reason of the development of the State: good life explains its existence. Similarly, "the lips are soft, fleshy, and able to part, both for protection of the teeth . . . and *still more* for the Good; for they are a means to the use of speech." [31] They developed, we may say, for protection: they exist for the sake of speech.[32]

In both of these ways, in insisting on the priority of the end, and in asserting that what animates development is not what animates completed result, Aristotle supplies the corrective of any view, based on modern theories of evolution, which would treat natural man as explaining political man. His teleology gives him the idea of development, but of development determined and coloured by a final cause. And it gives him further, and above all, an organic conception of the relations of the individual to the State. Since membership of a proper State is the end of human development, and since its end is the real nature or meaning of anything, it follows that man has his real meaning as a member of a State. In the State, and as a member of a State, he lives and has his being: without the State, and apart from the State, he has no meaning. This is the meaning of the famous phrase, "man is by nature a political being." His real "nature" or meaning consists in that citizenship of a πόλις, which is the end of his development.

---

[30] *De Gen. Animal.*, 778b 1–5.

[31] *De Part. Animal.*, ii., 659b 30.

[32] The thing as it develops is the "necessary" matter, which is moved immediately by necessity, as is the family association by the need of life, or the tissues which develop into the lips by the need of protection; but the thing as it stands developed has also an element "of supererogation," and matter of supererogation is moved by a final end, or a *good*. E.g., the developed State has an element of supererogation in its moral institutions, the reason for which is the final end of man, the human good; the lips, as a developed organ, have an element of supererogation in their power of speech, the reason of which is once more the human good; for speech, as we learn in the *Politics*, is the basis of justice. So too the human seed, "superfluous matter" remaining after the needs of nutrition (which led to its growth) have been properly satisfied, serves man for the final end of "partaking in the eternal and divine"; since the continuation of the race by the propagation of the species represents a certain attainment of immortality. True of Nature, this principle is also true of man: he may, for an immediate reason of necessity, do something which ultimately serves a final purpose of good; he may find a kingdom, when he is only seeking his father's asses.

Until he has attained this citizenship, he has not attained his nature, and he is not man in the full meaning of man. Complete *humanitas* implies *civitas;* and every proper man, as a man, is a citizen. As the end of his development is citizenship, so the end of all his action is "the political good." He *is*, only as a member of the State: he *acts*, only as a member of the State, and to promote its aim. The one proposition follows inevitably upon the other. It may seem at first sight as if the being and the action of the individual were limited by this way of thinking to a single aspect, and as if the right of the individual to a free and full development were consequently destroyed. But as we have seen in treating of Plato, such a *prima facie* view is quite unjustified. Teleology comes not to destroy, but to justify. "It was because Plato and Aristotle conceived the life of the πόλις so clearly as the τέλος of the individual, that they laid the foundation of all true theory of rights." For Aristotle "regards the State as a society of which the life is maintained by what its members do for the sake of maintaining it, by functions consciously fulfilled with reference to that *end,* and which in that sense imposes duties; and at the same time as a society from which its members derive the ability through education and protection to fulfil their several functions, and which in that sense confers rights." [33]

But while through his teleology Aristotle comes upon these two great conceptions—while it enables him to regard the State as a development and as an organism, it is nevertheless true that there are defects in his teleology, and that a defective teleology involves defects of political thought. Teleology taught him that there had been a development of the State: it did not teach him that there was a development still to come. On the contrary, it led him to see in the city-state the final goal and completion of all political progress, and to shut his eyes to the universal empire, which even in his own days was already beginning, and which was destined to endure as long as the name of the Roman Empire was used among men. Yet "the city-state, as he depicts it, without a Church, without fully developed professions, with an imperfectly organised industrial and agricultural system, and a merely parochial extent of territory, cannot be considered 'self-complete,' as he asserts it to be: perhaps, indeed, no single State can be held to be so." [34] While teleology thus appears as an enemy of progress, from another point of view it introduces a despotic and illiberal element into Aristotle's conception of politics. As it failed to give a *full* idea of development, so it fell short of supplying a *really* organic view of the State. The origin of this latter

[33] Green, *Principles*, § 39. At the same time, it is obvious from this passage that the teleological method leads to the emphasising of duties rather than rights; and a political science based on a teleological method begins from duties, as naturally as a political science which, like that of Spinoza, denies the doctrine of Final Cause, begins from rights (or rather powers).
[34] Newman.

defect is not far to seek. A true teleology regards the State as a scheme, and each individual as having a function in that scheme. It does not seek to differentiate degrees of value in those functions, or to distinguish between subsidiary and primary functions; nor does it therefore regard one function as a means to another, or one performer of function as the "instrument" of a higher performer. But it is easy to fall into a false teleology. A simple and crude form of false teleology is that which regards everything as meant for the service of man, and man as the final end to which everything else is a means. This is an *external* and unreal teleology, which makes objects subserve an end outside and foreign to themselves, and which splits asunder, instead of organically uniting, the scheme which it postulates. A true teleology must be *internal;* it must involve an immanent end, in working towards which the members of a scheme are united to one another in a common participation. Now it can hardly be denied that an external teleology creeps into Aristotle's conception of the State. He may regard the full citizens as united to one another in a common participation: he also regards a large class of non-citizens as subsidiary to them, and as means to an end external to themselves. A degradation of those who are not concerned in actively and immediately realising the end is a feature of his political philosophy. So far as the end is an object of active realisation by man, Aristotle tells us that it is a "function." Activity, or "energy," in the direct realisation of the State's function makes a man "part" of the State, or citizen; and those who do not actively aid such a direct realisation are not parts, but necessary material—not citizens, but drudges. Who then are those who actively contribute to that realisation, and who are those who do not? The end or function of the State is moral life: those who have the material wealth and the proper leisure to help forward that moral life are therefore citizens; and the artisan or labourer, who has neither the one nor the other, and cannot therefore contribute to an end demanding both, can never aspire to citizenship. Insistence on a teleological conception thus disfranchises all but the men of means and leisure. This conception is not peculiar to politics. The distinction between the "parts" which actively energise, and the necessary elements which passively contribute, is true of the human body. The anhomœomerous parts, or organs, like hand and foot, actively work, and are citizens, in the polity of the body: the homœomerous parts or tissues, like blood and sinews and bone, passively contribute, and are accordingly disfranchised.[35]

We have not yet exhausted the importance of the teleological conception in the field of politics. We have to notice a further development of that conception. To Aristotle the world is not an uncorrelated mass of separate movements towards separate ends: Nature is not episodic, not a num

[35] The parallel does not work properly, and there is an important difference.

ber of disconnected scenes, like a bad tragedy. There is to some extent a kingdom of ends: that which is the end of one activity may be itself the means to a still higher end. This view is stated of creation, in a somewhat external form, in the first book of the *Politics:* plants exist for animals, and animals for man. It is stated of the arts in the beginning of the *Ethics:* the art of bridle-making is subordinate to that of riding, that in its turn to the art of war, and that in its turn to political art. It helps Aristotle to a view of the State which makes it, not the one association and the sole end of man, as it had tended to become in Plato's hands, but the supreme association and the dominant end. The State is an association embracing other associations, like the family: its end of good life involves in itself other and subordinate ends, like that of mere life, or that of a common life of friendship. It is this conception of the State as embracing, not negating, other associations,[36] which gives to Aristotle's views much of their sanity and wholesome truth. The zeal of the State has not eaten him up, as it had Plato. Yet, on the other hand, while the teleological conception, in this form, helps Aristotle to save the household, it also helps him to preserve slavery. If the household is saved, as having an end subsidiary to that of the State, the slave is preserved, as having a means to the household's end. Teleology as a philosophical principle helps the practical principle of respect for the given to justify slavery as a natural institution. The slave is one who is necessary to the household's realisation of its end, and is also intended by his moral nature merely to serve as a means.

The conception of end has a still further use. It serves to classify States, and to classify them in order of merit. The "essence" of a thing lies in its end; and therefore in defining we must always give the end. Everything is defined by its function, we read in the *Politics:* definitions, we are told elsewhere, must not only state the facts, but also their cause.[37] An axe is defined by its function of chopping: we must not only say that it is made of iron, in a certain shape, but that it is made to chop. What is true of definition is applicable to classification; and as the State in general is defined by its function, as an association for good life, so will individual States be classified according to the exact kind of function they discharge. We shall have one class of States engaged in the pursuit of wealth; another aiming at liberty; a third with virtue for their goal. Nor does the end only give classification: it gives classification in order of merit. States are valued as they approximate to, or recede from, the normal end of virtue. The danger of this method of proceeding, this measuring of the lower by the higher, is, that in assuming the normal to be the natural and real, as he does, Aristotle falls, or seems to fall, into a confusion of the actual and the ideal which is apt to perplex the reader. That he does not also fall into a contempt for

[36] Cf. *Ethics,* 1160a 9–30.
[37] *De Anima,* 413a 13–15.

the actual, or despise the perverted States of his classification, is due to his knowledge of their working and his respect for existing institutions, which lead him, not to attempt to force perversions into the image of the ideal, but to reform them according to their own principles. But the conception of end is not only useful to the theorist in classification: it is not only the *criterion* used in the study. It serves the practical politician as a *standard* in actual life for the distribution of rewards: exactly as a citizen has actively contributed to the realisation of the function of the State, requital is measured back to him again for his contribution. Such reward or requital is made by the gift of office; and hence the end of the State determines the holders of its offices. As a criterion of classification, and as a standard of distribution, theoretically as well as practically, the conception of end is thus all-important for Political Science.

The conception of end has come before us in many names, and from many aspects. As "form," it represents the shape into which amorphous matter is moulded: as "Nature," it represents identification with that ideal, towards which all movement is directed. As "function," it is that full height of action, to participate in which constitutes partnership in the body politic; while the degree of participation in the function of the State is also the "standard" by which office is distributed. As "essence," the end has already presented itself as the content of definition and the criterion of classification: as "limit," we have still to notice, it determines the character of its means. Limit, a conception so dear to the Greeks in itself, that the infinite and illimitable were to them the synonym of evil, received a philosophical basis in the conception of end. The end must limit and define whatever serves as its means: a boat cannot be either a span or two furlongs in length, for in either case it will fail to discharge its end of sailing properly. A play must be neither too long nor too short to exhibit the change of the hero's fortunes, which it is the aim of tragedy to delineate. The same ideas are applied in the *Politics* to wealth, and even to the State itself. Wealth must be limited, because wealth is a "mass of instruments," a complex of means, "necessary for life, and useful for the association of the State or family." The State is equally limited in size by the necessity of discharging its functions: it must definitely stand between a minimum, constituted by the lowest number of citizens sufficient for the end of good life in a political community, and a maximum constituted by the greatest number of citizens whose faces it is possible to carry in mind, as the ruler must do in order to discharge his functions of command and judgment. And thus it is the conception of end, as issuing in limit, which involves Aristotle in these parts of his political philosophy which a modern most readily criticises— his reactionary economics, and his unprogressive politics; his belief in barter, his leaning to parochialism. Yet from another point of view one can readily sympathise with the doctrine of limit. The conception of limit readily passes into that of the "mean." The boat is limited by its end of sailing to a mean size: wealth is similarly limited to moderate possessions by the end of a virtuous life. Because it is best calculated to aid the realisation of some end, the mean comes to be viewed as in itself the best. Moral excellence lies in the cultivation of the mean of passion which lies between the two extremes—foolhardiness and cowardice, indulgence and asceticism—to which each passion is prone. And Aristotle's political aim, while ideally an "extreme" State where all are virtuous, tends to become in practice a "middle" State, in which neither rich nor poor, but the middle classes, are vested with ultimate power. In this way the conception of limit, if it makes for rigidity, makes also for moderation.

Here we may close our sketch of the bearing of a teleological method upon Aristotle's political thought. We should be mistaken in holding that this method had determined or originated all the views which we have attempted to bring under its scope. It is actual Greek practice, and contemporary Greek opinion, which form Aristotle's starting-point. It is they which give him his ideas of the proper size and constitution of the State; it is they which supply him with a classification of States; it is they which give him a distinction between subsidiary and disfranchised members of the State, and primary and enfranchised sharers in its life. What he does is to generalise and to rationalise all these data in the light of a doctrine of Final Causes; and in the light of that doctrine he occasionally corrects or modifies the opinions and practices on which his theory is based. But, as it stands, his whole system of thought is informed by a teleological conception of the world; and to that conception, as we have seen, objection may be taken on some of its sides. That is why a revolt against Final Causes marks the beginnings of modern philosophy, a revolt whose champion is Bacon in the sphere of science, and Spinoza in the province of human life. Yet science and politics have returned, and must return, to teleology. Science deals in the conception of organism, and organism, as we have seen, is a conception based on teleology: it is the conception of a whole whose parts can be seen to be "organs" to a common and single end. Nor can the ultimate conception of the State be other than the conception of a whole working for a single end, from which "all the body fitly framed and knit together through that which every joint supplieth, according to the working in due measure of each several part, maketh the increase of the body."

ARISTOTLE'S CONCEPTION OF THE UNITY OF THE STATE

So far, we have discussed the influence of Aristotle's teleology upon his conception of the State, and incidentally we have been led to speak of the conception of the State's unity, to which teleology leads. We may now consider more fully his views of the nature of unity, as further determining his conception of the State. We have to speak both of the formal character of the State's unity, as an "association" or "compound," and of its inward and spiritual meaning, as a friendship and society. Aristotle's theory of its formal character comes to light in the beginning of the second book of the *Politics,* when, in combating Plato's conception of political unity, he suggests his own. To Plato's favourite "oneness" he opposes his more moderate conception of "association." A city is not one in the identity of exactly similar members; it is one in the co-operation of dissimilar units. Here we touch the general question of the relation of universal to particular. Shall the one be destructive of the individual existence of the many, or shall the many retain that existence, while yet sharing in a common existence which "blends, transcends, them all"? In politics, as in metaphysics, the answer of Aristotle is cast in favour of the latter alternative. In metaphysics, he holds, the one does not exist above and beyond the many: it is in and among, in the sense that it is predicable of, all its individual constituents. In politics, the State does not tower above the individual to the negation of his individual self: it is an association of individuals bound by spiritual chains about a common life of virtue, while yet retaining the individuality of separate properties and separate families. In that life it is one body, "knit together through that which every joint supplieth"; but, though it is of the very essence of man that he should be a member of that body, its claims upon him are not unto the last surrender of every vestige of self.

The elucidation of Aristotle's view depends upon an understanding of the full doctrine of "association." An association must be composed of men diverse indeed in kind [38] (and this, we shall see, is of the essence of association), but yet so far alike as to be fairly equal; for master and slave cannot form an association. Each of these diverse, yet like and equal elements possesses his own specific advantage; and each naturally exchanges his own advantage, which his neighbour needs, for his neighbour's, which he needs himself. Differentiation, and a consequent exchange, are therefore of the essence of association. And thus it issues in a common action, which, in the sphere of ordinary labour, is the production of material wealth, but in that of political activity is the realisation of virtue. So far therefore the State, as an association, is a union of members of different aptitudes, mutually benefiting by the products of those aptitudes in the realisation of a common aim.[39] Of such associations there are various kinds. Each has its justice, regulating the mutual exchange of services: each its friendship, knitting the association together. All kinds of association are parts of the supreme association, which is the state. Other associations than this are di-

---

[38] *Ethics,* 1133a 17.
[39] This conception is not so far removed from that of Plato as Aristotle would lead us to believe: on the contrary, it is implied in the second book of the *Republic.* But Aristotle insists, as Plato hardly does, that an association is composed of equal members; and his conception of association has thus a democratic flavour which the Platonic conception does not possess.

rected towards some partial good, or temporary advantage: this aims at the whole good of man, for the whole of his life. Like other associations the State has its justice: it has also its friendship—a friendship which it is the great concern of the legislator to preserve, for it is the bond which knits the State in harmony.

But before we turn to justice and friendship, there is more to be said of the character of the formal unity of the State. In speaking of it as an association, we have not accounted for the presence of ruling and subject elements, which characterises the State, but is not involved in the conception of association. Yet we have already gone far enough to understand something of the criticism which Aristotle levels against Plato's conception of the unity of the State. Diversity, he argues, is as essential as unity; or rather, it is essential *to* unity. And therefore Plato's procedure in the *Republic* was self-destructive: he was so fixed upon his end, that he swept away the means. Pure unity, such as he desired, is best attained where there is but a single unit: as Plato himself dwarfs his State into a family or clan, so in strict logic, for perfection's sake, it should be dwarfed from a family into a single individual. And from yet another point of view the defect of conceiving the unity of the State as undifferentiated is equally apparent. One of the aims of political society, indeed *the* aim of political society, is "independence," [40] in the sense of satisfaction by that society itself of its own wants, material and moral. The greater the number of agents possessed of diverse capacities, the more likely are those wants to be satisfied, and independence to be attained; while a society of members all alike can only result in a single contribution and an imperfect independence. As against Plato, the criticism is not absolutely fair, for Plato had not said, as he is assumed to have said, that the State is constituted of like elements: on the contrary, he had insisted primarily on the differentiation of classes. Yet Aristotle is not entirely unjust in his criticism. If the classes of the State are differentiated, the members of the two ruling classes are indeed "unified" at the cost of all diversity.

But the full conception of the State's unity is not properly expressed by the term association. To express the State's unity adequately, we have seen that an additional category must be employed, which will do justice to the presence of authority and subordination in the State. The State is therefore classed as a "compound" (σύνθετον), or more precisely as an organic compound, or "whole" (ὅλον), in which the composition of the parts results not in their mere aggregation, but in a new identity.[41] As a "whole," it is viewed as composed of parts different in kind, which are subordinated one to another; for in all compounds which form a whole, there may be traced a ruling element and a ruled.[42] It is not, however, a whole in which

---

[40] αὐτάρκεια
[41] *Pol.*, 1274b 39–40.
[42] *Pol.*, 1254a 28–31.

the separate existence of the parts is lost: it is on the contrary a union of elements which still continue to subsist as parts of the new whole which they form. It is neither a mere compound of parts placed in juxtaposition and retaining their integrity, nor a whole constituted by the fusion of elements which lose themselves in the process: if, like the latter, it forms a new identity, like the former it is consistent with the continued existence of its separate parts. These parts are generally regarded as being the individual citizens, though Aristotle uses the word in a variety of senses, and sometimes means by it classes, sometimes households and villages. The whole conception is important as the basis of many conclusions. Because the State is a compound whole, Aristotle begins the first book of the *Politics* by an application of the analytic method. In the third book the problem of the State's identity is solved by considerations based upon this view. By it, again, the priority of the State to the individual is proved in the first book. For the whole is prior to the part, in the sense that the part cannot exist, unless the whole be presupposed; nor can the individual exist as a moral being apart from the presupposition of a State in which he is a part, and which is therefore "prior to him."

Hitherto the unity of the State has been regarded from a formal and external point of view. The *inner* unity of the State, like that of all associations, is to be found in the justice and friendship which unite its members. They give and receive, it may be according to the dictates of a justice which means even-handed requital, it may be in a spirit of generous friendship. In the *Ethics* justice and friendship are closely connected; but while justice is regarded as needing friendship in addition, friendship is viewed as of itself sufficient for the State in which it is found. *Ubi justitia, ibi amicitia; et potior amicitia.* But the true spirit of a political association, in Aristotle's general view, is nevertheless justice. Justice is "the political good": defined as a "reciprocal rendering of equal amounts," it is termed the "saviour of the State" (1261a 30). The life-breath of the State, we may say, is a justice which assures to each his rights, enforces on all their duties,[43] and so gives to each and all their own. Somewhat similarly in the *Republic* Plato had found in justice the harmonising quality, whereby, each "doing his own," the State was kept in equilibrium. Similarly again, in modern times, we find in the State a scheme of rights and duties resting upon justice—that habit of mind which leads us to respect rights and acknowledge duties. Yet behind justice, Aristotle tells us, there always stands friendship. Friendship follows on the feet of justice—and varies as it varies. There is little justice in a perverted State; and accordingly there is little friendship. There are different forms of justice in different constitutions; and accordingly there are different forms of friendship. In a State where

---

[43] *I.e.* by giving A a right, and also imposing on him the duty of recognising B's right, and *vice versa,* it enforces "a reciprocal rendering of equal amounts."

justice gives much to a small body of rulers, because they deserve much, there is a corresponding friendship as between inferior and superior. Where justice awards equally, there is a friendship of equals. Men do not merely live in a cold region of reasonable acknowledgment of the principle of requital. The relation to their fellows, which such acknowledgment means, involves a further and a warmer connection by ties of feeling and affection; and Aristotle can even speak of friendship in the *Ethics* as the bond of the State. The friendship which thus results within the association of the State expresses itself in various ways. (i) The "energy" of friendship is social intercourse. Its active expression involves more than a mere feeling; it means the sharing of a common life. One of the aims of the State, as an association of friends, is therefore social intercourse, such as is to be found in sacrifices and various ways of passing the time pleasantly together; and the State aims at securing not only life and good life for its members, but also social life (not only τὸ ζῆν and τὸ εὖ ζῆν, but also τὸ συζῆν). (ii) Again, where justice is even-handed, friendship will be generous. Justice may secure to each a private property: friendship will throw that property open. Thus, and thus alone, will the true rule of property—private possession, common use—be duly satisfied. (iii) But in still another way, friendship is a yet more vital factor of the State. The State is based on a common good, a good which is the same for each man, a good which each man can only attain for himself by promoting it in his fellows. Now friendship means that a man regards his friend as "another self," for whom, exactly as if he *were* himself, he wishes and does all that is good for his own sake—with whom, again, he shares the same preferences, the same pleasures, the same pains. The conception of a common good, the conception that the good of another is one's own good, these things are thus the essence of friendship, as they are of the State. If the State is to have political fellowship, it must possess the virtue of friendship. (iv) Finally, friendship is an essential part of happiness, of εὐδαιμονία, which is the good of the State. One must have friends for society's sake, if one is to have pleasure; and pleasure is part of happiness. Or, it is argued more esoterically, happiness is an energy, or more strictly the consciousness of an energy; and while energy is more possible to a man when working in company with friends, the consciousness of energy, which is true happiness, comes most easily when the energy is seen as active in the person of "another self," where it is most readily perceived. In all these ways, then, friendship is of the essence of political association—both as leading to social intercourse and the right use of property, and as making for political fellowship and full happiness.

The State has already been described as an association of associations. Each of the subordinate and subsumed associations has its justice and its friendship. Aristotle means, by the subordinate associations of which he speaks, the connections of husband and wife, of father and child, of brother and brother. In each of these connections there is a justice and a friendship. Husband and wife, for instance, mutually respect rights and acknowledge duties; and besides this justice, there is between husband and wife a friendship expressed in a common social life. But the family being included in the State, the justice of the family has become a part of the justice of the State: the rights and duties of the members of the family towards one another are guaranteed and enforced by the law of the State. Just because the family is a natural association, with its own justice, which the State has incorporated not to destroy but to confirm and guarantee, making that association part of itself, and that justice part of its own,—just for that reason is the integrity of the family preserved by Aristotle from the destruction with which it was menaced by Plato. Aristotle, indeed, could regard the various family relations as microcosms of the different kinds of States. The relation of husband and wife suggests to him an aristocracy; the husband rules by virtue of his merit, and assigns to the wife her due share, as the rulers in an aristocracy rule by the same title, and act together towards their subjects on the same principle. The relation of father and child suggests a monarchy: that of brother and brother a timocracy, as it is termed in the *Ethics*, or, as it would be called in the *Politics*, a "polity."

ETHICS AND POLITICS

It now remains to discuss the ethical conceptions which colour, and which dominate, the *Politics*. The *Ethics* and the *Politics* form a single treatise in Aristotle's conception, and the subject of that treatise is political science. We must therefore understand, first, what is the relation of political science to science in general; secondly, and particularly, how it stands related to ethics. The first book of the *Ethics* begins with a horizontal and a vertical arrangement of sciences. Horizontally, they are divided into theoretical sciences, which deal with objects unalterable by man, and therefore aim at understanding, and not at altering, those objects; and practical and productive sciences, which deal with objects alterable by man, and therefore aim not only at understanding, but also at altering, their objects. Theoretical science seeks to bring man into conformity with the immutable and eternal; and the name of that conformity is truth. Practical science attempts to bring external things into conformity with some principle in man disclosed by its investigations. Theoretical science therefore *analyses* its given material, until the mind absorbs that material in all its bearings—in its causes, its construction, its results—and is thus brought into that full conformity with the object of study, which is truth. Practical science *calculates* the means by which the external object shall be brought into conformity with the principle in man which it has elicited. The two thus employ different faculties. Of the two parts of the rational soul, theoretical science employs the scientific, practical faculty the calculative. The calculative faculty in the sphere of moral action is called moral prudence, or political faculty; the former term regards the individual and his welfare, the latter regards that of the State.

Before turning to the vertical division of sciences, one should notice the importance of this classification of political science among the practical sciences, and its divorce from the theoretical sciences of metaphysics, mathematics, and physics. It means that instead of analysing the facts of political life, and seeking, like physics, to classify and to explain, political science first discovers a principle—happiness, or the supreme good—and attempts to calculate the means by which human life may through the State be brought into conformity with this principle. This is the point at which Greek political science seems to part company so decidedly with that of modern times, as expounded for instance by Seeley, who would make political science an analysis and classification of the facts of history. But it must be admitted that this scientific method of dealing with political science is not alien to Aristotle himself. We have seen that he based his *Politics* on the facts of history, so far as to collect a record of a great number of Greek constitutions. The *Politics* itself is full of references to Greek history; and three of the books, at any rate, which deal with ordinary constitutions, have, along with their practical therapeutics, much that is of the nature of scientific analysis and classification. And indeed, Aristotle refuses to acknowledge any strict separation of theoretic from practical science. He says, indeed, that practical science aims not at knowledge, but at action; but this is an emphasis of his real point by means of a paradox. And his real point is, that practical science, through knowledge, influences practice, while theoretical science stops at knowledge. But both seek knowledge (1253b 16–18). Knowledge is the prior end even of practical science: that action flows from the knowledge acquired is a great thing—so great, that he sometimes makes it everything—but yet it is in a sense secondary. Hence in the *Politics* he contrasts the philosophic treatment of a practical science, aiming primarily at knowledge, with the merely utilitarian (1279b 13): the latter treatment hardly beseems the magnanimous and liberal soul (1338b 2).

To understand the full scope of political science, we must now turn to the vertical division, that is to say, to Aristotle's classification of sciences in a hierarchy, one subordinate to another, and all to a common end. Science differs from science in the dignity of the end it serves: political science is the greatest and most dignified of all practical sciences, because its end is the ultimate end to which all others are subservient, the end of man's life. For in man's action, as we saw implied in Aristotle's teleological conception of the world, there is always an end pursued: each action has its purpose (like each growth of Nature), and each purpose is subordinate to the one final and ultimate aim of all action, which is happiness. To act for this end, to act teleologically, is to act rationally: to act rationally, as we shall see, is to act morally. This end behind all ends thus makes morality possible. And as all other ends are subservient to this end, so are all other sciences to its science. Political science is a master-science, "architectonic" in its character, from which all other practical sciences take their cue. Are we then to conclude that ethics, which also discusses the Good, is one of these other sciences, and shall we say that ethics is a separate and subordinate science, treating of the end of the individual, while politics treats of the end of a whole society? Such is not Aristotle's view. He does not know ethics as a separate science: he has no word for ethics, as a branch of study distinct from politics. Politics *is* ethics: to treat the end of a society is to treat the end of an individual, for both have the same end. There is one end of man's action, happiness: there is one science of that end, politics. Whether man is considered as living a life in himself, or as living with the life of the State to which he belongs, he lives the same life, for the same purpose, in the same way; and there can be no distinct science, which treats him as living a life by himself, distinct from his life in the State. True, this one and indivisible life can be considered in two aspects: it can be considered as a condition of mind present in the individual, or as a political fact to be realised by the State; and corresponding to these two aspects, we get the two treatises, which we call the *Ethics* and the *Politics*. But the *Ethics* opens by telling us that its subject is politics: it is concerned with a man as the member of a πόλις, or ethical society. To such a man the State is everything. It tells him his good, and it employs the means which habituate him to its pursuit. And therefore the *Ethics*, as a treatise discussing the moral life of a πολίτης, must ultimately culminate in the *Politics*, as surely as the State is the great, the single means of the realisation of man's good. Conversely the *Politics* is indissolubly united with the *Ethics*. As the State was all in all to individual morality, so was its moral mission the whole duty of the State. It was through and through a moralising agent. Yet this belief in the identity of ethics and politics, this conception of the State's subordination to a moral purpose, is afterwards modified by Aristotle. Political science vindicates its independence of ethics in three books of the *Politics:* setting aside moral considerations, it discusses perverted constitutions, and the methods of their preservation. It seems to lose all ethical connection, though not its practical purpose, and to become a study of the character and the method of preservation of non-moral States.[44] But the close connection of ethics and politics is normal;

[44] Thus there would appear to be two kinds of political science—a science of the Ultimate Good, as pursued by the πόλις; and a science of the πόλις, even when it is *not* pursuing the Ultimate Good. Even in its higher sense, as the science of the Ultimate Good, political science may be said to have two aspects; and while at the beginning of the *Ethics* it regards the Good as social, and looks to the welfare of the State (in whose welfare the individual will share), at the end of the *Ethics* it seems rather to regard the Good as individual, and the State as a means to its realisation in the individual.

and in this respect again the course of modern political science has generally been contrary to Aristotle. Machiavelli, as he is the parent of the modern view of political science as a scientific induction from history, is still
more eminently the author of the divorce of politics and ethics. "It is frequently necessary for the upholding of the State to go to work against
faith, against charity, against humanity, against religion." That is to say,
the divorce appears in the shape of a liberation of the State from any ethical control, and this divorce appears to be confirmed to-day by German, if
not by English, political thought. It appears again, in regard to the individual, in the distinction which we make between private and public obligations, between obedience to the dictates of conscience, and obedience to
the commands of the State expressed in law. But it must always be remembered that such a distinction is foreign to Aristotle. It is *not* implied in the
separation of a treatise on the *Ethics* from the treatise on *Politics:* the same
word justice serves Aristotle, as it served Plato, for goodness and law-abidingness, for the virtue of man and the virtue of citizen.

We are now ready to discuss the exact way in which political science, as a practical science with an ethical purpose, works towards the
realisation of the end of human life. There are three stages in morality—
natural disposition, habitual temperament, and rational action, according
as natural instinct, or an external and habituating force, or the internal
conviction of reason, dictates and controls our behaviour. We are born
good, or we have goodness thrust upon us, or we achieve goodness. But
generally we are in the second stage, of an habitual temperament determined by the pressure of external forces, such as the opinion of our family
or country, which may indeed have become so inveterate, owing to repeated action in obedience to their dictates, as to be of the nature of internal forces. But even if they be internal, they are not assimilated. We have
absorbed them because we must, not because we willed to do so out of a
clear knowledge and a voluntary acceptance of their reason and purpose.
And as they are unassimilated, so they are unconnected. The commanding
forces within us are a chance congeries, united by the fact of their co-exis-
tence within a single personality, but not by any causal tie of reason. Political science in its widest sense teaches us to assimilate, because it teaches
us to unify, these commanding forces, as all issuing from the single compulsion of the one end of human striving—happiness, or the Good. And because such a union gives for the first time a clue for *self*-guidance—
because it enables a man to determine himself rationally in the light of a
principle—it lifts him to a higher stage of moral life. Progress in political
science is not so much to know more as to be better—not an increase of
knowledge, but of goodness through knowledge. It means self-knowledge,
and with that self-control: to be without that knowledge is not indeed to
be uncontrolled, but to be controlled from without. But it is not to all that
it is given to attain self-direction in the light of a principle. It is only to a
few men morally gifted by Nature, or carefully trained by man. The major-

ity must always remain in the state of creatures of habits which they do not understand. But even for them political science is still necessary. It does not minister to them directly an inward light, but none the less it guides them indirectly. They receive a guidance from without: they are led by those in whom that light is burning. The rulers of the State guide them towards their end by punishments and by rewards, by pain and by pleasure, acting upon their instincts because they cannot appeal to their reason, and supervising alike the education of the young and the habits of adult life. In this sense political science "lays down the laws of what is to be done, and what is not to be done."

It remains to inquire into the end, which whether it is present to us, or only to the statesmen who guide us, is always the clue of life. Aristotle discovers man's end by investigating his function.[45] That function is not life—for that is the function of all things that live, of plants and animals as well as men—but life of a peculiar sort, corresponding to the specific difference of man from other living things. Aristotle conceived, and was the first to conceive, that life was identical throughout organic Nature. But life has its different kinds.[46] There is the life of nutrition and of growth, with which the reproduction of the species is connected; and this, and this alone, is the life in which plants share. There is the life of sensation, involving the power of having images presented and consequently of feeling desire; and this, as well as the life of nutrition, is the life of animals. Lastly, there is the life of reasoning, peculiar to man, but combined in man with the preceding stages of nutrition and sensation, each higher stage always presupposing and containing the lower. But the lower life, when united with the higher, to some extent alters its character under the influence of the higher. Sensation in man is modified by the presence of reason; and the desire which springs from sensation is equally modified by the same influence. And thus, while the function of man is broadly and generally a life in which his complex powers of nutrition, sensation, and reason all come into play, it is specifically and properly a life of reason—not indeed pure reason (that is for higher beings than man), but reason permeating and controlling the physical elements to which it is tied. This is the function of man: this is happiness. Herein is virtue; for virtue consists, as Plato had said, in the proper discharge of function; and therefore the virtue of man lies in a life duly lived in accordance with reason. And so we come to a closer understanding of the work of the State in encouraging virtue. In individual men the reason which should control their being is involved in other elements of appetite and passion. These elements are not, indeed, entirely dissevered from or antagonistic to reason: reason modifies that with which it is combined, and the appetite of man is not the utter appetite of

---

[45] *Ethics,* 1097b 24 *sqq.*
[46] *De Anima,* ii., c. 2.

the beast. It partakes in reason: it hearkens to reason as a son to a father.[47] None the less, in any human soul reason is always adulterated: it is always mixed with passion. But the State in its ideal form is the vehicle of *pure* reason: the law of the State is reason without passion. Out of its purity the State is strong: in his complexity the individual is weak.

As the science of the Ultimate Good, political science would thus appear to be concerned with the direction of men towards a rational life. Such direction it gives in two ways. Some men it teaches to realise for themselves the end of life; and such realisation both unifies their character, and lifts their moral action to the plane of self-conscious direction by the light of an inner reason. But most men it aids indirectly and by means of the few it has taught; for the legislator and the statesman (of whom the former is the greater to Aristotle, as laying down the main principles, which the latter only applies in detail) determine for most men the end to be realised, and the means for its realisation. By political science they have learned to know both the end and the means: by political science they impart their knowledge to others. Political science, therefore, must needs be the master science, declaring what other sciences are to be studied, and by whom, and to what extent: it must needs have subject to itself the sciences which men most value, like economics, strategy and rhetoric. Hence domestic economy and the theory of education are both treated in the *Politics* as vitally connected with political science. It is by the State that the material outfit and the spiritual equipment necessary to the good citizen must both be regulated. Particularly is the education of its citizens the State's concern: as the end is one, so, it is argued, the education and the educational authority must also be one. Since education is *ethical,* a making of character (or ἦθος) rather than of intellect, the great ethical influence of the State must here if anywhere be omnipotent, and here if anywhere find its great mission. And so Aristotle argues at the end of the *Ethics* that paternal authority is insufficient for the moral training of youth. It has not force or power of compulsion, such as is vested in the law of the State; and while the young may hate the hand that chastens them for their own good, so long as it is the hand of a definite person, they cannot hate the impersonal State. To the State therefore, and to political science, which is the science of the State's action, must be assigned above all things the province of education, and the function of leading man towards the rational life which is his Ultimate Good. A treatise on political science must ideally be a treatise on the objects and methods of the education of man.

It has been suggested above that in modern times ethics and politics have been divorced, and that the sphere of ethics has been conceived as the separate sphere of the individual. None the less, we still conceive of the State as inculcating moral laws, and as entering to that extent upon the

[47] *Ethics,* 1102b 30–33.

sphere of ethics. "We differ from Aristotle not in our view of what is fundamentally important to the community, but in the line we draw between
things which the State can touch with advantage, and things which it
should leave alone." [48] The essential mission of the State is still ethical:
whatever else it may do, it is preeminently and particularly a moral force.
It is the expression of our will, as the doctors of the school of contract
taught; but it is further the expression of our moral will, as only one of
those doctors, Rousseau, was wise enough to teach. That the State is thus
concerned not merely with the life, but also with the good life, of its subjects, is already writ large in the statute book, and would be written larger
still, if reformers had their way. It can only be anticipated that the sphere
of the State's action will be widened. The old theory which confined the
action of the State to the protection of life and property was due to a re-
vulsion of feeling directed, not against the State itself, but against monarchical authority. Whig and Liberal theorists, from Locke downwards,
sought to save liberty, not only by trying to liberalise the government, but
also by trying to emancipate the individual. In our days the government is
liberalised, or at any rate popularised; and as a result there is no distrust,
but rather a demand for its action. The emancipation of the individual
seems an almost forgotten creed; and our modern danger is rather the opposite excess of collectivism. It seems to be expected of the State that it
shall clothe and feed, as well as teach its citizens, and that it shall not
only punish drunkenness, but also create temperance. We seem to be
returning to the old Greek conception of the State as a positive maker
of goodness; and in our collectivism, as elsewhere, we appear to be harking
"back to Aristotle."

If the State is, and seems likely to be still more largely, a moral force,
political science must always be closely connected with ethics. It is a science, which lacking a terminology of its own, has always had to borrow
from other sciences, and to be interpreted in alien terms. It has borrowed
from law, in the days of the theory of a social contract: it has borrowed in
our own times from biology—though the metaphor of the body politic is
very old and from psychology—though, again, in Aristotle we already get
some attempt at a "psychology of the crowd." But the only safe creditor of
political science is Ethics. Law can only explain the external: biology can
only afford a simile. The real explanation of the inner life of a group of
men in action must be accommodated to the explanation given of the inner
life of individual men in action. As Plato said, the letters are the same:
they are only written larger in the State. Ethics, with psychology as its
handmaid, must be our basis in any philosophical explanation of the State.

None the less, ethics hardly figures in our political science in the
same way as in that of Aristotle. The State cannot be said to habituate its

[48] Nettleship, *Lectures,* p. 144.

citizen actively in the ways of virtue. Once the State attempted the task in England, under the Commonwealth; and it raised up in one generation a crop of imitative hypocrites, and in the next a crew of reactionary debauchees. Ethical life, we feel, is nothing without spontaneity. Automatism has no moral value; and the end of legislation is to get rid of itself. The modern State sets itself therefore [49] to the removal of obstacles to a moral life. It enforces education, not so much to compel the father to perform a moral duty, as to remove from the son's path the obstacle to a moral life which ignorance involves. It seeks to make no man good by act of Parliament; but it does by act of Parliament see to it that every man shall have the chance of being good. Aristotle went further. He did believe in the direct enforcement of outward conduct, in forcing men to act habitually along certain lines. It was not that he was satisfied with the act alone: no man taught more than he that true morality is in the spirit; but he believed that to become habituated to a certain line of action *might* ultimately bring the corresponding spirit, and with it spontaneity of action. Habituation was, as it were, a ploughing and harrowing of the land for the seed, which it should afterwards receive and nourish.[50] It was similarly the aim of Laud, who acknowledged Aristotle as his master *in humanis*, to habituate men in conformity to a certain ritual as an avenue to the religious spirit.[51] But it must be admitted that self-direction by an indwelling spirit was, in Aristotle's opinion, reserved for the chosen few, *paucis quos . . . ardens evexit ad æthera virtus.* His State is one of men taught by an external force to follow a higher code than they could ever themselves conceive. It is the height of the ideal that is at fault: the means are inevitable if once the ideal is accepted.

In conclusion of this study of the relations of ethical and political sci-

---

[49] According to modern theory; but in practice, as we have just seen, men clamour for more.

[50] *Ethics,* 1179b 24–26.

[51] There is much in the theory of religion which lies behind Laudianism that is parallel to Aristotle. i. It postulates the need of habituation by means of a ritual which is charged with the beauty of holiness; and similarly Aristotle desired the habituation of youth by means of artistic influences. ii. In accordance with this postulate, it conceives man as necessarily a part of an ecclesiastical "association," and a member of a Church; and this conception of man as essentially bound to a group is peculiarly Aristotelian. iii. It believes in the *continuous* life of the Church, as a living development from the days of its Founder; and with this belief the Aristotelian view of the natural and unbroken development of the State may naturally be compared. As Laudianism is akin to Aristotelianism, so is Puritanism to the Cynicism which Aristotle rebuked. Puritanism believed in a personal religion, attained by direct contact of the soul with its God, as Cynicism in a personal morality, achieved by the wise man for himself by his own reason. And as Cynicism was a force hostile to "association," and disbelieving in the necessity of the State, so was Puritanism hostile to the conception of a "Church" in the sense of an indispensable and living group with a continuous history. Puritanism, indeed, believed in a congregation; but its conception of a congregation was individualistic. The congregation was somewhat mechanical, "made by hands" for the edification of its units.

ence, it remains to inquire into the relation between the two treatises of
Aristotle which deal with these sciences—the *Ethics* and the *Politics*. In a
sense these two works are parts of a single treatise, whose subject is political science in the higher meaning of that word. But the fact remains, that
we have two separate works, distinguished by many differences, and that
while Plato contented himself with treating politics and ethics in a single
treatise, Aristotle preferred to make a division for the purpose of his study
of human action. How shall we explain the difference between Plato and
Aristotle? How shall we account for the division which Aristotle makes?
Plato, as we have seen, felt strongly the connection between moral character and political environment. States, he believed, did not spring "from an
oak or a rock," but depended vitally on the characters of their members.
Writing a single treatise, he emphasised this interrelation as the vital truth
of the science of man. And again, the nature of his philosophic principles
impelled him in the same direction. Particular could not for him be separated from universal: the particular only existed so far as it "imitated" or
"participated in" the universal. To study it separately was to study nothing.
But man is the particular and the State is the universal in which he participates; nor can man be studied except in relation to the whole which gives
him meaning and existence. To Aristotle the relation between particular
and universal appeared in a different light: the individual had emphatically a real existence, and the universal was no divine "Abstraction" separate from the individual, but a concrete being immanent in the thing which
it informed. The study of the individual came naturally to Aristotle. He believes, indeed, in the vital connection between man and the State of which
he is a part; and no writer has emphasised more vividly the necessity of
the State for man's development. But none the less the individual comes by
his own in Aristotle's teaching; and one may cite, as a simple instance, the
vindication of the right of private property which appears in the second
book of the *Politics*. The individual self was to him a precious thing:
φιλαντία , the due respect of a man for his own true self, was not the least of
the moral virtues. It was inevitable that the ethical aspect of the individual
self should receive a separate treatment at Aristotle's hands, although he
well knows, and often emphasises, the necessity of a political environment
for the ethical life of the individual. And thus he writes a work on *Ethics*,
as a separate inquiry, but one so vitally connected with the inquiry of politics, that the two must always be "thought together," if we wish to arrive at
the truth of either. In the *Ethics*, morality is treated in connection with
psychology, as a state of the soul: it is viewed as a composition of the parts
of the soul into a habit of deliberate action, in which the supremacy of the
rational part is recognised. In the *Politics*, morality is regarded in connection with its environment: it is seen, in its *creation* by the educative influence of a political authority, and in its *action* in the proper field of its exercise. In a word, the *Ethics* are static in comparison with the *Politics*, the

Politics dynamic in comparison with the *Ethics;* but both are fundamentally ethical treatises, concerned with the theory of the moral life of man, · η‘ περὶ τὰ ἀνθρώπεια φιλοσοφία.

In this account of their relations, however, we are rather sketching the ideal which may have hovered before Aristotle, than the actual result which he has achieved. It is tempting to call the *Politics* the dynamics of morality, and to find in its teaching the complement of the statical treatment of the *Ethics;* but it is by no means entirely true. We do indeed find in the *Ethics* something of a progress towards a work on dynamics. Virtue, we soon find, is not achieved without a training in habits: to preach the truth of ethics is a thing of little avail, save for a fine character which Nature has endowed with a love for the "beauty of holiness." All must be trained in their youth: the majority must be coerced into goodness throughout life; fear is their motive, and punishment their spur. It is the training of the young that occupies Aristotle most at the end of the tenth book; and for its perfection he desires the State. Education is best when it proceeds from the State, both because it proceeds from rulers chosen for their goodness, and because it is nothing empirical, but the expression by a legislator, who has grasped the end of life, of the means which conduce to that end. The problem, which the last pages of the *Ethics* raise, is how to produce such a legislator. In words which recall his master Plato, Aristotle complains that the practical politician is an empiric, who cannot train another in his knowledge; and that the political theorist, like Isocrates, is not only unacquainted with practical politics, but also ignorant of what political science is, or with what it deals. The want of any proper treatment of "legislation" (in the sense of determination of the training which makes for a moral life), makes it incumbent upon Aristotle to attempt an inquiry, which shall complete the "philosophy of men." The statics have thus brought us to the door of dynamics. But the dynamics are by no means what we should expect.

In the first place, there is no neat suture of politics and ethics. We close the *Ethics* with the feeling, that a State is necessary for the education and habituation of the individual: we open the *Politics* to find that the individual is a part of the State, for which he was meant, in which alone he comes by himself, to which he is "posterior." It follows naturally upon this difference of tone, that while we leave the *Ethics* with the feeling that in the speculative life of each man lies the height and depth and breadth of his being, we begin the *Politics* with the sense, that, the individual being essentially a citizen, his essential life is that of civic action. This difference of spirit suggests of itself that the two courses of lectures were distinct in composition as well as in delivery. In a consecutive course there would have been some adjustment: it was natural not to trouble to tie the ends of thought together, when the two "inquiries" were separate. But the same difference of tone is apparent, not only in this want of adjustment of the beginning of the *Politics* to the end of the *Ethics*, but also in the body of either work. On the one hand, there are some questions which are treated in the *Ethics* in a different way from that in which the same questions are treated in the *Politics*. Particularly is the scheme of constitutions expounded in the *Ethics* different from the classification in the *Politics*. The perverted forms are more unreservedly condemned in the *Ethics:* a constitution called a "timocracy," which is regarded as based upon a property qualification, and as a near neighbour to democracy, apparently takes the place of the later "polity"; and the cycle of constitutional change suggested in the *Ethics* is distinct from any suggested in the *Politics*. Even the vital teaching of the *Politics*, that the State is a natural growth, seems contradicted by the language of the *Ethics*, which assigns to political societies an origin in compact, or more strictly, regards them as "appearing to be by contract." On the other hand, there are some questions treated in the *Politics*, which, judging by the *Ethics*, we should not expect to find treated there, or which, at any rate, we should expect to find treated differently. The marked attention paid in the *Politics* to perverted and non-moral forms of the State is not what we should expect, if the State is to be viewed as a moral institution; and it is perhaps still more striking, that some of the forms, which a perversion like democracy may assume, should be selected for praise. But, as we have already noticed, Political Science comes to mean something else in the *Politics* than it does at the beginning of the *Ethics:* it becomes a technical practical science, dealing with what is given and with all that is given (normal or abnormal); it loses its character of an ideal moral science, concerned with the nature and production of the highest type of character. Yet whatever the differences between the two, the *Ethics* are indispensable to the full understanding of the *Politics*. However much the argument may assume in its course a practical aspect, it still remains the fundamental characteristic of the *Politics*, that its author treats his subject ideally, from a moral point of view, in terms of ethics. If later generations were to approach that subject through Roman Law, he approached it as decidedly through the moral philosophy of Greece; and our approach to the study of Aristotle's *Politics* must similarly be made through the avenue of Aristotle's *Ethics*.

FORM AND TEXT OF THE *POLITICS*

To a modern reader, one of the striking things about the *Politics* is perhaps its form. Equally with the Platonic dialogue the Aristotelian monologue represents thought at work, and not the finished product of thought. The author has not thought out his chapters and his sections: he has not determined exactly what he is going to say in each: still less has he made sure, that the view enunciated in one passage is consistent with the view suggested in another. He is working his way to conclusions in the treatise it-self. The labour which should precede composition seems to be done in the very article of composition. A subject is dropped, because something said in the course of its discussion suggests a digression, and that another di-gression; and then it is resumed (if it is resumed at all) from some other point of view, without any attempt to link the second discussion to the first. Each view taken in its contexts, may seem convincing; but to attempt to co-ordinate two views on the same subject, enunciated in two different contexts, may involve violence to the one or the other. And then there are times when no view seems to be reached. Possible or probable solutions are suggested to some question; but each, it is found, has its difficulty, and none may be finally adopted. "He disputes subtilely to and fro of many points, and judiciously of many errors, but concludes nothing himself." [52] The reader of the *Politics* must determine not to expect consistency, still less certainty, but to content himself with being stimulated to think. He must take a view in its context: he must beware of quoting as Aristotle's view what is perhaps only a tentative solution, or what, again, may be some previous thinker's view, which is ultimately combated or modified.

The explanation of these characteristics of Aristotle's work seems most naturally to be found in the view, that it represents rather a lecture than a set work, and a lecture more by way of discussion, than of set enun-ciation. Postponing for the present this question, we may first of all notice the form which Aristotelian discussion takes. It is Aristotle's first object to collect the received views on the subject which he is discussing, whether they are the ordinary and accepted popular views, or those of previous thinkers. This is a procedure followed in theoretical works like the *De Anima,* but still more in practical treatises like the *Ethics* or *Politics.* Here it is popular opinion which is the fundamental basis of inquiry. For in sub-jects like these popular opinion is not simply what most people think about the subject of discussion, as it is in biology: popular opinion is itself the subject of discussion. Ethics deals with the types of character generally ap-proved by men's opinion: universal opinion is the test of ethical truth. Sim-ilarly, the subject of politics is no subject simply given, like the bones of an animal, to be treated in itself by the inquirer, without any necessary refer-ence to what any man ever thought of it before: its subject is political institutions moulded, worked and directed by men's minds—alterable by human thinking, and by human thinking made what they are. And thus while a theoretical science like physics, dealing with things eternal, need not so much be treated—though by Aristotle it *is* treated—with reference to previous research or opinions, a practical science like politics must al-ways be discussed with regard to opinions, because it is constituted by them. The opinions of the many or the wise are therefore the basis of dis-

---

[52] Filmer, *Patriarcha,* ii., c. 10.

cussion; but opinion needs correction or amplification, if not, as with the opinions of some thinkers, entire rejection. To examine opinion is to see difficulties or inconsistencies, statements that err by excess or defect, or statements that contradict one another. This is the stage of ἀπορία, in which thought is involved in an apparent *cul de sac*, from which some escape must be found. And here the second, or *a priori*, element of discussion enters. For Aristotle applies to opinion metaphysical principles of his own, principles elsewhere established, to elicit the deeper meaning of opinion, or to correct its errors. Seldom, if ever, is opinion rejected in the sphere of practical science. It is developed by criticism: its excesses or defects are qualified: its inconsistencies are reconciled by some proof, that either of the two contradictories represents one aspect of truth. The presence of these two elements—received opinion and metaphysical principle—has various results. It makes Aristotle's method of science neither inductive nor deductive, but "a continual and living play between both." It makes his style assume almost the form of a dialogue, in which popular opinion states its case, or previous thinkers urge their views, on the one side, and on the other Aristotle the metaphysician answers. There is a constant dialectic for the eliciting of truth. This is no eristic—no chopping of logic for the sake of confutation; on the contrary, Aristotle seeks to absorb what he can from previous opinion, and, even if he rejects it, to appreciate its better side by showing that its error is half a truth. It is an honest facing and weighing of all possibilities for truth's sake. But dialectic such as this, dialectic which almost leads to dialogue, reminds us naturally of Plato; and the suggestion comes readily, that enough of the spirit of Platonic dialogue had been imbibed, during those years of study under the master, to inspire, not only the exoteric discourses of Aristotle, but also his lectures in the inner school. Nor is the dialectic reminiscent only of Plato; it suggests the very process of the human mind in its normal working. Do we not all bring to the facts we are considering certain general conceptions, to which our experience and temper have brought us, and which we always tend to use as clues to the truth? These conceptions are our principles (ἀρχαί): conformity to them means for us the mental satisfaction which we call truth. Nor is the process by which these principles meet their material in the mind at all unlike dialogue. It is often a one-sided dialogue, in which the side that suits our principles says everything; but so is the Platonic dialogue too. Indeed, compared with Aristotle, Plato himself may sometimes seem, for instance in the *Laws*, less dialectician than preacher; and the peripatetic monologue, which has been contrasted with the Platonic dialogue, may appear the true dialogue.

It is this play of dialectic which leads to the constant use of the aporetic method—a tentative method of propounding a thesis, stating its difficulties, and working towards a solution of those difficulties before attempting to prove the thesis. Take, for instance, the thesis that the virtue of the good man is the same as the virtue of the good citizen. Aristotle, proceeding as he himself says by the aporetic method, suggests various difficulties in the way of this thesis. The State as an association is composed of dissimilar members: citizen differs from citizen. Different citizens have different virtues; but the good man has always the same kind of virtue, and the virtue of the good citizen is therefore *not* the same as that of the good man. But Aristotle suggests, in the form of a question, a tentative escape from this *impasse*. May it not be the case, that though *all* good citizens are not as good men, yet *some* citizens have the same virtues as they? Logically this is possible; and Aristotle proceeds to prove that it is in fact the case. The citizen who rules has political faculty: the good men moral prudence. But these virtues are really identical; and therefore the good citizen, *if he be a ruler,* is the same as the good man. The thesis is finally established, but only under limitations and with a qualification, which the use of an aporetic method has discovered.

We may finally notice the part played by analysis in Aristotle's procedure. This has been referred to his medical training; but, as we have seen, the Socratic tradition was *divide et intellige,* and analysis was a method inherited by Aristotle from his master. He speaks of it as his guiding method in the *Politics;* and his first procedure in the very first book is to employ the method of analysis for the understanding of the State. As a compound the State is analysed into its constituent units of family and villages, in order to attain a proper comprehension of its character, just as life is elsewhere considered in its divisions—nutritive, sensitive, rational—in order to attain an understanding of the principle of life in general. In other passages in the *Politics,* analysis is used to distinguish the several attributes of a subject, with the aim of eliminating its essential attribute, and thereby attaining a proper definition. Such an essential attribute is one which is true in every instance of a subject, and true of nothing but that subject. Hence in the third book, in discussing the essential attribute of the State, he dismisses successively the various attributes which his analysis gives—necessary aid to life, alliance, commercial union (c. ix.); habitation in a common city, intermarriage (c. iii.)—because all these are attributes of other things than the State. They are not true of the State specifically; and they are not essential attributes of the State. But the sixth and final attribute, a common interest in a good life, does characterise a State specifically: it is the essential attribute of the State; nor can a State be otherwise defined, than as an association, whose members are united by a common interest in a good life.

Dialectical, aporetic, analytic—such are the characteristics of Aristotle's method. And now it follows, in the light which these considerations furnish, to inquire into the text of the *Politics,* and the proper order of the eight books of which it is composed.[53] A treatise in which terms are carefully analysed, and in which difficulties are raised and considered, but not necessarily solved, suggests of itself the lecturer rather than the author. And such a suggestion receives confirmation from what we know, or can readily guess, of the philosophic schools, which arose at Athens in the fourth century. They depended simply on oral teaching, transmitted orally. A master relied on the living word, and sought to quicken men's minds rather than to leave written monuments. A pupil, who had heard and imbibed the teaching of his master, arose in his own day, to propound the same doctrine with more or less modification, as his greater or less originality suggested. Where the master had been an Aristotle, the divergence of his pupils would be but slight. This oral tradition, transmitted inside the school, would have one fixed and central point, which would preserve continuity and a certain stability. The original master must have made notes for his lecture: it is impossible that a teacher like Aristotle, covering such a wide range of subjects, and referring to so many facts as his political lectures, for instance, embrace, should ever have done otherwise. Such notes, whether in the master's own hand, or, as Shute prefers to think, in a good copy, would be treasured in the school: they would be treasured with the more veneration, the more scrupulous adherence to every word and syllable, as the school grew older and the prestige of the master became greater. It is likely that our text of Aristotle represents notes of this kind, thus carefully preserved. It is more likely than the view that it represents the notes of pupils. That view involves the difficulty of explaining how one pupil's notes became the *textus receptus,* when there would be numbers of versions: it involves the graver difficulty of accounting for the unity of style which pervades all the Aristotelian treatises—for though that unity may be explained by the assumption, that our text of all these treatises represents the notes of a single pupil, such an hypothesis is very improbable.

It has thus been assumed, on general grounds, that the Aristotelian works which we possess are not set compositions intended for publication and given to the world by Aristotle himself, as the Platonic dialogues had been by Plato; they are not writings for the world, but notes for a school. The assumption is supported by a variety of particular reasons. In the first place, we cannot explain the ignorance of the *Politics* which the world showed for some centuries after Aristotle's death, if we assume that it had been already published by Aristotle himself. Polybius would not have shown knowledge of the *Polities,* and ignorance of the *Politics,* if the latter had been accessible to him in the form of a book. This ignorance is however explicable if we assume, that the *Politics* was preserved esoterically in the school for some centuries, before it was given finally to the world. Secondly, the difference in style between Aristotle's set writings, and treatises

---

[53] For the history of the text I follow Shute, *History of the Aristotelian Writings.*

like the *Politics,* is so great, that one cannot hold the two to be in any way parallel. It is true that we have very little of Aristotle's set compositions by which to judge. The dialogues, and the set discourses like the *Protrepticus,* are lost. There is, indeed, the Ἀθηναίων πολιτεία ; and possibly the two books of the *Politics* which deal with the ideal State, forming as they do a decided exception to the rest in point of style, were published by Aristotle himself. A German critic speaks of the "masterly style" of the former [54]; and Shute points to the set avoidance of hiatus in the latter. No one would speak of the masterly style of treatises like the other six books of the *Politics,* or notice in them any particular avoidance of defects of style. But, apart from any judgment on this ground, we can use two other and perhaps more cogent reasons for regarding the Aristotelian works which we possess as no set compositions. The first is the high opinion entertained by antiquity of Aristotle as a writer, if that opinion may be taken to be represented by Cicero, who again and again praises the "eloquence," the "golden flow," of his style. The second [55] lies in the fact that Aristotle was at any rate versed in the theory of style. He had lived in an Athens where style was cultivated—where Isocrates taught and practised eloquence, and Plato chiselled his sentences to perfection; and he had put contemporary practice into theory in the *Rhetoric.* But the theory of the *Rhetoric* is not followed—it is consistently violated—by the practice of the *Ethics* and *Politics.* It would seem to follow, therefore, that we must regard the Aristotelian treatises as sets of notes—notes made by Aristotle himself for use in his lectures. As such, they were meant for an audience, which could be assumed, as it is constantly in so many words assumed by Aristotle, to know previously something of the main Aristotelian doctrines. The hearer of the opening lectures on ethics is required to know something of Aristotle's metaphysics, in order to understand his teleological point of view; of his logic, in order to appreciate his criticism of the "Idea of the Good"; and of his psychology, in order to follow his theory of man's highest Good. The same is true of the *Politics:* the political lectures imply a previous knowledge of the Aristotelian system, in the light of which they acquire a deeper meaning; while in every way they would naturally be vivified by a fuller, richer, and more explicit treatment in class.

It remains to determine the date of the publication of these sets of notes. It is possible, *a priori,* that it may have been some centuries after the lectures were delivered by Aristotle, when they were first given to the world as a published work. During those centuries the notes, in a form modified by the working of oral tradition, would be continuously delivered and expounded in the Peripatetic school at Athens, where they might be heard by all who cared to join the course. Among the Peripatetics there

---

[54] The Aristotelian authorship of the Ἀθηναίων πολιτεία is, however, dubious.
[55] Used by Oncken, *Staatslehre.*

would be no oblivion of Aristotelian doctrines; but for want of publication they would be unknown to a wider public. It is possible, however, that the lectures on politics may have fallen into desuetude: the city-state was dead, and men's minds were more set on the problem of individual happiness, as Stoic and Epicurean philosophy shows. Copies of some of the notes may have been procured for the Alexandrian library, and the notes of the *Politics* may have been among those which were copied. But according to the tradition of antiquity there was no real publication until shortly after 100 B.C., or almost two centuries and a half after Aristotle's death. Anxious for Greek authors with the anxiety of the modern Renaissance, the Roman Renaissance, which had developed under the patronage of the Scipios, now won for itself a published Aristotle through the instrumentality of Sulla,[56] who brought the Aristotelian books' to Rome, to be edited there by two Romanised Greeks. "From this time forward . . . Rome is the centre of Aristotelian culture, as Athens is of Platonic." [57] And at Rome a *published* Aristotle is the basis of this culture; while previously at Athens it had been an *oral* Aristotle, modified in the process of oral transmission, which had formed the basis of Peripatetic philosophy.

Several questions arise out of this theory. Does the text which we possess represent Aristotle's own notes, word for word, or have we a text modified in the course of tradition? Are the books, as we have them, of Aristotle's dividing? Did he leave them in our present order? Leaving, for the moment, the question of the absolute authenticity of our text, we may suggest that it is very unlikely that lecture-notes would be divided into books. They might be divided according to the terms in which they were delivered, or according to the main subjects they treated, but not according to books. The division into books would be made by editors, after the lecture-notes had been published in the form of a book, a form which would naturally suggest such a scheme of division. But if the later editors charged themselves with this function, may they not have ventured on more? May they not have altered the text itself? It is true that the Sullan editors had before them, if not Aristotle's autograph, at any rate the copy belonging to Theophrastus, his immediate successor, which, after having lain in oblivion for some time, had been lately recovered. On the other hand, they would also have the modified version of the Peripatetic school at Athens. It seems possible that if there were any lacunæ or obscurities in the former text, they may have been supplied, or elucidated, from the text of the Peripatetic version. It may be doubted if the respect of modern textual criticism for *ipsissima verba* would then be felt. At any rate the references in our present text, which allude to a past or promise a future treatment of some subject, would certainly appear to have been added by later editors. In the

---

[56] Apellicon had already begun a published Aristotle at Athens, before Sulla carried away his library to Rome.
[57] Shute.

light of these considerations, the problem of the proper order of the books becomes easy. In discussing that problem, we must first ask, what was the order left by Aristotle, and secondly, what was the order adopted by the editors. Now if the *Politics* formed a single body of lectures, it might be expected that there would be a single natural order left by Aristotle himself. But the *Politics* does not seem to form such a single body. There are three sets of lectures, on distinct subjects, in distinct styles. It is important, not only as regards the order of the books, but also for the general understanding of the *Politics,* to realise this division. There is, first, a set of lectures, general and introductory, which lays down the principles of political science and of "economy" as one of its branches (books i and iii), and criticises the suggestions of Aristotle's predecessors and the construction of the most generally admired of existing States (book ii). There is, secondly, a set of lectures practical and detailed (books iv–vi in the old order), discussing and classifying the actual constitutions of contemporary Greece; showing where they are wrong or likely to go wrong, and in what way they may be corrected; and suggesting in conclusion that a mixture of oligarchy and democracy is—for practical purposes, and as an average best —the proper aim of the statesman. The first of these sets is to the second, as a treatise on the principles of physiology to a manual of pathology. Lastly, there is a set of lectures on the ideal State (books vii–viii in the old order), discussing the best methods of realising the conclusions attained in the first set of lectures with regard to the purpose and aim of the State, and forming the positive or constructive side to the negative criticism which, in that set, Aristotle had passed on Platonic ideals and Spartan institutions.

Now it seems most likely that Aristotle left these three sets separate and distinct, and in no definite order relatively to one another. In our traditional text they stand to one another in the order in which they have just been mentioned. But that is not, apparently, the order in which they were placed by the editors who supplied the references. The references are inserted on the supposition that the lectures on the ideal State immediately follow the set of introductory lectures. Now as we have no original Aristotelian order, it seems best to follow the order which best suits the internal development of ideas. That order is the order which the editors who inserted the references had adopted. The lectures on the ideal State follow most naturally on the introductory lectures, which alike in their constructive principles and their destructive criticisms lay the foundations for the building of such a State. Thus the plan of the work would be (i) a beginning of preliminary principles and criticism (the first three books); (ii) a middle in which those principles and that criticism are used in the construction of an ideal State (the fourth and fifth books, traditionally arranged as the seventh and eighth books); (iii) lastly, an end, peculiarly Aristotelian in character, analysing and classifying the actual facts of Greek politics—accepting those facts as given, while yet seeking to modify them into something better; and applying to politics the favourite doctrine of a golden mean, in the suggestion of a State midway between democracy and oligarchy. This end would form books six, seven and eight—the traditional fourth, fifth and sixth. The further and less important question of order (whether a further rearrangement of the traditional order should be made in the three books which would now form the end, so that the old fourth should become the sixth, the old sixth the seventh, and the old fifth the eighth book) is perhaps too slight, and too dubious, to be discussed here. It is on the strength of the references that the change has been made; but they cut both ways. Hildenbrand argues that internal logic postulates the old order; and Newman preserves that order, while suggesting that the fourth and sixth books (of the traditional order—the sixth and eighth of the new) formed one treatise, into which the other book was intercalated.

But it cannot be said that even with this re-arrangement the *Politics* forms a complete and logically ordered treatise. It is obvious that the books on the ideal State are by no means finished. Something is said of its foundation: something, but not all that was intended, of its education; but there is little or nothing said of its constitution or of its laws. It may be, as has been suggested, that Aristotle, sober and practical by nature, soon tired of constructing an imaginary Utopia; or the composition may have been interrupted by other causes. In any case there is a lacuna. There is again a lacuna at the end of the set of lectures on practical politics—at the end of the last book of the *Politics,* in the revised order. One would have expected the discussion of the executive to be followed by a discussion of the judicature and the deliberative: the very words with which the book ends show that it is interrupted, and not finished. Besides these lacunæ at the end of two sets, there is also a large omission in the middle of one. In dealing with practical politics, it might seem that not only the constitution, but also the laws, would naturally have been discussed. In the *Laws* (the work of Plato which in many respects corresponds to this section of the *Politics*) they bulk largely. Aristotle himself had the greatest faith in laws: law, which is reason itself, is to him the only true sovereign. Indeed he practically promises to discuss legislation at the beginning of the three books on practical politics: it is part of political science, and the whole of political science must be fully discussed. There are thus three decided gaps in the *Politics;* and the plan of the whole work, had it ever been completed, would have been somewhat as follows.

First Set of Lectures

Prolegomena of Politics, or the theory of the State in general, including:

Book i—the State in its relation to the household and household management; and books ii and iii—the data for the construction of an ideal State. Of these two books the former discusses the best constitutions already suggested in theory or existing in fact, in order that, when they have been sifted, the residue may be absorbed into Aristotle's projected construction; the latter, the fundamental book of the *Politics*, discusses the definition and classification of States. Incidentally to this definition, the meaning of citizenship is elucidated; while in treating of classification, Aristotle discusses the standard for the distribution of office, which is the same as the criterion of classification. In both respects he lays down principles of great importance to a builder of States.

The second and third sets of lectures both deal with particular States, the second with a suggested ideal State, the third with actual States.

Second Set of Lectures

Suggested Ideal State   The first of the two books which deal with an ideal State begins with a short preface, on the nature of the best life which that State is to realise. It proceeds to postulate the elements of an ideal State, for which the founder must trust to fortune, *e.g.* the nature of the soil and the character of its people; and Aristotle then begins to discuss those elements, which it is within the province of human art to supply—discipline and instruction. He lays down the rules of discipline, beginning with the discipline of the body in tender years, and proceeding in the second book to deal with the discipline of the body of the young by gymnastics, and of their instincts by proper music—a subject which engages his attention for some chapters, and in the middle of which he suddenly breaks off this last set of lectures. The body and instincts have received their *discipline;* but nothing has been said of the *instruction* of the intellect by reason. And not only is the subject of education unfinished; but practically nothing is said of the constitutional arrangements of the ideal State, and nothing at all of its laws. The ideal State is altogether imperfect; and some account of the further stages of education, and of the State's legal and constitutional structure, would naturally have followed.

Third Set of Lectures

Actual States   The three books relating to these deal only with their constitutional arrangements; and it has been suggested that there is a gap of as many more books, which should have discussed their laws.

a. The first of the three books which discuss the constitutional arrangements of actual States analyses the existing governments of Greece, and suggests in the light of that analysis what is the best average constitution under actual conditions. It further indicates, in a brief passage, to what sort of populace each of the existing governments is suitable; and then proceeds to prepare the way for discussing the method of constructing these governments, by distinguishing the three powers of government, executive, judicature, and deliberative.

b. The second of these three books continues the preparation for construction, by discussing what are the causes which ruin or preserve the State in general, and existing States in particular. It is obvious that before one proceeds to construction (by putting the three powers together in various combinations), such a knowledge of preservative and destructive forces is necessary: one must know, for instance, before constructing a democracy, that to combine a democratic form of the executive power with a democratic form of the deliberative power ruins a State, since it makes it too extreme to survive.

c. The third of these books, naturally, after these preparations, proceeds to the construction to which they were preliminary. It does not, however, construct by suggesting combinations of the three powers, but gives broad principles, both for oligarchy and democracy, based on the conclusions gained in the preceding book, the main principle being, that in forming either constitution, men should be careful of pushing its characteristics to excess. There would naturally have followed next a detailed examination of laws from the same practical and mediatorial point of view; but the examination was never made.

5

The Quantification
of Aristotle's Theory
# of Revolution

FRED KORT

The decisive impact of classical Greek thought on medieval scholasticism and the Renaissance failed to prevent the general neglect of Aristotle's theory of revolution. The first noteworthy attempt to revive the theory must be attributed to an English political theorist of the seventeenth century, namely, to James Harrington. The subsequent prevalence of Aristotle's idea in American political thought, from the defense of an agrarian democracy by Jefferson to the crusade against trusts by Roosevelt and Wilson, can be explained in terms of Harrington's influence. Nevertheless, this conceptual persistence contributed little to the empirical verification of Aristotle's theory as a scientific hypothesis. Twenty-three centuries elapsed before the idea of the classical Greek philosopher was cast into a form which has

This article was originally published in *The American Political Science Review*, 46 (June 1952), 486–493. It is reprinted here with the permission of the author and of the publisher.

opened new avenues for investigation. The hypotheses on income and political disturbances of the contemporary American mathematician Harold T. Davis, which are based on Vilfredo Pareto's theorem of income distribution, are virtually a restatement of Aristotle's theory of revolution. In its ultimate perspective, the Pareto-Davis theory constitutes a quantitative presentation of a relationship that was conceived in qualitative terms during the fourth century B.C.

ARISTOTLE'S STATEMENT OF THE THEORY OF REVOLUTION

The diversity of the causes of revolution under different forms of government, which Aristotle discussed in the fifth book of the *Politics*, did not preclude his conviction that all revolutions originate in a condition of inequality: "In all these cases [whether sedition is directed against the constitution, or only towards its modification] the cause of sedition always is to be found in inequality—though there is no inequality [and therefore no justification for sedition] when unequals are treated in proportion to the inequality existing between them. . . ." [1]

A notion of equality in terms of natural rights is an idea that belongs to a later period in political thought and cannot be attributed to Aristotle. His concept of inequality must be understood in terms of the relative political and economic status of individuals, in terms of what he called "equality proportionate to desert." [2] Accordingly, a condition of inequality is created by a situation in which (a) groups that occupy a privileged political status do not enjoy a corresponding economic status, or (b) groups that have decisive economic advantages are deprived of corresponding political privileges. The result of this incongruity is a dominant consciousness of inequality, for which a remedy is sought in revolution. A consistent pattern of thought thus can be ascribed to the statement that "there is no inequality . . . when unequals are treated in proportion to the inequality existing between them." According to Aristotle, inequality between different strata of society is not a cause of revolutions; only inequality in the sense of an incongruity of the respective political and economic status within social classes is a factor which promotes political disorders. In its essential features, Aristotle's theory may be reduced to the proposition that whenever political and economic power are separated, a revolution is likely to occur.

[1] Ernest Barker, trans. *Politics* (Oxford, 1948), Bk. 5, Chap. 1, § 11. The portions in brackets are comments of the translator. The term "sedition" in Barker's translation should be noted. Benjamin Jowett uses the term "revolution." Barker prefers "sedition" as a translation of the Greek word *stasis* in order to do justice to the comprehensive meaning of *stasis*, which is not confined to armed rebellion. In view of the fact that the term "revolution" acquires a definite denotation in the Pareto-Davis theory, Barker's concept of "sedition" is helpful for the purpose of this inquiry.

[2] *Politics*, § 12.

An extensive illustration of Aristotle's general theory is found in his discussion of revolutions under democracies, oligarchies, aristocracies, kingships, and tyrannies. According to Aristotle, revolutionary changes in democracies are the result of political attacks upon the wealthy by the demagogues. The members of the propertied class unite under this challenge and overthrow the democratic institutions. Such a situation existed at Cos, where notables formed an alliance against the rising demagogues and abolished the democracy. Similarly, when the demagogues of Rhodes withheld funds which were due the trierarchs, the trierarchs combined and terminated the era of democratic government. In Heraclea democracy came to an end when the notables, exiled by the demagogues, returned and destroyed the democracy. A parallel situation existed at Megara. The demagogues expelled the notables in order to confiscate their property; however, the notables returned from their exile, defeated the people in a battle, and established an oligarchy. And the same fate befell the democracy at Cyme, which was overthrown by Thrasymachus.[3] It should be noted that in all of the foregoing instances political power was vested in a numerical majority, which supported the demagogues, whereas economic power resided with a few notables.

A similar separation of political and economic power is Aristotle's explanation of revolutionary changes in oligarchies. At Massilia, Istros, Heraclea, and in other city-states, he reported, the oligarchies were overthrown because only a few members of the economic elite held public office. The excluded members created disorders until they became office-holders. As a consequence, the oligarchy at Massilia was changed to a form of government that resembled a polity, at Istros it was transformed into a democracy, and at Heraclea it was extended to include six hundred members.[4] In the foregoing instances, political and economic power were separated, and revolutionary changes ensued. Aristotle also indicated that the existence of oligarchies could be undermined by the assumption of demagogic power by a member of the governing body. This was the case in Athens in the days of the Thirty and in the days of the Four Hundred, and it was also the case in Larisa.[5] The rising demagogues gained the support of the masses, and political power shifted from the privileged holders of public office to the popular majority; but the wealthy few—the former holders of political power—still retained economic power. The resulting separation of political and economic power led to a revolution. Other instances to which Aristotle referred show how competitive oligarchies were organized within the same city-state. Political and economic power were separated, and this condition promoted the ultimate destruction of the entire oligarchial system.

[3] *Politics*, Bk. 5, Chap. 5, §§ 1–4.
[4] *Politics*, Bk. 5, Chap. 6, §§ 2–3.
[5] *Politics*, §§ 6–7.

As in oligarchies, Aristotle saw revolutionary changes in aristocracies as caused by the concentration of political power in the hands of a wealthy elite, while other economically powerful groups do not have a commensurate share in government. This was the case in Sparta, where the illegitimate sons of Spartan peers, called the Patheniae, formed a conspiracy to overthrow the existing government. Their intentions were detected, and they were sent into exile to Tarentum.[6] A different situation existed at Thurii, where the concentration of economic power in the hands of the few was challenged by the ascending political power of the people. The ruling aristocracy had acquired more land than it was allowed to have by law, but, as the result of a war, the people had acquired virtual rather than nominal political power; they protested against the concentration of economic power in an elite, and forced the notables to abandon their excessive property.[7]

A detailed examination of Aristotle's discussion of revolutions under kingships and tyrannies does not seem to be warranted here. His general statement to that effect should suffice: "The aims pursued by revolutionaries, like the origins of revolution, are the same in tyrannies and kingships as they are under regular constitutions."[8]

The preceding account of Aristotle's historical illustrations should be sufficient to justify the initial inference made here regarding the essence of his theory of revolution: that whenever political and economic power are separated, a revolution is likely to take place. To be sure, nowhere in the *Politics* is his theory of revolution stated in this particular form. Nevertheless, the specific illustrations with which Aristotle supplemented his theory, added to his concept of inequality, hardly permit an alternative interpretation. Supplementary support for its validity can be obtained if the corollary of Aristotle's theory of revolution is considered, namely, the concept of constitutional stability in a polity. That an equitable political balance may best be maintained in a polity where economic and political power are unified, was a conclusion which Aristotle reached in the course of his extensive comparative study of governments. (The theory that democracy—polity in Aristotle's sense—is most stable wherever there is a strong middle class, is a contemporary version of the relationship originally ascertained by Aristotle.) "Constitutional stability," the concomitant phenomenon of a unification of political and economic power, and "revolutionary trends," the result of a separation of political and economic power, thus appear as conceptual manifestations of a consistently integrated pattern of thought. They are the product of Aristotle's inquiry, but their ideational basis was prevalent in the Athenian commonwealth even before Aristotle's time. According to Plutarch, their inception may be ascribed to Solon:

[6] *Politics,* Bk. 5, Chap. 7, §§ 1–2.
[7] *Politics,* § 9.
[8] *Politics,* Bk. 5, Chap. 10, § 14.

Solon, however, himself says that it was reluctantly at first that he engaged in the state affairs, being afraid of the pride of one party and the greediness of the other; he was arbitrator and lawgiver; the rich consenting because he was wealthy, the poor because he was honest. There was a saying of his current before the election, that when things are *even* there never can be war, and this pleased both parties, the wealthy and the poor; the one conceiving him to mean, when all have their fair proportion; the others, when all are absolutely equal.[9]

THE PARETO-DAVIS THEORY OF INCOME DISTRIBUTION AND POLITICAL DISTURBANCES

The familiarity of Pareto and Davis with Aristotle's theory of revolution would not justify the assumption that the two contemporary thinkers relied on the ideas of their classical predecessor. As a unified product of a related endeavor, the Pareto-Davis theory of income distribution and political disturbances indicates a development of thought which has maintained its independence from its precedents. Inasmuch as Pareto limited his analysis to income distribution, he apparently did not exhibit particular interest in the political implications of Aristotle's theory. Davis certainly is concerned with the ramifications of income distribution for politics, and there is evidence that he formulated his hypotheses with full knowledge of Aristotle's theory, but without reliance on this classical precedent.

The essence of Pareto's theorem is contained in the hypothesis that, in all places and at all times, the distribution of income conforms to a definite pattern, and that this relationship may be stated in the following mathematical terms [10]:

$$N = \frac{A}{x^a}$$

N represents the number of people whose income is equal to or higher than income denoted by x; A is a constant, depending upon the size of the economy; a is a parameter. If the logarithms of the values of N and x are graphically represented in such manner that the logarithms of N are projected along the vertical axis of the graph and the logarithms of x along the horizontal axis, the resultant curve is a straight line with a slope of $-a$. This curve represents the distribution of income.[11]

[9] *The Lives of the Noble Grecians and Romans,* trans. John Dryden and rev. Arthur Hugh Clough (Modern Library ed., New York, 1932), p. 104.
[10] Vilfredo Pareto, *Cours d'économie politique* (Lausanne, 1896–1897), Vol. 2, p. 306.
[11] Representative samples were found by Pareto in the income distributions of the following countries and cities during the specified periods: England, 1843, 1880, and 1894; Prussia, 1852, 1876, 1881, 1886, 1890, and 1894; Saxony, 1880 and 1886; Florence, the city and county of Perugia, Aconia, Arezzo, Parma and Pisa combined, and other Italian cities in combination (no dates specified); Augsburg, 1471, 1498, 1512, and 1526; Peru, at the end of the 18th century (*Cours* . . . , Vol. 2, p. 312).

Pareto failed to explore the political implications of variances in income distribution; but these neglected implications became the focal point in the inquiry pursued by Davis. The examination below in terms of graphical representation reveals that Pareto's original relationship encompasses various degrees of income concentration. Inasmuch as the numerical value of a determines the slope of the curve which represents income distribution, a high numerical value of a indicates a wide dispersion of income, and a low numerical value of a denotes a high concentration of income. Fig. 1 and Fig. 2 illustrate hypothetical situations of extreme values for a. In Fig. 1, where a approaches infinity, almost complete equality of income prevails. In Fig. 2, where a approaches 0, a very high concentration of income exists. In differentiating between various degrees of income distribution, Davis made a distinction between situations which may be identified with a *stable economy* and contrary situations, as shown by these two figures, which are characterized by a high concentration or wide dispersion of income. Fig. 3 represents graphically a *stable economy*; in this case, a is approximately 1.5. According to Davis, such stability in the economy of a society (*i.e.* a "normal" income distribution) is indicative of political stability; on the other hand, high concentrations or wide dispersions of income are correlated to political disturbances.

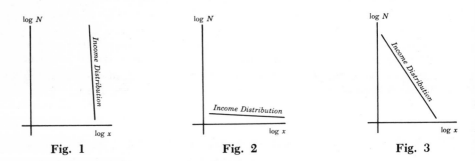

Fig. 1   Fig. 2   Fig. 3

To avoid the inverse relationship between values of a and the concentration of income, Davis introduced a new concept in his modification of Pareto's theory, namely, the *concentration ratio*.[12] Symbolized by ρ, the *concentration ratio* can be related to the parameter a by means of the following equation [13]:

[12] Harold T. Davis, *Political Statistics* (Evanston, Ill., 1948), p. 185. Davis points out that this concept originally was proposed by C. Gini in "Intorno alle curve di concentrazione," *Metron*, Vol. 9, 1932, Nos. 3–4, pp. 3–76.
[13] *Political Statistics*, p. 185. Davis uses a different notation in this formula; the parameter a is symbolized by ν. In order to maintain a consistent set of symbols, the formula has been modified here accordingly, and Professor Davis has approved the change for the purpose of this presentation.

$$\rho = \frac{1}{2a-1}$$

In accordance with this formula, the *concentration ratio* ρ varies from 0 to 1 as the parameter a varies from infinity to 1. With the aid of a simple process of substitution, it can be readily seen that a value of 0.5 for ρ corresponds to a value of 1.5 for a.[14] In other words, a *stable economy* is characterized by a *concentration ratio* ρ of 0.5 as well as by a parameter a of 1.5. Moreover, as a increases beyond 1.5, ρ falls below 0.5 and indicates a relatively dispersed distribution of income. On the other hand, as a decreases below 1.5, ρ rises beyond 0.5 and denotes a relatively high concentration of income.

The two main hypotheses that Davis formulated with the aid of the *concentration ratio* constitute a decisive amplification of Pareto's original theory: (1) whenever the *concentration ratio* exceeds a certain critical value above 0.5, *i.e.*, whenever a critically high concentration of income prevails in a society, a revolution is likely to occur; (2) whenever the *concentration ratio* is lower than a certain critical value below 0.5, *i.e.*, whenever income is dispersed beyond a certain critical minimum of concentration, a civil war is likely to take place.[15]

No claim is made by Davis that the relationships between income distribution and political disturbances have attained the status of scientific laws. They are presented in the form of hypotheses, with the definite understanding that their validity is contingent upon extensive empirical verification. To be sure, a noteworthy amount of empirical evidence has been obtained by Davis himself. He has interpreted the French Revolution of 1789, the Russian Revolution of 1917, and the Spanish Revolution of 1931 as situations which support the first hypothesis. All of these revolutions were preceded by an unduly high concentration of income and wealth, *i.e.*, the *concentration ratio* exceeded the critical value above 0.5. The Spanish Civil War of 1936–39 and the American Civil War serve as verifying instances for the second hypothesis. The latter event is of particular interest inasmuch as its detailed examination by Davis yields a *concentration ratio* of 0.20, a value that is definitely below the critical minimum of income concentration.[16]

[14]
$$\frac{1}{2a-1} = \frac{1}{3-1} = 0.5 = \rho.$$

$$(a = 1.5)$$

[15] *Political Statistics*, p. 195. The distinction which Davis makes between "revolution" and "civil war" obviously is the following: a revolution is a political disturbance that is created by an underprivileged majority; a civil war is a political disturbance that is initiated by a privileged minority.
[16] *Political Statistics*, pp. 195–202.

ARISTOTLE'S THEORY OF REVOLUTION RESTATED
IN QUANTITATIVE TERMS

The correspondence of the Pareto-Davis theory of income distribution and political disturbances with Aristotle's theory of revolution is exhibited by two fundamental parallels. First, Davis' concept of a *stable economy* is analogous to Aristotle's idea of a polity. A *stable economy* is characterized by a "normal" income distribution (a *concentration ratio* of 0.5), and no political disorders are anticipated. A polity finds its distinctive feature in the presence of a strong middle class, and constitutional stability is assured by a unification of political and economic power. Second, although Aristotle made no distinction between "revolution" and "civil war," it would be justifiable to identify his concept of "sedition" with both "revolution" and "civil war" as employed by Davis. On this basis, an agreement between the two theories under investigation can be established. The first hypothesis of Davis—*i.e.*, that whenever the concentration of income exceeds a certain critical point, a revolution is likely to occur—can be stated in Aristotelian terms as follows: Whenever a separation of political and economic power results from the fact that economic power is vested in the wealthy few, whereas *real* (not necessarily *nominal*) political power resides with the many, the holders of political power, in an attempt to eliminate the concentration of economic power in the elite, probably will advocate a revolution. The second hypothesis of Davis—*i.e.*, that whenever income is dispersed beyond a certain critical minimum of concentration, a civil war is likely to take place—would read in Aristotle's sense as follows: Whenever a separation of political and economic power exists because economic power has shifted to the many, whereas *real* (not necessarily *nominal*) political power is retained by the few, the few, in order to regain their economic power, will probably resort to a civil war.[17] In both cases, it is a separation of political and economic power which entails political disorders.

The validity of the Pareto-Davis theory is not a focal point of concern in this inquiry. It has been emphasized that Davis presented his observations in the form of hypotheses, that he obtained significant verifying instances in support of his hypotheses, but that he has not claimed the status of scientific laws for the relationships which he formulated. The relevance of his investigation which can be ascertained within the limits of the present inquiry manifests itself in two respects: (1) a qualitative relation-

---

[17] The distinction between *real* and *nominal* political power can be illustrated by the following examples: (1) During the Russian Revolution of 1917, *nominal* political power was vested in the Provisional Government; *real* political power resided with the soviets. (2) During the Spanish Civil War, *nominal* political power could be identified with the Republican Government; *real* political power would have to be ascribed to the supporters of Franco. In any case, *real* political power is the decisive criterion; for it is the residue of *real* political power which enables groups to commence a revolution or a civil war.

ship has been restated in quantitative terms; (2) the pertinence of a theory of the fourth century B.C. for contemporary problems has been established, and a new method for its investigation has been devised.

Aristotle, of course, conceived his theory of revolution in qualitative terms. He detected a cause of "sedition" in the separation of political and economic power, but he was not able to determine what degree of such separation would assume alarming proportions. The concept of the *concentration ratio* supplies numerical values for the critical points in the separation of political and economic power; *i.e.*, it specifies that if the separation of political and economic power has proceeded beyond certain values (above or below 0.5), political disturbances will ensue.[18] In this manner, the qualitative relationship which Aristotle formulated has been restated in quantitative terms.

The applicability of Aristotle's theory to contemporary situations appears to be beyond dispute if it is noted that Davis supported his hypotheses primarily by referring to events of the late nineteenth and early twentieth centuries. It is in this connection that the quantitative restatement of Aristotle's theory by Davis attains its full significance. To be sure, qualitative relationships can be empirically verified; Aristotle himself succeeded in obtaining verifying instances for his qualitatively conceived theory. The difficulty of dealing with qualitative relationships is to determine the pertinence of a particular situation to the general content of the hypothesis under investigation. For example, in order to appraise the adequacy of the American Civil War as a possible verifying instance for Aristotle's theory, it would be necessary to compare the degree of separation of political and economic power in that particular instance with the degree of separation envisaged by the theory. A comparison in qualitative terms would entail decisive handicaps. If, however, the degree of separation of political and economic power can be expressed in quantitative terms, the pertinence of the particular situation to the general content of the theory can be readily determined. The contribution of Davis, therefore, is a method of inquiry which immensely facilitates the ultimate verification (or possible refutation) of Aristotle's theory of revolution.

FURTHER READINGS FOR PART I

Thucydides

Brunt, P. A., "Thucydides: The Compassionate Scientist," *History Today*, 7 (December 1957), pp. 820–828.

[18] An index that would measure the distribution of political power in the same manner as the *concentration ratio* measures the distribution of economic power, would be an additional aid. Research in that direction would be an extremely difficult, but worthwhile, undertaking.

Cochrane, Charles N. *Thucydides and the Science of History*. New York: Oxford University Press, 1929.

Finley, Jr., John H. *Thucydides*. Cambridge, Mass.: Harvard University Press, 1942.

——. "The Unity of Thucydides' History," *Harvard Studies in Classical Philology*, Supplement Vol. I, pp. 255–297.

Fliess, Peter. *Thucydides and the Politics of Bipolarity*. Baton Rouge: Louisiana State University Press, 1966.

Grene, David. *Man in His Pride: A Study in the Political Philosophy of Thucydides and Plato*. Chicago: University of Chicago Press, 1950.

——. *Greek Political Theory: The Image of Man in Thucydides and Plato*. Chicago: University of Chicago Press, 1965.

Kateb, George. "Thucydides' History: A Manual of Statecraft," *Political Science Quarterly*, 79 (December 1964), pp. 481–503.

Westlake, Henry D. *Individuals in Thucydides*. New York: Cambridge, 1968.

Plato

Allen, R. E. "Participation and Predication in Plato's Middle Dialogues," *Philosophical Review*, 69 (April 1960), pp. 147–164.

——. "The Socratic Paradox," *Journal of the History of Ideas*, 21 (April–June 1960), pp. 256–265.

Barker, Ernest. *Greek Political Theory: Plato and His Predecessors*. London: Methuen, 1947.

Bigger, Charles P. *Participation: A Platonic Inquiry*. Baton Rouge: Louisiana State University Press, 1968.

Bluck, Richard S. *Plato's Life and Thought*. Boston: Beacon, 1951.

Bosanquet, Bernard. *A Companion to Plato's Republic*. New York: Macmillan, 1895.

Brumbaugh, Robert S. "A New Interpretation of Plato's Republic," *Journal of Philosophy*, 64 (October 1967), pp. 661–670.

Chance, Roger J. F. *Until Philosophers Are Kings*. London: University of London Press, 1928.

Chroust, Anton-Herman. "Plato's Detractors in Antiquity," *Review of Metaphysics*, 16 (September 1962), pp. 98–118.

——. "Who is the Platonic Philosopher-King?" *New Scholasticism*, 34 (October 1960), pp. 499–505.

Coleman, Winston R. "Knowledge and Freedom in the Political Philosophy of Plato," *Ethics*, 71 (October 1960), 41–45.

Crossman, R. H. S. *Plato Today*. New York: Oxford University Press, 1959.

Edelstein, Ludwig. "The Function of the Myth in Plato's Philosophy," *Journal of the History of Ideas*, 10 (October 1949), pp. 463–481.

Field, Guy C. *The Philosophy of Plato.* New York: Oxford University Press, 1956.

——. *Plato and His Contemporaries.* London: Methuen, 1948.

——. "Plato's Political Thought and Its Value Today," *Philosophy,* 16 (July 1941), pp. 227–241.

Foster, Michael B. *The Political Philosophies of Plato and Hegel.* New York: Oxford University Press, 1935.

Friedländer, Paul. *Plato.* New York: Pantheon, 1958.

Gorospe, Vitaliano R. "Plato's Natural-Law Theory in the *Republic,*" *The Modern Schoolman,* 43 (January 1966), pp. 143–178.

Gouldner, Alvin W. *Enter Plato: Classical Greece and the Origins of Social Theory.* New York: Basic Books, 1965.

Grant, G. P. "Plato and Popper," *Canadian Journal of Economics and Political Science,* 20 (May 1954), pp. 185–194.

Gregory, Sister M. John. "Myth and Transcendence in Plato," *Thought,* 43 (Summer 1968), pp. 273–296.

Gross, Barry. *The Great Thinkers on Plato.* New York: Putnam, 1968.

Johnson, Harold J. "Three Ancient Meanings of Matter: Democritus, Plato, and Aristotle," *Journal of the History of Ideas,* 28 (January 1967), pp. 3–16.

Johnson, J. Prescott. "The Ontological Argument in Plato," *The Personalist,* 44 (Winter 1963), pp. 24–34.

Kendall, Willmoore. "The People vs. Socrates Revisited," *Modern Age,* 3 (Winter 1958–1959), 98–111.

Laing, B. M. "The Problem of Justice in Plato's Republic," *Philosophy,* 8 (January 1933), pp. 412–421.

Levinson, Ronald B. *In Defense of Plato.* Cambridge, Mass.: Harvard University Press, 1953.

Maguire, Joseph P. "Plato's Theory of Natural Law," *Yale Classical Studies,* 10 (1947), pp. 151–178.

Merlan, Philip. "Form and Content in Plato's Philosophy," *Journal of the History of Ideas,* 8 (1947), pp. 406–430.

Morrow, Glenn R. *Plato's Cretan City: A Historical Interpretation of the Laws.* Princeton, N.J.: Princeton University Press, 1960.

Murphy, Neville R. *The Interpretation of Plato's Republic.* New York: Oxford University Press, 1951.

Nettleship, Richard L. *Lectures on the Republic of Plato.* New York: St. Martin's, 1929.

Popper, Karl R. *The Spell of Plato (The Open Society and Its Enemies,* Vol. I). Princeton, N.J.: Princeton University Press, 1950.

Rambrough, Renford. "Plato's Modern Friends and Enemies," *Philosophy,* 37 (April 1962), pp. 97–113.

Randall, John R. *Plato: Dramatist of the Life of Reason.* New York: Columbia University Press, 1970.

Sachs, David. "A Fallacy in Plato's 'Republic,'" *Philosophical Review*, 72 (April 1963), pp. 141–158.

Sayre, Kenneth M. *Plato's Analytic Method.* Chicago: University of Chicago Press, 1969.

Sibley, Mulford Q. "The Place of Classical Political Theory in the Study of Politics: The Legitimate Spell of Plato," in Roland Young (ed.), *Approaches to the Study of Politics* (Evanston, Ill.: Northwestern University Press, 1958), pp. 125–148.

Sparshott, F. E. "Plato and Thrasymachus," *University of Toronto Quarterly*, 27 (October 1957), pp. 54–61.

Steintrager, James. "Plato and More's Utopia," *Social Research*, 36 (Autumn 1969), pp. 357–372.

Strauss, Leo. *Natural Right and History.* Chicago: University of Chicago Press, 1953.

——. "On a New Interpretation of Plato's Political Philosophy," *Social Research*, 13 (1946), pp. 326–367.

——. *What Is Political Philosophy?* New York: Free Press, 1959.

Taylor, A. E. *Plato: The Man and His Work.* New York: World, 1956.

——. *Socrates.* New York: Doubleday, 1960.

Teske, Roland J. "Plato's Later Dialectic," *The Modern Schoolman*, 38 (March 1961), pp. 171–201.

Thorson, Thomas L., ed. *Plato: Totalitarian or Democrat?* Englewood Cliffs, N.J.: Prentice-Hall, 1963.

Voegelin, Eric. *Plato and Aristotle (Order and History*, Vol. 3). Baton Rouge, La.: Louisiana State University Press, 1957.

——. *Plato.* Baton Rouge, La.: Louisiana State University Press, 1966.

Walsh, W. H. "Plato and the Philosophy of History: History and Theory in the *Republic*," *History and Theory*, 2 (1962), pp. 3–16.

Wild, John D. *Plato's Theory of Man: An Introduction to the Realistic Philosophy of Culture.* Cambridge, Mass.: Harvard University Press, 1946.

——. *Plato's Modern Enemies and the Theory of Natural Law.* Chicago: University of Chicago Press, 1953.

Aristotle

Allan, Donald J. *The Philosophy of Aristotle.* New York: Oxford University Press, 1952.

Bluhm, William T. "The Place of the 'Polity' in Aristotle's Theory of the Ideal State," *Journal of Politics*, 24 (November 1962), pp. 743–753.

Chroust, Anton-Herman. "Aristotle's 'On Justice': A Lost Dialogue," *The Modern Schoolman*, 43 (March 1966), pp. 249–263.

Demos, Raphael. "Some Remarks on Aristotle's Doctrine of Practical Reason," *Philosophy and Phenomenological Research,* 22 (December 1961), pp. 153–162.

Foley, Leo. "The Metaphysical Evolution of Aristotle's Realism," *The New Scholasticism,* 34 (January 1960), pp. 62–78.

Grote, George. *Aristotle.* London: J. Murray, 1872.

Hamburger, Max. *Morals and Law: The Growth of Aristotle's Legal Theory.* New Haven, Conn.: Yale University Press, 1951.

Hardie, W. F. R. *Aristotle's Ethical Theory.* New York: Oxford, 1968.

——. "The Final Good in Aristotle's Ethics," *Philosophy,* 40 (October 1965), pp. 277–295.

Jaeger, Werner. *Aristotle: Fundamentals of the History of His Development.* New York: Oxford University Press, 1948.

Joachim, H. H. *Aristotle: The Nicomachean Ethics.* New York: Oxford University Press, 1955.

Long, Norton. "Aristotle and the Study of Local Government," *Social Research,* 24 (Fall 1957), pp. 287–310.

Marshall, John S. "Aristotle and the Agrarians," *Review of Politics,* 9 (July 1947), pp. 350–361.

May, William E. "Structure and Argument of the Nicomachean Ethics," *The New Scholasticism,* 36 (January 1962), pp. 1–28.

Monan, Donald J. *Moral Knowledge and Its Methodology in Aristotle.* New York: Oxford, 1968.

Moravesik, J. M. E. (ed.). *Aristotle: A Collection of Critical Essays.* Notre Dame, Ind.: University of Notre Dame Press, 1968.

Randall, John. *Aristotle.* New York: Columbia University Press, 1960.

Ross, W. D. *Aristotle.* London: Methuen, 1937.

Sherman, Charles L. "A Latter-Day Tyranny in the Light of Aristotelian Prognosis," *American Political Science Review,* 28 (June 1934), pp. 424–435.

Shuchman, Philip. "Aristotle's Conception of Contract," *Journal of the History of Ideas,* 23 (April–June 1962), pp. 257–264.

Taylor, A. E. *Aristotle.* New York: Dover, 1956.

Ward, Leo R. "Aristotle on Criteria of Moral Good," *Review of Politics,* 30 (October 1968), pp. 476–498.

Wheeler, Marcus. "Aristotle's Analysis of the Nature of Political Struggle," *American Journal of Philology,* 72 (April 1951), pp. 145–161.

Wheelwright, Philip. *Aristotle.* New York: Odyssey, 1951.

II

THE ERA OF EMPIRE: ALEXANDER THE GREAT, POLYBIUS, AND CICERO

6

Alexander the Great
and the Politics
of *Homonoia*

HENRY M. DE MAURIAC

I

In 336 B.C. Philip, King of Macedon, was murdered, and his twenty-year-old son, Alexander, ascended the throne.[1] During the next two years the young king disposed of his political opponents, consolidated his position as *Hegemon*

This article was originally published in *Journal of the History of Ideas,* 10 (January 1949), 104–114. It is reprinted here with the permission of the publisher.

[1] Alexander the Great was not without historians in his own day. Among them were Callisthenes, the philosopher who accompanied him and recorded events until the death of Darius; Ptolemy, one of Alexander's generals and later king of Egypt; Nearchus, the admiral of the fleet which sailed from the Indus River to the Persian Gulf; Onesicritus, a navigator with Nearchus; and Aristobolus, a companion of the king on the Indian expedition. In the fourth, or possibly the third, century B.C., Cleitarchus wrote a highly-colored and not-too-reliable version of Alexander's Asiatic conquests. All these sources are lost to us, and are significant only for their influence on later writers.

Probably the most trustworthy and definitive accounts of Alexander

of the Corinthian League, and prepared his armies for invasion of the Orient. By 334, the preparations being completed, Alexander the Great, with an army of 35,000, crossed the Hellespont. In the Battle of the Granicus River, his first against the Persians, he defeated an army under the leadership of the local satraps. In rapid succession he overcame a small but well-equipped force under the Great King, Darius, stormed Tyre, took Gaza, and proceeded to Africa and the Nile. After assuring himself of the loyalty of the Egyptians, he returned to Persia and defeated the main forces of Darius in the Battle of Gaugamela (331 B.C.). Because this battle broke organized Iranian resistance, it was the decisive engagement of the campaign. Darius was in full flight to Ecbatana and Bactria, where he was later murdered by the satrap Bessus. Although there were many difficult battles after Gaugamela, the Persians no longer presented a united front to the Macedonian invaders. Babylon fell without resistance; Susa and Persepolis, after short engagements. The remote eastern provinces of Bactria and Sogdiana were subjugated during the years 330–328, but only after bitterly-contested struggles with the local rulers. By 327 Alexander the Great was ready to invade India, an operation which occupied him for the three years 327–324. In 324 Alexander returned to Susa, where he turned his attention to the unfinished business of establishing a government, but the task was never completed. The thirty-three-year-old conqueror contracted a fever and died June 13, 323.

This review of the campaigns of Alexander, brief and inadequate as it is, illustrates the vast extent of his empire and the heterogeneous nature of the population. We are now confronted with the question: What was Alexander's relationship to Asia's lands and peoples? I think the best approach to the problem is through a discussion of Alexander's concept of the unity of mankind and through an examination of the organization of his empire.

---

appear in the *Anabasis* and in the *Indica* of Arrian (c. A.D. 150). So far as can be discerned, he relied for the *Anabasis* upon the accurate works of Ptolemy and Aristobolus, and for the *Indica* upon Aristobolus and Nearchus. Diodorus Siculus (c. 20 B.C.) drew upon Cleitarchus for his *Bibliotheca historica*. Of the extant books of this work, 11–20 are relevant to Alexander. Quintus Curtius (c. A.D. 42) also used Cleitarchus almost exclusively as a source for his *De rebus gestis Alexandri magni*. Justin (2d. century after Christ) also employed Cleitarchus for his *Historiarum philippicarum libri XLIV*, but derived the mass of his material from the now lost *Historiae philippicae et totius mundi origines et terrae situs* of Trogus (c. 10 B.C.?). Plutarch (c. A.D. 45–125) used Cleitarchus in his *Life of Alexander,* but with more discretion than most of his predecessors. It is noteworthy that the inaccuracies of Cleitarchus are generally reflected in the writings of those later historians who adopted his work as their chief source of information.

There are many modern writers who have made valuable contributions to our knowledge of Alexander. Most of them have not been mentioned here in footnotes. Two in particular, however, have written well on the general subject of Alexander's relations with the Greeks: Raymond Bugard, *L'expédition d'Alexandre et la Conquète de l'Asie* (Paris, 1937); and Victor Ehrenberg, *Alexander and the Greeks* (tr. Ruth Fraenke von Velsen; Oxford, 1938).

II

Greeks of the classical period, speaking very roughly, divided mankind into two classes, Greeks and non-Greeks; the latter they called barbarians and usually regarded as inferior people, though occasionally some one, like Herodotus or Xenophon, might suggest that certain barbarians possessed qualities which deserved consideration, like the wisdom of the Egyptians or the courage of the Persians. But in the third century B.C. and later we meet with a body of opinion which may be called universalist; all mankind was one and all men were brothers, or anyhow ought to be.[2]

The idea of the unity of mankind is sprung from the Greek concept of *Homonoia*. *Homonoia*, a difficult word to translate, means unity and concord, "a being of one mind together."[3] The Greeks recognized the desirability of *Homonoia*, but they interpreted it in a negative manner: the absence of faction fights. "There was hardly a trace as yet of the more positive sense which *Homonoia* was later to acquire, a mental attitude which would make war or faction impossible because the parties were at one."[4]

By proposing "to treat the whole Greek world as one and the futile wars between city and city as faction fights,"[5] Isocrates extended the meaning from the traditional Greek interpretation of unity and concord within a city. It was this extended concept of *Homonoia* which Isocrates presented to Philip, the concept which Philip adopted when he made himself *Hegemon* of the Corinthian League. Although Isocrates did not accept the Platonic contention that all barbarians were slaves by nature, he employed the Platonic idea that the Greek world should unite against the natural enemy, the barbarians. The barbarians in this case were the Persians, and Isocrates saw that the quickest and easiest path to Greek unity lay in a *holy war* against the Persians.

With the death of Philip the influence of Isocrates declined. Alexander, the pupil of Aristotle, naturally turned to the Aristotelian concept of *Homonoia*. "Aristotle told Alexander to treat Greeks as friends, but barbarians like animals; but Alexander knew better, and preferred to divide men into good and bad without regard to their race. . . ."[6] Alexander probably realized that it would be easier, by treating the inhabitants of a conquered country as free men rather than as slaves, to deal with the problems of administration. Radet supports this opinion, when he says that Alexander regarded the difference between one nation and another as *"moins une question de race qu'une affaire de culture."*[7] Although Alexander did not accept

---

[2] William Woodthorpe Tarn, *Alexander The Great and the Unity of Mankind* (Reprinted from *Proceedings of the British Academy,* XIX, 1933), 3.
[3] W. W. Tarn, 4.
[4] W. W. Tarn, 5.
[5] W. W. Tarn, 5.
[6] W. W. Tarn, 5.
[7] Georges Radet, *Alexandre Le Grand* (Paris, 1931), 45.

Platonic *Homonoia*, his theory of the unity of mankind was not inconsistent with the Platonic thesis that anything is possible, if the structure is harmonious and pleasing.[8]

Alexander's concept of the unity of mankind is well expressed in the following paraphrase of two passages from Plutarch: ". . . the first says that his intention was to bring about, as between mankind generally, *Homonoia* and peace and fellowship and make them all one people; and the other, which for the moment I will quote without its context, makes him say that God is the common father of all men." [9] Alexander's desire to accomplish this deed was intensified by his belief that he had a mission from the deity to harmonize mankind. Tarn is so impressed with Alexander's application of the principles of *Homonoia* that he concludes his monograph with these words: "Alexander for the things he did was called The Great; but . . . I do not think we shall doubt that this idea of his—call it a purpose, call it a dream, call it what you like—was the greatest thing about him." [10]

III

> In Macedonia he was and remained like Philip and his predecessors the king of the people and the army, beside whom the nation in arms preserved its old rights in the assembly of the army. To the Greeks of the Corinthian League he was the *Hegemon* with the rights and duties laid down by the Covenant of the League. As King of Persia he was to the Asiatics an absolute ruler in the sense of the Achaemenids, as whose successor he regarded himself after the death of Darius.[11]

Such was the position of Alexander when he set about the establishment of an administrative structure for his newly won Persian empire. Although he had certain commitments at home, he was responsible to no one but himself in the administration of the Persian and Indian areas of his empire. It appeared to him that this was an excellent opportunity for experimentation with his broad interpretation of *Homonoia*. He had the diversified population which made the experiment ideal, and he had the absolute power to see that his orders were promptly executed. In his mind the new empire was to be "Greco-Oriental in its very essence." [12] There was to be no small Macedonian ruling class as opposed to a large and unparticipating Iranian population. In so far as possible, it was to be a joint undertaking.

[8] Mikhail Ivanovitch Rostovtzev, *A History of the Ancient World*, I, "The Orient and Greece" (Oxford, 1936), 352.
[9] W. W. Tarn, 7.
[10] W. W. Tarn, 28.
[11] Ulrich Wilcken, *Alexander The Great* (New York, 1933), 245.
[12] M. I. Rostovtzev, "The Hellenistic World and Its Development," *American Historical Review*, XLI (January 1936), 234.

In the establishment of his rule Alexander the Great did not overlook the advantages of certain elements in the Persian method of handling the problem of a large empire. Particularly, he valued the organizational powers of the Persians and the efficiency of the Persian satrapies.[13] These he incorporated into his scheme of administration. Because he treated individual problems without regard for uniformity, it is difficult to make a detailed examination of the organization of the empire under Alexander. In general, however, it was his practice to appoint Iranians to the offices of satrap, and Macedonians to the new and especially created offices of taxation and finance. These two offices operated independently of one another, a feature which tended to minimize misuse of funds. In addition to these arrangements, he placed Macedonians at the head of the military forces in the satrapies. In this way he was able to employ, without endangering the military position of the conquering Macedonians, native Persians in the civil government of Persians. After his return from India, Alexander discovered that during his absence some of the Persian satraps had misbehaved. As a result, preferring to rely upon trusted Macedonians, after 328 he created no more oriental satraps. The important thing is not the element of failure, but the fact that Alexander attempted to achieve a measure of coöperation between Persians and Macedonians.[14]

The separate treatment of taxation and finance, "an absolutely original idea of Alexander's," illustrated his interest in the economic problems of the new empire.[15] The general effect of this innovation was the creation of taxation districts, usually comprised of several of the satrapies. In this manner he organized a highly centralized and efficient method of taxation and finance. He made further efforts to standardize the economy of the empire by reserving to himself the right of coinage in both gold and silver.[16] The standardization of the coinage and the centralization of the taxation and the finance structures indicate that Alexander the Great was aiming at the unification of his empire. He was so successful in these economic measures, especially in matters of transportation and communication, that he opened the way for safe intra-empire commerce, something which had never before been accomplished.[17]

In addition to these mechanical elements of administration, Alexander inaugurated a twofold civilizing policy. Reciprocal in nature, this policy was designed to acquaint the Persians with the culture of the Greeks, and the Greeks with the customs of the Persians. Although it must be said to Alexander's credit that the spirit of his plan was reciprocity, it must be

[13] M. I. Rostovtzev, 28.
[14] Gustave Glotz, Pierre Roussel, Robert Cohen, *Histoire Ancienne: Histoire Grecque,* IV, "Alexandre et l'hellénization du monde antique" (Paris, 1938), 232–242.
[15] Ulrich Wilcken, 254.
[16] Gustave Glotz, etc., 228–232.
[17] Gustave Glotz, 248.

further admitted that it degenerated into a program of indoctrination of the Persians with Greek ideas. This indoctrination particularly took the form of Greek art and literature. The effect of the Greek arts may be seen in the oriental architecture of later periods, which, centuries after the disintegration of Alexander's empire, still reflected the Greek influence. The civilizing program was further designed to benefit both Greeks and Persians through its scientific research, particularly in the fields of geography and cartography. The explorations which resulted from this interest were probably less important for what they revealed about geography than for their spreading of Hellenism. Because they were the centers of Greek culture and the crossroads of commerce, the cities which Alexander founded played an important rôle in the spreading of Hellenism.[18] The most sensational attempt to civilize and to educate both Greeks and Persians was probably the promotion of interracial marriage. Because it was an easy way to prevent revolt through fusion of racial stocks, Alexander was the outstanding proponent of this idea. Accordingly, in a mass marriage ceremony at Susa in 324 Macedonian soldiers and officers took Persian wives. Alexander himself had set the example for such marriages by marrying the reportedly beautiful Persian, Roxana, in 327.[19]

The policies of Alexander can be said to have had seven principal features: (1) shrewd attention to the welfare of the Persians, (2) respect for the Persian institutions, especially religion, (3) equal distribution of offices among Macedonians and Persians, with the Persians holding the civil positions and the Macedonians, the military, (4) the "gradual regeneration" of Persia rather than "progressive degradation," (5) free communication throughout the empire, (6) advocation of the blending of customs, (7) liberal extensions to the Persians of the privileges and advantages of his own country.[20]

IV

He must meet the orientals on their own ground; he must become their king in their own way. The surest means of planting Hellenism in their midst was to begin by taking account sympathetically of their prejudices. Alexander assumed the state of Great King, surrounded himself with Eastern forms and pomp, exacted self-abasement in his presence from oriental subjects, and adopted the maxim that the king's person was divine. . . . He hoped ultimately to secure uniformity in the relations of Macedonians and Persians to their king.[21]

[18] Ulrich Wilcken, 255–261.
[19] Ulrich Wilcken, 248. Cf. M. I. Rostovtzev, A History of the Ancient World, I, "The Orient and Greece," 351.
[20] (Anonymous) The Moral and Political Consequences of the Conquests of Alexander The Great (Oxford, 1841), 15–17.
[21] J. B. Bury, A History of Greece to the Death of Alexander The Great (London), 794.

Such was the position of Alexander as Great King of Persia. It was this course of action which he chose as the most satisfactory method of attaining the sought-after *Homonoia*.

There were two important difficulties in Alexander's approach as Great King. The first was his attempt to create an artificial social structure in which all races and nations held social equality with all others. As a result of this essay both the Macedonians and Persians, by reason of political influence and material wealth the predominant elements in the empire, were dissatisfied. The Persians were resentful, because they, the former ruling class of the Achaemenid Empire, were placed on the same social level with the Bactrians, Sogdians, Syrians, and other minority groups, whom they had traditionally considered inferior peoples.[22] The Macedonians, on the other hand, felt that Alexander, by granting to the Persians social equality with their conquerors, had forsaken them. This feeling was most obvious in the army, where Persians were brigaded with Macedonians.[23]

Alexander's army and his closest friends objected strenuously to his close association with the Persian Artabazus. This relationship between their king and a Persian politician the Macedonians regarded as a personal slight of the most obvious sort.[24] Furthermore, his partial adoption of Persian dress was a source of irritation to Alexander's men.[25] They also found his marriage to Roxana particularly distasteful. That Alexander, King of Macedon, should marry a barbarian they regarded as a repudiation of his birthright. The Macedonians did not relish the idea of a Persian-Macedonian heir to the throne. Only a Greek or a Macedonian woman would have been an entirely acceptable queen for Alexander.

Important as it was, this matter of social equality was only the surface manifestation of a far deeper Macedonian resentment, a resentment which springs from a series of events in the life of Alexander. This was the matter of the divinity of Alexander. Had it not been for this singular aspect of the king's character, it is probable that the Macedonians would have overlooked their other sources of dissatisfaction. In order to get to the roots of this problem, it is necessary to examine certain incidents which led Alexander to the idea of himself as a divinity, and to the application of these ideas to the exigencies of empire administration.

Rostovtzev makes a statement, which I consider highly significant: "We have no certain knowledge, but I am inclined to believe that Alexander ranked himself above ordinary mortals, not merely because he was a king and a distant descendant of Heracles."[26] This implies that Alexander might have considered himself a god, but points out that there is no con-

---

[22] Frederick Allen Wright, *Alexander The Great* (London, 1934), 160–161.
[23] Ulrich Wilcken, 250–251.
[24] F. A. Wright, 164.
[25] Ulrich Wilcken, 249.
[26] M. I. Rostovtzev, *A History of the Ancient World*, I "The Orient and Greece," 352.

clusive evidence. Rostovtzev's is a careful statement of the case, and I believe, for reasons that will become obvious later, that it is important not to
take dogmatically the position that he believed himself to be a divine
ruler.

In 333 Alexander the Great went to Gordion, where he cut the famous Gordian Knot. The legend was that the person who untied this knot
would rule Asia. At first the young conqueror attempted to untie it, but
failing, drew his sword and cut the rope.[27] The knot was untied and the oracle fulfilled. From this time on, according to orthodox opinion, he felt
himself destined to rule Asia, especially in the light of the fact that he
knew himself to be distantly descended from Heracles.

Probably the most important were the events which occurred in
Egypt during the last months of 332 and early in 331. An understanding of
these incidents requires a knowledge of the background.

The Persians had ruled over Egypt prior to the arrival of Alexander.

> In most countries Persian rule was comparatively just and humane, and of
> all the kings that followed after Cyrus only two were tyrants in the worst
> sense of the word. But, as it happened, these two, Cambyses and Artax-
> erxes III Ochus, were the only Persian monarchs who impressed themselves
> very clearly in the Egyptian imagination, and the impression was a painful
> one.[28]

By his sacrilegious conduct in connection with their divinities, Cambyses
had outraged the Egyptians; Ochus had oppressed and enslaved the people
far beyond the necessities of his tyranny. To the Egyptians Alexander was
a liberator. Consequently, Alexander was warmly welcomed and quickly
honored with the Egyptian regal titles. He became: Horus the Strong
Prince, the Protector of Egypt, the beloved of Ammon, the Chosen of Ra,
King of Upper and Lower Egypt, and the Mystically Begotten Son of Ra.[29]

The answers to Alexander's subsequent inquiries of the oracle at the
Temple of Ammon reflected the popular opinion throughout Egypt. Alexander, of course, encouraged this reflection with liberal gifts to the priests
and to the Temple; so it is not surprising that the oracle greeted Alexander
as the Son of Ammon. To the Greeks, who recognized Ammon as co-equal
with Zeus, the greeting meant that Alexander was the son of the most powerful of the gods. Furthermore, the oracle encouraged Alexander in his desire to be Great King of Persia. This encouragement appears to me to be
extremely important, because I think that it confirmed in his mind whatever ideas of mission he had previously held. I think also that it is this acquiring of a sense of mission which makes Rostovtzev's observation, that
Alexander ranked himself above ordinary mortals, so important. I believe

[27] J. B. Bury, 755–756.
[28] F. A. Wright, 109.
[29] F. A. Wright, 112.

that it was on the basis of this sense of mission that Alexander considered himself a super-normal human being.[30]

When Alexander returned from Egypt to defeat Darius at Gaugamela, he returned as the announced son of Zeus-Ammon. Had it not been for the fact that Darius and his predecessors were recognized by the Iranians as divine, this newly acquired attribute of divinity might never have become a matter of great importance. Alexander was also recognized as having certain qualifications for divinity. These qualifications, of course, resulted from: (1) his relationship to Heracles, (2) his cutting of the Gordian Knot, (3) the events at the Temple of Zeus-Ammon. These well-known events made it easy for Alexander to assume the attributes of Great King.

Tarn has crystallized the connection between the concept of Alexander, the divinity, and the concept of Alexander, the man with a mission:

> . . . he did say that all men were sons of God, that is brothers, but that God made the best ones peculiarly his own; he did aspire to be the harmonizer and reconciler of the world—that part of the world which his arm reached—he did have the intention of uniting the peoples of his empire in fellowship and concord and making them of one mind together; and when, as a beginning, he prayed at Opis for partnership in rule and *Homonoia* between Macedonians and Persians, he meant what he said—not partnership in rule only, but true unity between them.[31]

It seems to me that this statement complements Rostovtzev's point of view.[32] I believe that it is a legitimate conclusion that Alexander adopted the divinity of the Persian King to bring about his *Homonoia*, his prototype of "the more perfect union." [33]

In becoming Great King, Alexander also adopted the traditional rites and customs concomitant with oriental monarchy. This adoption caused him more trouble than any of his other political ventures. The Macedonians, upon whom he had to rely for support, felt that he had betrayed them and had deserted the Greeks in favor of the Persians. In particular, there was one aspect of Alexander's assumption of oriental divinity which was especially revolting to the Macedonians: the practice of *proskynesis*, prostration of the subjects before the Great King. The difference in the Persian point of view and the Greek opinion of this institution is the key to the problem. The Persians regarded the *proskynesis* as a salute to the king, but *"les Grecs considéraient la 'proskynèse,' non comme une sorte spéciale de salut, mais comme un honneur réservé aux dieux, tout au plus héros, qu' ils refuseraient aux vivants."* [34] Radet expresses it, *"la proskynèse . . . ne sert jamais pour honorer les hommes."* [35]

[30] See note 26.
[31] W. W. Tarn, 27–28.
[32] See reference on note 8.
[33] *The Constitution of The United States*, "Preamble."
[34] Gustave Glotz, etc., 136.
[35] Georges Radet, 257.

We are assured that Alexander did not attempt to practise oriental absolutism toward the Macedonians.[36] Actually, he did try it in one case, but it met with such universal disapproval that he never again attempted it. Even this one attempt seems to have been less one of exacting homage from the Macedonians than it was of rendering uniform the court ceremonials.[37] The Macedonians, however, considered the attempt the crowning act of tyranny. They recalled rather pointedly that the tyrannicides, Harmodius and Aristogeiton, were honored in Athens.[38] The result of this whole series of closely linked events, particularly the episode of Macedonian prostration, was an ever-widening gulf between Alexander and his army.

In the light of the arguments presented, I am able to reach only one conclusion. Alexander the Great did not become a god as an end in itself. He became a god in order to achieve an end, *Homonoia*. In this political move his strong army was his weakest link. He was never able to convince the Macedonians of the necessity of race fusion.[39] Alexander saw in the divinity ascribed to him through his descendance from Heracles and by the oracle of Zeus-Ammon, the great and convenient tool for the accomplishment of the task of unification, which he had proposed for himself. He was drawing on all the resources at his disposal in order to create an empire rich in *Homonoia*.

[36] Ulrich Wilcken, 250.
[37] J. B. Bury, 796–797.
[38] Georges Radet, 271.
[39] Ulrich Wilcken, 251.

7

Polybius
and the Roman State

FRANK W. WALBANK

I

It would be interesting, if it were possible, to discover who
first described the Romans as masters of the world. According to Polybius,[1] Scipio Africanus in his speech before
Zama promised his men that if they were victorious, they
would "gain for themselves and their country undisputed
command and sovereignty over the rest of the world." But
since Polybius says the same thing himself a chapter earlier [15.9.2], he may have attributed to Scipio sentiments
which he (or his source) later judged appropriate to the
situation.

After Magnesia, in 190–189 B.C., we find Rhodian and
Syrian spokesmen similarly addressing the Romans as "rulers and masters of the world," [2] and this is perhaps easier
to believe, since the defeat of Antiochus must obviously

This article was originally published in *Greek, Roman and Byzantine
Studies,* 5 (Winter 1964), 239–260. It is reprinted here with the permission of the author and of the publisher.

[1] 15.10.2 If not otherwise stated, references are to Polybius.
[2] 21.16.8 (Syrians), 23.4 (Rhodians).

have made a tremendous impact on the Greek east. In the negotiations which preceded the Syrian War the Romans had insisted that Antiochus should not cross over into Europe, and propaganda on both sides had created the impression that Rome spoke for Europe and Antiochus for Asia. Antiochus' defeat had thus left Rome mistress of both continents and so, since Carthage had already been humbled, of the whole world; or so it may well have seemed. At any rate, when Carneades, the leader of the New Academy, delivered his famous lecture on justice at Rome fifteen years later in 155 B.C., he could refer to the Romans as masters of the world, as if the phrase were a commonplace [3]; and twenty years later still, Tiberius Gracchus stirred his popular audience with references to these "so-called masters of the world, who do not possess a single clod of earth to call their own." [4]

Masters of the world— κύριοι τῆς οἰκουμένης; in this phrase we have the realisation of those Greek fears voiced by an Aetolian statesman as early as 217 at the peace conference of Naupactus [5.104], and the characterisation of a new period in Mediterranean politics in which the old Hellenistic balance of power was as dead as the dodo. It is of this new era of the world-power that Polybius is the historian and—if one can dignify him with such a title—the philosopher. His subject is precisely defined and a matter of concern to his contemporaries; he will discuss by what means and under what kind of constitution the Romans, in less than fifty-three years, have succeeded in subjecting nearly the whole inhabited world to their sole government—a thing unique in history [1.1.5].

As a statement of the central problem of Roman imperialism this may appear inadequate; it certainly by-passes most of the issues which are hotly debated in contemporary journals and monographs. Today we ask: in what sense were the Romans imperialists? Did they go to Greece as part of a plan of expansion or moved by sentiment? Did they win their empire in a mood of nervous aggression engendered by fear? Was the Senate blundering or Machiavellian? But these are issues in which Polybius is not interested. Consider, for example, his picture of early Roman expansion overseas. The Romans undertook the first war with Carthage in response to an appeal from some Campanian freebooters who had settled at Messana [1.10.2–11.3]; but no sooner had they taken Agrigentum in 262–261 than "they began [says Polybius at 1.20.1–2] to plan to drive the Carthaginians out of Sicily." The experience of the First Punic War and its perils so schooled the Romans that [1.63.9] "it was perfectly natural that they not only gained the courage to aim at universal dominion, but executed their

---

[3] *Cf.* Cic. *Rep.* 3.24, from L. Furius Philus' speech, which is based on that of Carneades.
[4] Plut. *Tib. Gracch.* 9.5; on the authenticity of these words of Gracchus (transmitted *via* Nepos) see P. Fraccaro, "Oratori e orazioni dell' età dei Gracchi," *Studi Storichi per l'Antichità Classica* 5 (1912) 423; Scullard, *JRS* 50 (1960) 64 n.1.

purpose." One war led to another. "I regard the war with Antiochus," writes Polybius [3.32.7], "as deriving its origin from that with Philip, the latter as resulting from that with Hannibal, and the Hannibalic War as a consequence of that about Sicily, the intermediate events, however many and various their character, all tending to the same purpose."

On this assumption *our* problem—Why did the Romans seek an empire?—hardly exists. It was perfectly natural—λίαν εἰκότως; or, as the Athenians had long ago observed at Melos,[5] "of the gods we believe, and of men we know, that by a necessary law of nature men rule wherever they can." This was not, of course, good enough for the Romans themselves. Their well-established tradition, that Rome fought only just wars, would have suffered rude violence from the acceptance of such a thesis; and fortunately by the second century, when the Romans found themselves on the defensive about their imperial motives, the Stoics were already at hand to help them out with the comfortable doctrine that the Roman empire was the reward of Roman virtue, and an instrument of justice benefiting ruler and ruled impartially.[6] Polybius was not blind to these considerations, and he has some pertinent remarks on Roman morals and Roman morale. But his primary concern was different. The question he asked was not "Why did the Romans acquire their empire?" but "How did they contrive to do it so successfully?"

The Hellenistic answer to this kind of question was regularly cast in one of two forms: either Fortune, Tyche, was the motive force directing events, or alternatively success was due to the transcendent power of some individual, a Philip or an Alexander. Polybius was a Greek and his history pays its due to the role of one determined man.[7] But he was also, first and foremost, a rationalist, and if he speaks of the rise of Rome to world power as an accomplishment of Fortune, he leaves it quite clear that this is not a formula designed to absolve him from the duty of explaining the process also in terms which a rationalist would find acceptable. He does not despise moral worth—far from it—nor does he underestimate what chance can do; but he rates higher than either the political acumen which can create a stable, imperialist state, and that is why after describing the catastrophe of Cannae, where Hannibal annihilated the best part of two consular armies, he breaks off his narrative to devote a whole book to the problem of the Roman constitution.

There may be something a trifle arid about Polybius' theorising, a lack of imagination, a tendency to schematise, to want an answer to everything. But he wrote on the spot, an intelligent man, himself a statesman and a general, in touch with those who controlled the realities of Roman

---

[5] Thuc. 5. 105.2.
[6] *Cf.* W. Capelle, "Griechische Ethik und römischer Imperialismus," *Klio* 25 (1932) 86–113.
[7] *Cf.* 1.35.4; 8.3.3, 7.7; 9.22.1, 22.6; 22.4.2.

political life, a man moreover with the fresh eye of a foreigner who looks at new institutions against the background of a different experience. At a time when the affairs of Greece and Rome were becoming inextricably intertwined, as they have been ever since, he stands out as an important witness whose evidence should not be neglected.

II

Born about the end of the third century at Megalopolis in Arcadia, Polybius devoted the first thirty years of his life to acquiring the education and the military and political experience of an Achaean statesman. His father was Lycortas, an eminent politician and a follower of the great Philopoemen. It was no doubt thanks to this connextion that Polybius was selected in 182 to carry Philopoemen's ashes to burial,[8] and sometime later he wrote his biography.[9] The boy's upbringing was coloured by the family's position as rich landowners. His interest in military matters is shown by his lost book on *Tactics* [*cf.* 9.20.4], and by many digressions in the *Histories* [10]; he was also devoted to riding and hunting—indeed tradition ascribed his death to a fall from a horse at the ripe age of eighty-two.[11] Admittedly, his knowledge of literature was not extensive; occasional quotations from the poets often suggest the use of a commonplace book.[12] His philosophic studies too were limited. Despite his use of the word "unphilosophical" as a term of abuse,[13] his references to Heracleitus, Plato, Aristotle and Demetrius of Phalerum provide no evidence that he had gone very deeply into any of these writers.[14] On the other hand he had obviously given close attention to his predecessors in the field of history, such as Timaeus, Phylarchus, Theopompus and Ephorus. This emerges very clearly from the strictures which he feels it his duty to pass upon most of them whenever an occasion offers.[15]

Of Polybius' career between Philopoemen's death and the Third Macedonian War only a little is known. But he was Cavalry Commander of the Achaean Confederation for the year 170–169, a critical moment in his country's history. Involved in an irksome war with Perseus of Macedonia, the Romans were irritably watching all Greek states for signs of disloyalty.

---

[8] Plut. *Philop.* 21.5.
[9] 10.21.5 f; it was the source of Plutarch's *Philopoemen*.
[10] *E.g.* 3.81.10, 105; 5.98; 10.16.1–17.5, 22–24, 32.7–33, 43–47; 11.25.6.
[11] Ps.-Lucian, *Macrob.* 23.
[12] See C. Wunderer, "Citate u. geflügelte Worte bei Polybios," in *Polybios-Forschungen* II (Leipzig, 1901).
[13] 12.25.6 (Timaeus); 36.15.5 (Prusias).
[14] *Cf.* 4.40.3, 12.27.1 (Heracleitus); 4.35.15, 6.5.1, 45, 7.13.7, 12.28.2 (Plato); 12.5.4 ff, 6al ff, 6b3 ff, 7.2, 7.4, 8 ff, 11.5, 23.8, 24.2, 31.16.3 (Aristotle); 29.21 (Demetrius).
[15] For attacks on Timaeus see Book 12 *passim;* on Phylarchus, 2.56.1–63.6; on Theopompus, 8.9–11; Ephorus is more gently treated, *cf.* 5.33.2, 12.28.10.

It was the tradition of Polybius' family to maintain an independent attitude vis-à-vis Rome, and in 170 B.C. independence among Greeks was a quality little respected by the Senate. In the purge which followed Perseus' defeat, Polybius found himself one of a thousand eminent Achaeans who were summoned to Rome, ostensibly for examination, and subsequently detained there without even the pretence of justice.

Once at Rome, Polybius was more fortunate than his colleagues. Soon after the internment began, and while he was still in the city, he had the good fortune to attract the attention of the eighteen-year-old Scipio Aemilianus. The acquaintance, which sprang out of "the loan of some books and conversation about them" [16] quickly ripened into friendship, and when soon afterwards the other internees were distributed among the municipal towns of Italy, Polybius received permission to stay on in Rome, where he became Scipio's mentor and close friend.[17] His position was now highly ambiguous. Technically a foreign internee,[18] he enjoyed friendship on equal terms with men like Aemilianus, his brother Q. Fabius, and the whole of that famous circle. Undoubtedly he felt flattered by this attention; and it is not wholly surprising that he responded sympathetically to the special virtues of Roman aristocratic character and tradition.

The majesty of the Senate,[19] that repository of political talent, directing an amenable people thanks to a moral prestige or *auctoritas* enhanced by the successful struggle against Hannibal, could not fail to impress the Achaean statesman, who was all too conscious of the unruliness of Greek popular assemblies. The author of the *Tactics* had already experience of the methods and discipline of the Roman army; the more he studied it, the greater grew his admiration. In their civil life, too, the Romans had avoided the errors of his compatriots. Their peculiar and somewhat sensational funeral customs were designed to inspire the young noble with a sense of duty, family pride and patriotism, and a determination to model his own conduct on that of such figures as Horatius Cocles [*cf.* 6.53.1–55.4]. A strong public opinion, reinforced by salutary sanction of the death penalty, inculcated strict standards of public honesty [6.56.1–5]; bribery, the most venial of Greeks sins, was virtually unknown.[20] Finally, Rome still possessed what the cynical and critical Greeks had so lamentably discarded, a state religion clothed in great pomp, and penetrating every aspect of private life with its reminders of the terrors and torments of Hades, so that any potentially unruly plebeians were kept in order and

---

[16] 31.23.4 ἔκ τινος χρήσεως βιβλίων καὶ τῆς περὶ τούτων λαλίας. Gelzer, *Kleine Schriften* III (Wiesbaden 1964) 178 n.133, following Leo, takes χρῆσις to mean "reading together," rather than "loan." The books were probably from Perseus' library, now the property of Aemilius Paullus (Plut. *Aem.* 28.1).

[17] 31.23 ff; Diod. 31.26.5; Vell. 1.13.3; Plut. *Mor.* 659F; Ps.–Plut. *Mor.* 199F.

[18] The Achaeans were κατεχόμενοι; *cf.* 30.32.8, 33.1.3; see Gelzer *loc. cit.* (n.16 above).

[19] On the Senate see 6.13.

[20] 6.56.2; later this integrity was less universal at Rome, *cf.* 18.35.

compelled by their fears to respect the sanctity of the oath [6.56.6–15].

To Polybius this all seemed most desirable. Gradually he cast aside his resentment and lurking hostility towards the state which, despite its *fides* and its *deisidaimonia,* had treated him and his colleagues so ill, and anticipating the role of a Smuts, became the interpreter, theoretician and philosopher of his adopted empire. He resolved in short to write a universal history which should explain by what means and thanks to what kind of constitution in a period of almost fifty-three years—from the outbreak of the Second Punic War to the victory over Perseus at Pydna—Rome had become mistress of the world.

III

This programme, it will be observed, is twofold—"by what means, and thanks to what kind of constitution," πῶς καὶ τίνι γένει πολιτείας. The means by which Rome rose to world dominion is the subject of Polybius' history as a whole: but his account of the Roman constitution is concentrated in Book 6. It is to that account I propose to devote the remainder of this paper.

The great importance which Polybius attaches to the constitution as a factor in Roman success illustrates that concern to find the best type of state which had been a Greek preoccupation at least since Herodotus composed his famous dialogue on the subject and put it into the mouths of the Persian nobles.[21] In the fourth century, Plato's *Republic* and *Laws* and Aristotle's *Politics* are only the most outstanding discussions of the ideal constitution; and the output went on into the Hellenistic age and beyond. Moreover, as Professor Sinclair has pointed out,[22] the Greek interest in utopias was never wholly divorced from reality; and this fact is illustrated not only by Plato's unhappy adventures in Sicily, but also from another aspect by Aristotle's comprehensive study of 158 existing constitutions, of which the *Constitution of Athens* survives as a solitary example.

Polybius himself devotes a substantial part of Book 6 to a comparison of the Roman constitution with those of Sparta, Crete and Carthage [6.43–56]. In other respects, however, he breaks new ground. His sixth book has suffered in modern times partly because it has survived only in fragments—though these are in fact substantial enough to permit a convincing reconstruction of the plan and even the details—and partly because the argument is itself complicated and attempts to combine within a single thesis elements which are not always fundamentally reconcilable.[23]

[21] Herod. 3.80–82.
[22] T. A. Sinclair, *History of Greek Political Thought* (London, 1952) 7.
[23] See Brink and Walbank, "The Construction of the Sixth Book of Polybius," *CQ* N.s.4 (1954) 97–122.

At bottom Polybius is always the teacher. He writes because he wants his readers to benefit from his work. Repeatedly he stresses the utility of what he is saying; and it is partly at least his didacticism which has led him to overelaborate his discussion of the Roman constitution. He wants this lesson in political science to be one which will not only explain why Rome has grown to what she is, but will also enable students and statesmen to forecast the future, whether at Rome or elsewhere; and he recognises the special difficulties which Rome presents. "In the case of . . . Greek states," he writes [6.3.1–3], ". . . it is an easy matter both to describe their past and to pronounce upon their future. For there is no difficulty in reporting the known facts and it is not hard to foretell the future by inference from the past. But about the Roman state it is neither at all easy to explain the present situation owing to the complicated character of the constitution, nor to foretell the future owing to our ignorance of the peculiar features of public and private life at Rome in the past." This passage commits Polybius to two tasks—an analysis of the Roman constitution as it functioned at the time of the Second Punic War, and an account of earlier Roman history. But if this account is to be of general application and relevant to other states, in short if any universal lessons are to emerge, then he must also show to what extent the development of the Roman state corresponds with the more general principles of political evolution.

At this point an obvious objection presents itself. Are there in fact any such general principles of political evolution? Polybius believes that there are, and he devotes chapters four to nine of Book 6 to their exposition. They are based, he claims, upon a general law of nature, the simple rule that all things have their beginnings, their growth, their perfection, their decline, and their end. This is a law which is valid for all mortal things. But its application to political development can be defined with greater detail and precision. The result is the remarkable system to which Polybius gives the name of the ἀνακύκλωσις τῶν πολιτειῶν,[24] the cycle of constitutions. According to this doctrine all constitutional development is in a circle. Originally mankind lives in a state of complete lawlessness, in herds like animals, for the sake of mutual protection. In such a society the man who excels in physique and courage becomes the natural leader, "as happens in the case of bulls, bears, boars, cocks and the like." Such a leader we term the monarch.

In the course of time, however, through a process which Polybius analyses in detail moral concepts arise along with feelings of sociability and companionship. When this happens and the "leading and most powerful man throws the weight of his authority on the side of such moral notions," the basis of his power changes from fear to respect; and instead of a monarch (μόναρχος) we speak of a king (βασιλεύς). In time however, the king's

[24] 6.9.10; cf. 5.4–9.9 for the detailed account.

descendants degenerate through yielding to their appetites and exploiting their position of privilege, and this sets up feelings of hatred, envy and resentment; the kingship has become a tyranny. The next stage is reached when the noblest, the most high-spirited and the most courageous unite to lead the people against the tyrant, to expel him and to substitute an aristocracy.

But once again, when the original liberators are succeeded by children who have had no experience of either misfortune or moderation, they in turn deteriorate, and by devoting themselves to the pursuit of gain, or to wine and rioting, transform an aristocracy into an oligarchy, until they are driven out by the angry commons, who now set up a democracy. Once more, however, when a generation grows up which does not remember the vices of the oligarchs, men again become selfish and eager for power; they are now so used to freedom and equality that they no longer value them. Demagogues arise who seek popular support by the giving of bribes, and the people are corrupted by receiving them. All turns into the rule of violence: under such leaders the people begin to massacre, banish and plunder, until they degenerate again into savages and so once more find their master. At this point the cycle begins all over again.

How precisely Polybius sought to reconcile this cycle with the simple law of birth, perfection and decline, of which he clearly considers it to be a special case, is a subject which deserves fuller discussion than it can be given here.[25] At some points it appears as though the biological idea is being applied to each separate stage in the circle, with three separate points of perfection in kingship, aristocracy and democracy, each in turn followed by its own decline and a new start with the transition to the next stage. Elsewhere the cycle as a whole appears to be regarded as following the biological principle, but never very adequately: with the mixed constitution regarded as the ideal form, it was difficult to find an alternative acme anywhere among the simple forms which the cycle offered.

Where Polybius found this theory is not known. He connects it with "Plato and certain other philosophers [5.5.1]"; and it is true that in Book 8 of the *Republic* [544c] Plato sets out an "order of states"—the best form (equated with aristocracy or kingship), the Cretan or Laconian form (equated with timocracy), oligarchy, democracy, and tyranny—with the implication that these develop one into another. But, as Aristotle observes in Book 5 of the *Politics* [7(5).12.1316al ff], Plato failed to close the circle with a change from tyranny to the best state; he also failed to show how the changes come about. Admittedly, *Republic* 8 is not the only passage in which Plato discusses the theory of constitutional change[26]; but nowhere do we find anything quite like the *anacyclōsis*, and it seems clear that de-

[25] For fuller discussion see the article quoted in n. 23.
[26] See also *Laws*, 3.677 A ff, 4.709 A ff, *Ep.* 7.326 B ff, *Polit.* 291 D–E.

spite Polybius' reference to Plato, the origins of this must be sought at a date later than the fourth century. In his valuable book *Metabole Politeion*, the Swiss scholar Ryffel has traced two distinct traditions within Polybius' *anacyclōsis*—a theory of the origins of culture going back to the sophists and, in particular, to Protagoras, and a theory about the causes of corruption in states. It seems, however, pretty certain that it was not Polybius who conflated these two themes, but that he borrowed the theory *in toto* from some immediate predecessor. Who that was we cannot tell. Panaetius of Rhodes, who is known to have been a member of the Scipionic circle, has been suggested,[27] and there is a case for seeing some Stoic influence in Polybius' theory. On the other hand, it also contains non-Stoic features, and since most philosophical schools were fairly eclectic in the second century B.C., the positive evidence for Panaetius is really very weak. On the whole, it is more likely that the origins of the theory lay in some popular philosophical milieu such as that which produced works like the pamphlets known as Pseudo-Hippodamus and Ocellus Lucanus.[28]

In any case, the important thing is the use Polybius made of it. Understanding of the Roman constitution, he had said, was handicapped by Greek ignorance of the Roman past. Unfortunately, the section of Book 6 in which he set out to remedy this gap has not survived except in a series of fragments. Something can be deduced from the second book of Cicero's *De Republica*, which certainly drew on Polybius' excursus on early Roman history; but it is not known how close the resemblance was. One fact seems to be well established. Cicero carried his account of Roman history down to the time of the Decemvirate, which undertook the codification of Roman law about 450 B.C.; and Polybius apparently did the same, since a fragment following immediately after the excursus [6.11.1] seems to refer to 450 as the date at which it ended. What was the significance of this date? It may, of course have been chosen because of the character of Polybius' sources. But it seems altogether more likely that it had a special importance in his interpretation of Roman history. Polybius' historical excursus—let us call it by the convenient and traditional title of the *archaeologia*—seems in fact to have been designed to lead up to the date at which Rome succeeded in emerging from the *anacyclōsis* by acquiring a constitution of a finer and more stable type. Within the *anacyclōsis* we have traced six forms of constitution (omitting the primitive monarchy which closed the circle). These are kingship, aristocracy and democracy, each followed by its respective perversion (παρέκβασις), tyranny, oligarchy and ochlocracy. "But it is evident," says Polybius [6.3.7], "that we must regard as the best constitution a combination of all the three above-mentioned varieties, since we have

---

[27] See references quoted in *CQ* 37 (1943) 85; Walbank, *Commentary on Polybius* I (Oxford, 1957) 644.

[28] See Walbank, *Commentary*, 644.

proof of this not only theoretically but in actual experience." This com-
bined, or mixed, constitution is the one found at Rome at the time of the
Hannibalic War, and it is in the possession of this that the strength of
Rome lies.

Thus the *archaeologia* served to illustrate the workings of the normal
constitutional cycle, the *anacyclōsis,* as it occurred at Rome, as well as to
show how the setting-up of a mixed constitution put the brake on that fatal
process. The surviving fragments, together with a cautious use of Cicero's
De Republica 2, suggest that in this version of early Roman history Romulus and his immediate successors filled the rôle of the king (whether or not
Romulus began as the primitive monarch is not clear), and that with Tarquinius Superbus kingship degenerated into tyranny. The explusion of Tar-
quin led to the setting up of an aristocracy with regular magistrates, and
this deteriorated into an oligarchy with the Decemvirate. At this point,
however, Rome diverged from the pattern. In the absence of substantial
fragments we cannot be certain to what extent elements of balance and the
mingling of the three forces—the one, the few and the many—appeared in
the earlier stages of the Roman constitutional evolution; but there is an interesting passage in Cicero [*Rep.* 2.42] in which he says that these three
elements *ita mixta fuerunt et in hac civitate et in Lacedaemoniorum et
Carthaginiensium, ut temperata nullo fuerint modo*—they were mixed,
both in this state (he means Rome under the kings) and in Sparta and in
Carthage, in such a way that there was no balance among them whatsoever. If this remark is based on Polybius, it suggests that the *archaeologia* traced, among other things, the gradual achievement of a balance between kingship, aristocracy and democracy, which finally came to fruition
after the Decemvirate, at a time when the normal working of the *anacyclōsis* would have led the observer to expect the emergence of a democracy.

Certainly the *archaeologia* was intended primarily to explain the
genesis of the Roman mixed constitution; and it is followed by a detailed
analysis of how that mixed constitution functioned in practice [6.11.11–
18.8]. The date with which Polybius is nominally concerned is the period
of the Second Punic War. The mixed constitution may have taken its
rise in 450, at the time of the Decemvirate, but it was at its height,
its acme, at the end of the third century B.C., when the Romans were
fighting Hannibal. In chapters 11 to 18, therefore, after some introductory
remarks, Polybius proceeds to list in order the powers of the consuls
(whom he takes to represent the kingly power), those of the Senate (or
aristocratic element) and those of the people, followed by an analysis of
the checks and limitations exercised against each of the three in turn. For
example, the consuls have almost unlimited power as commanders in the
field; but without the consent of the Senate they can get neither food nor
clothing nor pay for their troops; and on laying down office they have to

account for their actions to the people. The Senate has vast powers, including control of the treasury and a general supervision over serious cases requiring a public investigation throughout Italy; but a *senatus consultum* has to be confirmed by the people before the Senate can hold such an enquiry, and its proceedings are subject to tribunician veto. Finally, the people alone has the right to confer honours and inflict punishments; but in competition for public contracts—and here it is interesting to find Polybius identifying the people with the group which shortly afterwards emerged as the *equites*—they are wholly at the mercy of the Senate through its control of censorial contracts and the law courts.

After listing these and many other similar instances, Polybius concludes that "such being the power that each part has of hampering the others or cooperating with them, their union is adequate to all emergencies, so that it is impossible to find a better political system than this." For in time of danger from abroad, the three parts unite in the face of the common peril; and if in time of peace any element tends to become too predominant, the system of checks inherent in the constitution quickly restores the *status quo*.

This leads Polybius to a comparison between the mixed constitution of Rome and other noteworthy constitutions [6.43–56]. Athens and Thebes are both quickly dismissed. The success of those states was due to chance and circumstance, a rapid and ephemeral effulgence that was quickly quenched. Thebes owed everything to two men, Epaminondas and Pelopidas—a just criticism [6.43.6–7]; and once the era of Themistocles had passed, Athens displayed all the characteristics of a ship without a helmsman—a remark perhaps somewhat unfair to Pericles [6.44.2–3]. Crete is treated at greater length because Ephorus (and others according to Polybius) had commended it and compared it to Sparta; Ephorus' claim is rejected, since "it would be rare to find personal conduct more treacherous or public policy more unjust" than in Crete [6.47.5]. Plato's *Republic* is excluded from the comparison as a purely intellectual conception, not a real state [6.47.7–8]. Lycurgan Sparta is given high praise as a genuine mixed constitution—already in an earlier chapter Polybius had assumed that it stood on an equal footing with Rome in this respect [6.10.12–14]— but it is less well adapted to foreign conquest, and therefore, in view of Polybius' general standpoint in his *Histories*, inferior. "If anyone esteems it finer and more glorious," he remarks, ". . . to be the leader of many men, and to lord it over many and have the eyes of the world turned to him, it must be admitted that from this point of view the Laconian constitution is defective, while that of Rome is superior and better formed for the attainment of power" [6.50.3–4].

This leaves only Carthage; and in comparing the constitutions of Rome and Carthage, Polybius concludes that although Carthage was also a mixed constitution, at the time of the Hannibalic War this was already past its prime. By then the masses had acquired the chief voice in deliberation, whereas at Rome the Senate still kept control over this important aspect of policy. This conclusion is followed by a detailed examination of the two states [6.51–6], taking account of such matters as their skill in sea and land fighting and their morale; and in this connection we are given some interesting information about Roman customs and the relative behaviour of the two peoples in regard to the acquisition of wealth, and about religious observances. This all contributes to Polybius' general picture of Roman *mores* and the Roman constitution; and it now becomes apparent why Rome was able to beat Carthage and advance to the mastery of the known world.

In these final chapters the reader is brought back to the theme of prognostication. Polybius' purpose, like that of all the more reputable ancient philosphers, is didactic. As we saw, his essay was designed not merely to explain the growth of Rome, but also to enable his readers to forecast the future. What lessons have emerged from his analysis? First, the example of Carthage provides one warning. Carthage, like Lycurgan Sparta, was a mixed constitution, but at the time of Hannibal she had passed her prime; her constitution had not saved her, and presumably the Roman constitution would not ultimately save Rome either. A mixed constitution, so long as it functions and is maintained intact, can prevent political decay. But the mixed constitution is no more immortal than anything else. "That all existing things are subject to decay and change," writes Polybius in the last chapter but one of the book [6.57.1,5–9], "is a truth that scarcely needs proof"; and he goes on to say that "when a state has weathered great perils and subsequently attains to supremacy and uncontested sovereignty, it is evident that under the influence of long established prosperity life becomes more extravagant, and the citizens more fierce in their rivalry regarding office. . . . As these defects go on increasing, the beginning of the change for the worse will be due"—the change in tense is significant—"to love of office and the disgrace entailed by obscurity, as well as to extravagance and purse-proud display." The cause, he adds, will be the people, who for various motives give way to passion, reject authority, and demand the lion's share in everything. "When this happens, the state will change its name to the finest sounding of all, freedom and democracy, but will change its nature to the worst thing of all, mob-rule."

The lesson for Rome is explicit. The "change for the worse" is still happily in the future. But already Rome has won "supremacy and uncontested sovereignty," the Romans are "lords of the earth," κύριοι τῆς οἰκουμένης. Despite the temporary brake of the mixed constitution, the general trend of the *anacyclōsis* is unmistakable; and though in the chapter from which I have just quoted, Polybius slurs over the exact process by which a mixed constitution slides back on to the revolving wheel of change, the ultimate outcome, ochlocracy, is never in doubt.

IV

Does this mean that Polybius had a secondary purpose in Book 6, to proph-esy disaster to the Roman constitution and the Roman state? And if so, was this due to a later revision of his views? Many have thought so; and it has been argued that those parts of Book 6 which concern themselves with the *anacyclōsis* and the decay of the mixed constitution belong to a second layer added at a date when Polybius had awakened to the signs of corrup-tion in Roman society and had lost that earlier confidence which shaped the original concept of his *Histories*.[29]

To this hypothesis there are several objections. First: in so far as Po-lybius is concerned with foretelling the future development of Rome, this is a secondary purpose. The primary object behind Book 6 and the work as a whole was that enunciated at the outset and repeated in the last chapter of Book 39—to explain Roman success. Secondly, if at the end of Book 6 Po-lybius describes in terms which clearly apply to Rome the beginning of the decline from the mixed constitution, he makes it clear (as I have just pointed out) that this constitutional decline is still something in the future —a fact hard to reconcile with the hypothesis that it is part of a revised plan which Polybius has adopted because he has now come to recognize the beginnings of the process of decay going on around him.

According to that hypothesis Polybius was shaken by the events of 150 to 146—the wars with Carthage, Macedon and Achaea, and the de-struction of Carthage and Corinth—and began to condemn, or at any rate to distrust, Roman imperialism. The Third Punic War was preceded by a famous debate between Cato and Scipio Nasica on what ought to be done about Carthage, in which Nasica argued that the removal of all outside dangers must leave the road open to internal conflict and decay.[30] This, it is suggested, was the belief of Polybius; and in support of this thesis it is conveniently pointed out that Polybius' friend Scipio Aemilianus had wept tears beside the burning roofs of Carthage and quoted Homer—"a day shall come when Priam's holy city too shall perish"—in dismal foreboding for Rome itself [38.21–22]. According to an anecdote related by Valerius Maximus [4.1.10], when Scipio was censor four years later in 142 B.C., he made a significant change in the official prayer. This had formerly called upon the gods to "render the possessions of the Roman people ever greater and more ample"; Scipio, we are told, preferred to pray that "they should maintain them for all time undiminished." Here was evidence, it seemed,

---

[29] For bibliography see Walbank, *Commentary* I, 636.
[30] Plut. *Cat. Mai.* 27.3; App. *Lib. 69;* Diod. 34.33.4–6; see Gelzer, *Kleine Schiften* II, 39–72. It has recently been argued by W. Hoffman ("Die römische Politik des 2. Jahrhunderts und das Ende Karthagos," *Historia* 9 [1960] 309–344) that this debate is apocryphal; I hope to discuss this view, which I find unconvincing, elsewhere.

that Scipio, and so by implication his friend Polybius, was awake to the dire consequences of world dominion.

It is an interesting thesis; but it will not stand up to detailed examination. In the first place, it is reasonably certain that the anecdote in Valerius Maximus is completely apocryphal.[31] Secondly, Aemilianus' career shows him to have been the consistently loyal servant of the Senate in its policy of imperialism. From the day when he won the approval of Cato during his first command at Carthage to his destruction of the Spanish city of Numantia in 133, he acted like the true son of Aemilius Paullus, who in a carefully coordinated piece of frightfulness sacked seventy Epirote cities and enslaved 150,000 persons in a single hour. As a commentary on the toughness of both men it is perhaps also appropriate to recall that Aemilianus *exemplo patris sui, Aemili Pauli, qui Macedoniam vicerat,*[32] shared with his father the doubtful distinction of being the first Roman to introduce the custom of throwing deserters and fugitives to the wild beasts in a public show. As for Aemilianus' tears over Carthage, that was in the Hellenistic tradition; Antiochus the Great had wept [8.20.10] when his men brought in the traitor Achaeus bound hand and foot, "because," Polybius suggests, "he saw how hard to guard against and how contrary to all expectations are events due to Fortune." It did not prevent his acquiescing in the decision "to lop off Achaeus' extremities and then, after cutting off his head and sewing it up in an ass's skin, to crucify the body." Similarly Aemilius Paullus greeted Perseus after his surrender with tears in his eyes,[33] and delivered himself of a sermon at Perseus' expense. Hellenistic men were quick to weep and quick to recall the fickleness of Fortune; and Aemilianus prided himself upon his Hellenic culture. In terms of Roman policy, however, it meant just nothing.

The same conclusion holds good for his friend Polybius. Scipio Nasica had argued that Carthage must be maintained in existence so as to ensure internal harmony at Rome. Polybius, on the contrary, asserted that "when the Romans are freed from fears from abroad (τῶν ἐκτὸς φόβων)" and reap the consequent prosperity, any tendency to excess and disproportion is countered by the checks of the mixed constitution, which automatically restores the equilibrium [6.18.5–8]—an argument which reads very much like a reply to that of Nasica. Not the existence of a dangerous foe, but the maintenance of the mixed constitution is Rome's best protection against internal disruption. Indeed, if Professor Gelzer is right in attributing a passage in Diodorus to Polybius, as I think he is, the latter committed himself

---

[31] *Cf.* A. Aymard, *Mel. de la soc. toulousaine* II (1948) 101 f. In *JRS* 50 (1960) 68 n. 38, H. H. Scullard argues that Cic. *De Orat.* 2.268, which appears to imply that not Scipio but his colleague Mummius *condidit lustrum*, could in fact refer to Scipio; but he admits that this would be a somewhat strained interpretation.
[32] Livy, *Ep.* 51; Val. Max. 2.7.13.
[33] 24.20.1–4; Plut. *Aem.* 26.5.

to the view that "states who seek hegemony acquire it through courage and intelligence, increase their power by moderation and kindness towards men, but assure it by inspiring fear and consternation." [34] Sir Frank Adcock's comment is to the point: "Polybius probably yielded to the temptation to defend Roman frightfulness by treating it as though it followed some kind of natural law." [35] This again would point to an orthodox attitude towards Roman foreign policy.

On the other hand, it is certainly true that Polybius was not uncritical either of the Roman political system or of Roman society. But this fact cannot be used to sustain the theory of a change in emphasis in Book 6, because it is clear that his critical attitude dated from his first arrival in Rome, and no doubt from before then. The detailed chronology of the composition of Polybius' *Histories* is a subject of controversy [36]; it would, however, be generally agreed that he started the work shortly after his internment began. But already in Book 1 we find him asking why the Romans, now that they are masters of the world, are no longer able to put such large fleets to sea as they had done in the First Punic War [1.64.1–2], and he promises an answer in Book 6; unfortunately it has not survived. Here he points clearly to deterioration following upon the acquisition of world dominion; and in a later passage in Book 18, where he is discussing the fact that Romans are no longer proof against bribery,[37] he defines the period of moral change as that at which they began to undertake overseas wars—by which he seems to mean the second century wars in Greece and the Near East.

In detecting some moral deterioration from that time onwards, Polybius was of course neither alone nor particularly far-sighted. As early as 184 Cato's censorship had been celebrated by the setting up of a statue in his honour in the temple of Salus with an inscription stating that "when the Roman state was tottering to its fall, he was made censor and, by helpful guidance, wise restraints and sound teachings, restored it again." [38] The reference was to Cato's campaign against luxury and declining morals. Polybius cannot have been unaware of the controversies this had awakened, and he must therefore have known that the issue of moral decay at Rome had been a lively one sixteen years before he set foot in Italy. By 168 it must have been a commonplace.

Thus from the time he planned his history Polybius was conscious of some degree of decline since the great days of the Hannibalic War; he did not need the arguments of Scipio Nasica and the events of 146, still less the

---

[34] Diod. 32.2 and 4; see Gelzer, *Kleine Schriften* II, 64–65.
[35] F. E. Adcock, "Delenda est Carthago," *Camb. Hist. J.* 8 (1946) 127–128.
[36] See my discussion in *Commentary* I, 292–297; add H. Erbse, "Polybios-Interpretationen," *Philologus* 101 (1957) 277 ff; Gelzer, *Kleine Schriften* III, 209–210; T. Cole, "The Sources and Composition of Polybius VI," *Historia* 13 (1964) 440–486.
[37] 18.35; see above n. 20.
[38] Plut. *Cat.Mai.* 19.3; *cf.* Walbank, *Commentary* I, 647–648.

Gracchan catastrophe of 133, to convince him of this. Consequently, if despite this knowledge he could plan a work which was to explain Rome's imperial success by reference to the Roman mixed constitution, with its checks and its functional stability, there was nothing in the years during which he was becoming more and more identified with the ideals of the Scipionic group to lead him to change that emphasis.

In 150 Polybius returned to Greece; he was with Scipio at the fall of Carthage [38.21–22], and later did great service to his fellow-countrymen in Achaea by acting as mediator with the Romans after the disastrous Achaean War.[39] At some date after this—we do not know precisely when —he decided to extend the original plan of his history to go down to 146 instead of 168, in order that "contemporaries will be able to see clearly whether the Roman rule is acceptable or the reverse, and future generations whether their government should be considered to have been worthy of praise and admiration or rather of blame [3.4.7]." Once again Polybius strikes the didactic note. A lesson is to be learnt; and the many remarks hostile to Roman policy which occur throughout his narrative of the years 167 to 150, when as a detainee at Rome and a victim of Roman policy he was watching affairs from outside, detached and even cynical, might suggest that the verdict was to be given against Rome.[40] But this conclusion would be wrong. From 150 onwards, as the friend of Aemilianus and an active participant in what was going on in the next five years in Africa and Greece, Polybius' sympathies are increasingly with Rome. His account of the Third Punic War, the war with Andriscus and the Achaean War are all whole-heartedly pro-Roman in sympathy. Support for Andriscus is only explicable as a heaven-sent infatuation, *daimonoblabeia* [36.17.12–15]. The Carthaginians may have given posterity some grounds, however slight, to speak in their defence; the Greeks gave none, and it is a historian's duty to speak out in their condemnation without mincing words [38.1.5]. The commander Hasdrubal was wholly worthless; indeed the Greeks and Carthaginians were alike in their leaders at this time [38.7.1, 8.14]. Polybius had seen these things for himself, and he had seen them from the Roman camp; he had no illusions and no doubts. And, as we observed, where Romans did resort to frightfulness, he was inclined to condone it as the inevitable accompaniment of an empire which must be secured.

V

Of Polybius' later years we know little; but apparently he died in his own land. His long exile at Rome and his conversion to the *fatum Romanum* had left him a Greek at heart; and when one has made every allowance for

[39] See Walbank, *Commentary* I, 5 n. 8.
[40] Books 30–38 are full of remarks critical of Roman policy.

the influence of the Scipionic circle, his picture of the Roman state in Book 6 remains almost wholly the product of Greek political speculation. As we saw, the *anacyclōsis*, though it appears for the first time in its complete form in Polybius, can claim a long ancestry and a probable parentage in the popular philosophy of the Hellenistic age. The mixed constitution has equally venerable origins. Thucydides had praised Theramenes' constitution of 411 B.C. as a moderate combination as between the few and the many [8.97.2]; and Plato and Aristotle had both dealt with the theme at length, Plato applying it in particular to his interpretation of Sparta. As in the case of the *anacyclōsis*, Polybius' immediate source is obscure. Many scholars have thought of Dicaearchus, who wrote a work called the *Tripolitikos*. But we know that at some stage the Stoics also approved the mixed constitution, so certainty is impossible.[41]

Polybius' sources then must remain an open question. The novelty in his treatment lay in the application of Greek political theory to the realities of the Roman state. Admittedly, there is some creaking. As a definition of Roman government in the late third and early second centuries the mixed constitution is over-formal. It stresses an important aspect of the Roman character, its genius for compromise; but it neglects that elaborate texture of political life which ensured the domination of the noble class. The *anacyclōsis* too, put forward as the natural cycle of political evolution, is far too schematic to fit the history of any one state; and its fallacies had been pointed out long ago in advance by Aristotle, who observed, criticizing Plato, that in fact any constitution could turn into virtually any other [*Pol.* 7(5).12.1316al ff]. The real mainspring of Rome's imperial success lay in the domination of the Senate and in her flexibility and capacity for growth—a feature which had impressed Philip V of Macedon, who commented on it in a letter written to urge an intake of new citizens at Larisa several years before Polybius was born [*Syll.* 543]. This potentiality for growth and change was something which escaped Polybius entirely—and naturally so; for as a Greek of the upper classes he was conditioned both by philosophical traditions and by inclination to identify the ideal state with immobility and in political evolution to see nothing but the threat of disorder.

Yet in one respect he succeeded in throwing off the preconceptions of his theories. It is to his credit that he could point to the Roman constitution as the fruit of a long period of political development, which the Romans had attained "not by any process of reasoning"—the Greek way— "but by the discipline of many struggles and troubles and always choosing the best in the light of experience gained in disaster [6.10.13–14]." This diagnosis acutely characterizes the development of Rome; and as a piece of political analysis it is likely to outlive the elaborate scheme of the *anacy-*

[41] See Walbank, *Commentary* I, 640–641.

clōsis, the much-advertised science of prognostication, and the ingenious fiction of the mixed constitution.

Indeed this might well have been a convenient point to leave the subject—if it were not for the fact that ideas have their own history and ingenious fictions sometimes foreshadow realities. Polybius' sixth book as a whole has exercised an outstanding influence on later political thought. As we saw, Cicero drew on it for his *De Republica;* and though it had little relevance for the Roman Empire—Tacitus jeered at the mixed constitution as something easier to describe than to accomplish—we find it cropping up many centuries later in Machiavelli. The *Discourses on the First Decade of Livy* opens with a restatement of the theory of the *anacyclōsis* almost in Polybius' own words; and Machiavelli follows it with an account of the principles of the mixed constitution developed to fit his thesis of a balance of competing social and economic interests held in check by a powerful prince.

After Machiavelli the two main aspects of Polybius' theory, the cycle of development and the mixed constitution designed to slow down its effects, seem to have made their appeal in different quarters. To the historical philosopher, the *anacyclōsis* contained the attractive suggestion of a universal law of political development. Giambattista Vico in his *Scienza Nuova* sets out to reveal "the ideal, the eternal laws in accordance with which the affairs of all nations proceed in their rise, progress, mature state, decline and fall." Despite the profound difference of approach in Vico's devout attempt to reveal the design of God in human history, Polybius' influence is unmistakable. Similarly in more recent times, it is apparent that the vast structures raised by Spengler and Toynbee would not have borne quite the same appearance had Polybius' sixth book not survived at all.

It is however to the mixed constitution rather than to the *anacyclōsis* that statesmen and political scientists have turned in their search for the ideal state. As Sabine points out in his *History of Political Theory,*[42] the doctrine of the mixed constitution was not alien to the Middle Ages, with their notion of tempered monarchy and the division of powers which lay behind mediaeval constitutional practice. But quite apart from mediaeval influence, there is a direct debt to Polybius in the work of Machiavelli's contemporary, Francesco Guicciardini, who wrote of a *governo misto* made up of monarchy, oligarchy and democracy; and the same is true of the constitutional theory of John Calvin.

More interesting perhaps than either, because he interprets the idea of a mixed constitution less as a union of political forms than, like Polybius before him, as a system of mutual checks and balances exercised by various embodiments of political power—in this case between the legislative, the executive and the judiciary—is Montesquieu. Montesquieu saw this balance exemplified in Britain and made it (together with our climate!) the source

---

[42] G. Sabine, *History of Political Theory* (London, 1951) 278 ff, 471.

of English liberty. Whether he was right in so doing after 1688 and the assertion of parliamentary sovereignty is arguable; it has been suggested [43] that he was here following Locke and Harrington, and the already obsolete theories of his friend Bolingbroke, who in 1733 wrote that "it is by this mixture of monarchical, aristocratical and democratical power, blended together in one system, and by these three estates balancing one another, that our free constitution of government hath been preserved so long inviolate." [44]

Whatever the merits of Montesquieu's views on the English constitution of the eighteenth century, his theories were however destined to make their mark in English-speaking lands abroad. Bryce described the *Esprit des Lois* as the bible of eighteenth century political philosophy. Its influence can be detected in several American state constitutions of the late eighteenth century, for example in the Virginian Declaration of Rights of 1776 and the Massachusetts Constitution of 1780; and as a recent essay has pointed out,[45] the pages of the *Federalist* and the notes published by James Madison in 1836 show the great fascination which this work exercised over the members of the commission set up to study forms of government, ancient and modern, in preparation for the American Constitution of 1787. Thanks very largely to this influence of Montesquieu, the American Constitution is today the example *par excellence* of separated powers and an equilibrium based on checks and counter-checks. The legislative organs can block the executive, the executive the legislature; and the Supreme Court can—and frequently does—block both. It is a system which has been severely criticised on various occasions. John Adams, the second president, thought it of dubious efficacy and Jeremy Bentham feared it might lead to stagnation. It has certainly not done that; but to this day it is the cause of an element of uncertainty in American policy, which cannot be under-estimated as a factor in contemporary politics. For this feature, good or ill, we must, I suggest, reserve at least part of our thanks or execration for Polybius, whose essay on the constitution enjoyed by the κύριοι τῆς οἰκουμένης of his own time has thus by a strange and unexpected channel of transmission helped to shape the destiny of a people whose role in the modern world is perhaps not altogether dissimilar to that of the Romans in theirs.[46]

---

[43] G. Sabine, 472–473.

[44] Bolingbroke, *A Dissertation upon Parties:* Letter 13; from the *Craftsman* (1733–1734), quoted by Sabine.

[45] A. Delatte, *La constitution des Etats-unis et les Pythagoriciens* (Paris, 1948). See also on this topic G. Chinard, "Polybius and the American Constitution," *J. Hist. Ideas* 1 (1940) 40 ff; R. M. Gummere, "The Classical Ancestry of the United States Constitution," *American Quarterly* 14 (1962) 3–18. Gummere records the fact that "Thomas Jefferson sent from Paris to Madison, a former graduate of John Witherspoon at Princeton, and to George Wythe, a finished Greek and Latin scholar . . . copies of Polybius and sets of ancient authors."

[46] A lecture delivered at Duke University on May 5th, 1964, and at several other universities in the United States and Canada the same spring.

8

Cicero, *de re Publica II,* and His Socratic View of History

R. F. HATHAWAY

Historians of philosophy have long been aware that Cicero's *Republic* handles historical matters in an ambiguous and circumspect way, especially in the speeches of Scipio.[1] My first purpose is to show that the ambiguity derives from Cicero's true model in the dialogue, Socratic political philosophy, and not from the Stoic natural law teachings which Cicero puts in the mouths of Scipio and Laelius. It has

This article was originally published in *Journal of the History of Ideas,* 29 (January–March 1968), 3–12. It is reprinted here with the permission of the author and of the publisher.

[1] M. Pohlenz, "Cicero, *De republica* als Kunstwerk," *Festschrift für R. Reitzenstein* (Leipzig, 1931), 88, says that in the first book "gibt Cicero *bewusst* eine quasihistorische Darstellung" and "Historie in eigene Form *umsetz*" (emphases mine). Cf. H. H. How, "Cicero's Ideal in his *De republica,*" *JRS,* 20 (1930), 28. How claims that in the first two books Cicero is more dependent on Polybius than on Panaetius, and draws the inference from this that "Cicero's *Republic* is not philosophic and poetic, but real and historical" (26). How overlooks what Pohlenz saw, and forgets that Cicero's very use of Polybius and Panaetius is dependent on his choice of Scipio as a character, i.e., on a poetic choice. In general, it is very unclear what kind of "history" the *Republic* contains.

been noted recently that it is misinforming to call Cicero a simple adherent of the Stoic natural law teaching.[2] The problem is this. Cicero presents Scipio as the defender of the Roman polity, i.e., as defending the justice of its polity but never forgetting that it was most unjust at many times and in several respects. The keynote of Scipio's defense is his revelation, in the second book, of the *natural* cycle (*orbis*) of politics or of political matters, that is to say, of as much of natural order as Roman society could act upon. Like Socrates, Scipio seeks objects intelligible to the ordinary citizen. These intelligible objects he found in a certain account of Roman history and a certain treatment of the roots of Roman law. Into this account he inserts the Socratic themes, justice and statesmanship. Scipio's defense of the Roman polity and treatment of its history becomes Socratic, at least because it is motivated by Socratic ends. But one should go further. Scipio somehow manages to teach that Roman law or custom itself points to justice and the natural order without presuming that it and the natural order are in total harmony.[3] His whole treatment of history is Socratic, if by Socratic we signify the discovery of Socrates that despite the tension between nature and law there exists a natural articulation of justice and law. Cicero is, to put it briefly, the Socratic thinker who extended that discovery to include law in its historical framework, that is, in political tradition. How Cicero does this I shall attempt to show in what follows, beginning from the unique reference to "history" in the dialogue.

The term *historia* occurs only once in Cicero's *Republic*. At II, 33, in speaking about Ancus Marcius, the fourth ancient king of the Romans, Cicero makes Caius Laelius say, "This king indeed is praiseworthy, but Roman history is obscure if we know the mother of this king but are ignorant of his father." [4] At the very midpoint of his discussion of the roots of Roman law, Cicero notices the obscurity of *historia*. To this remark Scipio replies, "This is so, but from those times the names of such kings are almost the only things which are known." [5] This apology is followed without a break by a speech describing the "tremendous river of arts and sciences (*artes et disciplinas*)" which flooded Italy at the time of Ancus, when Roman history was "obscure." [6] What is the relation between the incursion

[2] Leo Strauss, *Natural Right and History* (Chicago, 1953), 155.
[3] A stylistic note may be of interest. Laelius, whose well-known epithet was "wise" (*sapiens*), sits in the center of the participants in the dialogue, while Furius Philus, the Academic sceptic, stands apart, the former representing Rome and its ancestral wisdom, the latter the dispassionate love of knowledge (e.g., of the celestial bodies about which he discourses at the beginning) and of justice. The position combining both, viz. Scipio's, is *philosophia* of the Socratic sort.
[4] Laudandus etiam iste rex; sed obscura est historia Romana siquidem istius regis matrem habemus, ignoramus patrem." *De re publica*, red. K. Ziegler (Leipzig, 1964) II, 33 (60, 24–26). Numbers in parentheses after citations of the *Republic* are Ziegler's pages and lines.
[5] II, 33 (60, 26–28).
[6] II, 34 (61, 1 ff.).

of foreign learning and our ignorance of certain historical facts? Laelius' original remark had come only just after a long enumeration of historical facts about Ancus Marcius.[7] It is safe to infer that Cicero knew more than "only names" about the period in question. The fact that the period was *the* period of ancient Roman conquest and territorial aggrandizement leads one to wonder whether Cicero believed certain facts too shameful to mention. But this may not be his only reason for finding Roman history obscure or remote; the incursion of foreign arts and sciences might be immeasurably more important with respect to his intentions in the *Republic* to transfer Socratic philosophy to Roman soil. In any case, the remark of Laelius is curiously inconsistent with Scipio's rejoinder and with the speech which follows.

Cicero was fully conscious of a tension between the native virtues of Rome and foreign arts. At II, 28 Scipio is interrupted by the young Manilius, who wishes to know whether the founder of Roman religion, Numa Pompilius, was taught by the Greek philosopher Pythagoras. Scipio reacts with indignation: Manilius' idea is based on false historical information. Pythagoras lived long after the time of Numa, the Moses of Rome. In refuting this "firmly rooted error" Scipio is represented as an arbiter of history. Manilius acquiesces and adds, "I am glad that we [Romans] got our culture, not from arts imported from overseas, but from the native virtues of our own people." [8] Scipio then makes a crucial promise: throughout the whole of his discourse (*oratio*) dealing with the ancient republic up to its "best condition" (*optimus status*), as it moved in its "natural course," he will demonstrate the truth of Manilius' statement. The Roman republic must be based on native, not on foreign, wisdom.

How far does Scipio's discourse on the republic up to its "best condition" extend? It extends up to the center of the passage at II, 33, the first allusion to an actual "flood" of Greek arts and sciences into Italy. Scipio's promise thus begins to break down at II, 33, the midpoint of the development of the ancient monarchy. The uncorrupted roots of Roman law are now brought into maximum confrontation with those Greek arts which included philosophy in its original form, pre-Socratic philosophy. Cicero seems almost to anticipate Rousseau's belief that the arts and sciences corrupt the good society, the old, small city. At this juncture, it is well to recall what Cicero thought about history and political philosophy.

The high calling of history as Scipio presides over its development contrasts strongly with Cicero's own explicit pronouncements. When begged by friends to write a history of Rome, he politely refused.[9] His reasons for refusing appear to lie in his devotion to Socratic philosophy. Socrates chose not to write, much less to write a history of Athens. The So-

---

[7] II, 33 (**60**, 14–24); cf. II, 5 (**48**, 19–20).
[8] II, 29 (**59**, 4–6).
[9] *De leg.* I, 5.

cratic Plato omits history in his system of education in the *Republic*. And although the Socratic philosopher Aristotle [10] was responsible for much of the best writing on ancient history, he confined his own historical research to his unpublished treatises. Cicero's *Republic* belongs to "the genus of books . . . written for the many which they [Socratic philosophers] called 'exoteric.'" [11] The curious handling of history in Scipio's speeches is due to the exoteric nature of the work. The ambiguity of the whole dialogue becomes clearest if one remembers that in the third book Cicero asks, "What could be more worthy of esteem than to join the study and knowledge of those [philosophic] *arts* to the handling and employment of important [political] affairs?" [12] So carefully does Cicero prepare us that we hardly note what he says about Scipio, Laelius, and Philus: they "added the *foreign* learning which originated with Socrates to the traditional customs of their own country and their ancestors." [13] Foreign arts, Greek arts, have become salutary rather than harmful. Scipio's discourse is the bridge from the distrust of all things foreign to admiration for Socrates and philosophy. The modern critique of Cicero as an ignoramus in political matters [14] stems in part from a refusal to come to grips with the Socratic element in his *Republic*. This is proved by the case of the third book, often read as expounding an early theory of historical "progress." [15] Commentators have been biased by a modern reading of the preceding book and Scipio's discourse, in which the primary intent is to give history a natural *telos* or hierarchy of political choices. Cicero did not believe in historical progress. He did believe in the evaluation of history by the lights of political philosophy.

Scipio's handling of Roman history depends throughout on his awareness of the tension between native and foreign wisdom. His promise to

---

[10] Cf. *De scientia politica*, ed. A. Mai (*Script. Vet. Nova Collectio* II, 571–609), V, 15: Socrates and his followers were "the lights in their day not only of Greece but also of all the world. To that company belong Plato, Xenophon, and *Aristotle*. . . . For Cicero is right in calling Socrates the founder . . . of general and true philosophy." (Italics mine.) Cf. *De or.* III, 16.

[11] *De fin.* V, 12.

[12] *De re pub.*, III, 5 (83, 22–25).

[13] *De re pub.* (83, 28–84, 1). This portrayal of Scipio, Laelius, and Philus suggests Plato's portrayal of Timaeus, Critias, and Hermocrates (*Tim.* 19b3f.) but not his portrayal of the interlocutors in his *Republic*. Does Cicero (who translated part of the *Timaeus*) conflate at the surface level Plato's *Republic* and *Timaeus* (and *Critias*)?

[14] According to Hegel, Cicero "had no knowledge of the nature of states and in particular not of the Roman State." *Vorlesungen über die Philosophie der Geschichte* II, 401 ed. Glockner. Cf. How, 35.

[15] Cf. III, 33 (96, 26sq.) with III, 1 in St. Augustine (82, 5–6 and cf. 82, 16–17). Cicero's point is that man's natural reason *at birth* only gradually attains its perfection. Cf. *De fin.* V, 55 "Omnes veteres philosophi, maxime nostri [i.e. Socratics], ad incunabula accedunt, quod in *pueritia* facillime se arbitrentur naturae voluntatem posse cognoscere." (Italics mine.) The idea of natural law itself contradicts a theory of progress. P. M. Valente, *L'Éthique stoïcienne chez Cicéron* (Thèse, Univ. de Paris, 1956), 366, says, "Posons le problème d'une autre manière, puisque ces considérations littéraires ne l'éclairent pas: le concept de loi éternelle n'interdit-il la notion de progrès?" Valente might have pursued certain "literary considerations" further than he did.

Manilius is explained by his early refusal (II,3) to follow the way of Socrates, the way of "inventing" (*fingere*) republics. For this he substitutes the way of the Roman Cato, returning to the "origin" of one's own republic.[16] "Old and useful things" replace Socrates' disinterested inquiry into justice and the *politeia* in which justice becomes visible. The way of Socrates is addressed to the young and at virtue; the way of Cato is addressed to the old and experienced and at utility.[17] Scipio, curiously, had been made to study under Cato as a boy and had discovered Socrates as a grown man.[18] With these two poles in mind, Cato–Socrates, we now reconsider the full meaning of the passage at II, 33 with its surrounding discourse.

The unique use of *historia* occurs after a list of the deeds (*facta*) of Ancus Marcius, the grandson of Numa: Ancus conquered the Latin tribes, annexed the Aventine Hills, divided the conquered territory, made the coastal plains and forest public domain, built and settled Ostia and reigned for twenty-three years. Laelius now emphasizes our ignorance of a single name, that of Ancus' father, and infers that Roman history is obscure. It seems that the old sage Laelius is worried about the break in the patrilineal tradition caused by this omission. The patrilineal line is surprisingly important in the *Republic*.[19] On the other hand, Cicero may here be silently indicating the shocking rise to power of an illegitimate son of the daughter of Numa, the Moses of Rome. Scipio's excuse for *obscura historia*, that we know "almost" only the names of the kings, is a calculated evasion, since it is precisely the name that is missing. The following speech of Scipio hastens to add a new dimension to this problem. During the reign of Ancus a "foreign way of life" was brought to Italy by a certain Demaratus of Corinth who had fled from Cypselus, a tyrant. Demaratus is said to have settled in the Etrurian city of the Tarquinii and to have married a Tarquinian woman and raised their two children in the Greek way.[20] One of his children, Lucius, who Cicero later implies employed the harsh methods of the Corinthians for obtaining cavalry supplies, when he became a king[21] not only educated his children also in the Greek way but even had

[16] II, 3 (47, 13–19).

[17] Cicero the consummate rhetorician was aware always of his audiences. Cf. Aristotle, *De arte rhet.* 1389a2–1390b11.

[18] II, 1 (46, 2 ff.). It must be remembered that Scipio's passion for Socrates derives from his love of Xenophon; Cicero adds the Platonic Socrates. His fidelity to the character of Scipio is proved, however, by his making Scipio distinguish between the Socratic and Pythagorean element in Plato; I, 16 (11, 24sqq.). Scipio is suspicious of Pythagoras (cf. p. 5, *supra*); he believes Pythagoras came to Italy only during the reign of the tyrant Tarquinius Superbus; II, 28 (58, 17–18).

[19] "Father" occurs thirty-six times in the dialogue but only sixteen times in the extant *Laws*. Down to the time of Lucius, of course, the people still used the ancient name *patres* for the senators or patricians. Cf. II, 56 (72, 14).

[20] II, 34 "omnibus eos artibus ad Graecorum disciplinam eru °'" (the form of the verb *erudire* unknown, Ziegler). The *disciplina* of the Greeks in the singular seems to mean simply παιδεία.

[21] II, 36 (62, 6–10). Cicero's silence about the connection between Corinthian exactions from widows and orphans and the Corinthian origins of Lucius' father (whom Cicero calls "liber ac fortis") underscores his mode of writing.

a Greek name. This name he changed to its Roman counterpart in order "to seem in all respects to imitate the customs of the (Roman) people." [22] Cicero not only knows many facts about the ancient kings which he does not divulge; he knows of their names and changes of names; he knows their intentions. A Greek stranger appears near Rome at the moment when a "tremendous river of arts and sciences" flowed from Greece. Demaratus symbolizes motion from Greece to Rome; the appearance of "art" and the change of names coincide.[23] In the preceding passage Scipio had pointedly praised the virtues of Numa and referred to the fact that foreign arts came to Rome only after and not during his reign. Numa symbolizes religious purity and ancient customs, the ancestral good; Demaratus symbolizes obscurity and the alteration of customs. Lucius, the Greek-educated son of Demaratus, himself bears the name Tarquinius, which points ahead to the horrors of the regime of Tarquinius Superbus and the decay of the monarchy. The arrival of Greek arts coincides with the transition from the ancestral good and the birth of tyranny; the arrival of a Greek philosopher coincides with the first *known* tyrant.[24]

Lucius was the first king to change his name in order to "seem" to agree with Roman customs; his most significant act as king was to change the name of the old Roman senators from "fathers" to "men of the more ancient families." [25] The break in the patrilineal line under Ancus is generalized under Lucius. The motion begun by Demaratus, meanwhile, culminates in the arrival of Pythagoras under Tarquinius, but Cicero is completely silent about this connection. The break in the patrilineal line at II, 33 is tacitly linked by Cicero to the gradual influx of Greek arts and sciences; but the appearance of Greek philosophy awaits the completion of this process. Philosophy presupposes a prior growth of the arts. The good Numa gives way to the wicked Tarquinius. The full discovery of natural law and philosophy occurs only at the end. What began as the return to the origins of one's own city ends as the discovery of the "natural motion" of political things. This Scipio calls "the crown of political judgment, the goal of my entire discourse." [26]

The result of Scipio's innocent return to the origins is intended to shock: opposites are brought into play, king and tyrant, the sight of the love of the people for the king and the "fathers" turning into hatred for the tyrant and his creature, the corrupted aristocracy.[27] The final result, how-

[22] II, 35 (61, 24–25). For the connection between "names" and custom, cf. I, 54 (33, 17) "nomen *quasi* patrium regis"; *De fin.* II, 12; *De nat. deor.* I, 84; II, 60, 61, 71; III, 44. On the alteration of names, *Academica* I, 25; on their invention, *Tusc. disp.* V, 10.

[23] "Names" conventionally honored do not always point to real "deeds"; cf. the transition *a fabulis ad facta* at II, 4 (48, 9).

[24] Cp. II, 44 (66, 5) with II, 47 (67, 14–15). The tyrant appears first simply as an "iniustus dominus"; only later is he called "dominus populi, quem *Graeci* tyrannum vocant." Only the Greeks call a spade a spade. Cf. also III, 23 (92, 1–3) and *infra*.

[25] II, 35 (61, 27–62, 1).

[26] II, 45 (66, 16).

[27] Cp. II, 23 (56, 4–10) with II, 46 (67, 3–11).

ever, is to direct one's attention to the center between these opposites, the "best condition" of the ancient monarchy or *res publica,* its condition under the reigns of Tullius Hostilius and Ancus Marcius. Tullius combined the arts of war (Romulus) with the arts of peace (Numa); Ancus perfected this combination by both extending the boundaries of the city and providing the conditions necessary for the existence of the arts and sciences. The precise center of Scipio's "natural motion" is the place where Cicero makes his unique reference to "history." The *obscura historia* of II, 33 therefore opens up a polarity of political principles; it opens the way to the philosophic questions of the third book. Moreover, it directs attention at the republic.[28]

The *obscura historia* at II, 33 creates a chain reaction: Demaratus passes on his Greek ways to Lucius, who alters Roman custom artfully; Lucius passes on his Greek education to Servius,[29] who himself came to power by means of a clever ruse. Servius, despite his many virtues, was the first king "to rule without the consent of the people." [30] Servius also was the king who first disciplined the people and formed the solid basis of the later patrician assembly by inventing the centuriate.[31] The most salutary means for preserving the republic was invented by a king. The chain reaction consists of a growing complexity in political affairs combined with the growing art of rule as such, under the influence of Greek ways. The whole complex "natural motion" as guided by one art, Cicero's art of writing, places vivid emphasis on the terror of tyranny under Tarquinius: the danger posed by a ruler lacking the art of rule after a long development of all the arts is absolute. Tarquinius tried to placate his conscience for his blood guilt by sending "magnificent gifts" to Apollo at Delphi.[32] The influence of Greek ways upon Rome has decayed into a degraded and degrading piety. Pythagoras arrives only now; philosophy, the highest art, is now needed. Natural law or the "natural motion" of politics emerges only after the breakdown of social order.[33]

---

[28] Scipio himself favored kingship; cf. II, 43 (65, 22–25) here considered the best of the simple forms of government.
[29] II, 37 (62, 24 ff.).
[30] II, 37 (62, 25).
[31] II, 39 (63, 18 ff.).
[32] II, 44 (66, 11–13).
[33] Scipio's "natural motion" or "orbit" might be diagrammed thus:

Tarquinius Superbus (II, 44–53)

Romulus (II, 1–24)

Servius Tullius (II, 38–43)

Numa Pompilius (II, 25–31)
"volat in optimum statum res publica"

"primus iniussu populi regnavisse traditur"

Tullius Hostilius (II, 31–33)

Lucius Tarquinius (II, 35–37)

Ancus Marcius (II, 33–34)
"historia . . . obscura est"

The introduction of Socratic themes can now be traced in the following sections of the dialogue. The first step is the juxtaposition of kingship and tyranny, which leads to the second, the problem of the royal art as political prudence or wisdom.[34] This leads inevitably to the broader question of the art of rule in a developed situation or statesmanship. The fourth and last step reached is the question of natural right,[35] the basis of philosophic statesmanship. Cicero, without evading history, turns antiphilosophic ire to philosophic purposes. How does he manage this? By giving educative example. Rome's own customs, not ingrafted traditions, point to eternal principles. This is Cicero's noble lie, a Socratic noble lie. Cicero was uniquely fitted to make this adaptation of his model on account of his lifelong acquaintance with the close relation between rhetoric and history.[36] But Cicero was aware of the relation between history and philosophy as well, a relation now almost impossible to recall in its classical sense, "history" in the sense of "inquiry" into the natural roots of things, into the origins.[37] Cicero's adaptation of his Socratic model is a complete synthesis of these two relations, of history akin to rhetoric and history akin to philosophy.[38] In Cicero history is restrained from becoming what it does under the terrors of the post-Augustan Empire, Tacitean political commentary. His vision of Tarquinius Superbus is forward-looking; he preserves a species of hope. To a Socratic the patrilineal tradition is bound to appear to be a kind of opinion; as opinion it is dependent on a certain species of history for its existence. History therefore is always a mixture of the clear and the obscure.

---

[34] II, 45 (66, 14sqq.).
[35] The third book. In Cicero's treatment these two steps appear almost as one and the same. The fragmentary fourth book might have gone on to discuss modes of education and the best regime, but this is difficult to decide from the available evidence.
[36] *De fin.* V, 7. The young Piso remarks of the Old Academy, "from their writings and principles" one can learn "all liberal arts, *all history, all eloquence.*" Cicero seems to have Aristotle in mind. Cicero's use of Stoic teachings through Scipio itself is rhetorical; Scipio was taught by the Stoic Panaetius who disagreed with only one statement of Plato (cf. *Tusc. disp.* I, 78–80). The Socratics were, broadly speaking, famous for debating the immortality of the soul and serenity; the Stoics, for debating fortitude and endurance of pain. Cp. Plato, *Menexenus,* 247b1–3 with Aristotle, *De arte rhet.* 1361a25–27.
[37] *De fin.* V, 7. "*Historia* is pleasing; we are accustomed to pursue it to the end . . . we strive (to know) the origins." *Historia* here is paralleled with astronomy, the investigation of celestial phenomena; one recalls that the *Republic* itself begins with an astronomical problem. The view of Philus transcends the vulgar sense of *historia* (tradition); he is the only one to suggest, for example, a distinction between what is by nature tyranny and what is by convention kingship (cf. III, 2392, 1–3), i.e., the copresence of and distinction between nature and convention. Scipio is aware of the distinction. In I, 56 (34, 8 f.) he accepts Critias' view of the political utility of the popular (conventional) belief in Jupiter. Critias, *Sisyphus Sat.* ed. Diels, II, 320, 1–321, 7. For the sense of *historia* as "inquiry" cf. *Tusc. disp.* I, 108 "Permulta alia colligit Chrysippus ut est in omni historia curiosus." This is the sense of the term in Plato, *Phaedo* 96a.
[38] This synthesis is the basis of Cicero's reply to the Epicureans, "in vestris disputationibus historia *muta* est." The comparison of *historia* to speech shows the relation to rhetoric.

In the *Republic* the rhetorician Cicero pleads the case for Rome itself.
Greek arts and sciences, nay, even philosophy, are all subservient to a form
of rhetoric. Cicero is the father of all moralizing history.

This would be sufficient if it did not lead to the persistent claim that
Cicero is a reactionary or a man who wanted to restore the purity of the
old regime.[39] We cannot stop to argue with this view, but it seems rather
to be the case that Cicero believed that the ancient ways of Rome point in
a dim way to certain true principles. His moderation, not his conservatism,
ought to be emphasized. However, this is not the gravest objection that
can be made to Cicero's adaptation of the Socratic teaching. Cicero did not
write a history of Rome, but he did bring history into his political philosophy. In so doing, he exceeds the bounds laid down by Plato.[40] The pursuit
of history knows no limits in practice; *historia* is an infinite field unless
pursued in the light of the ends and unchanging principles. Cicero, in
showing how Rome's own customs point to eternal principles, evokes the
vulgar notion of an "eternal Rome." Precisely because his rhetoric is successful, he blurs the issue of the mortality of all earthly cities; he makes us
believe that history culminates, in some sense, in Rome, that a mysterious
ratio pervades history, and even that history is not after all the realm of
chance. The vulgar interpretation has a way of winning. Neither Cicero
nor any of the ancient philosophers believed that history was "rational" or
pervaded by any rule of reason, but Cicero's vast influence on the modern
humanist revival [41] may have contributed to the rapprochement of history
and philosophy which completely revolutionized the ancient view.

---

[39] A. Michel, *Rhétorique et philosophie chez Cicéron* (Paris, 1960), 3, speaks of Cicero's
"idéal de restituer la tradition romaine dans sa pureté."

[40] Had he finished it the *Critias* would have been Plato's historical dialogue; his praise
of a just and good ancient Athens is related on the surface, to Cicero's praise of the just
and good ancient Rome in the *Republic*. Why is Critias, who may or may not be the
tyrant, unable to finish paying his debt to Socrates, a debt incurred in Plato's *Republic?*
The plan of Zeus is unfinished; there is no divine politics, no avenging God in Plato.
P. Shorey [*What Plato Said* (Chicago, 1934), 350] says the *Critias* is "Herodotean." In
general, Plato refused to write an account of Athenian history, an attitude which contrasts strongly with Aristotle's. Cf. K. von Fritz, "Die Bedeutung des Aristoteles für die
Geschichtsschreibung," *Histoire et historiens dans l'antiquité*, Entretien IV (Geneva,
1958), 83–145.

[41] The humanists supposedly did not have Cicero's *Republic* (which was not edited
until Cardinal Mai's edition in 1820), but they had other writings in which the same
synthesis is presented. This question, however, is an open one. Certain humanists, notably Juan Luis Vivès, testify to the presence of an unpublished copy of Cicero's *Republic*
which was jealously guarded by its owners. Cicero's indirect influence is most evident
in Jean Bodin, whose *Six Books of the Republic* is based on Cicero's dialogue (commonly called *de re publica libri sex*); Bodin's work, incorporating his earlier *Method for
the Easy Understanding of Historical Things*, is both the first modern synthesis of history and political philosophy and an attack on the foundations of ancient political philosophy.

FURTHER READINGS FOR PART II

Adcock, Frank E. *Roman Political Ideas and Practice*. Ann Arbor: University of Michigan Press, 1959.

Arnold, Edward V. *Roman Stoicism*. London: Cambridge University Press, 1911.

Barker, Ernest. *From Alexander to Constantine: Passages and Documents Illustrating the History of Social and Political Ideas, 336* B.C.–A.D. *337*. New York: Oxford University Press, 1956.

Chinard, Gilbert. "Polybius and the American Constitution," *Journal of the History of Ideas*, 1 (January 1940), pp. 38–58.

Clark, M. *The Roman Mind: Studies in the History of Thought from Cicero to Marcus Aurelius*. Cambridge, Mass.: Harvard University Press, 1956.

Cochrane, Charles N. *Christianity and Classical Culture*. New York: Oxford University Press, 1957.

Emmrich, Kurt. *Alexander the Great: Power as Destiny*. New York: McGraw-Hill, 1968.

Errington, R. M. "Cronology of Polybius' Histories," *Journal of Roman Studies*, 57 (1967), pp. 96–108.

Fisch, M. H. "Alexander and the Stoics," *American Journal of Philology*, 58 (1937), pp. 59–82, 129–151.

Fritz, Kurt von. *The Theory of the Mixed Constitution in Antiquity: A Critical Analysis of Polybius' Political Ideas*. New York: Columbia University Press, 1954.

Griffith, Guy T. (ed.). *Alexander the Great: The Main Problems*. New York: Barnes and Noble, 1966.

Hadas, Moses. *Hellenistic Culture: Fusion and Diffusion*. New York: Columbia University Press, 1959.

Hammond, Mason. *From City-State to World-State in Greek and Roman Political Theory Until Augustus*. Cambridge, Mass.: Harvard University Press, 1951.

Hicks, Robert D. *Stoic and Epicurean*. New York: Russell and Russell, 1962.

Milns, R. D. *Alexander the Great*. London: Hale, 1968.

Murray, Gilbert. *Stoic, Christian and Humanist*. London: G. Allen, 1940.

Poyser, G. H. "Ancient Light on a Modern Problem," *Hibbert Journal*, 51 (July 1953), pp. 338–342.

Richards, George C. *Cicero: A Study*. Boston: Houghton Mifflin, 1935.

Syme, Ronald. *The Roman Revolution*. London: Oxford University Press, 1962.

Tarn, William W. *Alexander the Great*. Boston: Beacon, 1956.

Usher, S. F. "Polybius and the Rise of Rome," *History Today,* 13 (April 1963), pp. 267–276.

Walbank, F. W. *A Historical Commentary on Polybius.* New York: Oxford University Press, 1957.

——. "Polemic in Polybius," *Journal of Roman Studies,* 52 (1962), pp. 1–12.

Zeller, Eduard. *The Stoics, Epicureans and Sceptics.* New York: Russell and Russell, 1962.

III

THE CHRISTIAN ERA:

ST. AUGUSTINE,

JOHN OF SALISBURY,

AND ST. THOMAS AQUINAS

9

St. Augustine's Theory
of Society

SIR ERNEST BARKER

I

St. Augustine was born (A.D. 354), and spent his life, in the eastern part of what is now the French province of Algeria; and for the last thirty-five years of his life he was bishop of what is now the French port of Bona. In his lifetime, and to the very year of his death (A.D. 430), when the Vandal Gaiseric began a Teutonic conquest, the land was part of the Roman province of Africa. St. Augustine was thus an "African"; and he shows in *The City of God* some traces of that nationalism which, in Africa as well as elsewhere, but perhaps more than elsewhere, emerged from the decline and fall of Rome. The Roman province of Africa, many centuries ago, had been governed by ancient Carthage; the language of ancient Carthage, Punic, still lingered in the province, and formed a vernacular basis of

This article was originally published in Sir Ernest Barker, *Essays on Government* 2d ed. (Oxford: Clarendon Press, 1945, 1951), pp. 234–269. It is reprinted here with the permission of the publisher, Clarendon Press, Oxford, England.

African nationalism. St. Augustine drew illustrations from the old speech: he urged on the Christian clergy of the province the need for acquainting themselves with it; and when he speaks, in *The City of God*, of the Punic Wars, he betrays a sympathy with the *victa causa* of Carthage.

The archaeological research of our own day proves more and more abundantly the culture of Roman Africa. Born among this culture, St. Augustine began to imbibe it at an early age. By the year A.D. 370, at the age of 16, he was engaged in study at Carthage. He mastered the Latin classics —particularly Cicero, Virgil, and the encyclopaedic Varro, whose *Antiquitatum Libri* (in forty-one books, now lost) is quoted again and again in *The City of God*. He also read (in translations) the *Categories* of Aristotle and many of the dialogues of Plato. He was particularly influenced by Plato; and one of the chapters of *The City of God* is headed: "Of the means by which Plato was able to gain such intelligence that he came near to the knowledge of Christ." He became a teacher of classical culture: he professed "rhetoric" at Carthage as early as 377, and was professing the same subject at Milan in 384. . . . And then, by the ways which he has himself described in his *Confessions*, he was led to the Christian cause. Henceforth there are, in a sense, two men in St. Augustine—the antique man of the old classical culture, and the Christian man of the new Gospel. It is the great fascination of *The City of God* (and particularly perhaps of the nineteenth book) that we see the two men at grips with one another. This is what makes the work one of the great turning-points in the history of human destiny: it stands on the confines of two worlds, the classical and the Christian, and it points the way into the Christian. For there is never a doubt, in all the argument, from the first words of the first chapter of the first book, of the victory of that "most glorious city of God" proclaimed, as with the voice of a trumpet, in the very beginning and prelude.

St. Augustine was baptized in 387 at the age of thirty-three. After an absence of five years in Italy, he returned to Africa in 388. Three years later, in 391, he was directly ordained a presbyter, omitting all minor orders; and he was set by his bishop (the Bishop of Hippo, which is the modern Bona) to expound the Gospel and to preach in his presence. He was thus directed, early in his career, to the task of Christian exegesis; and having a ready pen as well as an eloquent voice—burning, in every way, with a great gift and a fine passion of communication—he set to work on his lifelong task of justification and interpretation of the Christian faith. He was consecrated bishop in 395. His episcopal duties were far from light. For one thing, he had a heavy burden of judicial duties: the episcopal court, in the custom of the age, was a court of general resort, even for civil cases.[1] For another thing, he was organizing around him (as he had al-

---

[1] When St. Augustine (e.g. in Book xix. 6) speaks of the difficulties of the judge and "the error of human judgements when the truth is hidden," he is speaking from a full experience.

ready begun to do when he was first made presbyter) a community of clergy, or canons, living a common life under a rule; and he was thus occupied in the foundation of what, in the language of a later day, would have been called a religious order—a task which a St. Benedict or a St. Francis found engrossing enough in itself. But whatever the burden of his judicial work, and whatever his obligation to the clerical community gathered round him, he never ceased to write till the very year of his death. He began in 397 a work *De Doctrina Christiana:* it was not finished until 426. He began in 413 *The City of God;* and that too was not finished until 426. (We have to remember, in reading it, that it appeared, part by part, over a period of thirteen years; and then we can understand its length, its repetitions, its diffuseness, its lack of a single controlling scheme of arrangement. The bishop was giving to his flock and to the world—part by part, and section by section—the thoughts that had poured into a fermenting brain, the experiences which had filled a rich life, in the intervals between the publication of one section and the appearance of the next; and his flock, and the world of his readers, had come to expect their recurrent food in its season.) But the treatise on *Christian Doctrine* and that on *The City of God* are only two among a multitude of others. There are the *Confessions,* for instance, which were finished before 400; there are commentaries on Genesis, the Psalms, and the Gospel of St. John; there are homilies, *De Bono Conjugali* and *De Nuptiis;* there are treatises on Free Will and Predestination, the Trinity and the Grace of Christ; there are, at the end of his life, the *Retractationum Libri.* It was an indefatigable pen which finally ceased its work in the last days of August 430 in that city of Hippo in which he had spent more than half of the seventy-four years of his life. The city was being besieged by the Vandals as he died; and within five years of his death they had settled in a large tract of the Roman province, with their capital at Hippo. For his own city, at any rate, St. Augustine had been the "last of the Romans."

He was a man of vital personality, with an abounding gift of self-expression. One of his phrases, as Mr. Bevan has remarked in an essay on the "Prophet of Personality," [2] is the solemn and profound phrase, "abyssus humanae conscientiae," "the abysmal depths of personality." He knew the depths of the soul, and he could express its secrets, in a way which was new among the writers of the ancient world. He had at his command a remarkable style and a Latinity which was at once nervous, subtle, and sinuous. "We should perhaps never have dared to forecast," Mr. Bevan writes of his Latin, "how this speech of massive construction, made for rock-graven epigram or magisterial formula, could be used to convey the outpourings of mystical devotion, to catch the elusive quality of shadowy moods, to enter into the subtleties of psychological analysis." The glory of

[2] Essay VII in *Hellenism and Christianity.*

his Latinity, and of the vision which it expressed, was destined to work permanently on the imagination of all the Middle Ages. When Abelard sings his great hymn—

O quanta qualia sunt illa sabbata,
Quae semper celebrat superna curia,

he is borrowing the very words of St. Augustine, and particularly of that last chapter of the last book of *The City of God* which is entitled, "of the eternal felicity of the city of God and its perpetual Sabbath." And when Dante climbs into Paradise, he is following St. Augustine's footsteps.

It is tempting to quote some of the great sayings of St. Augustine.[3] "Thou has made us for Thyself, and our heart is restless until it find rest in Thee." "This is the sum of religion, to imitate whom thou dost worship." "A man shall say unto me, *Intelligam ut credam;* and I will reply to him, *Immo crede ut intelligas.*" "There is one commonwealth of all Christian men." "That heavenly city which has Truth for its King, Love for its Law, and Eternity for its Measure." "Whosoever reads these words, let him go with me, when he is equally certain; let him seek with me, when he is equally in doubt; let him return to me, when he knows his own error; let him call me back, when he knows mine." All these sayings show the man. Many of them became the great commonplaces of future ages. To remember them is to remember the essence of the writer's thought. Who can forget the deep meaning of his cry to God, "Da quod jubes—et jube quod vis"?

II

The occasion of the writing of *The City of God* was the sack of Rome by Alaric and his Goths in 410. The sack was not in itself the most terrible of visitations. Gaiseric and his Vandals sacked it again in 455, plundering at leisure for a fortnight. The Normans under Guiscard sacked it once more in 1084, and their ravages exceeded the ravages of Goths and Vandals. But the sack of A.D. 410 impressed the imagination of the age profoundly. Rome herself, intact from a foreign invader for nearly a thousand years—Rome, the founder, the mistress and the capital of the Empire—had fallen. She had fallen in the hour of the victory of Christianity; she had fallen (murmured those who clung to the ancient ways) in consequence of that victory. News of the fall of Rome had come flying over the seas to Carthage; and fugitives from Rome had come flying in the wake of the news. Here was a great question for Christian apologetics. Were the barbaric invasions

---

[3] They are collected in Bishop Welldon's edition of the *De Civitate Dei*, vol. ii, pp. 656–658.

and the decline of the Empire, which had just culminated in the resound-
ing crash of the "Eternal City," the result of abandoning the old civic gods
and the old civic faith? If they were not, what was their meaning, and
what "philosophy of history" could Christians produce to explain and justify the march of events? These were the questions to which Augustine
turned, and which formed the original inspiration of *The City of God.*

But a work which, as we have already had occasion to notice, took
thirteen years in composition, and eventually ran to twenty-two books, was
bound to transcend its original design. St. Augustine indeed deals with history in *The City of God;* but he left a good deal of the historical theme to
Orosius, a Spanish monk who had come to Hippo in 414 (the year after
The City of God had been begun) and was entrusted with the writing of
an *Historia adversus Paganos* by way of an appendix or corollary—not of
a very high order—to his master's work.[4] St. Augustine himself took a
higher flight. He had been drawn into a connexion with Volusianus, the
proconsul of Africa, a philosophical pagan engaged in the study of Christian evidences. The connexion gave a new theme and fresh motive to the
development of his treatise on *The City of God.* He was no longer only
concerned to provide a philosophy of history in answer to pagan murmurings; he was also concerned to provide a justification of the whole *philosophia Christi* in answer to the human philosophy of the ancient world. It
was this double purpose which determined the trend and the argument of
The City of God as the work developed down to 426.

St. Augustine himself has given his own account of the scope of his
work in a passage of the *Retractationum Libri.* The twenty-two books, he
explains, fall into two parts—which, as we shall see, correspond to the two
purposes of which we have spoken. The first part, embracing the first ten
books, falls itself in turn into two divisions. The first division (Books i–v) is
directed against the belief that human prosperity depends upon the maintenance of a civic worship of the many gods of the pagan pantheon; and in
particular it is intended to disprove the opinion that the prohibition of such
worship, which had been recently enacted by Gratian and Theodosius (c.
A.D. 380), was responsible for the late calamities—the barbarian invasions,
the decline of the Empire, and the sack of Rome. The second division
(Books vi–x) is directed against a more moderate trend of pagan belief and
opinion: it is intended to refute the thinkers who, admitting that calamities
were the inseparable and perpetual companions of humanity—admitting,
therefore, that the late calamities needed no special explanation of ancient
gods irate at the special oppression of their worship—nevertheless believed
that for the course of the life to come (if not for the course of this life) the

---

[4] "Orosius's cue was this: the world, far from being more miserable than before the ad-
vent of Christianity, was really more prosperous and happy. Etna was less active than
of old, the locusts consumed less, the barbarian invasions were no more than merciful
warnings." Dr. F. F. Stewart, in the *Cambridge Ancient History*, vol. i, pp. 576–577.

worship of the ancient gods had its own advantages. The argument of both the divisions of the first part is thus critical and destructive: it is an *argumentum adversus paganos*. But criticism was not enough: St. Augustine desired to be constructive as well as destructive; he desired not only to put to flight pagan murmurings about the sack of Rome, but also to draw over to the Christian side the thoughtful pagan (such as Volusianus) who was pondering the truth of Christian evidences. "As I did not wish," he says, "to be accused of having merely controverted the doctrines of others, without stating my own, this (that is to say, the statement of his own doctrines) is the theme of the second part of this work, which is contained in twelve books." This second part is divided by St. Augustine into three divisions. The first (Books xi–xiv) "contains the *origin* of the two cities, the City of God and the city of this world"; the second (Books xv–xviii) "contains their *process or progress*"; the third (Books xix–xxii) deals with "their appointed *ends*"—in other words, with the goal towards which they move and the consummation in which the logic of their process necessarily culminates.

III

St. Augustine, taking over the idea from the philosophers of antiquity, distinguishes four grades (or, we may say, concentric rings) of human society. The first is the *Domus* or Household. Above that, and wider than that, is the *Civitas*—which had originally meant the City, and the City-State founded upon and co-extensive with it, but had been extended (as Rome, for example, grew, and from a city became an empire) to mean the great State of many cities, and many tribes and kingdoms, united in a common allegiance to the person of a common ruler. Above the *Civitas*, and wider than it, comes the *Orbis terrae*—the whole Earth and the whole human society which inhabits the Earth. Finally, and widest of all societies, there is the Universe, *Mundus,* which embraces the heavens and their constellations as well as the earth, and includes God and His angels and the souls of the departed as well as the human society now sojourning upon the earth. In the light of this classification we may make some preliminary observations on St. Augustine's conception of the City of God.

Strictly, the City of God transcends the grade (or the concentric ring) of the *Civitas*. It belongs to the great society of the Universe; it is coextensive with the *Mundus*. But for centuries past, by a natural metaphor, the conception of *Civitas* (or πόλις) had been applied to the universal society; and such society had been regarded, and described, as a city. Men naturally sought to import the warmth and the intimacy of the close and familiar civic community into the Universe, as soon as they began to regard it as a unity or society; they felt that they had made themselves at home in the Universe when they had called it a "city," in which the Divine and the human dwelt together in a common "citizenship." The Stoics, about 300 B.C., had already begun to go this way; and indeed the Cynics had already trodden the way before them. They had spoken of the κοσμόπολις, the City which is as wide as the whole κόσμος (the Greek word for Universe which was translated by the Latin *Mundus*); and in the process of time, as we find in the *Meditations* of Marcus Aurelius (iv. 23), the very term "City of God" began to be applied to the Cosmos. Turning to it, the Emperor cries, "All fits together for me which is well-fitted for thee, O thou Universe; from thee are all things, in thee are all things, to thee come all things; the poet saith, 'Dear City of Athens,' but wilt thou not say, 'Dear City of Zeus'?" (ὦ πόλι φίλη Διός.) St. Augustine had thus the great phrase ready to his hand; but he had even more than the phrase. He had a picture, inherited from the past, of the lineaments of the City of God.

The picture was a double picture, and it had been painted by two men, both of whom came from the same corner of the Eastern Mediterranean.[5] One of them was Posidonius of Apamea, an eclectic philosopher who blended Stoicism with Platonism, and gave to the world of the first century B.C. (the world into which Christianity was born) its prevalent body of philosophic ideas. Mr. Bevan has described, in his book on *Stoics and Sceptics,* the picture which Posidonius drew of the Universe. The outer spheres of the Universe (the spheres of the fixed stars and the planets and the sun) were composed of pure ether; and this pure ether was the place of God, and indeed it was God. As you came inward, towards the earth, purity diminished with the admixture of baser substance; and from the sphere of the moon to the central earth there was an increasing degree of impurity. What happened within this Universe was simple. At death the soul of man (now a *daimon*) tried to fly away to the pure ether and to be with God. It got as far as its life on earth warranted; and so the inner Universe, between the earth and the outer spheres, was peopled with *daimones.* "You will see," Mr. Bevan writes, "that when the Stoic books talked about the world as one great city, of which gods and men were citizens, it was really a much more compact and knowable whole which was presented to their imagination than is suggested by the Universe to ours. Even to Posidonius, indeed, the spaces of the heavens were vast, as compared with the globe of earth; yet he could see the fiery orbs which marked the outer boundary of the Universe, *flammantia moenia mundi,* and there was nothing beyond it. . . . The whole of reality was contained for him within the envelope of

---

[5] It is one of the curiosities of history that three great thinkers came from the neighbourhood of the Gulf of Cilicia, and all went to Athens to learn or to teach. The first was Zeno, from Citium in Cyprus, who came to Athens about 300 B.C. and founded Stoicism. The second was Posidonius of Apamea, who was in Athens about 100 B.C. The third was St. Paul of Tarsus, who was preaching in Athens about A.D. 50. An Englishman can hardly refrain from adding the name of Theodore of Tarsus, who became Archbishop of Canterbury in A.D. 668, and organized the English Church. He, too, had studied in Athens, and was called "the philosopher."

fiery ether, one world, knit together by a natural sympathy between all the parts."

The other man who painted a picture of the City of God was St. Paul. A number of inspirations combined to produce his picture. In the first place he was a Jew, and he knew the City of Jerusalem; he knew, too, the old Hebrew dreams of the Holy City of Zion, to which all the nations should resort, and which should gather the world into its glory. Again he was versed (like St. Augustine himself in his day) in the teachings of the Greek philosophers; and a knowledge of Stoic philosophy peeps again and again through his Epistles. Above all he was an Apostle, and he knew the teaching of our Lord: he had received the gospel of the "Kingdom of Heaven," into which all men might enter by regeneration, if they believed in God and His Son and their belief were counted to them for "Righteousness." Under these various inspirations, but especially and particularly under the last, St. Paul spoke of a commonwealth (a πολίτευμα, or organized civic body) as "existing in the heavens," [6] and yet as including Christian believers here on earth who had attained (or, more exactly, had been given by the grace of God) the gift of "Righteousness." It is to that Divine commonwealth, or City of God, that all Christians really belong; and St. Paul thus speaks of them as fellow-citizens (συμπολίται) of the Saints.[7] But meanwhile Christians are also sojourning below in another polity; and in that other, or earthly, polity they may be called "strangers and pilgrims" [8] —or, as a Greek would have said, "resident aliens" (ξένοι μέτοικοι), who, belonging as citizens to another city, are temporarily resident as strangers in a foreign body of citizens. It is here, and in this picture (sketched with a few bold strokes) of the commonwealth in the heavens and the pilgrimage on earth, that we find, as it were, the original drawing from which St. Augustine painted the great canvas of *The City of God*.

We must pause, at this point, to notice some fundamental differences between the picture of St. Paul and the picture of Posidonius and the Stoics. For the latter there is really but a single city, reaching from earth to heaven—a city in which the baser sort (the *Stulti*, as the Stoics called them) will indeed occupy a far lowlier position, never attaining near to the outer ether, but which, none the less, includes the Divine and the *daimones* and all humanity in its wide embrace. St. Paul implies two sorts of cities—the Divine commonwealth in the heavens, and the human commonwealth on earth. (Just in the same way St. Augustine distinguishes the *Civitas Dei* and the *terrena civitas*.) And the reason for this distinction of the two sorts of cities is, in one word, "Righteousness." For the Divine city is the city only of the righteous; and no unclean thing may enter into it. Here, in this one word Righteousness, which in Latin is *Justitia*, we touch

[6] Phil. iii. 20.
[7] Eph. ii. 19.
[8] The words are those, not of St. Paul, but of St. Peter (1 Pet. ii. 11). I would add that I owe these references to Bishop Welldon's edition of the *De Civitate Dei*.

one of the great key-words of human thought—a key-word to the thought of
St. Augustine, a key-word to the thought of the Middle Ages. It is a word
which we must study; and we shall find that its study takes us back to
Plato.

Language plays great tricks with the human mind. Words of a mixed
and wavering content are the greatest of all tricksters. Among these words
is the Latin word *Justitia*. When the thought of the Greeks—the thought of
Plato and of St. Paul—came to the Latin West, there came with it the
word Δικαιοσύνη, which (so far as it has an equivalent in our language)
may be translated "Righteousness." The translation which it received in the
Latin language was *Justitia;* and that translation had large (and sometimes
disastrous) consequences in the field of theology and of moral philosophy.
It legalized a term which in the original Greek was something more than
legal; and a legal tone (a tone of wrongs, penalties, sanctions, and "justification") thus came to affect the thought of Latin Christendom. This had
not been the tone of Greek writers. Plato, for example, had written a dialogue called *The Republic, or Concerning Righteousness* (πολιτεία ἢ περὶ
δικαιογύνης); but the Right (τὸ δίκαιον) had meant for him the ideal good
of a society in the whole range of its collective life (and not merely in the
field of legal relations), and Righteousness had meant accordingly the ideal
goodness of a whole society in all its breadth. The idea of Righteousness in
Plato was a moral idea (which at its highest seemed to pass into a religious
idea) rather than an idea of law; and what is true of Plato is also true, and
even more true, of St. Paul and his use of the idea of Righteousness. It is
also true, as we must now proceed to show, of St. Augustine.

St. Augustine, as we have already had occasion to mention, was particularly influenced by Plato. He had read his dialogues in a Latin translation; he had read the Neoplatonists' interpretations of their master; and he
cites Plato again and again in the course of *The City of God*. We are here
concerned only with the influence of the Platonic conception of Righteousness, and that only as it bears on the social and political theory of St. Augustine; but the influence of Plato upon St. Augustine goes farther than
that. St. Augustine carried the *general* thought of Plato into his own *general* thought; and through him, as we shall later have reason to notice,
Plato influenced the subsequent course of Western theology throughout the
Middle Ages and down to the Reformation, which was indeed itself, in
some of its aspects, a return to Plato and St. Augustine. "The appeal away
from the illusion of things seen to the reality that belongs to God alone, the
slight store set by him on institutions of time and place, in a word, the
philosophic idealism that underlies and colours all Augustine's utterances
on doctrinal and even practical questions and forms the real basis of his
thought, is Platonic." [9]

In *The Republic* Plato had constructed an ideal city, based upon

---

[9] Dr. Stewart in the *Cambridge Modern History*, vol. i, p. 579.

Right and instinct with Righteousness, which might almost be described as a city of God, and is actually described by Plato as "laid up somewhere in heaven." This ideal city was to be a model; and looking upon it, and trying to copy it, men might blot out some features from their cities, and paint in others, until "they had made the ways of men, as far as possible, agreeable to the ways of God." [10] Over against the ideal city Plato had set, in the later books of *The Republic*, a description of the actual and earthly cities of men, tracing the progressive corruption of the ideal in their successive forms. The ground of the distinction and contrast was simple. In the ideal city there was Righteousness. Each of its citizens took his particular station; each of them performed—performed only, but performed to the best of his power—the appointed function of that station; and since Righteousness consisted in "performing the function of station" ($\tau\grave{o}$ $\alpha\grave{v}\tauo\hat{v}$ $\pi\rho\acute{a}\tau\tau\epsilon\iota\nu$), a city on such a foundation was Righteous. In the actual and earthly cities, on the other hand, Unrighteousness reigned; men departed more and more from their station, and encroached more and more on the stations of others; there was no order; there was no system of stations; there was no system of right relations duly based on a system of stations.

We may almost say that St. Augustine takes the Platonic distinction, and Christianizes it. Righteousness is lifted to a higher plane: it ceases to be a system of right relations between men, based on the idea of social stations, and it becomes a system of right relations between man and God (but also, and consequently, between man and man), based on the idea, first of man's faith in God's will for a system of right relations, and secondly of God's grace as rewarding such faith by creating (or rather restoring), through the "election" of the faithful, the system of right relations interrupted by sin but renewed by faith and election. *Ordo* is a great word in St. Augustine; and *ordo* is closely allied to what I have called a "system of right relations," [11] as that in turn is closely allied to, and indeed identical with, the idea of Righteousness. We can now understand St. Augustine's transfiguration of the old Platonic conception; we can understand his distinction of the City of God and the terrene city; we can understand his saying (iv. 4), "Remove righteousness, and what are kingdoms but great bands of brigands"? The City of God is the city of the righteous, a city pervaded by a system of right relations (*ordo creaturarum*) which unites God and His Angels and the Saints in Heaven with the righteous on earth. It is a city of the Universe (*Mundus*); and yet it does not embrace the whole Universe, for it excludes the fallen angels, the souls of the unrighteous, and the unrighteous who are living on earth. It is an invisible society: it cannot be identified with any visible society; it cannot, in strictness, be identified with the Church, because the Church on earth contains baptized members

[10] *The Republic*, 501 B–C.
[11] "Ordo est parium dispariumque rerum sua cuique loca tribuens dispositio" (xix. 12).

who belong to *its* society, and yet are not righteous, and cannot therefore belong to the society of the City of God. Look at the City of God in its earthly membership (remembering that this is only one part of the whole), and you will see that, so far as religious society on earth is concerned, the City contains most, but not all, of the members of the Church: you will see again that, so far as secular societies are concerned, the City "summoneth its citizens from all tribes, and collecteth its pilgrim fellowship among all languages, taking no heed of what is diverse in manners or laws or institutions" (xix. 18). Compare it then with its opposite, and you will readily see the nature of the earthly city. That again, in strictness, is no formal, visible, enumerable society. It is simply all the unrighteous, wherever they be in the Universe—the fallen angels, the souls of the unrighteous, the unrighteous who are living on earth. You cannot identify it with any actual organized society: you cannot, for instance, identify it with the Roman Empire. It is something more—it includes fallen angels as well as men; it is something less—it does not include the righteous, who are to be found in any actual State.

We can now see, as it were face to face, the lineaments of the City of God, "Two loves have created two cities: love of self, to the contempt of God, the earthly city; love of God, to the contempt of self, the heavenly" (xiv. 28). Of the heavenly city St. Augustine writes further in one of his letters (cxxxvii) saying, "The only basis and bond of a true city is that of faith and strong concord, when the object of love is the universal good, which is, in its highest and truest character, God Himself, and men love one another, with full sincerity, in Him, and the ground of their love for one another is the love of Him from whose eyes they cannot conceal the Spirit of their love" . . . . And these two cities, and these two loves, shall live together, side by side, and even intermixed, until the last winnowing and the final separation shall come upon the earth in the Day of Judgement.

Two things remain to be said—one concerning the State and its institutions in their relation to this distinction of the heavenly and the earthly cities; the other concerning the Church and its relation to the same distinction.

We might think, at first sight, that the State corresponded to, or was somehow identical with, the earthly city or some form of that city. But, as we have just seen, it would be as great a mistake (or an even greater mistake) to identify the earthly city with the Roman Empire, or any form of actual State, as to identify the heavenly city with the Catholic Church. The earthly city, like the heavenly city, is an ideal conception; or rather, and to speak more exactly, it may be called the ideal negation, or antithesis, of the ideal. It is a city of Unrighteousness. The actual State, as it really exists, is something different. It is not absolutely unrighteous. On the contrary, it has a sort of *Justitia* of its own; and not only so, but the citizens of the heavenly city avail themselves of the aid of this *Justitia* in the course of their pilgrimage, so that the State is thus, in its way, a coadjutor of the City of God.

In order to understand this view of the State we must make a distinction between absolute and relative righteousness. Absolute righteousness is a system of right relations to God—relations which are at once religious, moral, and, if you will, legal: relations which are, in a word, *total.* This system, or *ordo,* has not to reckon with, or to be adjusted to, any defects; it has not to reckon with, or to adjust itself to, the defect of sin, for sin has been swallowed up in faith and grace. Relative righteousness is a system of right relations mainly in the legal sphere, and it is a system of right relations reckoning with, and adjusted to, the sinfulness of human nature. It is the best possible, *granted the defect of sin;* but again, and just because that defect has to be assumed, it is only a second best. This is the basis of St. Augustine's conception of the State and all the institutions of the State— government, property, slavery. All of these institutions are forms of *dominium* of government over subjects, the *dominium* of owners over property, the *dominium* of masters over slaves. All *dominium* is a form of *ordo,* and to that extent good; but the order is an order conditioned by, and relative to, the sinfulness which it has to correct, and it is therefore only relatively good. The argument may be illustrated from the example of property. Ideally, for the righteous, all things are in common, and we read of the early Christians that "they had all things common." But sinfulness continues and abounds; and a form of sinfulness is greed. Partly to provide a punishment for greed, and partly to provide a remedy, private property becomes a necessity and an institution of the organized State. It is not *quod postulat ordo creaturarum;* but at any rate it is *quod exigit meritum peccatorum* (xix. 15). We may say, therefore, that property is an institution, not indeed of absolute, but at any rate of relative righteousness. We may even say that it is willed by God, who wills a relative righteousness where sin makes absolute righteousness unobtainable. What is true of the institution of property is true of the whole State. "God willed the State," in the view of St. Augustine (as afterwards in that of Burke); but he willed it *propter remedium peccatorum.*

The State, therefore, if it falls far below the heavenly city, may be said to rise above the earthly city of the unrighteous. It stands somewhere between the two, though it must be admitted that the language of *The City of God* often seems to suggest that the State and the earthly city touch and blend. From this point of view we can understand how St. Augustine can speak of the heavenly city as using the aid of the State. The State has its *ordo,* though it is not the order of creation: the State has its *pax,* though it is not the true and eternal peace. "Therefore the heavenly city rescinds and destroys none of those things by which earthly peace is attained or maintained: rather it preserves and pursues that which, different though it be in different nations, is yet directed to the one and selfsame end of earthly peace—provided it hinder not religion, whereby we are taught that the one highest and true God must be worshipped. Therefore, again, the heavenly city uses earthly peace in this its pilgrimage: it preserves and seeks the agreement of human wills in matters pertaining to the mortal nature of men, so far as, with due regard to piety and religion, it can; and it relates that earthly peace to the heavenly peace, which truly is such peace that it should be accounted and named the only peace of the rational creature, being as it is a most ordered and most concordant companionship in the enjoyment of God, and, again, in the enjoyment of one another in God" (xix. 17).

Here, it might seem, we touch St. Augustine's theory of the relation of Church and State. In a sense that is true, though we have to remember that, so far as our argument has hitherto gone, the Church and the heavenly city are not the same, and it is of the heavenly city that St. Augustine is speaking in the passage which has just been quoted. This much, at any rate, we may believe about the State, that it is not an unblessed or Satanic institution. It has its own "order": it has its own relative "righteousness." It is not a *magnum latrocinium;* for you *cannot* remove righteousness from it, and St. Augustine only said that kingdoms were great bands of brigands *if you remove righteousness.* Nor again was it founded by Satan (even though Gregory VII, at a far later date, might say in a hot moment that kings took their beginnings from those who were instigated by the prince of this world to desire dominion over their fellows); on the contrary, it is willed and intended by God. It can stand up, on its own basis, with its own justification, to aid the heavenly city. The State has thus assumed a clear character; but we are still left with the question of the position of the Church, of its relation to the distinction of the heavenly and the earthly cities, and, again, of its relation to the State.

We may begin by noticing that, at the time at which St. Augustine was writing, a distinction had already established itself between the Church in the East and the Church in the West. The Eastern Church had become something of the nature of a State-Church, with a reverential awe for its Emperor at Constantinople and a veneration for the memory of Constantine as "equal to the apostles." The Church of the West was far more independent. St. Ambrose had but lately rebuked and controlled the great Emperor Theodosius; the Pope at Rome, all the more as the Emperor had recently withdrawn to Ravenna, stood ready to assume the purple. Did *The City of God* prepare the way for the pretensions and the power of the medieval papacy? A great ecclesiastical scholar has written the words, "St. Augustine's theory of the *Civitas Dei* was, in the germ, that of the medieval papacy, without the name of Rome. In Rome itself it was easy to supply the insertion, and to conceive of a dominion, still wielded from the ancient seat of government, as world-wide and almost as authoritative as that of the Empire." [12] In what sense, if any, may it be said that *The City of God* was the germ of the medieval papacy?

What St. Augustine might be interpreted into meaning, or used to suggest, is a different thing from St. Augustine's own teaching. We may admit, and admit readily, that the whole picture of the *gloriosissima civitas Dei* might easily be transferred to the medieval Church and the papacy. After all, that Church was based on the "righteousness" of the *lex evangelica* (*Justitia* was the cry of Hildebrand, and his dying words were *Dilexi justitiam*); after all, it sought to spread the reign of "righteousness" by the action of its papal Head in every State and upon every Estate or condition of men: why should it not be counted the heir of *The City of God?* But we are here concerned with St. Augustine himself, living and writing in nationalist Africa (and no little of a nationalist himself, as witness his references to ancient Carthage) between the years 413 and 426. What was his actual conception of the Church, in his own day and for his own generation? [13]

We must turn to some of his other writings to get the outlines of his conception clear. He believed in a universal Church comparable to the moon; he believed in particular Churches (*particulatim per loca singula Ecclesiae*) comparable to the stars. He held that an especial authority resided in the particular Churches founded by the Apostles; and among these he recognized a primary or still more especial authority in the Roman Church. The Roman Church might therefore be particularly consulted for an authoritative pronouncement on disputed questions, though at the same time St. Augustine speaks of an appeal to "a plenary Council of the Church Universal." Roughly, we may say that he believes in a universal Church as a single unit of faith and Christian society: he believes in particular or local Churches as units of organization; he allows a special authority to some, and a still more especial authority to one, of these; but he has no single Church which is at one and the same time a unit of faith, of organization, and of authority.

We may now inquire into the relation of the universal Church, as a unit of faith, to the City of God. We can only say that the thought of St. Augustine about this relation varies, according as his thought glows into a fervour of incandescence, or restricts itself within the bonds of his theological logic. Logically, there is a difference between the Church and the City of God. Not all who formally belong to the Church as a unit of faith—not all who have been baptized and confirmed—are righteous; and the Church may thus contain members who are not also members of the City of God. But the fervour of faith may sweep away the difference; and there are pas-

[12] The late Mr. C. H. Turner in the *Cambridge Mediaeval History*, vol. i, p. 173.
[13] In seeking to answer this question, I have drawn on Appendix H of Bishop Welldon's edition.

sages in which the Church is made the same as the City of God. "The ark is a figure of the City of God on its pilgrimage in this world, *that is to say of the Church,* which is saved by the wood on which hung the mediator of God and men, the man Christ Jesus" (xv. 26). "Therefore even now the Church is the Kingdom of Christ and the Kingdom of the Heavens" (xx. 9). A number of other passages might readily be collected to the same effect. We can only say that the Church, as a unit of faith, sometimes glows with the greatness of the City of God, and sometimes falls short of that measure.

What, then, shall we say of the relation of Church and State? It is a question that hardly enters into St. Augustine's thought, in the form in which it presented itself to the Middle Ages, or presents itself to us to-day. There is no question, in *The City of God,* of any system of "concordat" between Church and State, or of any State "Establishment" of the Church, or of the superiority of the *sacerdotium* over the *regnum,* or of the power of the keys, or of the Donation of Constantine,[14] or of anything of the sort. The Church is a pilgrim society, living by faith and looking to the Hereafter. It lives on earth by the side of the State; it uses the *terrena pax* of the State; it acknowledges the divine institution and the relative righteousness of the State. But it simply moves as a pilgrim past the grandeurs and dignities of this world, "nihil eorum rescindens vel destruens, immo etiam servans et sequens," but always looking beyond, and always with eyes fixed elsewhere. What has a pilgrim to do with a king, except to acknowledge that he is king, to render to him due obedience in matters of worldly peace, and to pass on?

Yet there is a sense in which the doctrine of *The City of God* is inimical to the State, and even subversive of its existence. St. Augustine shifts the centre of gravity. The men of the ancient world had thought in terms of the *Civitas Romana* as the one and only society; they had deified the Roman Emperor as its living incarnation, and they had thereby given a religious sanction to its claims: they had pent all life—religion, politics, everything—in a single secular framework. Writing at a time when the framework seemed to be cracking and breaking, St. Augustine says, in effect: "This is not all; nor indeed is it the half of the matter. There is another and a greater society; and it is towards that society that the whole of creation moves." The ultimate effect of *The City of God* is the elimination of the State: it is the enthronement of the Church (or at any rate of the heavenly city which again and again is identified with the Church) as the one and only *final* society. Rome has fallen: Christ has risen. The process of history is a process making for His Kingdom. When we remember that St. Augustine himself, as a consecrated officer of the Church, was already doing justice from his own episcopal tribunal in all sorts of cases, and thus taking the place of the State in the great sphere of jurisdiction, we can see

[14] The idea of the Donation first emerges in the eighth century.

that the way was prepared, alike in his thought and his life, for the enthronement of the Church upon earth.

IV

The student who seeks to acquaint himself with the thought of St. Augustine may well be dismayed by the 1200 pages of a Latin edition of the *De Civitate Dei,* such as that which was published by Bishop Welldon in 1924. He may even be alarmed by the 800 pages of the English translation printed recently (1945) in Everyman's Library.[15] Perhaps he may be wise to steep himself in some single book of the twenty-two. The argument of *The City of God* is not a sustained argument in distinct and successive logical steps. Writing as he did in separately published parts, and repeating and reinforcing his cardinal views, St. Augustine may be studied, as it were, in a "sample." The sample will not give the whole of his thought; but it may indicate its general drift and tendency. Such a sample may be found in Book xix.[16]

The City of God, it was said above, "stands on the confines of two worlds, the classical and the Christian, and points the way forward into the Christian." The nineteenth book particularly illustrates this sentinel attitude. On the one hand, St. Augustine looks back upon the theories of classical philosophy in regard to the nature of the Supreme Good, and reviews the attempts of antiquity to construct a gospel of human happiness within the confines of our mortal existence; on the other hand, he looks forward to the peace and happiness of the heavenly city of God, alike in the time of its earthly pilgrimage and in the eternity of its perpetual Sabbath.

In the early chapters (1–3) St. Augustine, using, as he so often does, the compilation of Varro, begins by stating the best features of the theories of classical antiquity in regard to the nature of the Supreme Good. He finds these features represented in the opinions and doctrines of the Old Academy—that is to say, in the Platonic tradition. We may summarize these opinions and doctrines in two propositions. (1) The Supreme Good, in which lies happiness, is composed of the goods both of the body and of the mind; but since virtue, the highest quality of the mind, is incomparably the greatest of all goods, the life of man is most happy (and the Supreme Good is most perfectly attained) when he enjoys the possession of virtue, with the other goods of mind and body without which virtue is impossible.

[15] The translation printed in Everyman's Library is the Jacobean translation of John Healey, published in 1610. The editor of the text, the Rev. R. V. E. Tasker, has incorporated most of the corrections made in the later edition of 1620, and has added some further corrections and emendations.
[16] Mr. R. H. Barrow, in his "St. Augustine, *The City of God*" (1950), prints the Latin text of Book xix (with some few omissions), and an English translation facing the text, on pp. 62–133. He adds an analysis, and a full commentary, on pp. 177–263.

(The Christian answer to this theory is stated by St. Augustine in the fourth chapter.) (2) The happy life is social, and the Supreme Good can only be attained in society. Men desire the good of their friends: they desire that good for its own sake; they wish for their friends, for their friends' own sake, the good which they wish for themselves. Society thus arises, and appears in four grades—the grades we have already mentioned—the *domus,* the *civitas,* the *orbis,* the *mundus;* and society is essential to happiness. (To this line of thought St. Augustine cannot but give, as he says, a "far ampler approval"; and therefore, partly in agreement with it, and partly in correction of it, he devotes twelve chapters (5–17) to a consideration of society and its relation to the Supreme Good and the happiness of man. It is these twelve chapters which give to the nineteenth book its particular interest for students of the social and political thought of St. Augustine.)

In stating these two propositions, we have incidentally indicated the gist of the first seventeen chapters, which form more than two-thirds of the nineteenth book. But there is another and final section of the book which also bears particularly on St. Augustine's political theory. After three intervening chapters (18–20), which are partly occupied with some details of the opinions of the Academy, and partly with an insistence on the idea that Christian happiness is an anticipatory happiness (*spe,* as he says, rather than *re*), he starts, in chapter twenty-one, to discuss Cicero's definition of *populus.* It was natural that, after discussing *societas* in general, he should turn to a discussion of *populus* and *respublica;* and thus a final and peculiarly political section is added to the book (21–27). But there is a long theological digression early in the section (22–23, but particularly 23); and the conclusion of the section, rising to higher than political themes, first treats of the relations between religion and morality, and then ends with the end of the wicked.

There are three themes which emerge from this brief analysis of the nineteenth book. The first is St. Augustine's criticism of the moral theory of the ancient philosophers. The second is his own theory of *Societas.* The third is his definition of *Populus* and *Respublica.*

(1) His criticism of the moral theory of the ancient world begins in and ends with the affirmation of the opposing tenets of the Christian faith. "The City of God will make answer that eternal life is the Supreme Good, eternal death is the Supreme Evil; and it is therefore for the sake of gaining the one, and shunning the other, that we must live rightly." There can be no Supreme Good or Happiness in this life only—and it is to this life only that pagan philosophy has its regard. Sickness assaults the body: afflictions threaten the senses; insanity menaces reason itself; and even virtue, the highest reach of mere mortal faculty, is always a struggle against the lusts of the flesh—a battle, and not a felicity. One by one St. Augustine examines the four cardinal virtues of ancient theory—Temperance, Prudence,

Justice, and Fortitude—and of each in turn he proves that, so long as it is a merely mortal virtue, without the comfort of faith in God and the corroboration of the hope of eternal life, it must necessarily absent itself from felicity. Consider, he urges, Fortitude; consider its culmination in Stoic theory, which was a theory of Fortitude; and what do you find at its peak but Suicide, glorified as the last and greatest fling of the brave heart? And how can a theory which ends in *that* be a theory of the Supreme Good or of Happiness? This is a shrewd and vital criticism of the moral theory of the ancient world: the gaunt figure of Suicide standing on its summit is the index of its inherent inconsistency. "O vitam beatam, quae ut finiatur mortis quaerit auxilium"—"O strange Happiness, that seeketh the alliance of Death to win its crown." From the gospel of Death St. Augustine turns to point to the gospel of Life, the Life of Eternity. Seek the righteousness which comes from faith in God, and you shall have the hope of immortality; and in that hope you shall have both *salus* and *beatitudo*—the Salvation and the Happiness which philosophy seeks in vain. "Talis salus, quae in futuro erit saeculo, ipsa erit etiam finalis beatitudo." The supreme Good and Happiness are not in the Here and Now: they are in the Yonder and the Hereafter; it is in terms of eternal life alone that the "Good" of man can be understood, and won.

(2) The philosophers have said that the moral life is *vita socialis.* Therein they spoke wisely, and we may agree with their saying; for how could the City of God, itself a society, have its beginning, or its course, or its consummation, *nisi socialis esset vita sanctorum?* But if happiness be social, society (in itself) is not happiness; and St. Augustine (looking always to Eternity) proceeds to show the troubles and the misfortunes to which society is prone. He takes each of the four ranges of society. The domus, *commune perfugium,* has none the less its losses and griefs, its disputes and its angers. The society of the *Civitas* suffers from the problems of litigation and the perils of civil war. (On the problems of litigation St. Augustine, himself a judge, writes a pregnant chapter (6). How difficult it is for the judge to find the truth, and yet how necessary is his office; how gladly would he leave his bench, but how strictly is he constrained to his duty by human society, "which he thinks it a crime for him to desert"; how fervently can he repeat the Psalmist's cry to God, "*De necessitatibus meis erue me.*") On the city follows the *orbis terrae,* the third range of human society (7); and lo! the earth is full of misfortunes and troubles. The difference of languages has kept the human race sundered; and if the *imperiosa civitas* of Rome has imposed her own language on conquered nations through the peace of the great society she has achieved, the price of her achievement in the past has been war, as the price of its maintenance to-day is still war—war without, or war on the frontier: war within, or civil war, which the very extent of the Empire inevitably breeds. And if it be said that there is such a thing as "just war" (the Christian canonists were later to elaborate

a theory of *justum bellum*), it may also be said that even the just war is a "cruel necessity," unavoidable, indeed, if the unjust aggressor is to meet his due, but none the less, in itself, a trouble and a misfortune.

At this point St. Augustine turns aside to speak of friendship (8). It is a consolation and a delight; but when we give our heart to our friends, we give it over to perils. Our friends may suffer—and then we suffer; they may be corrupted—and then we suffer even more. The society of friends is precious, but it is as perilous as it is precious; and in it, as in all the three ranges of society through which the argument has run, there is no exemption from misfortune and trouble. Nor is there any exemption in the fourth and highest range of society, the *Mundus*, which brings us into the society of spirits (9). We cannot see the angels familiarly; and Satan sends false angels for our deception. It is these false angels, masquerading as gods, who have produced pagan polytheism. Even the true Christian, who has not yielded, like the pagan, to such guile, is never secure from the assaults of deception (10). . . . But the trouble from which he suffers serves only to whet the fervour of his longing for that final security in which peace— peace as complete as it is certain—is at the last to be found.

Peace now becomes the note of St. Augustine's argument (11). Society is a good thing; but we want a society free from trouble and misfortune; we want a society which is at peace. We may say therefore that the Supreme Good, which was defined before as eternal life, is also, and at the same time, peace (11). It is not idly, continues St. Augustine, that Jerusalem, which is the mystical name of the Heavenly City, should also signify peace; for the Hebrew *Salem* is the Latin *Pax*. And yet peace is not enough in itself to denote the Supreme Good (for peace may also exist in a lower sense); nor again is eternal life enough in itself (for we read of the eternal life of the wicked, which is the Supreme Evil); and we must therefore put both together, and define the Supreme Good as "Peace in Eternity" or "Eternity in Peace."

Having thus vindicated eternal peace as the Supreme Good, St. Augustine proceeds to show that the highest peace is but the finest music of a chord which runs through all creation (12). Peace is the diapason [17] of the Universe. Peace is the object of war: the breaker of peace desires peace— only a peace more after his own mind; conspirators and robbers need peace—if it be only peace with one another. The very animals seek peace and ensue it; and it is by the gate of their instinct for peace that they pass into the life of the herd or society, of which that instinct is the condition and (we may almost say) the origin. Man is especially moved by the laws of his nature to enter upon society and to seek peace with all men. It is only a perversion of a genuine instinct when a man seeks, by conquering and dominating others, to make his will their peace. Properly, naturally—

---

[17] Diapason, if we go back to the Greek, is ἡ διὰ πασῶν τῶν χορδῶν συμφωνία.

by the law of his nature, which is part of the universal law of all nature—man should seek to live in equality with others under the peace of God: improperly, unnaturally, violating that law, he seeks to make others live in inequality and subjection under a peace of his own imposition. But even in violating nature (that is to say, in instituting *dominium* over others to the end of securing an imposed peace), man does homage involuntarily to nature; and he does so because he seeks and ensues, in his own way, the peace which is nature's purpose and chord and law. "No man's vice is so much against nature that it destroys even the last traces of nature." This great phrase is like that of Shakespeare:

> There is some soul of goodness in things evil
> Would men observingly distil it out.

The free will of man cannot entirely defeat the purpose of nature; and all nature, as the creation of God, is intrinsically good. "Even what is perverse must be peaceably set in, or in dependence on, or in connexion with, some part of the order of things."

St. Augustine's idea of universal peace is thus closely connected with the idea of a universal order or law, proceeding from God and pervading creation. *Pax* and *ordo* go together; they are like obverse and reverse of the same coin. From the connexion of *pax* and *ordo* St. Augustine rises to one of the finest and most philosophical of his arguments (12, end). Imagine a living human body suspended upside down. It is a thing contrary to the order, the natural law, the peace of that body. Imagine the body left alone, day upon day, day upon day. Order, natural law, peace, all return. The body dies, dissolves, is resolved into the earth and air: it returns to its order, its nature, its peace. "It is assimilated into the elements of the Universe; moment by moment, particle by particle, it passes into their peace; but nothing is in any wise derogated thereby from the laws of that Highest and Ordaining Creator by whom the peace of the World is administered." The words (with their suggestion of the sovereignty of nature's great laws and the conservation of all nature's energy) have the ring of modern science [18]; but they have at the same time the solemn overtone of Christian faith.

We now see that many things work together, and are fused, in St. Augustine's thought. We spoke of righteousness as a system of right relations, an order; and St. Augustine himself (4) speaks of righteousness as a *justus ordo naturae*. Peace, too, is an order—the order of an "ordaining" God who pervades an "ordinate" creation, and always and in everything acts by law, in Heaven above and on the earth beneath. This order of peace is an order which everywhere, and in all creation, composes part to part (both

[18] See Dr. Cunningham, *St. Austin,* Appendix A (St. Austin and the Observation of Nature).

among things animate and among things inanimate) according to law; it is an order, therefore, issuing in society—the society of the whole articulated Universe as well as, and in the same way as, the societies of men. *Pax, ordo, lex, societas*—the words are like four bells ringing a peal in all the Universe. Burke, who knew the writings of the Fathers, has a noble passage in the *Reflections on the Revolution in France*, which is a modern counterpart of St. Augustine. *Pactum*, or contract, is his key-note rather than *pax;* but he makes *pactum* pervade the Universe just as St. Augustine made *pax.* "Each contract of each particular State is but a clause in the great primeval contract of eternal society, linking the lower with the higher natures, connecting the visible and invisible worlds, according to a fixed compact sanctioned by the invisible oath which holds all physical and all moral natures each in their appointed place." [19]

In the following chapter (13) St. Augustine proceeds to enumerate the phases and manifestations of peace. There is a peace of the body; a peace of the irrational soul; a peace of the rational soul; a peace of both body and soul in their union with one another. There is a peace between man and God, which is "ordered obedience in faith under eternal law"; there is a peace between man and man, which is "ordered concord"; and, as species of this latter, there are the peace of the household ("ordered concord of its members in rule and obedience") and the peace of the *Civitas* or State ("ordered concord of citizens in rule and obedience"). Finally, there is the peace of the City of God, "a most ordered and concordant companionship in enjoying God and one another in God"; and there is the universal peace of all things, which is "the tranquillity of order." This peace of order, in all the range of its phases and manifestations, is a system of righteousness; but it embraces even the unrighteous. They have, in one sense, gone out of the order; they are, in another sense, caught fast in the order. So far as they are miserable, and justly miserable, their misery is only the "return" upon them of the order which they have violated; so far as they are free from disturbance, it is because they are adjusted, by a sort of harmony, to the conditions in which they are placed; and in this way they possess a sort of tranquillity of order, and therefore a sort of peace. We may gloss this argument by saying that the institutions adjusted to unrighteousness (the State and its government, slavery, property) are institutions fundamentally righteous, because they represent the return—the inevitable return—of interrupted right and order and peace. Nothing can exist outside order. Nothing can be in its nature utterly bad.[20] God made creation, and made it good. If His creatures, by their will, introduce evil,

---

[19] Burke's *Works*, vol. ii, p. 368 (Bohn edition).
[20] "There cannot be a nature in which there is no good. Not even the nature of the Devil, in so far as it is nature [and therefore the creation of God], is evil; but perversity maketh it evil. . . . He abode not in the tranquillity of order; but he hath not therefore escaped from the power of the Ordainer."

the overruling order of His will returns, and instils good into that evil. The State is the return of the order of God upon the evil introduced by man's sin.

In the fourteenth chapter the argument begins to trend more definitely in a political direction, and the fifteenth and sixteenth chapters (more especially the former) contain some of the most essential elements in the political thought of St. Augustine. He goes back to one of the phases or manifestations of peace which he has mentioned in the previous chapter. The highest peace of man (considered, for the moment, simply as man) is the peace of his highest faculty. This is his rational soul; and its peace may be defined as an "ordered harmony of knowing and doing." Knowing precedes doing; but for any true knowledge man needs a Divine Master whom he can follow in certainty, and a Divine Helper whom he can obey in liberty. The Master and Helper has given us two commandments—that we should love God, and that we should love our neighbours as ourselves. It follows that we should serve and aid our neighbours to love God, since that is the greatest love and the highest service we can give them. If we do that, we shall be living in peace—which is "ordered concord," which again is "society"—with our neighbours. The rules of this society will be, first and negatively, to injure no man, and secondly or positively, to aid all men whom we can. The first circle of such society will be the family; and in the family there will be authority and subjection. But since the rule of the society is love, and love means service, any authority will only be a mode of service, and it will be exerted in the spirit of service. "They who exercise authority are in the service of those over whom they appear to exercise authority; and they exercise their authority, not from a desire for domination, but by virtue of a duty to give counsel and aid."

St. Augustine here started a line of thought which was long to endure. More than a thousand years afterwards, in 1579, the author of the *Vindiciae contra Tyrannos* echoed his words when he wrote, "Imperare ergo nihil aliud est quam consulere"; and a writer of our days has similarly said of the State, "It commands only because it serves." But St. Augustine has no sooner started this line of thought than he sees, and faces, a difficulty. He has been speaking of the circle of the family; and the family, in his day and generation, included slaves. Can the position of the slave be reconciled with the idea that authority is only a form of service? St. Augustine attempts an answer in the fifteenth chapter. The free society, in which *imperare est consulere*, is argued to be both the prescription of natural order and the rule imposed at the moment of creation. God gave the first man dominion only over the animal world. "He would not have reasonable man, made in His own image, to exercise dominion save over unreasoning beings: He set man not over man but over the beasts of the field. Therefore the righteous of the first days were rather made shepherds of flocks than kings of men, in order that God might, even after this manner, suggest what it is which is required by the order of created beings, and what it is which is demanded by the desert of sin." For there is a great gulf between these two things; and slavery is explained, and justified, by that gulf.

Slavery is the result of sin; and it is a condition rightly imposed on the sinner. It comes to pass by the judgement of God; it is justified by His judgement. There is even a sense in which it is the result, or rather the "return," of natural order. "No man, indeed, is a slave to man, or to sin, by the nature in which God first created man. But penal slavery is ordained by that law, which commands the preservation and forbids the violation of natural order." Thus even the unrighteous, as we have already had reason to notice, are caught fast in the system of righteousness; and even what seems the unnatural institution of slavery is but the "return" (in the form of retribution for "the desert of sin") of the order of nature. The question one naturally asks to-day (though St. Augustine did not pause to put it) is whether an actual slave has ever really committed any unrighteousness other than, or beyond, that committed by the rest of mankind? And if the answer to that question be "No," it is difficult to explain why he should be placed none the less in a totally different condition from other men.

But if slavery be a result, or a "return," of natural order, the true master of slaves must nevertheless look to their eternal happiness (16). He must serve and aid them (for they, too, are his neighbours) to love God; and meanwhile he may hope to be released from the burden of his mastership in the Hereafter. For it *is* a burden, in the same way and the same sense as St. Augustine has argued before that the office of judge is a burden: it involves, in the same way, the duty of discipline and the office of correction. The master, like the judge, may cry for deliverance (*De necessitatibus meis erue me*), "longing and praying to reach that heavenly home, in which the duty of ruling men is no longer necessary." (How often must any "administrator" echo that cry!)

We might expect, after this discussion of the household, to be carried into a discussion of the *Civitas* or State. But St. Augustine, omitting to speak of the *Civitas* at large in general terms, flies away at once, in a chapter (17) which concludes his long discourse on society, to a consideration of the heavenly city. His theme is its relations—its relations both of agreement and of disagreement—with the earthly city. It is, in a way, the theme of the relations of Church and State. In some things, says St. Augustine, "the things which are necessary to this mortal life" (roughly, we may say, the preservation of law and order), both cities can readily share together. The heavenly city (or, more exactly, the part of it which is now making its earthly pilgrimage) accordingly uses the earthly peace of the earthly city; its members enter into the agreement of wills concerning the things pertaining to mortal life; they obey the laws regulating these things, "that as mortality is common to both cities, so concord may be preserved between both in matters pertaining thereto." But there is a sphere of things, "the things pertaining to immortality," in which no concord is possible. Polytheistic thinkers have introduced supposed gods as civic deities into the affairs of the earthly city; and the heavenly city, devoted to the one true God, cannot therefore have any laws of religion in common with the earthly city. It has therefore followed the way of Dissent; it has trodden the hard road of Persecution—"until the days [they had already come in St. Augustine's time] when at length it may make the spirits of its adversaries recoil before the terror of its multitude."

(3) The final theme of the nineteenth book is the nature of a *Populus* and of the *Respublica* in which a *Populus* is organized. The theme, as we have already had occasion to notice, would naturally follow on the discussion of *Societas;* but in fact it is treated separately, and the chapters concerned with the theme are in the nature of an appendix. St. Augustine had promised, in an earlier book (ii. 21), to prove that, on Cicero's definition of the term, there had never existed a *Respublica* at Rome. What he has said in the nineteenth book about the heavenly city, as the only home of true Righteousness, reminds him of his promise, and he sets about its performance.

A *Respublica* is res *Populi:* what then is a *Populus?* In Cicero's definition it is "the union of a number of men associated by the two bonds of common acknowledgement of Right (*jus*) and common pursuit of interest" (21). It is the word Right, or *Jus*, which offends St. Augustine. In the Latin usage *Jus* is a legal term; and it signifies simply the body of legal rules which is recognized, and can be enforced, by a human authority. On the basis of this significance of *Jus* there is little in Cicero's definition with which we need quarrel. It might, perhaps, go farther; but it is correct enough so far as it goes. But St. Augustine had his own preconceptions; and they made him resolved to quarrel with Cicero's definition. With his mind full of the idea of Righteousness (the Greek Δικαιοσύνη, as it appears in Plato and in St. Paul), he twists the sense of *jus*. He identifies *jus* with *justitia;* he identifies *Justitia* with *vera justitia;* and he argues accordingly that "where there is no true righteousness, there cannot be a union of men associated by a common acknowledgement of Right." Here he has already departed far from Cicero's sense; but he proceeds to depart still farther. *Justitia*, he argues, is the virtue which gives to each his due. It must therefore include, and include particularly, the giving of His due to God. In other words, it must include true religion; for it is only true religion which gives to God His due. But if *Justitia* thus involves true religion, and if *Justitia*, as has already been assumed, is ncessary to the existence of a *Populus*, it follows that true religion is necessary to the existence of a *Populus*. The worship which gives to God His due is the *sine qua non* of the existence of a *Populus*, and therefore of a *Respublica*. It is therefore proven that, on Cicero's *definition*, there never existed a *Populus* at Rome; for the *populus Romanus* never gave God His due.

We may rejoin that this has only been proven on the basis of assumptions about the significance of *Jus* which Cicero would never have admitted. But if we make that rejoinder, we must also make an admission. We must admit that century upon century was destined to hold, and to hold tenaciously, the view which St. Augustine implies—the view that a people, in order to be a true people, must not only be a legal society, but also, and in the same breath, a religious society worshipping God in union and uniformity. This is the Elizabethan view, implied in the Act of Uniformity and expressed in the philosophy of Hooker: the commonwealth of the people of England must be a Church as well as a State in order to be a true commonwealth, and its members must be Churchmen as well as citizens in order to be truly members. Indeed, so long as a form of Establishment lasts, there still remains a relic of the idea that religion is necessary to the existence of a *Respublica*.

And yet St. Augustine is willing, after all, to allow that there may be a people without any confession of true religion. He had only set out to prove, and he was content with having (as he thought) proved, that *on Cicero's definition of the term* there could not be a people without a confession of true religion. *If* (he had argued) you say that there must be "common acknowledgement of Right," *then* there must be common acknowledgement of God, for *that* is involved in common acknowledgement of Right. But you need not say that there must be common acknowledgement of Right. You may pitch the key lower, and simply say that a people is "the union of a reasoning multitude associated by an agreement to pursue in common the objects which it desires" (24). On this definition the end and criterion of a people is not *Jus;* it is simply—whatever it is. On this definition, again, the objects desired may be higher or lower; and a people will be better or worse accordingly. On this definition, finally, the Roman people was a people, and the *Respublica Romana* a *Respublica;* but history shows the quality of the objects it desired, and history testifies how it broke again and again, by its civil wars, the agreement on which the salvation of any people depends. This is equally true of Athens and other States of antiquity. We may allow that they were "peoples": we must also allow that they were "cities of the ungodly, devoid of the truth of Righteousness." And therefore the conclusion of the matter is that, though a people may be a people without confessing the true God, no people can be a good people without that confession.

And so St. Augustine argues, in the last chapters of the book (25–27), that true virtue cannot exist apart from true religion. Indeed, virtue which does not come from the knowledge and love of God is a vice rather than a virtue; it is a matter of peacock pride and idle vainglorying. "Not from man, but from above man, proceedeth that which maketh a man live happily." And yet (the argument proceeds, as St. Augustine turns to the other side of the matter), even a people alienated from God, destitute as it is of virtue, has "a certain peace of its own, not to be lightly esteemed" (26). It is indeed to the interest of the Christian that it should have this peace; "for so long as the two cities are mixed, we too use the peace of Babylon." Here St. Augustine returns to the old problem of the relations of the heavenly and the earthly cities; but he adds a fresh tribute to the service and the claims of the earthly city when he cites the Apostle's exhortation to the Church to "pray for kings and those in authority." The peace of this world, after all, deserves its acknowledgement. Not but what the Christian, even in his world, has a peace of his own which is higher than the peace of this world—the peculiar peace of his faith (27). And yet even that higher and peculiar peace has its miseries, so long as it is enjoyed, precariously enjoyed, in this mortal life. Sin besets us always: even upon the brave fighter "subrepit aliquid . . . unde, si non facili operatione, certe labili locutione, aut volatili cogitatione, peccatur." (The words have a beauty and a subtlety beyond translation.) Only at the last "will there be such felicity of living and reigning as there shall also be serenity and facility of obeying; and this shall there, in all and in each, be eternal, and its eternity shall be sure; and therefore the peace of this beatitude, or the beatitude of this peace, shall be the Supreme Good."

V

We have seen the philosophy of sunrise seeking to dispel the philosophy of night. It only remains to say some words on the future influence of *The City of God*. It was studied by Gregory the Great: it was read and loved by Charlemagne, who believed that he had inaugurated the *Civitas Dei* upon earth. Abelard wrote hymns in the strains, and even the words, of the great prose of St. Augustine; and Dante, though he only refers to him twice in the *Divina Commedia*, uses his teaching in his *De Monarchia*.[21] But the deeper influence of St. Augustine is not to be traced in particular writers. It is to be traced in the general theory of the canonists and the general theological tradition of the Middle Ages.

One element in the theory of St. Augustine which particularly influenced the canonists was his teaching with regard to property—that by the natural order all things are enjoyed by the righteous in common: that private property is the result of sin; but that none the less it is justified (on that doctrine of the "return" or recoil of natural order of which we have spoken), because it is, after all, a remedy for sin, and because it canalizes,

[21] On Dante and St. Augustine, see Moore, *Studies in Dante*, I. One might have dreamed that Virgil would have been succeeded by St. Augustine (who, by the way, loved Virgil) when the end of the *Purgatorio* was being reached. But Beatrice appears instead to guide Dante upward to the Heavenly City. In the *Paradiso* Dante simply mentions St. Augustine as the founder of canons, by the side of St. Benedict the father of monks and St. Francis the founder of friars.

as it were, and reduces to order the greed of possession which came with sin. This teaching passed to Gratian and the canonists; and it gave them, as Dr. Carlyle has shown (*Medieval Political Theory in the West,* II. ii. 6), their technical doctrine in regard to property—that it is not a primitive or natural institution; that its origin must be sought in sinful appetite; that its title rests on the sanction of custom and civil law. It is tempting, but it is impossible in this place, to investigate the debt of Wyclif's theory of *Dominium* to the teaching of St. Augustine. It can only be said that Wyclif, in this as in other points of this theory, was steeped in St. Augustine, even if he carried the premises of his teacher to conclusions at which the teacher himself might have stood aghast.

If the teaching of St. Augustine certainly influenced the canonists' theory of property, it is a much more difficult thing to say how far his teaching influenced their theory of the relations of *regnum* and *sacerdotium.* Of this theme we have already spoken; and there is but little to be added here. It is sufficient to say that, between the time when St. Augustine finished *The City of God,* in 426, and the outbreak of the War of Investitures, in 1075, a whole stock of new weapons had been added to the armoury of polemics. There is the Gelasian theory of the parity or "diarchy" of the two powers (*c.* 500); there is the weapon of the "Donation of Constantine," fabricated about 760; there is the argument from the "Translation of the Empire," deduced from Charlemagne's coronation in 800; there are the theories drawn by later controversialists from the "Keys" and the "Two Swords" and the analogy of "Sun and Moon"; there is the application of feudal theory to the relations of Church and State. It was from materials such as these that the Middle Ages proper constructed a theory of the relations between *regnum* and *sacerdotium;* and the teaching of St. Augustine could only be one ingredient in a large and varied amalgam. It is tempting to trace a connexion between the saying of St. Augustine, "Remove righteousness, and what are kingdoms but great bands of brigands?," and the outburst of Gregory VII in his letter to Hermann of Metz, "Who can be ignorant that kings took their beginnings from those who by way of rapine, at the instigation of the prince of this world, desired to have dominion over their fellows?" But before we attempt to trace the connexion, or to conclude that St. Augustine taught Gregory VII that States were organizations of brigands, we must remember two things. The first is that, as we have already seen, St. Augustine taught nothing of the sort. The second is that the outburst of Gregory VII stands in isolation, and is contradicted by his other statements. Little can be made of the influence of St. Augustine in this particular connexion; and it must remain doubtful how much can be made of it in other respects. Scholars have differed upon the issue whether the teaching of St. Augustine tended, or did not tend, to depress the State and to promote the rise of a theocracy. Harnack has said, "He roused the conviction that the empirical Catholic Church *sans phrase* was the kingdom of God, and the independent State that of the Devil." [22] (This is a saying which cannot be justified.) Gierke has said, "The theory of *The City of God* left the worldly State practically destitute of importance, except in so far as it ranged itself, as a subordinate member, within and below the Divine State which was realized in the Church." (This is a saying, again, which the reader of St. Augustine's actual text can hardly accept.) Dubief has said (as it seems to me with more justice), "It is impossible to find in St. Augustine's words those comparisons between the spiritual power and the temporal power which are intended to establish the pre-eminence of the former above the latter, and denote the intention of subordinating the State to the clergy." Perhaps Ernst Troeltsch, in his massive way, gives the best and soundest view of the matter [23]: "St. Augustine admitted that view of the State and its laws which brings them both into connexion with natural law, but he confined that view within narrower limits than the other fathers: he wanted room for the possibility of irreligious Emperors (regarded as a visitation of God and a punishment of sin), and for the moral rejection of the powers that be in so far as they did not allow themselves to be guided by Divine Righteousness." There were, Troeltsch argues, two elements in the thought of the contemporary world. One was a belief in the *Naturrecht* of the State (in other words, a belief that it was based on what St. Augustine calls *naturalis ordo*); the other was the theocratic belief of a newly victorious religious society that its principles were the sovereign principles, and must therefore prevail even in the area of political organization. "The latter, as is well known, was particularly expounded by St. Augustine in his great work. But what is less noticed is that in it he also enunciated and maintained the former. In the irreconcilable struggle of the two points of view lies the double nature of the work of this great thinker—a work which, for this very reason, transmitted also to the future a double tendency. Theocracy and *naturalis ordo* are both made to consecrate the State: what the one cannot do the other will; and in any case the Emperor is primarily determined by his quality of existing *Dei gratia* and by his theocratic connexions. Yet the State itself remains, for all that, the incarnation of 'the world.' " After this account of St. Augustine's own position, Troeltsch turns to his influence on the Middle Ages. "Chrysostom, Leo I, Gelasius I, St. Augustine might indeed demand the theocratic subjection of the Emperor under the clergy, on the analogy of the Old Testament, and they might sketch the 'Programme of the Middle Ages.' But the programme was never realized at all in the East, and it was only realized in the West after five centuries had passed." When these five centuries had passed, and the realization of the programme was attempted,

---

[22] I have borrowed these quotations mainly from Bishop Welldon's edition, vol. i, pp. 51–52. The reference to Troeltsch is my own.
[23] I have translated or summarized four passages in his *Soziallehren der christlichen Kirchen*, pp. 168, 170, 191, 215.

St. Augustine's treasures of thought were used. But (and this is the important point), if "the harsh sayings of St. Augustine about the State were again brought into play, they underwent a radical intensification in the process; and an exorbitant exaggeration of emphasis was laid on the sinfulness of the State, on which St. Augustine had indeed laid stress, but behind which he had always recognized the existence of a basis of natural law."

The influence of St. Augustine on the theological tradition (as distinct from the social and political doctrines) of the Middle Ages is a vast theme, upon which we cannot embark, but which it would be almost a treason not to mention. St. Augustine enters into the *Summa* of St. Thomas; he influenced Wyclif profoundly; he influenced Luther no less profoundly. "The history of Church doctrine in the West," Harnack has said, "is a much disguised struggle against Augustinianism." This is a deep saying, and we must attempt to gloss it. St. Augustine, we may say, imbued as he was with Platonic philosophy, always believed in the unchanging perfection of a God who always and everywhere acted by law. In his theory, God is always determined (or to speak more exactly He always determines Himself) by *rationes exemplares* [24] (or, as Plato would have said, "ideas"); His relations to His creatures are always relations in the sphere of immutable order; any apparent change is a change not in God, but in the creature, and God must adjust Himself to the changing creature in order to remain unchanged in His own unchanging essence. Against this clear and pure rigour of an unanswering general order (the rigour which Wordsworth celebrates in His *Ode to Duty*), it was natural that those should revolt who wanted a mysterious and emotional world, rich in insoluble riddles, and needing a mediatory and miraculous Church to give a mystical clue. Such a revolt was that of the Nominalists of the later Middle Ages; and here we find one of those "much disguised struggles against Augustinianism" of which Harnack speaks. *Latet dolus in generalibus,* said the Nominalists; and they accordingly laid their emphasis on the Particular in its unique and concrete "reality." Their emphasis on the Particular led them to lay stress on individuality and personality, alike in man and in God; and their study of human individuality helped them to make some of the first modern researches in psychology. But the trend of their thought turned them also towards obscurantism. The individual became an ultimate mystery: God Himself became an inscrutably omnipotent individual, acting indeterminately by His individual will. The Nominalists thus came to magnify the authority of the Church as the only escape from "the burden of the mystery"; they believed in *fides implicita;* and in them may be traced the tendency of the over-subtle intellect to pass through obscurantism to the acceptance of mere authority. It was against the Nominalists that Wyclif and Luther were both in revolt; and they both went back to St. Augustine for comfort and coun-

[24] I have borrowed the phrase from Wyclif.

tenance. It would be too bold to say that St. Augustine inspired the Reformation. But it would perhaps be true to say that he took the sixteenth century back to the idea of a Divine general order of the Universe, and back to a conception of Righteousness based upon that idea.

10

Augustine's Political Realism

REINHOLD NIEBUHR

I

The terms "idealism" and "realism" are not analogous in political and in metaphysical theory; and they are certainly not as precise in political, as in metaphysical, theory. In political and moral theory "realism" denotes the disposition to take all factors in a social and political situation, which offer resistance to established norms, into account, particularly the factors of self-interest and power. In the words of a notorious "realist," Machiavelli, the purpose of the realist is "to follow the truth of the matter rather than the imagination of it; for many have pictures of republics and principalities which have never been seen." This definition of realism implies that idealists are subject to illusions about social realities, which indeed they are. "Idealism" is, in the esteem of its proponents, characterized by loyalty to moral norms and ideals, rather than to self-interest, whether individual or collective. It is, in the opinion of its critics, characterized by a disposition to ignore or

Reprinted with the permission of Charles Scribner's Sons from *Christian Realism and Political Problems,* pages 119–146, by Reinhold Niebuhr. Copyright 1953 Reinhold Niebuhr. Reprinted with permission of the author and of Faber & Faber, Ltd.

be indifferent to the forces in human life which offer resistance to universally valid ideals and norms. This disposition, to which Machiavelli refers,
is general whenever men are inclined to take the moral pretensions of
themselves or their fellowmen at face value; for the disposition to hide
self-interest behind the facade of pretended devotion to values, transcending self-interest, is well-nigh universal. It is, moreover, an interesting
human characteristic, proving that the concept of "total depravity," as it is
advanced by some Christian realists, is erroneous. Man is a curious creature with so strong a sense of obligation to his fellows that he cannot pursue his own interests without pretending to serve his fellowmen. The definitions of "realists" and "idealists" emphasize disposition, rather than
doctrines; and they are therefore bound to be inexact. It must remain a
matter of opinion whether or not a man takes adequate account of all the
various factors and forces in a social situation. Was Plato a realist, for instance, because he tried to guard against the self-interest of the "guardians"
of his ideal state by divesting them of property and reducing their family
responsibilities to a minimum? Does this bit of "realism" cancel out the essential unrealism, inherent in ascribing to the "lusts of the body" the force
of recalcitrance against the moral norm; or in attributing pure virtue to
pure mind?

Augustine was, by general consent, the first great "realist" in western
history. He deserves this distinction because his picture of social reality in
his *civitas dei* gives an adequate account of the social factions, tensions,
and competitions which we know to be well-nigh universal on every level
of community; while the classical age conceived the order and justice of its
polis to be a comparatively simple achievement, which would be accomplished when reason had brought all subrational forces under its dominion.

This difference in the viewpoint of Augustine and the classical philosophers lies in Augustine's biblical, rather than rationalistic, conception of
human selfhood with the ancillary conception of the seat of evil being in
the self. Augustine broke with classical rationalism in his conception of the
human self, according to which the self is composed of mind and body, the
mind being the seat of virtue because it has the capacity to bring all impulses into order; and the body, from which come the "lusts and ambitions," being the cause of evil. According to Augustine the self is an integral unity of mind and body. It is something more than mind and is able to
use mind for its purposes. The self has, in fact, a mysterious identity and
integrity transcending its functions of mind, memory, and will. "These
three things, memory, understanding, and love are mine and not their
own," he declares, "for they do what they do not for themselves but for me;
or rather I do it by them. For it is I who remember by memory and understand by understanding and love by love." [1] It must be observed that the

[1] *De Trin.*, 15.22.

transcendent freedom of this self, including its capacity to defy any rational or natural system into which someone may seek to coordinate it (its capacity for evil) makes it difficult for any philosophy, whether ancient or modern, to comprehend its true dimension. That is why the classical wise men obscured it by fitting its mind into a system of universal mind and the body into the system of nature; and that is also why the modern wise men, for all their rhetoric about the "dignity" of the individual, try to cut down the dimension of human selfhood so that it will seem to fit into a system of nature. This conception of selfhood is drawn from the Bible, rather than from philosophy, because the transcendent self which is present in, though it transcends, all of the functions and effects, is comprehensible only in the dramatic-historical mode of apprehension which characterizes biblical faith. Augustine draws on the insights of neo-Platonism to illustrate the self's power of self-transcendence; but he rejects Plotinus' mystic doctrine, in which the particular self, both human and divine, is lost in a vast realm of undifferentiated being.

Augustine's conception of the evil which threatens the human community on every level is a corollary of his doctrine of selfhood. "Self-love" is the source of evil rather than some residual natural impulse which mind has not yet completely mastered. This excessive love of self, sometimes also defined as pride or *superbia,* is explained as the consequence of the self's abandonment of God as its true end and of making itself "a kind of end." It is this powerful self-love or, in a modern term, "egocentricity," this tendency of the self to make itself its own end or even to make itself the false center of whatever community it inhabits, which sows confusion into every human community. The power of self-love is more spiritual than the "lusts of the body," of which Plato speaks; and it corrupts the processes of the mind more than Plato or Aristotle knew. That is why Augustine could refute the classical theory with the affirmation that "it is not the bad body which causes the good soul to sin but the bad soul which causes the good body to sin." At other times Augustine defines the evil in man as the "evil will"; but with the understanding that it is the self which is evil in the manifestation of its will. "For he who extols the whole nature of the soul as the chief good and condemns the nature of the flesh as if it were evil, assuredly is fleshly both in the love of the soul and in the hatred of the flesh." [2] This concise statement of the Christian position surely refutes the absurd charge of moderns that the Christian faith is "dualistic" and generates contempt for the body. It also established the only real basis for a realistic estimate of the forces of recalcitrance which we must face on all levels of the human community, particularly for a realistic estimate of the spiritual dimension of these forces and of the comparative impotence of "pure reason" against them. Compared with a Christian realism, which is

[2] *De Civ. Dei,* 15.5.

based on Augustine's interpretation of biblical faith, a great many modern social and psychological theories, which fancy themselves anti-Platonic or even anti-Aristotelian and which make much of their pretended "realism," are in fact no more realistic than the classical philosophers. Thus modern social and psychological scientists are forever seeking to isolate some natural impulse such as "aggressiveness" and to manage it; with equal vanity they are trying to find a surrogate for Plato's and Aristotle's disinterested "reason" in a so-called "scientific method." Their inability to discover the corruption of self-interest in reason or in man's rational pursuits; and to measure the spiritual dimension of man's inhumanity and cruelty, gives an air of sentimentality to the learning of our whole liberal culture. Thus we have no guidance amid the intricacies of modern power politics except as the older disciplines, less enamored of the "methods of natural science," and the common sense of the man in the street supplies the necessary insights.

II

Augustine's description of the social effects of human egocentricity or self-love is contained in his definition of the life of the "city of this world," the *civitas terrena,* which he sees as commingled with the *civitas dei.* The "city of this world" is dominated by self-love to the point of contempt of God; and is distinguished from the *civitas dei* which is actuated by the "love of God" to the point of contempt of self. This "city" is not some little city-state, as it is conceived in classical thought. It is the whole human community on its three levels of the family, the commonwealth, and the world. A potential world community is therefore envisaged in Augustine's thought. But, unlike the stoic and modern "idealists," he does not believe that a common humanity or a common reason gives promise of an easy actualization of community on the global level. The world community, declares Augustine "is fuller of dangers as the greater sea is more dangerous." [3] Augustine is a consistent realist in calling attention to the fact that the potential world community may have a common human reason but it speaks in different languages and "Two men, each ignorant of each other's language" will find that "dumb animals, though of a different species, could more easily hold intercourse than they, human beings though they be." [4] This realistic reminder that common linguistic and ethnic cultural forces, which bind the community together on one level, are divisive on the ultimate level, is a lesson which our modern proponents of world government have not yet learned.

[3] *De Civ. Dei,* 19.7.
[4] *De Civ. Dei,* 19.7

Augustine's description of the *civitas terrena* includes an emphasis on the tensions, frictions, competitions of interest, and overt conflicts to which every human community is exposed. Even in the family one cannot rely on friendship "seeing that secret treachery has often broken it up." [5] This bit of realism will seem excessive until we remember that our own generation has as much difficulty in preserving the peace and integrity in the smallest and most primordial community, the family, as in integrating community on the highest global level.

The *civitas terrena* is described as constantly subject to an uneasy armistice between contending forces, with the danger that factional disputes may result in "bloody insurrection" at any time. Augustine's realism prompts him to challenge Cicero's conception of a commonwealth as rooted in a "compact of justice." Not so, declares Augustine. Commonwealths are bound together by a common love, or collective interest, rather than by a sense of justice; and they could not maintain themselves without the imposition of power. "Without injustice the republic would neither increase nor subsist. The imperial city to which the republic belongs could not rule over provinces without recourse to injustice. For it is unjust for some men to rule over others." [6]

This realism has the merit of describing the power realities which underlie all large scale social integrations whether in Egypt or Babylon or Rome, where a dominant city-state furnished the organizing power for the Empire. It also describes the power realities of national states, even democratic ones, in which a group, holding the dominant form of social power, achieves oligarchic rule, no matter how much modern democracy may bring such power under social control. This realism in regard to the facts which underlie the organizing or governing power refutes the charge of modern liberals that a realistic analysis of social forces makes for state absolutism; so that a mild illusion in regard to human virtue is necessary to validate democracy. Realistic pessimism did indeed prompt both Hobbes and Luther to an unqualified endorsement of state power; but that is only because they were not realistic enough. They saw the dangers of anarchy in the egotism of the citizens but failed to perceive the dangers of tyranny in the selfishness of the ruler. Therefore they obscured the consequent necessity of placing checks upon the ruler's self-will. Augustine's realism was indeed excessive. On the basis of his principles he could not distinguish between government and slavery, both of which were supposedly the rule over man by man and were both a consequence of, and remedy for, sin; nor could he distinguish between a commonwealth and a robber band, for both were bound together by collective interest; "For even thieves must hold together or they cannot effect what they intend." The realism fails to

[5] *De Civ. Dei*, 19.5.
[6] *De Civ. Dei* 19.21.

do justice to the sense of justice in the constitution of the Roman Empire; or for that matter to the sense of justice in a robber band. For even thieves will fall out if they cannot trust each other to divide the loot, which is their common aim, equitably. But the excessive emphasis upon the factors of power and interest, a wholesome corrective to Cicero's and modern Ciceronian moralistic illusions, is not fatal to the establishment of justice so long as the dangers of tyranny are weighed as realistically as the dangers of anarchy.

Augustine's realistic attitude toward government rests partly upon the shrewd observation that social peace and order are established by a dominant group within some level of community; and that this group is not exempt from the corruption of self-interest merely because the peace of society has been entrusted to it. (One thinks incidentally how accurately the Augustinian analysis fits both the creative and the ambiguous character of the American hegemony in the social cohesion of the free world.) The realism is partly determined by his conception of a "natural order" which he inherited from the early Christian fathers, who in turn took it from that part of the Stoic theory which emphasized the primordial or primitive as the natural. This Stoic and Christian primitivism has the merit of escaping the errors of those natural law theories which claim to find a normative moral order amid the wide variety of historic forms or even among the most universal of these forms. The freedom of man makes these Stoic conceptions of the "natural" impossible. But it has the weakness which characterizes all primitivism, whether Stoic, Christian, or Romantic, for it makes primitive social forms normative. A primitive norm, whether of communal property relations or unorganized social cohesion, may serve provisionally as an occasion for the criticism of the institutions of an advancing civilization, more particularly the institutions of property and government; but it has the disadvantage of prompting indiscriminate criticism. This lack of discrimination is obvious in primitivistic Stoicism, in early Christianity, in seventeenth-century Cromwellian sectarianism, in Romanticism, and in Marxism and anarchism.

Augustine expressed this idea of a primitive social norm as follows: "This is the prescribed order of nature. It is thus that God created man. For 'let them,' He says, 'have dominion over the fish of the sea and the fowl of the air and over every creeping thing, which creepeth on the earth.' He did not intend that His rational creature, made in His image, should have dominion over anything but irrational creation—not man over man but man over beasts. And hence the righteous men of primitive times were made shepherds of cattle rather than kings of men." [7] This primitivism avoids the later error of the absolute sanctification of government. But its indiscriminate character is apparent by his failure to recognize the differ-

[7] *De Civ. Dei* 19.15.

ence between legitimate and illegitimate, between ordinate and inordinate subordination of man to man. Without some form of such subordination the institutions of civilization could not exist.

III

If Augustine's realism is contained in his analysis of the *civitas terrena*, his refutation of the idea that realism must lead to cynicism or relativism is contained in his definition of the *civitas dei*, which he declares to be "commingled" with the "city of this world" and which has the "love of God" rather than the "love of self" as its guiding principle. The tension between the two cities is occasioned by the fact that, while egotism is "natural" in the sense that it is universal, it is not natural in the sense that it does not conform to man's nature who transcends himself indeterminately and can only have God rather than self for his end. A realism becomes morally cynical or nihilistic when it assumes that the universal characteristic in human behavior must also be regarded as normative. The biblical account of human behavior, upon which Augustine bases his thought, can escape both illusion and cynicism because it recognizes that the corruption of human freedom may make a behavior pattern universal without making it normative. Good and evil are not determined by some fixed structure of human existence. Man, according to the biblical view, may use his freedom to make himself falsely the center of existence; but this does not change the fact that love rather than self-love is the law of his existence in the sense that man can only be healthy and his communities at peace if man is drawn out of himself and saved from the self-defeating consequences of self-love. There are several grave errors in Augustine's account of love and of the relation of love to self-love; but before considering them we might well first pay tribute to his approach to political problems. The virtue of making love, rather than justice, into the norm for the community may seem, at first blush, to be dubious. The idea of justice seems much more relevant than the idea of love, particularly for the collective relationships of men. The medieval tradition which makes the justice of a rational "natural law" normative even for Christians when they consider the necessities of a sinful world, seems much more realistic than modern forms of sentimental Protestantism which regards love as a simple alternative to self-love, which could be achieved if only we could preach the idea persuasively enough to beguile men from the one to the other. Augustine's doctrine of love as the final norm must be distinguished from modern sentimental versions of Christianity which regard love as a simple possibility and which think it significant to assert the obvious proposition that all conflicts in the community would be avoided if only people and nations would love one another. Augustine's approach differs from modern forms of sentimental perfectionism in the fact that he takes account of the power and persistence of egotism, both individual and collective, and seeks to establish the most tolerable form of peace and justice under conditions set by human sin. He inherited the tradition of monastic perfection; and he allows it as a vent for the Christian impulse toward individual perfection, without however changing the emphasis upon the duty of the Christian to perfect the peace of the city of this world. Furthermore, he raises questions about monastic perfection which, when driven home by the Reformation, were to undermine the whole system. "I venture to say," he writes, "that it is good for those who observe continence and are proud of it, to fall that they may be humbled. For what benefit is it to anyone in whom is the virtue of continence, if pride holds sway? He is but despising that by which man is born in striving after that which led to satan's fall . . . holy virginity is better than conjugal chastity . . . but if we add two other things, pride and humility . . . which is better, pride or humility? . . . I have no doubt that a humble married woman is to be preferred to a proud virgin . . . a mother holds a lesser place in the Kingdom of God because she has been married, than the daughter, seeing that she is a virgin. . . . But if thy mother has been proud and thou humble, she will have some sort of place and thou none." [8]

While Augustine's doctrine of love is thus not to be confused with modern sentimentalities which do not take the power of self-love seriously, one may well wonder whether an approach to politics which does not avail itself of the calculations of justice, may be deemed realistic. We have already noted that Augustine avails himself of the theory of the "natural law," only in the primordial version of the theory. If primordial conditions of a "natural order" are not to be defined as normative, the only alternative is to assume a "rational order" to which the whole of historical life conforms. Aquinas, in fact, constructed his theory of the natural law upon classical, and primarily Aristotelian, foundations. It was the weakness of both classical and medieval theories that they assumed an order in history, conforming to the uniformities of nature. Aristotle was aware of deviations in history, greater than those in nature; but he believed that there was nevertheless one form "which was marked by nature as the best." There is, in other words, no place in this theory of natural law for the endlessly unique social configurations which human beings, in their freedom over natural necessity, construct. The proponents of "natural law" therefore invariably introduce some historically contingent norm or social structure into what they regard as God's inflexible norm. That was the weakness of both classical and medieval social theory; and for that matter of the natural law theories of the bourgeois Parties of the eighteenth century, who had found that they regarded as a more empirically perceived "natural law"; but the mod-

[8] Sermon CCCIIV, ix, 9.

ern empirical intelligence was no more capable than the deductive rational processes of classical and medieval times to construct a social norm, not colored by the interests of the constructor, thus introducing the taint of ideology into the supposed sanctities of law. We must conclude therefore that Augustine was wise in avoiding the alleged solution of a natural law theory, which was the basis of so much lack of realism in both the classical and the medieval period, and which can persist today long after the Aristotelian idea of fixed form for historical events has been overcome, as the dogma of a religious system which makes its supposed sanctities into an article of faith. His conception of the radical freedom of man, derived from the biblical view, made it impossible to accept the idea of fixed forms of human behavior and of social organization, analogous to those of nature, even as he opposed the classical theory of historical cycles. Furthermore, his conception of human selfhood and of the transcendence of the self over its mind, made it impossible to assume the identity of the individual reason with a universal reason, which lies at the foundation of the classical and medieval natural law theories. It is in fact something of a mystery how the Christian insights into human nature and history, expressed by Augustine, could have been subordinated to classical thought with so little sense of the conflict between them in the formulations of Thomas Aquinas; and how they should have become so authoritative in Roman Catholicism without more debate between Augustinian and Thomistic emphases.

Augustine's formula for leavening the city of this world with the love of the city of God is more adequate than classical and medieval thought, both in doing justice to the endless varieties of historical occasions and configurations and in drawing upon the resources of love rather than law in modifying human behavior.

Every "earthly peace," declares Augustine, is good as far as it goes. "But they will not have it long for they used it not well while they had it." That is, unless some larger love or loyalty qualifies the self-interest of the various groups, this collective self-interest will expose the community to either an overt conflict of competing groups or to the injustice of a dominant group which "when it is victorious it will become vice's slave." Let us use some examples from current national and international problems to illustrate the Augustinian thesis. There is, or was, a marked social tension between the middle classes of industrial owners and the industrial workers in all modern industrial nations. In some of them, for instance in Germany and France, this tension led to overt forms of the class conflict. In others such as Britain, the smaller European nations and America, this tension was progressively resolved by various accommodations of interest. Wherein lay the difference? It did not lie in the possession of more adequate formulae of justice in some nations than in others. The difference lay in the fact that in some nations the various interest groups had, in addition to their collective interest, a "sense of justice," a disposition to "give each man his due" and a loyalty to the national community which qualified the interest struggle. Now, that spirit of justice is identical with the spirit of love, except at the highest level of the spirit of love, where it becomes purely sacrificial and engages in no calculation of what the due of each man may be. Two forms of love, the love of the other and the love of the community, were potent in short in modifying the acerbities and injustices of the class struggle. The two forms of love availed themselves of various calculations of justice in arriving at and defining their *ad hoc* agreements. But the factors in each nation and in each particular issue were too variable to allow for the application of any general rules or formulae of justice. Agreements were easier in fact if too much was not claimed for these formulae. Certain "principles" of justice, as distinguished from formulas or prescriptions, were indeed operative, such as liberty, equality, and loyalty to convenants; but these principles will be recognized as no more than the law of love in its various facets.

In the same manner the international community is exposed to exactly the tensions and competitions of interest which Augustine describes. There are no formulas of justice or laws which will prevent these tensions from reaching overt conflict, if the collective interest of each nation is not modified by its loyalty to a higher value such as the common civilization of the free nations. Where this common loyalty is lacking, as in our relation with Russia, no formula can save us from the uneasy peace in which we live. The character of this peace is just as tentative as Augustine described it. Whenever common loves or loyalties, or even common fears, lay the foundation for community, it must of course be our business to perfect it by calculations of justice which define our mutual responsibilities as exactly as possible.

It must be noted that the Augustinian formula for the leavening influence of a higher upon a lower loyalty or love, is effective in preventing the lower loyalty from involving itself in self-defeat. It corrects the "realism" of those who are myopically realistic by seeing only their own interests and failing thereby to do justice to their interests where they are involved with the interests of others. There are modern realists, for instance, who, in their reaction to abstract and vague forms of international idealism, counsel the nation to consult only its own interests. In a sense collective self-interest is so consistent that it is superfluous to advise it. But a consistent self-interest on the part of a nation will work against its interests because it will fail to do justice to the broader and longer interests, which are involved with the interests of other nations. A narrow national loyalty on our part, for instance, will obscure our long range interests where they are involved with those of a whole alliance of free nations. Thus the loyalty of a leavening portion of a nation's citizens to a value transcending national interest will save a "realistic" nation from defining its interests in such narrow and short range terms as to defeat the real interests of the nation.

IV

We have acknowledged some weaknesses in the Augustinian approach to the political order which we must now define and examine more carefully. Non-Catholics commonly criticize Augustine's alleged identification of the *civitas dei* with the visible Church. But we must absolve him of this charge or insist on a qualification of the criticism. He does indeed accept the Catholic doctrine, which had grown up before his day; and he defines the visible Church as the only perfect society. There are passages in which he seems to assume that it is possible to claim for the members of the Church that they are solely actuated by the *amor dei*. But he introduces so many reservations to this assertion that he may well be defined in this, as in other instances, as the father of both Catholicism and the Reformation. Of the Church, Augustine declared, "by faith she is a virgin. In the flesh she has few holy virgins" [9] or again: "God will judge the wicked and the good. The evil cannot now be separated from the good but must be suffered for a season. The wicked may be with us on the threshing floor . . . in the barn they cannot be." [10] The reservations which he made upon the identification of the Church and the kingdom laid the foundations for the later Reformation position. But these reservations about the sinners who might be present in the visible Church cannot obscure a graver error in his thought. This error is probably related to his conception of grace which does not allow for the phenomenon, emphasized by the Reformation, that men may be redeemed in the sense that they consciously turn from self to Christ as their end, and yet they are not redeemed from the corruption of egotism which expresses itself, even in the lives of the saints. This insight is most succinctly expressed in Luther's phrase *"justus et peccator simul"* (righteous and sinners at once). When Augustine distinguished between the "two loves" which characterize the "two cities," the love of God and the love of self, and when he pictured the world as a commingling of the two cities, he does not recognize that the commingling is due, not to the fact that two types of people dwell together but because the conflict between love and self-love is in every soul. It is particularly important to recognize this fact in political analyses; for nothing is more obvious than that personal dedication is no guarantee against the involvement of the dedicated individual in some form of collective egotism.

We have frequently referred to Augustine's definition of the "two loves" which inform the "two cities" of which "the one is selfish and the other social," the one loving self to the point of the contempt of God and the other loving God to the point of contempt of self. The question is whether Bishop Nygren [11] is right in defining the Augustinian conception

---

[9] Sermon CCXIII, vii, 7.
[10] *Comm. on Ps.* CXI, 9.
[11] Anders Nygren, in *Agape and Eros.*

of *amor dei* as rooted in a classical rather than a biblical concept.

In defense of Augustine it must be said that he is not insensible to the two facets of the love commandment and therefore does not define the *amor dei* in purely mystical terms as a flight from this world. He insists on the contrary that the *amor dei* is "social" and he offers the concord among brethren as a proof of the love of God. But nevertheless Nygren is right in suggesting that the thought of Plotinus has colored Augustine's conceptions sufficiently so that the *agape* of the New Testament is misinterpreted by Augustine's conception of *charitas* and *amor dei*. The *agape* form of love in the New Testament fails to be appreciated particularly in two of its facets: (a) the equality of the "two loves," the love of the neighbor and the love of God (enforced in the Scripture by the words "the Second is like unto it") is violated by Augustine under the influence of Plotinus even as a later medieval Catholic mystic, St. John of the Cross, violates it when he regarded the love of the creature as a ladder which might lead us to the love of God, but must be subordinated to the latter. Augustine wants us to love the neighbor for the sake of God, which may be a correct formulation; but he wants us to prove the genuineness of our love of God in the love of the neighbor, or by leading him to God. Thus the meeting of the neighbor's need without regard to any ultimate religious intention is emptied of meaning. The love of the neighbor is for him not part of a double love commandment but merely the instrument of a single love commandment which bids us flee all mortality including the neighbor in favor of the immutable good. (b) The second facet of the *agape* concept of the New Testament which tends to be obscured is the notion of sacrificial love, the absurd principle of the Cross, the insistence that the self must sacrifice itself for the other. It is not fair to Augustine to say that he neglects this facet of meaning for he seems to emphasize it so constantly. He comes closest to its meaning when he deals with the relation of humility to love. Yet it seems fair to say that he was sufficiently imbued by classical mystical thought forms so that the emphasis lies always upon the worthiness or unworthiness of the object of our love; the insistence is that only God and not some mutable "good" or person is worthy of our love. This is a safeguard against all forms of idolatry. But it does not answer another important question: when I love a person or a community do I love myself in them or do I truly love them? Is my love a form of alteregoism? The Augustinian *amor dei* assumes that the self in its smallness cannot contain itself within itself and therefore it is challenged to go out from itself to the most ultimate end. But it hardly reveals the full paradox of self-realization through self-giving which is a scandal in the field of rational ethics as the Cross is a scandal in the field of rational religion. Yet it is the source of ultimate wisdom. For the kind of self-giving which has self-realization as its result must not have self-realization as its conscious end; otherwise the self by calculating its enlargement will not escape from itself completely enough to be enlarged. The weakness of Augustine in obscuring these facets of the *agape* principle may be illustrated, without unfairness I hope, by referring to his treatment of family love. He questions the love of mate or children as the final form of love, but not for New Testament reasons. He does not say: "When you love your wife and children are you maybe really loving yourself in them and using them as the instruments of your self-aggrandisements?" He declares instead, in effect, you must not love your family too unreservedly because your wife and children are mortal. They also belong to the "rivers of Babylon," and, if you give them absolute devotion, the hour of bereavement will leave you desolate. Of course Augustine is too much the Christian to engage in a consistent mystic depreciation of the responsibilities and joys of this earthly life. After all, his whole strategy for the "commingling" of the two cities revolves around the acceptance of the ordinary responsibilities of home and state but in performing these tasks for the ultimate, rather than the immediate end. "What then?" he asks. "Shall all perish who marry and are given in marriage, who till the fields and build houses? No, but those who put their trust in these things, who prefer them to God, who for the sake of these things are quick to offend God, these will perish. But those who either do not use these things or who use them as though they used them not, trusting more in Him who gave them than in the things given, understanding in them His consolation and mercy, and who are not absorbed in these gifts lest they fall away from the giver. These are they whom the day will not overtake as a thief unprepared." [12] We must not, in criticizing Augustine for neo-Platonic elements in his thought, obscure the Christian elements which will be equally an offense to modern men who regard the world as self-sufficing and self-explanatory, who reject as absurd the Christian faith that there is not only a mystery behind and above the world of observed phenomena and intelligible meanings, but that it is a mystery whose meaning has been disclosed as a love which elicits our answering love. This modern generation with its confidence in a world without mystery, and without meaning beyond simple intelligibility, will not be beguiled from its unbelief by a reminder that its emancipation from God has betrayed it into precisely those idolatries, the worship of false gods, the dedication to finite values as if they were ultimate, of which Augustine spoke. But it must be recorded nevertheless as a significant fact of modern history. While it is an offense to regard communism as the inevitable end-product of secularism, as some Christians would have us believe, it is only fair to point out that the vast evils of modern communism come ironically to a generation which thought it would be easy to invest all the spiritual capital of men, who mysteriously transcend

[12] *Comm. on Ps.* cxx, 3.

the historical process, in some value or end within that process; and communism is merely the most pathetic and cruel of the idolatrous illusions of this generation.

We must be clear about the fact that all the illusions about man's character and history which made it so difficult for either the classical or the modern age to come to terms with the vexing problems of our togetherness, seem to stem from efforts to understand man in both his grandeur and his misery by "integrating" him into some natural or rational system of coherence. Thereby they denied the mystery of his transcendence over every process which points to another mystery beyond himself without which man is not only a mystery to himself but a misunderstood being.

We cannot deny that from a Christian standpoint the world is like a "river of Babylon" to use Augustine's symbol; and that Augustine is right in suggesting that ultimately we cannot find peace if we are merely tossed down the river of time. We must find security in that which is not carried down the river. "Observe however," declares Augustine in a simile which will seem strange to generations which have made the "rivers of Babylon," the stream of temporal events, into forces of redemption; but which will not seem so strange as the modern experience proves history as such to be less redemptive than we had believed. "The rivers of Babylon are all things which are here loved, and pass away. For example, one man loves to practice husbandry, to grow rich by it, to employ his mind on it, to get his pleasure from it. Let him observe the issue and see that what he has loved is not a foundation of Jerusalem, but a river of Babylon. Another says, it is a grand thing to be a soldier; all farmers fear those who are soldiers, are subservient to them, tremble at them. If I am a farmer, I shall fear soldiers; if a soldier, farmers will fear me. Madman! thou hast cast thyself headlong into another river of Babylon, and that still more turbulent and sweeping. Thou wishest to be feared by thy inferior; fear Him Who is greater than thou. He who fears thee may on a sudden become greater than thou, but He Whom thou oughtest to fear will never become less. To be an advocate, says another, is a grand thing; eloquence is most powerful; always to have clients hanging on the lips of their eloquent advocate, and from his words looking for loss or gain, death or life, ruin or security. Thou knowest not whither thou hast cast thyself. This too is another river of Babylon, and its roaring sound is the din of the waters dashing against the rocks. Mark that it flows, that it glides on; beware, for it carries things away with it. To sail the seas, says another, and to trade is a grand thing—to know many lands, to make gains from every quarter, never to be answerable to any powerful man in thy country, to be always traveling, and to feed thy mind with the diversity of the nations and the business met with, and to return enriched by the increase of thy gains. This too is a river of Babylon. When will the gains stop? When wilt thou have confidence and be secure in the gains thou makest? The richer thou art, the more fearful wilt thou be. Once shipwrecked, thou wilt come forth stripped of all, and rightly wilt bewail thy fate *in* the rivers of Babylon, because thou wouldest not sit down and weep *upon* the rivers of Babylon.

"But there are other citizens of the holy Jerusalem, understanding their captivity, who mark how human wishes and the diverse lusts of men, hurry and drag them hither and thither, and drive them into the sea. They see this, and do not throw themselves into the rivers of Babylon, but sit down upon the rivers of Babylon and upon the rivers of Babylon weep, either for those who are being carried away by them, or for themselves whose desserts have placed them in Babylon." [13]

Whatever the defects of the Augustine approach may be, we must acknowledge his immense superiority both over those who preceded him and who came after him. A part of that superiority was due to his reliance upon biblical rather than idealistic or naturalistic conceptions of selfhood. But that could not have been the only cause, else Christian systems before and after him would not have been so inferior. Or were they inferior either because they subordinated the biblical-dramatic conception of human selfhood too much to the rationalistic scheme, as was the case with medieval Christianity culminating in the thought of Thomas Aquinas? or because they did not understand that the corruption of human freedom could not destroy the original dignity of man, as was the case with the Reformation with its doctrines of sin, bordering on total depravity and resulting in Luther's too pessimistic approach to political problems? As for secular thought, it has difficulty in approaching Augustine's realism without falling into cynicism or in avoiding nihilism without falling into sentimentality. Hobbes' realism was based on an insight which he shared with Augustine, namely, that in all historical encounters the mind is the servant and not the master of the self. But he failed to recognize that the self which thus made the mind its instrument was a corrupted and not a "normal" self. Modern "realists" know the power of collective self-interest as Augustine did; but they do not understand its blindness. Modern pragmatists understood the irrelevance of fixed and detailed norms; but they do not understand that love must take the place as the final norm for these inadequate norms. Modern liberal Christians know that love is the final norm for man; but they fall into sentimentality because they fail to measure the power and persistence of self-love. Thus Augustine, whatever may be the defects of his approach to political reality, and whatever may be the dangers of a too slavish devotion to his insights, nevertheless proves himself a more reliable guide than any known thinker. A generation which finds its communities imperiled and in decay from the smallest and most primordial community, the family, to the largest and most recent, the potential world community, might well take counsel of Augustine in solving its perplexities.

[13] *Comm. on Ps.* CXXXVI, 3, 4.

11

John of Salisbury
and the Doctrine of Tyrannicide

RICHARD H. ROUSE
MARY A. ROUSE

The doctrine of tyrannicide is a well-known element of John of Salisbury's *Policraticus*.[1] Although John was not the first Western thinker to propose the legitimacy of tyrannicide, the fact that he was the first to expound the idea fully and explicitly entitles him to be called the "author" of the doctrine insofar as concerns twelfth-century Europe.[2] At various times from the thirteenth to the sixteenth century John is cited as authority by actual and would-be tyrannicides, and is condemned as such by their opponents.[3]

Reprinted, by permission, from *Speculum*, 42, 4 (October 1967), 693–709, published by the Mediaeval Academy of America, and with the permission of the authors.
[1] We wish to thank Professor R. D. Face of Wisconsin State College, Stevens Point, and Professor Brian Tierney of Cornell University who read this article in an earlier state and made suggestions for its improvement.
[2] C. H. McIlwain, *The Growth of Political Thought in the West* (New York, 1932), p. 323.
[3] For reference to specific instances, see J. Dickinson, trans., *The Statesman's Book of John of Salisbury* (Books 4–6, selections from 7 and 8 of the *Policraticus*; New York, 1927), pp. lxxiv–lxxv; E. F. Jacob,

The fact, then, that John of Salisbury defended tyrannicide is undeniably true; however, it is not the whole truth. John's exposition of tyrannicide contains many reservations, qualifications, and outright contradictions, including his reiteration of the traditional view that a Christian owes submission to the powers that be. Unfortunately most of the writers on this subject, whether students of John in particular or of mediaeval political theory in general, ignore the contradictions and regard John as an unequivocal advocate of tyrannicide. This assessment appears in studies of John of Salisbury ranging from the full-scale biography by Schaarschmidt to Huizinga's brief essay.[4] As one would expect, the treatment of John as a straightforward proponent of political assassination is emphasized in studies devoted to the history of the right of resistance; [5] and by means of more general surveys of political theory, including such standard works as McIlwain, Sabine, and the Carlyles, this oversimplification of John's position has been given wide currency.[6]

Those writers who do take cognizance of the contradictions are in disagreement when they attempt to explain why John's statement of the principle of tyrannicide contains these inconsistencies. Dunning, for example, says that John "fully [commits] himself to the pagan principle" of tyrannicide, and then recurs "to the primitive Christian idea" of submissiveness; which is to say, John's contradictions are explained by the fact that they are contradictory. Dickinson is at least frank in admitting that, for him, the entire *Policraticus*, including the doctrine of tyrannicide, is com-

"John of Salisbury and the *Policraticus*" (pp. 53–84 in *The Social and Political Ideas of Some Great Mediaeval Thinkers*, ed. F. J. C. Hearnshaw, New York, 1923), pp. 81 f; W. Ullmann, "The Influence of John of Salisbury on Medieval Italian Jurists, *EHR*, 59 (1944), 387.
[4] C. Schaarschmidt, *Johannes Saresberiensis* . . . (Leipzig, 1862), pp. 160, 349; J. Huizinga, "John of Salisbury: A Pre-Gothic Mind" (pp. 159–177 in his *Men and Ideas*, trans. J. S. Holmes and H. van Marle, New York, 1959), pp. 172 f. In addition see M. Demimuid, *Jean de Salisbury* (Paris, 1873), pp. 102–107; Jacob, p. 69; D. D. McGarry, trans., *The Metalogicon of John of Salisbury* (Berkeley and Los Angeles, 1955), p. xviii; R. L. Poole, *Illustrations of the History of Medieval Thought and Learning* (2d ed. rev., London, 1920), pp. 208 f.; Dorotea C. Macedo de Steffens, "La Doctrina del Tiranicidio, Juan de Salisbury (1115–1180) y Juan de Mariana (1535–1621)," *Anales de Historia Antigua y Medieval 1957–1958* (Buenos Aires, 1959), pp. 123–133, esp. p. 129; M. A. Brown, "John of Salisbury," *Franciscan Studies*, 19 (1959), 241–297, esp. p. 289. See also M. Chibnall, trans., *John of Salisbury's Memoirs of the Papal Court* (London, 1956), p. xv, where it is erroneously asserted that "to John only a usurper was to be regarded as a tyrant."
[5] See Johannes Spörl, "Gedanken um Widerstandsrecht und Tyrannenmord im Mittelalter" (pp. 11–32 in Bernard Pfister and Gerhardt Hildmann, *Widerstandsrecht und Grenzen der Staatsgewalt*, Berlin, 1956), pp. 21–26; Peter Meinhold, "Revolution im Namen Christi," *Saeculum*, 10 (1959), 390 f.
[6] McIlwain, pp. 322 f.; G. H. Sabine, *A History of Political Theory* (3d ed., New York, 1961), p. 247; R. W. and A. J. Carlyle, *A History of Mediaeval Political Theory in the West*, vol. III (New York, 1916), pp. 142–146. In addition see, for example, J. B. Morrall, *Political Thought in Medieval Times* (2d ed., London, 1960), p. 44; F. Kern, *Kingship and Law in the Middle Ages* (trans. S. B. Chrimes, Oxford, 1939), pp. 108 f.; J. Bowle, *Western Political Thought* (London, 1954 [1947]), p. 192.

posed of a "more or less confused mass of contradictory ideas." Dal Pra notes that John places certain limitations upon the method to be employed, but states that he maintains the legitimacy and the obligation of killing a tyrant. On the other hand, taking a passage of John's out of context, Ullmann even concludes that John at last "cancelled his previous remarks on the justness of murdering a tyrant."[7]

It seems reasonable to suppose that the problem of John's inconsistent treatment of tyrannicide to a large degree hinges upon the explanation of his motive for including the doctrine of tyrannicide in the *Policraticus;* since this doctrine was not, after all, a commonplace of twelfth-century political theory, there must surely be a reason why John took the trouble to raise the issue. Again, those few writers who deal with the subject present divergent views. For Webb, the question of motive is easily answered: the doctrine of tyrannicide is merely "a natural development of the republican rhetoric which [John] found in classical writers." Liebeschütz feels rather that John was impelled by recent events, that the doctrine of tyrannicide is an expression of retrospective indignation at the tyrannical behavior of certain nobles and mercenaries during Stephen's reign. Wieruszowski agrees that John was moved by recent events; but she suggests that it was the ecclesiastical policy of Roger II of Sicily which "may have dictated to him the passionate terms" in which he deals with tyrants and tyrannicide. Spörl states that John was motivated in large part by bitter resentment against the "Teutonic tyrant" Frederick Barbarossa as a result of the latter's stand in the disputed papal election of 1159; but this idea can surely be dismissed as a chronological impossibility.[8]

The main question, then, is why John proposed the principle of tyrannicide; and its corollary, why his statement of that principle was inconsistent. Through an examination of John's definition of *tyrant,* of John's attitudes pro and con on tyrannicide, and of the significance of the tyrant in John's conception of the commonwealth; and through an evaluation of the political realities of Angevin England, it can be shown that John's doctrine of tyrannicide was written as pure theory with a practical purpose; and that John's self-contradictions have their reasons.

[7] W. A. Dunning, *A History of Political Theories* (New York, 1923), pp. 187 f.; Dickinson, pp. lxvi–lxxxii; M. Dal Pra, *Giovanni di Salisbury* (Milan, 1951), pp. 140–142; Ullmann, p. 388. Hans Liebeschütz, *Mediaeval Humanism in the Life and Writings of John of Salisbury* (London, 1950), pp. 50–52, presents probably the most straightforward description of these contradictions.

[8] C. C. J. Webb, *John of Salisbury* (London, 1932), p. 66; Liebeschütz, pp. 52 f.; Liebeschütz, "Englische und europäische Elemente in der Erfahrungswelt des Johannes von Salisbury," *Die Welt als Geschichte,* 11 (1951), 38–45, esp. p. 41; H. Wieruszowski, "Roger II of Sicily, *Rex-Tyrannus,* in Twelfth-Century Political Thought," *Speculum,* 38 (1963), 46–78, esp. pp. 68–70; Spörl, pp. 21 f.; Spörl, "La Teoria del Tirannicidio nel Medioevo," *Humanitas: Rivista Mensile di Cultura,* 8 (1953), 1013. The *Policraticus* was completed July–Sept. 1159; John does use the term "Teutonicus tyrannus" with reference to Frederick, but only in letters written seven or eight years after this date; cf. epp. 218, 225, Migne, *PL,* cxcix.

First of all, if John is to advocate tyrannicide, he must distinguish between the tyrant and the legitimate ruler, the prince: "Between a tyrant and a prince there is this single or chief difference, that the latter obeys the law" while the former "brings the laws to nought." [9] While John on one occasion suggests that only a usurper can properly be termed *tyrant*,[10] he elsewhere makes it plain that a legitimate prince can turn into a tyrant if he uses his power to contravene the law.[11] So the distinction is clear-cut: a prince obeys the law, a tyrant does not. But John must be pushed for a further definition of terms: what does he mean by *the law*? Although John was never a formal student of law, his writings display a wide acquaintance with both Roman law and canon law.[12] The former he is presumed to have learned from the Bolognese master Vacarius, brought to England by Theobald, Archbishop of Canterbury; and the latter either at the papal Curia or during his years in Theobald's service.[13] However, it is neither the *Corpus Juris Civilis* nor the *Decretum* specifically which John has in mind when he says that the tyrant breaks "the law." Rather, John describes law with a rhetorical flourish as "the gift of God, the model of equity, a standard of justice, a likeness of the divine will, the guardian of well-being, a bond of union and solidarity between peoples, a rule defining duties, a barrier against the vices and the destroyer thereof, a punishment of violence and all wrong-doing." [14] More succinctly, he defines it as "the justice of God . . . [Whose] law is equity," equity being "a certain fitness of things . . . allotting to each that which belongs to him." [15] While this definition,

[9] Unless otherwise indicated, the notes for John's words and ideas refer to book and chapter of the *Policraticus*. The authoritative edition is that of C. C. J. Webb, *Policratici sive de nugis curialium et vestigiis philosophorum libri viii* (2 vols., Oxford, 1909). The translations used are those of Dickinson, cited above, note 3; and J. B. Pike, *Frivolities of Courtiers and Footprints of Philosophers* (Books 1–3, selections from 7 and 8 of the *Policraticus* [Minneapolis, 1938]). IV, 1: "Est ergo tiranni et principis haec differentia sola uel maxima, quod hic legi obtemperat. . . ." Webb, I, 235; Dickinson, p. 3; VIII, 17: ". . . tirannus nil actum putat nisi leges euacuet . . ." Webb, II, 345; Dickinson, p. 335.

[10] III, 15: Webb, I, 232; Pike, p. 211.

[11] VIII, 18, 20: Webb, II, 359 f., 373; Dickinson, pp. 352, 367 f.

[12] Webb has compiled an impressive list of citations in the *Policraticus* from both the *Corpus Juris Civilis* and the *Decretum* (II, 482 f., 486 f.). There are occasional citations from the former in the *Metalogicon*, and from both in letters John wrote during this period (John of Salisbury *Letters* . . . , vol. 1, ed. W. J. Millor and H. E. Butler, revised by C. N. L. Brooke [London, 1955]).

[13] *Letters*, pp. xx–xxiii.

[14] VIII, 17: "Porro lex donum Dei est, aequitatis forma, norma iustitiae, diuinae uoluntatis imago, salutis custodia, unio et consolidatio populorum, regula officiorum, exclusio et exterminatio uitiorum, uiolentiae et totius iniuriae pena." Webb, II, 345; Dickinson, p. 335.

[15] IV, 2: "Nec in eo sibi principes detrahi arbitrentur, nisi iustitiae suae statuta praeferenda crediderint iustitiae Dei, cuius iustitia iustitia in euum est, et lex eius aequitas. Porro aequitas . . . rerum conuenientia est . . . tribuens unicuique quod suum est." Webb, I, 237; Dickinson, p. 6. The sources of this definition of equity are discussed by Brooke, *Letters*, pp. xxi–xxii.

as with all attempts at definition of the "higher law," obviously invited dispute over interpretation and application in specific cases, it was nonetheless meaningful as a general concept. For in equating justice with equity —that "certain fitness of things" which consists of the prince's ruling impartially and rendering to each his due—John, for all his classical and biblical allusions, is essentially identifying justice with custom. When John writes that a tyrant rules contrary to the law, his readers understand him; he means a tyrant is a king who arrogates to himself powers, prerogatives, or possessions which have not traditionally belonged to the king. John does not use the words "customs of the realm" or "natural law" of course; rather, in the manner traditional for a Christian political theorist, he says that the law is "the gift of God." These, too, are words his readers understand.

Given the foregoing definitions, that the law is from God and that the tyrant is a ruler who flouts the law, it logically follows that "it is the grace of God which is being assailed, and that it is God himself who in a sense is challenged to battle." [16] What then must a Christian do if his ruler is a tyrant assailing God? John replies, in the same passage, "the tyrant, the likeness of wickedness, is generally to be even killed." [17] John maintains the legality of tyrannicide "according to both temporal and divine law." [18] In addition to its basis on authority, the legality of tyrannicide is demonstrable by syllogism: a tyrant is judged an enemy of the human race; it is lawful to kill a condemned enemy; therefore, it is lawful to kill a tyrant.[19] Not only is tyrannicide legal and logical, but it has a long-standing precedent in both secular and sacred history. John catalogs, first from Roman history, then from the Old Testament, the tyrants in turn and the violent end of each.[20] He has also, he says, written a book specifically "Of the Ends of Tyrants," a work not extant but seemingly an elaboration of the chapter of the *Policraticus* devoted to Roman tyrants.[21] Besides being legal, logical, and historical, tyrannicide is even a pious act, and one is justified in deceiving, flattering, and disobeying a tyrant, practices which constitute treachery if employed in dealing with a true prince.[22] "It is not merely lawful to slay a tyrant but even right and just," and, this is John's most ex-

---

[16] VIII, 17: ". . . planum est gratiam oppugnari et Deum quodammodo prouocari ad praelium." Webb, II, 345; Dickinson, p. 335.

[17] VIII, 17: ". . . tirannus, prauitatis imago, plerumque etiam occidendus." Webb, II, 345; Dickinson, p. 336.

[18] VIII, 17: ". . . tirannus secularis iure diuino et humano perimitur. . . ." Webb, II, 357; Dickinson, p. 349.

[19] VIII, 19: Webb, II, 371; Dickinson, p. 364.

[20] VIII, 19 and 20: Webb, II, 364–379; Dickinson pp. 358–374.

[21] VIII, 20: Webb, II, 373; Dickinson, p. 367. Webb (*John of Salisbury*, p. 68) doubts that John ever got around to writing the book.

[22] VIII, 20: Webb, II, 376 f.; Dickinson, pp. 370–372; III, 15: Webb, I, 232; Pike, p. 211; VI, 9: Webb, II, 23 f.; Dickinson, p. 201; VI, 12: Webb, II, 32 f.; Dickinson, pp. 212 f.

treme statement, he who does not take action against a tyrant "sins against himself and against the whole body of the secular state." [23]

This, in brief, is John's case for tyrannicide. If this were all he had to say on the subject, his doctrine would be truly anarchical, leaving every private citizen with the permission, indeed the encouragement, to be his own judge and executioner of any ruler who in his own opinion fits the description of a tyrant. But it is impossible to conceive of John of Salisbury as being in any sense a fanatic. To say that his moderation and lack of dogmatism are everywhere manifest in his writings, is scarcely too broad a generalization. John believes that moderation is the essence of virtue, whereas excess is a fault always to be avoided; and, in short, "nought is so splendid or so magnificent that it does not need to be tempered by moderation." [24] This policy of moderation might in a sense be called his philosophy; he proclaims himself to be an Academic [25] (after the fashion of Cicero and the Later Academy)—i.e., one who suspends judgment "in regard to things that are doubtful to a wise man." [26] But John cannot bring himself to be doctrinaire even in support of skepticism. He criticizes those Academics who were so skeptical as to doubt everything, even their senses and their memory; it is all right to "question as long as a matter remains obscure," but "as truth on the bases of probability" appears, a man should acquiesce.[27] John evinces this same moderation vis-à-vis many of the conventional beliefs of his day: Hunting is a frivolous practice which is to be condemned; "the activity, however, is laudable when moderation is shown." [28] Gambling is shameful; "there are, however, times when . . . games of chance are permissible." [29] The making of promises is risky business, and "not conducive to virtue"; "it may be, however, not merely permissible but even desirable to make a promise." [30] Concern with one's dress

---

[23] III, 15: "Porro tirannum occidere non modo licitum est sed aequum et iustum. . . . et quisquis eum [tirannum] non persequitur, in seipsum et in totum rei publicae mundanae corpus delinquit." Webb, I, 232 f.; Pike, pp. 211 f.

[24] IV, 9: Webb, I, 266 f.; Dickinson, p. 43; VIII, 20: ". . . nichil tam praeclarum est aut tam magnificum quod non moderatione desideret temperari." Webb, II, 373; Dickinson, p. 367.

[25] Prologus: Webb, I, 17; Pike, p. 10; Metalogicon, ed. C. C. J. Webb (Oxford, 1929), Prologus, p. 4; McGarry, p. 6; Letters, p. 214.

[26] Metalogicon II, 20, repeated IV, 31: ". . . in his que sunt dubitabilia sapienti. . . ." Webb, pp. 106, 199; McGarry, pp. 128, 251.

[27] VII, 2: Webb, II, 95–98; Pike, pp. 219–221; VII, 7: ". . . dum res obscura est, quaerat; dum probabiliter elucescit ueritas, adquiescat." Webb, II, 117; Pike, p. 239.

[28] I, 4: "Is uero modus laudabilis est, cum moderatione adhibita. . . ." Webb, I, 33; Pike, p. 25.

[29] I, 5: "Est tamen cum in aliqua specie sui [alea] licenter admittitur. . . ." Webb, I, 37; Pike, p. 28.

[30] III, 11 (entitled, "De . . . promissariis, et quod promittere non expediat ad virtutem"): "Fit tamen ut non modo licitum sit promittere sed et conducibile." Webb, I, 209; Pike, p. 190.

and appearance is vanity; "however, if moderation is displayed. . . ." [31]
And on and on, concerning use of food and drink, concerning frugality, education, the permissibility of suicide, the commendability of self-castration, the "universals" controversy, astrology, the worth of Aristotle—from topic to topic John proceeds to expound at length the traditional view of the Church (or of the schoolmen, whichever is applicable to the given topic), and then to conclude abruptly, often in the most startling *non sequitur* fashion, with a brief passage in which John the Academic appears and greatly modifies the overwhelming arguments assembled by John the Dialectician. As he himself says, the Academic "will not presume to state definitely what is true in each and every case." [32]

This non-dogmatic, or better anti-dogmatic, temperament is of course apparent in John's doctrine of tyrannicide just as in the rest of his writings. He does not present his case for tyrannicide in any consistent, integrated whole, as has been attempted above for the sake of demonstration. Instead, his remarks on tyrannicide are scattered in various parts of the *Policraticus;* and scattered with them are statements which soften, modify, or even contradict this doctrine. "None should undertake the death of a tyrant who is bound to him by an oath or by the obligation of fealty; use of poison as the instrument of death is unlawful; tyrannicide is to be effected "without loss of religion and honor." [33] The stipulation about "oath" and "fealty" rather effectively nullifies the legality of killing any tyrant except the ruler of a country other than one's own! Particularly would this be true in England, John's own country, where in theory every free man owed primary fealty to the king, be he tyrant or saint. But to continue, ignoring this technicality, as John himself does, "it is not well to overthrow [tyrants] utterly at once, but rather to rebuke injustice with patient reproof until finally it becomes obvious that they are stiff-necked in evil-doing." [34] So citizens are to wait until the last straw is added to their burden, and even then they are to kill tyrants only "if they can be curbed in no other way." [35] For there is another way in which tyrants can get their due; "wickedness is always punished by the Lord," sometimes through a human instrument, but sometimes with His own hand. Thus God has taken direct action in the

---

[31] VIII, 12: "Verum, si moderatio adhibeatur, in his interdum sensuum uoluptate uersari sapienti non arbitror indecorum. . . ." Webb, II, 315; Pike, p. 373.
[32] *Metalogicon* IV, 31: "Academicus uero fluctuat, et quid in singulis uerum sit diffinire non audet." Webb, p. 199; McGarry, p. 251.
[33] VIII, 20: "Hoc tamen cauendum docent historiae, ne quis illius moliatur interitum cui fidei aut sacramenti religione tenetur astrictus . . . Sed nec ueneni, licet uideam ab infidelibus aliquando usurpatam, ullo umquam iure indultam lego licentiam. Non quod tirannos de medio tollendos esse non credam sed sine religionis honestatisque dispendio." Webb, II, 377 f.; Dickinson, pp. 372 f.
[34] V, 6: ". . . non statim usquequaque deiciuntur, sed patienter corripitur iniustitia, donec fiat conspicuum eos pertinaces esse in malo." Webb, I, 300; Dickinson, p. 85.
[35] VIII, 18: ". . . honestum fuit occidere, si tamen aliter coherceri non poterat." Webb, II, 364; Dickinson, p. 356.

case of such infamous rulers as the Egyptian pharaoh and Nebuchadnezzar and the emperor Julian, and others "whose very names would fill a book." [36] If God is going to see to it that tyrants are punished, why does He bother to permit their existence in the first place? John's answer to this is the traditional one: tyrants are visited as punishment upon a sinful people, and only when the people repent are they permitted to "cast off the yoke from their necks by the slaughter of their tyrants." [37] Indeed, "tyrants are the ministers of God" who will cause the wicked to be punished and the good to be chastened and exercised.[38] All power is good, since all power is from God; hence power is "worthy of veneration even when it comes as a plague upon the elect." John quotes approvingly, "Who, therefore, resists the ruling power, resists the ordinance of God" (Romans XIII 2).[39] Surely, anyone attempting to put into practice John's advice regarding tyrannicide would, in the light of this last admonition, have qualms as to the safety of his immortal soul. Caught between the shame of sinning against himself and the state if he does not take direct action against a tyrant, and the spiritual disaster of resisting the ordinance of God if he does, this hypothetical Christian citizen might well sigh with relief upon reading that "the method of destroying tyrants which is the most useful and the safest, is for those who are oppressed to take refuge humbly in the protection of God's mercy, and lifting up undefiled hands to the Lord, to pray devoutly that the scourge wherewith they are afflicted may be turned aside from them." [40]

Seen in the context of the whole of John's concept of the correct Christian behavior toward tyrants, the doctrine of tyrannicide assumes a more cautious character, to say the least. And his entire discussion of behavior toward tyrants achieves its own proper perspective only when it is seen as merely a part of John's views on rulers in general. For the main literary function served by the tyrant in the *Policraticus* is as a foil to the prince; he is the "horrible example" of everything the prince is not. As to positive advice on what a prince should be, John cites two main authorities, one sacred, one secular. The first of these is Deuteronomy XVII 14–20, which John explains and elaborates in Book IV, chapters 4 through 12. The principal content of this discussion concerns itself with what might best be

[36] And even as it is, John has filled a chapter—VIII, 21: Webb, II, 379–396; Dickinson, pp. 375–393.
[37] VIII, 20: "Licebatque finito tempore dispensationis nece tirannorum excutere iugum de ceruicibus suis. . . ." Webb, II, 374; Dickinson, pp. 368 f.
[38] VIII, 18; Webb, II, 358; Dickinson, p. 350.
[39] VIII, 18; Webb, II, 359; Dickinson, p. 351; IV, 1: "Si itaque adeo uenerabilis est bonis potestas etiam in plaga electorum, quis eam non ueneretur, quae a Domino instituta est. . . ." Webb, I, 236; Dickinson, pp. 4 f.
[40] VIII, 20: "Et hic quidem modus delendi tirannos utilissimus et tutissimus est, si qui premuntur ad patrocinium clementiae Dei humiliati confugiant et puras manus leuantes ad Dominum deuotis precibus flagellum quo affliguntur auertant." Webb, II, 378; Dickinson, p. 373.

termed the private morality of the prince (though John himself would undoubtedly object to any distinction between "private" and "public" in a figure so essentially public as the prince). It consists of a series of admonitions: the prince should not be proud, nor adulterous, nor avaricious, nor too stern nor too lax; and he must know the laws in order to learn to fear God and keep His word.

Curiously enough, however, John does not mention tyrants, the opposite of princes, in this matter of individual spiritual development. Rather, the contrast between tyrant and prince is revealed when the relationship of the ruler to society—the prince *in* the commonwealth—is considered. John's exposition of this relationship is taken, he says, from the *Institutio Trajani* written by Plutarch for the edification of the emperor Trajan.[41] The idea put forth by John's "second authority" is the well-known concept of the commonwealth as a body "endowed with life by the benefit of divine favor," acting "at the prompting of the highest equity," and ruled by "the moderating power of reason." The head of the body is the prince; the soul, the clergy; the heart, the Senate (the prince's mature counselors); the eyes, ears and tongue, the judges and governors of provinces; the hands, the officials and soldiers; the sides, the prince's attendants or courtiers; the stomach and intestines, the financial officers and keepers of the privy chest (and to extend the analogy, John remarks with a twinkle in his eye that these organs are subject to indigestion and constipation); and the feet, the husbandmen.[42] Certainly the microcosm-to-macrocosm analogy was not new in descriptions of the commonwealth; but "it is John of Salisbury who first attempts to apply and work out the comparison in detail."[43] The centrality of this concept to John's entire political theory has always been recognized by students of the *Policraticus;* but the importance of the *Institutio Trajani* has been further enhanced, within recent decades. The nineteenth- and early twentieth-century scholars of John's writings have realized that the *Institutio* was not written by Plutarch, but by someone considerably later—whom, it was impossible to say, since there is no extant copy of the work. In 1943, however, Hans Liebeschütz argued convincingly that the "treatise" was an invention of John himself, a disguise donned to give the weight of classical antiquity to his own ideas. Saverio Desideri has contested this view, presenting a plausible case for fourth- or fifth-century authorship of the work; but even so, he concedes that John's use of it constituted a "rifacimento libero."[44] Therefore, here, in the truest

---

[41] The discussion of the *Institutio Trajani* is, in general, the basis of Books V and VI, and it is frequently referred to in the two concluding books, VII and VIII.
[42] V, 2: Webb, I, 282 f.; Dickinson, pp. 64 f.
[43] Jacob, p. 64.
[44] H. Liebeschütz, "John of Salisbury and Pseudo-Plutarch," *Journal of the Warburg and Courtauld Institutes,* 6 (1943), 33–39, argues thus: (1) that the plan of the pseudo-Plutarch fits John's schema just too perfectly; (2) that that which John claims to be Plutarch sounds no different from that which he admits to be John; (3) that no one else

possible sense, is John of Salisbury's own description of the state: The commonwealth is an integrated, organic whole, as much so as the human body itself; and the well-being of the entire commonwealth depends upon the proper performance by each part of its own proper function, just as the body depends upon all its organs to stay in their places and perform the tasks for which they were created.

Great is the responsibility of the head in John's commonwealth, for it has the task of constraining the other parts of the body to behave properly. With great responsibility, of course, comes great power. "On the prince fall the burdens of the whole community. Wherefore deservedly there is [divinely] conferred on him, and gathered together in his hands, the power of all his subjects. . . ." [45] The prince is the representative of the commonwealth, "in whose place he stands." [46] He is "representative" not in the democratic sense of the word, but rather in the sense that a guardian is the representative of his ward.[47] Since he "bears the public person," the prince also bears a sword and sheds blood blamelessly in protecting the commonwealth from evil-doers.[48] Indeed, in all public matters "his will is to have the force of a judgment; and most properly that which pleases him therein has the force of law." [49]

Thus the powers of the prince are vast. In connection with this fact, much has been made of the point that, nevertheless, John places the prince in a position subordinate to that of the Church.[50] Undeniably he does so.

seems ever to have seen this mysterious document, since all who cite it quote it from John; and (4) that the ideas of the pseudo-Plutarch bear unmistakable similarity to those John learned from Robert Pullen, his former master. A. Momigliano, "Notes on Petrarch, John of Salisbury and the *Institutio Traiani,*" *Journal of the Warburg and Courtauld Institutes,* 12 (1949), 189 f. questions these conclusions, but Liebeschütz's reply (p. 190) seems satisfactory. Liebeschütz's arguments have convinced E. H. Kantorowicz, *The King's Two Bodies* (Princeton, 1957), p. 94, note 20, and they are accepted without question by Chibnall, p. xv, and by Brown, p. 287. S. Desideri, *La "Institutio Traiani"* (Genoa, 1958), feels that Liebeschütz's hypothesis is a slur on John's *bona fides.* He, too, cites the Petrarch reference, but admits that this external evidence is not conclusive (p. 28). His argument rests instead upon textual criticism of the fragments reproduced in the *Policraticus;* and on this basis he has concluded that the treatise did indeed exist, that it was written in the fourth or fifth century by a pagan author, was extensively reworked by a Christian writer of the post-Carolingian period, and was then freely redone by John of Salisbury. The question of whether the treatise did exist, but underwent a "rifacimento libero" by John, as Desideri maintains (p. 47); or whether instead John combined genuine ancient exempla, drawn from various sources, to compose the "treatise" himself, as Liebeschütz contends, is largely a question of degree insofar as the present discussion is concerned.

[45] IV, 1: ". . . principi onera imminent uniuersa. Vnde merito in eum omnium subditorum potestas confertur. . . ." Webb, I, 235; Dickinson, p. 3.

[46] V, 2: ". . . cuius uice fruatur. . . ." Webb, I, 282; Dickinson, p. 64.

[47] V, 7: Webb, I, 308; Dickinson, p. 95.

[48] IV, 2: ". . . in eo personam publicam gerit. . . ." Webb, I, 238 f.; Dickinson, pp. 7 f.

[49] IV, 2: "Eius namque uoluntas in his uim debet habere iudicii; et rectissime quod ei placet in talibus legis habet uigorem. . . ." Webb, I, 238; Dickinson, p. 7.

[50] See, for example, W. Ullmann, *The Growth of Papal Government in the Middle Ages* (2d ed., New York, 1962), pp. 420–426; Webb, *John of Salisbury,* pp. 170–178.

For the clergy are the soul of the commonwealth, and John says (blithely mixing his analogy), "the soul is, as it were, the prince of the body." The prince is subject "to those who exercise [God's] office and represent Him on earth," whereas, as John has stated elsewhere, the Roman Church "is subject only to the judgment of God." [51] He takes the position, unusual for his time,[52] that all authority belongs to the Church; she confers the temporal sword on the prince, or rather employs it by his hand, since it is "unworthy of the hands of the priesthood," while she herself wields the spiritual authority.[53] Also in the troublesome question of interpretation of "the law," John gives the clerics the dominant position. The prince is to read the law "through the medium of the priest's tongue," and "in accordance with their preaching should the ruling power guide the government." [54] It is a mistake, however, to judge from these statements that John conceives of the prince as being forcibly held in line by ecclesiastical authority. For the prince, by definition, voluntarily rules according to law, according to the divine principle of equity; and the clergy, through making the law clear and intelligible to him, are merely aiding the prince to do that which he wishes to do. Elsewhere, John even implies that the prince himself can understand the law, and can govern "guided solely by the judgment of his own mind." [55] After all, in a properly-functioning body politic, the head and the soul are in concert, not at cross purposes. And the parts of the body shall certainly "function properly so long as they follow the guidance of the head, *and the head remains sane.*" [56]

Upon this basic premise, the "sanity of the head," rests the logic of John's entire concept of a Christian commonwealth; this premise denied, his theory of commonwealth becomes utterly unworkable. Herein lies the significance of the tyrant. Since John conceives of the prince as having great, and in a sense unlimited, power, it logically follows that the tyrant has, in direct proportion, great opportunity for evil-doing. A tyrant as head

---

[51] V, 2: ". . . anima totius habet corporis principatum. . . . Princeps uero . . . uni subiectus Deo et his qui uices illius agunt in terris. . . ." Webb, I, 282 f.; Dickinson, pp. 64 f.; Letter 124: ". . . [Romana ecclesia] quae solius Dei reseruatur examini. . . ." *Letters,* p. 206.

[52] The only other definite claim "that all authority, ecclesiastical or secular, belongs to the spiritual power" prior to John, is in the *Summa Gloria* of Honorius of Autun (Jacob, p. 79).

[53] IV, 3: "Est ergo princeps sacerdotii quidem minister et qui sacrorum officiorum illam partem exercet quae sacerdotii manibus uidetur indigna." Webb, I, 239; Dickinson, p. 9.

[54] IV, 6: "Legat itaque mens principis in lingua sacerdotis . . . quia praedicatione eorum debet potestas commissi magistratus gubernacula moderari." Webb, I, 255; Dickinson, p. 28.

[55] V, 6: "Dictum est autem principem locum obtinere capitis, et qui solius mentis regatur arbitrio." Webb, I, 298; Dickinson, p. 83; cf. IV, 6: Webb, I, 250 f.; Dickinson, p. 24.

[56] IV, I: ". . . ut omnia recte moueantur, dum sani capitis sequuntur arbitrium." Webb, I, 235; Dickinson, p. 3; italics added.

corrupts all parts of the body; and the result is a "commonwealth of the ungodly" aping the "civil institutions of a legitimate commonwealth," with a sacrilegious priesthood as its soul, and "its heart of unrighteous counselors"; "its eyes, ears, tongue, and unarmed hand are unjust judges, laws, and officials; its armed hand consists of soldiers of violence whom Cicero calls brigands"; and its feet are rebellious and disloyal husbandmen.[57] (John has been an eye-witness of the moral disintegration of a commonwealth afflicted with "insanity"; the reign of Stephen of Blois, which ended just five years before John is writing, can serve only too well as model for the sketch of the ungodly commonwealth.) The tyrant, using, or rather, abusing, the power of a prince, disregards right and justice.[58] He rules by force, not by law; and he is not satisfied until he has reduced the people to slavery.[59] As ward of the prince, the commonwealth is under his protection; but if the guardian be a tyrant, the commonwealth is at his mercy. The tyrant "will be the ruin of his people." [60]

What resolution for this state of affairs does John's concept of the commonwealth offer? In simple fact, it offers none. The commonwealth is a body with each part assigned its proper function; and John nowhere suggests that it would be "proper" for any presumptuous extremities or visceral organs to take it upon themselves to discipline the head. Such an idea is diametrically opposed to his political philosophy. Logically, if any part of the body were to discipline the head, it would be the soul, the Church. John has set up all the premises, but he does not draw the expected conclusion, either explicitly or implicitly. The closest he comes to doing so, is in his statement that the prince receives his sword from the Church, and that "he who can lawfully bestow can lawfully take away." [61] But with this quotation from Roman law, John lets the matter drop. He does not suggest any means by which the Church might effect the deposition of a tyrant; there is no plan for the taking away of the temporal sword, however "lawful" such action be for the Church. He certainly does not imply that the priesthood is commissioned, nor even permitted, to execute tyrants; wielding the bloody sword is "unworthy of the hands of the

---

[57] VIII, 17: "Habet enim et res publica impiorum caput et membra sua, et quasi ciuilibus institutis legittimae rei publicae nititur esse conformis. Caput ergo eius tirannus est imago diaboli; anima heretici scismatici sacrilegi sacerdotes . . . ; cor consiliarii impii, quasi senatus iniquitatis; oculi, aures, lingua, manus inermis, iudices et leges, officiales iniusti; manus armata, milites uiolenti, quos Cicero latrones appellat; pedes qui in ipsis humilioribus negotiis praeceptis Domini et legittimis institutis aduersantur." Webb, II, 348 f.; Dickinson, p. 339.

[58] VIII, 17: Webb, II, 347; Dickinson, p. 338.

[59] VIII, 17: Webb, II, 345; Dickinson, p. 335.

[60] V, 7: "Rex insipiens perdet populum suum . . . Cum in subiectos potestas saeuit, idem est ac si tutor pupillum persequatur, uel eum suo mucrone iugules, ob cuius defensionem ab eodem traditum tibi gladium accepisti." Webb, I, 308; Dickinson, pp. 94 f.

[61] IV, 3: ". . . eius est auferre qui de iure conferre potest." Webb, I, 241; Dickinson, p. 10.

priesthood." [62] The explanation of the fact that John makes no claim that the clergy may discipline the tyrant seems to be this: that "the head is quickened and governed by the soul" [63] only in the legitimate, godly commonwealth, not in the topsy-turvy commonwealth of the tyrant.[64] It is the proper function of the soul to govern the head; but if the head is not sane, no part of the body functions properly.

Since a "sane head" is the *sine qua non* to the viability of John's concept of commonwealth as macrocosm; and since there is no provision, indeed no possibility, for the restoration of that sanity, once lost, from within the commonwealth; it follows therefore that the solution must come from without. To drop the analogy: God, and God only, punishes tyrants. "All power is from the Lord God" [65]; and tyrants, even non-Christian tyrants, are frequently the ministers of God.[66] In the light of this statement, who but God can possibly have the authority to punish tyrants? God is inexorably thorough in giving tyrants their desserts. But He takes action through varied means; sometimes He makes use of the forces of nature, sometimes He sends an angel to do the task, sometimes He strikes a tyrant with disease, sometimes He even permits a tyrant to live long and die naturally, only to find that his soul is damned to eternal punishment [67]; and sometimes He uses a human hand. Here is the doctrine of tyrannicide reduced to its proper size; it is one weapon from the entire armory at God's disposal. When the doctrine is seen in this perspective, the reason for John's self-contradictory statement of it becomes obvious. Citizens are not empowered to slay tyrants at their own discretion; that power is God's. John takes pains to prove that tyrannicide is permissible and even, at times, an unavoidable duty; but God, not man, will say *whether* and *when* and *how*. John the Academic, who "will not presume to state definitely what is true in each and every case" [68] for any given subject, certainly is not going to attempt to state definitely the will of God in each and every case of rule by tyrant.

In summary, there are three basic factors in the relationship of the tyrant to John's concept of commonwealth: (1) that the commonwealth as an organism can operate properly only provided its head be a true prince; (2)

---

[62] IV, 3: Hunc ergo gladium [sanguinis] de manu Ecclesiae accipit princeps, . . . qui sacrorum officiorum illam partem exercet quae sacerdotii manibus uidetur indigna." Webb, I, 239; Dickinson, p. 9.

[63] V, 2: ". . . ab anima uegetatur caput et regitur." Webb, I, 283; Dickinson, p. 65.

[64] See, for example, the incident of priestly submission to Attila; IV, 1: Webb, I, 236; Dickinson, p. 4.

[65] IV, 1: "Omnis etenim potestas a Domino Deo est. . . ." Webb, I, 236; Dickinson, p. 4.

[66] VIII, 18: Webb, II, 359; Dickinson, p. 351.

[67] VIII, 21: Webb, II, 380–382; Dickinson, pp. 377 f.; VIII, 19: Webb, II, 362 f., 371 f.; Dickinson, pp. 355 f., 365 f.

[68] *Metalogicon* IV, 31: ". . . quid in singulis uerum sit diffinire non audet." Webb, p. 199; McGarry, p. 251.

that should the head, on the contrary, be a tyrant, an impasse results from the lack of any authority within the commonwealth qualified to remove him; and (3) that this conflict can be resolved only by God, Who may or may not choose to work through a human hand.

Finally, what was John's purpose in including a discussion of tyrannicide in the *Policraticus?* Obviously John had not the slightest intention that someone would read his book, be inspired thereby, and kill Henry II of England; aside from the fact that this would be a foolish and foolhardy notion for any subject of Henry's to propound, John still at this time (1159) had hopes that Henry, with the proper guidance, would prove to be the true prince that Stephen had so miserably failed to be. It is equally important to realize that John did not intend to suggest, even hypothetically, that assassination is the normal recourse against a wicked king; nor did he suppose that any such radical interpretation would be placed on his words by readers of the *Policraticus.* After all, John wrote the book for the royal chancellor Thomas Becket, Henry's closest and most trusted companion. And while John intended the *Policraticus* for Becket's personal edification, he hoped that his book would influence the king as well. As Liebeschütz says, John "desired that when the chancellor had been enlightened by study of his book, he would try to lead the youthful King back to the right path. . . ." [69] Moreover, John evidently intended that the *Policraticus* should influence the king directly. This is suggested in the *Entheticus,* the prefatory poem in which John instructs his book on its duties. For one thing, the form of the *Entheticus* is modeled on Ovid's introduction to the *Tristia,* which he was sending to Rome to plead his cause with Augustus; the analogy would seem to be that John hoped the *Policraticus* would reach his "Augustus," Henry II.[70] Stronger evidence is the fact that one passage in the *Entheticus* unmistakably reveals John advising his book on how to behave in the king's presence: "Do not display what may the prince's eye affront, on whom alone thy life and welfare hang; . . . what he forbids is wrong, what he enjoins is right; laws stand by him or fall. 'Tis virtue only pleases him and so by virtue only shalt thou please. . . ." [71] Mere prudence would dictate that John should not appear to the king as the proponent of a revolutionary doctrine; on the contrary, John was eager that his book should not offend at court. His dedication of the book to

---

[69] Liebeschütz, *Mediaeval Humanism,* p. 17.
[70] The *Entheticus* is described and discussed briefly in Liebeschütz, pp. 19 f., and Webb, *John of Salisbury,* pp. 22–24.
[71] "Non tamen ostendas, oculos quod principis urat, / A quo tota tibi uita salusque datur. / . . . Quod prohibet fieri, scelus est; quod praecipit, aequum: / Iuraque pro placito stantque caduntque suo. / Huic quia sola placet, sola uirtute placebis. . . ." Webb, I, 3, lines 3–9; Pike, p. 417. There is an abrupt shift here in John's narrative, for in the lines immediately preceding he has instructed the book to find Becket; however, the only conceivable interpretation of the terminology used in the lines quoted here and in those immediately following is that they refer to the king himself.

Thomas, and the passages in the *Entheticus* nominating the chancellor as the book's "guardian" against critics at court,[72] suggest that John wanted Becket to see to it that the *Policraticus* was favorably received. As an added precaution, before dispatching the *Policraticus* to Becket, John sent it to his closest friend Peter of Celle for Peter to remove passages which might give offense: "I should not like it to make me an enemy to the courtiers. I beg you to start on its improvement without delay, and as soon as it has received your castigation, send it back to your expectant friend."[73] These factors—the book's intended "reading public," and John's desire to avoid offending—clearly prove that John was not, even in hypothesis, propounding the doctrine of tyrannicide as a plan of action. The book's discussion of tyrannicide should not distract attention from the obvious fact that the *Policraticus* is, after all, a prince manual, as scholars have readily recognized.[74] It is what its pseudo-Greek title proclaims it: The Statesman's Book.

The main portion of the political theory of the *Policraticus* is positive in tone, intended to describe to the king and his chancellor the kind of commonwealth John hoped they would govern and the kind of prince he hoped Henry would be. But there is always the possibility, on the negative side, that any true prince may become a tyrant by deciding to rule contrary to the law of equity. Unfortunately, this possibility was disquietingly apparent in John's own particular true prince; John was definitely apprehensive concerning Henry II's future intentions toward the Church. In order to explain these fears, it is necessary to examine briefly the relationship between the Church and the Crown during the first years of Henry's reign, and to note the prospects for the future.

At the time of the completion of the *Policraticus* (late summer 1159) John was secretary to Theobald, Archbishop of Canterbury. John had held this post for a number of years (since 1154 at least, and possibly since as early as 1148),[75] and was a staunch supporter of the archbishop and of the rights of the See of Canterbury. From the very beginning of the reign, Theobald, who had used his quite considerable influence to promote the Angevin succession, had claims on Henry's gratitude. As added insurance of the king's goodwill Theobald secured the appointment of royal chancellor for his protégé, the Archdeacon of Canterbury Thomas Becket. There seemed to be good prospects for a period of amicable relations between

---

[72] Webb, I, 2, lines 1–6; Pike, pp. 415 f.

[73] Letter 111: "Nollem tamen quod me curialibus faceret inimicum. Precor ut eum incunctanter erudiatis, eumque expectanti amico remittite castigatum. . . ." *Letters*, p. 182.

[74] See, for example, W. Berges, *Die Fürstenspiegel des hohen und späten Mittelalters*, *M.G.H. Schriften* II (Stuttgart, 1938); W. Kleineke, *Englische Fürstenspiegel vom Policraticus Johanns von Salisbury bis zum Basilikon Doron König Jakobs 1* (Halle, 1937).

[75] C. N. L. Brooke presents the most convincing chronology of John's early years; *Letters*, pp. xii–xxiv.

Church and State; but the actuality proved disappointing to the Church.

For one thing, Becket's behavior disillusioned both Theobald and John. There is no need to detail once more the familiar story of Becket's shift of allegiance to his new royal master. His eager adoption of the more extravagant modes of court life seems to have dismayed his old friend John of Salisbury; for surely many parts of the *Policraticus* dealing with "the frivolities of courtiers" are friendly barbs aimed at Thomas.[76] The very elaborateness with which John exempts Becket from his criticism indicates a gentle irony: "I am not endeavoring to restrain you from clothing yourself gaily in gold embroidered raiment; from feasting sumptuously every day; from holding high office; . . . from humoring the times and even perverse morals, upright as you personally are in all matters; and from mocking a world which mocks its own cajolery. Though it has already caught many, you are too great to allow yourself to be caught by its snares." [77] As for Theobald, his sentiments toward Becket were those of a father for a wayward son; the depth of his feeling is revealed in his last letter to Thomas, asking, commanding, pleading (in vain) that Becket come to see him once more before he dies.[78] But more serious than these purely personal considerations is the fact that Becket proved a disappointment to Theobald and John in their endeavor to maintain ecclesiastical liberties. Theobald's intent when he obtained the chancellorship for Becket was that Becket should guard the interests of the Church; but with Thomas now seconding the king's opinion in all things, he obviously could not be depended upon to oppose any royal encroachment on ecclesiastical rights.

The See of Canterbury, then, would have to depend upon its own efforts to resist royal interference. Assuredly Theobald had proved competent to protect the Church's interests even during the uncertainties of Stephen's last years; but Theobald had been ill continuously since 1156, and by summer 1159 he knew he was dying.[79] At the time when he was completing the *Policraticus* John doubtless had this question weighing on his mind: who will protect the Church once Theobald is gone, if Henry should determine to violate the law of equity? In John's letters, whether written in his own or in Theobald's name,[80] he clearly reveals his anxiety for the

---

[76] *E.g.*, the discussion of hunting (I, 4), gaming (I, 5), indulgence in feasting (VIII, 10), extravagance in dress (VIII, 12).

[77] VIII, 25: "Nec inhibeo quin uestibus niteas deauratis circumdatus uarietate, quin epuleris cotidie splendide, quin primos honores habeas; . . . quin tempori sed et peruersis moribus, rectus tamen ut es ipse, in omnibus morem geras et suis lenociniis irridentem irrideas mundum. Maior enim es quam ut debeas aut possis (licet iam sic ceperit multos) capi tendiculis eius." Webb, II, 423 f.; Pike, p. 410.

[78] Letter 129, Abp. Theobald to Thomas Becket (c. Sept. 1160), *Letters,* pp. 224 f.; cf. A. Saltman, *Theobald Archbishop of Canterbury* (London, 1956), pp. 45, 168 f.

[79] Letter 22, Abp. Theobald to Thomas Becket (late 1156), contains many phrases showing that Theobald is already expecting death; *Letters,* pp. 35 f. and n. 2.

[80] See *Letters,* p. xxxviii, for a discussion of John's role in the writing of letters ostensibly by Theobald.

future—his fears that the king may "bring the laws to nought," tyrant-fashion, with regard to the Church.

In one letter to Henry there is a reference, with a vagueness no doubt deliberate, to unspecified persons "who, as is well known, are plotting" against Theobald and the Church; John goes on to say that Theobald, whose "days will be brief," is anxious about the church of Canterbury and that it would be most laudable if the king would "preserve that church unscathed." [81] A slightly later letter to Henry is more pointed in its expression of fears for the future and of hopes that the fears will prove groundless: "If you desire, or rather, since you desire that Christ should be propitious to you," seek the favor of the Church, for he who lacks the Church's favor "has the whole Trinity, his creator, for his foe." John is especially outspoken in the passage which follows: "The sons of this world counsel you to lessen the authority of the Church that your royal power may be increased. But assuredly they wrong your majesty and, whoever they may be, bring down . . . the indignation of God. . . . It is utterly iniquitous that you should impair the glory of your Benefactor and Lord. It is a sin that deserves punishment and assuredly its punishment shall be very bitter; or rather by God's blessing, the penalty shall be averted, since by God's blessing the crime shall be averted." [82] It is clear that John is not censuring Henry for a past breach of equity, but rather that he and Theobald are fearful for the future. Evidently they felt that Henry had designs upon the Church and was awaiting the proper moment to effect his plans—that he was, perhaps, simply biding his time until Theobald's death. (Modern scholarship, with the advantage of hindsight, would support their diagnosis.) [83] In fact, John explicitly suggests this to be the case, with regard to one specific matter: In a letter to Becket concerning an election to the vacant See of Exeter, John says, "If you delay to give effect to this petition until the king comes home, [the archbishop] will think that you are seeking to delay the matter until his death." [84]

[81] Letter 116, Abp. Theobald to King Henry II (early 1160): "Et sunt nonnulli eorum, sicut celebre est, in insidiis personae aut ecclesiae nostrae. . . . Amodo enim iam breues erunt dies nostri. . . . Nec est quod uestram magis deceat excellentiam, quam ut eam [ecclesiam Cantuariensem] seruetis indempnem." *Letters*, p. 191.

[82] Letter 127, Abp. Theobald to King Henry II (June–July 1160): "Si uultis, immo quia uultis Christum habere propitium, sponsam eius (quae est ecclesia . . .) studeatis habere propitiam. Nam cui deest gratia ecclesiae tota creatrix Trinitas aduersatur. Suggerunt uobis filii saeculi huius ut ecclesiae minuatis auctoritatem ut uobis regia dignitas augeatur. Certe uestram inpugnant maiestatem et indignationem Dei procurant quicumque sunt illi . . . ; poena dignum est et proculdubio poena acerbissima punietur, immo Deo propitio non punietur quia ipso propitiante non fiet." *Letters*, p. 220. We know from John's own testimony that the language employed in this case is his own; see Letter 128, John to Thomas Becket (*c*. September 1160), *Letters*, p. 221.

[83] Cf. Z. N. Brooke, *The English Church & the Papacy* (Cambridge, 1952), p. 189.

[84] Letter 128: "Noueritis autem quia, si distuleritis usque ad aduentum domini regis petitionis effectum, eo ipso putabit quod in mortem eius dilatio quaeratur." *Letters*, p. 223. In this particular case John's suspicion was unfounded; Theobald's candidate received royal approval just before the archbishop's death.

An attempt to connect the views quoted above with the doctrine of tyrannicide in the *Policraticus* may seem to be weakened by the fact that these letters postdate 1159. However, they are all written within the twelve months following John's completion of the *Policraticus,* and it seems unlikely that there had been a sudden change in Church-State relations during this period.[85] Much rather, the opinions expressed in the letters represent a sentiment of disquiet and distrust of the Crown which had been growing at Canterbury for three or four years.[86] This sense of foreboding even appears in the *Policraticus* itself, in a cryptic passage which constitutes one of the very few topical references in that work: At the end of a chapter devoted to praising the past deeds of the young king, John concludes that his own talents will be unequal to describing Henry's greatness, "if his future course shall be long and prosperous according to the measure of the grace which has been bestowed on him in the past. However, the period which marks the end of a man's youth is looked upon by some with suspicion, and may it prove that the fears of the good are groundless!" [87]

The precise reasons for these fears are hard to determine. Perhaps they represent in large measure mere surmise on John's part, based on his realization that Henry II, especially when compared with Stephen, was a strong king—strong, and thus potentially difficult, from the Church's standpoint. However, there are certain actions of Henry's prior to the completion of the *Policraticus* which may have seemed to John indicative of tyrannical tendencies. For one thing, John was in serious disfavor with the king from autumn 1156 until Easter 1157; while the exact cause of Henry's anger is unknown, John indicates in his correspondence that the king was indignant over John's defense of ecclesiastical liberties.[88] In describing his plight, John implies that Henry constantly interfered with the freedom of canonical elections and with the functioning of ecclesiastical courts: "If the English Church ventures to claim even the shadow of liberty in making elections or in the trial of ecclesiastical causes, it is imputed to me. . . ." [89] (While scholars today may dispute the validity of this accusation, particu-

---

[85] Of course, there is the papal schism dating from the double election in September 1159; while the concerns evidenced in the quoted passages refer specifically to the problems of the English Church, surely the anxiety at Canterbury must have been increased by the lack of a recognized head of the universal Church.

[86] That is to say, at least since the time of John's disgrace in 1156.

[87] VI, 18: ". . . si iuxta praecedentis gratiae cursum sibi diu successerint prospera. . . . Ceterum adolescentiae exitus aliquibus suspectus est, et utinam frustra a bonis timeatur." Webb, II, 54; Dickinson, p. 237.

[88] Letter 19, John to Peter abbot of Celle (autumn 1156), *Letters,* pp. 31–32. The dating of this fall from grace, a major revision in the chronology of John's life and writings, was accomplished by Giles Constable, "The Alleged Disgrace of John of Salisbury in 1159," *EHR,* 69 (1954), 67–76; Constable's findings are summarized by Brooke, *Letters,* Append. II, pp. 257 f.

[89] Letter 19: "Quod in electionibus celebrandis, in causis ecclesiasticis examinandis uel umbram libertatis audet sibi Anglorum ecclesia uendicare, michi inputatur. . . ." *Letters,* p. 32.

larly when applied to the first years of Henry's reign,[90] the only fact which is relevant for our purposes is that John believed the accusation to be true.) Besides the questions of Church elections and ecclesiastical jurisdiction, John was also concerned with Henry's infringement of the Church's financial rights, as exemplified by the levy of 1159. For the purpose of his Toulouse campaign Henry assessed not only the ordinary tax, the scutage, which the Church had paid previously in 1156 (with perhaps some minor grumbling)[91]; he also, "contrary to ancient custom and due liberty," levied an arbitrary "contribution, or rather exaction" from the Church, which totaled four times the amount of the scutage proper. As John complained, the Church had not even the slim consolation of sharing this burden with the lay lords; the arbitrary tax fell on Church fees only.[92] Certainly if equity consists of "allotting to each that which belongs to him," then John as a churchman considered Henry's action in levying this tax a breach of equity. Knowledge of these previous royal transgressions undoubtedly contributed to John's premonition of future royal assaults upon ecclesiastical rights.

Therefore, in writing the *Policraticus*, John felt it his duty to inform rulers in general, but obviously Henry II in particular, that princes do not break the law of God with impunity; that God always punishes wickedness, without fail. As it has been shown above, tyrannicide is but one of God's weapons. However, John is being realistic when he chooses this particular weapon to emphasize. Henry was no Louis VII, to be panicked easily into penitence. He was not one to quiver with terror over the threat of divine thunderbolts or the distant prospect of eternal damnation. But tyrannicide is something else again; to speak of God's directing possible human action against him was to speak in terms that Henry understood.

Thus, John of Salisbury's doctrine of tyrannicide is both theoretical and practical. The doctrine of tyrannicide is purely theoretical, in the sense that John was not proposing it as a plan of action. But it is theory with this practical purpose, that John hoped thereby to convince Henry that, for his own good, he must rule in accordance with the law. The doc-

[90] Cf. Z. N. Brooke, pp. 189, 198 f.; H. G. Richardson and G. O. Sayles, *The Governance of Mediaeval England* (Edinburgh, 1963), Ch. XVI, "Church and State in the Twelfth Century," especially pp. 302 f.
[91] Letter 13, John to William bishop of Norwich (spring–summer 1156), indicates some sort of mild protest to the king on this occasion; *Letters,* pp. 21 f.
[92] Ep. 145, John to Bartholomew bishop of Exeter (1166): ". . . Tolosam bello aggressurus, omnibus contra antiquum morem et debitam libertatem indixit ecclesiis, ut pro arbitrio eius, satraparum suorum conferrent in censum, nec permisit ut ecclesiae saltem proceribus coaequarentur in hac contributione uel magis exactione tam indebita quam iniusta." Migne, *PL,* cxcix, 134. It should be noted that John is writing here with the advantage of seven years' hindsight; however, Liebeschütz, *Mediaeval Humanism,* p. 14, believes that "this judgment is certainly not a projection into the past of experiences in the period of Becket's struggles with the king." The details of the levy of 1159 are worked out by J. H. Round, *Feudal English* (London, 1909), pp. 275–279.

trine of tyrannicide is a symbol (not the only one, but the one most easily understood in human terms) of the fact that, though God acts in mysterious ways—ways so mysterious that John cannot give a consistent, uncontradictory statement of them—He invariably *does* act against tyrants.

12

St. Thomas Aquinas
as a Political Philosopher

MAURICE CRANSTON

Lord Acton once spoke of St. Thomas Aquinas as "the first Whig." It is a striking phrase, and one still often finds it quoted in textbooks and in candidates' answers to questions about Aquinas in examinations in the history of political thought. But it is not a remark that stands up to much reflection. Aquinas believed, assuredly, in freedom and natural rights and government by consent; but there is no clear evidence that he thought men had a right to rebellion; he explicitly rejected the theory of the social contract; and as for the "natural right" that interested the Whig theorists most—the right to property—Aquinas denied that it was, strictly speaking, a natural right at all.

One thing Aquinas undoubtedly was, and that is a Christian philosopher; and, indeed, he is by common consent the greatest of Christian philosophers. Many of his ideas were anticipated by other medieval writers but, even so, he gave to Christian civilization a systematic and rational philosophy of a kind it had not known before, and

This article was originally published in *History Today*, 14 (May 1964), 313–317. It is reprinted here with the permission of the author.

one that the greater body of Christian, and especially Catholic speculation has continued ever since to use as a basis of departure. Before Aquinas started teaching in the thirteenth century, the main stream of Christian thought had been anti-rationalistic, if not anti-philosophical. Religion was seen to be based on faith, and reason was thought to be inimical to faith. Aquinas set out to reconcile faith and reason, and to do so by forging a union of Christian revelation with Greek philosophy, and notably with Aristotle, of whom a knowledge had been revived in Europe, thanks largely to the work of Arab scholars.

Aquinas was born in 1225, or thereabouts, into a noble Italian family at Roccasecca near Aquino. As an undergraduate at the then newly founded university of Naples, he resolved to enter the Dominican Order. His family objected, but Aquinas persisted, and he went to Paris to study under the most eminent of Dominican scholars, Albertus Magnus. Albertus had a prodigious knowledge of all the then known Greek, Roman and Arabic philosophies, and was the author of commentaries on each of the recognized books of Aristotle. Aquinas learned all that Albertus had to teach, and then followed his footsteps in the career of a university scholar; he taught at the universities of Cologne, Rome, and Naples as well as Paris, and had some experience of service in the Papal Court. He was less than fifty years of age when he died, leaving a voluminous number of writings on theological and philosophical subjects.

These works are written in the scholastic form, in which the argument is developed in a series of proposals and objections. This does not make for easy reading. Besides, Aquinas used the method of dictation to a secretary, and his style lacks the elegance of the earlier divines.[1] There is also some uncertainty, in such works as his commentaries on Aristotle, as to whether Aquinas is merely paraphrasing the original or indicating his own agreement. Moreover, there are still doubts as to which parts of the works traditionally ascribed to Aquinas were genuinely his. He is, therefore, one of the most difficult philosophers to write about with confidence; and any short sketch of his views must inevitably be a crude one.

Aquinas' political philosophy, like his metaphysics and ethics, was the fruit of his union of Christian with pagan theories. In the process, he rejected one central notion in traditional Christian thinking about the state and enlarged another. The notion he rejected was one that had been laid down nine centuries before by the greatest of his predecessors, St. Augustine: namely, that political societies came into being only as a result of the Fall of Man, and were devised as an artificial corrective to sin. Against this belief, Aquinas put forward the Aristotelian theory that man is by nature a political and social animal. Society, on this view, is prior to the individual. Man was designed by nature to live in community; to live, that is to say,

[1] See T. Gilby, *Principality and Power*, 1958, pp. 272–274.

not only in a family, but under common government with his neighbours in a state. Men, for Aquinas, are thus united by nature; societies were not introduced either by conquest or by a social contract; they do not exist simply to preserve tranquillity or protect interests; they exist because men are naturally members of one another, and because men's nature is such that a truly human life is impossible for man unless he lives as a member of a political community.

For Aquinas to say, as a Christian, that men were designed by nature for society is equivalent to saying that they were so designed by God; and, recognizing this, Aquinas went on to repudiate a further Augustinian notion: the notion that all terrestrial cities are pervaded by evil, so that all Christian hopes for life in a good society must be laid up in the world to come. Aquinas believed that justice could be made to prevail in this world; that the political community had its own dignity and honour; and that it was possible to speak of a Christian order for the government of man on earth.

Aquinas was not, however, like some of his contemporaries, a champion of theocracy. He had no wish to see priests as secular princes, or the Pope as the political emperor of Christendom. The fellowship of the Church was, of course, more exalted in his eyes than the community of the state, but he considered that the province of religion was plainly distinguishable from the province of politics, and that the arts of statesmanship and law required a different skill from the vocation of holy orders. Besides the fellowship of the Church was universal, and Aquinas followed Aristotle in thinking of the state as something limited in size and number of inhabitants. Hence, although there was only one Church, there were, and should be, many states. In thinking thus, Aquinas revealed himself not only an Aristotelian but also a man of the modern world—a world in which the old Christian ideal of a universal holy empire had perished in face of the reality of ever more vigorously independent nation states.

And yet in this Aquinas was in no sense a mere reviver of Aristotle. For he improved on Aristotle's notion of the state as a natural institution by incorporating an idea that, though not Christian in origin, had become a crucial notion in Christian thinking: that of Natural Law. His point here is not difficult to follow. It is natural for men to live under government; but governments do not fully conform to nature unless they are just: and the criterion of justice is something laid down by the Creator, and visible to the eye of reason in all men. In other words, the positive law of states must conform to those fundamental moral principles traditionally known as Natural Law. Aristotle himself sometimes spoke of Natural Law, but he did not mean what Aquinas meant when he used the same term; and Aristotle had no conception, as Aquinas had of natural rights. Aristotle's thinking was shaped by the *ethos* of the city state; the good man is the good citizen; the moral law is the command of society—a view that leaves little room for discussing whether society itself is right or wrong. But even Aristotle was not content with this; nor, indeed, were certain other Greeks. Sophocles' play *Antigone*, for example, turns on a dispute between King Creon, who expounds the view now known as legal positivism, and Antigone, who defends what was later known as natural law and natural rights. Creon claims that the law is the voice of the sovereign, and must always be obeyed; Antigone insists that the positive law is not valid if it is contrary to the "edicts of heaven" or denies the fundamental rights of man: in the play, she claims that her brother has a natural right to burial. Antigone's view, astonishing to many of Sophocles' contemporaries, became fashionable with the Stoic philosophers after the breakdown of the city states, and passed through Rome to Christianity. The attraction of such a notion to Christians is obvious; for Natural Law can be understood as divine law, about which the Church, as opposed to the State, can speak with authority; and once the Church is recognized as the ultimate arbiter as to what is just and unjust, its superiority over the state, and its authority to criticize the state, is logically entailed.

Aquinas articulated a more elaborate theory of Natural Law than any of his predecessors. Not that it is without a certain ambiguity; and part of its ambiguity stems from the dual role that is assigned to Nature in Aquinas' theory. Natural Law for him is both descriptive and normative, both biological and moral. Nature is everything that *is*, apart from what is artificial; but Nature is also everything that *should be*. There is a Natural Law, which prevails; and a Natural Law that commands: the Natural Law of science and the Natural Law of ethics. The Natural Law of science puts men into society; but the Natural Law of ethics demands that every society shall be a just one. Men cannot help living in communities; that is part of the human condition. But men, who have free will, must by their own efforts order their societies justly, and bring their community into harmony with Nature's ends.

Aquinas distinguishes Natural Law from Eternal Law as well as from positive law; and it is not always easy to follow him in some of the distinctions he makes between the natural and supernatural. For example, he shows how Nature ordains that men and women shall unite in families and reproduce their own kind; but, at the same time, he insists that the vocation of the priesthood, which entails a renunciation of this natural way of life, is somehow of higher moral value. Aquinas is strongly opposed to those Christian intellectuals, however, who would like to see the clergy enact the role of Platonic guardians in a society governed by "philosophers." Aquinas, like Aristotle, has no patience with such utopian dreams; he believes in "natural" forms of government, which have been experienced in history.

Moreover, although he repudiates the theory according to which all societies derive from a social contract, Aquinas still looks for a marked contractual element in the actual constitution of a just society. "Properly a

law is first and foremost an ordinance for the common good; and the right
to ordain anything for the common good belongs either to the whole multitude or someone who represents the whole multitude." [2] This is not to say
that Aquinas was a democrat, for he was not. He thinks the best earthly
city will be, like heaven itself, a monarchy. But he insists that government
must be representative; it must rest on consent; indeed, Aquinas goes so far
as to recommend that the monarchy should be elective. At the same time,
he assigns a special function of leadership and administration to an aristocracy. Here, again, we can see an echo of Aristotle's idea of a "mixed constitution," with elements of monarchy, aristocracy and democracy combined.

Although Aquinas has a great deal to say about how a just society
should be arranged, he never forgets that certain governments in the real
world are tyrannical. He is far from suggesting that a Christian is obliged
only to obey the edicts of a truly Christian, or just government. For obedience to governments is part of the natural order of things; and it is only if
a ruler issues an edict that is manifestly at variance with Natural Law that
the Christian may disobey. Unjust laws have no moral validity. Aquinas is,
in fact, reluctant to give the name "law" to any edict that is contrary to the
basic principles of justice: "Laws of this kind are acts of violence rather
than laws . . . they do not bind in conscience unless observance of them is
required to avoid public scandal or public disturbance." [3]

The reservation about "public scandal" and "public disturbance"
makes it hard to decide how far Aquinas was willing to concede the right
of revolt against tyranny; but plainly Aquinas did not think any considerations, other than prudence, obliged men to obey a tyrant. Even so, he saw
that prudence was an important virtue in political life. "Prudence applies
principles to particular issues; consequently it does not establish moral
purpose, but contrives the means thereto." [4] He would not have approved
of reckless resistance to tyranny, or of foolish "civil disobedience."

Aquinas never enumerated the "natural rights of man" in the style of
later philosophers; nor would he have agreed with those who, like Locke,
summed up those rights as the rights of life, liberty and property. The right
to life Aquinas certainly believed in; and, indeed, he gave it a richer content than Locke did. For Locke the right to life meant only the right to be
preserved from acts of aggression by others. But for Aquinas the right to
life meant the right to a decent or honourable way of living. It also entails
the *duty* of self-preservation. Thus, whereas Locke explicitly denied that
the right to life meant that a starving man had the right to steal a loaf of
bread, Aquinas maintained that it was no theft for a starving man to help
himself to bread that belonged, in positive law, to another.[5]

[2] *Summa Theologica*, II–I, 90, 3.
[3] *Summa Theologica*, Ia, IIae, 96, 4.
[4] *Summa Theologica*, IIa, IIae, 47, 7.
[5] *Summa Theologica*, IIa–IIae, 66, 2. See also Gilby, p. 156.

Aquinas, in fact, was unwilling to regard the right to property as one of the natural rights of man at all. There was, assuredly, such a thing as the right to property; but this was an *addition* to Natural Law, a device of prudence, and based on the purely utilitarian consideration that private property was conducive to economic growth and the common good. A true natural right, such as the right to life, was therefore far more compelling in morality than this additional right; hence the justice of the starving man's claim to take what he was not given. Aquinas reveals an even more marked dissent from later Whig or bourgeois theory by reaffirming the old Christian teaching that usury is wrong; and he gives a good Aristotelian reason for doing so. "To lend money at usury is grave sin . . . because it is against natural justice. For someone who lends money on the understanding that he will receive it back, and in addition makes a charge for the use of it . . . is selling the same thing twice, and this is plainly contrary to natural justice." [6]

Aquinas, again, never speaks of the "natural right to liberty" in the manner of the Whig theorists. Liberty he was inclined to regard rather as a feature of a justly ordered commonwealth than as an inalienable right of the individual. Indeed, it was part of his purpose to show, against some of his more individualistic and anti-political predecessors, that liberty and government go together, and the subordination of one man to another in a political community should not be confounded with the subjection of one man to another in the institution of slavery. And he maintains that liberty is successfully combined with government whenever the man who rules directs others to act, either in ways that are conducive to their own personal good or to the good of all. For, in this way, the ruler is instructing the people to act as they themselves would wish to act; and thus there is brought about in a properly governed society a harmony between what men want to do and what they ought to do, between natural drives and Nature's ends.

[6] *Disputations*, XIII, *de Malo*, 4.

13

St. Thomas Aquinas
on Political Obligation

A. P. D'ENTRÈVES

If political institutions are an aspect of "natural" morality, this means that the justification of the State and the ground of political obligation must be sought in the very nature of man. This is precisely the leading idea which St. Thomas derives from Aristotle. Few expressions are repeated so often, every time St. Thomas approaches the problem of politics, as that *homo naturaliter est animal politicum et sociale (ut Philosophus dicit, ut probatur in I° Politicae,* etc.). The words are significant. William of Moerbecke, whose Latin translation of the *Politics* was the source of St. Thomas's knowledge of Aristotle's work, had translated the Aristotelian expression πολιτικόν ζῷον with the words *animal civile*. St. Thomas maintained this expression in his Commentary on the *Politics,* but he constantly used *animal politicum et sociale* in all his other works. It is not so much a question as to whether they are a more correct rendering of Aristotle's thought. What is interesting is the empha-

This exerpt was originally published as part of the Introduction to A. P. d'Entrèves (ed.), *Aquinas: Selected Political Writings,* trans. J. G. Dawson (Oxford: Basil Blackwell & Mott, Ltd., 1949), pp. vii–xxiii. Reprinted by permission.

sis which is laid upon the social character of politics. Man is a political animal because he is a social being. This means that the State must have its roots in social experience, that it cannot be, or cannot be solely, the creation of human will. The State is not a work of art, but a historical product. It is the highest expression of human fellowship. All that pertains to that fellowship is natural to man. All that renders it possible is open to rational enquiry and susceptible of rational justification.

St. Thomas never tires of emphasizing the importance of the political nature of man. In one place he describes man as subject to a *triplex ordo*, divine law, reason, and political authority. If man had been by nature a solitary animal, the order of reason and that of revealed law would have been sufficient. But man is a political being. It is necessary, if he is to attain his proper end and the highest forms of life and of virtue, that he should share in political life, that he practice the *virtutes politicae*.[1]

The doctrine of the political nature of man has an immediate bearing upon the treatment of political obligation. It implies that the historical origins of the State must not be confused with the problem of its rational justification. Whatever the earliest conditions of mankind, political relationship is its "natural" condition. It is therefore quite pointless to argue about the causes of some supposed change in human conditions, and to seek in them an explanation and justification of the State and political institutions. There is no place in such doctrine for a contrast between "nature" and "convention." There is no need for a social contract. St. Thomas makes full use of Aristotle's notion of man as a political animal. He does not hesitate in breaking away, when necessary, from the tenets of earlier Christian writers. His difficulties are clearly apparent in his careful discussion of the state of nature and of the natural equality of men. Stoic and Christian philosophy had been strangely consonant on this point. The teaching of the Fathers left no doubt as to the conditions in which mankind had originally been placed by God. St. Augustine, in a famous passage which St. Thomas did not fail to remember, had stated that God had made the rational man to be the master of animals, not of his fellowmen, thus showing by visible signs what is the proper order of nature and what are the consequences of sin.[2] The same conception was repeated by Gregory the Great, and by St. Isidore of Seville, a Christian writer of the beginning of the seventh century, whose great work of compilation was constantly referred to by medieval writers. The older doctrine of the law of nature, laid down by some of the Roman lawyers and transmitted in Justinian's *Corpus Juris,* had also emphatically asserted the natural freedom and equality of all men, contrasting the institutions which can be referred to the *ius naturale* with those which are grounded upon the *ius gentium* and on human conventions.

[1] S. *Theol.,* 1a2ae, LXI, 5.
[2] *De Civitate Dei,* XIX, 15.

Here again St. Thomas did not directly and categorically contradict these conceptions. His answer to the difficulty raised by two contrasting modes of thought shows his effort of adaptation and is a typical instance of scholastic subtlety. But the distinction which makes the answer possible is important and has important results. Yes, God has made man to his image and likeness. Had men remained in the state of innocence the more jarring inequalities between them, such as the distinction between masters and slaves, would not have existed. But even in the state of innocence the fundamental difference between man and man would have been apparent; for, as Aristotle points out, men are not equal, but unequal. Everything is clear if we distinguish between two different sorts of subjection. Slavery—the *subiectio servilis* in which man is degraded to a tool—is undoubtedly contrary to nature, and can therefore only be explained as a consequence of sin. But political relationship—the *subiectio civilis* of man to man which is necessary for the attainment of the common good—is not a consequence of sin, for it is founded upon the very nature of man. Authority and obedience would still have been required even if the state of innocence had been preserved. The reason for this is again that, according to Aristotle, man is a social and political animal. Society would not be possible without authority, and without those who are more wise and righteous having command over the rest. The idea of sin, without being rejected, is confined to narrow limits, merely to explain certain inevitable hardships of social and political experience, such as slavery, the penal character of laws, or the existence of unjust rulers. It has no part in the rational justification of the State, because political obligation is inherent in man's nature. Man is unthinkable without the State, because it is only in the State and through the State that he can achieve perfection.

But at this point another difficulty was bound to arise, perhaps even more serious. Surely a doctrine such as the one which we have analyzed ran counter to some very old and deep *motifs* of Christian experience. If man can only achieve perfection in the fellowship of other men, what about hermits and saints? There is an interesting passage in the Commentary on the *Politics* about this. St. Thomas is commenting here on the Aristotelian doctrine of the "monstrous" condition of man deprived of society and isolated from political life. He finds it necessary to make an express reservation with regard to asceticism, in favour of the idea of a higher degree of perfection to be attained by retiring from the world rather than by participating in it. But he is at pains to emphasize the exceptional character of a life of this kind, and the necessity, for the attainment of such an ideal, of more than human capacities. "If any man should be such that he is not a political being by nature, he is either wicked—as when this happens through the corruption of human nature—or he is better than man—in that he has a nature more perfect than that of other men in general, so that he is able to be sufficient to himself without the society of men, as were John the Baptist and St. Anthony the hermit."[3] The Aristotelian doctrine has opened up new perspectives. The idea of the social and political nature of man leads to an emphatic assertion of the full and harmonious integration of individual life in the life of the community. "All men being a part of the city, they cannot be truly good unless they adapt themselves to the common good."

It is upon the ultimate meaning of this "integration" that we must focus our attention. What are the real implications of so much emphasis laid on the common good as being greater, and indeed more divine (*maius et divinius*) [4] than that of the single individual? Does it not imply in some way a belittlement of human personality? Can it not lead to a complete absorption of individual life in that of the State? We are clearly here faced with that "organic" conception of the State which Gierke stressed as one of the essential features of medieval political theory: and an organic conception can only mean that the State, as the whole, is prior to its parts, that the end of the individual is subordinate to that of the community, that, in fact, the individual has no independent meaning nor value apart from the whole of which it is a part. Such views seem hardly compatible with the Christian conception of the absolute value of human personality. They tend to make the State a sort of Leviathan, which devours its components. They conjure up the notion of the "mortal God" in a Hegelian sense, still more than in Hobbes's familiar wording. It is interesting to find that they are by no means a modern invention. Historians have coined the expression "political Averroism" to indicate the direction in which medieval Aristotelianism was moving. The impact of Averroist ideas has been clearly traced back in Marsilius of Padua, and even in Dante. It is therefore of the greatest importance that we should interpret St. Thomas correctly on this momentous issue. But this is far from being an easy task. For there is no doubt that he conceives of the State as an organism,[5] of the individual as subordinate to the community, and of the common good as the supreme value to which all others are instrumental.[6] He repeats and endorses the Aristotelian statement, that the family and all other groups differ from the city not only in size, but "specifically," and derives from it the conclusion that "the common welfare is different in nature from that of the individual, just as the nature of the part is different from that of the whole." [7]

We have, however, only to look a little more deeply into the matter in order to realize to how many cautions the "organic" conception of the State is subject in St. Thomas's interpretation. To begin with, the unity

---

[3] *Comm. on the Politics*, lib. I, lectio 1.
[4] *De Regimine Principum*, I, ix.; also in S. *Theol.*, 2a2ae, XXXI, 3, and *Summa contra Gent.*, III, 17.
[5] S. *Theol.*, 1a2ae, LXXXI, 1: ("*secundum quod in civi[li] bus omnes homines qui sunt unius communitatis, reputantur quasi unum corpus, et tota communitas unus homo*").
[6] S. *Theol.*, 1a2ae, XC, 3; cp. also *Summa contra Gent.*, III, 17.
[7] S. *Theol.*, 2a2ae, LVII, 7.

which is achieved through any form of human association is a unity of a very peculiar kind. "It must be noted"—we read in the first chapter of the Commentary on the *Ethics*—"that this unity which is the political community or the unity of the family, is only a unity of order and not an unconditional unity. Consequently the parts which form it can have a sphere of action which is distinct from that of the whole; just as in an army a soldier can perform actions which are not proper to the whole army. At the same time the whole has a sphere of action which is not proper to any of its parts: as for example the general action in battle of the entire army; or again, like the movement of a ship which results from the combined action of the rowers." This seems to exclude that the grouping together of men should be creative of a new and separate being, different in substance from the parts that compose it. The rôle of the individual is neither minimized nor denied; it is simply enhanced and brought as it were upon a higher plane. The integration of the individual in the whole must be conceived as an enlargement and an enrichment of his personality, not as a degradation to the mere function of a part without a value of its own. Above all, the difference between the end of the individual and that of the whole does not imply a difference in the standards by which both can and must be judged. Ultimately these ends are one and the same.[8]

Thus could the interplay of man and society be assessed and the value of individual personality secured with all due concession to the new conceptions which were revealed from the reading of Aristotle. A solid safeguard was provided by natural law. Though the emphasis is never on "natural rights" in the modern sense, the action of the State is delimited by objective rules of justice which ensure the respect of the fundamental demands of the Christian conception of human personality. It is further delimited by the fact that the laws of the State cannot aim at making men perfectly virtuous. They are confined to pass judgement only upon external actions.[9] The spirit of Christian individualism remains unabated. The individual can never be entirely absorbed by the State. Something in him is reserved for a higher end. The value of the single soul is sealed by the price of Redemption.[10] No human authority can be absolutely binding in conscience. And a higher authority is given to man, which rises high above the authority of the State and of all other earthly power. It is the authority of the Church, which has its source directly from God and finds its justification not only in Scripture, but in that very progression of ends which inspires St. Thomas's whole treatment of Ethics.

Thus in the end does St. Thomas's theory of politics lead us back to medieval theocracy. The State is no longer denied any right of existence. But it must fit into the scheme of a hierarchical and graded society, and

---

[8] *De Regimine Principum,* I, xiv.
[9] *S. Theol.,* 1a2ae, 96, 2 and 3; C, 9.
[10] *S. Theol.,* 1a2ae, XXI, 4, and CXIII, 9, ad 2um.

accept its subordinate part. We can now measure all the distance which separates St. Thomas's from the modern conception of politics. It is unfortunate that he should not have left us a systematic treatment of the problem of State and Church. But a clear account of his doctrine is to be found in the fourteenth chapter of the *De Regimine Principum*. It is the doctrine of the necessity of a dual direction of human affairs, of the insufficiency of the *humanum regimen* and of its completion through the *divinum regimen*. This duality is reflected in the distinction between the *regnum* and the *sacerdotium*. It is the traditional doctrine, which had found its solemn expression in the famous letter of Pope Gelasius I to the Emperor Anasthasius at the end of the fifth century, and had been enshrined in the great collection of Gratian towards the middle of the twelfth century. What is new and startling is its development on the basis of the Aristotelian theory of ends. It is with a view to the full attainment of human ends, culminating in the *fruitio divina,* that the necessity of the two powers is shown. The duality converges into unity in Christ, who is both *rex* and *sacerdos*. In this world the two powers are committed separately, the one to earthly kings, the other to priests, and principally to the Roman Pontiff, "so that temporal affairs may remain distinct from those spiritual." But the different value of the ends necessarily implies a subordination of the one power to the other, of the *regnum* to the *sacerdotium*. Hence it follows that to the *Summus Sacerdos,* the successor of Peter and Vicar of Christ, "all Kings in Christendom should be subject, as to the Lord Jesus Christ Himself."

However clear and definite in its outlines, this doctrine is far from being free of all ambiguities. Let us remark for one thing that St. Thomas does not conceive of a relation between two different societies, between State and Church in any modern sense, but of a distinction of functions (*gubernationes, regimina, ministeria, potestates*). We are entirely on the lines of what historians have called the Gelasian doctrine, the doctrine of the distinction and interrelation of two great spheres of human life within one single society—the Christian society, the *respublica christiana*. But it is the relationship itself that leaves the field open to uncertainty. What does the necessary "subjection" of all temporal rulers to the authority of the Pope really amount to? If we relate the doctrine laid down in the *De Regimine Principum* with other passages from St. Thomas's other works,[11] and especially if we compare it with the extreme claims of what we may call the "theocratic" doctrine proper, such as set forth by Boniface VIII and his supporters, we are inclined to appreciate its moderation. There is no mention of the *plenitudo potestatis,* of a direct sovereignty of the Pope in temporal matters. The subordination or *subiectio* of the civil to the spiritual power of which St. Thomas speaks, is such only with regard to the end. It comes much nearer to the *potestas indirecta,* the typical doctrine of

---

[11] *Comm. on the Sentences,* book II, dist. xliv, q. 3, a. 4; and S. *Theol.,* 2a2ae, CXLVII, 3.

the post-Tridentine Church, although this doctrine represents an adaptation to social and political conditions greatly different from those of the Middle Ages, and implies the definite abandonment of the medieval idea of the unity of the two societies, the Church and the State. But it is this unity that matters. The spiritual and the temporal spheres are not independent. "The temporal power is subject to the spiritual as the body to the soul," [12] as philosophy is to theology, as the natural is to the supernatural. It is all right to speak of an indirect power, inasmuch as "the spiritual Prelate should interest himself in temporal affairs with respect to those things in which the temporal power is subject to him or in matters which have been left to him by the secular power." But when we come to examine the actual working of this indirect power, we do not only find that, as could later be said of the Jesuits, what is granted with one hand is immediately withdrawn with the other. We also find that the matters which the State is supposed to leave to the Church are precisely those which the modern man has struggled for centuries to secure against the interference of Church and of State alike: such as the pursuit of truth and the worship of God according to his conscience. There is no room for religious freedom in a system which is based on orthodoxy.

The theory of St. Thomas is the theory of the orthodox State. We are apt to forget it. We have grown so accustomed to the threat which comes from the State, that we are only too ready to hail the Church as the champion of freedom. Medieval intolerance had at least one great advantage over modern totalitarianism. It subtracted entirely the definition of orthodoxy from the hands of the politician. It put a bar on Erastianism. It would never have allowed that "the General Will is always right." It was an intolerance of a different and more noble brand. But it was intolerance all right, and a thorough, totalitarian intolerance. I am not drawing a fanciful picture. I would like to refer the reader to the little treatise *De Regimine Judaeorum*. Here is a picture of a society thoroughly Christian, led by the two authorities to the attainment of the ultimate goal. The fact that this society is a society of the faithful does not exclude that there may be infidels among them. But, as such, they are not members of the society proper. They are *qui foris sunt*, without the community altogether. However, "we must bear ourselves honestly, even to those that are outcasts." They must be tolerated. They must even be respected. The great spirit of Christianity speaks in the words: "Gentiles and Jews . . . should in no way be constrained to embrace the faith and profess belief. For belief depends upon the will." But the Jews are and remain outcasts in the Christian community. Their rites, which after all bear testimony to our faith, may be allowed, in the same way as prostitution is allowed to avoid greater evils. But they must be obliged to bear some special sign to distinguish them

[12] S. *Theol.*, 2a2ae, LX, 6.

from the Christians. They should be compelled to work for their living rather than be allowed to live in idleness and grow rich by usury.

The unhappy lot of the Jews is a paradise compared with that of the heretic or the apostate. They had at one time accepted the faith and professed it. They must be "constrained, even physically, to fulfil what they have promised and to observe what once they accepted for ever." Their sin is one which can hope for no pardon. "If it be just that forgers and other malefactors are put to death without mercy by the secular authority, with how much greater reason may heretics not only be excommunicated, but also put to death, when once they are convicted of heresy." But the Church is merciful. She will not condemn heretics unless they remain pertinacious. She will even go so far as to tolerate their rites when they are in very great numbers or in the case that their suppression should be a cause of discord or of scandal. Yet the principle of intolerance is unflinchingly maintained. It casts a sinister light upon this part of St. Thomas's teaching. There can be no doubt as to the ultimate meaning of the indirect power and the separation of spiritual and temporal matters. In theory the power of the Church is purely spiritual. Her weapons are not temporal weapons. But they carry a temporal weight because of the subservience of the State to the higher direction of the Church in all temporal matters. By the sentence of excommunication the heretic is not only separated from the Church. He is passed on "to the secular judgement to be exterminated from the world by death."

Very little seems to be left at this point of all the effort to secure an independent and proper platform to the State and to politics. And yet here is the final paradox: indeed, not a paradox at all, but a strictly logical consequence of the accepted premises. Political authority has a value of its own, independent of religion. It has such value as the expression of a natural and rational order. This implies that even a non-Christian State is endowed with a positive value, over and against St. Augustine's conception of the pagan State as the embodiment of the *civitas terrena* and a work of sin. But though based on the very nature of man, political obligation cannot avoid being subordinate to religious obligation. It is a question of interpreting correctly the fundamental principle that Grace does not abolish Nature, but perfects it. Let us quote St. Thomas again, for his words are better than any commentary. "We must note that government and dominion depend from human law, but the distinction between the faithful and infidels is from divine law. The divine law, however, which is a law of grace, does not abolish human law which is founded on natural reason. So the distinction between the faithful and the infidel, considered in itself, does not invalidate the government and dominion of infidels over the faithful. Such right to dominion or government may, however, with justice be abrogated by order of the Church in virtue of her divine authority; for the infidel, on account of their unbelief, deserve to lose their power over the faithful, who are become the sons of God. But the Church sometimes does and sometimes does not take such steps." It is a momentous step and such as to make the holder of the spiritual power hesitate before taking it. But its very possibility makes in certain cases the final decision inevitable. It is in the power of the Church to release those bonds of allegiance to the State which are founded in Nature. These bonds can and must be released whenever a danger threatens religion. Christian rulers must know the price of having embraced the faith, of being a part of the Christian republic. Political obligation ultimately rests upon religious obligation. "It is not the province of the Church to punish infidelity in those who have never embraced the faith, according to what the Apostle says, 'What have I to do to judge them that are without?' But the infidelity of those who have once embraced the faith, she may punish by judicial sentence; and it is just that they be punished by loss of the right to rule believers. For this could lead to widespread corruption of the faith: as it is said, 'the apostate breeds evil in his heart, and sows discord,' seeking to detach men from their faith. And therefore, as soon as a ruler falls under sentence of excommunication for apostasy from the faith, his subjects are *ipso facto* absolved from his rule, and from the oath of fealty which bound them to him." St. Thomas lays down with uncompromising clearness the principles which underlie the medieval conception of the State. The student of history will have little difficulty in providing the necessary illustrations of its practice.

FURTHER READINGS FOR PART III

St. Augustine

Battenhouse, Roy, ed. *A Companion to St. Augustine*. New York: Oxford University Press, 1955.

Brooks, Edgar H. *The City of God and the Politics of Crisis*. New York: Oxford University Press, 1960.

Brown, Peter R. L. *Augustine of Hippo: A Biography*. Berkeley: University of California Press, 1967.

Caldwell, Caylon L. "Augustine's Critique of Human Justice," *A Journal of Church and State*, 2 (May 1960), pp. 7–25.

Cantor, Norman, and Peter L. Klein, eds. *Medieval Thought: Augustine and Thomas Aquinas*. Waltham, Mass.: Blaisdell Publishing Co., 1969.

D'arcy, M. C., ed. *Saint Augustine*. New York: World, 1957.

Deane, Herbert A. *The Political and Social Ideas of Saint Augustine*. New York: Columbia University Press, 1963.

Figgis, John N. *The Political Aspects of St. Augustine's City of God*. London: Longmans, 1921.

Gilson, Étienne. *The Christian Philosophy of St. Augustine*. New York: Random House, 1960.

Hartigan, Richard S. "Saint Augustine on War and Killing: The Problem of the Innocent," *Journal of the History of Ideas*, 27 (April–June 1966), pp. 195–204.

Howie, George. *Educational Theory and Practice in St. Augustine*. New York: Teachers College Press, 1969.

Lacey, Hugh M. "Empiricism and Augustine's Problems About Time," *Review of Metaphysics*, 22 (December 1968), pp. 219–245.

Mommsen, Theodor. "St. Augustine and the Christian Idea of Progress: Background to the City of God," *Journal of the History of Ideas*, 12 (July 1951), pp. 346–374.

Nash, Ronald H. *The Light of the Mind: St. Augustine's Theory of Knowledge*. Lexington: University Press of Kentucky, 1969.

O'Connell, Robert J. *St. Augustine's Early Theory of Man*. Cambridge, Mass.: Belknap Press, 1968.

Pope, Hugh. *St. Augustine of Hippo*. London: Longmans, 1954.

Portalie, Eugene. *A Guide to the Thought of Saint Augustine*. Chicago: Regnery, 1960.

Sontag, Frederick. "Augustine's Metaphysics and Free Will," *Harvard Theological Review*, 60 (July 1967), pp. 297–306.

Versfeld, Marthinus. *A Guide to the City of God*. New York: Sheed and Ward, 1958.

John of Salisbury

Liebeschütz, Hans. *Medieval Humanism in the Life and Writings of John of Salisbury*. London: University of London Press, 1950.

Webb, Clement C. J. *John of Salisbury*. London: Methuen, 1932.

St. Thomas Aquinas

Brennan, Robert E., ed. *Essays in Thomism*. New York: Sheed and Ward, 1942.

Chesterton, G. K. *St. Thomas Aquinas*. Garden City, N.Y.: Doubleday, 1956.

Copleston, Frederick C. *Aquinas*. Baltimore, Md.: Penguin, 1955.

D'arcy, Martin. *St. Thomas Aquinas*. Glen Rock, N.J.: Newman Press, 1955.

D'Entrèves, A. P. *The Medieval Contribution to Political Thought*. New York: Oxford University Press, 1939.

Donohue, John W. *St. Thomas Aquinas and Education*. New York: Random House, 1968.

Farrell, Walter. *A Companion to the Summa*. New York: Sheed and Ward, 1939–1942.

Ferraro, Joseph W. "Marxism and Thomism: Some Reflections on the Basis
    for A Dialogue," *International Philosophical Quarterly*, 10 (March 1970),
    pp. 75–101.
Ford, Lewis S. "Tillich and Thomas: The Analogy of Being," *Journal of
    Religion*, 46 (April 1966), pp. 229–245.
Gilby, Thomas. *The Political Thought of Thomas Aquinas*. Chicago: Uni-
    versity of Chicago Press, 1958.
———. *Principality and Polity: Aquinas and the Rise of State Theory in
    the West*. London: Longmans, 1958.
Gilson, Étienne. *The Christian Philosophy of Saint Thomas Aquinas*. New
    York: Random House, 1956.
Grabmann, Martin. *Thomas Aquinas: His Personality and Thought*. New
    York: Longmans, 1928.
Heath, Thomas R. "St. Thomas and the Aristotalian Metaphysics: Some
    Observations," *New Scholasticism*, 34 (October 1960), pp. 438–460.
Jaffa, Harry V. *Thomism and Aristotelianism: A Study of the Commentary
    by Thomas Aquinas on the Nicomachean Ethics*. Chicago: University
    of Chicago Press, 1952.
Kenny, Anthony. *The Five Ways: Saint Thomas Aquinas' Proofs of God's
    Existence*. London: Rutledge, 1969.
MacGuigan, Mark R. "St. Thomas and Legal Obligation," *New Scholasti-
    cism*, 35 (July 1961), pp. 281–310.
Maritain, Jacques. *St. Thomas Aquinas*. New York: World, 1958.
Mihalich, Joseph C. *Existentialism and Thomism*. New York: Philosophical
    Library, 1960.
O'Connor, Daniel J. *Aquinas and Natural Law*. New York: Crowell-Collier-
    Macmillan, 1968.
Raeymaeker, Louis de. "What St. Thomas Means Today," *The Review of
    Politics*, 20 (January 1958), pp. 3–20.
Ruby, Jane E. "The Ambivalence of St. Thomas Aquinas' View of the Rela-
    tionship of Divine Law to Human Law," *Harvard Theological Re-
    view*, 48 (1955), pp. 101–128.
Stevens, Gregory. "Moral Obligation in St. Thomas," *The Modern School-
    man*, 40 (November 1962), pp. 1–21.
Thiry, Leon. "Ethical Theory of Saint Thomas Aquinas: Interpretation and
    Misinterpretations," *Journal of Religion*, 50 (April 1970), pp. 169–185.
Turner, Walter H. "St. Thomas's Exposition of Aristotle: A Rejoinder,"
    New Scholasticism, 35 (April 1961), pp. 210–224.
Walker, Leslie J. "Aquinas," *Philosophy*, 10 (July 1935), pp. 279–288.

IV

THE CONCILIAR ERA:

MARSIGLIO OF PADUA,

DANTE,

AND WILLIAM OF OCCAM

14

Marsiglio of Padua
and Dante Alighieri

MARJORIE REEVES

Marsiglio and Dante were almost contemporaries. Dante
was ten or more years the elder but died younger
(1265–1321), so that Marsiglio, born between 1275 and
1280 and dying in 1342 or 3, had a longer span of life. In
background and in some of the political experiences which
formed them there are close parallels, yet the political
thought into which those experiences crystallized was as-
tonishingly different. This sharp contrast invites exploration, not so much in hope of explanation, as from desire to
savour more fully the distinctive quality of each.

Each was born and brought up in an Italian city-
state which had not yet succumbed permanently to the sig-
nory of one family and which prized its republicanism
deeply. Florence at this time was busy reshaping its constitution in accordance with the shift of political power towards the major and median guilds. From the constitu-

This article was originally published in Beryl Smalley (ed.), *Trends
in Medieval Political Thought* (Oxford: Basil Blackwell, 1965), pp.
86–104. It is reprinted here with the permission of the author and of
the publisher.

tional experiments which reached a climax in 1293–95, the Signoria, consisting of Priors chosen from the guilds, emerged as the chief instrument of political power. In contemporary Padua power still remained with the *Concilium maius* of one thousand citizens—with a property qualification—and the chief administrative officer was still the Podesta, elected by the *Concilium maius*. At a time when new men were jostling for position, both cities clung to liberty, but neither achieved equilibrium.

There is a significant divergence in the education of the two men. Dante, as we know from his own analysis of his experience, was at one stage of his growth fascinated by the Lady Philosophy and followed her closely:

> And as it is wont to chance that a man goeth in search of silver and beyond his purpose findeth gold, that which some hidden cause presents, not, I take it, without divine command; so I, who was seeking to console myself, found not only a cure for my tears, but words of authors, and of sciences and of books, pondering upon which I judged that Philosophy who was the lady of these authors, of these sciences and of these books was a thing supreme; and I conceived her after the fashion of a gentle lady, and I might not conceive her in any attitude save that of compassion; wherefore the sense for truth so loved to gaze upon her that I could scarce turn it away from her; and impelled by this imagination of her, I began to go where she was in very truth revealed . . . so that in a short time . . . I began to feel so much of her sweetness that the love of her expelled and destroyed every other thought.
>
> *Convivio*, ii, 13, tr. P. Wicksteed

Marsiglio, on the other hand, was for some time chiefly interested in the natural sciences and medicine. He was in Paris from 1312 to 1313 and *c.* 1320 to 1326, when he was giving lectures on natural philosophy and studying medicine. This difference in academic taste we shall find reflected in the modes of thought of the two men. Yet both display a common characteristic in that the pursuit of learning was interrupted by political activities. Dante's name appears in the Florentine records as a participant in city councils a number of times between 1295 and his exile in 1302. Marsiglio at some period turned from the study of "nature" to become involved in the politics of Can Grande della Scala and Matteo Visconti. Both returned to paths of study—Dante because his exile shut the door on any satisfactory political activity, Marsiglio apparently by choice. Both, as we shall see later, got once more caught up in political strife, this time at the imperial level.

The experience of life in a city-state engendered in both these thinkers one over-riding political concern which at times seems to become an obsession: the paramount importance of finding the cause of civil strife in communities, of striking at this root evil in human society and of discovering the true formula for peace. Moreover, the common conditions of politics in thirteenth-century Italian city-republics meant that both discovered one of the major causes of civil strife in the "invasions"—or conversely in the immunities—of the Church. On the one hand, ecclesiastical authorities from the pope downwards were claiming increasing rights of intervention in the civil sphere; on the other hand, clerical immunities from civil control threatened to ham-string political authority. Thus we find in Dante a mounting resentment against the disastrous role of the Church in politics, a resentment underlined by Boniface VIII's intervention in Florentine affairs, with its fatal consequence of exile for Dante. As for Marsiglio, during his lifetime there was a continual struggle in Padua against clerical immunity from civil jurisdiction and clerical control over the laity, a struggle which found expression both in the bitter complaints of chroniclers and civil legislation against these privileged persons. It is not surprising that in his mind the clergy came to constitute the primary obstacle to peace in the state.

Finally, both men were impelled to distil their political experience into a work of political philosophy. Both, in their works, assumed the passionate role of a political reformer, and both, at some stage, pinned their faith on an emperor as the agent of political regeneration. There has been controversy about the date of Dante's *Monarchia*,[1] but the most generally accepted view places it somewhere between 1309 and 1313, that is, during the Emperor Henry VII's expedition to Italy.[2] Dante supported this attempt of imperial authority to reassert control over Italy with great passion: he burnt all his political boats, heaped reproaches on Florence for resisting Henry, and—since the expedition failed—rendered his own sentence of exile irrevocable. We do not know when Marsiglio began the *Defensor pacis*[3] but he tells us that he finished it on June 24, 1324.[4] Thus it was not conceived, like Dante's work, in a moment of political crisis, but thought out in the comparative remoteness of the Paris schools. His author-

[1] See the critical edition by G. Vinay (Florence, 1950). All quotations in this essay are given in the translation of D. Nicholl and C. Hardie, *The Monarchy and Three Political Letters* (London, 1954).
[2] On the dating of the *Monarchia*, see C. Hardie, *Note on the Chronology of Dante's Political Works* in the translation cited in note 1, pp. 117–121; U. Cosmo, *A Handbook to Dante Studies* (trans. D. Moore, Oxford, 1950), pp. 107–108.
[3] The most easily available critical edition of the *Defensor pacis* is that of C. Previté-Orton (Cambridge, 1938). It has been studied in detail and translated by A. Gewirth, *Marsilius of Padua: The Defender of Peace*, Vol. I. *Marsilius of Padua and Medieval Political Philosophy* (New York, 1951): Vol. II. *The Defensor Pacis* (New York, 1956). Copyright 1951 by Columbia University Press, New York. It will be obvious that I have drawn heavily on these two authorities. All quotations from the *Defensor pacis* are given in Gewirth's translation.
[4] Previté-Orton has distinguished two groups of MSS, a French and a German, and has detected in the German group revisions which Marsiglio was making down to 1329 (pp. xxvi–xli).

ship became known in 1326; the book was declared heretical and Marsiglio was forced to flee to the court of the Emperor Lewis of Bavaria.[5] Among Marsiglio's Paris contacts had probably been a group of Spiritual Franciscans, including Ubertino da Casale. These became curious allies in the attack upon clerical wealth and privilege and both Marsiglio's political polemic and the Spirituals' religious denunciation were utilized by Lewis of Bavaria in his offensive against Pope John XXII. So Marsiglio found himself, like Dante, supporting an imperial expedition to Italy in 1327. In Rome there was a brief make-believe of putting Marsiglio's political doctrines into practice, but this was quickly over. After the debacle Marsiglio spent the rest of his life in exile at the court of Lewis.

Thus there are striking parallels between the experiences of these two men, but even more striking is the sharp divergence of their thought. Broadly similar experiences drove them in diametrically opposite directions. In turning now to look briefly at Dante's political philosophy, we shall leave on one side problems of its development through various phases, selecting only a few main points which remain more or less constant and which will point up our contrast with Marsiglio. In the first place, seeking for the root of this great over-riding evil of civil strife, Dante found it in the sin of *cupiditas* to which all human beings are so prone. Quoting from Aristotle he affirms that "the greatest obstacle to justice is cupidity" (*Monarchia*, i, c. ii). The "invasion" of that which is not one's own brings untold evil consequences. This view is carried to such lengths that even the physical expansion of a thriving city like Florence is denounced by Dante's ancestor, Cacciaguida, in *Paradiso*, xvi, instead of being regarded as a sign of healthy vitality. But the greatest example of cupidity is found by Dante in the papacy—taking from Constantine that which was not her own, grasping the sword as well as the crook, invading the civil sphere at every turn: [6]

> . . . your avarice grieves the world, trampling on the good and raising up the wicked. . . . You have made you a god of gold and silver. . . . Ah, Constantine, to how much evil gave birth, not thy conversion, but that dower the first rich Father had from thee!
>
> *Inferno*, xix, 104–117

> Thou canst plainly see that ill-guiding is the cause that has made the world wicked. . . . Rome, which made the good world, used to have two

---

[5] Implicated with Marsiglio in the condemnation of the *Defensor pacis* was his friend John of Jandun; both fled together. The question of the latter's share in writing the treatise remains uncertain. Previté-Orton (pp. xxv–xxvi) thought his influence was "more pervasive than local," and that "the main author seems . . . to be Marsilius." Gewirth regards Marsiglio as the sole author, "John of Jandun and the *Defensor Pacis*" in *Speculum*, xxiii (1948), pp. 267–272.

[6] Translations from the *Divina Commedia* are given in the version of J. Sinclair (London, 1939).

suns, which made plain the one way and the other, that of the world and that of God. The one has quenched the other and the sword is joined to the crook, and the one together with the other must perforce go ill.

Purgatorio, xvi, 103–111

Justice is only possible when greed has been utterly removed and greed is only removed when nothing is desired. This is a possible state of mind only for one who possesses all, that is, a universal monarch. In him alone can perfect justice be achieved, for he alone is free from all cupidity:

> But when there is nothing to be desired there can be no cupidity, because the passions cannot remain when their objects have been eliminated. But the Monarch has nothing to desire, since the ocean alone is the limit of his jurisdiction—unlike other princes . . . whose jurisdictions are limited by one another's frontiers. It follows that of all mortals the Monarch can be the purest incarnation of justice.

Monarchia, i, c. ii

So Dante arrives at the concept of universal monarchy as the only cure for civil strife.

This desire to end civil strife is not just a negative impulse. Dante starts the argument of the *Monarchia* from the perspective of the ideal goal of human civilization as a whole. This goal is to realize the specific potentiality of humanity, as distinct from that of animals in general, and this he defines as the potentiality or capacity of intellect. To achieve this, universal peace is necessary and, as we have seen, the elimination of strife can only be achieved under unity of rule:

> For, if it is agreed that mankind as a whole has a goal (and this we have shown to be so), then it needs one person to govern or rule over it, and the title appropriate to this person is Monarch or Emperor. Thus it has been demonstrated that a Monarch or Emperor is necessary for the well-being of the world.

Monarchia, i, c. 5

Dante goes on to elevate the argument for universal monarchy above the level of civil necessity to that of cosmic and divine perfection. The whole heavens are ruled by a single motion and, on this pattern, the whole human race should be ruled by one ruler and one law. Moreover, humanity comes nearest to achieving its goal when it most resembles God. God is absolute unity. Therefore the human race is most God-like when it is most one, and it follows that when it is subject to one prince it most resembles God.

Dante, you will observe, has elevated the "end" of political life into a final or ideal "end." But very clearly he also has another final "end"—the

goal of mankind on the supernatural plane. Thus he conceives of two beatitudes towards which mankind strives:

> . . . it follows that man's ultimate goal is twofold—because since man is the
> only being sharing in both corruptibility and incorruptibility, he is the only
> being who is ordered towards two ultimate goals. . . . Unerring Providence
> has therefore set man to attain two goals: the first is happiness in this life,
> which consists in the exercise of his own powers and is typified by the
> earthly paradise; the second is the happiness of eternal life, which consists
> in the enjoyment of the divine countenance (which man cannot attain to of
> his own power but only by the aid of divine illumination) and is typified by
> the heavenly paradise.
>
> *Monarchia,* iii, c. 16

The one "end" is made plain by human reason, that is, by the direction of
philosophy; the other is only attained by the guidance of the Holy Spirit.
Progress towards the one is directed by the emperor, towards the other, by
the pope.

This is a strange conception: it seems to postulate two final ends to
be reached by distinct and different means. Dante almost commits himself
to belief in two completely independent planes of human existence. Here
lies his most individual political thought. He is driven to it by his conviction that, for the proper fulfilment of the earthly beatitude, the political
ruler must not be subordinated in any way, *qua* ruler, to the pope. His
own political experience forced this separation upon him, while the claims
of the canonists forced him to make it as absolute as possible in order to
bar the way to their invasions. We see his strong feeling that the developing claims of ecclesiastical lawyers were a major cause of strife in his attack upon the Decretalists in Book III of the *Monarchia.* Indeed, the whole
of the Third Book is devoted to proving that the authority of the Roman
monarchy is derived directly from God.

This is a great assertion of Christian humanism: the belief in an ultimate value on the strictly human level of existence which is given and
blessed by God. Yet it would have been unthinkable for Dante—even the
Dante of the period before the *Divina Commedia*—to have conceived of
the purpose of human life solely in terms of earthly felicity. His second
goal of eternal beatitude is axiomatic. Can he, then, sustain two absolute
ends right through the argument of the *Monarchia?* In the last chapter he
reiterates Man's two ends and reasserts his belief in the independence of
the temporal monarch whose authority is received "directly and without
intermediary, from the source of all authority." Yet in the end the dichotomy *must* be transcended. After all, Dante admits, mortal felicity is, in a
certain sense (*quodammodo*), ordained to serve immortal felicity. The
Roman monarch must, therefore, acknowledge that he is subjected *in ali-
quo* to the Roman pontiff.

> Caesar, therefore, is obliged to observe that reverence towards Peter which
> a first-born son owes to his father; so that when he is enlightened by the
> light of paternal grace he may the more powerfully enlighten the world, at
> the head of which he has been placed by the One who alone is ruler of all
> things spiritual and temporal.
>
> *Monarchia,* iii, c. 16

Thus, in spite of his efforts to create an absolute division between the two,
Dante at the last opens a door through which the ecclesiastics could once
more invade the political territory.

Marsiglio's argument contrasts with Dante's in a most illuminating
way. He starts from the same purpose of opposing the mounting arrogance
of papal claims, through which the papal *plenitudo potestatis* is seen as
above and inclusive of all other powers. His declared and immediate purpose, as expressed in the first chapter of the *Defensor pacis,* is to refute
"this perverted opinion . . . pernicious to the human race." But he sets
about his task quite differently. Dante shared with his antagonists a mode
of thought which began with an ideal framework of universal order and
worked back to institutions and political practice. The papalists, of course,
saw this order in terms of one organic hierarchy of powers crowned by the
papal *plenitudo potestatis,* whereas Dante and other anti-papalists sought
to diversify the order, Dante himself going so far as almost to create a
dualism of orders. But he still thought in terms of ideal orders, of goals and
ends. The weakness of this mode of thought is clear from the concluding
sentences of the *Monarchia:* so long as one thought in these terms, one end
must ultimately be declared final and, since there could be little doubt in
men's minds as to which end was absolutely final, Dante is forced to admit
a breach in his defences through which the papalists could reclaim the
whole position.

Marsiglio makes a radical break with this tradition of thinking in
terms of ideal orders and ultimate goals. He starts from the opposite end:
the natural desires of men. For him the "natural" is the primitive, not the
perfected; it is the original endowment of Man, an endowment shared in
part with the animals. He has constantly in mind the biological image of a
living organism which he can apply either to the individual or to the state,
and his language frequently suggests biological or even medical categories.
Thus normal healthy men and animals have natural desires which are only
perverted if the organism is sick or defective:

> All men not deformed or otherwise impeded naturally desire a sufficient life
> and flee and avoid what is harmful thereto; which has been admitted not
> only concerning man but also concerning every genus of animals.
>
> *Defensor pacis,* I, iv, § 2

The state, too, can be seen as a well-balanced animal organism—and here Marsiglio is taking a point from Aristotle:

> Let us assume with Aristotle . . . that the state is like an animate nature or animal. For just as an animal well disposed in accordance with nature is composed of certain proportioned parts ordered to one another and communicating their functions mutually and for the whole, so too the state is constituted of certain such parts when it is well disposed and established in accordance with reason. The relation, therefore, of the state and its parts to tranquillity will be seen to be similar to the relation of the animal and its parts to health.
>
> *Defensor pacis*, I, ii, § 3

Again, he likens discord or strife to the illness of an animal and speaks of diseased governments. Many examples of this use of medical or biological metaphor can be found in Marsiglio's work.

Thus Marsiglio places politics within a biological context and starts his analysis from instinctive desires. Where Dante sees the meaning of politics in terms of a progression towards man's true nature which is his end, Marsiglio sees it as a series of consequences following from a biological drive which is his predetermined beginning. His political doctrines follow with a kind of inevitability which is new because it derives from beginnings, not ends. Here the contrast between the two thinkers is reinforced by the striking difference of the analogies they use: whereas Marsiglio, envisaging his perfect state, thinks of the healthy animal organism, Dante, seeking for a symbol of ideal political harmony, finds it in the divinely-ordered and immovable hierarchy of the cosmos.

But now we meet a difficulty in Marsiglio's reasoning. Like Dante he was, as we have said, obsessed by the evil consequences of civil strife. The theme of conflict pervades the whole *Defensor pacis*, with its constant references to contentions, injuries, disputes, strifes. But Marsiglio is forced to begin by accepting conflict as "natural." Naturally each individual man pursues his own private desire for the sufficient life, and equally naturally he will pursue it too far, so that clashes between warring desires will inevitably arise. Dante can sit in moral judgement on the sin of cupidity: Marsiglio must start from an instinct to desire in excess which is a biological consequence of the nature of Man: "Without . . . correction the excesses of these acts would cause fighting . . . and finally the . . . loss of the sufficient life" (I, v, § 7). He finds the origins of the state, therefore, not in the need to realize a perfected end, but in the necessity of modifying and controlling natural desire for the sufficient life in the very interests of achieving that sufficient life. Moreover, his experience of city economics shows him that division of labour and co-operative functioning make for a more sufficient "sufficient life." So, in his account of the origins of the state, Marsiglio accepts the limitation of natural desire in the interests of avoiding harm and making life easier:

> Men had to assemble together in order to attain what was beneficial through these arts and to avoid what was harmful. . . . Men, then, were assembled for the sake of the sufficient life, being able to seek out for themselves the necessaries enumerated above and exchange them with each other. This assemblage, thus perfect and having the limit of self-sufficiency, is called the state. . . . For since diverse things are necessary to men who desire a sufficient life . . . there had to be diverse orders or offices of men in this association. . . .
>
> *Defensor pacis*, I, iv, § 3, 5

Once this position is accepted, the state becomes a necessity because all or most healthy men will recognize that their private desire has been incorporated into the public aims. Because men desire the sufficient life, it will follow that "all or most men" will "wish for a law appropriate to the common benefit of the citizens" (I, xii, § 8). The people's will must be accepted and the individual will rejected because the former aims at the common benefit with the same necessary biological drive as the latter aims at its private benefit.

Precisely because conflict is so natural, it is of paramount importance to prevent, over-ride and suppress it, so that the common benefit, that modicum of natural life alone possible, can be salvaged from destruction. The most urgent purpose of government is not to lead the good life but to coerce members into a "due proportion." For conflicts will inevitably arise:

> Because among men thus assembled there arise disputes and quarrels which, if not regulated by the norm of justice, would cause men to fight . . . and thus finally would bring about the destruction of the state, there had to be established in this association a standard of justice and a guardian or maker thereof.
>
> *Defensor pacis*, I, iv, § 4

Marsiglio is haunted by the danger of the destruction of the state and with it of the only possible formula for the sufficient life. This dominates his thinking. The highest authority must be accorded to the government because it alone has the necessary means to prevent descent into anarchy. Thus political necessity rather than noble ends gives the state its *raison-d'être*. There is little need here to point up the contrast with Dante.

It is true that Marsiglio does set forth his "end" in his concept of the sufficient life, but this is pitched in a far lower key than Dante's two beatitudes. Marsiglio, of course, takes the idea of a political "end" from Aristotle, but he makes an important shift of emphasis from final to immediate ends. When he comes to explore the meaning of the sufficient life in the civil community, he does, it is true, move beyond animal sufficiency to include activities which he can describe under the heading of "living well":

> Those who live a civil life not only live, which beasts and slaves do too, but they live well, having leisure for those liberal functions in which are exercised the virtues of both the theoretic and the practical soul.
>
> *Defensor pacis*, I, iv, § 1

Now the interesting thing here is that, although his civil happiness includes theoretical aspects, it puts them on the same level as practical activities. There is no hierarchy of ends or values. The sufficient life for men consists in realizing all the values which they naturally desire, and all aspects of civil life—moral, intellectual and theological, as well as practical and economic—evolve from the original natural impulse. We realize the levelling effect of Marsiglio's conception when we compare his view of the purposes of peace with Dante's. To the Florentine the noble end of peace is to enable the human race to realize the whole power of possible intellect. The Paduan simply enumerates the advantages of peaceful co-operation in society:

> . . . the mutual intercourse of citizens, their intercommunication of their functions with one another, their mutual aid and assistance . . . the power . . . of exercising their proper and common functions, and also the participation in common benefits and burdens. . . .
>
> *Defensor pacis*, I, xix, § 2

Both have an Italian civic background and it is noteworthy that only one incorporates it into his idea of peace. This sharp contrast perhaps gives us the most central point of divergence between Dante and Marsiglio, for whereas Dante's aspiration to achieve the possible intellect leads him straight forward to the single monarch as the only means to this end, Marsiglio's spread of varying civic values without distinction of grade is the basis of his republicanism. The qualities of his sufficient life are minimal enough to be desired and attained by a large proportion of the people, whereas a hierarchy of ends presupposes that only an élite will reach the highest.

The people, then, associate naturally for economic and social activities, impelled to this action by basic biological needs. There is no indication that Marsiglio conceives of men as desiring each other's company for its own sake. The state is a group of men forced into association with each other by elementary necessities. It consists of six principle parts: farmers, mechanics or artisans, bankers, judges or rulers, soldiers, priests. The chief aim of political life is the "good disposition" of all the parts, so that they may function easily within the whole. The meaning of peace is interpreted in an entirely secular and external sense—simply as smooth inter-relations. Marsiglio resolutely turns his back on any concept of peace "in the inward parts," for the state is concerned with outward acts alone, in so far as they affect other people. "Transient" actions, i.e. acts that pass over into effects on others are to be distinguished from "immanent" acts, i.e. motivations which do not reveal themselves in external deeds; the state can take cognizance of the former only, for the latter are not within its competence.

This has a direct bearing on Marsiglio's treatment of Law. Like a condition of inward peace and the existence of "immanent acts," he recognizes the reality of divine law. But it is irrelevant, because it does not impinge directly on the externalized relationships which form the civil life. So he refuses to discuss it:

> I shall discuss the establishment of only those laws and governments which emerge directly from the decision of the human mind.
>
> *Defensor pacis,* I, xii, § i

Human law must be a coercive command which affects outward acts. Precisely because the essential basis of human law is not reason but coercive command, Marsiglio defines the law of the state as the command of the whole body of citizens, for, though it may not express the highest reason, only the whole has the right to coerce each member. Thus we reach Marsiglio's famous concept of the whole people as Legislator. The state must rest, not on a higher law, but on the positive will of a human agency and Marsiglio postulates with great force that this must be the people—the "primary and proper efficient cause of law" (I, xii, § 3). The people, then, constitutes the Legislator and this he endows with a kind of sovereignty unparalleled in medieval political thought. The Legislator elects the deliberative experts who propose the laws, discusses and judges the adequacy of their proposals and stamps them with its coercive command which alone makes them law.

You will notice here that the exercise of reason and expertise does enter into the drafting stage of law-making. The question arises as to whether Marsiglio believes in simple majority opinion at the promulgating stage. This would be out of keeping with the whole medieval way of thinking in terms of group opinion, especially strong in civic communities. Marsiglio does define the people as the *universitas civium*—as if he were going to proceed by counting heads—but he adds the important qualification "or the weightier part of it" (I, xii, § 3–5). His discussion of this concept of *valentior pars* is most illuminating. His criteria for determining it include both quantitative and qualitative factors, the recognition of majority opinion and the weighting by wealth, experience, function, etc. In fact, looking more closely at Marsiglio's thought at the point, it seems that his units of opinion are not the individuals of a modern democracy but functional groups of people. All groups must, however, share in forming the will and there is an almost modern note in his passionate defence of the rightness of the many as against the wisdom of the few. Whilst the wise and experienced may guide in the initial stages of law-making, the ordinary good sense and judgement of average citizens is needed to make good enactments:

> That at which the entire body of citizens aims intellectually and emotionally is more certainly judged as to its truth and more diligently noted as to its common utility. For a defect in some proposed law can be better noted by the greater number than by any part thereof, since each whole . . . is greater in mass and in virtue than any part of it taken separately. Moreover, the common utility of a law is better noted by the entire multitude because no one knowingly harms himself. . . .
>   . . . For most of the citizens are neither vicious nor undiscerning most of the time; all or most of them are of sound mind and reason and have a right desire for the polity and for the things necessary for it to endure. . . . For although not every citizen nor the greater number . . . be discoverers of the law, yet every citizen can judge what has been discovered and proposed to him . . . and can discern what must be added, subtracted or changed.
>
> *Defensor pacis*, I, xii, § 5 and xiii, § 3

Naturally, of course, there will be some wrong-headed citizens who lack the good sense to see where their well-being lies. It is characteristic that these "deviationists" (as I think Marsiglio would have called them to-day) are described, not as sinners, but as "deformed." There is no question but that they must be coerced into agreement.

The people elects the ruler or government and delegates its executive authority to this chosen power. Marsiglio is quite clear that the only basis of legitimate rule is the will of the people: it cannot be any personal qualities of wisdom or experience, however desirable these are in themselves:

> It now remains to show the efficient cause of the ruler, that is, the cause by which there is given to one or more persons the authority of rulership which is established through election. For it is by this authority that a person becomes a ruler in actuality and not by his knowledge of the laws, his prudence or moral virtue, although these are qualities of the perfect ruler. For it happens that many men have these qualities, but nevertheless, lacking this authority, they are not rulers. . . .
>
> *Defensor pacis*, I, xv, § 1

The people must correct, punish or depose the ruler if he infringes the law. Above all, the ruler cannot make the law—for a very illuminating reason: that the one or the few must inevitably seek to pervert the law to private interests against which the only safeguard is the many. This stands in sharp opposition to Dante's argument for the single ruler—that he alone, possessing all, is free from the perverting corruption of cupidity.

To Marsiglio, with his emphasis on an externalized peace, the primary function of the government is the judgement of disputes and the prevention of "impediments" to the smooth working of the state. This is a negative and limited function, yet of vital importance. The ruler is strictly controlled by the people but, because the preservation of peace is the primary purpose of the state, the ruler must himself tightly control all parts of the community to ensure the preservation of the state. He has, for instance, the right to direct the citizens' choice of occupation and to regulate economic activity. There is a constant flow of authority from the people to the ruler and from the ruler to groups and individuals. Once again we find Marsiglio using the biological analogy when he describes the ruler as the heart of an animal:

> Consequently the action of the ruler in the state, like that of the heart in the animal, must never cease. . . . For the command and the common guardianship of the things which are lawful and prohibited . . . must endure at every hour or minute and whenever anything unlawful or unjust is done, the ruler must completely regulate such acts or must perform the preliminary steps towards such regulation.
>
> *Defensor pacis*, I, xv, § 13

Finally, we must look briefly at two special problems (out of many) in Marsiglio's thought: his approach to the Church/State controversy and his attitude towards the concept of universal government. The whole argument in Discourse I is designed as a foundation on which to build the special argument of Discourse II concerning the position of the Church. The last chapter of the first discourse is entitled *On the efficient causes of the Tranquillity and Intranquillity of the City or State, and on that singular cause which disturbs States in an unusual way; and on the connection between the first Discourse and the Second.* It is clear that to Marsiglio the Church, with its immunities and extra-territorial jurisdictions, constitutes the chief impediment to tranquillity in the state. The papacy in particular is "the efficient cause of civil strife." Here, of course, the Italian city-state experience comes out most strongly:

> There is, however, a certain unusual cause of intranquillity or discord of cities or states. . . . This cause has for a long time been impeding the due action of the ruler in the Italian state, and is now doing so even more; it has deprived and is still depriving that state of tranquillity . . . ; it has vexed it continually with every evil . . . and misery. . . . (It is) a singular impediment because of its customary hidden malignity. . . . This cause arises because the bishops of Rome therefore assumed for themselves this universal coercive jurisdiction over the whole world under the all-embracing title "plenitude of power" which they assert was granted by Christ to St. Peter

and to his successors. . . . so those who call themselves vicars of Christ and of St. Peter have this plenitude of coercive jurisdiction limited by no human law.

Defensor pacis, I, xix, § 3, 4, 9

In Discourse II Marsiglio expatiates eloquently and at great length on the machinations of the bishops of Rome—how by their stealthy double-dealings they have been creeping up on rulers to usurp their jurisdictions, how this "pernicious pestilence" has spread, how they have wormed their way through all the states of the world to subject all governments to them.

Marsiglio builds his attack on the papacy and its protagonists on his completely secular approach to the state in Discourse I. Here all the problems of civic life, including those of the Church, are examined solely in the light of reason and common experience, excluding all considerations of faith or eternal ends. Thus the Church is, in the first place, an organ of a secular state designed to contribute to its smooth functioning, and the priesthood, therefore, must receive its status from the secular authority. Instead of the familiar division into State and Church, Marsiglio sees only one state with two parts to it: the *pars principans* (ruling part) and the *pars sacerdotalis* (priestly part). Since civil peace is Marsiglio's central concern and this can only be achieved by secular authority, the government must form the primary part and the clergy must be subordinated to it. Here he strikes at the root of the papalists' position, namely, their claim that the pope alone is the ultimate guardian of the divinely-ordained ends which govern the whole life of man and that he alone could fully implement them. Marsiglio overturns this by denying the relevance of eternal ends to the organization of the civil community and by concentrating on immediate means rather than ultimate ends. His means of preserving civil peace really becomes a this-worldly end, cut off from eternal values.

As a functioning part of the state, the priesthood has an important role; it must, therefore, be established by the government and hold its temporal possessions under governmental control. It is hardly necessary to add that all clerical immunities, in Marsiglio's view, must be eliminated, since they destroy the unity of the state through an unordered plurality of government. Divine law is irrelevant because it is coercive only in a future world and therefore is really not law at all in this world. Thus coercion in matters of faith cannot be exercised by the Church, but only by the ruler or the Legislator, and this only in the interests of civil peace, not to ensure correct belief. Once again, we see that the state is concerned solely with "transient" acts. The priests may teach divine law and administer the sacraments, but where divine law impinges on the outward acts of men, the power to enforce it belongs solely to the secular agents of human law who have the monopoly of coercive power, "for the office of coercive rulership over any individual, of whatever condition, or any community or group

does not belong to the Roman bishop or any other bishop or priest as such
. . ." (*Defensor pacis*, I, xix, § 12).

Since the Church is treated as a social organism it is easy to see how
Marsiglio arrives at his definition of it as the "universitas fidelium"—the
whole people in its religious activity, just as the Legislator is the whole
people in its law-making capacity. It is the *universitas fidelium*, therefore,
which must elect the priesthood, define articles of faith through its elected
General Council, elect a head-bishop, control excommunication and so on.
It is astounding that Marsiglio should thus, with one stroke of the knife,
cut away the whole structure of priestly powers. One can see the preparation for this in Marsiglio's civic background and in the desperate secularism he develops in face of mounting ecclesiastical claims, yet, none the
less, this claim for the *universitas fidelium* remains one of those leaps in
original thought which surprise whenever the historian meets them. It introduces a kind of medieval "congregationalism" which is unique.

The paradox is that, over against this democratic socialized Church
which strikes so modern a note, Marsiglio sets an extreme other-worldly
ideal for the priesthood which betrays the influence of some of the most
rigorous medieval idealists, the Spiritual Franciscans. On the one hand, the
Church is a social institution, functioning in a this-worldly context and, as
such, requiring the priesthood to contribute to the sufficient life of civil society and even to participate as part of the people in the coercive authority
of the state. Yet, on the other hand, in Discourse II Marsiglio makes it
plain that because the clergy are dedicated to other-worldly ends, they
ought to refuse to take part in secular responsibilities. For the divine law
they serve has no coercive force in this world. Christ said: *My kingdom is
not of this world;* therefore, says Marsiglio, by Christ's counsel and example they must refuse such rulership. He goes further—and here surely one
hears the echo of the Spiritual Franciscans—in asserting that the clergy
must renounce riches and ambition and all the secular values which characterize the state; in opposition to these they must practice poverty and
humility, they must preach contempt of this world's values, they must exhort men to pursue those of the world to come. Marsiglio seems here to set
up two contrary systems of values which he does not attempt to make compatible. Theoretically he never resolves the dichotomy, but practically he
gets the priests out of their dilemma, for since, he argues, the Legislator
has the plenitude of power, it can give the priests power to participate in
government. The Legislator's authority can be limited by nothing, and certainly not by the other-worldly allegiance of the clergy.

Thus, in the long run, Marsiglio has to admit that there is a realm of
eternal values which does impinge on his domain of secular values in the
problem of the priesthood. Like Dante, there are for him, after all, two
ends. Here, however, we reach the most striking contrast in their two
methods of handling the problem of Church and state. Dante, like Marsig-

lio, affirms the reality of the temporal end in its own right, but his two beatitudes are, in the long view, united in one, for the lines of both are extended beyond this world's horizon to their meeting-point in the unity of
God. He cannot resist putting the temporal in the context of the eternal
and this is the undoing of his argument. His whole case for the independence of the secular ruler collapses since the beatitude which belongs to
the eternal order must govern the temporal which is ultimately subsumed
into it. To Marsiglio the horizon of this life cuts the two ends sharply
apart. The civic end is severed at that point, but in this life it is absolute.
The eternal end is certainly to be recognized here as a kind of invisible
line running through the consciences of men and, especially, the loyalties
of priests, but it does not exist here in external acts, for it has no coercive
force: its realm is the next world. Thus Marsiglio is able to give complete
sovereignty to the authority responsible for this world's ends, not because
it is higher but because in this life it alone has coercive force.

We can only look briefly at Marsiglio's approach to the concept of
universal government. Discourse I seems to make it plain that Marsiglio
can only conceive of the unity of the state in terms of a republic in which
the whole people can be the Legislator. He would seem to be utterly opposed both to the idea of universal government and to the concept of monarchy which went with it. Even though he allows for various forms of state,
the image of the Italian city-state seems to be before his eyes most of the
time. Unlike Dante, he dismisses universal government as something which
"merits a reasoned study, but is distinct from our present concern" (*Defensor pacis,* I, xvii, § 10). Yet in the second Discourse Marsiglio seems to be
thinking in far wider terms: the *universitas fidelium* is a world-wide
Church and the ruler so frequently mentioned in opposition to the pope is
not the head of a city-state but the emperor. One can even at times detect
a swing from republicanism towards absolutism. Is there really a change
between the two Discourses? When in Discourse II Marsiglio turns the attack directly on the pretensions of the bishops of Rome, he is forced to
counter the universalism of those claims by something correspondingly
worldwide. His answer is the General Council to which he gives universal
legislative powers in religious matters. But when we examine this we find
that it still rests on the popular authority of all the separate human legislators:

> And now I am going to show that the principal authority . . . for such de-
> termination of doubtful questions belongs only to a general council com-
> posed of all Christians or of the weightier part of them, or to those persons
> who have been granted such authority by the whole body of Christian be-
> lievers. The procedure is as follows: Let all the notable provinces or com-
> munities of the world, in accordance with the determination of their human
> legislators whether one or many, and according to their proportion in quan-
> tity and quality of persons, elect faithful men, first priests and then

non-priests, suitable persons of the most blameless lives and the greatest experience in divine law . . . they are to assemble at a place which is most convenient . . . where they are to settle those matters pertaining to divine law which have appeared doubtful. . . . There too they are to make such other decrees with regard to church ritual or divine worship as will be conducive to the quiet and tranquillity of the believers.

Defensor pacis, II, xx, § 2

Because it derives from all the peoples this General Council becomes the faithful human Legislator with universal coercive powers:

. . . to the faithful human legislator which lacks a superior belongs the authority to give a coercive command or decree ordering that all men alike, priests and non-priests, observe the general council's decisions, regulations and judgements, and to inflict punishment in person or in property, in this world, on transgressors of its command. . . .

Defensor pacis, II, xxi, § 4

Both the international extent of the "pernicious plague" he is fighting and the very universality of the Faith itself, seem to edge Marsiglio in Discourse II away from his ingrained small-scale republicanism towards the world state. Yet he goes unwillingly. Fundamentally the two Discourses are not out of harmony with each other. To the universalism of the papal *plenitudo potestatis* he opposes a consensus of human opinion which still reflects the common sense and judgement of "the whole body of believers or their weightier part." Where Dante sees universal monarchy as a theological idea mirroring divine unity, Marsiglio sets up the faithful human Legislator as an expression of the *universitas fidelium*. The common experiences of Italian city-politics and papal monarchy could not have driven two men in more opposite directions.

15

William of Occam
and Higher Law

MAX A. SHEPARD

William of Occam has fittingly been called the "most subtle doctor of the Middle Ages." Despite this fact, or perhaps because of it, the vast political writings [1] of this famous fourteenth-century scholastic have been surprisingly neglected by modern students, particularly in England and the United States. It is commonly agreed that among general philosophers of the Middle Ages this "second founder of nominalism" is surpassed by St. Thomas Aquinas alone. Surely, therefore, the presumption is reasonable that the encyclopedic mass of Occam's political writings conceals many "diamonds in the rough," only awaiting discovery. The present writer hopes that he may throw some light on

This article was originally published in *American Political Science Review*, 26 (December 1932), 1005–1023, and 27 (February 1933), 24–38. It is reprinted here with the permission of the publisher.
[1] They cover about 900 folio pages in Goldast's *Monarchiae*, Vol. II, and are exceeded by those of no other medieval political writer, unless it be St. Thomas Aquinas. Other political works published since Goldast considerably increase this amount. See Scholz, *Unbekannte Kirchenpolitische Streitschriften* (Rome, 1911), Vol. I, pp. 141–189; Vol. II, 392–480.

certain important problems discussed by Occam, especially that most significant one of a "higher" or fundamental law.

An impression seems prevalent in many quarters that Occam obtained most of his political ideas from his famous contemporary, Marsiglio of Padua, who has established himself among modern students as the really great political genius of his times. Without detracting from Marsiglio's well-deserved fame, we are quite unable to accept this view. On the contrary, Occam, as might be expected of such a great general philosopher, can stand upon his own feet, and his political theory in many respects exhibits characteristics entirely independent of any Marsiglian influence. Riezler's hypothesis of a mutual interaction between the two is probably correct.[2]

Nor is the allegation tenable that Occam's writings are so diffuse, obscure, and self-contradictory that his own opinion on important questions can never be ascertained satisfactorily.[3] It is true that Occam habitually presents all sides of the questions he discusses, and in certain instances specifically disclaims any intention of setting forth his own views.[4] But a careful analysis of Occam's actual words will usually reveal his meaning and the position which he occupied on the questions under debate. With respect to the idea of the higher law, there is a body of remarkably clear and self-consistent doctrine which can justly be designated as Occam's own. Indeed, by the aid of his sound, if often tedious, dialectical method, Occam attained a synthetic grasp, a profundity, and an originality equaled by few, if any, other writers of the Middle Ages. It is high time that his piercing intellect receive due recognition.

If we are to concentrate our attention on Occam's theory of a higher law, the first question naturally is: What do we mean by "higher law"? For the purposes of this discussion, the term may be defined as those rules of social conduct conceived of as limiting determinate authority and as laying down the conditions under which such authority must be exercised. It is "higher" because it is above the legal rules emanating from such political authority. Determinate political authority is public-legal control exercised by a *clearly recognizable, definite man or body of men.* John Austin's sovereign is, by this definition, a "determinate political authority." The higher law thus becomes those rules, springing in large part from a source or sources distinct from such sovereign or other definite political authority, which limit its jurisdiction. In John Dickinson's phrase, the higher law is the "law behind law," the law behind the rules laid down by any definite,

[2] Sigmund Riezler, *Die Literarischen Widersacher der Päpste,* p. 274.
[3] See W. A. Dunning, *Political Theories, Ancient and Medieval,* p. 245; Paul Janet, *Histoire de la Science Politique,* Vol. I, pp. 485–595; and R. L. Poole, *Illustrations of the History of Medieval Learning and Thought,* p. 244.
[4] Cf. *Octo Quaestiones,* Book VIII, chap. 5, printed in Melchior Goldast's *Monarchiae* (Frankfurt, 1668), Vol. II, p. 393. Hereafter, Goldast, Vol. II, will be cited simply by pages.

tangible center or complex of governmental control.[5] The vast, amorphous populace, the "people" or "society," is not a determinate political authority. On the other hand, any identifiable center of public-legal control, such as emperor, pope, king, feudal lord, municipality, general council, organized estates, or other legislative body, acting as or for the people, falls within this category. Custom, if it is conceived of as limiting all determinate political authority, "natural law," and "divine law" are ordinarily higher law. Statutes or decrees, on the other hand, are generally civil, or lower, law. We propose, then, to consider Occam's theory of the relation of determinate political authority and the law it lays down to the higher law. This will inevitably involve a careful investigation of the nature, sources, and branches of the higher law, as well as the question of whether it really is law or merely "morality." Finally, also, the problem of sanctions in Occam's theory must be faced. How far must men obey rules violating higher law? Can any machinery be invoked against a recalcitrant ruler or ruling body? Surely no more fundamental political or legal problem could occupy the minds of medieval thinkers, and none has more far-reaching implications for the history of political thought or for modern constitutional doctrine.

Occam does not, of course, nicely label and catalogue his theory of higher law as such. It must never be forgotten that his writings are primarily "tracts for the times," polemics written to defend the Emperor Lewis of Bavaria against his arch-antagonist Pope John XXII (*circa* 1330). Occam focuses attention upon the extent and limits of papal power and its relation to temporal authority. However, he drops many incidental, though highly important, remarks concerning the latter, so that we can piece together a quite systematic theory concerning it also in relationship to higher law.[6] In this period, the Papacy is indeed as politically important as the Empire or national kingdoms. Many disputes involved secular control exercised or claimed by the Pope; moreover, discussions of the nature and limits of his purely spiritual powers and of his relation to the church councils furnish instructive analogies, applicable *mutatis mutandis* to the temporal authorities.

For Occam, as for most of the great medieval thinkers, all laws, jurisdictions, and authorities come from God in the same sense in which the Apostle Paul spoke when he said that "there is no power except from God."[7] Occam would, however, have been the first to recognize that this

---

[5] See John Dickinson, "The Law Behind Law," 29 *Columbia Law Review*, 113–146 and 285–319. Dickinson does not believe it advisable or correct to designate "higher law" as real law today, although he admits that it was law in the Middle Ages. See his *Administrative Justice and the Supremacy of Law in the United States*, p. 84. The present writer agrees completely as far as the Middle Ages are concerned.

[6] Many readers will perhaps be surprised to discover that Occam, though called upon to defend the Emperor with the "pen, instead of the sword," no more envisaged an absolute and unlimited imperial power than a papal one.

[7] *Opus Nonaginta Dierum*, chap. 88, p. 1146.

settles few problems. In any question of conflicting laws or authorities, we need to know what law or set of laws takes precedence, what precepts come most directly from God. In the elaborate feudal hierarchy in which Occam lived, the burning questions obviously turn upon this matter of mediation. The laws coming immediately from God must take precedence over those coming only mediately from him.

Occam designates those rules coming most directly from divine revelation, without the intervention of any human will, as divine law, *lex divina*, or *lex Dei*. Such law relates primarily, if not exclusively, to spiritual matters and overrules any contrary human law, no matter by whom promulgated.[8] If, for example, a king, or other authority, should order the worship of Mohammed or the observance of the laws of the Jews, his subjects would never be excused from their sin if they obeyed. Everyone capable of reason is expected to know that divine law stands over mortal law.[9] No mortal can command obedience in subversion of divine law,[10] which includes the *lex Christiana*, or evangelical law,[11] the law contained in the Holy Scriptures [12] and the law ordained by Christ.[13] Under divine law, the Pope has the power of intervening in temporal matters when subversion of the Christian faith is threatened. Occam qualifies this papal prerogative, however, very strictly. It may not be exercised regularly and directly, but only in exceptional cases and in special circumstances, and when all lay authorities fail to perform their duties.[14] Although divine law is immutable, Occam hints in one place that it may not all be eternal; some provisions were promulgated only for the benefit of bygone ages and have lost their significance today.[15]

Next to divine law comes natural law. This contains provisions conceived of as immutable and binding on every human authority and individual. Unlike divine law, it does not come through special revelation, but is implanted by God in all men's hearts so that "he who runs may read." We constantly find *ius naturale* and *ratio naturalis* linked together, which shows us that Occam held to the time-honored ancient and medieval tradition of eternal, immutable principles of nature, discoverable by the use of reason.[16] Gierke regards Occam as a member of that school which saw the essence of natural law in will rather than reason, and which identified it with the divine command or will. In this respect he contrasts him with Aquinas, whom he considers much more inclined to emphasize the reason

---

[8] *Dialogus,* Part III, Tractatus II, Liber II, chap. 4, p. 904.
[9] *Dial.,* Part I, Liber VI, chap. 47.
[10] *Dial.,* Part I, Liber VI, chap. 47.
[11] *Dial.,* I, VI, 47, p. 51.
[12] *Dial.,* I, VI, 100, p. 630.
[13] *Dial.,* III, I, I, 16, p. 786.
[14] *Dial.,* III, I, I, 16, p. 786.
[15] *Dial.,* III, I, II, 20, p. 808.
[16] *Dial.,* I, VI, 62, p. 568.

immanent in the Being of God as the source of the law of nature. According to Gierke, Occam's views proceed from pure nominalism, Aquinas' from realism.[17] He does not, however, cite any supporting passage from the author for his interpretation. Our own conclusion is that no really essential difference exists between Occam and Aquinas on this point, and that it is on the whole erroneous to extend the nominalistic-realistic schism to embrace their respective theories of natural law.[18] To be sure, Occam linked up natural law with God, as he did all law, directly or indirectly, mediately or immediately. But so did Aquinas, and so did all the other great medieval thinkers. The evidence goes to show that he had a clear distinction in mind between divine law and natural law and that, when he did link the two together, he characterized both types of law as "right reason" rather than "divine will." [19] The distinction which Occam himself drew is that natural law, together with positive human law, regulates the temporal affairs of men without the interposition of any divine revelation; whereas spiritual matters are controlled to a considerable extent by such revelation [20] or by divine law in its strictest sense.

Unmistakably, Occam regards all inferior human laws as subject to correction and rejection by natural law, just as much as by divine law. "No

---

[17] *Political Theories of the Middle Ages* (Maitland trans.), pp. 172–173, note 256.

[18] Indeed, the general similarity of their two theories of natural law is quite noticeable and remarkable. Occam borrowed a great deal from Aquinas and must thank the master for many of his underlying ideas about and classifications of law. Aquinas furnished the general lines within which Occam, and indeed all his successors, moved. How far Occam was from a mere plagiarist, however, will become evident to anyone who makes even the most superficial examination of their writings. In countless places Occam refines and subtly develops ideas present, if at all, only in the most rudimentary form in the master. His ever-awe-inspiring ability to draw acute distinctions well merits for him the title of *subtillismus doctor,* and his synthetic grasp is second only to Aquinas'. Perhaps Occam's greater stress on the *jus gentium,* as a legal category which did allow for particularistic variations from ideal norms, is some evidence of his nominalistic bias. But the point cannot be pushed very far. Occam also emphasized the ideal and immutable elements of natural law, while, on the other hand, Aquinas was too great a thinker not to realize the importance of *jus gentium* as a means of adapting ideal norms to practical circumstances. The similarity of the two theories, their oneness on many critical points, deserve, in our opinion, much greater stress than their differences. This is but another and striking testimonial to the widespread, deeply rooted, and unwavering medieval belief in and consciousness of a higher law above all human persons and authorities, a veritable "law behind law." Here were two philosophers standing at the opposite poles of realism and nominalism in their general philosophies and their *Weltanschauungen,* yet agreed in their fundamental presuppositions concerning natural and divine law. It would appear that Occam, despite his radical nominalism, could not divorce himself from the ingrained legal thinking of centuries, as summed up in the *Summa Theologica* of Aquinas. Without in any way disparaging the former's tremendous contributions, immense ability, and marvelous keenness, we cannot help feeling that Aquinas was the more consistent and that his realism (or in modern terminology, idealism) is a truer philosophical expression of the legal ideas which both men held in common than Occam's nominalism. This only makes the extreme importance, fixity, and intensity of medieval higher-law notions the more evident.

[19] *Dial.,* I, VI, 47, p. 551.

[20] *Dial.,* III, II, II, 4, p. 904.

just positive law can be contrary to natural law." [21] Nor is it correct to interpret this as a merely moral obligation, without legal significance or
binding force. The higher law is quite as much law as the lower positive
law, indeed more so, just because it is "higher," and any conflicting lower
law is no law at all. This is made plain in unequivocal language. To be
sure, no one can disobey laws laid down by superior authority at will (ad
libitum), but such disobedience is not only justified, but indicated as a
duty, if lex superior or ratio evidens can be shown to be on the side of him
who disobeys. "And the reason of this is because there can be no law
which is openly repugnant to superior law or to reason, whence any civil
law whatsoever which is repugnant to divine law or obvious reason is not
law, and in the same manner the words of canon or civil law, in case they
are repugnant to divine law, i.e., Holy Scriptures, or to right reason, are
not to be observed." [22] All human authority, not excepting emperor and
pope, is limited as a matter of course by the higher natural law.[23] This is
indeed a self-evident proposition and the foundation stone of Occam's
whole system. No human power can break unbreakable natural law. Such a
possibility does not enter his mind.

These statements, though forceful and clear-cut, do not exhibit any
great originality. It is in connection with the further elaboration of the subject that we first encounter Occam's subtle ability to draw fine distinctions
which mark real differences, and which he made because he recognized so
profoundly the unending complexity of human affairs and the necessity of
adapting theories to fit the practical conditions of the times. He distinguishes three senses in which we may use the term "natural law," and these
we must keep clearly in mind if we are to understand Occam. In the first
sense, natural law is "that which conforms to natural reason, which in no
case fails." He has, and we have, thus far been using the phrase in this
sense, in emphasizing the binding character of natural law as against all
human and subordinate authority. In the second sense, natural law is a
purely ideal concept. "It is that which must be observed by those who employ natural equity alone, without any human custom or constitution." [24]
No people today really lives by natural equity alone. Since the fall of man,
or as a result of original sin—in other words, since man is not perfect—we
can only expect at most a distant approximation to it. Taken in this second
sense, therefore, natural law has a directive or normative force only, not a
binding one. We can call it law only in the case of an ideally perfect community. These two categories correspond to distinctions laid down by St.
Thomas Aquinas between the immutable and mutable parts of natural law,

[21] Dial., I, VI, 100, p. 629.
[22] Dial., I, VI, 100, p. 630.
[23] For the Emperor, cf. Dial., III, II, II, 26, p. 922–923; and for the Pope, Dial., III, II,
I, 23, pp. 891–892, and Octo Quaestiones I, chap. 2, p. 315.
[24] Dial., III, II, I, 10, p. 878.

between the unchangeable principles and the directive demonstrations of that law,[25] although Occam worked out the theory in much more detail. Natural law in the first sense is immutable, in the second, changeable, although the change should be as slight as is consistent with actual conditions and needs. As examples of natural law in the first sense, Occam gives us the rules that "thou shalt not commit adultery," "shalt not lie," and the like.[26] "Thou shalt not worship a foreign god" is also included in this category.[27] The two leading rules of natural law in the second sense are "property is common to all" and "all men are free," about both of which we shall have something to say later. The practical importance of the rule against adultery or "breaking the marriage vow" can be seen from Occam's specific illustration.[28] Questions of adultery and matrimony pertain to secular jurisdiction as far as natural law is concerned and to ecclesiastical as far as divine law is involved. Since natural law does not forbid a man to have several wives (and it upholds the sanctity of the vow), it follows that no secular ruler can punish polygamy as adultery. The ecclesiastical judge may, however, punish it with severe penalties because polygamy is a crime against divine law.[29] Here we have a clear and concrete example of the binding force of natural law upon a secular ruler, as well as further evidence of a distinction between divine and natural law.

Occam's peculiar genius comes most clearly to the fore in his treatment of natural law taken in the third sense, or *jus gentium*, a category which had caused Aquinas a considerable amount of difficulty. We have seen that natural law in the second sense, as a normative principle of natural equity, is not immutable; that it is possible to "establish that something be done contrary to that law." [30] Now, in the third sense, natural law includes those deviations from pure natural law in the second sense, and this is *jus gentium*, together with other human law. "In the third sense, natural law is called that which is derived from the *jus gentium* or from *any human act* by evident reason, unless by the consent of all who are interested the contrary is established; this may be called natural law by supposition." [31] As a matter of fact, we have really moved a long way from pure natural law in making this jump to *jus gentium* and to other human law, and Occam knows it. He really regards *jus gentium* much more as human law than as natural law. In a most important and original passage, he tells us that we must distinguish between human laws of which "certain

[25] *Summa Theologica*, Part II, Vol. I, Qu. 94, Arts. 5–6.
[26] *Dial.*, III, II, III, 6, p. 932.
[27] *Dial.*, III, II, I, 10, p. 878; cf. above note 9.
[28] Cf. Dorner, "Das Verhältnis von Kirche und Staat nach Occeam," *Theologische Studien*, 1885 (1–2), the best treatment of Occam's political theory of which we are cognizant.
[29] *Dial.*, III, II, II, 16, p. 915.
[30] *Dial.*, III, II, III, 6, p. 933.
[31] *Dial.*, III, II, III, 6, p. 933. Occam's great debt to Aquinas will be obvious to anyone who reads the *Summa Theologica*, II, I, Qu. 94, Art. 5.

ones are laws of emperors and other persons and of particular communities subjected to the Emperor; these laws may be called civil laws; certain are in a sense proper to the entire community of mortals, which seem to pertain to the *jus gentium,* which in a sense is natural and in a sense human or positive." This *jus gentium,* or "higher human law," clearly binds the Emperor and is above all civil law or enacted law.

> The Emperor is never bound of necessity, even if it is proper for him to live, by his own laws, *provided* those laws are kept which pertain to the *jus gentium,* for the reason that all nations (*gentes*) and especially all rational people use such law, just as the Emperor is bound to the same. Whence generally he is not permitted to prohibit occupation of land, wars, captivities, servitude . . . and other things which seem to pertain to *jus gentium.*[32]

One can see from this that Occam was an eminently practical person. Recognizing that he confronted a "condition, and not a theory," he refused to confine the discussion of higher-law limits on authority to ideal principles of pure equity. In a rough and imperfect world we can still retain important limits on imperial, or other determinate, political authority and yet meet the facts of life halfway. *Jus gentium* is the nearest approach to ideal justice attainable, "taking men as they are and not as they should be." It contains principles which are in general to be obeyed by all rulers and subjects. They can, however, be modified by human beings, under exceptional circumstances, since *jus gentium* is human law. *Jus gentium* is always subject to modification by the consent of all mortals who can establish the contrary as law.[33] Even the Emperor can break *jus gentium* himself in exceptional cases, when the common good demands it, but it must be particularly noted that Occam hedges this authority in on all sides.[34] The criteria of the common good or of the general utility always here condition the exercise of imperial power. These points will become much clearer when we observe them later in their concrete content.

We have seen that Occam feels that natural law, taken in its first sense, does not afford sufficient restraint on the Emperor or king, and, on the other hand, is too practical to give the ideal principles of natural equity more than directive force as against them. Therefore, he interposes higher human law as a further limit, following pure natural law respectfully, though at a distance. *Jus gentium,* he says, was introduced through human addition, after original sin or the fall of man.[35] We must be quite clear as to what Occam meant by these words.

---

[32] *Dial.,* III, II, II, 28, p. 924.
[33] *Dial.,* III, II, II, 28, p. 924. This is a theoretical statement of the famous medieval principle of "quod omnes tangit ab omnibus approbetur." See also *Dial.,* III, II, III, 12. p. 942. Note that the "consent of all mortals" is not a determinate political authority.
[34] *Jus gentium* is never fully to be abrogated. *Dial.,* III, II, III, 12, p. 943.
[35] *Opus Nonaginta Dierum,* chap. 92, p. 1150.

Although original sin was to the medievalist a burning reality, the words translated into modern language mean that modifications in pure natural law have to be made because of the actual conditions of the times and the imperfect character of human nature. Ideals must compromise with practical realities if any progress is to be made toward their realization. "A leader must be out in front, but not too far." This does not make *jus gentium* inequitable or unjust. On the contrary, it is human nature (man's "sinful" character) or practical circumstances that are responsible for the inequity or injustice, not the legal rules which are adapted to do everything possible to minimize injustice, to approximate ideal equity, and to promote the general welfare in an imperfect world. As Occam puts it:

> The custom (*consuetudo*) of the *ius gentium* is contrary to that natural equity which existed in the state of innocence, and indeed to that natural equity which ought to exist between men following reason in all things. To the natural equity which exists among men prone to dissension and acting badly, that custom is not contrary; and thus the contradiction is according to nature,[36] and not according to human morals, because such custom is not iniquitous or evil.[37]

In this sense, Occam was right in calling *jus gentium* natural. To be sure (and perhaps here his fundamental philosophical nominalism gives the key to his attitude), he saw the impossibility of extolling as a reality a set of ideal norms having no relation to the facts. But he could not fail to note, as one great fact, that men are constantly striving to approximate justice no matter how imperfect the realization.[38] Or, to sum it up in the admirable synthetic phrase of the great German jurist, Rudolf Stammler, he recognizes a "natural law with variable content." [39]

As we shall see later in more detail, private property rights are ordinarily subsumed under the *jus gentium*. By bringing such rights as these under this law, Occam, as far back as the fourteenth century, anticipated the modern critics of the natural-rights school. They quite properly point the finger of scorn at men like Locke for maintaining the inviolability of private property as a principle of immutable natural law, as a natural-legal right of the individual anterior to all society. The rights which Occam recognized under the *jus gentium* are not immutable, inviolable natural rights. They are rights, which, though generally invariable, can be adapted to changing circumstances, can be suspended under emergency conditions, just because they are essentially human and social, even though they embody the ceaseless striving of the human spirit toward the greatest attaina-

[36] Here meaning the ideal state of things.
[37] Here meaning the ideal state of things.
[38] Cf. the famous couplet: "Ah! but a man's reach should exceed his grasp. Or what's a heaven for?"
[39] *Theory of Justice,* passim.

ble natural justice. To coin a phrase, we encounter here not natural-legal rights, but "social-legal rights." We use both the words "legal" and "social." For Occam, *jus gentium* is law just as much as natural law (first sense) and, as far as legal validity is concerned, differs from the *jus civile* (or enacted law of emperors, kings, or of the state) only in being on a higher plane. Most significant is the characterization "social." These rights arise out of human relationships in society, as distinguished from human political relationships. They limit generally, and except in extraordinary cases, emperor, king, councils, assemblies, and in fact every determinate political authority. They are not political creations of state or government, but are prior logically, legally, and often temporally, to the state regarded as the embodiment of determinate governmental authority. Unless we draw this distinction between the state and society, we completely fail to grasp the drift of Occam's theory.

This theory of the *jus gentium* as developed by Occam brings to full completion a movement of thought, the faint beginnings of which can be traced at least as far back as the Roman period. Cicero, the most acute of the Roman political philosophers, seems to have distinguished between *jus gentium* and *jus naturale*,[40] although not very clearly. The whole tenor of his thought warrants the conclusion that he regarded natural law as true law, since human law is merely embodied natural law and no state is conceivable except a just one, founded on law.[41] The best Roman jurists also seem to have distinguished between *jus gentium* and *jus naturale,* although Maine implies that they did not.[42] It will be recalled also that Seneca, the Stoic, extols a primitive state of innocence and points to private property, slavery, and government (institutions which, as we shall see, Occam brings under *jus gentium*) as inevitable consequences of the fall of man and the depravity of human nature.[43] Seneca is not entirely clear as to whether these institutions are themselves conventional examples of man's sinful character or natural in the sense of being the best remedies for it. The latter is the more likely interpretation, but Seneca never clearly faced the question. This problem caused the Christian fathers more concern than any other. Whether they considered the conventional institutions arising out of the fall as just or unjust is not an easy question, although the former view again seems the better.[44] The whole matter bears directly on theories of the social compact. The one line, taken by Sophist and Epicurean writers, and which has a modern representative in Hobbes, regards the state as purely conventional, purely a man-made affair, formed entirely irrespective of

[40] See his *Partitiones Oratoriae,* chap. 37, sec. 130–131.
[41] *De Republica,* I, 25.
[42] See Maine, *Ancient Law,* p. 46, and cf. Carlyle, *Medieval Political Theory,* Vol. I, Part II, chap. 3, and passages cited from Roman jurists.
[43] Carlyle, Part I, chap. 2.
[44] Whether St. Augustine regarded justice as essential to the state is a much mooted point. We can only note the controversy here.

principles of justice. The other view, starting from the Stoics (if not with Plato and Aristotle), and shared by most modern social-contract writers, including Locke and Rousseau, considers the state, although man-made, as natural in the sense of a more or less perfect embodiment of and striving toward eternal principles of natural justice. Obviously, Occam, with his theory of *jus gentium*, falls in the second group.

Gratian, the great canonist of the twelfth century, distinguished between natural law and custom, the *jus gentium* being included in the latter.[45] The exact position, however, of this extremely bothersome category in Gratian's theory is uncertain. His pupil Rufinus, was somewhat explicit. After the fall, Rufinus tells us, man "stirred up the dying embers of the science of justice," which taught him to form treaties of concord and to enter into pacts "which indeed are called *jus gentium* because almost all nations employ them." [46] Here again the inchoate idea of a "natural law with variable content" appears.

St. Thomas Aquinas, in the next century and less than a hundred years before Occam, anticipates the latter's theory most nearly. He clearly distinguishes between *jus naturale* and *jus gentium*, classifying the latter, like Occam, under "human law," and, like him, deriving it from natural law. Aquinas specifically states that *jus gentium*, although contained under human positive law, proceeds from natural law just as "conclusions from principles." "It is in a certain sense natural to man, according as it is rational and derived from natural law, whence men easily consent to it; it is distinguished, however, from natural law, especially from that common to animals." [47] Building upon this basis, Occam worked out the whole thing in much more detail.

Occam's *jus gentium* bears a very striking resemblance to medieval customary law. He apparently recognized this, at least unconsciously. Like *jus gentium*, medieval custom is man-made and is generally regarded as unchangeable, but in practice is capable of being modified to a degree to meet changing social realities. Undoubtedly some theory of the identification of custom and the *jus gentium* was in the back of Occam's mind. Any human law, higher than the enacted will of a king, pope, emperor, or feudal assembly, must be custom. Occam does, indeed, speak in one place of a "consuetudo juris gentium," or "custom of the *jus gentium*," [48] and when he says that "*jus gentium* can never be fully abrogated but only for time," [49] he must have had some idea of custom in view. This is the only rational explanation when we consider that he regarded *jus gentium* as human, and

---

[45] See Carlyle, Vol. II, Part II, chap. 4.
[46] Carlyle, Vol. II, Part II, chap. 4., citing the *Summa Decretum*, Preface.
[47] *Summa Theologica*, II, I, Qu. 95, Art. 4.
[48] *Opus N. D.*, 92, p. 1150.
[49] *Dial.*, III, II, III, 12, pp. 942–943.

not divine or natural, law in any strict sense. Finally, he says that it is a principle of *jus gentium* that "what touches all should be approved by all," [50] and that, since *jus gentium* is human law, "by the consent of all mortals acting contradictorily the contrary may be kept for law." [51] Both these last quotations strongly suggest medieval customary law. In general, unanimity was a fundamental principle in the Middle Ages; every member of the community was supposed, at least theoretically, to have a voice in matters affecting fundamental laws or customs. Occam would, of course, have been the last to carry out the principle to its ultimate and logical conclusion. In extraordinary or emergency situations, as we shall see later, he allowed a majority vote (perhaps fictitiously regarded as cast for all) to decide, the general welfare overriding individual desires. In such emergency instances, he allowed determinate political authority—king, emperor, pope, or council—to change the *jus gentium*. But he envisaged no absolute power. All authority, for him, had to act reasonably and in relation to special circumstances and cases, not arbitrarily. Ordinarily his *jus gentium*, like medieval customary law, was regarded as unchangeable or changeable only by the consent of all mortals, a process much more nearly resembling an unconscious, communal act than a consciously interposed legislative or constitutive act. Although this theory no doubt under-estimates the importance of change and evolution in the law, it seems to have developed in very large measure out of a real factual situation. No social or legal growth ever remains static. Certainly custom in the Middle Ages did not. The change, however, was so slow and gradual as to be almost invisible. At any given time, and by any given body of men, it was not deemed possible to do more than modify bits of custom, to bring new facts under old principles, to provide for exceptional circumstances, or to act so as to make the whole body of the law more self-consistent. The men of the Middle Ages (with Occam at their head) would have stood aghast and uncomprehending if confronted by the modern idea of a sovereign constitutive or legislative assembly. They could not conceive of a body theoretically able to change the whole body of existing law at will and overnight. The broad river of medieval custom wells up from many different sources and is fed by many different tributary streams. These include courts, kings, wise men, councils, popes, emperors, ecclesiastics, gilds, the sworn inquest of the countryside, and other institutions much less tangible and ponderable though no less significant. Perhaps all may be subsumed under the broad general category of the "sense of right of the community." Nowhere does the legal hierarchy pyramid to a single absolute and legally omnipotent sovereign head, be he regarded as a man, a body of men, or any definable

[50] *Dial.*, III, II, III, 12, p. 942.
[51] *Dial.*, III, II, II, 28, p. 924.

combination of political organs or authorities. Only by the most imperceptible, if inexorable, of processes can this river of custom change its channel or be diverted from its bed.

Occam's largely implicit, but partly conscious, identification of *jus gentium* with custom can be found to a much less extent in previous writers. Cicero,[52] Gratian,[53] and Aquinas [54] seem to share this view, though they do not develop its consequences. The civil and canon lawyers also discussed custom at some length, but, for the most part, instead of identifying it with *jus gentium,* they assigned it to a place subordinate to enacted civil law or legislation. This attitude clearly shows their servile dependence upon Roman law, and their failure to take sufficient account of the actual conditions in the medieval legal world. Indeed, these lawyers always allowed a later enacted law, if explicit enough, to override an earlier conflicting customary law.[55] Only the great feudal lawyers, such as Bracton, and the feudal custumals, such as Beaumonoir's, definitely recognized feudal customary law as a higher law, setting bounds to enacted law.[56] But these lawyers did not take the further philosophical step of linking up custom with *jus gentium* and of thus developing a theory of "natural law with variable content." [57] Occam, indeed, came nearer to considering *jus gentium* as higher customary law than any other medieval writer we have observed.

This category of *jus gentium* constitutes the very core of his theory of higher law. A clearer comprehension of this truth will result from a consideration of the detailed and consistent application which he made of his principles. We turn, then, to his theories of the origin of political power, of private property, and of liberty.

All temporal government rested, for Occam, ultimately upon the consent of the governed. The community, or *communitas,* of the realm establishes and elects the national king, and the *communitas,* or *universitas,* of all mortals elects the Emperor; these are principles following directly from *jus gentium.*[58] If it is objected that "all political authority comes from God," the answer is that it "comes from God, but not solely from God. Imperial power comes from God through the mediation of men." [59] Occam even gives us an embryonic governmental contract theory in asserting that

[52] *Partitiones Oratoriae,* 137, sec. 130–131.
[53] Gratian, *Decretum,* VI, sec. 1.
[54] *Summa Theologica,* II, I, Qu. 95 and 97.
[55] Cf. Sigmund Brie, *Die Lehre von Gewohnheitsrecht,* passim. This statement, of course, leaves out of account higher natural and divine law which might come in to reёnforce the prior customary law.
[56] For Bracton, see C. H. McIlwain, *Magna Carta and Common Law,* p. 35, citing Folio 1B; and for Beaumonoir, see sec. 1514 (Salmon ed., pp. 264–265).
[57] The only hint of such a linkage is Bracton's famous statement: "Non sub homine sed sub Deo et lege."
[58] *Dial.,* III, II, III, 12, p. 942; III, II, III, 6, p. 934; III, II, I, 29, p. 902.
[59] *Dial.,* III, II, I, 8, p. 876; *Dial.,* III, II, I, 26, p. 899.

"it is a general pact of human society to obey its kings and more generally its emperor in those things which make for the common utility." [60] Thus the Romans saw the importance from the point of view of the common utility of the entire world of having one emperor govern all mortals. At this time, the necessity for peace and security overbalanced all else, and the consent of a majority of the people sufficed to start the government going.[61] Chaos had to be avoided at all costs. To make the government thus established entirely just and legal, the later consent of the whole world was necessary. Occam's true thought seems clearly, however, that, considering the anarchic conditions at the time of the institution of the Roman government, such "majority rule" was the nearest approach to justice then possible.[62] Ordinarily, such a cavalier disregard of the desires of the minority on such a great question would never be allowed by Occam.[63] The beauty of the *jus gentium* as human law, however, is that under extraordinary circumstances normally unbreakable principles of *jus gentium*, like this one of *quod omnes tangit ab omnibus approbetur,* can be broken or modified. Of course, the majority has no absolute power to override a minority in such a matter, but can act so only under emergency or exceptional circumstances. Its action must always, furthermore, meet the test of natural law, divine law, and the general standard of the common good.

From this theory of the origin of government, definite human-legal restraints (*jus gentium*) upon political authority can easily be postulated. These are in addition to those necessarily following from divine and natural law. The Emperor, for example, in relation to his subjects and their property, can only do those things which further the common utility.[64] Nor can he destroy the *imperium,* or political jurisdiction, in which he "lives, moves, and has his being," and "whatever works toward the destruction of the *imperium* does not hold as a matter of law (*de jure*)," so that such illegal imperial act may be revoked by a successor.[65] Emperors must, of course, in general obey the *jus gentium,* although in special cases, when the common utility would suffer prejudice by maintaining those rules, they may derogate from it.[66] Occam does envisage the historical existence of monarchies in which the king, unrestrained except by natural and divine law, ruled according to his own will, unbound by "any purely positive human laws or customs (*consuetudines*)." [67] In such a government, *jus gentium* would not restrain the king. However, Occam carefully distinguishes

[60] *Dial.,* III, II, II, 28, p. 924.
[61] *Dial.,* III, II, I, 27, p. 900.
[62] *Dial.,* III, II, I, 27, p. 900.
[63] Cf. A. L. Lowell's "consensus" as necessary to create a real public opinion. *Public Opinion and Popular Government,* passim.
[64] *Dial.,* III, II, II, 27–28.
[65] *Dial.,* III, II, I, 18, p. 887.
[66] *Dial.,* III, II, II, 28, p. 924.
[67] *Dial.,* III, I, II, 6, p. 794.

this form of government from the generally prevailing type of his own day and suggests that perhaps (*forte*) it can be found no longer anywhere in the world. In the second or "modern" form of government, "even if in a sense one man rules according to his own will,[68] yet he is bound by certain human laws and customs, which have been introduced, which he is held to maintain, and is obliged to swear and promise to maintain."[69] Again we discern in the back of Occam's mind a linking up of the higher law, or *jus gentium*, with fundamental medieval customary law. What are these "certain human laws and customs" if not the equivalent of Occam's *jus gentium?* We know that he did not deem emperor or king legally bound by laws of their own making, or by civil law in the strictest sense. *Jus gentium* is the only alternative. Occam's mention of the oath taken by the king can have only one meaning. This refers to the familiar coronation oath by which kings swore to observe and rule by the fundamental laws and customs of the realm. It will be recalled that Occam was an Englishman, even though like many of his fellow-countrymen he preferred to live on the Continent. Very probably he had in mind the English coronation oath. Of course, the higher customary law in England would be the common law itself, particularly as embodied in such provisions as Chapter 39 of Magna Carta.

Occam's greatest vacillation occurs over the burning question of whether or not the Holy Roman Emperor is the temporal lord of the whole world. It seems clear that he recognizes a large measure of *de facto,* if not *de jure,* independence in the national kingdoms, and in one place he boldly says that a *de facto* situation might just as well be recognized as *de jure.*[70] From the point of view of higher law, the thing to determine is simply what the community of mortals desires: Does it still want to recognize the Emperor as the *de jure* world-sovereign or does it sanction a splitting up into separate national kingdoms, in each of which the community of the realm elects the king or regulates his succession to the throne? Perhaps Occam's vacillation is due to his uncertainty as to just how the community of mortals, or "public opinion," stands on this question. Or he may not have wanted to offend his sponsor, the Emperor Lewis of Bavaria.

Even though the community of mortals can substitute legally independent national kingdoms for a universal empire, it ought not to disturb existing arrangements (i.e., modify the *jus gentium*) except for just cause and with all due respect to vested rights. The qualification here introduced of reasonable cause shows how far Occam was from recognizing any arbitrary or absolute power anywhere on earth. Even the community of mortals cannot disturb the existing legal situation in which it had originally acquiesced or which it had tacitly sanctioned (a universal empire with the

[68] That is, if we may interpret, he is not bound by his own laws. Cf. note 32 above.
[69] *Dial.,* III, I, II, 6, p. 795.
[70] *Dial.,* III, II, I, 10, p. 878, and III, II, II, 5 and 7, pp. 905 and 908.

right of election vested first in the people of the city of Rome, later in the college of the German *Kurfürsten*) except for just cause. Such cause would be guilt on the part of the electors or manifest public utility or necessity.[71] Arbitrary upsetting of the legitimate rights of imperial electors would redound to the "detriment of the entire community of mortals." [72]

Although Occam occupies himself principally with the question of papal authority, we can only touch upon it here. His strong conciliar tendencies are well-known, and in them he resembles Marsiglio of Padua and such earlier writers as John of Paris and Durandus de Mende the Younger. Occam believed that every papal right, beyond the Pope's purely spiritual authority (*potestas ordinis*) coming directly from God, springs from the consent of the community of the faithful, or from human law and custom. The community, generally acting through the general council of the church or the college of cardinals, not only elects the individual pope but also has the right to depose him if he acts heretically or illegally. It cannot, however, act arbitrarily or transmute the institution of the papacy, as such, into an aristocracy or democracy, because of obvious higher law limitations.[73]

Regularly, the Pope possesses no temporal power, although he is exempt from temporal laws or laws of general councils which would impair his purely spiritual functions.[74] However, he possesses a strictly qualified right to intervene in temporal matters when the Christian faith is threatened gravely and laymen do not do their duty. Under such special circumstances, divine law gives him wide prerogatives over temporals.[75] Similarly (and this is only another striking example of Occam's consistent relativity), the Emperor and other laymen have a limited right of intervention in spiritual matters, if it is for "the common utility of the church." They can, of course, not assume purely spiritual functions (*potestas ordinis*), but only administrative control (*potestas jurisdictionis*).[76]

In the purely spiritual sphere, the Pope is limited not only by divine and natural law but also in fifteen other specifically enumerated matters. Among these restraints upon papal jurisdiction, Occam mentions, as outstanding, acts of "supererogation." Ordinarily, and in the absence of sin on the part of the subject or obvious reasons of utility or necessity, the Pope cannot compel temperance, fasting, virginity, or marriage.[77] This is strikingly analogous to the modern opposition to sumptuary legislation. The

[71] *Octo Quaes.*, V, 3, p. 382, and *Dial.*, III, II, I, 29, p. 902.
[72] *Dial.*, chap. 31.
[73] *Dial.*, III, I, I, 17, p. 786; III, I, II, 27, p. 816; III, II, I, 19; III, II, II, 1; *Octo Quaes.*, II, chap. 1.
[74] *Octo Quaes.*, 1, 7, p. 322; and I, 8, p. 324.
[75] *Dial.*, III, I, I, 16, p. 786.
[76] *Dial.*, III, II, III, 4, p. 929.
[77] *Dial.*, III, II, I, 23, p. 892; III, II, II, 27 p. 923; III, II, III, 7, p. 935; III, II, I, 16, p. 786; *Octo Quaes.*, I, 7, p. 322; *De imperatorum et pontificum potestate* (Brampton ed.), pp. 58–59.

above bare outline should at least make clear how expressly Occam considered the authority of the Pope limited by a higher law.

It is in connection with Occam's elaborate theory of property that we
can most readily grasp the importance of his theory of higher law, particularly as embodied in the *jus gentium*. We must, therefore, investigate this
subject in considerable detail.

In Occam's view, God is originally the source of all property. But, as
in the case of law and government, this is true only in the most general
and indirect sense. Most property rights arise from human law and only
mediately from God, although in a few special cases such rights follow directly from special divine ordination or from *lex divina*.[78] Occam cites a
passage from St. Thomas Aquinas (*Summa Theol.*, II, II, Qu. 44, Art. 2)
stating that separate possessions are not according to natural law but are
founded upon human or positive law, and are added to natural law
through the exercise of human reason.[79] In the primal condition of mankind, or in the state of innocence in the Garden of Eden, all property was
common and none was discrete or private. Before Eve came, Adam had
only a *de facto* right of user and no greater right of private property than a
sole remaining monk would have in the property of a monastery.[80] The
natural condition of innocence, in which a law higher than any of purely
human creation makes all things common, corresponds to a state of affairs
in which Occam's natural law (second sense) prevails. He specifically in-
forms us, indeed, that "in the second sense of natural law, and not the first,
all things were common, . . . and if after the fall all men had lived according to reason, all things would have been held in common, since private
property was introduced on account of iniquity." [81] Communal ownership
could not possibly exist by natural law in the first sense, for in that case
nothing could have been licitly appropriated privately either by *jus gentium* or by *jus civile*. We must remember that natural law, taken in the first
sense, is immutable, invariable, and indispensable.[82]

Private property, then, results from human legal dispensation. It rests
upon a "coherently heterogeneous" system of private rights (*proprietas*)
and immunities replacing an "incoherently homogeneous" *dominium* vested
in the entire community. To a large extent, private property rests upon a
basis quite distinct from strictly civil law, or the law of kings, emperors,
and other political authorities. It is founded upon a human law anterior to
the law of any kings.[83] This can only mean logically that such rights of pri-

---

[78] *Opus Non. Dier.*, chap. 88, p. 1147.
[79] *Opus Non. Dier.*, chap. 88, p. 1146.
[80] *Opus Non. Dier.*, chaps. 26 and 27, p. 1073 ff.
[81] *Dial.*, III, II, III, 6, p. 932.
[82] *Dial.*, III, II, III, 6, p. 932.
[83] *Opus Non. Dier.*, chap. 88, p. 1147.

vate property are based on the *jus gentium*, the only kind of human law which stands above strictly civil law. "Private property rights [*dominia rerum* is here used as the equivalent of *divisio rerum*] were acquired outside of civil judgment by human law." As St. Isidore says, *"jus gentium* is the occupation of seats [*occupatio sedium*] etc. . . . By the *jus gentium* not only forms of action but also the occupation of seats was introduced." [84] Division of *dominium* into separate parts was introduced through human addition, and consequently by human law. This custom of the *jus gentium* [*consuetudo iuris gentium*] "is contrary to that natural equity which existed in the state of innocence, and indeed to that natural equity which ought to exist between men following reason in all things." The custom, however, is not contrary to that natural equity existing between men prone to dissension and to acting badly. The contradiction is according to nature, not human morality.[85] Here we can see clearly Occam's practical bent. He was willing to adapt norms of ideally pure natural law to the exigencies of social relations not illuminated exclusively by the white light of reason, and to accept *jus gentium* as a law good in so far as man's imperfect character and condition permits goodness. In short, we see here a "natural law with variable content," applied specifically to the fundamental question of private property.

What, then, is the position of emperors and kings[86] in relation to rights of private property? We have seen above that the Emperor is ordinarily bound by *jus gentium*.[87] It follows that normally he cannot arbitrarily deprive individuals who have rights in private property by the *jus gentium* (i.e., most individuals) of those rights. Occam unequivocally opposes those who claim that the Emperor can do everything in temporal matters not against divine and natural law, and who cite the much-mooted Roman-law maxims of *"imperator legibus solutus est," "quod principi placuit legis vigorem habet,"* and *"error principis facit jus"* in support of their claims. The Emperor, though not bound by his own law, must keep *jus gentium*, as higher human law, unless he sees that keeping it derogates from the common utility.[88] In relation to the goods of his subjects, he can do only those things that further that common utility.[89] He has no absolute rights over subjects; they would be his slaves if he could make them do anything except what is contrary to natural and divine law.[90] The Emperor is not sole lord of all temporal property, but he is lord in such a way that

[84] *Opus Non. Dier.*, chap. 91, p. 1149. Aquinas again had this theory of property as an institution of *jus gentium* in rudimentary outline, as did John of Paris.
[85] *Opus Non. Dier.*, chap. 92, p. 1150.
[86] The principles applying to the two are identical. *Dial.*, III, II, II, 25, p. 922.
[87] See *Dial.*, ff. 22, 26, p. 1013.
[88] *Dial.*, III, II, II, chaps. 26 and 28, pp. 922 and 924.
[89] *Dial.*, III, II, II, chap. 23, p. 921. Cf. also John of Paris.
[90] *Dial.*, III, II, II, chap. 27, p. 923.

"he can use them [temporals] and apply them to the common utility whenever he shall see that the common welfare takes preference over private interest. Of things pertaining to others, he has *dominium* in so far as he is able for cause and for the common utility of the people, and on account of the delicts of their possessors, to take such goods away from them and to appropriate them to himself or give them to others. Because, however, he cannot do this at his own arbitrary discretion, but as a consequence of the guilt of the possessors or for cause, to wit, the common utility, he does not have arbitrary *dominium* in them."

The Emperor certainly possesses some strictly private property which he can use and control in any way that he chooses, no matter how arbitrary. Besides this class of property and the property of private citizens, there is a category of state property over which the Emperor possesses a far from absolute authority. Occam's distinction is quite clear. "In certain immovable things, however, he does not have the right and *dominium* thus absolutely, because he cannot sell, give, bequeath, or alienate them, just as in the case of the *imperium* and the kingdoms [*regna*], the alienation of which would redound to the notable detriment of the realm [*imperii*], and which therefore he cannot alienate. If he alienates *de facto*, such alienation does not hold *de jure*, but everything is to be revoked to the jurisdiction of the realm [*jus imperii*], and he should be held to make restitution if he can. Nevertheless, in a sense he is lord of all such things, in so far as he can sell and defend them, and use them for the common utility, and in so far as no other man is deemed to have any right in them." [91]

Here the imperial rights over state property, or the fiscus, are treated as property rights, but as strictly limited property rights. This assimilation, or partial assimilation, of the *imperium,* or legal authority of the Emperor, to a limited property right (limited *dominium*) shows the importance of understanding Occam's theory of property.[92] Inevitably in the Middle Ages rights of private property carried with them (at least for the upper levels of the feudal hierarchy) a large amount of political and legal jurisdiction. In the light of this fundamental feudal principle, it is essential to ascertain Occam's theory of the incidents of the *dominium* inhering in emperors and kings. If we found that he recognized the Emperor's unlimited *dominium* in goods, it would be logical to infer that he placed no restraints upon his absolute power, except those resulting from divine and natural law. As a matter of fact, we have already found just the opposite to be the case. The *jus gentium* so strictly limits any imperial rights inhering both in the private property of individuals and in the common property of the state that Occam can say, in relation to these kinds of property, that, "taking the

---

[91] *Dial.*, III, II, II, chap. 23, pp. 920, 921. Cf. Bodin's prohibition of the *leges imperii* against alienation of the royal domain. *De Republica,* Book I, chap. 8.
[92] This assimilation appears clearly in the *Octo Quaes.*, II, chap. 1, where he discusses the origin of the "*proprietas* of the supreme lay authority."

term 'property' most strictly and properly, the supreme lay authority has no property." [93]

We must not, however, neglect the other side of the shield. Private individuals are normally immune from arbitrary interference by the Emperor in their property rights, but they have no absolute, eternal, never-variable immunities. Here again the fundamental relativity of Occam's point of view unmistakably crops out. Since property rights are based on human law, they can be modified or destroyed by that law, including the laws of kings and emperors, not by any arbitrary and ordinary process, but for legitimate cause, when exceptional circumstances warrant it, when the public welfare demands it, or when the individual concerned is guilty of a crime. In other words, unless we seriously misinterpret Occam, we are dealing here with an embryonic conception of eminent domain, or better still (since he does not mention compensation) with a rudimentary idea of police power. Indeed, we have before us one of the forerunners of the due process clauses of the federal [94] and state constitutions in the United States. It is an even clearer case of the foreshadowing of these modern constitutional provisions than Chapter 39 of Magna Carta, because Occam is dealing specifically with property rights. These modern rules constitute real legal restrictions on legislative power enforceable by the courts. The individual's rights are not absolute, but they are none the less real. The deprivation can occur only by "due process of law," and that means that some statutes, purporting to take away private property, are legal and some illegal. We have here a real legal limitation on determinate political authority.

It may indeed be argued that today the constitutional amending authority can override these constitutional limitations. The point is that in Occam's time no such legally constituted amending authority existed. Emperor and king were for him the highest determinate political authorities (except under very extraordinary circumstances), and he regarded both as bound by the *jus gentium*.

The history of the theory of private property expropriation through political authority has been treated in considerable detail by G. Meyer.[95] Both *Glossators* and *Post-Glossators* split on the matter, some holding, like Martinus and Baldus, that the Emperor had complete, or practically complete, *dominium* in his subjects' goods; others, like Bulgarus and Bartolus (and the weight of authority rests on this side), holding that expropriation could occur only *ex justa causa*.[96] The latter jurists, more impliedly than

---

[93] *Octo Quaes.*, II, 2, p. 336.
[94] Fifth Amendment: "No person shall be deprived of life, liberty, or property without due process of law." The Fourteenth Amendment extends the prohibition to the states.
[95] *Das Recht der Expropriation*, pp. 76–108.
[96] *Das Recht der Expropriation*, Martinus received a horse from the Emperor for his answer, while Bulgarus, who gave the contrary opinion, disconsolately philosophized: "Amisi equum, quia dixi aequum, quod non fuit aequum."

expressly, seem to base private property upon the *jus gentium*.[97] Bartolus develops such a theory at some length and appears to be in complete accord with Occam.[98]

This discussion of Occam and of the medieval lawyers concerning the right of the Emperor to expropriate private property must arrest our attention. As we have noted, it exhibits the clearest analogies to the present ever-recurring arguments and cases. Where we speak of "due process of law," the medieval writers talked about *justa causa*. We characterize, as did they, a certain confiscation as justified on grounds of "public policy" (*utilitas*). Or we, as they, condemn it as against "natural justice." To the question of what law shall serve as a basis for property rights, or to the query of why or when they should be respected, we are unable to furnish more satisfactory answers than the medievalists. Some writers and lawyers would today interpret the phrase "due process of law" so loosely, or the words "public utility" so inclusively, as to justify any executive or legislative exercise of the police power. They would probably find an ardent supporter in Baldus, who made *justa causa* equivalent to "any conscious desire" on the Emperor's part. But we think we are correct in concluding that the weight of authority lies on the other side, and the generally prevailing opinion, then as now, gives a real meaning to the concept of "due process of law." Be the determinate authority Emperor or Pope, President or Congress, it must submit to real limitations. These may be ill-defined, but they are none the less real. Congress and the state legislatures have discovered to their sorrow that it is possible to go beyond what the courts deem "reasonable limits." But even beyond this "rule of reason" there seems to exist an ineradicable conviction that the notion of property involves some fundamental, no matter how vaguely defined, which no earthly authority has the competence to touch. In a very real sense, and with abiding constancy, both modern lawyers and medieval legists seem to believe, implicitly or explicitly, that property is a right based upon and protected by a higher law. The fact that with such unanimity writers appeal to a standard of "reasonableness" or "public utility," and look upon property as based upon some fundamental or natural law, is one of tremendous significance. That significance seems to us to be that rulers, in order to stay within the limits of legality, have had to act inside bounds of what we today call "fair play." Of course, people will fiercely disagree as to the exact scope of the field within which acts of authority are fair. But there is almost unanimous agreement that things near the center of the circle are fair and that extensions which include matters lying far outside are manifestly unfair. Most of the argument will occur over the delimitation of the circumference of the circle,

[97] *Das Recht der Expropriation*, p. 91, citing Gloss ad L 2 Code (1, 19).
[98] It is interesting to note that Meyer, preoccupied with the jurists, does not once mention Occam, despite the fact that his theory has a much broader philosophical basis than that of the legists.

but that does not decrease the abiding significance and stabilizing influence of the very important sphere of agreement at the center.[99] To us, the ideal of justice (reasonableness, due process of law, or just cause) as related to such a matter as private property seems of extreme importance as a limitation, a goal, a stabilizer, and a great moderating force. A problem such as that of private property clearly demonstrates the permanent and practical significance of this great imponderable.

The meaning or content of the concept "property" has inevitably changed from age to age. This was bound to happen as the particular social and economic order which gave rise to this or that form of property-holding altered. Moreover, different ideas of "what is for the public utility" or "what is a reasonable encroachment" have been held by different writers in different countries and at different epochs. It is the beauty of the theories of such men as Aquinas, Bartolus, and Occam that they recognize this inevitable demand of change and variation and avoid the pitfall which trapped the later natural rights school. Locke, for example, regarded private property as a primitive, natural right anterior to the state, and to be logical he had to consider the function of civil law as exclusively one of protection and preservation of that natural right. Modern critics, in legitimately attacking this absolutistic idea of property, have gone to the other extreme and have based property rights entirely on civil law or the will of the state, meaning organized political authority. Occam puts these rights on a social basis, as logically, and often temporally, prior to state law. Instead of natural-legal rights inherent in the individual, he extols what we may call social-legal rights inherent in society.[100] This enables him both to retain real legal limits on state power and to grant the right of the state or government, if the general welfare imperatively requires it, and if the state's action accords with justice, to override human property rights not eternally immutable. Again we can only say that we discern here a "natural law with variable content."

The distinction between society and state, between community and government, is of transcendent importance. Occam certainly recognized it, even if in an inchoate and unconscious form. In one most noteworthy passage, he says that "the Emperor has no greater authority in temporals than the people [*populus*] had, since the Emperor has his authority from the people . . . because the people could not transfer more jurisdiction or authority to the Emperor than it had." But the people never had such plenitude of power that it could "impose on every one of the people everything not contrary to divine or natural law, because it could not order those things which did not have to be done of necessity." [101] In other matters, the consent of all is required. Now, it is submitted that we have here a distinc-

[99] Cf. Walter Lippmann's spheres of anarchy and spheres of agreement.
[100] Cf. *Dial.*, 26, p. 1015.
[101] *Dial.* III, II, II, 27, p. 923.

tion between the state, or *populus* (political authority or government) and society, or *communitas,* at least embryonically present. The *populus,* prior to the transfer of its authority to the Emperor, was the highest organized, determinate political entity. It was society organized to act as a unit; it was the state.[102] Clearly, according to Occam, the *populus* has or had no unlimited power. Does not this mean that the state has no unlimited power? The *populus* (a legally determinate political authority) transferred to the Emperor (another legally determinate political authority) all the legal power that it had. Neither is unlimited. Both can override property rights, but only by "due process of law" and for the general welfare. Any change in property relationships in the ordinary course of things, and when no question of the general welfare arises, can take place only by the "consent of all," i.e., *not* by a conscious, political act, but by a communal, social one. Once communal ownership is split up into private property by the *jus gentium,* society has an interest in keeping existing arrangements and vested rights normally intact. Of course, no individual obtains an absolute *carte-blanche* with his piece of private property. The community preserves the public interest by acquiescing in the establishment of a political authority (*populus, imperium,* emperor) with limited legal competence to override private rights in cases where the general welfare imperatively requires it. Occam's thought in this matter is by no means thoroughly conscious or self-consistent. But certainly some such distinction as the modern one between society or community on the one hand and state or government on the other lay in the back of his mind.[103] At times he seems to slide over the distinction and to identify or confuse *communitas* with *populus.*[104] But, in general, I think he considered the *populus* bound by the *jus gentium,* the *communitas* free from it and able, acting by that customary process of the "consent of all mortals," to change it.

If the Emperor has no absolute rights in the property of his subjects, it is for Occam *a fortiori* true that the Pope has none in the temporal possessions of the Church, and certainly none in the goods of private laymen. He has only a right of user in temporal goods necessary to perform spiritual functions, the title to such goods vesting in the *ecclesia, congregatio fidelium,* or whole body of faithful, clerics and laymen, men, women and children. This papal right may, however, become very sweeping and involve confiscations, depositions, and the transfer of realms, but only when

---

[102] Cf. Cicero's famous definition of the state, *De Rep.* I, 25: "Respublica res populi; populus autem non omnis hominum coetus, quoque modo congregatus, sed coetus multitudinis juris consensu et utilitatis communione sociatus."

[103] This distinction forms the cornerstone of all truly consistent modern pluralistic theories of the state.

[104] *Dial.,* III, II, II, 24, p. 921, where he cites St. Augustine and talks about the *populus* transferring to the Emperor all power to make human laws. This is impossible according to the above cited passage (p. 31), which clearly implies that the *populus* did not, and does not, have authority to make all human laws.

spiritual interests are threatened and laymen fail to fulfill their legitimate duties. The same principles apply to every other link in the ecclesiastical hierarchy, not excepting monasteries. Occam got into trouble, not only with the Pope but also with his own Franciscan order, by refusing to recognize that it had more than a right of *de facto* user in the temporal goods it administered. He argued that monks were, or should be, more perfect than other men, and should not contaminate themselves, even collectively, with property, but should live according to natural law (second sense) where all property is common to mankind. His logic seems quite unassailable.[105]

Occam's theory of liberty and slavery is in all essentials similar to his theory of property. Although by natural law, in the second or normative sense of "natural equity," all men are free, slavery arises legitimately enough under the *jus gentium*.[106] However, that law does not make all men slaves, and the Emperor or king most emphatically cannot treat free men as slaves. The ruler dares not order freemen to give up their goods at his bidding unless he can show grounds of public utility. Slaves and freemen are not held to equal obedience.[107] The legally limited character of imperial authority is again clearly evident here.

This brings us to a last and most interesting example of higher law in Occam's theory, one which is today very much *à la mode*. It seems that Occam refused to grant the Emperor the authority to order fasting (*jejunare*) or to prohibit wine-drinking (*bibere vinum*). No subject need obey his illicit and unjust commands, and commands to fast or forbidding the drinking of wine are just that, since they do not pertain to the office of the Emperor.[108] The analogy between this limitation and modern opposition to legislative enactments or constitutional amendments embodying so-called sumptuary legislation cannot be missed.[109] The restriction probably is best classed under *jus gentium* rather than under eternally immutable natural or divine law, although Occam does not definitely say so. Normally[110] and regularly, at any rate, interferences with wine-drinking would not be condoned by Occam. His highest determinate political authority (the Emperor) is limited in these sumptuary matters by a law higher than his own. His office or scope of authority, as legally constituted, includes no right to legislate on these subjects. Six hundred years after Occam, the almost identical problem reappeared in relation to the Eighteenth Amendment to the Constitution of the United States, which seeks, in effect, to forbid the

---

[105] *Octo Quaes.* I, 17, p. 333; I, 7, p. 322; *Opus Non. Dier.*, 3, 1006; 8, 1026; *Dial.*, III, I, I, 16, p. 786.
[106] *Dial.*, III, II, III, 6, p. 932–933.
[107] *Dial.*, III, II, II, 27 and 28, pp. 923 and 924; III, II, II, 20, p. 918; *Octo Quaes.*, VIII, 3, p. 385.
[108] *Dial.*, III, II, II, 20, p. 918.
[109] For the Pope, cf. *Dial.*, ff. 22, vol. 26, p. 1023.
[110] Occam might have approved of war-time prohibition.

drinking of wine in this country. In the National Prohibition Cases,[111] Elihu Root, counsel for the plaintiff-in-error, argued that the highest determinate public-legal authority in the United States, the amending authority (two-thirds of each House of Congress and the legislatures in three-fourths of the states), had no legal right to adopt such an amendment. The amending authorities provided for in Article V of the Constitution, he said, are only agents of the people. They must act within their authority, and that "authority does not embrace the right under color of an amendment to adopt mere sumptuary laws which are not constitutional laws in truth or essence." To be sure, Mr. Root admitted that the "people acting by the same means as were employed in the adoption of the Constitution" could have adopted the amendment. We submit that the "people" in this sense, even if regarded as acting legally and not revolutionarily, is not a *determinate* public-legal authority. The Supreme Court decided against Mr. Root, but the issue remains as far from settled as ever.

Sanctions play a less important rôle in the medieval legal framework than in the modern. Many of the rules of conduct which the medievalists emphatically regarded as law, and not merely as moral injunctions, had no very well worked out or consciously perfected machinery of enforcement. But Occam does envisage cases in which political authorities would refuse to obey the higher-law restraints upon their conduct, and has something to say about the action to be taken in such cases. Although he concerns himself principally with sanctions against illegally acting popes, he also discusses the matter as it relates to emperors and kings. In the first place, he clearly allows a right of passive resistance against an emperor who acts illegally. "No one ought to obey in illicit and unjust things." Subjects are held to obey only in those "things which are necessary to ruling justly and expediently the people subjected to him (i.e., the Emperor)." [112] However, our author goes farther than mere passive resistance. For example, in discussing the respective merits of monarchy and aristocracy, he states that "it would be easier for the people [*populus*] to correct one governor [*rectorem*], if in any way he should act exorbitantly, so that he should be removed, than several." [113] Although the king ordinarily is superior to the whole realm, yet under some circumstances (*in casu*) he is inferior to the realm; because in case of necessity it can depose the king and detain him in a castle; and this right it has from natural law.[114] He even hints at a right of tyrannicide in emergencies. Here perhaps we can see his nominalism emerging as opposed to the realism of Aquinas, who permitted only collective action against a tyrant. He says that it is not miraculous that casually the Pope uses the material sword against the Emperor, "because

[111] 253 U. S. 350 (1919).
[112] *Dial.*, III, II, II, 20, pp. 917–919.
[113] *Dial.*, III, II, I, 13, p. 881.
[114] *Octo Quaes.*, II, 7, p. 341.

indeed casually [*casualiter*] a rustic [*rusticus*] can use the material sword against the Emperor." [115]

The nominalistic and individualistic tendencies in Occam have led some writers to ascribe to him distinctly anarchistic leanings. Dorner believes that his enunciation of the right of individual disobedience in cases where the Emperor commands something contrary to the common welfare is a dangerous proposition offering no guarantee against the dissolution of the state. The individual is left the final judge, and a right of revolution is recognized. "If the representative of the state—the prince—does not represent its interests in a legal manner, then the people can get rid of him [are not obligated to obedience]. One must be struck by the fact that Occam, who usually is concerned with the most subtle juristic investigations, here lays little weight upon giving to the legal order of the state the necessary formal guarantees." [116] This is "permanent revolution," and Occam recognizes it even more clearly than the Reformation recognized the right of resistance. This critic believes that Occam should have pointed out more energetically that law is the only sanction against arbitrariness. [117]

We do not believe that the above interpretation offers a true understanding of Occam's theory. He was miles removed from anarchy. To be sure, his system recognized (as so many magnificent political theories before and since) the individual conscience as the ultimate forum for determining the duty of obedience. But a yawning chasm separates him from anarchy or any other theory tending toward the dissolution of the state. No man can be an anarchist who regards coercion as the principal function and prerogative of the state as clearly as did Occam. The "rule of princes" (*regimen principum*) is instituted, he says, so that evil men may be coerced and that good men may live quietly. [118] A government (*principatum*) is constituted principally to correct and punish delinquents. [119] To be sure, he recognizes a right of revolution, but he also emphasizes the duty of obedience. The secular authority must be obeyed unless his command clearly goes against natural or divine law or the common good. [120] Individuals may resist, but ordinarily the Emperor can with perfect legality put down their resistance. The standard by which the individual must decide whether or not to resist must lie in his own conscience and his own interpretation of the higher law, but the standard by which society as a whole will decide upon the legality of his resistance must be found in the generally prevailing ideas of higher law or in the interpretation of the wisest men acting for the community. The individual may judge for himself (he conceivably may

[115] *Octo Quaes.*, VIII, 5, p. 385.
[116] *Octo Quaes.*, p. 687.
[117] *Octo Quaes.*, p. 720.
[118] *Dial.*, III, II, I, I, p. 871.
[119] *Octo Quaes.*, III, 6, p. 352.
[120] *Octo Quaes.*, I, 10, and *Dial.* I, VI, 110, p. 630.

even be alone on the side of God), but if he guesses contrary to the prevailing view he will receive little mercy, and society may compel him to conform.

However, Occam thought of the broad principles of the higher law as ordinarily evident enough to any man acting reasonably and with a mind unwarped by passion or prejudice. If, for example, an emperor arbitrarily deprives a man of his property, an uprising in which the ruler is deposed and another substituted must obviously be righteous. More than that, it is legal, not merely morally justified, because Occam, in common with most medievalists, thought of the higher law as real law and not merely morality. Modern critics have assumed that the higher law is a totally, or almost totally, undefined substance which permits unlimited opportunity for honestly differing individual judgments. Occam had fewer doubts about it. Ordinarily, he believed, higher law commands us to obey regularly established authority. Ordinarily, too, the higher-law limits on that authority are apparent enough, so that honest and righteous men can tell when the ruler is acting illegally and when disobedience is justified. Appeal is taken, not from the law to something outside the law, as Dorner seems to assume, but from one body of law to another and higher body of law. Why should we assume the complete indeterminateness and haziness of the latter when Occam erects his whole structure of political and ecclesiastical authority upon it? Surely, in these days of "nullification," it can scarcely be contended, except for the purpose of making political capital, that widespread disobedience to one kind of law, or so-called law, constitutes the repudiation of all law or refusal to submit to any kind of control. At any rate, recognition of the right of contingent revolution by Occam is not the equivalent of anarchy.

The question of sanctions against a recalcitrant or heretical pope, although it bulks very large in Occam's works, since he designed them primarily as literary weapons against Pope John XXII, can only be touched upon. The Pope does not regularly have to submit to human judgment; however, "casually, if he is effected a heretic or appears incorrigible in any *crime* which scandalizes the Church (or if he usurps the jurisdiction of temporal rulers),[121] he is subjected to human judgment and ought to be judged by men and to suffer due penalty according to law [*de jure*]." [122] Occam makes elaborate provision for the machinery to be invoked against a guilty or heretical pope.[123] The investigation and punishment of such a pope pertains primarily to the whole body of the faithful. Since, however, this amorphous group cannot usually meet together in one assembly, it pertains secondarily to a general council acting for the whole Church. "If all

---

[121] *Octo Quaes.*, I, 16, p. 333.
[122] *Dial.*, III, I, I, 17, p. 787.
[123] *Dial.*, I, VI, chaps. 13, 47, 57 ff., 74 (on the right of disobedience to a pope's commands which violate natural and divine law).

clerics should be damnably negligent, it would pertain to laymen." [124] In
other words, Occam refuses to put any absolute legal power to judge an
heretical pope in a general council, made up of clerics and laymen, because it might in certain circumstances be as depraved as he. In fact, any
determinate center of authority may at times err; only the whole militant
ecclesia, or body of faithful, is immune from error.[125] This last statement
means merely that somewhere in the whole body of believers there will be
people having law and truth on their side. The general council is not always to be taken as acting for the entire congregation (*universalis congregatio*), because it may err. It might happen that pope, cardinals, prelates,
clerics, princes, and potentates (*potentes*), as well as general councils,
would be infected with heresy. Then appeal would have to lie to the consciences of the "simple and poor" laymen still remaining true to the
faith.[126] Occam carries out the argument to its logical conclusion. Sometimes we might even have to fall back on women [127] and, in the most extreme case, on children.[128] These statements should at least indicate how
emphatically he regarded any conceivable determinate center of authority
as bound by a higher law. All determinate agencies claiming to act for the
whole community must act within the bounds of this law. All may conceivably err and, if they do so, their commands do not hold. No absolute legal
authority exists anywhere on earth.[129]

Most of our discussion of higher-law limits on determinate authority
has been confined to emperors, kings, and popes. This is because ordinarily
they are, for Occam, the highest tangible centers of political jurisdiction.
General councils convene, as we have seen, only under exceptional circumstances, or when popes, emperors, or kings fail to perform their functions
or act illegally. Councils meet only for special purposes,[130] and even in
connection with these special matters they are not infallible or absolute.

The one thing that stands out like a beacon-light in Occam's political
theory is the fact that he considered all human authorities, agencies, or
persons as bound by and acting within the limits of a law emanating from
a source higher than their own individual wills. This dominant *motif* forms
an ever-present undertone, harmonizing and integrating all the complex
and (on the surface) apparently unconnected or irreconcilable opinions
which he enunciates. He conceived of this higher law as, in part, com-

---

[124] *Dial.*, I, VI, 57, p. 561. A general council may be summoned *in casu* without royal
authorization. *Dial.*, I, VI, 84, p. 602.
[125] *Dial.*, I, V, 25, p. 494.
[126] *Dial.*, I, V, 28, pp. 497–498; and cf. the distinction (p. 351 above) between state
and society. Here we have the same thing even more clearly expressed for the spiritual
sphere.
[127] *Dial.*, I, V, chap. 32.
[128] *Dial.*, I, V, 35, p. 506.
[129] Cf. also R. L. Poole, p. 243.
[130] *Dial.*, III, I, II, 19, p. 804.

pletely above the power of man to affect in any way whatsoever, as containing unbreakable principles of divine and natural justice. In large measure, however, he regarded it as a higher human law, or as *jus gentium*, ordinarily immutable, or changeable only by the slow customary process involved in the concept of the "consent of all mortals," but capable of adaptation or suspension to meet special cases and conditions. Even in the last instance, however, no absolute prerogatives were allowed. The authority desiring to dispense with *jus gentium* always had to point to the necessity of acting contrary to it in order to further the common good. A higher law always endured to restrain and measure the exercise of authority by any individual will or any determinate political agency. Relativity, not absolute sovereignty, is the true touchstone to Occam's theory.

FURTHER READINGS FOR PART IV

Allen, J. W. "Marsilio of Padua and Medieval Secularism," in F. J. C. Hernshaw, ed. *The Social and Political Ideas of Some Great Medieval Thinkers*. London: Harrap, 1923, pp. 167–191.

Bayley, Charles C. "Pivotal Concepts in the Political Philosophy of William of Ockham," *Journal of the History of Ideas*, 10 (1949), pp. 199–218.

Davis, Charles T. *Dante and the Idea of Rome*. New York: Oxford University Press, 1957.

D'Entrèves, A. P. *Dante as a Political Thinker*. Oxford: Clarendon Press, 1952.

——. *The Medieval Contribution to Political Thought: Thomas Aquinas, Marsilius of Padua, Richard Hooker*. New York: Humanities Press, 1959.

Emerton, Ephraim. *The Defensor Pacis of Marsilio of Padua: A Critical Study*. Gloucester, Mass.: Peter Smith, 1951.

Flick, Alexander C. *The Decline of the Medieval Church*. New York: Knopf, 1930.

Gewirth, Alan. *Marsilius of Padua: The Defender of Peace*. New York: Columbia University Press, 1951–1956.

Gilson, Étienne. *Dante and Philosophy*. New York: Harper & Row, 1963.

Lenkeith, Nancy. *Dante and the Legend of Rome*. London: University of London Press, 1952.

Lewis, Ewart. "The 'Positivism' of Marsiglio of Padua," *Speculum*, 38 (1963), pp. 541–582.

Offler, H. S. "Origins of Ockham's Octo Quaestiones," *English Historical Review*, 82 (April 1967), pp. 323–332.

Previté-Orton, C. W. *Marsilius of Padua*. London: Milford, 1935.

Rolbiecki, John J. *The Political Philosophy of Dante Alighieri*. Washington, D.C.: Catholic University of America Press, 1921.

Sigmund, Paul E., Jr. "The Influence of Marsilius of Padua on XVth-Century Conciliarism," *Journal of the History of Ideas*, 23 (July–September 1962), pp. 392–402.

Singleton, Charles S. "Dante and Myth," *Journal of the History of Ideas*, 10 (October 1949), pp. 482–502.

Stewart, H. L. "Dante and the Schoolmen," *Journal of the History of Ideas*, 10 (June 1949), pp. 357–373.

Tierney, Brian. "The Canonists and the Medieval State," *Review of Politics*, 15 (1953), pp. 378–388.

———. *Foundations of the Conciliar Theory: The Contribution of the Medieval Canonists from Gratian to the Great Schism*. Cambridge: University Press, 1955.

———. "Ockham, the Conciliar Theory, and the Canonists," *Journal of the History of Ideas*, 15 (1954), pp. 40–70.

Ullmann, Walter. *The Origins of the Great Schism*. London: Burns, Oates, and Washbourne, 1948.

V

THE CHRISTIAN

REFORM ERA:

LUTHER AND CALVIN

16

Politics and Religion:
Luther's Simplistic Imperative

SHELDON S. WOLIN

I

The encounter between the human mind and the outside world is the essence of speculation. The dramatic element in the encounter has been provided by man's assertion that mind is capable of comprehending and ordering the world about him. This same "epistemological presumptuousness," which we associate instinctively with the spectacular successes of the natural sciences, has also been implicit in the enterprise of political theory. Here, too, the claim is that the human intellect can understand all of the complex interrelationships of a political order. In some ways this claim is even more assertive than that of the natural scientist. The theorist seeks not only to analyze and explain certain phenomena, but to prescribe more satisfactory patterns.

Given the complexity of the subject matter of politics

This article was originally published in *American Political Science Review*, 50 (March 1956), 24–42. It is reprinted here with the permission of the author and of the publisher.

and the finite character of the human mind, it is not surprising that the ideas of political theorists lend themselves to diverse interpretations at the hands of later commentators. Disagreement in interpretation, however, can take one of two forms: it may turn on a question concerning a particular idea, meaning, or emphasis; or it may find the interpreters taking diametrically opposed positions concerning the basic tendency of a given set of political ideas. An example of the first type would be the interpretation of Locke's theory of property. The second type, which is apt to be more embittered, is illustrated by the current controversy over Plato. The case of Luther also falls under this second category. One product of the remarkable renascence in Lutheran studies over the past half-century has been a wide disagreement over the political tendencies of Luther's ideas. One group has tended to identify Luther with the stirrings of democracy and individualism associated with the Reformation, while another has taken the opposite position that his ideas directly fostered state absolutism in politics and state control of churches.[1] Both groups have been inclined to stress different aspects of Luther's thought. The image of Luther the libertarian has been constructed mainly out of the materials of his religious ideas; Luther the absolutist has been fashioned primarily from his political writings.

In both instances, however, something less than full justice has been done to the unity of Luther's thought. Moreover, the sharp contrast between the two images evokes the suspicion that each has been, to an extent, artificially contrived. This points to the possibility, which we wish to explore here, that Luther's political authoritarianism was closely related to the so-called "democratic" aspects of his religious ideas. By examining the inner relations between the two, some glimpse of the unity, if not the consistency, of Luther's thought is possible. By way of a *caveat*, the unity in question is not to be found in the systematic character of Luther's thought; if his theology was formless, we can expect at least the same in his politics. The two sides of Luther's thought were unified, first, by the way in which his political ideas presupposed his religious beliefs and by the extent to which the one "fed," so to speak, on the other; and, second, by a common impulse or imperative which was at work in both his religious and his political thinking. This aspect we shall call the "simplistic imperative": the

[1] The following are representative of those writers who see in Luther's writings various liberal or democratic ideas: James Mackinnon, *Luther and the Reformation,* 4 vols. (London 1925–1930), Vol. 2, pp. 93–97, 331; Werner Elert, *Morphologie des Luthertums,* 2 vols. (Munich, 1932), Vol. 2, p. 296; John T. McNeill, "Natural Law in the Thought of Luther," *Church History,* Vol. 11, pp. 211–228 (Sept. 1941). Representative of those who link Luther to absolutism are: Lord Acton, *Essays on Freedom and Power,* ed. Gertrude Himmelfarb (Boston, 1948), pp. 69, 94–96; John Neville Figgis, *Studies of Political Thought from Gerson to Grotius, 1414–1625,* 2d ed. (Cambridge, 1931), Lecture III; Pierre Mesnard, *L'essor de la philosophie politque au XVI*[e] *siècle,* 2d ed. (Paris, 1952), pp. 229–235; Ernst Troeltsch, *The Social Teachings of the Christian Churches,* trans. Olive Wyon, 2 vols. (London, 1931), Vol. 1, p. 532.

desire to reduce "reality" to its simplest components by sloughing off the complications which appear to obscure "reality" and to have no integral relationship with it. In its religious form, the imperative grew out of Luther's insistence that "the word of God, which teaches full freedom, should not and must not be fettered." [2] In its political form, it worked to release secular authority from traditional restraints and inhibitions.

Before turning to these problems, a preliminary difficulty must be disposed of. It has been argued by some commentators that Luther's thought, from beginning to end, was motivated solely by religious concerns and that, therefore, his outlook was fundamentally non-political. In the words of one recent writer, Luther "was first of all a theologian and a preacher," hence "he never developed a consistent political philosophy and knew little about the theories underlying the formation of national states in western Europe." [3] While it would be fruitless to deny the primacy of theological elements in Luther's thought, it is misleading to conclude on that account that politics was an alien concern. Luther himself held no such modest view of his own political acumen. Prior to his own writings, he declared, "no one had taught, no one had heard, and no one knew anything about temporal government, whence it came, what its office and work was, or how it ought to serve God." [4] Underlying this exaggeration was the implicit assumption that a religious reformer could not avoid political speculation. The extraordinary intermixture of religion and politics in that period compelled him to think about politics and even to think politically in religious matters. It was at once Luther's insight, as well as the source of a good many of his later difficulties, that he understood that religious reforms could not be undertaken in utter disregard of political considerations. It was exactly this lesson which many of the sectarians ignored at great cost. The problems in Luther's political thought were not the product of a monumental indifference toward politics, but arose from the "split" nature of a political attitude which oscillated between a disdainful and a frenetic interest in politics and sometimes combined both.

While the historical entanglements of politics and religion in the sixteenth century contributed in no small measure to Luther's political

---

[2] *Reformation Writings of Martin Luther*, ed. Bertram Lee Woolf (London, 1952), Vol. 1, p. 345. Only the first volume has thus far appeared. Hereinafter this will be cited as Woolf, Vol. 1. Reprinted by permission of the Philosophical Library, New York.
[3] Harold J. Grimm, "Luther's Conception of Territorial and National Loyalty," *Church History*, Vol. 17, pp. 79–94, at p. 82 (June, 1948). Substantially the same point is made by John W. Allen, *A History of Political Thought in the Sixteenth Century*, 2d ed. (London, 1941), p. 15; and by Preserved Smith, *Life and Letters of Martin Luther*, 2d ed. (Boston and New York, 1914), pp. 214, 228; and Mackinnon, Vol. 2, p. 229. Ernest G. Schwiebert has argued that Luther wrote essentially as a theologian, but that his political ideas derived largely from mediaeval sources. See "The Medieval Patterns in Luther's Views of the State," *Church History*, Vol. 12, pp. 98–117 (June 1943).
[4] *Works of Martin Luther*, ed. Charles M. Jacobs, 6 vols. (Philadelphia, 1915–1932), Vol. 5, p. 81. Hereinafter this will be cited as *Works*.

consciousness, an even more influential factor lay in the nature of the religious institutions which he attacked. His great anti-papal polemics of 1520 were directed against an ecclesiastical institution which, to the sixteenth-century mind, had come to epitomize organized power. The nature of the Papacy invited an indictment framed in political terms. Luther's writings of 1520 provide impressive evidence that he clearly recognized the issue to be one involving the power of an ecclesiastical polity. In the first place, the vocabulary employed was heavily sprinkled with phrases and imagery rich in political connotations. The sacramental practices of the priesthood were attacked as "oppressive" (*tyrannicum*) in that they denied the believer's "right" (*ius*) to full participation. The Papacy was denounced as the "tyranny of Rome" (*Romanam tyrannidem*), a "Roman dictatorship" (*Romana tyrannis*), to which Christians ought to "refuse consent" (*nec consentiamus*). The demand was then raised for the restoration of "our noble Christian liberty." "Each man should be allowed his free choice in seeking and using the sacrament . . . the tyrant exercises his depotism and compels us to accept one kind only." [5]

The political note became more pronounced as Luther went on to accuse the Papacy of ecclesiastical tyranny: the Papacy had arbitrarily legislated new articles of faith and ritual. When its authority had been challenged, it had sought refuge in the argument that papal power was unbound by any law. Moreover, the temporal pretensions of the Papacy had not only endangered the spiritual mission of the Church, but also damaged the effectiveness of secular authority by confusing secular and spiritual jurisdictions.[6] The usurpation of temporal power had permitted the Popes to advance their temporal claims under the guise of a spiritual mission, and, at the same time, to pervert their spiritual responsibilities by treating them politically. On this latter score, the sale of indulgences, the annates, the proliferation of the papal bureaucracy, and the control over ecclesiastical appointments had as their objective, not religious considerations, but the enhancement of the political power of the Papacy. The Pope had ceased "to be a bishop and has become a dictator." [7]

During these early years Luther was prepared to accept the perpetuation of the Papacy on a reformed basis. His criticisms were founded on the assumptions that religion and politics constituted two distinct realms within the *corpus christianum;* that each realm required its own form of ruling authority; and that while rulership might be either of a religious or of a political type, it ought not to be both. Despite these distinctions, Lu-

---

[5] ". . . cuique suum arbitrium petendi utendique relinqueretur, sicut in baptismo et potentia relinquitur. At nunc cogit singulis annis unam speciem accipi eadem tyrannide . . ." *D. Martin Luther Werke* (Weimar Ausgabe, 1888—), Vol. 6, p. 507; Woolf, Vol. 1, pp. 223–224.

[6] Woolf, Vol. 1, pp. 127–128, 162.

[7] Woolf, Vol. 1, p. 224.

ther's program for papal reform carried strong political overtones in that it was basically a demand for ecclesiastical constitutionalism and owed not a little to conciliarist inspiration.[8] The Pope was to exchange the role of despot for that of constitutional monarch. Henceforth his power was to be bounded by the fundamentals of Christianity and he could no longer legislate new articles of faith. Thus the teachings contained in Scripture were to be observed in much the same way as a fundamental law: they performed the function of a doctrinal constitution limiting the power of the popes.[9] To the papal argument that such institutional tinkering was blasphemous in that it would allow unclean hands to tamper with a divine institution, Luther responded that the Papacy itself was of human fabrication and hence susceptible of improvement.

The political element in Luther's case received further emphasis in the remedies he prescribed for dealing with a Pope who refused to recognize the bounds of his authority. If a Pope persisted in violating the clear injunctions of Scripture, then Christians were obligated to follow the fundamental law of Scripture and to ignore the papal commands.[10] Parenthetically it should be noted that this was the same formula employed later by Luther in dealing with secular rulers whose commands ran counter to Scripture. But in one particular Luther was prepared to counsel measures more drastic than anything he proposed against secular rulers. In an argument more political than scriptural, he contended that the Papacy might be forcibly resisted. "The Church has no authority except to promote the greater good." If any Pope were to block reforms, then "we must resist that power with life and limb, and might and main." [11]

Although Luther later retracted this and other more sanguinary exhortations,[12] the political element reached a climax when Luther prescribed for the condition *in extremis* where the Papacy blocked all efforts towards reform. Secular authorities possessed the right and the responsibility to initiate the processes of reform:

> Therefore, when need requires it, and the pope is acting harmfully to Christian well-being, let any one who is a true member of the Christian community as a whole take steps as early as possible to bring about a genuinely free council. No one is so able to do this as the secular authorities, es-

---

[8] Luther had read and admired Gerson, D'Ailly, and Dietrich of Niem. He does not appear to have been acquainted with the conciliarist side of Occam's thought. For a general discussion of these matters see Mackinnon, Vol. 1, pp. 20–21, 135; Vol. 2, pp. 228–229.

[9] Woolf, Vol. 1, pp. 224–225; *Works*, Vol. 1, p. 391; *Luther's Correspondence and Other Contemporary Letters*, ed. Preserved Smith and Charles M. Jacobs, 2 vols. (Philadelphia, 1918), Vol. 1, p. 156.

[10] Woolf, Vol. 1, p. 121.

[11] Woolf, Vol. 1, p. 123; *Werke* (Weimar Ausgabe), Vol. 2, pp. 447–449.

[12] For a further discussion see Roland H. Bainton, *Here I Stand: A Life of Martin Luther,* Mentor edition (New York, 1955), pp. 115–116; Ernest G. Schwiebert, *Luther and His Times* (St. Louis, 1950), pp. 464 ff.

pecially since they are also fellow Christians, fellow priests, similarly religious, and of similar authority in all respects.[13]

Despite the acerbity displayed in Luther's writings of this period, their revolutionary quality was blunted by the reliance on conciliarist arguments. He looked to a combination of secular initiative and conciliar reforms to restore the purity of the Papacy. In place of papal supremacy he relied partly on the older notion of the conciliarists that the Church was a *societas perfecta,* a self-sufficient society containing its own authority, rules, and procedures for regulating the common spiritual life of its members. According to this conception, the Church contained within itself the necessary resources for remedying any ills or grievances which might afflict it.

These conciliarist arguments worked to obscure two emergent aspects of Luther's thought: the reliance on secular authority and the bias against institutions. As long as he placed his hopes in a Church Council as the agency of reform, the secular ruler was reduced to secondary importance. But once this avenue of reform was closed off, the choice was automatically narrowed down to the secular ruler. When this stage was reached, the idea of the Church as a *societas perfecta* was dropped; the revitalization of its spiritual life was now held to depend on an external agency.

Similarly, as long as Luther adhered to a conciliarist position, and as long as he attributed some utility to the Papacy, the revolutionary quality of his theory of the Church would remain muted. But once he had broken with Pope and Council, the doctrine of the "priesthood of all believers" would assume central importance and the Lutheran conception of the Church would become clearer. Both of these developments, the reliance upon secular rulers and the Lutheran idea of the Church, were interrelated dialectically, in that Luther's quest for the "real" in religious experience led him to dismiss ecclesiastical institutions and to magnify the political institutions of the ruler. It is only partly correct to attribute Luther's emphasis on secular authority to the desperate plight of a reformer who had no alternative but to appeal to that quarter. Nor is it correct to view his extreme utterances during the Peasants' War as marking a sudden discovery of the absolute power of secular princes. There is sufficient evidence to indicate that he held a high opinion of secular authority before the peasant outbreaks. Instead, the emphasis on secular power should be viewed as the outgrowth of the deepening radicalism of his religious convictions, which lent additional weight to a pre-existing respect for the power of temporal rulers.

Once this is grasped, Luther's later dilemma becomes more understandable: the secular powers, whose assistance he had invoked in the

[13] Woolf, Vol. 1, pp. 122, 167.

struggle for religious reform, began to assume the form of a sorcerer's apprentice threatening religion with a new type of institutional control. The sources of this dilemma lay in the disequilibrium which had developed between his theory of the Church and his theory of political authority. In the early years of his opposition to the Papacy, he did not disavow the central argument of the papalists that spiritual affairs required a ruling head. Thus, although he disagreed with the papalists over the nature of that office, his thinking preserved the mediaeval tradition of a distinctive set of ecclesiastical institutions which might offset the thrusts of temporal powers. But as his views matured into a flat rejection of the Papacy and of the entire hierarchical structure of the Church, the whole idea of a countervailing authority was naturally dropped. The tie between religious beliefs and religious institutions was severed; at this stage of his thought Church organization was regarded as an impediment to true belief. Concurrently with these developments in Luther's conception of the Church, his doctrine of political authority had evolved towards a more enlarged view of the functions and authority of rulers. The rulers were now entrusted with some of the religious prerogatives previously belonging to the Pope.[14] Thus while institutional authority was being erased in the religious sphere, it was being underscored in the political.

It was at this point that the supreme difficulty arose. In his later years Luther began to pay increasing attention to the need for religious organization, a need which he had earlier minimized. But for practical reasons this could not be accomplished except by calling in the secular authorities whose power he had consistently exalted. The institutional weakness of the Church made it no match for the secular power which Luther had rationalized. The end-product was the territorial Church (*Landeskirche*).

Luther's elevation of political authority, then, was closely connected with his idea of the Church. The latter, in turn, was an outgrowth of his conception of religion; hence something must be said about his religious doctrines and their bearing upon his ecclesiasticism and politics.

In Luther's theology, the supreme vocation of man consisted in preparing for God's free gift of grace. Religious experience centered around an intensely personal communication between the individual and God; the authenticity of the experience depended upon the uninhibited directness of the relationship. Good works, therefore, were irrelevant, for they involved

---

[14] In this connection Luther's letter to John, Elector of Saxony, was significant: "There is no fear of God and no discipline any longer, for the papal ban is abolished and everyone does what he will. . . . But now the enforced rule of the Pope and the clergy is at an end in your Grace's dominions, and all the monasteries and foundations fall into your Grace's hands as the ruler, the duty and difficulty of setting these things in order comes with them." Smith and Jacobs, Vol. 2, p. 383. On several occasions Luther was to lament the release of the rulers from papal controls. See *Works*, Vol. 4, pp. 287–289.

relationships with men and things. Similarly, the ministrations of an ecclesiastical hierarchy and the full sacramental system were both useless and
dangerous; they only multiplied the intermediaries between God and man
and raised the inference that there existed a substitute for faith. In sum, everything which stood between God and man had to be eliminated; the only
true mediators were Christ and Scripture.

Against this backdrop Luther's famous metaphor of the "three walls"
surrounding the Papacy was symbolic of the dominant driving force in his
religious thought: the compulsion to erase and level all that interfered with
the right relationship between God and man. The significance of this "simplistic imperative" lies in the variety of ways in which it was expressed:
political, intellectual, as well as religious. Intellectually it took the form of
a nearly total rejection of the mediaeval philosophical tradition. It was not
a rejection steeped in ignorance, but one flowing from a deep conviction
that centuries of philosophy had worked to pervert the meaning of Scripture and to support the pretensions of the Papacy.[15] The influence of Aristotle was declared to be pernicious; the christianized Aristotelianism of
Aquinas was condemned as an "unfortunate superstructure on an unfortunate foundation." [16] Impatient with the "Babel of philosophy," with its endless and subtle disputations concerning substance and accidents, Luther
called for a return to the unglossed wisdom of Scripture and the Word of
God.[17] In this connection his radicalism was also turned against the *corpus*
of traditional knowledge represented by the teachings of the Church Fathers, the pronouncements of the Councils, and the doctrines of the canonists. The Catholic conception of accrued historical wisdom, painstakingly
built up through centuries of interpretation, Luther matched with the un-
complicated, direct knowledge of the humble believer.[18] "The simple faith"

[15] Luther's long apprenticeship in scholasticism is discussed in Mackinnon, Vol. 1, pp.
10–27, 50 ff.
[16] Woolf, Vol. 1, pp. 225, 227–229; Smith and Jacobs, Vol. 1, pp. 60, 64, 78, 150,
169–170, 359.
[17] Luther's distinction between Scripture and the Word of God is analyzed by Rupert
E. Davies, *The Problem of Authority in the Continental Reformers* (London, 1946),
pp. 31 ff.; and by Troeltsch, Vol. 2, p. 486. In connection with Luther's quest for the
"original" meaning of Scripture, it might be added that he was aided by contemporary
humanist scholars, such as Reuchlin and Erasmus, who were seeking to recapture the
true meaning of Scripture by means of philological researches.
[18] Woolf, Vol. 1, pp. 227–229. These sentiments were underlined in Luther's *Letter to
the Christian Reader* (1522): ". . . when I compare scholastic with sacred theology, that
is with Holy Scripture, it seems full of impiety and vanity and dangerous in all ways to
be put before Christian monks not forearmed with the armor of God." Luther then
turned admiringly to Tauler and the *Theologia Germanica* and raised the hope that
under the influence of the mystics "there will not be left in our earth a Thomist or an
Albertist, a Scotist or an Occamist, but only simple sons of God and their Christian
brothers. Only let not those who batten on literary dainties revolt against the rustic dic-
tion, nor despise the coarse coverings and cheap garments of our tabernacle, for within
is all the glory of the king's daughter. Certainly if we cannot get learned and eloquent
piety, let us at least prefer an unlearned and infantile piety to an impiety which is both
eloquent and infantile." Smith and Jacobs, Vol. 2, pp. 135–136. Compare Augustine,
Epistle 138, 4–5.

of the people was held to be more reliable; instead of chasing philosophical hares, it was content with the knowledge which comes from faith.

Thus the end-point of the revolt against the authority of philosophy
and received wisdom was a religious primitivism, flaunting simple faith
against philosophical complication, breaking "the images of ancestral wisdom" in the name of a return to original Christianity. This "simplistic imperative," with its bias against "man-made" rules and rites, appeared as a
kind of revival of the ancient controversy between "nature" and "convention" with scripturalism replacing nature as the basic norm. Like the ancients, Luther was beset by a deep urgency to erase historical accretions in
order to commune with an underlying truth. Characteristic of his search
for purity were his remarks on the confused state of marriage laws:

> . . . any and all of the practices of the Church are impeded, and entangled,
> and endangered, on account of the pestilential, unlearned, and irreligious,
> man-made ordinances. There is no hope of a cure unless the whole of the
> laws made by men, no matter what their standing, are repealed once for
> all. When we have recovered the freedom of the Gospel, we should judge
> and rule in accordance with it in every respect.[19]

The impulse towards simplification was also manifested in Luther's as-
sault on the mediaeval conception of the Church. Again the emphasis was
put on leveling the "walls" which stood between the believer and the object of his beliefs. The whole of the ecclesiastical hierarchy, with its niched
gradations of authority and function, was to be razed. Since the plain
meaning of Scripture could be understood by the average man, sacerdotal-
ism was superfluous; there could be no distinctions among believers:

> We all have the same authority in regard to the Word and sacraments, al-
> though no one has a right to administer them without the consent of the
> members of his church, or by the call of the majority (because, when some-
> thing is common to all, no single person is empowered to arrogate it to
> himself, but we should await the call of the Church). . . . When a bishop
> consecrates, he simply acts on behalf of the entire congregation, all of
> whom have the same authority. They may select one of their number and
> command him to exercise this authority on behalf of the others.[20]

The radical egalitarianism implicit in the doctrine of the priesthood
of the believers was not dictated by any necessary relationships among the
believers themselves. Rather, it grew out of Luther's conviction that faith
could be attained only by individual effort and that, therefore, the "Christian liberty" of the believer must be unbound by externals. Faith could not
be created or instilled by an external agency, whether sacerdotal or political; it was an inward disposition of the individual inclining him towards

[19] Woolf, Vol. 1, p. 303.
[20] Woolf, Vol. 1, pp. 318, 114.

God.[21] The reward of faith was membership in the invisible communion of Christians, the *corpus mysticum* ruled by Christ:

> There is no superior among Christians, but Christ Himself and Christ alone. And what kind of authority can there be where all are equal and have the same right, power, possession, and honor, and no one desires to be the other's superior, but each other's inferior? One could not establish authority where there are such people, even if one would, since their character and nature will not permit them to have superiors, for no one is willing or able to be the superior.[22]

The "true" Church, then, was not to be located in any physical assemblage of offices, nor was it to be identified with any hierarchical institution. The Church consisted simply of "an assembly of hearts in one faith. . . . This unity is of itself sufficient to make a Church." [23]

Although Luther consistently denied that the equality of the believers eliminated the necessity for a trained ministry, this denial in no way minimized the revolutionary character of his attack on ecclesiasticism. The priest had been transformed into a minister, that is, one who administered, expounded, and explained the Word.[24] The loss in status was accompanied by a drastic change in the relationship between minister and congregation. Unlike the priest, the minister could not draw upon the mysterious sources of authority flowing from a centuries-old tradition. Stripped of the *mystique* of office, the minister faced his congregation as a *primus inter pares*. The office itself was no longer consecrated by the representative of a powerful ecclesiastical institution; it was derived from the consent of the *pares*. Since the minister was the creature of consent, not of authority, he could be removed from office by those who had selected him.[25]

Underlying the equality among the believers and the whittling down of the role of the minister were certain assumptions about the capacity of the believers to recognize truth: ". . . each and all of us are priests because we all have the one faith, the one gospel, one and the same sacrament; why then should we not be entitled to taste or test, and to judge what is right or wrong in the faith?" [26] From this followed Luther's demand that the "second wall," symbolizing the papal claim to be the final interpreter of doctrine, be swept aside. The papal position, as Luther instinctively recognized, was grounded in a kind of christianized Platonism which asserted that disputed truths could be resolved only by a specially endowed intelligence.[27] Against this "aristocratic epistemology" Luther advanced a "demo-

---

[21] Woolf, Vol. 1, p. 113.
[22] *Works*, Vol. 2, p. 262.
[23] *Works*, Vol. 1, p. 349.
[24] Woolf, Vol. 1, pp. 115, 247, 249, 318, 367; *Works*, Vol. 3, pp. 326–328.
[25] Woolf, Vol. 1, pp. 115, 117, 181; *Works*, Vol. 4, pp. 79, 82.
[26] Woolf, Vol. 1, p. 120; *Works*, Vol. 4, pp. 76–77.
[27] Woolf, Vol. 1, pp. 119–120.

cratic" one which averred both the right and the ability of the congregation to judge religious teachings. He adopted this conclusion partly from a
profound conviction concerning the primacy of the direct communion between God and the individual soul; and partly from a conviction that the
individual conscience could not be forced into salvation.

Nostalgia for the apostolic simplicity of the primitive Church did not
blind Luther to the fact that a near-anarchistic form of church organization
was an inadequate prescription for an actual congregation whose members
dwelt in varying states of grace and faith. At an early stage in his writings
he began to elaborate the distinction between the "visible" and the "invisible" Church. The former consisted of those Christians whose weak faith ne-
cessitated a visible form of organizational structure. Unity had to be created externally by human art. The "invisible" Church, in contrast, derived
its unity from faith; it was largely independent of organization and regulations.[28]

In his later years Luther came to be more impressed with the value
of "distinguishing marks," even for the invisible Church.[29] This was less
significant, however, than his growing reliance upon secular authority to
police the visible Church and to insure a degree of religious uniformity.
Given this development, the Lutheran conception of political authority assumes crucial importance; for a religion which had denied itself the power
of an ecclesiastical organization was now confronted by, and invited the
assistance of, political rulers who were unhampered by the traditional restraints of religious institutions. To appreciate the new theoretical setting
within which temporal authority was now to operate, something must be
said concerning earlier Christian attitudes towards the political order and
the office of ruler.

II

From its early beginnings the Christian attitude concerning politics had
been complicated by a persistent impulse towards disengagement from the
world. The scriptural warning that "My Kingdom is not of this world" was
later systematized by Augustine into the tense symbolism of the *civitas dei*

[28] *Works,* Vol. 1, pp. 349–357.
[29] Compare *Works,* Vol. 1, p. 361; Vol. 4, p. 75; Vol. 5, pp. 27–87; Vol. 6, p. 148. Lu-
ther's theory of the Church has been discussed by Karl Holl, "Luther," *Gesammelte
Aufsätze zur Kirchengeschichte* (Tübingen, 1923), Vol. 1, pp. 288 ff.; Troeltsch, *op. cit.,*
Vol. 1, pp. 477–494; William A. Mueller, *Church and State in Luther and Calvin*
(Nashville, 1954), pp. 5–35; Wilhelm Pauck, "The Idea of the Church in Christian His-
tory," *Church History,* Vol. 21, pp. 191–213, at pp. 208–210 (Sept. 1952); Lewis W.
Spitz, "Luther's Ecclesiology and His Concept of the Prince as *Notbischof,*" *Church
History,* Vol. 22, pp. 113–141 (June 1953); John T. McNeill, "The Church in Sixteenth
Century Reformed Theology," *Journal of Religion,* Vol. 22, pp. 251–269 (July 1942).

and the *civitas terrena*. And despite the impressive effort of Aquinas to fashion a comfortable accommodation between the political order and the divine, the mystics and the monastics survived as eloquent witnesses to the strain of *incivisme* in Christianity. Moreover, this hostility towards the political order had been implicit from the beginning, when Christianity had directly challenged the classical assumption concerning religion and the political order. Classicism had judged religion largely from the viewpoint of its political and social utility. Religion had been expected not only to contribute to civic cohesiveness, but also to infuse the whole of man's political and social conduct in such a way that the believer would be a better citizen by virtue of his beliefs. For classicism, then, the value of a religion had been analyzed in terms of citizenship; the problem had been that of the citizen as a believer and not, as was to be the case with Christianity, the believer as a citizen.

In contrast, Christianity had come proclaiming the irrelevancy of political criteria to religious truths. Its avowed intention was to disentangle religion from its political context. This apolitical bent in Christianity was strikingly developed by Augustine in Books VI and VII of the *De civitate Dei*.[30] Christianity, he insisted, did not represent merely another "civil theology"; it came not to rescue a corrupt society, but to prepare men for the permanent estate of eternity. On the basis of this formulation, the relation between religion and politics was reversed. Instead of religion functioning as a support for the political order, the role of the political order was conceived to be one of securing the conditions of peace which would enable men to pursue unhindered their primary vocation of spiritual salvation. Although the responsibility for order was conferred upon the state, this did not imply, for Augustine, any positive control of or intervention into essentially religious matters. One of the primary aims of Augustine was to rid Christianity of the political interference typified by the policy of Theodosius. The state might assist religion by protecting the faithful from the contaminating influences of heresy, but the continuous supervision of religious life belonged to the Church. The spiritual needs of man were to be administered by a government reared on spiritual foundations.

In Luther the impulse towards disengagement took a quite different form. Where Augustine had relied upon the Church as the main aid to individual salvation and had relegated the state to the role of guardian of order, Luther felt constrained to call upon secular power to help Christian souls in gaining release from the tyranny of the organized Church. One fundamental reason for the different roles assigned government by Augustine and Luther is to be found in the different historical positions occupied by each. Augustine's thinking was deeply tinged by the millennial hopes

[30] This aspect of Augustine is brilliantly described in Charles Norris Cochrane, *Christianity and Classical Culture* (New York, 1944), pp. 359 ff. Also see the remarks of Eric Voegelin, *The New Science of Politics* (Chicago, 1952), pp. 81–84.

common in the early centuries of the Christian era. It was natural for him to adopt a time-perspective oriented towards the future. Although, in contrast to the expectancies of some of the early Christians, Augustine minimized the imminence of the millennium, the notion of a future pregnant with the promise of deliverance remained a vivid element in his thought.[31] The thousand years intervening between Augustine and Luther could not but have a sobering effect on Christian optimism. What had been a beckoning future for the one became, for the other, an interminable present calling for a certain resignation on the part of the believer. The muted eschatology of Luther contributed in an important way to his marked antipathy for history. After the days of apostolic simplicity had been passed, history had become a record of the degradation of the Word. Consequently, the theological and ecclesiastical legacy of these centuries must be dismissed. On the basis of these beliefs, Luther's time-perspective was reflective of a compelling urgency to return to a more primitive state of Christian perfection; it was part of a radicalism oriented towards recapturing the authentic Christian elements of the distant past; it lacked the vivid awareness of a future dimension.

These contrasts in time-perspectives were closely related to some important differences in the political ideas of Augustine and Luther. While Augustine had punctured the classical notion of the autonomy and self-sufficiency of the political order, he had not left the political order dangling in limbo. It was an integral part of the whole *ordo* of Creation and contributed its share towards the preservation of the total harmony. For Augustine the concept of a divine order symbolized more than an ingenious blend of diversities: it was a *concordia* moving towards consummation. Accordingly, the political order, integrated as it was into a cosmos full with meaning and direction, acquired a rooted stability, a sustenance drawn from the nature of Creation itself. Thus, even though the political community was destined to be superseded at the climax of history, until that time it participated in the perfection written into the very essence of things.[32]

Luther, however, departed significantly from the Augustinian conception of *ordo*. For Augustine *ordo* had operated as a principle immanent in the whole of Creation; therefore, any association, even a non-Christian one, possessed value to the extent that it secured peace and tranquillity.[33] Lu-

---

[31] *De civitate Dei*, XX. See also the remarks of Heinrich Scholz, *Glaube und Unglaube in der Weltgeschichte* (Leipzig, 1911), pp. 109 ff.

[32] The concept of *ordo* is most extensively discussed by Augustine in *De civitate Dei*, XIX, 11–18. Pertinent in this connection are: R. H. Barrow, *Introduction to Saint Augustine, The City of God* (London, 1950), pp. 220–260; Sir Ernest Barker, "St. Augustine's Theory of Society," in *Essays on Government*, 2d ed. (Oxford, 1951), pp. 245–248; Étienne Gilson, *Introduction à l'étude de Saint Augustin*, 3d ed. (Paris, 1949), pp. 237–238.

[33] *De civitate Dei*, XIX, 24.

ther, on the other hand, reduced "order" from an immanent to a formal principle without real viability:

> Order is an outward thing. Be it as good as it may, it can fall into misuse. Then it is no longer order but disorder. So no order has any intrinsic worth of its own, as hitherto the Popish Order has been thought to have. But all order has its life, worth, strength, and virtue in right use; else it is worthless and fit for nothing.[34]

In abandoning the concept of *ordo* as the sustaining principle within a larger pattern of meaning, Luther deprived the political order of the moral sustenance flowing from this more comprehensive whole. The lack of integration between the political order and the divine order produced a marked tension within Luther's conception of government. The political order appeared as a distinctly fragile achievement, precarious, unstable, and prone to upset. At the same time, the vulnerability of this order created the need for a powerful, repressive authority. In other words, it was not the political order itself which was sustained by a divine principle; it was the secular power upholding order that was divinely derived. It was no idle boast of Luther's to assert that he had praised temporal government more highly than anyone since Augustine.[35] Such praise was necessary once the political order had been extracted from its cosmic context. The divine element in political authority was inevitably transformed from a sustaining principle into a repressive, coercive one.

Luther's attachment to temporal authority, then, was not the product of a particular stage in his development, but was rooted in the conviction that the fallen world of man was fundamentally orderless. Order had to be imposed:

> Let no one think that the world can be ruled without blood; the sword of the ruler must be red and bloody; for the world will and must be evil, and the sword is God's rod and vengeance upon it.[36]

Significantly, Luther singled out, as the first "wall" to be leveled, the papal claims to a temporal jurisdiction. His logic here displayed the same impulse as his religious theorizing: just as the believer's free access to Scripture was to be secured from papal interference, so the secular ruler was to be unhampered in his efforts to achieve order:

> . . . the social corpus of Christendom includes secular government as one of its component functions. This government is spiritual in status, although it discharges a secular duty. It should operate, freely and unhindered, upon

[34] *Works*, Vol. 6, p. 186.
[35] *Works*, Vol. 5, pp. 81–82.
[36] *Works*, Vol. 4, p. 23. On this same point see: Vol. 3, pp. 231–233; Vol. 4, pp. 28, 248–253, 266–269, 299 ff.; Vol. 5, p. 38; Vol. 6, p. 460.

all members of the entire corpus, should punish and compel where guilt deserves or necessity requires, in spite of pope, bishops, and priests; and whether they denounce or excommunicate to their heart's desire.[37]

The long scholarly disputes over whether or not Luther preserved the mediaeval conception of a *corpus christianum* has served to obscure the profound changes he made in the content of that concept.[38] The emphasis on secular authority was accompanied by other doctrinal changes which enhanced that authority still further. At the same time that Luther was undercutting the sacerdotal hierarchy by the idea of the priesthood of all believers, he was elevating the status of rulers by clothing it with a sacerdotal dignity: rulers "are priests and bishops too." [39] The sharp line between clergy and laity was erased, and priest and peasant were placed on a level of equality in relation to secular jurisdiction.[40] The estate of Christendom had fallen to new trustees: the princes "discharge their office as an office of the Christian community, and for the benefit of that community. . . . Each community, council, and administration has authority to abolish and prevent, apart from the knowledge or consent of pope or bishop, anything contrary to God, and hurtful to man in body and soul." [41]

The significance of the role assigned to political authority lay not so much in its broad mandate, nor in its responsibilities for religious reform, but rather in the fact that its power was now to be exercised in a context where papal institutions had been deprived of divinity and power. The secular ruler alone derived his powers from God; the power of the papacy, in contrast, had resulted from strictly human contrivings, or, worse, from the machinations of the Antichrist.

III

Luther's view of political authority was not all of one piece; it varied depending on whether the issue was primarily religious or political. When temporal government was called upon to assist in furthering religious reforms, it was viewed as a positive and constructive agency. But in its more secular and political role, government appeared as essentially negative and repressive. In the one area it was treated as the sole alternative for initiating reform; in the other as the sole alternative to anarchy.[42] The link which

---

[37] Woolf, Vol. 1, p. 117; Mesnard, pp. 204–217.
[38] There is a recent discussion of this problem in Spitz, pp. 118 ff., and see the references cited there. In addition there are some interesting remarks in Friedrich Meinecke, "Luther über christliches Gemeinwesen und christlichen Staat," *Historische Zeitschrift*, Vol. 121, pp. 1–22 (1920).
[39] Woolf, Vol. 1, p. 114.
[40] Woolf, Vol. 1, pp. 114–115, 129–130, 141, 147, 226–227, 232, 275.
[41] Woolf, Vol. 1, p. 167.
[42] *Works*, Vol. 3, p. 235; Vol. 4, pp. 289–291.

bound together the two views of political authority was Luther's demand that rulers be released from pre-existing restraints in order to accomplish their work. We have already examined this element in connection with Luther's attack on the Papacy; it reappeared when he considered the secular activities of government. Finding the same confusion and complexity in the laws of society as had prevailed in religious matters, Luther advocated a characteristically simple and radical solution:

> . . . the body politic cannot be felicitously governed merely by rules and regulations. If the administrator be sagacious, he will conduct the government more happily when guided by circumstances rather than by legal decrees. If he be not so wise, his legal methods will only result in harm, since he will not know how to use them, nor how to temper them to the case in hand. Hence, in public affairs, it is more important to make sure that good and wise men are in control than that certain laws are promulgated. Men of this kind will themselves be the best of laws, will be alert to every kind of problem, and will resolve them equitably. If knowledge of the divine laws accompanies native sagacity, it is obvious that written laws will be superfluous and noxious.[43]

The only restraints operating on the ruler, other than those of his own conscience, came from the exhortations of the ministers; since the ministers no longer spoke as the representatives of a powerful ecclesiastical establishment, the effectiveness of this restraint would be problematical.

Although some commentators have shown that Luther never intended to emancipate the secular authorities from the dictates of natural law and reason, this proves only that Luther was not Machiavelli. For the point is that natural law becomes a mere set of moral homilies when it is translated into a context where the power of the rulers alone has been elevated above all other institutional rivals and where allegiance to the other great power institution has been condemned.

The situation thus created was ripe for a collision between the two entities which Luther, by analogous arguments, had sought to set free. On the one hand there was the secular ruler, unrestrained by the pressures of competing institutions, and on the other the Christian congregation seeking divine grace, unaided and unguided by sacerdotal institutions. Luther, however, often wrote as though the former never presented a threat to the

---

[43] Woolf, Vol. 1, p. 298. It is true that Luther occasionally praised customary law, but a close examination of the context of the argument shows that he was contending that customary laws were better adapted to local conditions than imperial laws, and not that customary laws were salutary restraints. McNeill, "Natural Law in the Thought of Luther," *loc. cit.,* has underlined the role of natural law and reason in Luther's writings, but again the context was one where Luther was asserting that natural law and reason or equity allowed the ruler to override existing laws or customs. Natural law, in other words, played a liberating as well as a restraining role in Luther's thought. See Woolf, Vol. 1, p. 187; *Works,* Vol. 6, pp. 272–273. One of the few occasions wherein Luther cited Aquinas for support involved an argument in favor of an unlimited secular power in times of emergency. See *Works,* Vol. 3, p. 263.

latter. The true believer was a subject of the Kingdom of God, where Christ alone ruled. "Therefore, it is not possible for the secular sword and law to find any work to do among Christians, since of themselves they do much more than its laws and doctrines can demand." [44] If all men were to become true Christians, secular government would be unnecessary. Government was justified by the existence of the large masses of the unrighteous and unregenerate; in the absence of coercion, men would be at each other's throats and society in chaos. "For this reason God has ordained two governments; the spiritual, which by the Holy Spirit under Christ makes Christians and pious people, and the secular, which restrains the unchristian and wicked so that they must needs keep the peace outwardly, even against their will." [45]

Even if the secular rulers, whose characters Luther frequently criticized, were to overstep their bounds and issue commands contrary to Scripture, no real harm could be done to the true Christian. Government, laws, and the ways of society could affect the physical goods of man, but never the vital center of his soul:

> When we consider the inner, spiritual man and see what belongs to him if he is to be a free and devout Christian, in fact and in name, it is evident that, whatever the name, no outer thing can make him either free or religious. For his religion and freedom, and, moreover, his sinfulness and servitude, are neither bodily nor outward.[46]

"Christian liberty," then, was the state enjoyed by the believer who had severed his external dependencies and had oriented his soul towards a complete submission to God. Although he could be expected to do more than his social and political obligations required, his ultimate salvation was in no way implicated in the world; his good works in the world were the consequence of his faith, and his faith could never be the result of his works. "You have the kingdom of heaven; therefore you should leave the kingdom of earth to any one who wants to take it." [47]

The doctrine of Christian liberty was modified by Luther in the light of his experiences during the Peasants' War. The basic question raised at that time was whether the spread of lawlessness might eventually undermine the peace of the faithful and thereby interfere with the quest for salvation. The pressure of events forced Luther to soften the distinction between the Kingdom of God and the kingdom of the world. If the rebellious peasants were to gain the upper hand "both kingdoms would be destroyed

[44] *Works*, Vol. 3, p. 234.
[45] *Works*, Vol. 3, pp. 235–236.
[46] Woolf, Vol. 1, pp. 357–358; *Works*, Vol. 3, p. 235; Vol. 4, pp. 240–241; *Werke* (Weimar Ausgabe), Vol. 1, pp. 640–643.
[47] *Works*, Vol. 3, pp. 248, 239–242; Vol. 6, pp. 447 ff.; Woolf, Vol. 1, pp. 234, 357, 368–370, 378–379.

and there would be neither worldly government nor Word of God, but it would result in the permanent destruction of Germany. . . ." [48] If both the Kingdom of God and the kingdom of the world possessed a common need for order, as Luther admitted, then the true believer could not be as indifferent towards the political order as the doctrine of Christian liberty implied. Religion and politics were more closely intertwined than the theory of the two kingdoms inferred. Luther's theory of government, then, came down to this: temporal authority could insure outward peace for the true believer; it could never affect his internal virtue. For the unbeliever, government could impose external order and external virtue. Government existed "in order that the good may have outward peace and protection; and that the wicked may not be free to do evil, without fear, in peace and quietness." [49]

Certain confusions began to appear in Luther's thought, however, when he attempted to relate his doctrine of government to the problems of obedience and freedom of conscience. Sometimes he argued that authority could not coerce the consciences of the believers; and this was consistent with his teaching that externals could not affect the liberty of the Christian man. At other times he insisted that government ought not to coerce consciences. This could only mean logically that freedom of conscience was useful primarily for the unrighteous who might some day be led back to the fold.

The same difficulty reappeared when Luther allowed that men need not obey when a ruler commanded contrary to the teachings of Scripture.[50] But this could involve only the true believer, for he alone possessed a conscience guided by Scripture. At the same time, he alone owned a conscience which could not be harmed by external actions.

The contradictory elements were present in other aspects of Luther's teaching on this same general subject. Earlier he had urged that the secular rulers apply force against the Papacy, yet he overwhelmingly maintained that secular rulers ought not to be resisted for any cause. Thus political authority might resist religious authority on either political or religious grounds, while religious authorities might never resist political authority on either religious or political grounds. The final incongruity appeared during the Peasants' War when Luther advocated the right of anyone to kill a rebellious peasant. Thus a rebel might be slain by anyone, a tyrant by no one.[51]

[48] *Works*, Vol. 4, p. 220; Smith and Jacobs, Vol. 2, p. 320.
[49] *Works*, Vol. 6, p. 460; Vol. 3, pp. 231–232; Vol. 4, pp. 23, 28; Smith and Jacobs, Vol. 2, p. 492.
[50] *Works*, Vol. 1, p. 271; Vol. 3, pp. 255–256.
[51] *Works*, Vol. 1, pp. 262–264; Vol. 3, pp. 211–212; Vol. 4, pp. 226–228. Some commentators have made a great deal of the joint declaration of 1531, wherein Luther sanctioned resistance to the Emperor. But when this is measured against the main body of his writings, its evidential value is small. Moreover, it would seem that the declara-

IV

Luther has frequently been criticized by later writers for promoting the cause of political absolutism. Figgis, for example, coupled Luther with Machiavelli and treated their ideas as two sides of the same coin.[52] While this view is correct in emphasizing the extreme lengths to which Luther went in releasing temporal rulers from previous restraints, it tends to view the problem primarily in terms of moral and religious restraints. Actually, Luther consistently upheld the right of Christians to rebuke the excesses of princes, and his own writings testify to the extent to which he followed that advice. If we are to look for the fundamental weakness in Luther's thinking, it is to be sought in his failure to appreciate the importance of institutions. His obsession with religious simplicity caused him to ignore the role of religious institutions as political restraints. The social consequences of a weakly organized religion were apparent in his own day. At moments of political and social crisis he was unable to appeal to any effective religious organization to act as mediator. During the Peasants' War he was compelled to entrust the whole cause of peace to the princes, despite his own conviction that all of the wrongs were not entirely on one side. In trying to get out of this predicament Luther succeeded only in making the Christian ethic appear irrelevant to the logic of the political order: "The sayings on mercy belong in God's kingdom and among Christians, not in the kingdom of the world. . . ."[53]

The quest for simplicity also had its effects when Luther considered political institutions. Here it took the form of accepting authority rather than rejecting it. From a few ingenuous ideas about authority, order, and social classes Luther fashioned a political doctrine of stark simplicity, unrelieved by the shadows of qualification. It was designed essentially to impress on princes the desirability of paternal rule and on subjects the wickedness of disobedience. Just as his religious teachings emphasized the single relationship of a believer who throws himself on God's mercy, so the political order was stripped of nearly all except the single relationship between ruler and ruled. In both cases the moral impotence and sinfulness of man was the source of his dependence.[54] But the peculiarity of the relationship between political superiors and their inferiors was that so much of it remained unpermeated by religious values. Religious considerations en-

---

tion was largely the work of Melanchthon. Luther affixed his own signature only after a great deal of agony and self-searching. A year previously he had warned against resisting the Emperor. See Mackinnon, Vol. 4, pp. 25–27.

[52] Figgis, pp. 55–61.

[53] *Werke* (Weimar Ausgabe), Vol. 18, p. 389.

[54] Tillich has remarked that "Christian pessimism with respect to human nature has helped a great deal to bring about the alliance between Christianity and authority." "The Gospel and the State," *Crozer Quarterly*, Vol. 15, pp. 251–261, at p. 258 (Oct. 1938).

tered only at the extremities of the relationship: the ruler held his authority from God, while the subject was under a divine injunction to obey rulers in every conceivable *political* circumstance. No provision was made for the other complex relationships in a political order. The political relationship, like the religious, was a personalized rather than an institutionalized one.

In this connection Luther's doctrine of Christian liberty and his defense of disobedience on religious grounds did little to redress the balance against the secular ruler. Both of these ideas had been hollowed of their political content. "True" liberty had been transformed into an internal state of faith, while obligation was disconnected from political relationships and made to apply solely to religious issues; in political matters men had to obey unquestioningly.

The foregoing points to the conclusion that the problem presented by Luther was not one arising from the divorce between politics and religious values, but from the political irrelevancy of the Christian ethic. While Luther certainly assumed that Christian values, such as love, neighborliness, and charity, would exercise a salutary influence in society and politics, he failed to show their viability in dealing with problems other than those located at the elementary level of the household and the neighborhood. The Christian ethic might well be applicable at the intimate, personal level, and yet be quite irrelevant for the relationships created by a complicated political order. Luther remained unaware of this difficulty, because he reduced political relationships to a single form. Something of the political inadequacy of the Christian teaching was glimpsed by Luther himself. In the tract *On Trading and Usury* (1524) his argument began by laying down the strict Christian teachings on the subject; soon, however, he was led to admit that the Christian ethic was of little utility here inasmuch as most members of society did not act as Christians. His solution was to abandon the Christian argument and to invoke, instead, the coercive arm of government. The argument ended on the note that the world would be reduced to chaos if men tried to govern by the Gospel.[55]

These doubts about the political effectiveness of Christian teachings had their roots in the fundamental ambiguity characteristic of the thinking of many of the early reformers. On the religious side they advocated the most uncompromising and radical reforms, while on the political side they enjoined quietism. Luther, for example, vehemently rejected any hierarchical distinctions among Christian believers; yet he assumed that a social hierarchy was natural and necessary.[56] He eloquently defended the sanctity of the individual conscience; yet he unhesitatingly accepted the institutions of serfdom. He admitted that some of the grievances of the peasants were justified, but counseled the peasants against attaching much value to mate-

[55] *Works*, Vol. 4, pp. 16–22.
[56] *Works*, Vol. 4, pp. 240, 308; Vol. 5, pp. 43 ff.

rial concerns. He was willing to raise fundamental questions about every form of religious authority, but towards political institutions he was quite unsceptical, even when he doubted the morals and motives of rulers. His thought represented a striking combination of revolt and passivity.

The split character of Luther's thinking is all the more striking, because embedded in his religious ideas were the rudiments of a theory of responsible government: the idea of the consent of the congregation, the responsibility of the ministry, and the right of each member to interpret the basic law. Nevertheless, it would be misleading to conclude, as some writers have, that Luther's religious ideas presaged later democratic ideas. It is necessary to be clear about what type of democratic theory is at issue. Luther's religious ideas bear no kinship to the liberal-democratic tradition later associated with Locke, Jefferson, and the *Federalist Papers*. If there is to be a relationship, it is with that democratic primitivism which searches obsessively for the pristine expression of the people's will and judges government by the faithfulness with which it reflects that will; which exhibits a deep impatience with all intermediary, representative institutions; and which chafes under all traditional legal and institutional restraints. In this equation, the intermediary institutions play the role of Luther's pope: an artificial fabrication designed to frustrate the faithful members of the congregation. The accent is on simplification, for the people have as little need for complicated political arrangements as Luther's true believer has for a visible Church. In both instances the quest is for personal identification: the believer with his God, the citizen with his government.

17

Calvin and the Reformation: The Political Education of Protestantism

SHELDON S. WOLIN

The purpose of this essay is to draw attention to two aspects of the political ideas of the sixteenth century Reformation which were important to the development of the Western tradition of political theory. First, like all great transformations, the Reformation stimulated the rethinking of much that had been taken for granted. In terms of political ideas, this centered around a developing crisis in the concept of order and in the Western traditions of civility. The criticism of the papacy by the early reformers had really amounted to a demand for the liberation of the individual believer from a mass of institutional controls and traditional restraints which hitherto had governed his behavior. The medieval Church had been many things, and

This article was originally published in *American Political Science Review*, 51 (June 1957), 428–453. It is reprinted here with the permission of the author and of the publisher.

among them, a system of governance. It had sought, not always successfully, to control the conduct of its members through a definite code of discipline, to bind them to unity through emotional as well as material commitments, and to direct the whole religious endeavor through an institutionalized power structure as impressive as any the world had seen. In essence, the Church had provided a rationalized set of restraints designed to mould human behavior to accord with a certain image. To condemn it as the agent of the Antichrist was to work towards the release of human behavior from the order which had formed it. This liberating tendency was encouraged by one of the great ideas of the early reformers, the conception of the church as a fellowship bound together by the ties of faith and united in a common quest for salvation. But the *Genossenschaft*-idea lacked the complementary notion of the church as a *corpus regens,* a corporate society welded together by a viable structure of power. The inference remaining was that men could be fashioned to live in an orderly community without the serious and consistent application of force.

The second aspect of Reformation thought to be examined concerns the nature and source of political ideas. The crisis just mentioned cannot be properly understood if we take a narrow view of what is "political" in a set of ideas. Statements may be politically significant, yet not issue from a "political" theory. When the men of the Reformation put forward competing ideas of the church, they were not, so to speak, engaging in a form of immaculate conception and stating their ideas independently of common modes of thought and experience. In the act of projecting their ideal religious orders, the reformers were ineluctably led not only to draw upon the available experience concerning the political and social order, but also to use the language of political and social thought. These considerations point to the likelihood that Reformation ideas of a religious society would evoke many remainders of a political society, and, conversely, that conceptions of the political order would share many of the categories of religious thinking.

Once this is appreciated, it is possible to uncover a whole range of relevant and influential political ideas in the religious writings of the Reformation, even though these ideas were not always cast in the strict language of politics. In the case of the reformers' attack on the papacy, for example, the issue of man as an institutional being, entwined in an elaborate network of duties, privileges, and relationships, was not the less political for being formulated in a semi-political way. Again, the raging disputes over the "proper form of church government"—itself a revealing bit of common usage—can easily be made more meaningful if for "believer" we substitute "citizen," for "discipline" we substitute "power." In summary, the student of the history of political ideas does well to take seriously Hooker's phrase "the laws of ecclesiastical polity."

I

Calvin's thought is particularly revealing of the interpenetration of political and religious modes of thought. The mixture of two is essential in understanding his crucial role in furthering the political education of Protestantism. On the religious side, his ecclesiology was a systematic elaboration of the principle that a church-society would remain incomplete and ineffective if it did not possess an institutional structure which could articulate its life. The community of believers was not enough; the additional element of power was needed to insure the coherence and solidarity of the community.

On the political side, the problem of order could be attacked only if the political community itself were regarded as worth saving. So long as men believed with Luther that government was a mighty engine of repression and that the political order was superfluous for the true Christian, so long would the political community remain in limbo.[1] To restore the discredited community was the first necessity.

While it would be extreme to conclude that Calvin presided over the "liquidation in the Reformation," [2] there can be no denying that his emphasis on structure and organization, on controlling the impulses liberated by the Reformation, inaugurated a new phase of the movement. The individual was to be reintegrated into a double order, religious and political, and the orders themselves were to be linked in a common unity. The discontinuity between religious obligations and restraints and their political counterparts was to be repaired; Christian virtue and political virtue were to move closer together. The order that emerged was not a "theocracy," but a corporate community that was neither purely religious nor purely secular, but a compound of both.

The restorative work of Calvin was most clearly displayed in his theory of the church, for it was in this area that the anti-institutional bias of the early reformers had been most evident. In his theory the idea of the church had two aspects, the church visible and the church invisible. The latter he defined as "the society of all the saints, a society spread over the whole world, and existing in all ages, yet bound together by the one doctrine, and the one Spirit of Christ. . . ." [3] The visible church, on the other hand, stood as a concession to human frailty. Since it included "many hypocrites" and many members in varying degrees of faith, its existence was attended by more tangible marks than the preaching of the Word and the administration of the sacraments. Its location was not universal but spe-

[1] *Works of Martin Luther,* ed. Charles M. Jacobs, 6 vols. (Philadelphia, 1915–1932), Vol. 5, p. 81, hereafter cited as *Works.*
[2] P. Imbart de la Tour, *Les origines de la Réformation,* 4 vols. (Paris, 1905–1935), Vol. 4, p. 53.
[3] "Letter from Calvin to Sadolet," *Tracts Relating to the Reformation,* trans. by Henry Beveridge, 3 vols. (Edinburgh, 1844), Vol. 1, p. 37.

cific; its unity was not guaranteed by grace, but required a definite and in-suring structure of offices; so its concord was not spontaneous, but was the calculated product of discipline. The visible church, in short, was a kind of second-best form of church polity accommodated to the weaknesses of man's nature. At the same time, Calvin repeatedly warned that the dispari-ties in perfection between the visible and the invisible church could never justify men in forsaking the visible form out of a desire to avoid contamina-tion. "A departure from the church," he declared, was a "renunciation of God and Christ," "a criminal dissension." [4] Just as Aristotle had believed that every imperfect polity was capable of being improved, so Calvin be-lieved that every visible church could be reformed by judicious measures.

The end at which such measures should aim was unity. This was the distinguishing mark of any society, visible or invisible, religious or civil. The solidarity of each type of society, however, was differently expressed. The unity of the invisible church, for example, was not the product of human art, but the result of the secret election of God which had predes-tined the membership for salvation. The unique destiny of the saints, how-ever, did not detract from the fact that they lived a social life. In their communion they formed a universal society; the bonds of community came from a common love of Christ.[5]

For the visible church, too, Christ served as the central point of loy-alty, the object of continual and ultimate commitment from which the unity of the whole derived. The force which conserved the society of be-lievers was not produced from the controlling center of a pope who acted as trustee for the *corpus Christianum*. Instead the cohesive force came from a mystical spirit working through the members who had joined with Him to form a *corpus mysticum*.[6] In the sacrament of the Last Supper the so-ciety possessed a unifying symbolism, which not only pointed towards the divine element which lay at the vital center of society, but towards the sus-taining principle of love which nourished the common identity of the mem-

---

[4] *The Institutes of the Christian Religion,* trans. by John Allen, ed. by Benjamin B. Warfield, 2 vols. (Philadelphia: Presbyterian Board of Christian Education, 1936), Vol. 2, pp. 281–283 (IV, i, 8–10). Hereafter this will be cited as *Inst.* and all translations, except where indicated, will be from it.

[5] "For unless we are united with all the other members under Christ our Head, we can have no hope of the future inheritance. . . . But all the elect of God are so connected with each other in Christ, that as they depend upon one head, so they grow up to-gether as into one body, compacted together like members of the same body; being made truly one, as living by one faith, hope, and charity, through the same Divine Spirit, being called not only to the same inheritance of eternal life, but also to a partici-pation of one God and Christ . . . the saints are united in the fellowship of Christ on this condition, that whatever benefits God confers upon them, they should mutually communicate to each other." *Inst.,* Vol. 2, pp. 271–272 (IV, i, 2–3).

[6] *Commentaries on the Epistle of Paul the Apostle to the Romans,* trans. by John Owen (Edinburgh, 1849), p. 458. Hereafter this will be cited as *Commentaries on Romans*. On this same point see Josef Bohatec, *Calvins Lehre vom Staat und Kirche* (Breslau, 1937), p. 271.

bers. The sacramental rite signified a common good which the participants shared with and through Christ. And the common love of Christ became the actuating principle compelling the participants to share this good with their fellows: they could not love Christ without loving each other; and they could not injure each other without injuring Christ.[7]

The second primary bond which worked to unify the visible society was of a doctrinal kind. Through the constant preaching of the ministry and the arduous effort of the members to model themselves to an image of perfection, the teachings of Scripture would come to be an infusive force penetrating the most intimate areas of human conduct.

But while the preaching of the Word and the sacramental rites were sufficient to establish the existence of the invisible society, the visible society, containing as it did members in varying states of belief and unbelief, required additional aids. Unlike the invisible society, the visible lacked the unity of a common destiny, hence it had to create its unity by means of a coercive structure. Stated somewhat differently, the sacraments and the Word could provide a "social" unity for the visible church, but they could not provide the ecclesiastical government, the element of power, which was necessary for dealing with the heterogeneous nature of the members. The disparate character of the membership, some destined for salvation, others for damnation, could be moulded to unity only by a definite set of controlling institutions, an ecclesiastical polity designed to spread and enforce the Word, effect order, promote cohesion, and insure regularity in church decisions. In sum, the visible church had to be equipped with the proper instrumentalities of power.

To the extent that the visible church required institutions, laws, and governing officials it belonged to the realm of human art; and to that extent it challenged the ecclesiastical legislator to make of it *une église bien ordonnée et reglée*. While it could never achieve the perfection of the invisible society of the elect, it might aspire to a special excellence of its own. At the same time, the architect of the church did not have a perfectly free hand in executing the grand design. He was limited by the injunctions of Scripture and by the reverence which ought to be accorded a divinely ordained institution. He did not create the idea of the church or its purposes. His task was to imitate, as far as the puny art of man allowed, the divine order which controlled the universe; to blend diversity into ordered harmony and individuality into a common good; to arrange the institutions

---

[7] ". . . such care as we take of our body, we ought to exercise the same care of our brethren, who are members of our body; that as no part of our body can be in any pain without every other part feeling corresponding sensations, so we ought not to suffer our brother to be afflicted with any calamity without our sympathizing in the same." *Inst.*, Vol. 2, pp. 696–697 (IV, xvii, 38). A supplementary bond was also provided by the sacrament of baptism which initiated the member into the "society of the church." *Inst.*, Vol. 2, pp. 583, 611 (IV, xv, 1; xvi, 9).

and offices of the church so that the whole would function with the coherence of a living body.[8]

In drawing attention to the structure of the church, its "constitutions" and "offices," Calvin was rediscovering what the Roman Church had always practiced and the early reformers had nearly always forgotten: that a religious society, like any other society, must find support in institutions; and that institutions, in turn, were aggregates of power. Many of the reformers, in their eagerness to condemn the "worldly power" of the medieval Church, seemed to believe that there was another kind of power, "spiritual" power, which ought to be the proper mode for expressing the authority of a religious society. Luther, for example, always drew a sharp contrast between the two forms of power, "spiritual" and "secular," and emphatically denied that there were any elements common to both.[9] "Spiritual" power emerged as something *sui generis*. It was visualized as a form of suasion over the consciences of the believers. It was the kind of influence represented by the ministerial functions of preaching and discipline. The extent to which "spiritual" power was becoming "psyche-centered" was best represented by Luther's teaching on the church's power of excommunication or the ban. He insisted, first, that this power, while it could be used to banish members from the fellowship of the church and its sacraments, could not carry with it any civil disabilities or penalties.[10] Again, while the ban could exclude an individual from the "outward, bodily and visible fellowship," it could not affect "truth and righteousness [which] belong to the inner spiritual fellowship . . . they dare not be surrendered for the sake of the external fellowship, which is immeasurably inferior, nor because of the ban."[11] Thus Luther's belief in the superiority of religious truth and faith over institutional forms helped to transform the concept of "spiritual" power from what it had been in the medieval Church. It surrendered its commanding, coercive and final character and took on what Hobbes would have called a "ghostly" form.

In Calvin's case, however, the rediscovery of institutional life led to a rejection of the antithesis between the two types of power and of the assumption which underlay it. Civil government and ecclesiastical government did not symbolize distinctions of kind, but of objectives. Their natures, therefore, were more analogous than antithetical. A spiritual polity (*spiritualis politia*) bore the same necessary relation to the life of the church as the civil government to the life of civil society.[12] The governors

[8] *Commentaries on Romans,* pp. 458–459.
[9] *Works,* Vol. 4, pp. 234–237; and see the Augsburg Confession (1530), Pt. II, art. VII in Philip Schiff (ed.), *The Creeds of Christendom,* 3 vols. (New York, 1877), Vol. 3, p. 58 ff.
[10] *D. Martin Luthers Werke* (Weimar Ausgabe, 1888–), Vol. 30, Pt. II, pp. 435, 462.
[11] *Works,* Vol. 2, pp. 37–38, 52.
[12] Note the analogies drawn by Calvin between religious and political institutions; *Inst.,* Vol. 2, p. 483 ff. (IV, xi).

of the church, too, must be well-versed in "the rule and law of good government," because such knowledge was essential to preserving any kind of order. Order, which Calvin defined as "a well-regulated polity, which excludes all confusion, incivility, obstinacy, clamours, and dissensions," was therefore a central objective of religious as well as civil polities.[13]

In Calvin's view, order was not a self-sustaining condition which, when once established, would continue from the momentum of its own perfection. It required a constant exercise of power. Just as the order of the universe was preserved by an active God so the human order must be supported by a steady force if its coherence was to be maintained.[14] Wherever there was order, there was power. Hence the kind of power which sustained a religious order might carry the adjective "spiritual," yet this did not transform it into a species of compulsion radically different from that present in the civil order. Spiritual power, in other words, constituted a specialized, not an etherealized, aspect of power applied to religious ends.

Admittedly Calvin frequently appeared to be arguing a sharp antithesis between secular and spritual power; it was, he declared, "a Jewish folly" to confound the two. Spiritual government was concerned with "the inner man" and with his preparations for eternity; civil government, on the other hand, regulated "external conduct" and "the concerns of the present state." [15] Nevertheless, if Calvin's distinctions are examined more closely it becomes apparent that the difference between the two powers was not one of substance but of application. In a highly revealing passage in the *Institutes* Calvin remarked that "it was usual" to distinguish the two orders by the words "spiritual" and "temporal"; and, while this was proper enough, he preferred to call "l'une Royaume spirituel, et l'autre Civil ou politique" (*regnum spirituale, alterum regnum politicum*).[16] In avoiding the usual pejorative contrast between "spiritual" and "secular" and by declaring each of them to be a *regnum,* Calvin was pointing to the fact that the coercive element was common to both governances. The differences between them lay in their range of objects or jurisdiction.

That spiritual power did not represent a difference in kind is further supported from another direction. One of the primary motives which had led Calvin to draw the distinction in the first place had been polemical. He had sought to defend power against those who had rejected it in the one form or the other. On the one hand, some of the radical sectarians, in the name of "Christian liberty," had taught that the true believer was totally

---

[13] *Inst.,* Vol. 2, pp. 477–483 (IV, x, 27–29; IV, xi, 1).
[14] *Inst.,* Vol. 1, pp. 52, 218, 220, 232 (I, ii, 1; xvi, 1–3; xvii, 1). The substance of these passages is that God is not "idle and almost asleep" but "engaged in continuous action."
[15] *Inst.,* Vol. 2, pp. 89–90, 770–771 (III, xix, 14; IV, xx, 1).
[16] *Calvani Opera,* ed. G. Baum, E. Cunitz, and E. Reuss, 59 vols. (Braunschweig, 1863–1900), Vol. 2, pp. 622–623; Vol. 4, p. 358 (*Inst.,* III, xix, 15). These volumes from part of the *Corpus Reformatorum,* and hereafter they will be cited as *Opera.*

absolved from the commands of political authority. At the other extreme, and equally dangerous in Calvin's eyes, were "the flatterers of princes" who would have so magnified the power of civil magistrates as to destroy the integrity of the spiritual power. Against the one extreme Calvin asserted the value of the civil order of all men and its right to command Christians in particular; against the other he affirmed the independent power of the church and its claim over a particular jurisdiction. In short, Calvin's distinction between the two powers was intended to preserve the power of each and to refute the notion that spiritual power was merely a form of insubstantial persuasion. Moreover, when Calvin defined the spiritual government as the means whereby "the conscience is formed to piety and the service of God" and the civil government as that order which "instructs in the duties of humanity and civility," he did not mean that the spiritual government alone was concerned with conscience while the political government alone regulated "external" conduct. As we shall note later on, the civil government was concerned with conscience, but of a different kind. It had a positive duty to promote and shape a "civic conscience," or what the ancients had called "civic virtue." Conversely, the spiritual government, in discharging its functions of preaching and instruction, was also expected to help form civil manners, to correct "incivility," in short, to influence "external" conduct. The conclusion towards which all these considerations pointed was that "man contains, as it were, two worlds, capable of being governed by various rulers and various laws." [17] In both worlds, Calvin conceived man to be a creature of order, subjected to restraints and controlled by power.

Calvin divided the power of the church into three aspects. The first, the power over doctrine, was limited by the injunction that "nothing ought to be admitted in the church as the Word of God, but what is contained first in the law and the prophets, and secondly in the writings of the apostles. . . ." [18] But in its relationship to the members of the church it took on a more positive aspect. The power to preach and expound an unchanging body of truths was a method for strengthening the collective identity of the community by keeping before the members the object of their common allegiance.

Closely connected with this theme was Calvin's insistence that the interpretation of Scripture be confined strictly to the appropriate officers of the church. Here Calvin was motivated to some degree by the threat to unity present in the Reformation principle of putting the Bible in the hands of Everyman. This might lead, as Calvin well recognized, to as many private images of God as there were believers. Hence Calvin's insistence on the primacy of a uniform public truth and the centralization of its

---

[17] *Inst.*, Vol. 2, p. 90 (III, xix, 15).
[18] *Inst.*, Vol. 2, pp. 422–423 (IV, viii, 8).

interpretation in the ministry had a social as well as religious purpose: to preserve the communal foundations of belief against the disintegrating effects of private visions.[19]

The second aspect of ecclesiastical power centered in the ability to make laws (in legibus ferendis; ordonner loix et statuts). In his discussion of this power Calvin was at his subtlest and most legalistic. He wanted to discredit the papal use of the legislative power without discrediting the power itself. In line with the first objective he contended that the papacy had abused the legislative power by enacting new rules of faith which had created unnecessary anxieties for believers. The popes, in other words, had trenched upon the sanctity of the individual conscience. In the course of Calvin's argument the claims of conscience came to be clothed with an almost sovereign immunity. Since Christ had been sent to free the Christian conscience from the burdens of error and superstition in order that men might more easily accept His teachings, it followed that "in matters that were left free and indifferent" no authority could legislate new barriers between the believer and the scriptural promise. "Our consciences have to do, not with men, but with God alone." [20]

Having demolished the Roman case, Calvin could only salvage the same power for his own church by modifying the dogma of conscience. For this purpose the proper starting point was not conscience but order. "In every human society some kind of government is necessary to insure the common peace and maintain concord." The nature of government required "some settled form" or procedures to expedite its transactions "decently and in order." But militating against any settled arrangement were such vagaries as the "diversity in the manners of men," the "variety in their minds," and the "repugnance in their judgments and dispositions." To overcome these anarchic forces, laws and ordinances were needed as "a kind of bonds," and once these controls had been established their existence would play a vital part in preserving the order of the church. "The removal of them would unnerve the church, deface and dissipate it entirely." Thus the legislative power, while not essential to the salvation of the believer, was fundamental to the preservation of the religious society. It was rescued by Calvin, not for the sake of the individual conscience, but for the sake of protecting the community against the strayings of the liberated conscience.[21]

The third aspect of the church's power, and "the principal one," was jurisdiction. This power was "nothing but the order provided for the preservation of spiritual polity." [22] Its scope extended from the humblest mem-

---

[19] Inst., Vol. 1, p. 74 (I, v, 11).

[20] Inst., Vol. 2, p. 452 (IV, x, 5).

[21] Inst., IV, x, 27. Here I have followed the translation of Henry Beveridge in his edition, 2 vols. (Grand Rapids, Mich., 1953), Vol. 2, p. 434.

[22] Inst., Vol. 2, p. 439 (IV, xi, 1), Beveridge translation. Calvin consciously sought to widen the power of jurisdiction by tracing it back to the Jewish Sanhedrin and thereby capitalizing on the extensive authority of that body.

ber of the congregation up to the highest political officers. Its preeminence came from the fact that it dealt with the most fundamental problem of order, namely, the discipline of the members.

> For, if no society and no house . . . can be preserved in a proper state without discipline, this is far more necessary in the church, the state of which ought to be the most orderly of all. As the saving doctrine of Christ is the soul of the church, so discipline forms the ligaments which connect the members together, and keep each in its proper place . . . Discipline, therefore, serves as a bridle to curb and restrain the refractory, who resist the doctrine of Christ; or as a spur to stimulate the inactive; and sometimes as a father's rod with which those who have grievously fallen may be chastized in mercy, and with the gentleness of the Spirit of Christ.[23]

Calvin's emphasis upon discipline makes it obvious that he saw in it another method for controlling the liberated conscience.[24] By means of discipline the believer was to be reinserted into a context of restraints and controls; he was to be reshaped into a creature of order. This was to be accomplished by minutely regulating his external conduct and by indoctrinating him in the basic teachings of the religious society. And buttressing this comprehensive system of controls was the supreme sanction (*severissima ecclesiae vindicta*) of excommunication. In Calvin's system excommunication implied a great deal more than the mere severance of external ties. The expelled were condemned to a life without hope, a life outside the circle of fellowship:

> . . . there is no other way of entrance into life, unless we are conceived by [the church], born of her, nourished at her breast, and continually preserved under her care and government until we are divested of this mortal flesh and "become like the angels" . . . we must continue under her instruction and discipline to the end of our lives . . . Anyway from her bosom there can be no hope of remission of sins or any salvation . . . It is always fatally dangerous to be separated from the church.[25]

Although Calvin denied that the power of jurisdiction was comparable in coercion to the punishing sword of the state, it is difficult to see how a power which could expel the already anxious believer from the circle of the faithful was in any way inferior to the strongest weapons at the disposal of civil rulers. The severity which marked this power was not attributable to any "Catholic" tendencies in Calvin's thought; rather it testified to his conviction that the problem of order was crucial. The solution, ac-

---

[23] *Inst.*, Vol. 2, pp. 503–504 (IV, xii, 1).

[24] See the discussion of Pierre Mesnard, *L'Essor de la philosophie politique au XVIe siècle*, 2d ed. (Paris, 1952), p. 283 ff.

[25] *Inst.*, Vol. 2, pp. 273–274 (IV, i, 4). It is important to note that the ultimate power of excommunication was placed specifically in the hands of the higher officers of the church, that is, the pastors and the Council of Elders. The power was specifically excluded from the province of the magistrates and the congregation.

cording to Calvin's logic, demanded the use of positive power on the part of the church in order to refashion Protestant man into a creature of order, or more accurately, to make him conform to a Christian image of civility.

The contrast between this conception of the role of the church and Luther's was not produced simply by Calvin's willingness to restore a three-term relationship of God-church-believer for the simpler notion of Luther. The real contrast took shape from Calvin's effort to recapture an older conception of the community as a school of virtue and the vital agency for the realization of individual perfection. If we compare, for example, Calvin's symbolism of the mother-church with the passages in Plato's *Crito* where Socrates declares he would rather take the hemlock than betray the *polis* which has nurtured him to dignity, a striking similarity in outlook emerges. This is not to say that Calvin, as the representative of sixteenth century French humanism, was intent on reviving in some mimetic sense the classical conception of the community. It is only to indicate that Calvin's conception of a church-society stood as the culmination of a long intellectual process, extending back to the beginnings of Christianity, whereby the idea of the community as the custodian of virtue had been translated from a political to a religious setting. The church and not the city became the vital medium for human improvement, the symbol of human destiny: "to the end of time," wrote Augustine, "as a stranger upon the earth, suffering the persecutions of the world and receiving the consolation of God, the Church travels onwards." [26]

While Calvin retained the Christian idea of the superior virtue of religious society, he reformulated it in a way which was different from both the medieval and the Lutheran conceptions of the church. In adopting the Lutheran idea of a community-in-fellowship Calvin departed from the dominant medieval tradition; in enveloping that community within a structure of power he departed from Luther. The final result pointed at a church which was to be something more than a community and something more than a christianized *polis*. At its deepest level the church cohered as a *corpus mysticum*, but on top of this mystic foundation Calvin erected a set of institutions to articulate and enforce a distinctive way of life. The tight corporate quality of the whole recalled the ancient *polis*, yet the underlying element of mystery was a reminder of that transcendent strain utterly alien to the classical community. The church heralded the triumph of God—and here Calvin followed an old Christian belief; it pointed towards a perfection in eternity, and not within the time-space limits of the *polis*. Citizenship in the church-society did not connote participation in offices, but participation in a pilgrimage which would ultimately transcend history.

Despite the fact that Calvin placed a high value on community life

[26] *De Civitate Dei*, Lib. XVIII, cap. 51.

and the institutions of the church, he was not insensitive to the danger that institutional means might become elevated into ultimate ends. As a safeguard against this possibility he insisted that the power of the church was limited, that the authority of Scripture was superior to that of the church, and that faith stood above both men and institutions:

> Ours is the humility, which beginning with the lowest, and paying respect to each in his degree, yields the highest honor and respect to the church in subordination, however, to Christ the church's Head; ours is the obedience, which, while it disposes us to listen to our elders and superiors, tests all obedience by the Word of God.[27]

II

To an important degree the institutional structure which Calvin proposed for the government of the church was fashioned to overcome the difficulties encountered by the Lutherans and Anabaptists. The Lutheran church appeared increasingly vulnerable to political pressures, while the Anabaptist congregations seemed to have escaped the world only to be troubled by internal disorders. Thus the one church was plagued by political interference, the other by the confusions of congregational democracy. To meet these problems Calvin proposed that the best church polity should aim at self-sufficiency, but without divorcing itself from the life of political society; it should follow the Reformation principle of bringing the members into the active life of the church, but without entrusting them with the close supervision of affairs; it should provide for strong leadership and direction within the church, but without restoring the pope. In tracing out a solution in these terms, Calvin produced a political theory of church government.

Calvin was particularly sensitive to the charge that, under the guise of attacking the papacy, he had reintroduced a new hierarchy. He tried to counter this by arguing that a church modeled on the *Institutes* could not be hierarchical because none of its offices could claim an authority independent of Scripture. Hierarchy, in his definition, was equivalent to arbitrariness; a chiseled structure of offices was not bad in itself, as long as it did not culminate in a single, preeminent human authority. Calvin, in short, was not so much anti-hierarchical as anti-monarchical.

Of the major offices outlined by Calvin the two most important were the pastorate and the Elders (*les Anciens*). Under the Genevan system the Elders were laymen elected by the secular civic Council; together with a selected number of ministers, they formed the Consistory, the chief organ of church discipline.[28] The pastors were unquestionably the most powerful

[27] *Inst.*, Vol. 1, pp. 35–36 (Ded. Epist.), 86–87 (I, vii, 1–2); Vol. 2, pp. 417–419 (IV, viii, 2–4); "Letter to Sadolet," *Tracts*, Vol. 1, p. 50.
[28] Herbert D. Foster, "Calvin's Program for a Puritan State in Geneva," *Collected Papers of Herbert D. Foster* (privately printed, 1929), p. 64; Emile Doumergue, *Jean Cal-*

agency and the nerve-center of the whole system. They were to be nomi-
nated, in the first instance, by their fellow-ministers, and then passed on by
the Council. The names which survived were then submitted to the congregation for its approval or rejection. The procedures whereby the pastors
were selected provides a good illustration of the role allotted the congregation in Calvin's scheme: the membership could ratify or reject decisions;
they could not formulate policy. Calvin looked upon the actions and the
decisions of the church as being primarily institutional products. They
were the results of prescribed procedures and of the actions of certain
designated officers and agencies. Above all, these methods were the
guarantee that order and regularity would prevail in church affairs; they
were the alternatives to the confusion and disorder of popular control.
The element in Calvin's church which most corresponded to popular
participation occurred at what we could call the "social" or sacramental
level. It was through the symbolism of the sacraments and the preaching
of the Word, and not in the making of "political" decisions in the church,
that the members enjoyed the shared intimacies of community.

These aspects of Calvin's system formed a sharp contrast to certain sectarian ideas—also hinted at by Luther on occasion—that the
ministers of the church were agents of the community, hence subject to
recall, and that some of the powers of the church, such as excommunication or expulsion, were to be wielded by the whole membership. For
Calvin the powers of the church resided "partly" in the pastors and "partly"
in the councils of the church. But the officers of the church, even though
elected by some of the members of the congregation, were not to be considered agents of the community, but instruments of the Word of God the
maker of all things (*instrumento artifex*).[29]

While the role of the congregation was hollowed of most of its substance, the pastorate, as the symbol of the common social purpose—"the
principal bond which holds the believers together in one body"[30]—was
exalted:

---

vin. Les hommes et les choses de son temps, 7 vols. (Lausanne, 1899–1928), Vol. 5, p.
188 ff.; Mesnard, p. 301 ff.

[29] In Doumergue's magisterial work on Calvin there is a spirited defense of the thesis
that Calvin's theory of the church embodied a strong "representative" element. Yet
Doumergue's argument is weakened by his failure to ask: what and whom do the officers of the church represent? He is content, instead, to indicate the several passages
where Calvin provided for congregational approval of certain church officers. The difficulty here is that election is not the same as representation, especially when it is not
accompanied by a power of recall. Hence even though Calvin declared that the ministers constituted a *corpus ecclesiae repraesentans* (*Opera*, Vol. 14, p. 681), his meaning
was that the ministers represented the purposes of the church as defined by Scripture.
He did not mean that the ministers represented the wills or separate interests of the
members of the congregation, hence Doumergue's attempt to relate the Calvinist theory
of the church to modern representative government is not convincing. See his discussion, Vol. 5, pp. 158–162.

[30] *Inst.*, Vol. 2, pp. 318–319 (IV, iii, 2); see also *Inst.*, Vol. 2, p. 317 (IV, iii, 1).

Here is the supreme power (*summam potestatem*) with which the pastors of the church . . . ought to be invested: that by the Word of God they may venture to do all things with confidence; may constrain all the strength, glory, wisdom, and pride of the world to obey and submit to His majesty; supported by His power, may govern all mankind, from the highest to the lowest . . . may instruct and exhort the docile; may reprove, rebuke, and restrain the rebellious and obstinate; may bind and loose; may discharge their lightnings and thunders, if necessary; but all in the Word of God.[31]

This last phrase—"all in the Word of God"—was the crucial qualification to Calvin, for it transformed what might have been a roving mandate into a species of limited power. Despite its central position in Calvin's scheme, the pastorate was not an office possessed of unlimited possibilities. It did not belong to that tradition wherein the holders of power might freely shape the passive mass of the governed, restrained only by the malleability of the human materials. In certain aspects Calvin's conception of the role of office in an organized community veered towards the Platonic tradition of the philosopher-ruler as the objective agency for an eternal truth which he served but did not invent. In its ideal form, the office of pastor, like that of the philosopher-ruler, remained undisfigured by the personality or bias of the incumbent. A pastor who strayed beyond the objective teachings of Scripture profaned his office. The pastors were enjoined to "bring forward nothing of themselves, but speak from the mouth of the Lord" and "speak nothing beside His Word."[32] The pastor must labor, then, as a selfless demiurge, a dedicated artisan at the service of the Word. His power was not personal but institutional.[33]

Nevertheless, qualifications attached to Calvin's conception of this key office removed it at certain points from the Platonic tradition. The Platonic ruler symbolized the unbroken trinity or virtue, knowledge, and power; if perfect knowledge were perfect virtue, then these must be allied to perfect power. But Calvin's pastor was deficient in all three: the elect symbolized virtue, and there was no guarantee that the pastor *qua* pastor belonged to this group; greater knowledge of Scripture he might have, but it would have been blasphemous to assert that this represented a perfect knowledge; and while he possessed great power and influence over the congregation, he was far from having a monopoly in these matters. The pastor, in short, was a leader, not a ruler. It was the highest office possible in a community without a head, without a single human center of direction and control.

[31] *Inst.*, Vol. 2, p. 424 (IV, viii, 9).
[32] *Inst.*, Vol. 2, p. 417 (IV, viii, 2).
[33] The authority and dignity of the pastoral office, according to Calvin, belonged not "to the persons themselves, but to the ministry over which they were appointed, or to speak more correctly, to the Word, the ministration of which was committed to them." *Inst.*, Vol. 2, p. 424 (IV, viii, 9). American constitutional lawyers will recognize in this a forerunner of the role the Supreme Court in the nineteenth century claimed for itself when interpreting the Constitution in the exercise of its power of judicial review.

When this conception of the pastoral office is placed alongside the other elements of Calvin's ecclesiology, such as the passive role of the congregation and the repeated emphasis on institutional structure; and when these in turn are combined with his unvarying belief in the binding objectivity of Scripture, then the fundamental motivation becomes clear: to make of the church and its officers a selfless instrument for advancing the Word. So obsessive was this master-idea that in the end the church stands as a kind of granite edifice, an inhuman monument. Its structure has been built to anticipate and counter the threat of human discretion. Wherever the human element, like some wayward and mercurial spirit, sought escape from the institutional processes in order to assert its own individuality, it was met by Calvin, lying in wait with the exacting measure of Scripture.

The obverse side to Calvin's conception of the church was that it marked the Protestant rediscovery of the institutional dimension. In developing his ideas on this subject Calvin touched upon a whole range of topics, including the nature of power, the functions of office, the bonds of community, and the role of membership. The totality of these problems constituted more than a theory of an ecclesiastical polity; it was nothing less than a comprehensive statement covering the major elements of a political theory. Here was a vision of a rightly-ordered society and its government; here, in the sacramental mysteries and in the preaching of the Word, lay a new symbolism, a new set of sustaining "myths" to cement the society together; here, in the tight discipline enforced by the church, was the shaping hand to mould the members to a common outlook and instruct them in the lessons of a common good; and here in the promise of salvation was the perfecting purpose towards which the particular wills of the members were to be bent. The central message of the whole was of man's necessary relationship to a determinate order.

III

The transition from Calvin's religious to his political thought was not abrupt. The same categories of analysis and modes of thought which had informed his religious writings are found in his political theory. For Calvin, political and religious thought tended to form a continuous realm of discourse. The major unifying element was the general concept of order which was a premise common to both religious and political society. This unity of outlook is worth emphasizing, because it is in sharp contrast with that of the early reformers. In the thinking of Luther and the Anabaptists the political and religious categories, far from being united by any internal connection, faced each other in a posture of dialectical tension. The hostility of many of the early reformers towards the political order created a kind of fault line between their political and religious modes of thought.

When they described the nature of the church or the holy life of the believers, their words and concepts evoked a picture of a good society, united in holy fellowship and living a life of harmony. It was the imagery of minds which had glimpsed a transcendent kingdom. But when they turned to consider the kingdom of the world, the categories shifted abruptly and the imagery darkened. For language and concept were no longer dealing with the church, the vessel of God's grace, but with the state, the weapon of His awful vengeance. Love, brotherhood, and peace, those immanent forces in the life of the church, trailed off into wistful hopes when confronted with political society. As part of the kingdom of the world, political society was a realm where conflict and violence rumbled below the surface, ready at any moment to erupt into bloodshed and disorder. Political authority naturally tended to be pictured as a mighty engine of repression—"smite and smite, slay and slay" Luther had exhorted the princes during the Peasants' War—designed to enforce peace and to protect the Christian remnant from the terrors of the world. Such a government aimed not at virtue, but at keeping men from each other's throats; mankind had never really given up the Hobbesian state of nature. In this view, an extreme tension persisted between the nature of man and the requirements of order. Political society marked a condition of "fallen nature" where sinful man strained impatiently at the restraints imposed by authority and restlessly searched for the chance to break through.

Yes it is a picture with a striking incongruity between the Christian cosmology and the Christian sociology; the one positing an omnipotent God ordering all of creation towards harmony, the other painting society as a dark, disordered mass trembling on the brink of anarchy and seemingly outside the beneficent order of God. In the thought of some of the early reformers, political society could be likened to a realm where the cosmic writ did not run. But while the moral status of government had shrunk, its power had been exalted even to the extent of entrusting it with religious responsibilities.

The task Calvin undertook was to reconcile the several opposites created by the split-vision of the early reformers. He had to resolve the conflict between the Christian cosmology and its sociology; he had to reestablish the moral status of the political order, but without making it appear as a substitute for religious society; he had to soften the black-and-white contrast between the two forms of society. The over-all method Calvin employed for bringing the two societies into some kind of congruence was to treat them both as subject to the general principle of order. Order became the common center to which the problems of the two societies, as societies, were to be referred. Political society was to be rescued from limbo by being restored to a wider, ordered frame. It was to become a part of the Christian cosmology. For Calvin the governance of God was displayed in His total command over all that occurred within His domain: "not a drop of rain falls, but at the express command of God." [34] His mastery extended also to history and society; He visited judgment on the affairs of men, punishing the wicked, elevating the just and protecting the faithful. The plenitude of His power, therefore, excluded the disruptive influence of contingency and chance. He "regulates all those commotions in the most exact order, and directs them to their proper end." [35]

As part of this divine economy, civil government could no longer be viewed as a mere agency of repression or as "a polluted thing which has nothing to do with Christian men." [36] It has been designed by God to preserve and to improve the creatures with whom He had covenanted. Government was elevated into an educative agency "by which a man is instructed in the duties of humanity and civility, which are to be observed in an intercourse with mankind." [37] But if the function of government were raised above mere repression, then evidently the nature of man must contain something beyond an irrepressible inclination towards disorder. And although Calvin stood second to none of the reformers in his low estimate of man's nature,[38] we find him, nevertheless, attaching an important qualification. The minds of all men contained "general impressions of civil probity and order"; they exhibited "an instinctive propensity to cherish and preserve society." [39]

By returning to the older political tradition which had pictured man as a creature destined for order, Calvin was able to recapture for his own purposes the idea of political society as the fulfillment of certain desirable tendencies in men. Political society, far from being a Procrustean bed which cut ungovernable humanity to the pattern of obedience, was now advanced to a divinely-ordained agency for man's improvement. "The authority possessed by kings and other governors over all things upon earth is not a consequence of the perverseness of men, but of the providence and holy ordinance of God." [40] Government was "equally as necessary to mankind as bread and water, light and air, and far more excellent." [41]

---

[34] *Inst.*, Vol. 1, p. 223 (I, xvi, 4).
[35] *Inst.*, Vol. 1, p. 233 (I, xvii, 1).
[36] *Inst.*, Vol. 2, p. 771 (IV, xx, 2).
[37] *Inst.*, Vol. 2, p. 90 (III, xix, 25).
[38] "Had we remained in the state of natural integrity such as God first created, the order of justice would not have been necessary. For each would then have carried the law in his own heart, so that no constraint would have been needed to keep us in check. Each would be his own rule and with one mind we would do what is good. Hence justice is a remedy of this human corruption. And whenever one speaks of human justice let us recognize that in it we have the mirror of our perversity, since it is by force we are led to follow equity and reason." *Opera*, Vol. 27, p. 409. See also *Opera*, Vol. 7, p. 84; Vol. 49, p. 249; Vol. 52, p. 267; and the discussion in Chenevière, *La pensée politique de Calvin* (Paris, 1937), pp. 93–94.
[39] *Inst.*, Vol. 1, p. 294 (II, ii, 13).
[40] *Inst.*, Vol. 2, p. 774 (IV, xx, 4).
[41] *Inst.*, Vol. 2, p. 90 (III, xix, 15); Vol. 2, p. 771 (IV, xx, 2).

Concurrent with the restored status of political society and the reinvestment of man with a political nature, the ends of the political order took on a loftier dignity. The office of the magistrate aimed not merely at the preservation of life, but at "the enactment of laws to regulate a man's life among his neighbors by the rules of holiness, integrity, and sobriety." [42] Through the pursuit of these ends the political order was linked with the higher purposes of religious society. Nevertheless, this union did not obliterate the integrity or the distinctiveness of the political order. It still had a unique role to play. It outfitted men with a type of civility and discipline which could not be gained elsewhere. The charge that Calvin was intent on stamping society with a Christian image, or on purging it of its distinctively political attributes, does less than justice to his basic intent. If the matter is analyzed merely in terms of certain "higher" and "lower" values, then there can be no denying Calvin's conviction that political society ought to promote the "higher" ends of Christianity—*ad majorem Dei gloriam.* To be a good citizen was not an end in itself; one became a good citizen in order to be a better believer. Nevertheless, the ends of political society were not exhausted by its Christian mission. Government existed to promote "decency" as well as "godliness," "peace" as well as "piety," "moderation" as well as "reverence." In other words, government existed to promote values which were not necessarily Christian, even though they might be given a Christian coloration; they were values which were necessary for order and, as such, a precondition for human existence. Civil government, then, was to promote the values which sustained order; it was to *civil*-ize men, or, in Calvin's words, "to regulate our lives in a manner requisite for the society of men, to form our manners to civil justice." It followed that when the spiritual and the political jurisdictions were rightly constituted the two orders were "in no respect at variance with each other." [43]

In a striking passage condemning the sectarian animus against the political order, Calvin summarized the value of political society and underscored its vital role in the Christian economy:

> For that spiritual reign, even now upon earth, commences within us some preludes of the heavenly kingdom, and in this mortal and transitory life affords us some taste of the immortal and incorruptible blessedness; but the end of this temporal regime is to foster and maintain the external worship of God, the pure doctrine and religion, to defend the constitution of the church in its entirety, to adapt our conduct to human society, to shape our manners in accordance with civil justice, to create concord among us, to maintain and preserve a common peace and tranquillity. All these things I confess would be superfluous if the kingdom of God, as it now exists within us, extinguishes the present life. But if it is the will of God that we should wander upon earth while aspiring towards our true country, and if such

---

[42] *Inst.*, Vol. 2, p. 90 (III, xix, 15); Vol. 2, pp. 772–773 (IV, xx, 3).
[43] *Inst.*, Vol. 2, p. 772 (IV, xx, 2).

aids are necessary to our journey here; then those who would take them from man deprive him of his humanity.[44]

The values of unity and cohesion, so prominent in Calvin's discussion of the church, were evident also in his conception of the political community. The unity of the political order, however, was not that of the *corpus mysticum*. Political unity would draw sustenance and support from the mystic solidarity of Christians—"Christians are not only a body politic, but they are the mystical and spiritual body of Christ,"[45]—but the more immediate source of cohesion would be in the political society itself.[46] There was a kind of natural unity arising from man's innate instinct towards an ordered life in society, and there was a kind of artificial unity which could be induced by the institutions of society. The full unity of the society was the product of an alliance between nature and art. For the individual member it meant an education in order, that is, the acquisition of a set of civil habits which would simultaneously support civilized life and satisfy one of man's basic instincts.

While civil law and political institutions were two of the main agencies of stability and order, these same ends were also served by the system of vocations. A graduated social hierarchy, clearly defined in terms of offices and obligations, was but the civil counterpart to the divine principle which sustained the universe. Far from being a divisive force, distinctions of status and eminence were not only inevitable, but, in a Christian society, salutary. They had been instituted by God to prevent men from wallowing in "universal confusion." They outfitted the individual with a sort of social map, a sense of direction "that he might not wander about in uncertainty the rest of his days." [47]

Man's education to membership in an ordered community was furthered from still another source. The life of the church was an intensely social one, and in the element of love, which bound the fellowship together, it possessed a powerful cohesive whose influence would carry over to blunt the sharp edges of the social hierarchy. Love became the basic

[44] *Inst.*, Vol. 2, p. 772 (IV, xx, 2). I have slightly changed the translation; see the text in *Opera*, Vol. 2, p. 1094. In connection with this point it is interesting to note how Calvin reversed the usual argument and asserted that obedience to human superiors helped to habituate men to obedience to God. *Inst.*, Vol. 2, p. 433 (II, viii, 35).
[45] Cited in Doumergue, Vol. 5, p. 45.
[46] Compare Calvin's use of the *corpus mysticum* to that of the fifteenth century writer Sir John Fortescue, *De Laudibus Legum Anglie*, edited and translated by S. B. Chrimes (Cambridge, 1949), cap. xiii. The whole problem of the influence of the Eucharist on political ideas remains to be explored. Some suggestive points are to be found in two articles by Ernst H. Kantorowicz, "*Pro Patria Mori* in Medieval Political Thought," *American Historical Review*, Vol. 56, pp. 472–492 (April 1951), and "Mysteries of State: An Absolutist Concept and Its Late Mediaeval Origins," *Harvard Theological Review*, Vol. 48, pp. 65–91 (Jan. 1955). Fundamental for this problem is Henri de Lubac, *Corpus Mysticum*, 2d ed. (Paris, 1949).
[47] *Inst.*, Vol. 1, pp. 790–791 (III, x, 6).

fusing force which blended the private goods of individuals into a common good for the whole society:

> . . . no member [of the human body] has its power for itself, nor applies it to its private use, but transfuses it among its fellow members, receiving no advantage from it but what proceeds from the common convenience of the whole body. So, whatever ability a pious man possesses, he ought to possess it for his brethren, consulting his own private interest in no way inconsistent with a cordial attention to the common edification of the church . . . whatever God has conferred on us, which enables us to assist our neighbor, we are the stewards of it, and must one day render an account of our stewardship.[48]

IV

Calvin's claim that there was a kind of virtue attainable only in a political order raised still another set of problems. If virtue implied knowledge—and Calvin assumed with the ancients that it did—then was it possible to have political knowledge and, if so, how reliable was it?

Calvin agreed that there was such a form of knowledge. It was located in the province of "terrestrial knowledge" (*l'intelligence des choses terriennes*), a knowledge "which relates entirely to the present life" and "in some sense is confined within the limits of it." The highest type of knowledge was "celestial knowledge" which pertained to "the pure knowledge of God, the method of true righteousness, and the mysteries of the heavenly kingdom." [49] The inferiority of political knowledge was the result partially of its association with lesser objects and partially of its reliance on the imperfect instrument of reason. Reason, like the rest of man's nature, had been ineradicably corrupted by the Fall. There was, however, an important qualification: the corruptive effects of Adam's apostasy were partial, not total. Man's rational understanding had been crippled but not annihilated. "Some sparks continue to shine in the nature of man, even in its corrupt and degenerate state, which prove him to be a rational creature. . . ." And while reason could not lead man to spiritual regeneration or to "spiritual wisdom," it might usefully serve him in political society.[50]

Proof of a natural relation between reason and political life was to be found in man's "instinctive propensity towards civil society." "This," Calvin declared, "is a powerful argument that in the constitution of this life no man is destitute of the light of reason." [51] Man was not rational and therefore social; he was social and therefore rational. More important, Calvin

---

[48] *Inst.*, Vol. 1, p. 757 (III, vii, 5).
[49] *Inst.*, Vol. 1, p. 294 (II, ii, 13).
[50] *Inst.*, Vol. 1, pp. 295–296 (II, ii, 14–15); pp. 298–299 (II, ii, 17–18); p. 366 (II, v, 19).
[51] *Inst.*, Vol. 1, p. 295 (II, ii, 13).

claimed that reason could elicit political truths, an assertion which he supported by the writings of the classical pagan authors. Where Luther had venomously condemned the "harlot reason" and had likened previous political philosophy to an Augean stable awaiting only the cleansing broom of the Wittenberg Hercules, Calvin moved to restore something of the classical relationship between reason and politics and something of the reputation of the classical philosophers: "shall we deny the light of truth to the ancient lawyers, who have delivered such just principles of civil order and polity?" [52] Calvin strongly agreed that natural reason would play men false if they attempted to convert it into a vehicle of spiritual salvation, yet this did not prevent a kind of kinship between the political wisdom in the Christian precepts, such as that contained in the second table of the Decalogue, and the political insights of natural reason. Both types of wisdom had a common origin in the will of God. Thus the principles of reason were not to be viewed as a human invention *ab nihilo* but as deductions from the moral dictates which God had "inscribed" and "engraven on the hearts of all men":

> Since man is by nature a social animal (*homo animal est natura sociale*), he is also inclined by a natural instinct to cherish and preserve society. Accordingly, we see that there are some general precepts of honesty and civil order impressed on the understanding of all men. For this reason there is no one who does not recognize that all human associations ought to be ruled by laws, and there is no one who does not possess the principle of these laws in his own understanding. For this reason there is a universal agreement among nations and individuals to accept laws, and this is a seed planted in us by nature rather than by a teacher or legislator.[53]

But since this universal moral law of conscience was too dim to illumine men's actions with any consistency, God had supplemented it by the Decalogue, which declared "with greater certainty what in the law of nature was too obscure. . . ." [54] When thus reinforced by the Decalogue, the moral law could function as the Christian version of natural equity which was "the same for all mankind." It was to be the informing standard for a rightly-ordered community, "the scope, and rule, and end of all laws." [55]

The qualifications which Calvin attached to the moral law were consistent with his conviction that a perfect knowledge of politics could not be achieved independently of the Christian teaching. Lacking the Christian wisdom, political knowledge possessed only a limited integrity of its own. The insufficiency of political reason in Calvin's system formed a logical parallel to the limited ends pursued by the political order itself. The sights

[52] *Inst.*, Vol. 1, p. 296 (II, ii, 15).
[53] *Inst.*, Vol. 1, p. 306 (II, ii, 13). The translation has been slightly changed; see the text in *Opera*, Vol. 2, p. 197.
[54] *Inst.*, Vol. 1, p. 397 (II, viii, 1).
[55] *Inst.*, Vol. 2, p. 789 (IV, xx, 16).

of political society were pitched lower because the virtue at which it aimed was a virtue of the second order. The chief end of man was to know God, and to achieve this end men had to be regenerated—"depart from ourselves" and "lay aside our old mind, and assume a new one." But the task of fashioning the "new man" was not assigned to the political order. Its business was to shape men to the habits of civility and order; it could not cure souls. Just as rational knowledge was lower than celestial knowledge, and just as the ends of civil society were inferior to those of religious society, so civic virtue stood beneath the perfect virtue taught by Christianity.

But having noted these distinctions in values, it is important not to translate them into antitheses. Although Calvin believed that a Christian foundation was a prerequisite for a well-constituted civil polity, there was no equivocation on his part about the essential value of the polity itself.

V

The consistency of Calvin's political and ecclesiastical thinking was nowhere more clearly evidenced than in the discussion of the office and duties of the civil magistrate. The same impulse which had dictated Calvin's conception of the pastoral office reappeared in the magistracy. Even the language he used to describe the civil governor—"sacred ministry," "vicar of God," "minister of God"—left the unmistakable impression that Calvin was less concerned to depict a political office as such than to create a political analogue to the pastorate. In both cases there was a single-minded concentration on the impersonal nature of the office, that is, on the institution. In both cases the personality of the occupant was absorbed into the office itself. Both magistrate and pastor were intended to be selfless instruments of a higher purpose and subordinated to a written law. Where the pastor was enjoined to add nothing of himself to the office or to the preaching of the Word, but to be only *"la bouche de Dieu,"* the magistrate too was to be depersonalized, but in relation to the civil law: "the law is a silent magistrate, and a magistrate a speaking law." [56]

The parallel between the two offices was expressed in still another way. Both were enveloped by an impressive *mystique* which aimed not only at discouraging disobedience in the respective societies, but also at awing the office-holder as well. Both of these elements are necessary to an understanding of Calvin's theory of political obedience. The distinctive emphasis in this doctrine lay in its insistence on active, affirmative allegiance to the ruler, and not merely a willingness to obey his commands.[57] The

---

[56] *Inst.*, Vol. 2, p. 787 (IV, xx, 14). The phrase is derived from Cicero, *De Legibus*, III, 1.2 and is related to the classical tradition of the ruler as *lex animata*; see Erwin R. Goodenough, "The Political Philosophy of Hellenistic Kingship," *Yale Classical Studies*, Vol. 1 (1928), p. 55 ff.

[57] See Mesnard, pp. 285–289; Chenevière, p. 298.

reverence of subjects towards their ruler ought to be rooted in conscience, not fear. At the same time, however, the loyalty of the subjects should be directed at the office rather than at the individual magistrate. The civic commitment was institutional and not personal. At bottom this institutional allegiance ran to the broad purposes of the society, to the civilized ends secured by the political order. Those who weakened the fabric of order were classed as "inhuman monsters," "the enemies of all equity and right, and totally ignorant of humanity." [58]

For his part, the magistrate symbolized, not mere power, but the permanent ends of society. His functions were to preserve order and a "temperate liberty"; to enforce justice and righteousness; and to promote peace and godliness.[59] He did not stand as the representative of the interests or opinions of particular groups, classes, or localities, but of a set of purposes which he served but had not originated. And since none of these ends were possible without order, the basic task of the magistrate was to insure that this condition prevailed. The pressing importance of order drew from Calvin the admission that even tyrants "retain in their tyranny some kind of just government. There can be no tyranny which does not in some respects assist in consolidating the society of men." [60] The tyrant was connected to the cause of order by his mere possession of power. The price of cohesion and unity was the active exercise of power, and this minimum condition could be fulfilled by a tyrant. "There is much truth in the old saying that it is worse to live under a prince through whose levity everything is lawful, then under a tyrant where there is no liberty at all." [61] Even the lawful ruler must, therefore, assert his power affirmatively; had not Jeremiah urged "execute ye judgment and righteousness"?

While at one level the allegiance relationship depicted by Calvin was essentially political, between ruler and ruled, at another level it transcended the political and implicated both parties in a relationship with God. The ruler was a transient occupant of a divine office, and owed a responsibility to God for the faithful discharge of his trust. On the other side, the subjects were bound to obey the commands of a divinely authorized agent. Allegiance, therefore, was both a political and a religious duty. At the human level it supported the civilized ends of society; at the ultimate level it was a search for a right relationship with God.[62]

---

[58] *Opera,* Vol. 52, p. 267.
[59] *Commentaries on Romans,* p. 481.
[60] *Commentaries on Romans,* p. 480.
[61] *Commentary on the Book of Psalms,* trans. James Anderson, 5 vols. (Edinburgh, 1845–1849), Vol. 3, p. 106; *Inst.,* Vol. 2, pp. 801–802 (IV, xx, 27).
[62] Given the lofty ends served by allegiance—"God had not intended men to live *pêle-mêle"* (*Opera,* Vol. 51, p. 800)—it is not surprising to find Calvin hostile to contract theory. This was not owing to any desire on his part to release rulers from their obligations, but rather to his belief that social duties ought not to be the subject of a crude bartering arrangement. *Inst.,* Vol. 2, pp. 801–802 (IV, xx, 27).

In the case of the tyrant the religious element was, in a sense, dominant. He was the agent of God's wrath sent to scourge the community for its sins; his coming ought to provoke a sense of collective guilt among the people, causing them to search their consciences for the sins they had committed.[63] The relationship between citizen and tyrant, then, belonged not to the political but to the "celestial" category, because the concept of sin, which connected tyrant and subject, was not a political conception at all.[64] And despite Calvin's intention of making obedience to tyrants appear more palatable, the effect of his reasoning was to underscore the extraordinary nature of tyranny and to isolate it from the normal political relationships. The tyrant might be elevated to a divine instrument sent *"pour châtier les péchés du peuple,"* [65] yet this very mission made him an essentially apolitical figure. Sin was a theological and not a political relationship.

This tendency towards placing the tyrant outside the usual political relationships cropped out again when Calvin came to consider the problem of obedience. In obeying the tyrant, the loyal subject was viewed as discharging an obligation to God rather than one deriving from the general ends of society. Obedience, however, was limited by the dictates of conscience, that is, by another extra-political factor. While conscience created a direct relationship between the individual and God, and thereby circumvented the political relationship between subject and ruler, it offered, nevertheless, a powerful threat to the unlimited claims of the tyrant. Conscience was essentially a religious conception and owed its beginnings to religious controversies, but it could be turned to political advantage without straining its fundamental meaning. For, in one sense, conscience was a response to power; it had to do with the individual as the object of compulsion in a governed order. Yet whether the protesting conscience felt imperiled by papal or civil power, it retained a saving relationship with God. In one sense Calvin's "court of conscience" pointed the individual away from the "political"; in another, it was obviously designed for the politically involved citizen. The citizen who, on strictly religious grounds, disobeyed a command which ran contrary to Scripture was, in Calvin's view, not only fulfilling his obligation to God, but also reminding the ruler of the true nature of his office. Calvin's conception of resistance was that of a selfless service designed to preserve the integrity of political institutions from the errors of temporary office-holders.[66]

While there was nothing novel in the proposition that scriptural injunctions prevailed over political commands, Calvin displayed a greater sensitivity than most reformers to the political implications of religious resistance. It was this which eventually led him to formulate a theory of re-

[63] *Inst.,* Vol. 2, p. 805 (IV, xx, 32).
[64] *Inst.,* Vol. 2, p. 790 (IV, xx, 16); p. 798 (IV, xx, 24).
[65] "Catechism of 1537," *Opera,* Vol. 22, p. 74.
[66] *Inst.,* Vol. 2, p. 805 (IV, xx, 32).

sistance which was political rather than religious in its motivation. He allowed that the estates or specially designated magistrates might "oppose the violence and cruelty of kings." By virtue of their position, these agencies had a positive obligation to protect popular liberties:

> . . . if they connive with kings in the oppression of the humble people, their dissimulation is not free from nefarious perfidy, because they maliciously betray the liberty of the people, while knowing, that by the ordinance of God, they are its protectors.[67]

Near the end of his life Calvin began to veer, hesitatingly to be sure, towards an acceptance of the idea that the coronation oaths and the laws of a country formed a system of agreements which might be defended against an arbitrary ruler:

> . . . certain remedies against tyranny are allowable, for example, when magistrates and estates have been constituted and given the care of the commonwealth: they shall have power to keep the prince to his duty and even to coerce him if he attempt anything unlawful.[68]

Two aspects of this deserve underlining. First, Calvin's declaration that the estates and inferior magistrates were entrusted with a divine responsibility contrasts with Luther's tendency to elevate rulership above all other offices. And consistent with this had been Luther's strong scepticism concerning the legitimacy of the estates as restraining organs.[69] Calvin, on the other hand, by breaching "the divinity that doth hedge a king," had created a rival agency, armed with the only credentials that most men of the period would respect, a divine ordination. The second important aspect of Calvin's resistance theory was its mention of the strictly political ends served by the organs of resistance: the protection of "the liberty of the people," "the care of the commonwealth." The effect of this was to provide a balancing parallel to the theory of allegiance. For the same reason that men obey authority in order to preserve the civilizing purposes supported by the political order, so the specified organs of the community might have to disobey in order to preserve that order.

While none of these considerations worked to dislodge either the primacy of the religious motive in Calvin's thought or the priority held by spiritual values, they did signify his rediscovery of political complexity. More than any other contemporary reformer, he was supremely sensitive to the plurality of relationships and obligations operating in a political community. Among most of the reformers the general tendency had been to reduce the manifold complexity of politics to a simple connection between

---

[67] *Inst.*, Vol. 2, p. 804 (IV, xx, 31); *Opera*, Vol. 4, p. 1160.
[68] *Opera*, Vol. 29, pp. 557, 636–637; Chenevière, pp. 346–347.
[69] *Works*, Vol. 5, pp. 51–52.

ruler and ruled or between both of them and God. Calvin, however, avoided this simple explanation and emphasized instead the triangular relationship of ruler, people, and the law. The connecting link between ruler and citizen was not a direct one, but occurred through the mediating agency of the law.[70] From the standpoint of the ruler this had the effect of adding one more obligatory element to his office: he owed responsibilities to the people, to God, to the law, and to the whole range of purposes proper to a rightly constituted society. The sum total of these obligations formed a premise which made the act of resistance a logical possibility within the Calvinist system and not, as many later commentators would have it, a matter of geographical accident.

VI

Calvin's conception of the church and of civil society, taken together, marked the Protestant rediscovery of the idea of the institutionalized community. It had been the genius of early sixteenth century Protestantism to create the notion of the cohesive religious association; but the failure to equip the religious fellowship with the necessary institutional structure had threatened the fellowship with dissolution from within and encroachment from without. While there can be no denying that the institutional hostility of the early reformers was nourished by a deep desire to prevent religious feeling from being stifled by ecclesiasticism, they failed to grapple with the fact that, as long as the church was bound to this world, it would have to face the threat of rival institutions powerfully organized. The strength of Calvin's position lay in its realization that the precondition for the survival of the community of believers was a strongly structured church government: a sense of institutions must be combined with a sense of community.

Similarly, where the early reformers expressed an indifference to the political order or else viewed it solely as a repressive agency, Calvin reasserted its value and denied that its essence consisted in coercion. In short, Calvin's emphasis on a strong church and on the dignity of political society was designed for a double purpose: to make the church safe in the world and the world safe for the church. In reorienting Protestantism towards the world, Calvin stands as the Protestant counterpart to Aquinas. Like Thomas he labored to reintegrate the political order with the order of grace, but unlike Thomas he had the further task of showing that the church could contribute to the order of civil society without perverting its own nature. The ethos created by the church was to be a *civil*-izing one, one which habituated the liberated Protestant to a life under order and discipline. In Calvin's system the church became the agency for resolving

---

[70] *Inst.*, Vol. 2, pp. 773, 787 (IV, xx, 3, 14).

the uneasy tension encouraged by the early Reformation belief that man was a divided being dwelling partly in a society of faith ruled by Christ and partly in civil society ruled by temporal authority. In resolving the bifurcated existence of man, Calvin returned to the substance, but not the form, of the medieval idea that human existence, whether lived at the spiritual or "material" level, was an existence preeminently social and ordered. No abrupt transition separated both aspects of existence, because in both of them man was a creature accustomed to the power and restraints of institutions and to a life of civility.

The result of these labors was not only to impart to Protestantism a depth of political understanding it had previously lacked, but to place the new movement on a more equal footing with the political sophistication of Catholicism. From the time of the first political repercussions of Protestantism, Catholicism had claimed to be more congenial to the requirements of civil society. In one sense this claim was profoundly true. Under the government of the Church the believer had been accustomed to the patterns of "civil" behavior enforced by church discipline, and was therefore prepared for the life of civil society. Once this is recognized it is easy to see that the emphatic insistence of the early reformers on an almost unqualified obedience to civil rulers was but a crude effort to overcome the political superiority of Catholicism. It was crude because it assumed that the habits of civility could be summed up so easily. Calvin's contribution was to see that the habits of civility needed by the church were also essential to civil life; the essential demands of order were the same for both societies. The interlocking of the religious and civil orders in Calvin's system was simply the fulfillment of two dominant impulses in man, one religious, the other social, and both united by the need for order.

Two elements in the Calvinist conception of order held radical implications for the future. The first was the notion that a society could be at once well-organized, disciplined, and cohesive and yet be without a head. While all Protestants were necessarily anti-monarchical in their belief that a religious society could flourish without a papal monarch, Calvin was unique in being able to describe the institutional substitutes for the pope. The political application of these beliefs awaited the English civil wars of the seventeenth century, but the distaste for secular monarchy was already in evidence in Calvin's own writings.[71]

The other potentially explosive idea lay in Calvin's belief that a community rested on an active membership. The unity which flowed from participation was the Calvinist answer to the papal theory that unity could only be guaranteed by the single will of the pontiff. Moreover, participation was an equalizing conception because the nature of the good at which

[71] *Opera,* Vol. 43, p. 374; and the discussion of John T. McNeill, "The Democratic Element in Calvin's Thought," *Church History,* Vol. 18, pp. 153–171 (Sept. 1949).

the society aimed was one intended for all the participants: the body of Christ knew no distinctions in value among the members. Once this concept of participation was given a political twist, it would be but a short step from Geneva to the English Levellers and to Colonel Rainborough's claim that the "poorest he that is in England hath a life to live, as the greatest he . . . every man that is to live under a government ought first by his own consent to put himself under that government." [72] To view such a step as the radical transformation of essentially religious notions would be to miss the whole meaning of Calvin's system. It was a system which needed no "transforming" in order to bring out a political implication, because the political element had been present from the start. At the very moment that Calvin grasped the importance of order the political theme was incorporated into the main body of writings and reached its fullest expression in the Calvinist conception of the church-society. To the extent that the church was a governing order, fully institutionalized and equipped with power, it possessed many of the qualities of a political society.

If we accept the view that Calvin's notion of the church was in some degree a species of political theory, additional light can be thrown on the relationship between Christianity and the development of Western political thought. One of the most important effects of Christianity had been to discourage the classical quest for an ideal state. To the Christian persuasion the attempt to build an eternal polity, untouched by the corrosions of time, had appeared as an act of *lèse-majesté,* an attempt to emulate the omnipotence of God. A writer like Aquinas, for example, might devote considerable attention to the best form of government, yet this was a far cry from the Platonic vision of a total regeneration of man through political means. The true Christian counterpart to the absolutely best societies projected by Plato and Aristotle was to be found in Augustine's City of God. The ideal society existed beyond and not within history; it was a society transcendental, not empirical. The powerful hold which this idea was to gain over the Western imagination had the effect of etherealizing the old classical idea of the best society into the idea of the kingdom of God. Only occasionally did the older notion reappear in the sublimated form of More's *Utopia* or Campanella's *City of the Sun.*

In Calvin's writings, however, the idea of the best society reemerged, but in a distinctively Christian rather than classical way. The church and the civil society were both viewed as social orders embodying certain values, yet the church was the better society on several counts. Its mission was loftier, its life more social, and its virtues of a higher dignity. The sacramental bond provided a kind of unity which the civil order could never attain: "every one imparts to all in common what he has received from the Lord." [73] In civil society, on the other hand, the necessary precondition

[72] A. S. P. Woodhouse (ed.), *Puritanism and Liberty* (London, 1938), p. 53.
[73] *Commentaries on Romans,* p. 459.

was that "men should have peculiar and distinct possessions." [74] The ethical pattern, the *justum regimen,* of the one society was to be sought in Christ, while the other society could never aspire to a good greater than external piety. The one society aimed at salvation and repentance; it was *"un vray ordre";* the other was concerned only with the public side of man. The one, in short, was the good society, the other a necessary but inferior society.

But while the church stood as the better society in comparison to the state, the church itself was only the best realizable society, not the absolutely best. Above the visible society of believers was the church invisible and eternal, the pure communion of saints. When compared to this society, the visible church was a *"res carnalis"* confined within the limits of time and space. But while the best society could not be realized by men on earth, it was not entirely disconnected from what men could achieve. A rightly ordered church and civil society could follow the same doctrine which inspired the life of the saints; and if their endeavors fell short of the standard of the best society, they might still achieve something of inestimable value, a whispered intimation of immortality.

FURTHER READINGS FOR PART V

Luther

Atkinson, James. *Martin Luther and the Birth of Protestantism.* Harmondsworth: Penquin, 1968.

Bainton, Roland. *Here I Stand: A Life of Martin Luther.* New York: New American Library, 1955.

Boehmer, Heinrich. *Martin Luther: Road to Reformation.* New York: Meridian, 1957.

Bornkamm, Heinrich. *Luther's Doctrine of the Two Kingdoms in the Context of His Theology.* Philadelphia: Fortress Press, 1966.

Cranz, Ferdinand E. "An Essay on the Development of Luther's Thought on Justice, Law and Society," *Harvard Theological Studies,* 19 (1959).

Erikson, Erik H. *Young Man Luther.* New York: Norton, 1958.

Feuerbach, Ludwig A. *The Essence of Faith According to Luther.* New York: Harper & Row, 1967.

Fife, R. H. *The Revolt of Martin Luther.* New York: Columbia University Press, 1957.

Forell, George. *Faith Active in Love: An Interpretation of Principles Underlying Luther's Social Ethics.* New York: American Peoples' Press, 1954.

[74] *Inst.,* Vol. 2, p. 272 (IV, i, 3).

———. "Justification and Eschatology in Luther's Thought," *Church History*, 38 (June 1969), pp. 164–174.

Grimm, Harold J. "Luther's Conception of Territorial and National Loyalty," *Church History*, 17 (June, 1948), pp. 79–94.

Miller, Arlene A. "Theologies of Luther and Boehme in the Light of Their Genesis Commentaries," *Harvard Theological Review*, 63 (April 1970), pp. 261–303.

Mueller, William A. *Church and State in Luther and Calvin*. Nashville, Tenn.: Abingdon, 1954.

Pelikan, Jaroslav J. *Spirit versus Structure: Luther and the Institutions of the Church*. New York: Harper & Row, 1968.

Ritter, Gerhard. *Luther: His Life and Work*. New York: Harper & Row, 1963.

Schwiebert, Ernest G. *Luther and His Times*. St. Louis, Mo.: Concordia, 1950.

———. "The Medieval Patterns in Luther's Views of the State," *Church History*, 12 (June 1943), pp. 98–117.

Simon, Edith. *Luther Alive: Martin Luther and the Making of the Reformation*. Garden City, N.Y.: Doubleday, 1968.

Trinkhaus, Charles. "The Religious Foundations of Luther's Social Views," in J. H. Mundy, R. W. Emery, and B. N. Nelson, eds. *Essays in Medieval Life and Thought*. New York: Columbia University Press, 1955, pp. 71–87.

Calvin

Battles, Ford L. "Against License and Luxury in Geneva: A Forgotten Fragment of Calvin," *Interpretation*, 19 (April 1965), pp. 182–202.

Breen, Quirinus. *John Calvin: A Study in French Humanism*. Hamden, Conn.: Archon Books, 1968.

Casteel, Theodore W. "Calvin and Trent: Calvin's Reaction to the Council of Trent in the Context of His Conciliar Thought," *Harvard Theological Review*, 63 (January 1970), pp. 91–117.

Harkness, Georgia. *John Calvin: The Man and His Ethics*. Nashville, Tenn.: Abingdon, 1958.

MacKinnon, James. *Calvin and the Reformation*. London: Longmans, 1936.

NcNeill, John T. *The History and Character of Calvinism*. New York: Oxford University Press, 1954.

———. "The Democratic Element in Calvin's Thought," *Church History*, 18 (September 1949), pp. 153–171.

Mosse, George L. *Calvinism, Authoritarian or Democratic?* New York: Holt, Rinehart and Winston, Inc., 1957.

Walzer, Michael. "Exodus 32 and the Theory of Holy War: The History of a Citation," *Harvard Theological Review*, 61 (January 1968), pp. 1–14.

VI

PRECURSOR

OF THE MODERN ERA:

MACHIAVELLI

18

Machiavelli

FRIEDRICH MEINECKE

Whatever the circumstances the business of ruling is . . .
always carried out in accordance with the principles of
raison d'état. Raison d'état may be deflected or hindered
by real or imaginary obstacles, but it is part and parcel of
ruling. It is not realized, however, as a principle and an idea
until a particular stage of development has been reached;
namely when the State has become strong enough to break
down those obstacles, and to lay down its own unqualified
right to existence in the face of all other vital forces. An account of this process from the standpoint of universal history
would have to embrace and compare all cultures; it would
have to begin by examining the idea of *raison d'état* in the
ancient world, and analysing its relationship with the spirit
of that epoch. For both the free city-states and the monarchies of antiquity are teeming with the problems of *raison
d'état* and with attempts to formulate it. In the dialogue
between the Athenians and the citizens of Melos, given by
Thucydides in Book 5 (chap. 85 ff.), the harsh and fright-

This article was originally published in Friedrich Meinecke, *Machia-
vellism*, trans. Douglas Scott (New Haven, Conn.: Yale University
Press, 1957), pp. 25–48. It is reprinted here with the permission of
Yale University Press and Routledge & Kegan Paul Ltd.

ening aspects of *raison d'état* and power politics are stated very succinctly.
In his *Phoenician Virgins*, Euripides makes Eteocles say: "For if one must
do evil, then it is good to do it for the sake of authority; but otherwise one
ought to act rightly." [1] In Book 5 of his *Politics*, Aristotle gives a picture of
the rationally conceived way in which a tyrant can rule. In Book 3 of
De officiis, Cicero discussed fully from the Stoic point of view the conflict
between morality and what is useful to the State, and stated regretfully:
Utilitatis specie in republica saepissime peccatur (chap. 11).[2] The great historical works of Tacitus are steeped in the idea of *raison d'état;* as evidence of
this we may quote one statement, from the lips of Cassius in Book 14 of the
*Annals: Habet aliquid ex iniquo omne magnum exemplum, quod contra sin-
gulos utilitate publica rependitur.*[3] Subsequently, after he had been repub-
lished by Justus Lipsius in 1574, Tacitus became the great teacher of *raison
d'état* (though not to any great extent for Machiavelli, who drew chiefly
on Livy, Aristotle and Xenophon); then for a whole century there
blossomed a literature of Tacitists [4] who exploited him politically. Justus
Lipsius himself put together his grammar of politics (*Politicorum sive civilis doctrinae libri sex, qui ad principatum maxime spectant,*[5] 1589) entirely
out of maxims from antiquity, principally from Tacitus; he thus made
available a mine of information (which is still valuable today) about the
opinions of the ancient world on the subject of *raison d'état*. And even if
the ancients had not coined for it any particular expression which was in
general use, yet we frequently meet with *ratio reipublicae* in Cicero, and
ratio et utilitas reipublicae in Florus.[6]

Polytheism and a secular view of human values were what nourished
raison d'état in antiquity. At the period when the city-state was flourishing,
the thing most worth living for was the State itself. The ethics of individual
and of national conduct thus coincided, and so there was no conflict between politics and ethics. There was also no universal religion, to try and

[1] Εἴπερ γὰρ ἀδικεῖν χρή, τυραννίδος πέρι κάλλιστον ἀδικεῖν τἄλλα δ'εὐσεβεῖν χρεών.
[2] "In a republic mistakes are most often made under the ruse of expediency."
[3] "Exemplary punishment always contains an element of injustice, but wrongs against
individuals are outweighed by the advantage to the state as a whole."
[4] Boccalini will serve us later as an example of these. As an expression of the high opinion in which Tacitus was held, the words of Gabriel Naudé in his *Bibliographia politica*
(edition of 1642, p. 233) may be reproduced: *At vero, quoniam sedet ipse velut omnium
princeps ac imperator in orchestra, aut potius sedem sibi facit in machina, ex qua cum
stupore et admiratione politicas difficultates componit, virtutum suarum majestate omne
fastigium humanum excedens, certe consultius esse mihi persuadeo, non hunc tenui ser-
mone velut hominem, sed eloquenti silentio Deitatis instar venerari,* etc. On the Tacitists, see p. 247 of the same, and Toffanin, *Machiavelli e il Tacitismo,* 1921. An intelligent and informative book, but one which exaggerates the significance of Tacitus for
Machiavelli.
[5] *The Six Books of Politics or Civil Doctrine, Which Especially Pertain to the Rule.*
[6] *Cicero ad Plancum* (Bk. 10 *ad fam. epist.* 16): Do not wait upon the Senate, let yourself be the Senate, *quocunque te ratio reipublicae ducet sequare. Florus,* Bk. 1, chap. 8,
speaks of the seven kings of Rome *tam variis ingenio, ut reipublicae ratio et utilitas
postulabat.*

restrict by its commands the free exercise of State powers. The national religion which existed tended rather to favour this free exercise, by glorifying heroism. As the city-state began to dissolve, the heroic ideal passed over into the new form which power assumed in the State where men struggled fiercely, each for himself; this was the State of the ruthless man of power, classically portrayed by Plato in Callicles of the *Gorgias*.[7] Altogether the ancient conception of *raison d'état* remained at this time firmly fixed in personalities, and served to vindicate the mode of action which was forced on contemporary rules by pressure of the situation. It never seemed to rise (or at least not at all consistently) towards the conception of a supra-individual and independent state personality, which would stand over against the actual rulers of the time.[8]

An epilogue and a final crushing judgment on the ancient view of *raison d'état* was given by Christianity, when Augustine said: *Remota justitia quid sunt regna nisi magna latrocinia*.[9] The new universal religion set up at the same time a universal moral command, which even the State must obey, and turned the eyes of individual men on other-worldly values; thus all secular values, including heroism as the herald of power politics and *raison d'état*, were caused to give ground. Then in the Middle Ages Germanic jurisprudence combined with Christian ethics in keeping down the State. The State certainly existed in the Middle Ages, but it did not rank supreme. Law was set above it; it was a means for enforcing the law. "Politics and *raison d'état* were not recognized at all in the Middle Ages." Naturally, of course, the general practice was different from this theoretical view. Therefore, "since there was no place in the legal and constitutional theory of mediaeval times for the demands of policy, these forced their own elemental way out." [10]

But in the later Middle Ages these irregular outlets began to be regularized. The struggle between Church and Papacy fostered the conscious power politics of great rulers like the Emperor Frederick II and Philip IV of France. The Emperor Charles IV in Germany and King Louis XI in France were examples of a thoroughly unscrupulous and rational art of government, based on their own authority. Even the Church itself, by its inner transformations, by the progressive permeation of the Papacy with worldly political interests, by the often very utilitarian approach of the Church Councils, and by the rational perfecting of Papal finance, paved

[7] Compare now Menzel, *Kallikles*, 1923; and the stimulating Berlin University lecture of 1924 by Werner Jaeger, on the ethics of the Greek State in the age of Plato.
[8] Kaerst, *Studien zur Entwicklung u. theoret. Bergründung der Monarchie im Altertum*, p. 10 f.
[9] "With justice gone, kingdoms are nothing but great frauds." *De civitate Dei*, IV, 4; for the correct meaning of the remark, cf. Bernheim, *Mittelalterliche Zeitanschauungen usw.*, 1, 37.
[10] F. Kern, *Recht und Verfassung im Mittelalter*, Histor. Zeitschr., 120, 57 and 63 f., a fundamental essay.

the way for a new spirit in the art of government. The strongest motive for this, however, still lay in the incipient growth of national States, and in the struggles of the more important dynasties, whose possessions had been amassed by feudal methods, to safeguard these possessions by non-feudal means, by adhesive methods of government. The universal ideas of this mediaeval *corpus christianum* moved continuously towards a new centre of Will concentrated in the State.

Late mediaeval thought began further to distinguish the ideal law of Nature from statute law, and thereby to diminish the influence which Germanic jurisprudence had hitherto exerted on the State. "Henceforth the power of the State is set above statute law, and comes under natural law. Thus it is no longer the case that every insignificant individual right is placed outside the grasp of the State; it is only the great fundamental principles of Natural Law that remain beyond its reach." [11]

Here and there at this time one notices a few basic admissions of the new conception of necessity of State. In the fourteenth century Philipp von Leiden, a priest in the service of the Count of Holland, wrote *de cura reipublicae et sorte principantis* [12]; he advanced the proposition that a territorial ruler ought to revoke a privilege which he had granted to a single town or to a single person, if it was injuring the *publica utilitas*.[13] In an even more general manner Jean Gerson declared in 1404 that if any laws conflicted with the aim of maintaining the peace (which was the supreme purpose of the State in the Middle Ages), then the laws ought to be interpreted more in accordance with that aim, or they would have to be completely abolished, since *necessitas legem non habet*.[14] Even more audacious was a certain doctor of theology in the service of the Duke of Burgundy, named Jean Petit. In a long and exceedingly sophistical dissertation, which he delivered in Paris in March 1408, he defended his master for having caused the murder of Duke Louis of Orleans; and he went on to say that promises and alliances between noblemen did not need to be kept, if keeping them would entail injury to the ruler and to the commonwealth. He even said that to keep such promises would be completely against the laws of God and Nature.[15]

A systematic search among the sources and authors of the late Middle Ages would probably discover still further opinions of this kind, and thus throw light on the gradual and continuing loosening up of the me-

---

[11] Kern, p. 74.
[12] "On the administration of the republic and duty of the ruler."
[13] v. Below, *Territorium und Stadt,* p. 190, and H. Wilfert, *Philipp von Leiden,* 1925.
[14] "Necessity has no law." Platzhoff, *Die Theorie von der Mordbefugnis der Obrigkeit im 16. Jahrhundert,* p. 27; cf. also Gierke, *Althusius,* 279, and v. Bezold, *Aus Mittelalter und Renaissance,* p. 257 f. (on Pontano).
[15] *"La quinte verité en cas d'aliance, seremens et promesses, est des confédéracions faictes de chevalier à autre en quelque manière que ce soit et puist estre, s'il advient icellui pour garder et tenir tourne ou préjudice de son prince, de ses enfans etd la chose publique, n'est tenu de les garder. En tel cas seroit fait contre les lois naturelles*

diaeval feudal barriers. But a theory on a grand scale has not yet grown up out of it.

Nevertheless the modern Western world has inherited one legacy of extraordinary importance from the Christian and Germanic Middle Ages. It has inherited a sharper and more painful sense of the conflict between *raison d'état* on the one hand, and ethics and law on the other; and also the feeling which is constantly being aroused, that ruthless *raison d'état* is really sinful, a sin against God and divine standards, a sin against the sanctity and inviolability of the law of the good old times. The ancient world was already familiar with these sins of *raison d'état,* and did not omit to criticize them, but without taking them very much to heart. The very secularity of human values in the ancient world made it possible to view *raison d'état* with a certain calmness and to consider it the outcome of natural forces which were not to be subdued. Sinfulness in antiquity was still a perfectly naïve sinfulness, not yet disquieted and frightened by the gulf between heaven and hell which was to be opened up by Christianity. This dualistic picture of the world, which was held by dogmatic Christianity, has had a deep influence even on the period of a Christianity that is growing undogmatic; and it has given the problem of *raison d'état* this deeply felt overtone of tragedy, which it never carried in antiquity.

It was therefore a historical necessity that the man, with whom the history of the idea of *raison d'état* in the modern Western world begins and from whom Machiavellism takes its name, had to be a heathen; he had to be a man to whom the fear of hell was unknown, and who on the contrary could set about his life-work of analysing the essence of *raison d'état* with all the naïvety of the ancient world.

Niccolo Machiavelli was the first to do this. We are concerned here with the thing itself, not with the name for it, which he still did not possess. Machiavelli had not yet compressed his thoughts on *raison d'état* into a single slogan. Fond as he was of forceful and meaningful catch-words (coining many himself), he did not always feel the need to express in words the supreme ideas which filled him; if, that is, the thing itself seemed to him self-evident, if it filled him completely. For example, critics have noticed that he fails to express any opinion about the real final purpose of the State, and they have mistakenly deduced from this that he did not reflect on the subject.[16] But, as we shall soon see, his whole life was

et divines." La chronique de Monstrelet p. p. Douet-d'Arcq, 1857, I, 215 f. (Bk. I, chap. 39). In the same 2, 417 (Bk. I, chap. 113) the unfavourable verdict of the Paris theologians: *Ceste assercion touche à la subversion de toute la chose publique et de chascun roy ou prince,* etc. But the Council of Constance did not dare to condemn out of hand Jean Petit's doctrine of tyrannicide. v. Bezold, *Aus Mittelalter und Renaissance,* p. 274. On Jean Petit, cf. also O. Cartellieri, *Beiträge zur Geschichte der Herzöge von Burgund V., Sitzungsber. d. Heidelb. Ak.,* 1914.

[16] Heyer, *Der Machiavellismus,* 1918, p. 29; cf. also A. Schmidt, *N. Machiavelli und die allgemeine Staatslehre der Gegenwart,* 1907, p. 104.

bound up with a definite supreme purpose of the State. And in the same way his whole political way of thought is nothing else but a continual process of thinking about *raison d'état.*

Machiavelli's system of thought was brought into being by an absolutely special and sublime, and at the same time extraordinary, conjunction of events: the coinciding of a political collapse with a spiritual and intellectual renaissance. In the fifteenth century Italy enjoyed national independence, and was, in the pregnant words of Machiavelli (*Principe,* chap. 20), *in un certo modo bilanciata* [17] by the system of five States which kept each other within bounds: Naples, the Papal States, Florence, Milan and Venice. There was growing up in Italy, fostered by all the realistic elements in Renaissance culture and directly promoted by the arrangement (which was just coming into fashion) of having permanent embassies, a form of statecraft which was carried on according to fixed and definite rules. This statecraft culminated in the principle of *divide et impera*, it taught that everything ought to be considered with a view to its usefulness, it surmounted all religious and moral limitations in a naïvely playful manner, but itself functioned by means of relatively simple and mechanical operations and thought-processes.[18] Only the catastrophes which overtook Italy after 1494, with the invasion by the French and the Spanish, the decline of Neapolitan and Milanese independence, the precipitate change in the form of government in Florence, and most of all the collective impact of foreign countries on the entire Apennine peninsula—only these catastrophes succeeded in maturing the spirit of politics to that point of passionate strength, depth and acuteness, which is revealed in Machiavelli. As a secretary and diplomat of the Florentine Republic until the year 1512, he learnt everything that Italian statecraft had achieved up to that time, and he was also beginning already to shape his own original thoughts on the subject. What caused them to pour out suddenly after 1512 was the crushing fate which overtook both him and the republic in that year. As a member of the party which had been overthrown and was being temporarily persecuted, Machiavelli, in order to re-establish himself, was forced to seek the favour of the new rulers, the Medicis, who were once more in power. Thus a conflict arose between his own personal and egotistical interests, and the ideals of republican freedom and the city-state which he had held up to now. It is indeed the greatness of Machiavelli that he strove now to settle this conflict, and bring it to a final issue. Against the obscure and not particularly attractive background of his own naïve and unscrupulous egoism, there came into being the new and masterly reflections on the relation between republic and monarchy, and about a new national mission of mon-

[17] "Balanced in a certain way."
[18] How the new calculating and rational spirit also arose simultaneous in economic life, particularly in the two mercantile States of Venice and Florence, is shown by L. Brentano, *Die Anfänge des modernen Kapitalismus*, 1916. Cf. v. Bezold, p. 255 f.

archy; it was in a context of all this that the whole essence of *raison d'état,* compounded of mingled ingredients both pure and impure, both lofty and hateful, achieved a ruthless expression. He had reached his fortieth year— the age at which productive scientific minds often give of their best—when after 1513 he wrote the little book about the prince. and the *Discorsi sopra la prima deca di Tito Livio.*

A spiritual and intellectual renaissance must also, as we said, have been a formative influence. Machiavelli did not by any means absorb the whole of the Renaissance movement. He did not share its religious needs, or its urge towards speculative philosophy; and, although unconsciously steeped and bathed in its aesthetic spirit, he still did not value its artistic attempts particularly highly. His passionate interest was the State, the analysis and computation of its different forms, functions and conditions for existence; and thus it was that the specifically rational empirical and calculating element in Italian Renaissance culture reached its peak in him. But a mere cool consideration of questions of political power would not have signified any complete spiritual and intellectual renewal. The faith and energy necessary to sustain it, and out of which the ideal of a rebirth could grow, were, so far as Machiavelli shared in them, of ancient origin. The spirit of antiquity was certainly not signalized in him (as it was in so many humanists of the Renaissance) by a merely learned and literary regeneration, with the bloodless rhetorical inspiration of a schoolmaster. Often his enthusiasm for the heroes and thinkers of antiquity shows a somewhat classicist lack of independence and judgment. But in the main the element of antiquity in him rose anew out of the tradition and hereditary feeling, which in Italy had never been entirely lost. In spite of his outward respect for the Church and for Christianity (frequently mingled with irony and criticism), and in spite of the undeniable influence which the Christian view had on him, Machiavelli was at heart a heathen, who levelled at Christianity the familiar and serious reproach (Disc., II, 2) of having made men humble, unmanly and feeble. With a romantic longing he gazed towards the strength, grandeur and beauty of life in antiquity, and towards the ideals of its *mondana gloria.*[19] He wanted to bring back once again that united strength of sense and intellect in the natural genuine man, where *grandezza dell'animo* and *fortezza del corpo*[20] combined together to create heroism. He broke then, with the dualistic and onesidedly spiritualizing ethic of Christianity, which depreciated the natural impulses of the senses. Although indeed he retained some of its structural ideas about the difference between good and evil, he strove principally for a new naturalistic ethic which would follow the dictates of nature impartially and resolutely. For whoever follows these dic-

[19] "Worldly glory."
[20] "Greatness of the spirit and strength of the body."

tates (as he said once) can find no fault in carrying on lighthearted amo-
rous affairs in the midst of serious business—even Nature is full of change
and contradiction.[21]

This kind of naturalism can easily lead to a harmless and unreflecting
multiplicity in the question of human values. But (in spite of the offering
which he gladly brought to the altar of Venus) Machiavelli concentrated
all his real and supreme values in what he called *virtù*. This concept is exceedingly rich in meaning, and although it was taken over from the tradition of antiquity and humanism, it had been felt and elaborated in a quite
individual manner; ethical qualities were certainly embraced in it, but it
was fundamentally intended to portray something dynamic, which Nature
had implanted in Man—heroism and the strength for great political and
warlike achievements, and first and foremost, perhaps, strength for the
founding and preservation of flourishing States, particularly republics.[22]
For in the republics, of which Rome in its great republican period seemed
to him an ideal example, he saw the conditions most favourable for the
generation of *virtù*. It therefore embraced the civic virtues and those of the
ruling class; it embraced a readiness to devote oneself to the common
good, as well as the wisdom, energy and ambition of the great founders
and rulers of States. But the *virtù* which the founder and ruler of a State
had to possess counted for Machiavelli as *virtù* of a higher order. For in
his opinion this kind of *virtù* was able, by means of appropriate "regulations," to distil out of the thoroughly bad and wretched material of
average specimens of humanity the other kind of *virtù* in the sense of
civic virtue; to a certain extent the latter was *virtù* of a secondary
quality, and could only be durable if it was rooted in a people whose
spirit was naturally fresh and unspoilt. This separation of *virtù* into
two types, one original and the other derived, is of exceptional significance
for a complete understanding of the political aims of Machiavelli. For it
shows that he was a long way from believing uncritically in the natural
and imperishable virtue of a republican citizen, and that he viewed even
the republic more from above, from the standpoint of the rulers, than from
underneath, from the standpoint of broad-based democracy. He appreciated the proverb, which was popular in his time, that *in piazza* your
opinions were not the same as they were *in palazzo* (Disc., II, 47). His republican ideal therefore contained a strain of monarchism, in so far as he
believed that even republics could not come into existence without the
help of great individual ruling personalities and organizers. He had learnt
from Polybius the theory that the fortunes of every State are repeated in a
cycle, and that the golden age of a republic is bound to be followed by its
decline and fall. And so he saw that, in order to restore the necessary

[21] To Vettori, 31st Jan. 1515. *Lettere di Mach. ed. Alvisi.*
[22] Cf. the work of E. W. Mayers mentioned by me, *Machiavellis Geschichtsauffassung
und sein Begriff virtù,* 1912.

quantum of *virtú* which a republic had lost by sinking to such a low point, and thus raise up the State once again, there was only one means to be adopted; namely, that the creative *virtù* of one individual, of one *mano regia*, one *podestà quasi regia* (Disc., I, 18 and 55),[23] should take the State in hand and revive it. Indeed he went so far as to believe that for republics which were completely corrupt and no longer capable of regeneration, monarchy was the only possible form of government. Thus his concept of *virtù* formed a close link between republican and monarchical tendencies, and, after the collapse of the Florentine Republic, enabled him without inconsistency to set his hopes on the rule of the Medicis, and to write for them the Book of the Prince. In the same way it made it possible for him immediately afterwards to take up again in the *Discorsi* the strain of republicanism, and to weigh republic and monarchy against one another.

Moreover his own special ethic of *virtù*—a product of the joyous worldly spirit of the Renaissance—begins now to throw light on the relation in which he stands to the ordinary Christian, and so-called genuine, morality; this relationship has been the cause of much dispute and a continual subject of reproof to Machiavelli. We have already remarked that he retained the basic Christian views on the difference between good and evil. When he advocated evil actions, he never denied them the epithet evil or attempted any hypocritical concealment. Nor did he dare to embody direct traits of morally wicked behaviour in his ideal of *virtù*. In Chapter 8 of the *Principe*, which deals with Agathocles, he says that to murder one's co-citizens, to betray one's friends, to be lacking in loyalty, piety and religion, cannot deserve the name of *virtù;* these things can achieve mastery, but not glory. And yet in Agathocles, who behaved in this way, he recognized at the same time a real *virtù* and *grandezza dell'animo*, i.e. great virtues of a ruler. The ethical sphere of his *virtù* therefore lay in juxtaposition to the usual moral sphere like a kind of world of its own; but for him it was the higher world, because it was the vital source of the State, of the *vivere politico*, the supreme task of human creativity. And because it was for him the higher world, so it could be permitted to trespass and encroach on the moral world in order to achieve its aims. These encroachments and infringements, these "sins" in the Christian sense, never ceased to be judged by him as immoral, and did not indeed constitute *virtù* itself—but they could in the last resort (as we shall soon see more clearly) arise out of *virtù*.

Let us first look more closely at his theory of *virtù*, and at the striking mixture of pessimism and idealism, of mechanistic and vitalistic elements, which go to compose it. In the *Discorsi* (I, 4), he says that of their own accord men will never do anything good, unless they are driven to it by some "necessity." Hunger and poverty, he goes on, make men industrious, and laws make them good. The penalties imposed on any infringement of the

---

[23] "Royal hand [person], one quasi royal power."

laws lead on towards a recognition of justice. For him, therefore, moral goodness and justice were produced and could be produced by the constraining power of the State. How high his opinion was of the State, and how little he thought of individual human beings! But this rigid positivist causal nexus was relaxed through the medium of *virtù*, and by a belief in the creative powers of great men, who, through their own *virtù* and the wise regulations which they made, were able to raise up the average level of humanity to a new, secondary form of *virtù*. Then too it was another mechanistic and fatalistic belief of his that, since the world always remained the same and all things were repeated in a cycle, *virtù* did not exist in the world in unlimited supply, but was passed round in the world continually, and now this, now that people was privileged to possess it. This was echoed by Hegel three hundred years later when, in his theory about the "dominant peoples of world history" (who are entrusted by the World Spirit from time to time with the task of directing its affairs in the world), he made the fatalistic element part of a sublime philosophy of progress and ascent. Machiavelli however contented himself with stating resignedly that only in ancient times did it happen that a single nation was blessed with a preponderance of this *virtù*; in modern times it was divided up amongst a number of nations. This brings out very clearly the similarity and the difference between the centuries. Surrounded by the collapse of the political world in which they lived, both thinkers cast longing eyes on the representatives of strength and efficiency in world history—Hegel with an optimistic belief in progress, the result of the century of the Enlightenment, Machiavelli with the old belief in the everlasting similarity of historical life, a belief which had always been fostered by the Christian disdain for this world and which the vital energy of the Renaissance had not been able to break down. But this vital energy was still strong enough not to lose courage even amid the collapse and in the face of the contempt of humanity, and strong enough to watch out for fresh *virtù*. For the development and creation of *virtù* was for Machiavelli the ideal, and completely self-evident, purpose of the State. To raise his own nation by means of *virtù* from the low point to which it had sunk, and to regenerate the State, if this was still possible (he continually wavered between doubting this and believing it), became his life interest. But this new political idealism was not indeed burdened with the serious problematical element which was inherent in the character of *raison d'état*. This brings us nearer to our real task.

It was certainly impossible, once the moral and religious bond had been severed which held together the mediaeval Christian ideal of life, to set up immediately a new worldly system of ideals which would have the same inner unity and compactness. For, to minds freshly released from the restraints of the Middle Ages, so many provinces of life were now opened up simultaneously that it was not possible at once to find a distinctive point of view, from which the secularized world could be grasped and comprehended once again as a harmonious unity. One made discoveries, first in one place, then in another; one devoted oneself enthusiastically and often quite wholeheartedly to the discovery of the moment and became so completely taken up with it, that one had no opportunity to examine the contradictions and discrepancies between the experiences one had newly acquired and the human values which had held up till now. Machiavelli possessed this one-sided passion for discovery to an extraordinary degree. He threw himself on his particular aim of the moment in such a way that occasionally all he himself had previously thought and said was entirely forgotten. In a quite undaunted, now and then almost fanatical manner, he deduced the most extreme, and sometimes the most terrible consequences from the truths which he had found, without ever testing their reaction on other beliefs he held. In the course of his experimental discoveries he was also fond of changing his standpoint, and identifying himself for the moment with widely different interests in the political struggle, so that for each interested party, whether it be a prince or an enemy of princes, he could devise some powerful remedy, some *medicina forte* (and wherever possible a *regola generale*). His occasional recipes, then, should often be taken as having a certain degree of relativity. And these tendencies of his should be kept firmly in view.

The most serious discrepancy in his system of thought—a discrepancy which he never succeeded in eliminating and which he never even tried to eliminate—lay between the newly discovered ethical sphere of *virtù*, and of the State animated by *virtù*, on the one hand, and the old sphere of religion and morality on the other. This *virtù* of Machiavelli was originally a natural and dynamic idea, which (not altogether unhappily) contained a certain quality of barbarity (*ferocia*); he now considered that it ought not to remain a mere unregulated natural force (which would have been in accordance with the spirit of the Renaissance) but that it ought to be raised into a *virtù ordinata,* into a rationally and purposively directed code of values for rulers and citizens. The *virtù ordinata* naturally set a high value on religion and morality, on account of the influence they exerted towards maintaining the State. In particular, Machiavelli spoke out very forcibly on the subject of the indispensability of religion (Disc., I, 11 and 12); at any rate, he was strongly in favour of a religion which would make men courageous and proud. He once named "religion, laws, military affairs" together in one breath, as the three fundamental pillars of the State. But, in the process, religion and morality fell from the status of intrinsic values, and became nothing more than means towards the goal of a State animated by *virtù*. It was this that led him on to make the double-edged recommendation, which resounded so fearsomely down the centuries to come, inciting statesmen to an irreligious and at the same time dishonest scepticism: the advice that even a religion tinged with error and deception ought to be supported, and the wiser one was, the more one would do it (Disc., I, 12). Whoever thought like this was, from a religious point of view, completely adrift. What final certainty and sure foundation was there left in life, if even an unbelieved and false religion could count as valuable, and when moral goodness was seen as being a product of fear and custom? In this godless world of Nature man was left alone with only himself and the powers Nature had given him, to carry on the fight against all the fateful forces wielded by this same Nature. And this was exactly what Machiavelli conceived his own situation to be.

It is striking and forceful to observe how he strove to rise superior to it. On the one side *fortuna*, on the other *virtù*—this was how he interpreted it. Many people today (he says in chap. 25 of the *Principe*), in the face of the various blows of Fate and unsuspected revolutions we have experienced, are now of the opinion that all wisdom is entirely unavailing against the action of Fate, and that we must just let it do what it likes with us. He admits that even he himself has occasionally felt like this, when in a gloomy mood. But he considered it would be lacking in *virtù* to surrender to the feeling. One must rouse oneself and build canals and dams against the torrent of Fate, and then one will be able to keep it within bounds. Only half our actions are governed by Fortune; the other half, or almost half, is left to us. "Where men have not much *virtù*, then *fortuna* shows its strength clearly enough. And because it is full of change, so there are numerous changes in republics and states. And these will always go on changing, until sooner or later there will come a man who so loves antiquity, that he will regulate *fortuna;* then it will not be able to show every twenty-four hours how much it is capable of accomplishing" (Disc., II, 30). *Fortuna* has got to be beaten and bruised like a woman one wants to possess, and boldness and barbarity will always be more successful there than coldness. But this boldness has got to be united with great cunning and calculation, for each situation of fate demands a method specially suited for dealing with it. He began to meditate very deeply on just this particular problem, for it showed up very clearly both the powers and the limitations of *virtù*, and of humanity altogether. The individual agent cannot escape the nature he is born with. He acts in such and such a way because this nature requires it. Hence it arises that, according to the disposition of Fate, this same method which his character dictates will turn out well one day, and badly the next (Disc., III, 9). An insight of this kind could lead back to fatalism. But the effect on him of all these doubts and impulses was like the bending of a taut-strung bow. He let fly his arrows with all the more force.

Enemies learn to use each other's weapons. *Virtù* has the task of forcing back *fortuna*. *Fortuna* is malicious, so *virtù* must also be malicious, when there is no other way open. This expresses quite plainly the real spiritual origin of Machiavellism: the infamous doctrine that, in national

behaviour, even unclean methods are justified, when it is a question of winning or of keeping the power which is necessary for the State. It is the picture of Man, stripped of all transcendent good qualities, left alone on the
battlefield to face the daemonic forces of Nature, who now feels himself
possessed too of a daemonic natural strength and returns blow for blow. In
Machiavelli's opinion, *virtù* had a perfectly genuine right to take up any
weapon, for the purpose of mastering Fortune. One can easily see that this
doctrine, which appeared so dualistic on the outside, had really sprung
from the background of a naïve Monism, which made all the powers of life
into forces of Nature. It now became a presupposition for the discovery
which Machiavelli had made about the essence of *raison d'état*.

But in order to make this discovery, yet another theory was needed
—one which he thought out and applied just as clearly and consistently as
he did the theory of the struggle between *virtù* and *fortuna*. This was the
theory of *necessità*. *Virtù, fortuna* and *necessità* are three words which keep
on sounding again and again throughout his writings with a kind of brazen
ring. These words, and perhaps also the refrain of the *armi proprie* (which
sums up the demands he made on the State in the way of military matters
and power politics), show his ability to condense the wealth of his experience and thought, and how the rich edifice of his mind rested on a few,
quite simple, but solid pillars. For him *virtù* and *necessità* were related in
a way very similar to that in which, in modern philosophy, the sphere of
values is related to the sphere of causal connection; i.e. where the causal
connection provides the means and possibility of realizing the values. If
virtù was the vital power of men, a power which created and maintained
States, and gave them sense and meaning, then *necessità* was the causal
pressure, the means of bringing the sluggish masses into the form required
by *virtù*. We have already heard how he traced back the origin of morality
to "necessity." We have discussed fully (so he says in the *Discorsi*, III, 12)
how useful *necessità* is for human actions, and to what glory it can lead on.
And (as several moral philosophers have written) the hands and speech of
Man—which are the two principal tools for his ennoblement—would
never have functioned completely, and human achievements would never
have reached their present high level, if they had not been pushed to it by
necessità. The old military commanders recognized the *virtù di tal
necessità* and used it to instil into their soldiers the dogged spirit of combat,
when they planned to put them in a situation where they would *have* to
fight. Come with me, a Volscian leader shouts to the soldiers round him,
in Livy (4, 28), *virtute pares, quae ultimum ac maximum telum est,
necessitate superiores estis.*[24] These were words to warm Machiavelli's
heart. The more *necessità* there is, he insists in the *Discorsi*, I, 1, the more

---

[24] "In courage you are equal, in desperation, which is the ultimate and greatest weapon,
you are superior."

virtù there will be also, and *necessità* can bring us to many things, which reason is not strong enough to drive us to (Disc., I, 1). And alongside the conception of *virtù ordinata* he placed the equally characteristic conception of *necessità ordinata dalle leggi* (Disc., I, 1) [25] as engendering first-class human material for the State. Thus it is always a question of following the natural forces of life, but also at the same time of regulating them by means of reason. If one were to adopt for a moment the unlovely nomenclature of "-isms," one could call his system a triad of naturalism, voluntarism and rationalism. But without his belief (rooted in universal history) in the positive *blessing* of *necessità*, without the real warmth which he gave it, he would never have come to proclaim with such determination and conviction that which one can call the *curse* of *necessità*, of necessity of State.

One more trait of his personality must have contributed: namely, the quite unconventional and at the same time radical nature of his thought, which never shrank back before any abyss. Certainly his contemporaries too had long learnt never to shrink back before any moral abyss, and to wade quite cheerfully through any filth. For if it had not been for the general stultifying of moral feeling in life, and without the examples offered by the Papacy from the time of Sixtus IV and Alexander VI, with his frightful son Cesar Borgia, Machiavelli would never have had the milieu required for his new ideas about the use of immoral methods in politics. They were indeed not new as regards content; but they were new in the sense that he dared to express them, and to combine them into a system which embraced a universal outlook. For up till now theory had only limped after practice. The selfsame humanists who, like Pontanus at the court of Naples, saw clearly all the dark side of the new statecraft, were indeed prepared to permit cunning and deception when it was for the good of the community; but after that they fell back once more on the formal pattern of the figure of the Prince, filled in with classic phrases.[26] If I am to offer something really useful, says Machiavelli, it seems to me more suitable to follow the real truth of things, rather than the imaginary picture one has of them. Many people have imagined for themselves republics and principalities, the like of which one has never seen or even thought possible; for the difference between what one actually does and what one ought to do is so great that whoever, in considering how people ought to live, omits to consider how they behave, is riding for a fall. That is to say, the man who makes it a rule in all circumstances to perform nothing but good actions, is bound to go under amongst so many who are evil. Therefore it is "necessary" for a prince, if he is to maintain his position, to learn also how not to be good, and then to utilize or not utilize this knowledge, as *necessità* prescribes.

[25] "Ordered necessity of law."
[26] Benoist, *L'Etat italien avant Machiavell. Revue des dux mondes,* 1st May 1907, p. 182; cf. Platzhoff, p. 28.

FRIEDRICH MEINECKE   415

It is worthy of notice that Machiavelli did not introduce near the beginning of his essay on the Prince this new principle of method—a principle which was to break fresh ground for so many centuries, and which was so purely empirical and so completely free from presuppositions. He does not bring it in till much further on, in Chapter 15. For he himself underwent development, during the course of his work on the book. Chapter 15 belongs (as we have tried to prove elsewhere [27]), not to the original conception of the *Principe*, but rather to an extension of it which probably came soon afterwards. Henceforth he always exercised the new principle, which was closely akin to the aesthetic honesty and directness of Florentine art. Then, when he was in the full spate of work, he suddenly became conscious that he was treading new paths. It was the climax of his life, and at the same time also a turning point for the history of European thought. And in this matter history of thought touched very closely upon the history of nations; they were both struck by the *same* electric shock. Even if the statesmen themselves learnt nothing new from it, the very fact that it was *being taught* was still new. For it was not until after it had been grasped as a principle that the historical tendencies achieved their full power of impact, and reached the stage when they could be called ideas.

But the initial application of the new scientific method, and its effect on historical life, were frightful and shattering. A prince must also learn how not to be good—this was the requirement of *necessità*, by which all human life was governed and constrained. But it was quite another matter to decide whether, on the one hand, the moral law should be broken only in the practice of politics, or whether, on the other hand, it was permissible to justify (as from now on became possible, and in fact more and more tended to happen) such an infringement by the plea of an unavoidable "necessity." In the first instance the moral law itself had, in its sanctity as a supra-empirical necessity, remained entirely unimpaired. But now this supra-empirical necessity was broken down by an empirical necessity; the force of evil was fighting for a place alongside that of good, and was making out that it was, if not an actual power of good, then at least an indispensable means for obtaining a certain kind of goodness. The forces of sin, which had been basically subdued by the Christian ethic, now won what was fundamentally a partial victory; the devil forced his way into the kingdom of God. There now began that dualism under which modern culture has to suffer: that opposition between supra-empirical and empirical, between absolute and relative standards of value. It was now possible for the modern State, following its own inmost vital impulse, to free itself from all the spiritual fetters that had constrained it; it was possible for it, as an independent power acknowledging no authority outside this world, to effect

---

[27] *Klassiker der Politik Bd. 8, Machiavelli, Der Fürst*, etc., Introduction, pp. 32 ff. I was not convinced by Chabod's counter-arguments in "*Archivum Romanicum*."

the admirable accomplishments of rational organization, which would have been unthinkable in the Middle Ages, but were now due to increase from century to century. But it already contained the poison of an inner contradiction, from the very moment it began its ascent. On the one hand religion, morality and law were all absolutely indispensable to it as a foundation for its existence; on the other hand, it started off with the definite intention of injuring these whenever the needs of national self-preservation would require it. But surely (it will be asked) Machiavelli must have felt this contradiction, and the serious consequences it was bound to have?

He was not able to feel it, for the reason that his cast-iron theory of *necessità* concealed it from him, or because (as he believed, at least) the theory of *necessità* resolved the contradiction. The same force which impelled princes to refrain from being good under certain circumstances, also impelled men to behave morally; for it is only from necessity that men perform good actions (*Principe*, chap. 23). Necessity was therefore the spear which at the same time both wounded and healed. It was the causal mechanism which, provided that *virtù* existed in the State, saw to it that the necessary morality and religion were present, and that any failings in that respect were made good. Thus the theory of the struggle between *virtù* and *fortuna*, and the theory of *necessità*, worked together very closely to justify the prince in the use of underhand measures, and to prevent this from being harmful in his opinion.

For all the time Machiavelli held firmly to the absolute validity of religion, morality and law. Even in the most evil and notorious chapter of the *Principe*, Chapter 18, which justifies breach of contract, and declares that a prince (and especially a new prince), for the purpose of maintaining the State, "is often obliged (*necessitato*) to act without loyalty, without mercy, without humanity, and without religion"—even in this chapter he still emphasizes that a prince, when he *can*, should not leave the path of morality, but only that he should, in case of necessity (when *necessitato*), also know how to tread the path of evil. Bad indeed was the infamous advice which he gives here: that it is not necessary for the prince to possess all the good moral qualities of loyalty, sincerity, etc., but that he must always appear to have them, because the former case, in which they would always be exercised, would be harmful, but the latter case where he appeared to have them would be useful. With this he helped to make any hypocritical scoundrel secure on a throne. It would throughout have been perfectly in keeping with his purposes and with the main line of his thought, to demand from the prince himself a certain inner moral restraint, even if it were united with the power to take upon himself, in a case of necessity of State, the entire conflict between State-interest and individual morality, and thus make a tragic sacrifice. But perhaps this kind of solution to the problem (one which Frederick the Great was to give later on) was still entirely alien to the intellectual climate of the period and to Machiavelli's own way of thought. The ability to think in terms of inner conflicts, violations and tragic problems, presupposes a more modern and sophisticated mentality, which perhaps only began with Shakespeare. It was in the spirit of the time to delight in tracing precise and rectilinear paths; and in opposition to the straight path of Christian morality Machiavelli laid down another path, just as straight in its own way, a path which was directed exclusively towards the goal of what was useful for the State. He then proceeded, with a pleasure which was characteristic of him, to draw from it the most extreme consequences.

But was it then, one cannot help challenging him once more—was it then really the well-being of the State, which he had in mind when he wrote the *Principe*? Or was it merely a breviary for the Medicis, whose favour he needed and to whom he dedicated the book, in order to found for himself a new principality by recommending the methods of the frightful Cesar Borgia? We have tried to prove elsewhere [28] that this interpretation is much too narrow. The personal and contemporary political motives which induced him to write the book are undeniable; but from far back there also entered in his entire philosophy of the State, and also his longing to see Italy freed from the Barbarians. Cesar Borgia, with his rational exercise of cruelty and bad faith, must certainly have offered a model for the practical methods of power politics in the situation as it then existed. But the ideal and supreme pattern for the new princes in Italy must have been the great national liberators and founders of States, such as Moses and Cyrus, Theseus and Romulus. The whole book from beginning to end, even including the last chapter (which is sometimes erroneously taken to be an appendix and not an integral part of the book), grew up out of one uniform and fundamental conception, and is built up on the great theme of the struggle between *virtù* and *fortuna*.

It is certainly true that, as regards its technical chapters, the *Principe* can easily arouse the feeling that Machiavelli is only watching out for the personal advantage of the prince. In this respect Machiavelli yielded to his passion for one-sided emphasis and excessive subtlety in dealing with the *thema probandum* of the moment. But if his work is taken together with the *Discorsi* and the other writings and treated as a whole, then this impression entirely disappears. One sees clearly what is the real central idea in Machiavelli's life: namely, the regeneration of a fallen people by means of the *virtù* of a tyrant, and by means of the levering power of all the measures dictated by *necessità*.

This is what is peculiar to Machiavelli, and at the same time constitutes the historical power of his work—the fact that he, the first person to discover the real nature of *raison d'état*, did actually succeed in taking the measure of all the heights and depths to which it led on. He knew its

[28] In the Introduction to vol. 8 of *Klassiker der Politik* already referred to.

depths, which lead down to the bestial element in Man—"thus it is necessary for a prince, that he should have a proper understanding of how to
make use of the brute as well as the man" (*Principe*, chap. 18). He could in
the process, as we already saw, when drawn on by his deep-rooted passion
for analysis, sink much more deeply into the filth of bestiality than was
strictly necessary in order to make a proper use of that bestiality. He knew
also that a case of necessity of State (where perhaps a republic which is
threatened by dangerous neighbours might be obliged to adopt a policy of
conquest) did not represent merely a simple factual necessity, but contained in addition certain elements of power-drive and power-appetite—
"molestation by others will give rise to the desire and necessity for conquering" (*la voglia e la necessità dello acquistare,* Disc., II, 19) [29] But he
despised a mere insensible greed for power, the *brutta cupidità di regnare*
(Disc., III, 8), and he always returned once more to the utilitarian middle
way of *raison d'état*. Keep your head clear, he advised, so that you only
wish for what is attainable; do not become presumptuous after victory, but,
if you have a stronger opponent, take care to make peace at an opportune
moment (Disc., II, 27). Nor should you exasperate an enemy with threats
or insult him in words; threats make him more cautious, while insults will
increase his hatred (Disc., II, 26). To draw hatred on oneself without getting any benefit from it, is indiscreet and unwise (Disc., III, 23). Under no
circumstances should a system of government be built up on a permanent
hatred amongst the people. It would be better even to provoke an attack
from the nobles, because there are only a few of them, and they can therefore be more easily subdued; but even here he advocated a rationally balanced procedure, "to refrain from reducing the nobles to despair and to
satisfy the people" (Princ., chap. 19).

Political utilitarianism was also at the same time a policy of relativity. Nowadays, he taught, it is necessary to pay attention to the subject
peoples, because the peoples are of more significance than the armies. The
Roman emperors, on the other hand, had to accommodate themselves to
the soldiers rather than the people, because the soldiers could do more at
that time than the people could (Princ., chap. 19). Fortified castles may be
useful or not, according to the state of the times; but not to be hated by
one's people is better than any fortified castle (Princ., chap. 20). But each
thing always has concealed in it some special evil that is peculiar to it
(Disc., III, 11); therefore whenever one is acting in accordance with *raison
d'état*, one must always be conscious of the spheres of uncertainty, of
change, and of two-fold consequences, in which it works. "No State ought
to think that it can adopt a course which is absolutely secure, but it ought
to reflect rather that all are doubtful; because it is in the order of things,

[29] Cf. also *Principe*, chap. 3: *È cosa veramente molto naturale et ordinaria desiderare di
acquistare, e sempre quando li uomini lo fanno che possano, saranno laudati e non bia-
simati.*

that one can never avoid an evil without running into another one. Wisdom therefore consists in distinguishing between different qualities of evil, and in accepting the lesser evil as a good" (Princ., chap. 21).

As we have already seen, he adopted a relativist view, when considering the various forms which the State could take. The contrast between the monarchist bias in the *Principe* and the republican tinge of the *Discorsi* is only apparent. The quantity of *virtù*, which existed in a people, was the factor that decided whether a monarchy or a republic was the more suitable. So it was only consistent that, for his disjointed times, he demanded a monarchical despot and took this to be a necessity of State. The fact that the thing he was asking for might cut both ways was perfectly clear to him; he knew quite well that the tool of monarchical power, which with supreme art he was putting into the hands of the prince, could be misused in the interests of a purely personal greed for power. One can understand why he does not proceed to treat this problem in the *Principe*. But in the *Discorsi* he gives it quite openly as his really sincere opinion, that only in a republic can it be ensured that public good will take precedence of private advantage, and thus make it possible for the State to achieve greatness (Disc., II, 2). With the passionate exaggeration into which he sometimes fell, he was capable of laying down, with reference to a city-state ruled by a prince, the following proposition: that what the prince did for his own advantage, would in most cases injure the State, and that what he did for the benefit of the State, would injure him.[30] Yet immediately afterwards he went on to modify his own crude conception, and contrasted the barbaric type of oriental ruler with the pattern of the Western prince; in that, if the latter be of a normal human stamp, then he will have a uniform paternal love for the cities which come under his care, and he will leave their old constitutional arrangements undisturbed. It is also in the essence of Machiavellian *raison d'état*, as one can see, that with regard to the inner life of the State it should still wish to behave in a relatively conservative and considerate manner.[31] But ruthless acts of interference, when they were necessary to protect power against direct threats, were not thereby excluded. Certainly there also appeared on the horizon of his political imagination the wish-fantasy of a great regenerator of fallen States, "who, either through his own *virtù*, or by means of the *virtù* of a regulation" (i.e. of a general reform), would breathe new life into these States. The practical needs and possibilities of his time, however (and he generally based his calculations on these), did not go beyond the suppression of actual resistance inside the State, i.e. did not go beyond a rational and at the same time thorough opposition, by direct and indirect means, to all

[30] His reference for this is to Xenophon's treatise *de tyrannide*—it is (as shown by Ellinger, *Antike Quellen der Staatslehre Machiavellis, Zeitschr. f.d. ges. Staatswissenschaften* Bd. 44, 40) the dialogue *Hieron*, which has been ascribed to Xenophone.

[31] Cf. the advice in chap. 3 of the *Principe:* "in newly conquered countries with the same language, the laws and taxes ought not to be changed."

conspiracies. The aims of the later type of absolutism, with its levelling tendencies, were still completely foreign both to himself and to his time. Machiavellism had certainly opened up the road which led to them, but they themselves had not yet come in sight. It is for this reason that we see no signs in Machiavelli of *raison d'état* taking precedence over statute law, which in the seventeenth century (as we shall see presently) was to constitute the principal importance of *raison d'état*. On the contrary a fundamental respect for the existing laws was part of the very essence of his rational autocracy. "It is well that princes should know that, in the very hour when they begin to break the laws, and disturb old arrangements and customs under which men have long lived, in that hour they begin to lose the State" (Disc., III, 5).

All this shows that he moved on the ethical heights of a *raison d'état* which within the limits of his time could only have limited aims indeed, but which was capable of a vital consciousness of the good of the community, the *bene commune* of the whole people. And ultimately he was even capable of rising to the highest ethical feeling which is possible for action prompted by *raison d'état*; this sacrifice consists in taking on oneself personal disgrace and shame, if only it offers a means of saving the Fatherland. Occasionally he would express it in the very same breath with his prosaic utilitarianism: "It will always be difficult to win the masses over to such conclusions as these, which appear to indicate cowardice and defeat, but do in reality signify salvation and gain" (Disc., I, 53). But the heights and depths of his *raison d'état* are united in the most powerful manner by that phrase, which is to be found at the end of his *Discorsi* (III, 41), and which must surely have sounded in the ears of a certain great German statesman during the First World War: that one may save the Fatherland even *con ignominia*. "When it is a question of saving the Fatherland, one should not stop for a moment to consider whether something is lawful or unlawful, gentle or cruel, laudable or shameful; but, putting aside every other consideration, one ought to follow out to the end whatever resolve will save the life of the State and preserve its freedom."

It has been the fate of Machiavelli, as of so many great thinkers, that only one part of his system of thought has been able to influence historical life. It is true that he exerted a powerful and lasting influence through his new method of building politics upon a foundation of experience and history—although even this did not immediately replace the previous scholastic and humanistic methods, but only, through the course of nearly two centuries, intermingled with the older methods, and was able gradually to supersede them. But his ideal of *virtù* soon faded; because the heathen mood of the Renaissance, from which it had sprung, was not able to survive in the period which followed the *sacco di Roma*. And with that too the ethical aim of his statecraft, the idea of regeneration, paled into insignificance. Attention was indeed paid to his republican ideals, but they were misinterpreted in many ways, as for instance in the opinion which was soon expressed that, by giving a sincere picture of the *Principe* he had wanted to unmask tyranny and give a warning against the danger he was pointing out.[32] But generally speaking he was seen first and foremost as having prepared the poison of autocracy; as such, he was publicly condemned and secretly made use of. As we have seen, Machiavelli is to blame for this himself, on account of his method of isolating in a one-sided manner whatever problem he happens to be dealing with at the moment. The chief thing was, however, that the idea of political regeneration was altogether beyond the capabilities and the wishes of the peoples and the rulers of that time, and hence it fell to the ground. The struggle which was to rage around religious values took up entirely all the higher spiritual power of men; and Machiavelli's ancient heathen idealism of the State was no longer understood by the men of the Counter-Reformation period—not even by the Free-thinkers, who took over the secular spirit of the Renaissance. But they very well understood the ancient heathen realism of his statecraft. And here it is very clearly demonstrated how much can be added to the mere naïvely-functioning forces of life by a spiritual and intellectual shaping. The intellectual formative power, finding Machiavellism already in existence, rendered it far more effective in influence, by making it into a well-reasoned, compact, and elegantly polished system. A plant which had been growing wild and spreading in all directions, and which was very poisonous and at the same time potentially curative in its effects, became to a certain extent cultivated, and thus perfected and its influence greatly multiplied. His theory combined absolutely convincing evidence that political life had always seemed to be of just this character and no other, and had probably always seemed like this, together with the pressure of *necessità* that a prince who does not wish to be ruined must behave like a fox among foxes, *vulpinari cum vulpibus*. And in this *necessità* one could also feel obscurely (it was the sole ethical element in Machiavelli's thought which produced any after-effect) some higher kind of justification for immoral political behaviour in the eyes of the moral conscience. Then the newly-animated Christian conscience of every creed rose up in opposition to this; and so there began that spiritual and intellectual struggle around the subject of Machiavellism, which we are going to describe. Later on we shall have to return once more to Machiavelli, when our task will be to consider the subsequent development of certain fertile conceptions, contained in his theory of *raison d'état;* these conceptions pointed forward to a more individualizing treatment of the State in historical and political thinking. It only remains now for us to give the most important

[32] This was the opinion already in the Giunta Edition of the *Principe* in 1532; Burd in the introduction to his edition (1891), p. 36.

concrete facts in connection with the spread of his theory, and with the
condensing of it into the catchphrase *ragione di stato*.[33]

The *Principe* was first circulated in manuscript. It was first put into
print by Blado in Rome in 1532. This was followed by countless reprints.[34]
In 1531 Blado also prepared the first edition of the *Discorsi*, which was
likewise reprinted over and over again. In 1552 the first published *Index li-
brorum prohibitorum* from Rome placed the entire writings of Machiavelli
on its list. But already in the following year there appeared at Basle the
first Latin translation of the *Principe*. It was impossible to prevent his
books from spreading.

The catchphrase of *ragione di stato* must have begun to take on very
gradually, beginning in the third decade of the 16th century. Guicciardini,
who was so close in spirit to Machiavelli, had already spoken once of the
ragione e uso degli stati [35]; but he used the phrase in such a way that it was
doubtful whether he was already using it to apply to a distinct concept.[36]
It has therefore been believed that the first evidence of a distinct theory of
ragione di stato is to be found in an anonymous book of memoirs, dating
from 1525. This is a mistake.[37] Therefore, until further evidence is forth-

---

[33] *Raison d'état*

[34] Cf. Gerber, *Niccolò Machiavelli, die Handschriften, Ausgaben und Übersetzungen
seiner Werke*, 1912.

[35] *Raisons et usages des états.*

[36] In a dialogue on the constitution of Florence (between 1523 and 1527), *Opere ine-
dite*, 2, 212; cf. Barkhausen, *Fr. Guicciardinis politische Theorien usw.*, 1908, p. 89.
Guicciardini here recommended that all the Pisan prisoners should be killed, in order to
weaken the city. Though this might not be a Christian idea, it was required by *ragione
e uso degli stati.*

[37] On pp. 529–533 of his *Secrets d'Etat de Venise* (1884), Lamansky published an anonymous and undated piece, which came from a manuscript of the seventeenth or eighteenth century belonging to Barozzi, the director of a Venetian museum; the anonymous
piece is entitled *Che si possa dai principi insidiare alla vita degli adherenti dei nemici
loro*. In connection with a supposed plot on the part of the Marchese Pescara (who died
in 1525), a general of Charles V, on the life of Duke Ercole of Ferrara, a supporter of
the King of France, the question is discussed of whether and to what extent there was
any foundation to the Duke's complaint about this plot. It is asserted in the process
that *la prudenza politica o ragione di stato, che noivogliamo chiamarla* did mean that a
ruler should set the preservation or aggrandisement of his *stato* before anything else, *e
di qua nasce, che tutto quello, che si opera con quello fine, si dice ragione di stato etc.
Questa prudenza però, non obligata ad altro, che al servitio, alla sicurtà et alla perpe-
tuatione del dominare, interpreta le leggi, altera le consuetudini, muta i costumi e quasi
arbitra dispone*, etc. Pescara's plot was not to be condemned, and individual plots of
this kind were not so bad or so destructive as war, which caused the death of many innocent persons. The only ground for complaint which Duke Ercole had was that Pescara, who was an Italian and a relative, had behaved in so unchivalrous a manner towards him. If this writing was contemporary, as Platzhoff (*Theorie von der
Mordbefugnis der Obrigkeit im 16. Jahrhundert*, p. 31) supposes, or in any case originated at the very latest in 1525 among the retinue of Pescara, then it would constitute
for us the first important evidence of a complete theory of *ragione di stato*. But more
than twenty years intervene before the next mention of *ragione di stato*, and further
decades elapsed before the theoretical discussion of *ragione di stato* was initiated by
Botero in 1589. I have the definite impression that the account presupposes this theo-

coming, we are bound to accept the view (which was already shared by Italian writers about *ragione di stato* in the seventeenth century [38]) that the archbishop and humanist Giovanni della Casa, about the middle of the sixteenth century, was the first to testify with any certainty to its existence as a distinct catchphrase.

It is instructive to see in what connection it occurred, and the comments he had to make on the subject. In 1547 Piacenza had fallen into the hands of the Emperor, who held on to it and refused to give it back to his son-in-law, Duke Octavio Farnese of Parma. So it occurred that in one of the following years della Casa (who was in Venice as papal nuntius in the service of Pope Paul III, the grandfather of Duke Octavio) requested the Emperor Charles V, in a very skilfully composed address, to hand back Piacenza.[39] Della Casa said that, although one might claim it would be contrary to the *ragione degli stati* [40] to do so, yet this opinion was in no way Christian or humane. It would be as if fairness and honour were only rough workaday clothes which one could not wear on grand occasions. It was precisely in the important questions of life that reasonableness ought to prevail. Whoever was acting contrary to it, particularly in affairs of State, was acting against Nature and against God. If the reason which guided States was only to serve purposes which were useful and profitable, and was to despise every other law, where then would be the difference between tyrants and kings, between men and beasts? It was all very well to create this title of *Utile ragion di stato*. But in doing so one created two kinds of reason—one of them crooked, false and unbridled, good for any robbery and infamy, which was given the name of *Ragion di stato* and entrusted with the government of States; the other plain, straightforward and steadfast, which had been entirely ousted from the business of ruling

---

retical treatment. The relationship of *ragione di stato* to positive law, the conception of it as *arbitra*, the efforts to define it precisely, the distinction and juxtaposition of a *ragione di guerra e di stato*, etc., are different traits which recur over and over again in the literature of *ragione di stato* after Ammirato (for whom, see chap. 6). It seems to me highly improbable that in 1525 a thinker would have been acquainted with all the problems which were modern in 1600. The account is also lacking in direct contemporary atmosphere. In general, it bears a more literary character. It treats the fall of Pescara as a text-book example, in the same manner as Paruta and Boccalini (who also dealt with the fall of Pescara on one occasion) were afterwards fond of taking instances from the past and discoursing on them as text-book cases. And lastly, the introduction to the account indicates that the author had already been in the habit of speaking on this subject occasionally—in short, it is obviously a fragment taken from a longer political treatise written by one of the practically innumerable political authors who wrote about statecraft around 1600. —Moreover nothing has become known from any other source about a plot by Pescara against Duke Ercole. M. Brosch, who had a thorough knowledge of the period, and on whom Platzhoff relied, assumed a sceptical attitude towards the anonymous author.

[38] Chiaramonti, *Della ragione di stato*, 1635, p. 10 Cf. Ferrari, *Hist. de la raison d'état*, p. vi.
[39] Edition of the *Opere della Casa's* of 1707, Vol. 2, 125 ff.
[40] *Raisons d'états*

States, and restricted to the mere discharge of judicial matters. And now he sought to put the Emperor in a frame of mind where he would find it impossible to act in accordance with this abominable doctrine.

It is true of course that, in the quarrel over Piacenza between Emperor and Pope, both sides used against each other all the arts of Machiavellian politics. In 1547 Pier Luigi Farnese, the father of Octavio, was murdered on the instigation of the imperial Governor of Milan. But that gave rise to a vengeful desire among the Farnese family to use the most evil measures against the Emperor. In the very well composed address this was concealed by the delicate and skilful *raison d'état* of the papal diplomat. But the whole rift, which had appeared between men's thoughts and their actions, could be glimpsed in the obscure background of his words.

19

The Perspective
of Art

CHARLES S. SINGLETON

It will be well, at the outset, to make clear the meaning of
the title and to place the subject; for such terms as "art"
and "perspective," in this particular company at least, may
easily be taken in quite other meanings than are here intended. I must at once declare (and I hope I disappoint no
one) that I shall not be speaking here about art of the kind
which our chairman is interested in collecting in his museum, nor of perspective as it is taught in the classrooms at
the Fogg—at least not primarily in those senses. Both
terms are here intended in a much broader meaning:
"perspective" simply in the sense of "angle of vision"; and
"art" in that much more inclusive sense which it had had
for as many centuries before the Renaissance as may be
counted from (at least) Aristotle to Thomas Aquinas; art,
that is, as any activity concerned with *making*. And, as

This article, a paper read before a meeting of the ACLS Renaissance Group, guests of the Fogg Art Museum of Harvard University,
was orginally published in *The Kenyon Review*, 15 (Spring 1953),
169–189. It is reprinted here with the permission of the author and
of the publisher.

will soon be evident, I am interested in this broad conception of art not merely in so far as art may be distinguished by its particular aim and *object,* but as its distinction from other forms of human activity may be affirmed with respect to the *subject* of the action, the maker, the agent, the artist. You will readily recognize the distinguishing features of art so intended as I quote from the *Ethics* of Aristotle and from the *Summa Theologica* of Thomas Aquinas.

In the *Summa,* as you may recall, Aquinas becomes concerned with art in connection with the subject of the virtues, and specifically in conjunction with the virtue of Prudence—mainly, we gather, because his master the Philosopher had in the *Ethics* considered Art in connection with Prudence. Thus, Aquinas, calling his own tune as usual by way of objections raised, brings in the question of Art as distinguished from Prudence: "Art does not require rectitude of the appetite." This is a point of signal importance in the definition of that activity as we are here concerned with it. Art does not require rectitude of appetite. Prudence does.

The essential distinction between the two we get more clearly by turning to Aquinas' *Commentary* on Aristotle's *Ethics* at that particular paragraph which the statement just quoted from the *Summa* had in mind: "Wherefore [says Aquinas in his gloss] Prudence, which is concerned with man's good (humana bona), of necessity has the moral virtues joined with it. . . . Not however Art, which is concerned with exterior goods (bona exteriora)."

Such brief quotations are nearly enough to give us our bearings with respect to the particular concept of art that we are here to attend to: partly because in our time we have heard a good deal about it from certain neothomists, have seen it brought to bear on the question of modern French poetry, and even on the movie industry. Thus, our general familiarity with the conception, as we meet it in Aquinas who is following Aristotle, makes it possible to get it before us with dispatch.

Art is an activity which is not concerned with rectitude of the appetite, as is prudence, because it is essentially an action passing into outward things; whereas the action of prudence is essentially one abiding in the agent. Here at bottom there is that essential distinction of two kinds of action which Aristotle had made, and Aquinas, in his turn, had stressed: a distinction between *agere* and *facere, doing* and *making.* We may return to the same point in the *Nicomachean Ethics* whence I quote:

> . . . *making* and *acting* are different; so that the reasoned state of capacity to act is different from the reasoned state of capacity to make. Hence they are not involved one in the other; for neither is acting making nor is making acting. Now since architecture is an art, and is essentially a reasoned state of capacity to make, and there is neither any art that is not such a state nor any such state that is not an art, art is identical with a state of capacity to make. . . . *Making* and *acting* being different, art must be a matter of making, not of acting.

Aquinas has rephrased this in the *Summa Theologica* under the question "Whether prudence is a distinct virtue from art," where, referring to the above passage, he observes, in his Reply, as follows:

> The reason for this difference is that art is the "right reason of things to be made"; whereas, prudence is the "right reason of things to be done." Now *making* and *doing* differ, as stated in *Metaphysics* IX, 16, in that *making* is an action passing into outward matter, e.g., to *build*, to *saw*, and so forth; whereas *doing* is an action abiding in the agent, e.g., to *see*, to *will*, and the like.
>   . . . Consequently it is requisite for prudence . . . that man be well disposed with regard to the end; and this depends on the rectitude of his appetite. . . . On the other hand, the good of things made by art is not the good of man's appetite, but the good of those things themselves: wherefore art does not presuppose rectitude of the appetite.

And a little further on: "The various kinds of things made by art are all *external to man.*"

This distinction between *doing* and *making* as two kinds of action is one which we have pretty well lost sight of, I think. And we realize this when we take note of the examples of *doing* which are cited: to *will*, to *hope*, to *see*. And since, in a moment, I shall be turning to Machiavelli's speculations on political action, it may be well, with the unfamiliar distinction fresh in mind, to ask here which kind of action, *political* action is. Is it *making* or *doing?*

We have Aquinas' clear answer to the question, and it is one faithful to Aristotle's thought. I quote from Aquinas' *Commentary* on the *Politics:*

> So our present science (politics) is a practical one; for reason not only knows but creates the City. Furthermore, reason can operate about things either as *making something* (per modum factionis), in which case its action passes on to some external material, as we see in the mechanical arts of the smith and the shipwright; or by *doing something* (per modum actionis), in which case the action remains intrinsic to the agent, as we see in *deliberation, making choice, willing,* and all that pertains to moral science. It is clear that political science, which is concerned with the ordered relationship between men, belongs, not to the realm of *making* or factitive science, or mechanical art, but rather to that of *doing* or the moral sciences.

This leaves no doubt whatever. In this conception, political action belongs not to the category of *making*, but to that of *doing*. We shall see that Machiavelli shifted the categories.

Prudence and Art, then, are both concerned with practical matters and both with a good. Prudence—and, as we see, political action—with the good of the agent, first of all: *bonum operantis;* and art with the good of that which is made: *bonum operis.*

Now, I am quite as much interested in the figure of the agent, the craftsman, the artist, as he is seen to act within the frame of this conception of action, as I am in the *object*. And for that reason I venture to indulge in another quotation from Aquinas. Again, from the *Summa*, from a context where discussion turns on the intellectual virtues:

> I answer that art is nothing else but the right reason about certain works to be made. And yet the good of these things depends not on man's appetitive faculty being affected in this or that way, but on the goodness of the work done. For a craftsman, as such, is commendable, not for the will with which he does a work, but for the quality of the work. Art, therefore, properly speaking is an operative habit. And yet it has something in common with the speculative habits. . . . For as long as the geometrician demonstrates the truth, it matters not how his appetitive faculty may be affected, whether he be joyful or angry; even as neither does this matter in a craftsman, as we have observed.

It is well that these distinctions and this particular conception of art can be so familiar to this audience that I may dispense with more quotations to make clear what I intend by my title: the perspective of art. As is now more than clear, I mean, a mode of action conceived as being in the order of making because passing into external matter; and consequently viewed as having its end and its good in that external goal; a mode of action, in short, which is extra-moral, amoral, and is recognized as such in the philosophy of a medieval Christian theologian. A matter which holds for you no surprise at all; but one which, I may report from the classroom, does awaken a considerable surprise in younger ears: that a theologian of those dark ages before the Renaissance should be able to entertain in his thought the concept of such an amoral perspective of action as that which he calls art, comes as something of a shock and an eye-opener to many of them. They are much taken when they are brought to read in the *Summa*, and in the context of this matter, such words as the following, for instance:

> Art does not require of the craftsman that his act be a good act, but that his work be good. . . . Wherefore, the craftsman needs art, not that he may live well, but that he may produce a good work of art.

And one always feels that the shock is (as most shocks in education, at least, are) a valuable one. For some, it is a first lesson in how a perspective of Greek philosophy can be carried in solution in a medieval Christian philosophy pure and unmodified.

This little frame of action, this perspective of art, one would expect to be in a position of some stress and challenge within that total frame of thought in which a concern for salvation, a concern for soul, for *bona humana*, was, to be sure, not exclusive, but certainly dominant. The perspective seems to express, in the figure of the craftsman, a certain *nonchalance du salut*. Of course, within the frame of Aquinas' thought one does not feel any strain. The perspective of art finds its place there as do all other things, and in its proper place is its peace. But, we readily conceive that it would be quite another matter were this perspective somehow to be projected into the meditations, say, of a St. Bernard of Clairvaux. He would indeed be much less readily inclined to entertain it. He would brush it aside as intolerable, for clearly the perspective of art is a mode of action conceived as lying entirely to one side of the drama of salvation in which, willy-nilly, we all have roles and from which none of us is excused. With respect to that engulfing frame and that drama, the perspective of art represents a *truancy,* a play to one side of the great upward thrust toward the completion and perfection of man in man, and of man above man. It is a mode of action concerned not at all with the *good of the actor* which in a Christian time must mean salvation of the soul.

Having before us now art as a mode of action so conceived, I am interested in turning forthwith to consider Niccolò Machiavelli's views on the matter of *political* action; in particular, to turn to what will readily be granted to be a characteristic and dominant pattern in his thought. One quotation from his *Discourses* will single out that pattern for your immediate recognition. In the 26th Chapter of that work, concerned mainly with republics, but in which the author of the *Prince* is not at all inclined to forget his interest in princes, we read:

> Whoever becomes Prince of a City or State, especially if the foundation of his power is feeble, and does not wish to establish there either a monarchy or a republic, will find the best means for holding that principality to organize the government entirely anew . . . ; that is, he should appoint new governors with new powers and new men, and he should make the poor rich, as David did when he became king. . . . Besides this, he should destroy the old cities and build new ones, and transfer the inhabitants from one place to another; in short, he should leave nothing unchanged in that province, so that there should be neither rank nor grade nor honor nor wealth that should not be recognized as coming from him. He should take Philip of Macedon, father of Alexander, for his model, who, by proceeding in that manner, became from a petty king, master of all Greece. And his historian tells us that he transferred the inhabitants from one province to another, as shepherds move their flocks from place to place. Doubtless these means are cruel and destructive of all civilized life, and neither Christian nor human and should be avoided by everyone. In fact, the life of a private citizen would be preferable to that of a king at the expense of the ruin of so many human beings. Nonetheless, whoever is unwilling to adopt the first and human course must, if he wishes to maintain his power, follow the latter evil course.

It is doubtful that one could produce a more typical slice from out of Machiavelli's manifold speculations on the gaining and the maintaining of power. Here we begin characteristically with an indefinite pronoun subject, "whoever" (*chi* in Italian). And we get, through this introduction of the pronoun, the statement of a general rule for action with regard to a particular situation. From this we come to the specific supporting example in history—here Philip. Then, for a moment at least, there is judgment pronounced on the action (and that is why I choose this passage rather than one in the *Prince* where the judgment would be carefully omitted): "Doubtless these means are cruel and destructive of all civilized life and neither Christian nor human and should be avoided by everyone."

Then, following the moment of judgment, that striking and most familiar turn of thought—return of thought in this case—which we recognize at once for Machiavelli's. We come back to the "whoever": Nonetheless, whoever is unwilling to adopt the first and human course must, if he wishes to maintain his power, follow the latter evil course." We see clearly what happens: by this last turn of thought, we are returned to the particular perspective from which the statement of the general rule is given, to the "whoever wishes" angle of vision—and we look from there. Looking from there, we no longer *go behind* the will to maintain power at any cost, neither do we in any way transcend it.

In the syntax of this Florentine's thought there is no element more common than this clause beginning with the pronoun *chi—whoever*—followed by a verb of volition. Either it is a "whoever" clause or it is an "if" clause, and that verb of desiring everywhere writ large. We readily see why this is so. Such a construction is the very instrument, the dialectic pattern, by which Machiavelli casts the action contemplated into the perspective of art. The "if" clause gives us precisely such a frame, staging that perspective in which an agent looks to an action which is to pass into outward matter, which must impress there a particular form and maintain that form. We do not go behind the will to question its direction. Or rather, having our passage from the *Discourses* in mind, we might say that for a moment we can and do stand in judgment on this action. But then, suddenly, we pivot again on that *whoever* and we slip back into the perspective of art. The *surrender* to the particular pattern of it is what is so striking. "Nonetheless whoever wishes . . . ," and there we are, looking along an angle of vision which is completely unconcerned with anything except *finis operis,* the work to be done. It is happening on almost every page of Machiavelli's writings on politics.

I shall be far from the first to remark how frequent is the metaphor of the work of art (in our broader sense) in the *Prince* and in the *Discourses.* I cite only two from the many instances of it. From the *Discourses:*

> The Roman people, then, admiring the wisdom and goodness of Numa, yielded in all things to his advice. It is true that those were very religious times, and the people with whom Numa had to deal were very untutored and superstitious, which made it easy for him to carry out his designs, *being able to impress upon them any new form.* And doubtless if anyone wanted to establish a republic at the present time he would find it much

easier with the simple mountaineers, who are almost without civilization, than with such as are accustomed to live in cities where civilization is already corrupt; *as a sculptor finds it easier to make a fine statue out of a crude block of marble than out of a statue badly begun by another.*

Not only does the figure of the Prince as artist come out very clearly in such passages, but (as part of the same perspective) a concern with the nature of the artist's materials. In our engineering schools we have a standard course usually entitled "the strength of materials." A good part of Machiavelli's writings could stand under such a heading.

Or, to take another example from the *Prince* where we follow the brief course of that shooting star named Cesare Borgia, the metaphor of the architect and the builder emerges time and again:

> For, as we have said, he who does not lay his foundations beforehand may by great ability do so afterwards although with great trouble to the *architect* and danger to the *building*. If then one considers the procedure of the Duke, it will be seen how firm were the *foundations* he had laid to his future power.

And earlier in the treatise where we consider the issue of *virtù* versus *fortuna* in such great figures as Moses, Cyrus, Romulus, and the like, we read: "And in examining their life and deeds, it will be seen that they owed nothing to fortune but the opportunity which gave them *the matter to be shaped into what form they thought fit.*"

"Matter to be shaped into what form they thought fit." The perspective of art is the perspective of *homo faber*. Clearly *homo faber* is the role in which Machiavelli is forever casting his hero. In five years Cesare Borgia lays his foundations admirably well. And as we follow him, it is the edifice to be built, the soundness of the structure, that concerns us. Any question of the good—of the moral good—is completely excluded. Like Cesare's eye, our eye is held fixed, in this desperate struggle, upon the structure to be fashioned.

Indeed we may pause to reflect that the word *virtù* which continues to give the translators so much trouble (and will continue) finds its true meaning in Machiavelli's usage only within the frame of the perspective of art. For, to come back to that distinction between two modes of action, *making* and *doing*, it should be clear that *virtù* may look along either way, and along either way find a meaning. In Machiavelli it is only along the way of *making*, where *virtù* is consequently the power essentially to make, to impress a form upon matter, durably—or as durably as possible. *Virtù* is the power of the sculptor, of the forger.

As we all very well know from that famous chapter of the *Prince* where the treatise turns to consider the qualities a ruler ought to have, Ma-

chiavelli was clearly aware of breaking with the traditional line of speculation on rule and rulers:

> It now remains to be seen what are the methods and rules for a Prince as
> regards his subjects and friends. And as I know that many have written of
> this, I fear that my writing about it may be deemed presumptuous, differ-
> ing as I do, especially in this matter, from the opinions of others. But my
> intention being to write something of use to those who understand, it ap-
> pears to me more proper to pursue the effectual truth of the matter than its
> imagination; many have imagined republics and principalities which have
> never been seen or known to exist in reality; for how we live is so far re-
> moved from how we ought to live, that he who abandons what is done for
> what ought to be done, will rather learn to bring about his own ruin than
> his preservation.

Even as it is with the term *virtù*, so it is with *effectual truth*, the key
term in this passage (and one also troublesome to translators and commentators): that is, we can understand the meaning of *verità effettuale* only
within the frame of that same dominant pattern in Machiavelli's thought,
the perspective of art. For within that pattern, as we know, it is precisely
the issue, the result, the product, *bonum operis*, which is contemplated,
and that alone. By the product is the truth of the rule given to be measured and judged. It is really not a term that ought to give much trouble.
It is merely a question of seeing the frame of reference by which it finds its
meaning. In Aristotle's *On the Heavens*, I find a passage which could serve
as an excellent gloss to this test of Machiavelli's for truth:

> In the confidence that the principles are true they are ready to accept any
> consequence of their application. As though some principles did not require
> to be judged from their results and particularly from their final issue. And
> that issue, in the case of productive knowledge [what better term for
> Machiavelli's "effectual truth"?] is the product.

All too often one hears that Machiavelli is one for whom the end justifies the means. This is not quite right. To say *justify* is to run the risk of
admitting the idea of justice which is quite excluded from the perspective
of art. Better say, the means are judged from and by the end.

With effectual truth (productive knowledge), we come to the necessity of a distinction which to my mind is too often not made. Up to this
point we have been looking mainly at Machiavelli's hero, the maker, the
artist. But what of Machiavelli himself, he who is casting this hero in this
particular role and who here speaks out about his concern with a particular kind of truth? How do we place *Machiavelli* with respect to the frame
of art? Is he too in that perspective? Clearly not, for in that frame there is
no question of truth but only of production, of result. The role of Machiavelli the author is not that of *homo faber*, but of *homo sapiens* or *sciens*.

The Prince is an artist but Machiavelli himself is a scientist, staking *his* reputation on an accumulated store of knowledge which is productive knowledge—"know how."

Machiavelli is very much the experimental scientist, finding his laboratory either in the contemporary arena of political struggle or in history, ancient or recent. In those two fields, past or present, he sets up his experiment. There, like a true scientist, he is interested in the particular instance only in so far as it may disclose a general principle. Cesare Borgia or Numa Pompilius, it does not matter: either, or many another, will serve the purpose. Both are pawns for the experimental scientist. Have not all readers of Machiavelli felt how his heroes have no inside?—a passing proof of which fact being our total lack of any sense whatever of tragedy at the death of Cesare Borgia. It matters little to us that his career is so prematurely ended, when his foundations are barely laid; and if he had been strangled by Vitellozzo instead of its being the other way around, it would still have made little difference to us. We are never really inside Cesare, because Cesare has no inside. He is only a particular outpost of observation in the field of political action, from which post the scientist can make observations leading to general principles: a means, like all the other figures who move as artists through these pages, an instrument by which Machiavelli can survey some particular sector of concrete reality "out there," some real situation. And always we are moving toward the "regola generale," our direction is from the particular to the general. But we come to the particular already having the desire for the general. Otherwise it would never yield it. In the exposition, of course, it will often be the other way around. We shall *begin* with the statement of a *regola generale*, with that indefinite "whoever" clause or that "if" clause with its verb of volition.

Nothing is more impressive in Machiavelli's thought than the way in which he can move about on the whole field of political action—that field for which alone he was born, as he puts it in a famous letter—looking now over the shoulder of this player in the terrible game, and now over the shoulder of that player, sizing up the chances of success, now from here and now from there. It is that freedom of his from any commitment to any particular cause which is so striking.

Near the beginning of the *Prince* we come to a characteristic passage. Machiavelli has begun to treat of mixed monarchies and foreign invasions; and, for a moment, turns to consider the case of Louis XII of France and his invasion of Italy:

> But let us return to France and examine whether it did any of these things; and I will speak not of Charles, but of Louis as the one whose proceedings can be better seen, since he held possession in Italy longer; you will then see that he did the opposite of all those things which must be done to keep possession of a foreign state. King Louis was called into Italy by the ambition of the Venetians who wished by his coming to gain half of Lombardy.

I will not blame the King for coming nor for the part he took, because *wishing* to set his foot into Italy and not having friends in that country and, on the contrary, the conduct of King Charles having caused all doors to be closed to him, he was forced to accept what friendships he could find and his scheme would have speedily been successful if he had made no mistakes in his other proceedings.

"I will not blame the king for coming into Italy." But why will Machiavelli not blame Louis? In a final chapter of this work he will condemn him and all other invaders of Italy most vehemently, exhorting his young Medici prince to seize the country and free her from these barbarians. But we know the answer to the question. It was not from any such position in patriotism that Machiavelli had worked as scientist to accumulate his great store of effectual truths. Not in any commitment to a cause had he worked, but precisely in complete freedom from any commitment. And here with Louis we note the pattern of thought that we met in the passage in the *Discourses*. Here is the familiar perspective of art: Louis contemplating a line of action by which he may gain power and impose his will upon a certain material—in this case, Italy. And as we hold to that perspective, of course we do not blame Louis. We do not go back of that will to question it or judge it. We do not demand that the action be a *good* action.

What we are observing is that Machiavelli the scientist is quite as free as is his projected hero, the artist. Indeed, it is important to note that what they have in common, these two, projector and projected, is precisely what they stand free from. The hero in the role of *homo faber*, in the frame of art, is free from any concern with moral good, with soul, with inward things or last things, with salvation. And this by definition. This is as it should be with *homo faber*. But so too is this mind that projects this action and speculates on it, this Machiavelli who casts that hero in such a role, using him as the instrument of his science. In the order of knowing, even as in the order of making, a complete freedom from concern with inward things. Like the artist, the scientist is turned entirely toward "bona exteriora," quite away from "bona interiora." The perspective of effectual truth in the order of knowing is completely faithful to that of art in the order of making.

This is so entirely the case that it becomes almost too easy a matter for us to take our own measure of Machiavelli's rupture with traditional speculation on political order, on rule and rulers. There could be no more effective way of taking this measure perhaps than to imagine that, early in the *Prince*, Socrates and his group of the *Republic* were somehow permitted to break in upon the discussion, so that it is turned into a dialogue. We can readily see what would begin to happen. Soon the course of dialectic would begin to shift, a new drift and sea change would begin to prevail, subtle perhaps at first. For we should begin to get such questions as those voiced in the *Republic* by Adeimantus and Glaucon, following Thrasymachus' sally: "You appear rather, Machiavelli (we hear some one say), to have no care or thought about us: whether we live better or worse for not knowing what you say you know, is to you a matter of indifference."

The new tide would begin soon to get the whole discussion over on other grounds, ideas of justice and injustice, wisdom and the good, would come in. We hear another voice: "But whether the just have a better and happier life than the unjust is a further question which we also propose to consider. I think we ought to examine further, for no light matter is at stake, nothing less than the rule of human life." Or here now is Glaucon saying: "Setting aside their rewards and results, I want to know what these things are in themselves, and how they work inwardly in the soul." And here is Adeimantus:

> No one has ever adequately described, either in verse or in prose, the true essential nature of either justice or injustice abiding in the soul and invisible either to any human or divine eye. Or shown that of all things in a man's soul which he has within him justice is the greatest good and injustice the greatest evil. . . . I would ask you to show not only the superiority which justice has over injustice, but what *effect they have on the possessor of them.* . . . I would ask you in your praise of justice to regard one point only: I mean the essential good and evil which justice and injustice *work in the possessors of them.* . . . And therefore I say not only prove to us that justice is better than injustice, but show what they either of them do to the possessor of them, which makes one to be a good and another an evil, whether seen or unseen by Gods and men.

But by this time Niccolò Machiavelli is quite ready to quit the room in complete disgust. For these questions, these desires to know such things, are completely disrupting the method of his science, collapsing his instrument, the perspective of art. Over the frame of that perspective is written: Abandon concern with these inward things, you who enter here.

May I be permitted one more quotation from Aristotle? I cannot but think it quite relevant since it concerns the matter of truth in practical matters, which remains ever close to the matter of effectual truth and politics. Indeed, it comes in that concluding part of the *Ethics* where that work appears to be looking already toward the treatise on Politics:

> The truth in practical matters is discerned from the facts of life; for these are the decisive factor. We must therefore survey what we have already said, bringing it to the test of the facts of life. And if it harmonizes with the facts we must accept it, but if it clashes with them we must suppose it to be mere theory.

Very close indeed to what Machiavelli was saying when he spoke of his break with the tradition. "Mere theory" sounds very much like *his* label for those imagined republics and principalities which never existed. And

Aristotle's "truth in practical matters," this "test by the facts of life" which he sets up, seems most like Machiavelli's effectual truth.

But is not this "test by the facts of life" one to which every age subscribes, from Aristotle to Machiavelli, and from Machiavelli to us? Do not all, in all times, generally agree? Yet what are these facts? There is very much the rub. And there precisely is the importance of the kind of pattern of thought that I have wanted to examine here: a perspective of art, a most valuable instrument because by means of it a selection may be made upon the total facts of life, by which our concern with these facts is so framed as to *leave out* as well as to *admit*. By that tool our attention can be directed and confined to certain aspects only of the total field of vision; confined, in this particular mode, to *bona exteriora* and to the form to be imprinted thereon; leaving out all concern with *bona interiora* and what is good or not good for the agent.

It is all very well to say approvingly with Bacon that Machiavelli deals with what men do, not with what they ought to do. We are merely taking Machiavelli on his own terms, in putting it so. We are simply agreeing with him in his *initial selection* of the facts of life, agreeing with him to leave out all concern with that other form of action which is *doing* and not *making*, which abides in the agent—but is surely as much a part of the facts as is the other.

Back along the way we were observing, it seemed to me, something of importance in that point seen in common between the projector and the projected, between the scientist and the artist, in their common freedom from concern with interior things, in their common extroversion. We were seeing how the perspective of art is the mutual bond and negotiable tie between an order of knowing and an order of making, the common frame on which they agree, saying just what they do agree should be left out of the picture: and shall we call *that* "concern with soul"?

The problem of science as it arises—(let us not say *in the Renaissance*, for that is begging the question, since we shall know the Renaissance by this very arising)—the problem of science as it arises in the Middle Ages and in the total frame of thought of that time, is *the problem of confining the attention*. If we come to this matter from the other side in time and out of the total medieval frame, we see that modern science can only arise and develop if the attention can be confined. But how shall this be done? The perspective of art is the clearest example I know, of one way: that "whoever" clause or that "if" clause in Machiavelli, by which a particular interest and angle of vision is set up. A circle is drawn. We agree to limit our attention to these confines. And the remarkable thing about it with Machiavelli is that this is a construction put upon a *human* activity—human actors are here staged and framed—actors who presumably have insides, who know and have access to and some concern with *bona interiora*.

In saying this I am thinking of the great difference of the problem for Machiavelli and for Galileo, one an observer of the movements of men, the other of stones and stars. Clearly there is a radical difference in the nature of what moves on their two contemplated fields. Stones and stars have no inside to be gotten out of them and you would therefore think it easier for Galileo, in that his field is already cleared for purposes of science in a way that Machiavelli's can be only after the application of the eliminating and excluding perspective of art. But we know of Galileo's struggle to clear his field, or to claim it as one, by nature, cleared. Somehow, even though stones and stars have no inside to be gotten out of the picture, stones and stars did have a way of carrying along with them, still clinging to them, an attachment to soul, a concern, in the spectator, with *bona interiora*. There are many eloquent passages in the *Dialogue of the Two Principal Systems*. We have time for only one.

Simplicio is holding to the old view (of course, and what is a Simplicio for?) that the heavenly bodies are smooth orbs, eternal, inalterable, incorruptible, quite out of reach of all sublunar physics. And Sagredo, speaking for Galileo, is meeting this view head on and most vigorously:

> I cannot without great wonder, I will say, repugnance of mind, hear it attributed to natural bodies as a great honor and perfection that they are impassable, immutable, inalterable, etc., and, on the contrary, hear it considered a great imperfection, to be alterable, generable, mutable, etc. As for me, I hold the earth to be the most noble and admirable by reason of so many and such diverse alterations, mutations, generations, which take place in her incessantly. And if, without being subject to any mutation whatever, she had been a vast desert of sand or a mass of jasper, or if in the time of the deluge the waters that covered her had frozen and she had remained an immense crystal globe where no thing ever was born or altered or changed, I would consider her an ugly body, useless, full of idleness and in a word, superfluous, as though being no part of nature. . . . Those who so much extol incorruptibility, inalterability, etc., bring themselves to say these things, I believe, out of a great desire to live a long time and out of the fear they have of death; and they do not consider that if men were immortal they had no business coming into the world. These persons would deserve to meet with a Medusa's head that would transform them into statues of jasper or diamond, so that they might become more perfect than they are.

Sagredo, alias Galileo, has put his finger squarely on the point. In the eye which had contemplated those heavenly bodies as Simplicio still persisted in doing, there was an ever present (though often unconscious) concern for soul, concern with last things, with escape out of flux to eternity; "desire to live a long time and fear of death," Sagredo puts it scornfully. Those orbs, to such an eye, had been symbols. They had pointed beyond themselves. We remember Dante's *stelle*, ever pointing upward and beyond, ending each of the three canticles of a journey to God.

But Galileo's science, even as Machiavelli's, requires that concern with soul be kept out of the picture. This means, for Galileo, getting symbolism out of nature and keeping it out. Simplicio, let us say, had double vision (though he may not have known it and might well protest that it was simply *whole* vision.) Sagredo and Salviati are trying to school him in single vision, or what is for him, partial vision. The purposes of the new science require that the attention be confined, so as to exclude concern with soul. The new science requires that the mind learn to remain within the enclosure of partial vision, which has made a selection out of the field of total concern. But the new science of nature could not use the perspective of art (since it was not dealing with men) and had to resort to other dialectical stratagems.

I leave Galileo for a moment to meet a question which I feel has been left open along the way. The considerable time which was taken in my beginning to find and distinguish the perspective of art in the thought of Thomas Aquinas must have left you wondering what I intended to make of the fact that we *then* find that frame of thought in Machiavelli. Am I suggesting that Machiavelli was a student of the *Summa?* And that he took the conception from there, gleefully saying, "Ah, here's something I can use!" But I know that you do not think I mean this. What then is the connection or interest?

Clearly the interest is in a pattern of thought which confines the attention so as to exclude concern with the inner man. And this, within the frame of a medieval philosophy where that pattern is not thought applicable to politics. Then, as we look beyond, it is no question of influence. We simply meet the pattern in Machiavelli and recognize it—and see that with him it *is* applied to politics. It is the same pattern, but now it is put upon an area of human activity where it had not been allowed in the thought of Aquinas following Aristotle. Now, it is not only the shift in the categories, in the application, that I would point to; though it would be difficult to exaggerate the implications of that fact, the signal therein contained of revolution in the history of thought. It is not only the new, the revolutionary, that I would point to, but the old and the continuing as well. The Middle Ages knew the perspective of art (unless we are going to claim Aquinas for the Renaissance); that perspective had been contained by a medieval philosophy where it was part of a whole fabric. The instance is most familiar and *that* is our interest in it. How often, how at every turn the historian of the Renaissance is meeting up with just this situation! A mode of thought, a mould of thought, which is no achievement of the Renaissance. There it is before. And the particular application and the exclusive and *excluding* cultivation of that mode which *is* the achievement of the Renaissance. Modern science and much of Renaissance art are the abundant fruits out of that cultivation.

Galileo could not use the perspective of art and curiously enough, though he was not dealing with men, Galileo had a harder time than did Machiavelli in the battle for that selected world of partial vision, the battle to get concern with the inner man out of the contemplated field. Galileo may not have felt entirely sure of his victory. But we who come after know that the victory was sure, though it was not his alone. For there were many minds working to that same end. There, in the same decade, was Descartes putting a seal upon it in his philosophy, finding *res cogitans* quite excluded from *res extensa*. And beyond Descartes lies the overwhelming triumph of the single and purified vision of science—and of Newton's sleep.

Meanwhile the inner man, the cultivation of *bona interiora* in the perspective of prudence, is left to men of letters, the humanists. Perhaps it is appropriate, on this anniversary, to recall that Leonardo prided himself on *not* being one of them. For the men of letters were already settling for what was left over from the whole field of vision on which a perspective of art (or its equivalent) was making a selection, staking out a claim which science would continue to think was much the better part.

20

Machiavelli's Concept
of Virtù Reconsidered

NEAL WOOD

Although much has been written on the question of Machiavelli's use of *virtù*,[1] some of it illuminating, little effort has been made generally to evaluate the concept in a rigorous fashion, for example, by a careful study of the con-

This article was originally published in *Political Studies*, 15 (June 1967), 159–172. It is reprinted here with the permission of the author and of the publisher, Clarendon Press, Oxford, England.
[1] Listed below are the discussions of *virtù* of twenty commentators on Machiavelli, all either written in English or translated into English. They include students of literature, historians, philosophers, political scientists. Some are specialists on Machiavelli and the Renaissance; others are generalists.

    J. W. Allen, *A History of Political Thought in the Sixteenth Century* (London, 1928), pp. 457, 472, 477; L. Arthur Burd, "Florence (II): Machiavelli," *The Cambridge Modern History* (Cambridge, 1902), Vol. I, p. 210; Herbert Butterfield, *The Statecraft of Machiavelli* (New York, 1962), p. 39; Ernst Cassirer, *The Myth of the State* (Garden City, N.Y., 1955), pp. 198–203; Federico Chabod, *Machiavelli and the Renaissance,* tr. David Moore (London, 1958), pp. 40–41, 95–96; Francesco DeSanctis, *History of Italian Literature,* tr. Joan Redfern (New York, 1931), Vol. II, pp. 549–550, 553, 559, 563–564, 583–585; Allan H. Gilbert, *Machiavelli's Prince and Its Forerunners* (Durham, N.C., 1938), pp. 68, 110, 147, 207–208; Felix Gilbert, "On Machiavelli's Idea of Virtù," *Renaissance News,* IV (1951), pp. 53–54; *Machiavelli*

text of usage. Where analysis of this kind might be expected, analysis is not forthcoming. Moreover, few scholars seem to have pondered the exact nature of the relationship of *virtù* to the other elements of Machiavelli's thought, to have probed its role in his total intellectual perspective.

One of the more notable exceptions to the general lack of analysis in discussions of *virtù* is J. H. Whitfield's admirable essay, "The Anatomy of Virtue." [2] Professor Whitfield's conclusions rest upon careful linguistic evaluation. His argument goes thus. The most commonly held view, which originated with Francesco DeSanctis, is that *virtù* is force and energy of mind used for good or bad purposes. By holding this position, DeSanctis and his emulators proclaim that Machiavelli abandons moral virtue. In reply, Whitfield denies (1) that this is a correct representation of Machiavelli's stand; (2) that his use of language is precise and systematic; (3) that a single doctrine of *virtù* can be discovered in his works. The ambiguity of *virtù* is due to the different meanings given to the word by Machiavelli, and they cannot be reconciled by a single comprehensive meaning. Machiavelli sometimes uses *virtù* as virtue, in opposition to vice (*vizio*) and vileness (*viltà*), as he also employs other terms to denote moral goodness such as *bontà*, and good (*buono*), and honest (*onesto*), in contrast to bad (*cattivo*) and wicked (*tristo*). Although his most frequent antonym of *virtù* is fortune (*fortuna*), indolence (*ozio*) and fury (*furore*) are also used as opposites. Again Machiavelli occasionally adopts the current biological designation of *virtù* as life-force. *Virtù* also sometimes stands for bravery and valour. Finally Machiavelli often uses *virtù* as if it were the Latin *virtus*, energy of will, manliness, excellence, and the plural of *virtù* to correspond with the Latin plural, *virtutes*, good actions or qualities. Of these two, the latter tends to be a more stable usage in Machiavelli's writing. In addition Machiavelli seems to have followed a special use by Cicero of *virtus*, and a meaning similar to that of Cicero given by Dante to *virtù*, a kind of energetic decisiveness. Hence Machiavelli's well-known condemnation of the middle way, of indecisiveness, of inactivity; but he always prefers the good use of energy, for

and Guicciardini: Politics and History in Sixteenth-Century Florence (Princeton, 1965), pp. 179–200; Hiram Haydn, *The Counter-Renaissance* (New York, 1960), pp. 426–427, 441–442; Friedrich Meinecke, *Machiavellism*, tr. Douglas Scott (New Haven, Conn., 1957), pp. 31–44; Leonardo Olschki, *Machiavelli the Scientist* (Berkeley, 1945), pp. 27, 35–36, 40–41; John Plamenatz, *Man and Society* (London, 1963), Vol. I, p. 29; Gerhard Ritter, *The Corrupting Influence of Power*, tr. F. W. Pick (Cowley, Oxford, 1952), pp. 20, 30–40, 189; George H. Sabine, *A History of Political Theory* (New York, 3d ed., 1961), pp. 344–346; Charles S. Singleton, "The Perspective of Art," *The Kenyon Review*, XV (1953), pp. 172–173, 178; Leo Strauss, *Thoughts on Machiavelli* (Glencoe, Ill., 1958), pp. 47, 162, 216–217, 227, 242–257, 263–269; Pasquale Villari, *The Life and Times of Machiavelli*, tr. Linda Villari (London, 1904), Vol. I, pp. 92, 106, 146, 221, 301–302, 514–516; Leslie J. Walker, *The Discourses of Niccolò Machiavelli* (New Haven, Conn., 1950), Vol. I, pp. 99–102, 116–117, 133; J. H. Whitfield, *Machiavelli* (Oxford, 1947), pp. 92–105; Sheldon S. Wolin, *Politics and Vision* (Boston and Toronto, 1960), pp. 200, 215, 229–231, 236–238.

[2] Whitfield, pp. 92–105.

example, as a contribution to the common good, to the wicked use of energy. Hence, Whitfield succinctly indicates some of the difficulties and the pitfalls in the assessment of Machiavelli's meaning.

While I certainly agree with Professor Whitfield that Machiavelli's use of *virtù* is highly ambiguous, and that no simple formula will do justice to his meaning, I wish to argue that the very plurality of meaning suggests a special meaning. In order to advance this hypothesis, I shall attempt to compile a catalogue of Machiavelli's men of *virtù*. The conclusions of this effort will then be related to Machiavelli's fullest discussion of *virtù*, that contained in the *Arte della guerra*.

I

The following, therefore, is a list of the fifty-three individuals specifically referred to as virtuous by Machiavelli in *Il Principe* and the *Discorsi*.[3] I make no claim that the list is definitive; a few names may have been overlooked.

Aemilius Paullus	Manlius Capitolinus
Aeneus	Manlius Torquatus
Agesilaus	Marc Antony
Agathocles	Marcus Aurelius
Alexander the Great	Marcus Cato the Elder
Antonius Primus	Marcus Cato the Younger
Aratus	Mohamet the Turk
Camillus	Moses
Carmagnola	Mucius Scaevola
Cesare Borgia	Oliverotto da Fermo
Cincinnatus	Ottaviano Fregoso
Coriolanus	Papirius Cursor
Cyrus the Great	Pelopidas
David	Philip of Macedon
Decius Mus the Elder	Pompey
Decius Mus the Younger	Regulus Atilius
Dion	Romulus
Epaminondas	Septimius Severus
Fabricius	Scipio Africanus the Elder
Francesco Sforza	Solon
Gonzalo de Córdoba	Tempanius
Hannibal	Themistocles
Hiero	Theseus
Horatius	Timoleon
Julius Caesar	Tullus Hostilius
Junius Brutus	Valerius Corvinus
Lycurgus	

[3] The texts of *Il Principe*, *Discorsi*, and *Istorie Fiorentine*, are those of Machiavelli, *Opere*, ed. Mario Bonfantini (Milan and Naples, 1954). The Arabic numerals in citations refer to the pages of this edition.

Leo X, Numa Pompilius, and Savonarola have been omitted from the list. In *Il*

The compendium of names is enlightening for several reasons. First, it confirms what is most obvious even to the casual reader of *Il Principe* and the *Discorsi:* Machiavelli's heroes are largely ancients. *Virtù* is attributed to six contemporaries only: Carmagnola, a noted *condottiere* who served Milan and Venice; Cesare Borgia, brilliant and iniquitous soldier-son of Pope Alexander VI; Francesco Sforza, founder of the Duchy of Milan; Gonzalo de Córdoba, the Spanish conqueror of Naples; Oliverotto Euffreducci, tyrant of Fermo; Ottaviano Fregoso, Genoese patriot.[4] Second, among the ancients over half are Romans, a predominance quite in keeping with Machiavelli's view that Rome possessed more *virtù* than any other state. Third, the large majority of Roman heroes lived prior to the outbreak of the first Punic War, after which time, Machiavelli believes, corruption began gradually to set in. Likewise, most of the non-Roman ancients lived before this period. Both these facts simply reflect Machiavelli's faith in the great concentration of *virtù* in the ancient Mediterranean world before the establishment of the Roman Empire. Fourth, and most important from the standpoint of our problem, is the fact that the heroes, ancient and modern, are men of action, not philosophers or men of learning. The only ones who can possibly qualify for the latter category are Marcus Aurelius and Solon. Marcus Aurelius was a competent administrator who faced almost impossible practical problems and ably led his forces in battle. Solon was a citizen-soldier, a commander in the field and a statesman, as well as a man of letters. Moreover, not only is everyone on the list a man of action, but also of a particular type of action. They are warriors, soldiers, generals. The five contemporaries are all in this category. Renowned generals, Epaminondas, Philip of Macedon, Alexander the Great, and Hannibal, are among the non-Roman military figures. The Roman heroes are primarily citizen-soldiers, among whom, of course, are the virtuosi in the art of war, Scipio Africanus and Julius Caesar.

Does Machiavelli consider any of these individuals more virtuous than others, and if so who are they and how does he describe them? Some of the figures are simply virtuous; others possess so much *virtù* that they are able to accomplish successfully this or that extremely perilous undertaking. The *virtù* of a small minority is superlative. Belonging to this latter group are the great founders, Moses, Cyrus, Romulus, and Theseus. In his discussion of new states that have been formed on the basis of the *virtù*

Principe, XI, 39, Leo is praised as a man of infinite *virtù* and goodness, but Machiavelli must be writing with tongue in cheek. Although Machiavelli refers briefly to the *virtù* of Numa Pompilius, the successor of Romulus, the emphasis is upon his goodness and prudence, not his *virtù*. He is only able to rule successfully and to strengthen the Roman constitution by introducing the fundamental Roman religious institutions because of the respite secured through the great *virtù* of Romulus. See *Discorsi,* I, xi, 124; xix, 143–144. Machiavelli refers only to the reflection of *virtù dello animo* in Savonarola's writings, perhaps a way of intimating that the priest's actions lacked *virtù*. See *Discorsi,* I, xlv, 186; III, xxx, 387.

[4] *Principe,* VII, 22; XII, 42; *Discorsi,* I, xxix, 156; xxiv, 287.

and arms of a single individual, Machiavelli contends that of all such men, these four founders are *li più eccellenti*.[5] And again he refers to their *eccellente virtù*. Of the four only Moses and Romulus are specifically termed virtuous in the *Discorsi;* Moses in passing, while the exploits of Romulus and his claim to eternal glory are fully analysed.[6] Next to the founders, if not equal to them in *virtù*, are three exceptional military commanders: Camillus, and those superb antagonists, Scipio Africanus and Hannibal. Camillus, Machiavelli avers, is one of the most memorable of Romans. Rome was brought back to her original principles and saved from an early corruption by an extrinsic blow of fortune, the invasion of the Gauls in 392 B.C. At the time of disaster, it is the *virtù* of Camillus that rallied his fellow citizens, freed his city, and saved the republic.[7] Machiavelli cites the military *virtù* of Camillus, twice mentions his *virtù* and *bontà*, and asserts that he is *buono* and *savio*.[8] Moreover, Machiavelli calls him the most prudent of all Roman captains.[9] Both Scipio and Hannibal are men of extraordinary and excessive *virtù*.[10] The prudence of Scipio and his other memorable virtues are emphasized.[11] Hannibal, despite his ruthless cruelty, in marked contrast to the humaneness of Scipio, possesses infinite *virtù*.[12] Three other persons whose *virtù* is exceptional but not the equal of that of Camillus, Scipio, and Hannibal, are the two Roman commanders, Manlius Torquatus and Valerius Corvinus, and the Emperor, Septimius Severus.[13] Each of these ten of the most virtuous of the virtuous are warriors. Four are founders, five, including one of the founders, Cyrus, are brilliant commanders, and one, Septimius Severus, is an exceptionally able soldier who seized power and retained it throughout his life, albeit in a most despotic fashion.

Who are the men who lack *virtù?* Here our analysis is confronted by a major obstacle, because, upon the basis of Machiavelli's writings, it is impossible to compile a comprehensive list of such a kind. I should again stress that my previous list consists only of the individuals specifically described by Machiavelli as virtuous. It would be utterly fallacious to infer that all the countless others mentioned, but not so described, are in his mind deficient in *virtù*. He is not the meticulous author of a scientific treatise that can be read in this manner. Undoubtedly he fails to include the names of some whom he considers virtuous, and neglects to refer to the *virtù* of some whom he does include. Moreover, no man is absolutely virtuous, or without virtue, and somewhere between the two extremes is a

[5] *Principe*, VI, 18–19.
[6] *Discorsi*, I, i, 92–93; xix, 143–144.
[7] *Discorsi*, I, viii, 113.
[8] *Discorsi*, III, i, 310; xxiii, 375; xxx, 386–387.
[9] *Discorsi* III xii, 354.
[10] *Discorsi*, III, xxi, 369–370.
[11] *Discorsi*, I, xxix, 157.
[12] *Principe*, XVII, 55.
[13] *Principe*, XIX, 64; *Discorsi*, I, x, 121; III, xix, 366; xxii, 373.

range of varying degrees of *virtù*. That A is more virtuous than B, but less so than C, does not necessarily signify that B, any more than A, is without *virtù*. Machiavelli's impressionism is of little aid in sorting out these problems. Finally the difficulties are compounded by the absence of any single word or phrase employed consistently to denote the opposite of *virtù* or its absence. About the best one can do is to examine each case, to study the author's remarks, and then to draw up a rather sketchy list of those who most obviously are the men of least *virtù*.

If we begin with the ancients, we find several categories of such individuals. First, there are the tyrants of antiquity, about whom Machiavelli is often critical: Pisistratus of Athens, Aristotemus of Epirus, Nabis of Sparta, Phalaris of Agrigentum, Dionysius II of Syracuse.[14] But, as we have seen, not all tyrants are without *virtù*, for example, Agathocles, Septimius Severus, and Oliverotto da Fermo.[15] The difference seems to be that the latter were able to crush their foes, and proved to be strong, vigorous, and decisive leaders. Both Agathocles and Severus died natural deaths. The last king of Rome, Tarquinius Superbus, is certainly viewed by Machiavelli as a tyrant of little *virtù*.[16] Nevertheless, Numa Pompilius, successor to Romulus, is a good king without great *virtù*, who makes important contributions to the commonwealth. Non-Roman kings like Solomon, Rehoboam, and Sultan Bazaret are good, not virtuous men, men of peace, not war who, with the exception of Rehoboam, are fortunate enough to succeed rulers of *virtù*.[17] Machiavelli has little regard for despotic princes, many of whom were legitimate, who proved ineffectual in their struggles with leaders and peoples of *virtù*: Croesus of Lydia, Darius III of Persia, Antiochus III of Syria, Philip V of Macedon and his son, Perseus.[18] Another category includes Roman citizens who attempted to overthrow the republic: the sons of Junius Brutus, Spurius Maelius, Appius Claudius and Quintus Fabius of the Decemvirate.[19] But Coriolanus, Manlius Capitolinus, and Julius Caesar, all guilty of treasonable actions, are virtuous.[20] Citizens who prove deficient on the field of battle also belong to the list: Sergius and Virginius, Varro, M. Centenius Penula, Lucius Minucius, and Marcus Minucius.[21] Yet Fabius Maximus, highly successful in his tactics against Hannibal, is never referred to as a man of *virtù*.[22] The Roman emperors make up a last category.[23] Of them only Marcus Aurelius and Septimius Severus are desig-

[14] *Discorsi*, I, ii, 98–99; x, 119; xxviii, 154; III, vi, 327–328.
[15] *Principe*, VIII, 28–31; XIX, 62–67; *Discorsi*, I, x, 121.
[16] *Discorsi*, III, ii, 314–315; iv, 317–318; v. 318–320.
[17] *Discorsi*, I, xix, 143–144.
[18] *Principe*, III, 10; IV, 16; XXI, 73; XXIV, 78–79; *Discorsi*, Ded., 88; II, x, 244–245; III, xxxv, 401.
[19] *Discorsi*, I, xxxv, 168–169; xlii, 183; III, i, 311; iii, 316; viii, 341; xix, 366–367.
[20] *Discorsi*, I, viii, 113; x, 119, 122; xxxiii, 164; III, i, 311; viii, 341–343; xiii, 354–355.
[21] *Discorsi*, I, xxxi, 160–161; liii, 200; III, xxv, 378.
[22] *Discorsi*, I, liii, 200–201; III, ix, 344–345; x, 346–349.
[23] *Principe*, XIX, 62–67; *Discorsi*, I, x, 120–122.

nated virtuous. The rest are termed either good or bad. Among the former are Galba, Titus, Nerva, Trajan, Hadrian, Antoninus Pius, Marcus Aurelius, Pertinax, Alexander Severus. It is not obvious that any, other than Marcus, are virtuous. The bad include Nero, Caligula, Vitellius, Commodus, Julianus, Septimius Severus, Caracalla, Macrinus, Heliogabulus, Maximinus. Of these only Septimius appears with any certainty to be virtuous.

Our task with the moderns would seem to be simplified, since *virtù* is such a rare quality among them, a point frequently stressed by Machiavelli.[24] A list of the notables of little *virtù* would evidently include some of the reigning monarchs, probably the French kings, Louis XII, and Charles VIII; and the Holy Roman Emperor, Maximilian I.[25] Ferdinand V of Spain, Francis I of France, Henry VIII of England, are ciphers on this score.[26] Most of the churchmen, especially Alexander VI and Julius II, are of little *virtù*.[27] If the flattery of Leo X is discounted, Machiavelli has a good word for only one modern pope, Sixtus IV.[28] Next would come most of the Italian princes of his lifetime: the Sforzas of Milan, d'Estes of Ferrara, Gonzagas of Mantua, Guidobaldos of Urbino, Manfredis of Faenza, Malatestas of Pesaro, Bentivoglis of Bologna and so on.[29] Particularly repellent to Machiavelli are the petty tyrants like Giovanpaolo Baglioni of Perugia and Pandolfo Petrucci of Siena.[30] One such figure, however, Oliverotto Euffreducci of Fermo, he describes in terms of his *virtù e scelleratezze*, comparing him to Agathocles, because in one daring and savage stroke he eliminates all who might oppose his seizure of power and subsequent rule, including his uncle and protector.[31] Florentines fare poorly at the hands of Machiavelli, and his attitude toward the Medici is at best lukewarm.[32] His city has produced good, law-abiding citizens like Savonarola and Soderini, who, however, do not possess sufficent *virtù* to contend with the corruption of their age.[33] As Machiavelli laments, only one hope for Italy, in the person of Cesare Borgia, has appeared in recent times, and he was struck down by *fortuna* at the very outset of his career.[34] In a final category fall the military commanders. At least among the Italians, with

---

[24] For example, *Principe*, XXVI, 83–85; *Discorsi*, I, Proemio, 90; II, Proemio, 218–221; *Istorie Fiorentine*, I, xxxix, 616–618; *Arte della guerra*, Proemio, 326; I, 331–333; Text is that of Machiavelli, *Arte della guerra e scritti politici minori*, ed. Sergio Bertelli (Milan, 1961).

[25] *Principe*, III, 6–7, 13; XI, 37; XII, 40; XVI, 52; XXIII, 76–77.

[26] *Principe*, I, 5; XVI, 52; XXI, 71–72; *Discorsi*, I, xxi, 146; xxiii, 149; xxix, 156.

[27] *Principe*, II, 6; III, 12–13; XI, 37–38; XXV, 81–88; *Discorsi*, I, xii, 127–128; xxvii, 153; III, ix, 345.

[28] *Principe*, IX, 37.

[29] *Principe*, II, 6; III, 7, 11; XIX, 60–61; *Discorsi*, II, xxiv, 286–287.

[30] *Principe*, XX, 69; XXII, 75; *Discorsi*, I, xxvii, 153; III, vi, 322, 335, 337–338.

[31] *Principe*, VIII, 29–31.

[32] *Principe*, IX, 34; *Discorsi*, I, viii, 115; xxxiii, 164; liii, 201–202; III, vi, 322, 334, 339–340; xv, 359; xvi, 361–362.

[33] *Discorsi*, I, xlv, 186; III, iii, 316–317; ix, 345; xxx, 387.

[34] *Principe*, XXVI, 83.

the exception of Borgia, Carmagnola, Oliverotto, and Sforza, all are evidently without much *virtù*, for they form a fraternity that simply plays at war.

I conclude, therefore, that Machiavelli's men of *virtù* are predominantly warriors who triumph in circumstances of extreme danger, hardship, and chance. Success is not always proof of *virtù*, but if one fails, he must do so in a glorious fashion as Leonidas did at Thermopylae, or Cato the Younger at Utica. *Virtù* is most typically exhibited by an individual who (1) founds a commonwealth and secures it, or inherits a commonwealth and secures it; (2) conspires to seize power and, having seized it, secures it; (3) preserves or extends a commonwealth by organizing an army and commanding it, or by commanding an army already organized.[35]

II

Since Machiavelli employs *virtù* chiefly to characterize warriors, the next logical step would appear to be an examination of *virtù* in relation to war and military activity. A convenient beginning is provided by Machiavelli's general view that the ancients are more virtuous than the moderns. The key to Machiavelli's explanation may be the relation between the two terms, *ozio,* meaning indolence, idleness, a lack of energy, and *necessità,* or necessity. In the opening of the *Discorsi* he affirms that men act either through necessity or choice.[36] Greater *virtù* occurs when human actions are determined by necessity. An extremely fertile site for a city will produce *ozio* in a people.

However, rather than prescribing a sterile site for a city, Machiavelli advocates a fertile location, such as the one chosen by Romulus, in order that a large population may be supported. The laws for the fledgling state will be designed to serve as a substitute for the *necessità* of a hostile physical environment. Artifice will discourage *ozio,* and hence promote *virtù.* Machiavelli claims that such a course of action is taken by the wisest of legislators. Later he repeats his initial precept by saying that men do not act good (*bene*) except under necessity.[37] When men have some choice in their conduct, the result is confusion (*confusione*) and disorder (*disordine*). Hunger and poverty make men industrious and the laws make men good (*buoni*). Necessity, which produces *virtù,* therefore, can result either from the natural environment or from the artifice of skillfully devised and vigorously executed laws. In both passages Machiavelli identifies *virtù* with conventionally virtuous conduct (*bene, buono*), but *ozio,* not *vizio* or *cattivo,*

---

[35] These criteria are suggested by the remarks in *Principe,* XXIV, 78; *Discorsi,* I, x, 118–119; III, xiii, 356.
[36] *Discorsi,* I, i, 92–93.
[37] *Discorsi,* I, iii, 100–101.

is the opposite. Likewise in Machiavelli's fullest treatment of necessity, *virtù* does not appear.[38] A prudent commander will place his troops in a situation of necessity, so that they must either fight with determination and courage, or perish. Accordingly, the leader must also take care to avoid placing his enemy in a similar circumstance. Here, Machiavelli obviously identifies virtuous behaviour with the vigorous and courageous action of men whose only alternative is death.

Machiavelli writes that had Rome been more peaceful (*quieto*) she would have been weaker (*più debole*), and hence would never have attained grandeur and glory.[39] And then he adds that if a state is so favoured by Heaven as never to be involved in war, *ozio* will make the people effeminate or divided. Again there is no word of *virtù*. In order to show that Machiavelli is actually discussing *virtù*, and its opposite *ozio*, I must refer to parallel passages in the *Asino d'oro*, and the *Istorie Fiorentine*. In the former work Machiavelli contends that *virtù* produces peace (*tranquillità*), and from peace arises *ozio*, the destroyer of country and city.[40] *Virtù* usually returns in times of civil disorder (*disordine*), and order is restored. Since nothing is stable in the world, the cycle will evidently be repeated. In the *Istorie Fiorentine* the contention is that peace (*quiete*) springs from *virtù*, and *ozio* follows peace.[41] Disorder and ruin are the consequences of *ozio*. But from ruin, order can arise and with it *virtù*, bringing *gloria* and *fortuna*. The basic formula then of the cycle in each work is as follows:

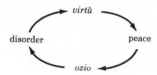

I think that Machiavelli's meaning may be summarized in the following way. Necessity generates *virtù*. War is a condition of necessity that produces *virtù*. Without war a people become indolent, weak, and effeminate, and lose their *virtù*. Although law is a kind of artificial necessity, which makes men industrious, thrifty, and respectful of authority, Machiavelli never argues that law can be a substitute for the necessity of war in rendering men virtuous. Laws must always be framed, applied, and executed by men. How is law itself to force the lawmaker to be prudent and watchful, and the magistrate to be vigorous? In order to clarify the relationship between *virtù*, *necessità*, and war, I must refer to a section in the *Arte della guerra*, Machiavelli's only complete and lucid treatment of the

---

[38] *Discorsi*, III, xii, 351–354.
[39] *Discorsi*, I, vi, 107–109; also II, xxv, 371.
[40] *Asino d'oro*, V, 831, in *Tutte le opere storiche e letterarie di Niccolò Machiavelli*, ed. G. Mazzoni and M. Casella (Florence, 1929).
[41] *Istorie Fiorentine*, V, i, 773.

subject.[42] This passage offers an explanation for remarks at the beginning of the second book of the *Discorsi*, to the effect that good and evil are roughly equal in the world, but that at certain times the good tends to be concentrated in a particular people, country or area. The words used are *buono* and *cattivo*. Then, in pursuing the idea, Machiavelli substitutes *virtù* for *buono*, and contends that it was first concentrated in Assyria, that it next passed to the Medes, then to Persia, and on to Italy. After the disintegration of Rome, *virtù* was dispersed and distributed among several peoples and countries: France, the Mohammedans, the Germans. Now in the *Arte della guerra*, the explanation is given for the unique concentration of *virtù*—and *virtù* not *buono* is the word used throughout—in the ancient world, and for the great number of virtuous men among the ancients in contrast to the few existing in his day. Machiavelli's use of *virtù* in the passage in the *Arte della guerra* apparently indicates that *buono* in the discussion in the *Discorsi* is not meant to convey the impression of conventional moral virtue, a further example of the Florentine's imprecise handling of words.

The argument in the *Arte della guerra* begins with the statement that many more renowned men of war (*uomini eccellenti in guerra*) lived in ancient Europe (evidently Italy and Greece) than in Africa and Asia. In Europe there were few kingdoms and numerous republics, while only one or two very large kingdoms and a handful of republics existed in Africa and Asia. The condition for many virtuous men is many states. If few states exist, virtuous men are few in number. Moreover, men can display *virtù* only when they are employed and encouraged by their sovereign. But since monarchs fear the *virtù* of their subjects and republics recognize the *virtù* of their citizens, where there are more republics than monarchies, and particularly where there are many republics, there must be many virtuous individuals. But why are many states the condition for many men of *virtù*? Machiavelli's explanation is that if many states exist, conflict and contention, the struggle for existence, will be much more acute than if the world consists of only a few states. Survival under conditions of perpetual tension and warfare requires *virtù*, which is recognized and honoured. Each state, living in continual fear of the other, is obliged to keep up its military discipline and organization. *Virtù*, therefore, is the consequence of the necessity of war and defence, which, in turn, results from the great number of republics.[43] Once Rome conquered the world, fewer and fewer virtuous men appeared. A single empire replaced the many small republics. Peace was established, and the Romans themselves were not anxious to encourage or reward the *virtù* of any of their newly conquered subjects. As Rome be-

---

[42] *Arte della guerra*, II, 392–396.
[43] One can infer from the passage that the *equality* of many small states produces a condition of total and perpetual war, a real Hobbesian state of nature. Machiavelli's formulation, however, is never explicitly in these terms.

came corrupt, the whole world was corrupted, and with the disintegration of the empire, the original *virtù* of the separate parts was never recovered.

Machiavelli then stresses another factor, crucial to the existence of so much *virtù* in ancient Italy and Greece. In so doing he clearly reveals the close relation between *necessità* and *virtù*. The mode of life (*modo del vivere*) of the ancients differed considerably from that of the moderns, because of the difference between the religion of the two eras, between paganism and Christianity. Pagan religion imposed upon the ancients the absolute necessity of self-defence, much more so than in the modern world in which Christianity has humanized war, because the pagan religious values helped to make war a ruthless, cruel, and bloody activity. The defeated in battle were either killed or enslaved. Captured cities were demolished and the inhabitants dispersed. In the modern world, however, because of the effect of Christianity, war is not such a fearsome and brutal thing. Survival is no longer so difficult and tenuous since conflict between nations has ceased to mean total annihilation for the loser. The result has been a decline of military discipline and organization, and a decrease in *virtù*. In fact, Machiavelli concludes that so little *virtù* remains, that *fortuna* now governs the affairs of men.

At the core of the passage in the *Arte della guerra*, is the distinction between the values of paganism and Christianity. Fortunately Machiavelli specifically treats the subject in the *Discorsi*.[44] That the matter is considered in the second book may be significant, for here Machiavelli devotes his enquiry to the external affairs of the Romans, their treatment of subject peoples, military organization and methods. In addition, the second chapter follows Machiavelli's contention that Roman conquests rested more upon *virtù* than upon *fortuna,* the reference being specifically to Roman military prowess. Machiavelli begins his treatment of religion by stating that the ancients placed the greatest value upon the honour and glory of this world, whereas Christianity disparages worldly things. In ancient times, men of action, like military commanders and rulers, were the most esteemed. The Christian ideal, by contrast, is the man of contemplation. Fierceness (*ferocità*) and bravery (*gagliardia*) are the traits cherished by paganism, humility (*umilità*) by Christianity. Consequently, paganism produced men of great spirit (*grandezza dello animo*) and endurance of body (*fortezza del corpo*). Christianity does emphasize endurance, more for the purpose of withstanding suffering, than for the encouragement of the performance of vigorous deeds. The *modo del vivere* of the modern world for which Christianity has so largely been responsible has made men weak (*debole*) and effeminate (*effeminato*), and has allowed them to become the prey of the wicked (*uomini scelerati*). Machiavelli concludes that the pernicious effect of Christianity upon human attitudes and actions has

[44] *Discorsi*, II, ii, 227–228.

been due to its interpretation by men of evil (*viltà*), in accord with *ozio* rather than *virtù*.

III

As Professor Whitfield has indicated, Machiavelli gives to *virtù* so many meanings, that no single one of them can do justice to them all. Moreover, he follows and mixes several traditional usages. But I wish to argue further that this very variety of meanings, far from ruling out the use of *virtù* in a special sense, makes it possible. Obviously, I do not mean to say that whenever Machiavelli speaks of the *virtù* of an individual, he intends the special sense, but only when he uses the term in certain ways. Take, for example, these meanings: foresight, self-discipline, constancy, strength of mind, fortitude, determination, purposefulness, decisiveness, manliness, bravery, boldness, vigour. Just because Machiavelli may associate these different meanings with *virtù* in different contexts, does not exclude the notion of a special sense. Each is different, yet if I can demonstrate that they all have something in common, that there is a unity in the plurality of usage, then to speak of a special sense of *virtù* is quite appropriate. I maintain that these different specific meanings do, in fact, have a common feature, which is not simply trivial. In other words we can speak legitimately of Machiavelli's "concept of *virtu*," and by recognizing its nature, we can advance our understanding of his thought as a whole. The clue to the special sense, so conceived, lies first in Machiavelli's ascription of *virtù* to warriors, and second in his explanation of the relation between *virtù* and war.

Quite often in referring to the *virtù* of an individual, Machiavelli seems to be thinking of a mode of conduct most typically manifested by the soldier in combat. Battles and campaigns are highly fluid situations of the greatest uncertainty, in which the severest hardships and the most pressing physical dangers are confronted, endured, and mastered, if victory is to be gained. To Machiavelli war is the archetypal contest between *virtù* and *fortuna,* between all that is manly, and all that is changeable, unpredictable, and capricious, a struggle between masculine rational control and effeminate irrationality. War is the supreme test of man, of his physique, of his intellect, and particularly of his character. War is a complex art in which force, guile, and persuasion must be maintained in an ever workable combination. In war the best laid plans go astray. The cautiously and skillfully executed manoeuvre may meet with unexpected accident. Certain victory may suddenly become the possibility of disaster. As the tide of battle changes adversely, as the peril mounts, and as the sand of time runs out, at such unnerving moments, the *virtù* of the captain is on trial. His character, his self-confidence, strength of will, fortitude, and courage, become of greater importance than his brains and bodily strength. Cunning and prowess of arms will be of no avail where there is a failure of nerve. Against overwhelming odds, the leader often must discard his carefully prepared battle plan, and rally his forces by a determined and audacious improvisation. How many times has victory been snatched from defeat by a great general, and how often has the moral victory and the glory gone to him, even in defeat!

Machiavelli believes that the characteristics of war are also those of particular kinds of non-military situations. The founder, the prince, the magistrate, the political conspirator may be actors in circumstances with similar features. Success in these circumstances will depend upon the same qualities displayed by the victorious warrior in battle. Indeed politics is a kind of war, and civil society is essentially a battleground for individuals and parties struggling for power. The traditional distinction between friend and foe used to describe the relation between the citizen and his city's enemy is now applied by Machiavelli to relations between fellow-citizens. The model of civic life is always military life, the model of civic leadership is always military leadership. Founding a new commonwealth, the reform of a corrupt state, conspiracy for the overthrow of government, the prevention of conspiracy, are fundamentally military situations, as appraised by Machiavelli. *Virtù*, therefore, is a set of qualities, or a pattern of behaviour most distinctively exhibited under what may be described as battlefield conditions, whether actual war or politics provide the context. Machiavelli's *politico* is cast in the mould of the warrior, and the standard of excellence of one is not so different from that of the other.[45]

Three other problems in connection with *virtù* can now be touched upon: (1) the source of *virtù;* (2) the relation between princely and civic *virtù;* (3) the relation of *virtù* to civic corruption. Princely *virtù* is an inborn and natural characteristic, shaped, however, by education; while civic *virtù* is the result of the right kind of education, organization, and discipline. *Fortuna*, of course, has an important part in the existence of both kinds of *virtù*. That a particular person is born with the qualities necessary for extraordinary leadership, and that he lives in a time and place in which he can distinguish himself by means of these qualities, are the work of *fortuna*. To an important extent, whether a people are virtuous or not is also dependent upon *fortuna*. Without the requisite conditions of necessity no type of civic education will for long secure the *virtù* of a people. But in the absence of proper education and organization, the necessity of circumstance will either overwhelm and destroy a people, or considerably reduce their effectiveness. Furthermore, whereas the context of necessity may result from *fortuna*, a certain kind of education and organization can help to generate and maintain the necessity so fundamental to *virtù*. Conditions of

---

[45] An expanded version of this interpretation is found in my introductory essay to the revision of Ellis Farneworth's translation, *The Art of War* (Indianapolis and New York, 1965) (Library of Liberal Arts).

war and struggle between peoples will be perpetuated as long as men are trained to be warriors, are imbued from birth with military values, and live in states that are organized for aggrandizement.

The distinction between the *virtù* of the leader and the *virtù* of a people seems to be one of degree rather than kind, a point made clearer by reference to Machiavelli's military model. The rank and file, the non-commissioned and commissioned officers, and the commander possess certain qualities in common because all are soldiers, engaged in the same kind of activity under the same conditions. Machiavelli's special sense of *virtù* refers to a style of conduct of all warriors, from the simple soldier to the great general. They are all members of an army, which is a rationally organized, hierarchical institution. Ideally, the commander by reason of his position at the top of the hierarchy is a better soldier than those below him in the pyramidal structure. Theoretically, if not always in practice, position in the hierarchy corresponds to merit. The commander, therefore, should be more of a soldier than his subordinates and should possess more *virtù* than they do. In a disciplined, well-ordered army *virtù* is manifested in the way all members from the top to the bottom command and execute commands. An army is not an obedience machine set in motion and kept in motion solely by the commands of the prime mover, the general. The commander himself must obey and execute orders, and right down the hierarchy are areas of discretion that entail initiative and command. At the top, general objectives are determined and tactics are decided upon by the commander and his staff, in accordance with the discretion allowed them by, for example, the civil authorities. But these rules, devised for a particular military operation, can be only of the most general nature if they are to be applied successfully, and in the application, during the course of changing battle conditions, they will be modified and even discarded. Here so much depends upon how the commander's subordinates use their discretionary powers. Here the foresight, purposefulness, determination, vigour, courage, in short the *virtù* of all the soldiers, commanders and subordinates, is put to the supreme test. The *virtù* of the commander in initiating, planning, and directing the total operation is similar to, if greater than, the *virtù* of the lieutenant on a small sector of the front, in initiating, planning, and directing an attack against an enemy strong point that is proving troublesome, or the *virtù* of the rank and filer in executing his lieutenant's scheme. Likewise in a well-ordered commonwealth citizens at all levels as well as the civic leaders will have certain qualities in common, *virtù*. The citizen will show his *virtù* in the style in which he performs his tasks, the way he executes his civic obligations, and dedicates himself to the common good. Such a citizen is not one who blindly obeys, but who demonstrates initiative by using his discretionary powers in certain ways and not in others.

Consequently, I have in effect answered the last of the questions, the relation between civic *virtù* and corruption. A people, with the very best of intentions, may wish to live in peace, to respect authority, and devote themselves to the common good. Unless they are vigorous, determined, and courageous, unless they are virtuous, the best of intentions will avail them very little. Civic corruption is a condition of *ozio* and the decline of *virtù*. A unified, patriotic, and energetic people are virtuous. The opposite is corruption. A virtuous leader may rule a corrupt people, as did Caesar. A wise leader like Soderini may attempt to reform a corrupt people, and will fail because of a lack of *virtù*. A virtuous and unwise leader may fail, like Manlius Capitolinus, in his efforts to seize control of a virtuous people. Under certain conditions a wise and good leader without *virtù*, a Numa, may successfully rule a virtuous people. Finally leaders who are neither virtuous nor wise cannot expect much success or security in seeking to rule a corrupt people, as Machiavelli believed the history of his own age so pointedly illustrated.

FURTHER READINGS FOR PART VI

Anglo, Sydney. *Machiavelli: A Dissection*. New York: Harcourt, 1970.

Baron, Hans. "Machiavelli: The Republican Citizen and the Author of 'The Prince'," *English Historical Review*, 76 (April 1961), pp. 217–253.

Burnham, James. *The Machiavellians*. New York: John Day, 1943.

Butterfield, Herbert. *The Statecraft of Machiavelli*. New York: Crowell-Collier-Macmillan, 1962.

Cassirer, Ernst. *Myth of the State*. New York: Oxford University Press, 1946.

Chabod, Federico. *Machiavelli and the Renaissance*. Cambridge, Mass.: Harvard University Press, 1958.

Cochrane, Eric W. "Machiavelli: 1940–1960," *Journal of Modern History*, 33 (June 1961), pp. 113–136.

Fleisher, Martin. "Trust and Deceit in Machiavelli's Comedies," *Journal of the History of Ideas*, 27 (July 1966), pp. 365–380.

Germino, Dante. "Second Thoughts on Leo Strauss's Machiavelli," *Journal of Politics*, 28 (November 1966), pp. 794–817.

Gilbert, Allan H. *Machiavelli's Prince and Its Forerunners*. Durham, N.C.: Duke University Press, 1938.

Gilbert, Felix. "The Concept of Nationalism in Machiavelli's Prince," *Studies in the Renaissance*, 1 (1954), pp. 38–48.

———. "The Humanist Concept of the Prince," *Journal of Modern History*, 11 (December 1939), pp. 449–483.

———. *Machiavelli and Guicciardini: Politics and History in Sixteenth-Century Florence*. Princeton, N.J.: Princeton University Press, 1965.

———. "Machiavelli: The Renaissance of the Art of War," in Edward M.

Earle, ed. *Makers of Modern Strategy.* Princeton, N.J.: Princeton University Press, 1944, pp. 3–25.

Guicciardini, Francesco. *Maxims and Reflections of a Renaissance Statesman.* New York: Harper & Row, 1965.

Hale, John R. *Machiavelli and Renaissance Italy.* New York: Crowell-Collier-Macmillan, 1960.

Ingersoll, David E. "The Constant Prince: Private Interests and Public Goals in Machiavelli," *Western Political Quarterly,* 21 (December 1968), pp. 588–596.

——. "Machiavelli and Madison: Perspectives on Political Stability," *Political Science Quarterly,* 85 (June 1970), pp. 259–280.

Kraft, Joseph. "Truth and Poetry in Machiavelli," *Journal of Modern History,* 23 (1951), pp. 109–121.

Landi, E. "The Political Philosophy of Machiavelli," *History Today,* 14 (August 1965), pp. 550–555.

Mattingly, Garrett. "Machiavelli's *Prince:* Political Science or Political Satire?" *The American Scholar,* 27 (1958), pp. 482–491.

McCoy, Charles N. R. "The Place of Machiavelli in the History of Political Thought," *American Political Science Review,* 37 (August 1943), pp. 626–641.

Merleau-Ponty, Maurice. "A Note on Machiavelli," in *Signs.* Evanston, Ill.: Northwestern University Press, 1964, pp. 211–223.

Olschki, Leonardo. *Machiavelli the Scientist.* Berkeley, Calif.: Gillick Press, 1945.

Ridolfi, Roberto. *The Life of Niccolo Machiavelli.* Chicago: University of Chicago Press, 1963.

Strauss, Leo. *Thoughts on Machiavelli.* New York: Free Press, 1958.

Tsurutani, Taketsugu. "Machiavelli and the Problem of Political Development," *Review of Politics,* 30 (July 1968), pp. 316–331.

Voegelin, Eric. "Machiavelli's Prince: Background and Formation," *Review of Politics,* 13 (April 1951), pp. 142–168.

Waley, Daniel P. "The Primitivist Element in Machiavelli's Thought," *Journal of the History of Ideas,* 31 (January 1970), pp. 91–98.

Whitfield, John H. *Machiavelli.* Oxford: Blackwell and Mott, 1947.